SILENT WARRIORS

Submarine Wrecks of the United Kingdom

VOLUME TWO

SILENT WARRIORS

Submarine Wrecks of the United Kingdom

VOLUME TWO

RON YOUNG & PAMELA ARMSTRONG

The
History
Press

First published 2009

The History Press
The Mill, Brimscombe Port
Stroud, Gloucestershire, GL5 2QG
www.thehistorypress.co.uk

British Library Cataloguing in Publication Data.
A catalogue record for this book is available from the British Library.

ISBN 978 0 7524 4789 6

Printed in Great Britain

CONTENTS

*This book is dedicated to Colin Smith (15 April 1935–16 June 1955)
and Gus Britton MBE (9 September 1922–21 July 1997)*

Two British Submariners and Silent Warriors

Above: Gus Britton on HMS *Tribune*. (Courtesy Imperial War Museum)

Left: Colin Smith. (Courtesy of Ray Smith)

ACKNOWLEDGEMENTS

THE AUTHORS OWE A GREAT DEAL OF THANKS TO THE FOLLOWING
PEOPLE AND ORGANISATIONS

Nelson McEachan and June Dillon and the staff at the UK Hydrographic Office, Taunton.

Michael Lowrey of Charlotte, North Carolina, USA, lecturer, author, naval historian and researcher of First World War U-boats.

Dr Axel Niestlé of Dabendorf, Germany; naval historian, author and researcher.

Brian D. Head: Lt Cdr, RD★, RNR (Rtd) Submarine Museum Committee Chairman.

Dennis Feary, RN Submarine Museum volunteer, who is a member of The Archive Working Party RNSM. They 'looked-up' what the regular staff don't have the time to do. With Brian D. Head as the chairman, the group help with archiving material and anything they are asked to do. Dennis is updating crew names and the Memorial Book in the Museum – hence the work is on-going.

John Eade of Perth, Western Australia. Born in Barking, Essex in 1946, John also spent many years living on the Isle of Wight, before moving to Australia. Unfortunately MND forced early retirement and now he spends most of his time researching in maritime history, especially in the Royal Navy Submarine Service.

Yves Dufeil of Martigues, France, author, First World War U-boat and maritime researcher.

Terry Whalebone from Bolton, ex-Maritime Marine officer, maritime historian and researcher.

Ian Spokes, author of the *1901 Great Storm*, maritime historian and shipwreck researcher, sadly now deceased.

Billy McGee, maritime historian and researcher of merchant ship crews.

Roger Griffiths, alias Hollywood, maritime historian and researcher.

Roger Jordan, author and maritime researcher.

Andy Mair for the additional information on HM S/M *Safari*.

Bill and Eva Ternström-Lidbetter-Sessions, authors of the SS *Ada*'s last voyage in 1917.

Steven Charles re: *U 1063*.

Jürgen Meyer-Brenkhof, Fregattenkapitän a D (Commander in German Navy with 34 years' active service) for information about Rudolph Wieser and translating Rudi's letters.

Rudolph Wieser, Matrosenobergefreite and survivor of *U 1195*, sadly now deceased.

Thomas Krispin of Wiesbaden near Frankfurt.

Ian Smythe, Edmonton, Canada for his photos of the rescue of crewmen from *U 1209* by HMCS *Ribble*. His father was Stoker J.E. Smythe from Edmonton, Alberta and served on *Ribble* from its commissioning in July 1944 until it was decommissioned in June 1945.

Bruce Barr of Dunstaffnage Marine Laboratory, Oban.

Rainer Bruns, U-boat researcher.

Platon Alexiades from Badgley, Montreal, Canada for assistance with *Safari* attacks.

Simon Schnetzke, First World War U-boat researcher and historian.

Colin Armstrong.

Jan-Olof Hendig of Sweden, ship researcher.

Maurice Voss, ship researcher.

Kendall McDonald of *DIVER* magazine and author/historian.

Wayne Acourt.

Herbert Karting of Itzehoe, a retired Elbe-Pilot and author of *German Coastal Sailing-Vessels*, five volumes of 'German schooners'.

Paul Sutton.

Gillian Hughes.

Sandra and Peter Gradwell.

Oliver Meise of Marburg, Germany; online dive magazine Taucher.net.

George Robinson from Cottingham, near Hull.

Roy Martin of Southampton, author of *Salvors Risdon Beazley* and researcher.

Matt Storey.

Ray and Mary Smith of Sunderland; Ray's brother Colin died on HM S/M *Sidon*

Dave Howell.

Walter Leotta, 13900 Biella, Italy for help with Italian vessels and *Safari*.

Davie McClymont.

Jöm Jensen.

Pat and Ian Forbes.

René Alloin, French ship researcher.

Theodor Dorgeist of Westfalen Freiberuflicher, maritime historian and researcher.

David Parkinson.

Dave Barlow.

Mr Heinz Thois, chairman of U-boat Memorial Foundation Council.

Herr Karl Schmeink and the Kiel U-boat Comrades Association.

The Bremen U-boat Comrades Association.

Axel van Eesbreek from Much, Germany, maritime researcher.

Richard Driver from the USA for First World War submarine photos.

George Malcolmson and the staff of the RN Submarine Museum.

Klaus-Peter Pohland of Gaillon, France.

Howard Cock and the enthusiastic guys who run www.ubootwaffe.net.

Hubertus Weggelar.

Guy AB Knapton of Lasne, Belgium, 12 miles south of Brussels.

Captain W.L. Hume, M.N.I. (Rtd) Cowes, Isle of Wight.

Newcastle Central Library.

Sander Kingsepp.

Jean Michel Forsans of Marseille, ship researcher.

The Mitchell Library, Glasgow.

Tyne Wear Archive.

The Barrow Branch of the Submariners Association.

Siri Holm Lawson of www.warsailors.com.

Portree Library.

Bob Baird, Scottish maritime researcher and author.

Interviews carried out with the following British veterans by Pamela Armstrong: ex-TI Bill Treble (*Umpire*), ex-CERA Rob Roy McCurrach (*Unity*, *Safari*), ex-CPO Bernard Cranmer (*Sealion*), ex-CERA Ernie Buckingham, ex-CPO Raymond Fry and Signalman Gus Britton (*Truculent*), Stoker Con McCabe (*Sturgeon*), Stoker Taff Harper (*Seal*).

David Asprey, ship researcher and historian.

Volksbund Deutsche Kriegsgräberfürsorge.

Commonwealth War Graves Commission.

Karl-J. Schmeink, Webmaster.

Alan Roberts.

Alain Croce from Ensues la Redonne, France.

Rolf Kristensen, Åsgårdstrand, Norway.

Mats Karlsson, of Köping, Sweden.

Torsten Hagnéus, Vastra Frolunda, Sweden.

Arie Visser, Holland.

Oliver Lörscher, ship and U-boat researcher, historian.

Adrian Vicary for ship photographs.

Trevor Hallifax, originally from Grimsby, but now resides in Ash Vale, near Aldershot.

Mikael Svensson, Museiassistent/Assistant, Göteborg, Maritime Museum, Sweden.

Rose Young – Ron Young's wife – for proofreading the book.

Kevin Belcher for *U 995* photos.

FOREWORD

BY DR AXEL NIESTLÉ OF DABENDORF, GERMANY

For a long time recreational divers and naval historians had almost nothing in common. Technical limits from diving gear previously restricted recreational divers to comparatively shallow waters close to the shoreline, which usually had not seen much naval action. Instead, naval history was written at military academies, universities or private offices, using official documents or oral recordings stored at archives or other places. In cases where contemporary records are lacking or incomplete, the precision in the accounts on naval actions or operations often decreased markedly and confirmed truth was replaced by various degrees of guesswork. Of course, it was not ill will on the part of the historians, but simply lack of information, which sometimes led them to dreadful distortions in the narrative of historical events. The operational history of the German U-boat campaign around the British Islands during both world wars in the twentieth century offers a splendid example for this. With a high percentage of U-boats lost with all hands and official records often destroyed or lost to wartime action, documentation of the German part necessarily remained fragmentary. Not surprisingly also, the final fate of many U-boats lost in British coastal waters remained obscure or without proof.

However, in recent times naval history increasingly benefited from the discoveries and information forwarded by the ever-growing number of recreational divers, now perfectly equipped to explore the seabed down to depths previously out of reach. Sixty years after the last war, many of the wartime wrecks are still preserved in surprisingly good condition. Therefore diving offers a completely new source of additional historic information for naval historians. Taking into account the various problems encountered to reach a correct assessment for anti-submarine actions, the simple discovery of a U-boat wreck in a certain place can already offer great help in the evaluation of individual attacks. With both divers and historians interested in identifying wrecks, a mutual basis for cooperation is presented. Wreck exploration by experienced divers combined with the expertise of historians has already resulted in numerous wreck identifications over the last years and a more precise understanding of events otherwise to be left obscured in the shadows of history.

Ron Young and Pamela Armstrong are providing a highly welcome encyclopaedia on charted and recorded U-boat and submarine wrecks around Britain, combining detailed historical information on the individual vessels and their final fate with a fresh account on the present condition of the wreck if it has been already located and examined by divers. Meticulously giving the archive sources for the information provided on the subject, readers are entitled to further check or crosscheck the details presented on the subject. With a fair number of recorded submarine wrecks still un-located today, the series of books should also be taken as a guide to plan future diving expeditions. The large number of naval personnel who perished, or went missing aboard the many submarines now lying strewn on the seabed around Britain, deserve that their final fates and resting places are correctly recorded for their ancestors and history. However, divers should never forget that many of the wrecks are now official war graves and should be treated with decent respect.

Opposite: Diesel engine room of *U 995*, a Second World War Kriegsmarine Type VIIC/41 U-boat. (Courtesy Kevin Belcher of Swindon)

GLOSSARY

A/S	Anti-Submarine.
AA	Anti-Aircraft.
AEG	electric motors manufactured by Allgemeine Elektricittäts-Gesellschaft.
AFA	Batteries manufactured by Accumlatoren-Fabrik-Aktiengesellshcaft.
AK	highest speed available – '*ausserste kraft!*'
ASCO	Anti-Submarine Control Officer responsible for working a ship's anti-submarine weapons, providing technical advice when required.
ASDIC	An acronym derived from 'Anti-Submarine Detection Investigation Committee' – SONAR being the American term adopted by the British from the late 1950s. Underwater acoustic detection equipment. In effect an instrument which transmits an acoustic pulse in water and measures distances in terms of the time for the echo of the pulse to return; used to detect submarines. ASDIC could accurately record the range and direction of an enemy vessel. ASDIC had the potential to be baffled by the sound of rushing water (if the hunting ship steamed at more than 18k), by differing water densities, by wrecks, rocky sea beds and by shrimps making their habitual clicking noise. Hunter-killer groups occasionally attacked unfortunate whales in error.

A school for training ASDIC operatives was established at Portland in Dorset in the mid-thirties. The overwhelming majority of Second World War U-boats featured in the book were first detected by ASDIC sets. Basically ADSIC was a submarine detection device housed in a dome under the hull of an A/S vessel or submarine. In active mode it transmitted a narrow beam of sound in the form of a series of impulses which produced a 'ping' or echo from any solid object detected within a maximum range of 3,000 yards from the transmitter. The signal thus produced could enable a skilled operator to deduce the accurate range and bearing of a U-boat. ASDIC could be used passively in hydrophone mode to detect propeller noise. In this mode the device could interpret bearing but not range.

From August 1944 British warships were fitted with two ASDIC sets '144-5Q' and '147B'.

Set 144-5Q consisted of:

A range recorder providing an echo plot

A bearing recorder – speed and course to be followed

Automatic control training gear – in some advanced warships, both the helmsman's gear and the captain's bearing instrument were connected to the ASDIC sets. In effect, during the latter stages of an attack, the hunting warship was steered automatically by the ASDIC gear.

Set 147B consisted of:

A depth oscillator

A depth recorder – automatic depth plotter

144-5Q was used, in general, for obtaining initial contact, determining course to steer then time to fire. 147B detected the depth of the target. The Depth Charge Pattern Control System fitted into the most modern warships was capable of delivering the *coup de grâce* by means of the automatic firing of projectiles.

ASV   Air to surface radar installed in Allied aircraft from 1942. ASV Mk 1 operated on a 1.4m band. The Germans retaliated by fitting their boats with *FuMB Metox* R600 radar detector sets to warn of approaching aircraft. For a time U-boat losses decreased but the Allies introduced ASV Mk III better known as H2S in 1943. H2S operated on a 9.7cm frequency and was far superior to its predecessors. U-boat losses rose alarmingly but the Kriegsmarine believed these losses were due to the radiating properties of the *Metox* R600 radar detector sets now in general use. *Metox* was quickly replaced by *Wanz G1* (which was inferior to the H2S sets used by the Allies due to its narrower wavelength). Only the introduction of *Naxos* (FuMb 7) in conjunction with *Wanz* G2 sets in November 1943 enabled the U-boats to keep pace with the Allies in the technological war. In April 1944, the combination of *Mucke* (FuMb 25) and *Fliege* (FuMb 24) sets replaced this arrangement.

AUDs   Deliberations of the Anti-Submarine Assessment Committee which can be found in the National Archive, Kew, London. The Committee was made up of experienced naval officers, personnel from naval intelligence and by 1944/45 the naval contingent was joined by an increasing number of 'pointy heads' or weapon technology scientists. Every escort group claiming a submarine sinking was required to submit a full report detailing the incident and citing the evidence for a successful attack. The AUD Committee would judge the claim on the evidence provided. The burden of proof for a classified sinking was high – hence Allied warships had little option to resort to 'can opener' attacks in order to gain recognition for a successful attack.

Aal   German slang for torpedo (eel).

Agrufront   *Ausbildungsgruppe für Front-U-Boote* – unit for training submarines to be used operationally, in what were known to the British as 'working up' exercises.

Alberich   Special rubber covering to protect the U-boats from ASDIC.

Aphrodite   By suspending aluminium strips from a hydrogen-filled balloon, a Second World War U-boat, already aware of radar emissions via its *FuMb* or *Wanz* set, could create false radar echoes and fool a hunting group by releasing an *Aphrodite* balloon before diving in a windward direction. The balloons (which were fitted with an anchoring device) were filled from hydrogen tanks fitted to the casing. The balloons took up space within the U-boat which was required to surface in order to release them. *Aphrodite* had a marked tendency to become entangled on the *wintergarten* guns and antennae. In the well-patrolled waters around the British coast, radar operatives were ultimately able to distinguish the echoes given off from an *Aphrodite* balloon from a U-boat from the appearance of multiple echoes. The device was therefore of limited usefulness.

Auxiliary Patrol   In 1914 the commitments faced by the Royal Navy saw its resources stretched as never before. There had been a modicum of pre-war organisational planning but both British and German navies underestimated the threat of the submarine. On 4 August 1914 British trawlers were barred from the fishing grounds in order to be made available for naval service. By the end of hostilities some 39,000 British fishermen (49 per cent) were engaged in naval patrols. The Auxiliary patrol bore the brunt of A/S patrols in British coastal waters, thus freeing the RN for more specialised tasks. Two thousand Auxiliary Patrol men died on active service.

Five thousand British trawlers or drifters were actively engaged in Auxiliary Patrol work, one quarter in minesweeping duties. Trawlers were fitted with naval surplus six- or three-pounder guns. Often these guns could not be properly elevated or depressed. The training given to the crews was as rudimentary as their armament. Nevertheless what the auxiliary patrol men lacked in skill, they made up for in enthusiasm (reports from exasperated RNR officers suggest often serious problems of discipline. British fishermen were not the kind of men to tamely follow Kings Regulations).

The primary function of the auxiliary A/S patrol was to keep U-boats submerged, driving them into minefields or alerting escorts or minesweepers to their presence. At the outbreak of war the British coast was divided into twenty-one patrol areas. The essential unit of each patrol was the trawler section, typically four trawlers serving under the command of a retired RN officer on a steam yacht. The yacht officers were drawn from the RNR, their expertise was often augmented by a sprinkling of trained RN gunners. Unless involved in a special operation, the trawlers tended to retain their peace time crews. By the summer of 1918, the increasing availability of potent depth charges, serviceable hydrophones and fast motorboats all added to the efficiency of the Auxiliary Patrols. By the end of hostilities this improvised navy had shown its worth.

BBC	Electric motor manufactured by Brown, Boveri & Cie.
BdU	*Befehlshaber der U-Boote* (Commander-in-Chief of Submarines).
BEM	British Empire Medal.
BM	Royal Humane Society's Bronze Medal awarded for saving life at sea
Balkon Gerat	See *GHG*.
'to Bat'	RN Submarine slang. When a boat was said to have 'batted', it had been lost with all hands.
Beam	The greatest width of the boat/ship.
Billet	British submarine patrol zone.
Blowers	Precious compressed air was used sparingly. Once ballast tanks had been blown and the boat had reached a state of neutral buoyancy, the supply of compressed air was turned off and pumps known as 'blowers' were used to rid the boat of excess water.
Boat/*Boot*	The submarine. Submariners of all nations tend to regard calling a submarine a 'ship' or a 'sub' as deeply offensive. A submarine has one deck. It is therefore a boat.
Bold	An acoustic decoy designed to baffle ASDIC detection. The device was ejected by U-boats and known to the British as SBT – Submarine Bubble Target. The name deriving from 'Kobold' – a goblin frequenting Nordic myth. Each *Bold* canister contained a mixture of calcium and zinc. The round canister was ejected from a re-loadable mechanism adjacent to the stern torpedo (known officially as *Rohr 6*, or more irreverently by the crew as the *Pillenwerfer* or pill-chucker). A hydrostatic valve on the canister controlled the entry of salt water. Five to ten minutes after ejection,

a mass of hydrogen bubbles would be produced. To the ASDIC operator on a British A/S vessel, this mass bore every resemblance to a dived U-boat travelling on a steady course. Thus the hunters would be duped into attacking a mass of bubbles while their prey made its escape. *See* 'Doppler'.

Bridge

The location from which a vessel is steered and its speed controlled

Bugtorpedoraum or ***Bugraum***

the fore ends/torpedo stowage chamber of a U-boat. Domicile of the '*Lords*'.

'Bunting Tosser'

RN Submarine slang for a signalman.

Bulkhead

A structural vertical partition separating compartments. The submarines featured in this book were generally fitted with three main bulkheads.

C–in–C

Commander-in-Chief.

CO

Commanding Officer.

Camel

Cylindrical lifting vessel used in salvage operations. Discarded submarines were often converted to harbour camels (*see* vols 3 and 4).

'Can Opener'

RN slang describing the routine (but highly distasteful) practice carried out following a submarine 'kill'. The AUD Committee demanded incontrovertible proof of the destruction of a U-boat. General service responded by targeting a suspected U-boat wreck with a barrage of depth charges sufficient to shatter the pressure hull with a view to 'liberating' human remains. It was not unheard of for human remains to be fished out and placed in bottles of formaldehyde prior to being handed to the ship's doctor for analysis.

Casing

The outer protective skin of a submarine, free flooding in many places.

Coaming

A vertical piece around the edge of a hatch, etc. to prevent the ingress of water.

Control Room

The nerve centre of a submarine corresponding to the German *zentrale*.

DAMS

Defensively Armed Merchant Ship (army or navy gunners attached to merchant ships during the First World War).

DBS

Distressed British Seamen.

DC or **Depth Charge**

The evolution of the depth charge is described in vol.1. It is sufficient here to add that experiments carried out on *D1* at HMS *Vernon* in the spring of 1918 indicated that a depth charge would have to detonate within 50ft (15.24m) of a submarine to cause significant damage. Inter-war experimentation reduced this distance to between 25ft and 30ft.

In the Second World War the British relied on the old Mk VII depth charge, fitted with a pistol to guard against premature detonation. Each canister contained 300lb of amatol. In the early stages of the War, six depth settings were provided between 50ft and 500ft. The depth charge was normally discharged in patterns of five, three from rails at the stern at a spacing of 150ft and two charges being thrown from the beam.

The Mk VII depth charge sank at the rate of 10ft per second in order to allow the hunting vessel to draw clear before detonation. Early in the war it was decided that a faster sinking rate was required to provide a second, deeper layer to the DC pattern. A ballast weight of 140lb was added to one end of the Mk VII depth charge which gave it a sinking weight of 16ft per second. This was known as the Mk VII heavy. The pattern was altered to provide for the ejection of one heavy DC along with every standard Mk

VII. The heavy was provided with depth settings between 140ft to 550ft. Some vessels were fitted to fire DCs in intermediate positions within the pattern shown above, to ensure greater coverage. From January 1943 minol replaced amatol as the DC explosive of choice. By the end of the war DCs were capable of detonating at 1,500ft. Four patterns could be discharged successively with 2 minute reloading delays. Ultimately the Depth Charge Pattern Control System was introduced. Connected to the ASDIC sets, this system facilitated the automatic release of DCs or Hedgehog projectiles at the most appropriate times. Allied experiments carried out after the Second World War suggested that a DC containing 320lb of minol would have to detonate within 25ft of a U-boat to rupture the pressure hull. A DC exploding within 50ft (7.62m) could cause sufficient damage to force the U-boat to surface. Cumulative damage was therefore always a better bet than a direct hit. The Allies estimated that 158 U-boats had been destroyed by DC (42.8 per cent) though this figure is now open to question.

DD list
RN 'Discharged Dead' list, compiled by officialdom in the aftermath of loss. RN DD lists tend to record only naval personnel. For instance the DD listing compiled following the sinking of *M2* ignores several seconded RAF who also died on the submarine.

DEMS
Defence Equipped Merchant Ship (army or navy gunners attached to merchant ships during the Second World War).

DF
Direction finding.

DSEA
Davis Submerged Escape Apparatus. Closed circuit breathing set (based on the Fleuss-Davis breathing set) patented in 1929. The set was standard British escape apparatus from 1932 to 1951.

DSM
Distinguished Service Medal.

DSO
Distinguished Service Order.

DT-Gerat
Dezimeter Telegraphie or Teknik early series of German radars using 80cm band.

Displacement
The weight of water displaced by a floating vessel, or the vessel's weight.

'Dockyard Matey'
RN slang for civilian shipyard worker or docker.

Doppler effect
Bold frustrated many RN A/S hunts. From the late summer of 1944 RN ships were equipped with ASDIC sets capable of registering 'doppler' effect. Now the hunters could determine the range, bearing and movement of an underwater contact *relative to the ASDIC equipped vessel*. In other words the RN could discriminate between a stationary *Bold* canister and the impulse produced by a real U-boat.

Drager* set or *Tauchretter
Oxygen breathing set based, like the British DSEA, upon the Fleuss-Davis closed circuit principle. The KDM ordered the first sets in 1912 and the design remained in use until 1945.

'Drip'
RN slang – to frequently complain.

Drop keel
Disposable keel fitted to British submarines.

EG
British escort group – usually destroyers, corvettes or frigates.

Elektra-Sonne
A crude predecessor of the American Loran A (and later C) and the British Decca Radio Navigation System. A master transmitter in Thuringia supported by several slave transmitters as far apart as Spain and Norway sent timed signals, which could be received by *schnorchelling* U-boats at periscope depth. Interpolation of the relative bearing lines enabled navigators to obtain a reasonably accurate fix. U-boats operating submerged for extended periods arrived at the R/V points off their Norwegian ports with navigational errors of less than 5 miles by relaying solely on the *Elektra-Sonne* system.

Evasion techniques   These varied significantly. What follows is a translation from a KDM manual issued to U-boat commanders (and said to have been one of the documents recovered from *UB110*. *See* vol.1):

PROCEDURE WHEN PURSUED WITH HYDROPHONES

1. A rough sea is the best natural protection.
2. The reduction to a minimum of the sounds caused by your own boat is an effective protection.
    (a) Connect the vertical rudder and hydroplanes for hand working.
    (b) Stop your ballast and trimming pumps. Use compressed air in lieu.
    (c) Let your main motors run at the lowest possible number of revolutions, stopping frequently. Keep the boat trimmed on the periscope.
3. Proceed at a depth of 45m (148ft).
4. It is better to keep near the coast than out in the open sea in cases where the depth is greater than 70m (230ft).
5. Lying on the bottom is a good way of evading hydrophone pursuit, provided that the hull is absolutely tight. No leakage of air, and, above all, no oil bubbles.
6. Make the most of the time when your pursuer is going ahead, in order to increase your distance from him. The submarine must, however, stop frequently to listen, even at the risk of not increasing her distance from the enemy so rapidly.

When attacked and forced to submerge, a submarine may:

    (a) Attempt to escape by proceeding at maximum speed.
    (b) Proceed at slow speed.
    (c) Proceed slowly, stopping and balancing occasionally to listen, or to synchronize with stops of hunting units.
    (d) Bottom, usually in water 40 fathoms (73m) or less.
    (e) Adopt a stopped trim.

When making an attack on a vessel or convoy, a submarine normally must submerge a considerable distance away, and then manoeuvre while submerged for position. This may require the use of high speed and consequently exhaust much of her battery power. By day in crowded waters, or in localities where our own submarines operate, or our patrols are thick, the enemy must spend most of the daylight hours submerged, and devote much of the night to recharging batteries. Recharging may be done while proceeding on the surface at moderate speed.

It should be noted that much of this advice was equally valid during the Second World War. In both wars, U-boat skippers learned how to take advantage of the 'blind time' between depth charges rolling off the deck of a ship and the subsequent explosion. During this time the hunting vessel would inevitably lose ASDIC contact. The U-boat skipper would order '*ausserste kraft*' accompanied by a dramatic alteration in course and depth in the hope of shaking off the hunter at this critical moment. Methods of foiling an ASDIC hunt in the Second World War varied but one technique commonly used was to remain at periscope depth, keeping the stern directed towards the hunting vessel, thus providing the smallest possible target. The escaping U-boat would attempt to keep to a straight course wherever possible rather than zig-zagging. If certain of having been observed, the U-boat would dive deep but not on its original course. Many U-boat commanders preferred to dive under convoy's track in order to baffle ASDIC operators. The most skilled submarine commanders, British and German, were able to use prevailing conditions to their advantage such as the varying densities of water or the presence of a rocky seabed, all of which would interfere with the acoustic transmissions of hunters.

FaT   *Flachenabsuchender Torpedo or Federapparat Torpedo* – German torpedo used against convoys. Ideally the U-boat would position itself ahead of an oncoming convoy or at a 90° angle to a passing convoy. Initially following a straight course after firing, the FaT

	would adopt a wandering course, punctuated by regular 180° turns until a ship was struck.
FdU	*Führer der U-Boote* – Flag Officer (Submarines) responsible for a given geographic area. Korvettenkapitan Herman Bauer was appointed as FdU during the First World War until June 1917, when he was replaced by BdU Michelsen.
FuMb	*Funkmessbeobachter* – Radar detector set. It was the responsibility of the radio operator to tune his set into a variety of wavelengths by manually turning a dial on the *Metox* set. Approaching aircraft were indicated by interruptions on a line displayed on the cathode ray tube oscilloscope. From August 1943 the *Wanz* sets replaced *Metox*.
FuMo	*Funkmessortungs Geracht* – Radar. The German version of radar was known as 'GSR' to the British and this term appears in Admiralty accounts. From March 1944 U-boats were fitted with FuMo 61 *Hohentweil*-U (Owl) a large 'mattress' radar antenna which fitted in an extension built into the port side of the conning tower. This radar operated at 54cm. It was effective against aircraft between 15 and 20km. The set was unreliable in detecting low-flying aircraft because the low station of the antenna resulted in the sea causing interference.
Fathom	Measure of distance – 6ft (1.82m).
Fessenden equipment	A somewhat primitive device enabling submarines to communicate underwater using morse code. A steel plate was affixed via a tightly coiled spring to the casing of the submarine. When the telegraphist pressed his morse code keys, an electric current caused the plate to vibrate, thus making the transmission audible to other vessels – including the enemy…
Fliege (fly)	Replaced *Naxos* radar detection sets in April 1944. The *Fliege* system covered a wavelength between 8 and 20cm. A cross fertilisation between FuMB *Mucke* (gnat) and *Fliege* was known as *Tunis* or FuMB 26. This arrangement became standard U-boat radar detection equipment in the last two years of the war.
Fore-ends	The section of a submarine forward of the conning tower and control room. The fore-ends contained the tubes and the torpedo stowage chamber. It was also home to the junior rates.
Foxer	Anti-acoustic torpedo gear used by the Allies to combat the *Gnat*.
Freeboard	The distance between the waterline and freeboard-deck/gunwale of a boat or ship.
Fuel/Cap	Fuel Capacity.
Funkpeilrahmen	The circular loop found on the conning tower of U-boats primarily used for taking directional bearings but also for receiving *Goliath* VLF transmissions. This D/F loop was used to receive medium-wave transmissions and to determine the direction of their origins. This loop reinforced the powerful Telefunken E381 'S' all-band receiver. Local communication between U-boats was carried out on the medium-range band. When not in use the loop retracted into a convenient slot built into the conning tower faring.
GHG	*Gruppenhorchgerat* or 'Group Listening Device' was a fixed hydrophone array arranged in the form of twenty-four (earlier U-boats carried eleven) sound heads on each side of the forward dive planes. Direction finding worked best when the target was beam-on to the U-boat. The more accurate *KDB* was introduced to compensate for the known shortcomings of the *GHG* system. *GHG* sound heads were found to be highly vulnerable to damage during a depth charge attack. A later device known as *Balkon Gerat*

was a circular fitting edged with twenty-four sound heads, welded into the extreme bow of the boat. Sound sources could be determined with remarkable accuracy over a wide arc using this device.

GL u. Co.   Electric motor manufactured by Garbe, Lohmeyer & Co.

GSR   Group Search Receiver for detecting radar transmissions. British term for FuMo radar fitted in U-boats.

GW   Germaniawerft.

Gamma patrol   A/S sweep routinely carried out by Escort Groups.

General Service   Submariners term for the surface navy.

Gnat   Allied term for the German T5/T5a acoustic torpedo or *Zaunkonig* (wren because the torpedo 'sang' as it sped towards its target – usually a warship pursuing at high speed). The *Zaunkonig*, introduced in the autumn of 1943, tended to be loaded into the stern tube for obvious reasons. A cornered U-boat was a dangerous beast. The torpedo was designed to run a straight course for 400m, thereafter it would lock on to the loudest screw noise, invariably a warship closing at high speed. Just in case, U-boat commanders were recommended to dive 60ft then adopt silent routine. The development of the *Zaunkonig* may be a reason why quarter was rarely shown in the closing stages of the undersea war. In time Allied warship commanders countered the Gnat threat by streaming Foxer and mounting attacks at slow speed.

Goliath   German scientists discovered that VLF (very low frequency) transmissions could be received by a dived U-boat. Messages sent by the massive *Goliath* transmitter built at Kalbe were capable of being received by the U-boats Telefunken all-band receiver. Crews described these messages as having been 'sent by Goliath'.

HA   Howitzer. The British armed larger decoy vessels with two versions of the 7.5in gun: the smooth-bore version known as a 'bomb thrower' and the rifled bore version. The latter was particularly useful because it was capable of firing a round that could travel 20ft under the water before exploding. Alternatively the marque could fire a large, penetrating projectile at a range of 300 yards.

HE   Hydrophone effect – the sound of a propeller cutting through water as detected by the hydrophone operator. Fixed shore-based hydrophones designed to monitor minefields were first developed in 1916, Portland being the *alma mater* of hydrophone development. Ship-borne hydrophones were introduced in 1915 – the PGS or portable general service hydrophone. The PGS was suspended by a crane over the side of a vessel to a depth of 30ft. The PGS could only be used if the ship's machinery was shut down, otherwise the operator could not distinguish between the sound of intruder HE and the ship's own background noise. The hydrophone operator rotated a wheel until the sound of intruder screws was heard with equal strength in both ears then the bearing was read off the dial attached to the wheel and plotted. A problem arose with the '180° error', in other words the operator was unable to determine from which side of the head the noise was coming. The mark 1 and mark 2 portable directional hydrophone (PDH) was introduced in 1917 and largely removed the 180° error. In addition it was possible to use the set with the vessel travelling at low speed.

Passive ASDIC transmissions largely fulfilled the same functions during the Second World War.

HF/DF   High-frequency direction finding. U-boats habitually made wireless transmissions when sighting or shadowing convoys, reporting weather conditions etc. In so doing, the Germans took a calculated risk. They realised that Allied shore stations would detect these transmissions and that just two shore stations taking cross bearings were capable of locating a U-boat. The dominant assumption in Kriegsmarine circles was that these 'fixes' were inaccurate. By late 1942 the Allies had produced a high-frequency ship-borne direction finder (HF/DF or 'huff duff'). By taking bearings via triangulation, U-boats could be located with great accuracy. In short, any U-boat transmitting near an Allied convoy could be 'fixed' in more ways than one. Indeed Staff Kapitan Hans Meckel (the staff officer responsible for U-boat signals) warned German intelligence late in 1942 that the Allies had such a device in their armoury, however no action was taken on his report.

HMCS	His Majesty's Canadian Ship.
HMT	His Majesty's Armed Trawler.
HSD	Higher submarine detector – an operative's role, not a machine.
HTP	High Test Peroxide.
Handelskrieg	The concept of war on merchant ships.
Hawser	Steel cable.
Heads	Toilet (RN).
Hedgehog	The A/S Experimental Establishment at Portland had long given consideration to attacking a submerged submarine by means of charges thrown ahead of the ship (*see* Evasion techniques). The 'blind time' between losing ASDIC contact, the charges sinking to firing depth and the ultimate explosion, was appreciated by both the British and their German U-boat opponents alike. In February 1942 Hedgehog – an ahead thrown contact weapon was developed in earnest. British warships were equipped with two Hedgehog mortar guns. Hedgehog had a sinking rate of 42ft per second which cut down significantly on the 'blind time' associated with depth charge attacks. Hedgehog projectiles were fired fixed elevation, twenty-four spigot mortars, possessing an average range of 275 yards. The missiles produced a 'Star of David' pattern ahead of the attacking ship. The fuse was armed after travelling 10ft through the water at high speed. A Hedgehog attack was normally carried out with the hunting vessel steaming slowly in such a way that the target bore straight ahead. The hunter would fire, sometimes automatically, at the moment the correct range was reached. Hedgehog was not considered to be effective against deep targets.
Hohentwiel	See *FuMo*.
KDB	*Kristalldrehbasis Gerat* – Rotating 'T'-shaped hydrophone mechanism found just after the foremost bollards on the bow casing of a U-boat. *KDB* produced far superior direction-finding bearings than *GHG*, particularly when the quarry was off the bows. However the operation of KDB required the U-boat to travel at low speeds.
KDM	*Kaiserliche Deutsche Marine*.
KTB	*Kriegstagebuch* – German war diary or boat/ship's log.
LB	Length/Beam/Draught.
LBDH	Length/Beam/Draught/Height.
LuT	*Lagenunabhängiger Torpedo* – 'bearing independent torpedo'. Armed with a 280 kilo warhead, the torpedo was designed to run into a convoy at 90°, prior to following a ladder like course. This course would be followed until the torpedo struck home.
Leigh Light	An 80 million candlepower light fitted in British coastal command aircraft. The Light was used to illuminate a surfaced U-boat or a *schnorchel*.

Leitmotif   Recurring theme.

Long haul route   *Nordweg* – the route north around Scotland, sometimes via the Fair Isle gap but the safer route was north of the Shetlands. This route made for longer travelling time but the route was far safer that the shorter but infinitely more dangerous run through the Channel.

m   Metre.

MAD   Magnetic airborne detector. The presence of a U-boat caused variations to the earth's magnetic field. MAD equipped aircraft flying at 100ft could detect a submarine up to 300ft below the surface. It was in effect a flying indicator loop. MAD was installed in Liberators, Catalinas and Short Sunderlands. In tracking a submerged U-boat the MAD aircraft flew in circles on each side of the probable course of the submarine, dropping a marker during each circle. Towards the completion of the fourth circle, the aircraft would automatically (or manually) release a 'retro bomb' rather like a rocket-propelled Hedgehog.

MAN   Diesel engines manufactured by Maschinefabrik-Augsburg-Nürnberg

MiD   Mentioned in Despatches.

ML   Motor launch.

Mm   Millimetre.

Mowt   Ministry of War Transport.

Magnetometer   an instrument for measuring the magnitude and direction of a magnetic field and an instrument used for finding metal/wreckage underwater by means of a electronic 'fish' towed behind a boat/ship.

Mines   (First World War) – Britain had prepared for a war against surface ships rather than submarines. At the outset of the First World War British mines were deficient in terms of both their firing and mooring devices, both the 'service mine' and the Elia design being unfit for purpose. On 2 October 1914 the British laid an anti-submarine minefield across the Dover/Calais line of the English Channel. On 4 February 1915, following the first phase of unrestricted submarine warfare, this field was augmented by a second stretching between Dunkirk and Elbow Bay, Broadstairs.

Despite an awareness of the poor quality of British mines, the KDM responded by fitting U-boats with hydroplane guards, jumping wire and net cutters.

In 1917 scientists working at HMS *Vernon* were able to study examples of the German 'E' mine. The result was the British 'H2' mine introduced in November. In fact the British had been sowing significant deep coastal minefields since May 1917. The East Anglian coast was protected by a barrage of 416 mines laid north of the Outer Gabbard, with a further field of 419 mines between the Galloper and the Gabbard. The east coast protective barrage was gradually extended northwards; a field of 486 mines blocked the Humber. Additional large minefields protected Robin Hood's Bay and Scarborough.

Eight thousand and nine mines were sown on the south coast alone. Large, deep minefields were laid at locations where U-boats were known to attack. Between June and November 1917 the minelayers *Wahine* and *Angora* laid 510 mines off Portsmouth, 520 off Portland, 780 off Beachy Head, 300 off the Lizard, 340 in Mounts Bay, with a further 680 off Plymouth and Prawle Point. In early 1918 sophisticated controlled minefields were laid off Dungeness, Folkestone, Start Point, Harwich, Burnham on

Crouch, Sunderland, the Tyne and Blyth. The Scottish bases were protected by controlled minefields at Broughty Ferry, Cromarty, Hoxa, Scapa and no fewer than four in the Forth. The story of the Folkestone-Griz Nez Barrage is told in vol.1, the Northern and North Channel barrage is described in vol.4.

Mucke

Gnat or Fu Mb 25 radar detector set – not to be confused with the Gnat torpedo.

Naxos

German radar detector introduced from November 1943 to guard against aircraft equipped with the ASV III radar introduced by the Allies with its 9.7cm wavelength. *Naxos* aka *Timor* was capable of operating on a handy 8-12cm wavelength.

Nauen

Code name for one of the slave transmitters used by the *Elektra-Sonne system*.

Nautical mile

Approximately 6,076ft or 1,851.96m.

Net Barrage

From the outbreak of hostilities in 1914 until mid-1917 British anti-submarine defence largely revolved around net barrages of one sort or another. British experimentation concerning the effi-cancy of mine barrages had been cut short by the 1904 *A1* disaster, consequently, defences were ill prepared. First of all an abortive attempt was made to block Folkestone and the Griz Nez sector of the Channel using a fixed defence in the form of a heavy net boom. The scheme was cancelled in May 1915 and replaced by a less ambitious plan to place a net boom across the Downs, which was completed in April 1915. The British turned to indicator nets. Each heavy net panel was fitted with a buoy, designed to indicate if the net had been fouled by a U-boat. Net panels of lengths vary-ing from 30 to 120ft were suspended from kapok-filled buoys. The indicator net defences laid across the Channel and the Irish Sea between 1914 and 1916 looked convincing on charts but in reality the nets were too heavy. The buoys became waterlogged and the nets harmlessly sank to the bottom.

In February 1915, in response to the first phase of unrestricted submarine warfare, the first anchored indicator net boom was run out between the North Goodwin Sands to Dunkirk. A second fixed barrier stretched from the Kentish Knock to the North Goodwin Lightship and a third blocked the mouth of the Thames. In the one instance when the net proved its worth, *U 8* was detected while attempting to pass through the Channel-anchored indicator net boom. The boat fouled the net and destroyer patrols correctly read the signs (vol.1). Not only did the nets have a tendency to sink, attempts to mine the approaches to the anchored net boom were undone by the Channel currents sweeping the mines into the nets. Moreover as the anchored indicator nets projected above the sur-face, U-boat *obersteurrmen* habitually used them as navigational aids. The favoured route of crossing these barriers was simply to wait until the combination of high tide and Channel current simply swept the surfaced U-boat across.

Following the German declaration of unrestricted submarine warfare, trawlers of the Auxiliary Patrol were handed the thankless task of towing drift nets in the hope of snaring the odd U-boat in the Channel and in the Irish Sea. Once encountered, the U-boats merely dived beneath them. An interesting variation on the drift net defence was improvised in the crucial North Channel (vol. 4) between Kintyre and the Antrim coast. It was planned that any U-boat seeking to run the North Channel and attack Liverpool/ Glasgow shipping routes would be forced to remain dived for 30 miles. Batteries would thus be exhausted. The boat would surface to recharge batteries in a sector where an armed patrol was waiting to pounce. This device was no more successful than the boom defence had been, leading to its abandonment at the end of 1915.

In late 1915 the British experimented with EC nets fitted with sea mines. In the autumn of 1916 they completed a continuous 28-mile-long EC net barrage between Dunkirk and the Goodwin Sands. For the sake of preserving merchant shipping, the buoys marking the net were required to be lit, once again providing the KDM boats with a most useful navigational aid. The lightweight nets collapsed or became torn. Sometimes unstable mines exploded while being handled by Auxiliary Patrol crews. The electrical circuits within the mines shorted, mines detonated by unfortunate whales and dolphins were not replaced. The nets never quite reached the sea bed, nor were they strong enough to withstand the cutters fitted to U-boat bows. The KDM quickly assembled a chart of safe routes under and over the Dunkirk/Goodwin barrage.

In retrospect it can be seen that during this early phase of the First World War, reliance upon net-based defences was futile, however it is interesting that Admiralty later returned to the fixed net deterrent in late 1917 as the surviving Nab Tower demonstrates. Admiralty had faced a sharp learning curve but valuable lessons had been learned and they would be put to good effect in the last two years of the war. It should also be noted that *Korvettenkapitan* Bauer overestimated the value of explosive net defences, a factor that caused him to (temporarily) bar his U-boats from using the Channel as a transit route on 12 April 1915, ordering his boats to use the *Nordweg* instead.

Nordweg	The outward route from the German North Sea coast around the northern coast of Britain, then travelling southwards off the west coast of Ireland. The English and Bristol Channels could be thus reached via a far safer route than running the Folkestone-Griz Nez mine barrage (*see* vol. 1).
OOW	Officer-of-the-Watch.
Op/R	Operational Range.
Observant	The standard RN anti-submarine hunting technique. The hunting vessel adopts a 'square' course around a suspect contact. Each straight length is systematically lengthened on each run as the ship describes a series of concentric squares. This was sometimes referred to as 'boxing'. Once ASDIC contact was re-established, one warship would slow down, turning bow-on to the contact, the crew listening intently on hydrophones. Meanwhile the remaining warships manoeuvred to adopt an attacking course. News of the contact was transmitted to other EG groups (as the BdU Diary testifies such messages were often detected by other German units too) who would rapidly close off potential escape routes.
'Oggin'	RN slang for sea.
PS	*Pferdestärke*, German standard for horsepower.
Pairs	Literally 'Lords' – German slang for U-boat seamen (*matrosen*) generally found in the *Bugtorpedoraum* or colloquially '*Bugraum*'.
Pier Head Jump	British submarine flotillas maintained pools of specialist officers and ratings. Should a regular crew member 'go adrift' or fall sick, a member of the 'spare crew' would be given a last minute 'pier head jump' to take his place.
Pressure hull	The vital inner protective membrane of a submarine. A submarine with a leaking pressure hull was in dire straits.

Props   Propellers.

'Q' Ships   Armed vessels, often crewed by RNR personnel, disguised as
                     merchantmen. The U-boat campaign of the First World War has
                     been divided into four phases:

1) 4 August 1914–3 February 1915 – the purely military phase,
2) 4 February 1915–18 September 1915 – the first phase of unrestricted submarine warfare,
3) 19 September 1915–30 January 1917 – the so called 'lost
   opportunity' phase,
4) 31 January 1917–11 November 1918 – the second phase of
   unrestricted submarine warfare.

This time structure is important because the use of decoys was
only viable until February 1917 when the KDM finally took the
muzzles off and U-boats commenced to attack merchants without
warning, using torpedoes launched from periscope depth. From
this point onwards the ratio of decoys lost to U-boats destroyed
was five to one against.

The first decoy experiment was the 'C' Class submarine/trawler
combination which achieved mixed success in 1915. The experiment ended when a trawler inadvertently dragged a submarine
through a minefield (*see* vols 1 and 4). The destruction of HMS
PRIZE and her heroic crew (*see* vol. 2) indicates that submarine/
Q-ship combinations were organised in the western approaches
during the summer of 1917 at least.

RDF   Radio direction finding – better known as Radar. Type 286 M sets
                     were installed in British warships as early as 1941, having previ-
                     ously been used in aircraft. The sets were introduced to submarines
                     in 1942–1943. The early British sets transmitted at 214 megaherz
                     or megacycles. At this frequency the transmit/receive ariel was a
                     cumbersome affair which had to be trained by hand. Not only was
                     there a 'blind' area astern, for instance a target travelling across the
                     stern would involve frantic rotation to recapture it, but coastlines
                     appeared as arcs rather than as detailed profiles. Small targets did not
                     even register. Centrimetric radar sets known as SJ were gradually
                     introduced in Allied ships from 1943 onwards. Power driven, they
                     gave an all-round scan and produced superior target definition.

Radar operatives, often known as 'wireless mechanics', were
highly regarded. Only 50 per cent of entrants passed the initial
exams. Training took place at Holyhead, Adrossan, Campbeltown
and Glasgow. Submarines temporarily stationed in Loch Foyle
performed the role of intruder U-boats for the radar ops to
practise upon.

RNR   Royal Naval Reserve. War diluted the resources of the Royal Navy.
                     The RN had long relied on RNR as a source of personnel in time
                     of war, particularly experienced officers. Many merchant navy
                     officers had served one year in the RN in peacetime and were
                     granted an RNR commission in wartime. Prior to the Second
                     World War, RNR officers were paid an annual retainer of £25
                     per year. Warships battled with the sea far more often than they
                     confronted U-boats. The skills of RNR personnel were essential.

RNVR   Royal Naval Volunteer Reserve. This force consisted mainly of
                     younger men with shore-based professions but with a love of
                     the sea. A significant percentage were experienced yachtsmen.
                     Many of the ratings were highly educated potential officers and

a commission within the RNVR was highly prized. During the First World War it was said that RNR personnel were sailors trying to become gentlemen and that RNVRs were gentlemen trying to become officers. What is certain is that in the last two years of the Second World War, the RNVR produced most of the junior officers who were required to specialise in gunnery, navigation, communications and radar. By 1943 RNVR officers began to be awarded their own commands as the escort forces expanded.

Recorder trace   *See* ASDIC.

'Room 40'   A top secret department within Admiralty set up during the First World War under electronics expert Sir Alfred Ewing (responsibility later passed to Cdr M. James of British Naval Intelligence). The staff of Room 40 comprised of naval technology experts and senior academics. The Naval Intelligence Division established a series of wireless direction finding stations along the British coast, designed to take cross bearings on W/T transmissions from both merchants and U-boats. Lt Hope ran the deciphering section within Room 40. W/T traffic in the Heligoland Bight was particularly useful as the deciphering team could tell very quickly when the High Seas Fleet had put out from the Jade basin due to the warnings given out to civilian maritime traffic, ordering them to keep away. Room 40 was thus able to visualise enemy movements at any given time. British movements preceding the Hartlepool Raid, encounters at Dogger Bank in 1914 and indeed Jutland in 1916 were both pre-empted by Room 40 intelligence gathering. As files in the National Archive demonstrate, Lt Tiark of Room 40 had a very accurate picture of where Bauer's U-boat flotillas were at any given time. Tiark routinely tracked U-boats from departure to return and could anticipate a likely operational zone. The Germans responded by changing cypher codes and signals on a regular basis but by studying the wavelengths, the length of signals and the DF bearing of the senders, Hope and his people were able to send a steady and accurate flow of intelligence to C-in-C Grand Fleet and the Operations Division of Admiralty.

Runddipol   Permanent radar detector antenna used by the *Wanz* radar detector sets installed in U-boats after 1943. The Kriegsmarine feared that the Allies were able to home in on radiation emissions; *Wanz* was believed to radiate less than other versions.

S/Sp   Surface Speed.

SBT   Submarine Bubble Target – the British term for *Bold*.

SM U-boat   *Seiner Majestät U-Boot* (His Majesty's Submarine).

SNO   Senior Naval Officer (RN).

SS   Steam ship.

SSW   Electric motor manufactured by Siemens-Schuckert-Werke.

Sub/R   Submerged Range.

Salvage blow   Valve fitted to submarines specifically to enable air to be blown in to the tanks from an outside source and so assist in salvaging the boat. Salvage blow valves were removed in the 1930s. Thereafter the term referred to an emergency operation carried out by a stricken submarine to force air from its tanks with a view to powering it back to the surface.

Schnorchel   A tube device enabling the operation of a dived submarine powered by a fuel-powered engine, using air supplied from the surface. This Dutch design was further developed by the Germans and came into service in February 1944. *Schnorchel*-equipped boats could travel at speeds of up to 8k. Higher speeds were often achieved but a dangerous wake (accompanied by unwelcome vibrations) often resulted. The standard procedure was to drive the boat on one diesel engine running at 3-4k, while the other was used to power the batteries. Hydrophone checks were made every 20 minutes or so. Three hours of *schnorchelling* could charge the batteries of a Type VII U-boat for a whole day.

Schnorchelling removed the imperative to surface and charge batteries a night, a necessity that had dominated submarine operation up to this point. This was a vital capability in view of the enemy-dominated waters these U-boats were operating in post 'D-Day'. Two types of *schnorchel* heads were fitted, the ball-float type or *kugelschwimmer* and the rarer cylindrical ring float or *ringschwimmer*. This is no mere technical detail, the *schnorchel* head provides a useful means of identifying wrecks. A *schnorchelling* school was established in Horten, Norway to train crews in the handling of this useful device. The snort mast was designed to work with the exhaust mast half a metre underwater. If this depth increased or trim was lost, there was every possibility that the counter pressure would force the diesels to discharge exhaust gases, including carbon monoxide, back into the boat. The head of the snort was often covered with an anti-radar coating known as *Tarnmatte*. This coating, a combination of synthetic rubber and iron oxide powder, was capable of masking the presence of a raised snort head from the Allied H2S 10cm aircraft radar.

Seemannstod	Literally seaman's death – the ultimate fate of the loyal sailor. Romanticised heroic death in battle with more than a flavour of Wagnerian *Gotterdamerung*.
SM	First World War U-boats (*Seiner Majestät U-Boot* or His Majesty's Submarine).
S/M	Submarine.
Sonar buoy	A passive ASDIC device embedded in a buoy dropped by aircraft. When the buoy hit the water, the hydrophone would deploy and the ASDIC would transmit any U-boat sounds picked up by the hydrophone back to the aircraft.
Spare Crew	British submarine flotillas maintained a pool of specialist personnel, for example there were spare crew ERAs, spare crew torpedomen and spare crew officers. Should any crew man fail to turn up on patrol, an appropriate member of the spare crew pool would be given a 'pier head jump' and ordered to join the submarine at harbour stations.
Spartacists	Leftist subversives who attempted to infiltrate German institutions such as the KDM with a view to fomenting revolution in 1918. It was commonly believed that communist-inspired *maschinisten* were at the heart of the famous fleet mutiny.
Squid	Hunting and destroying U-boats became increasingly mechanised by the closing stages of the Second World War. From August 1944 Hedgehog firing mechanisms were connected to the ASDIC gear enabling the depth to be pre-set at the last possible moment before discharge. In fact the firing process became increasingly automatic. The result was the Squid system. Squid was fitted to new-build ships. The weapon consisted of two three-barrelled mortars fitted into a frame which could be rotated through 90° for loading (which was automatic). A Star of David pattern resulted.

The time-fuse gave detonation settings from 20-900ft. Twin Squid ripple fired from the starboard mounting, first to explode at 50ft below the target simultaneous with the port mounting fired

50ft above. Each pattern was triangular, with the outboard side of the triangle fore and aft, the total pattern being the Star of David. HMS *Loch Killin* is credited with one of the earliest Squid 'kills' using this system in 1944. Squid was arguably the deadliest A/S weapon in the armoury.

Stick Slang for periscope, both RN and German.

Subsmash post 1932 the Admiralty code used to alert the fleet that a British submarine was missing.

Tadpole German nickname for UB1 Class.

Tauchretter *See Drager.*

Thetis A radar decoy buoy carried by later U-boats. The Thetis 2c buoy was carried in three pieces in the U-boat fore ends for later assembly on deck. A series of antennae radiated from the assembled buoy, which were capable of foiling the metric frequency of aircraft borne ASV radar but not the more sophisticated H2s.

Trim If a submarine was in perfect longitudinal and lateral balance it was said to be 'in trim'. Obviously trim changed as torpedoes were fired, stores were loaded or even when personnel moved around the boat. A badly trimmed boat might show its periscope or even its stern to an enemy. Maintenance of trim was of crucial importance and (RN) was the responsibility of the First Lieutenant and the Stoker PO. Using graphs and tables these men calculated the amount of water to be admitted or expelled from the tanks in order to maintain correct trim.

Trimmed down State in which a submarine's tanks were flooded until a state of neutral buoyancy was reached. The advantages of a low profile could be combined with the obvious ones of diesel propulsion. Only the conning tower would show above the surface, thus hiding the submarine from view. However the submarine was vulnerable should it suddenly enter a patch of denser water.

Trot Manoeuvre carried out by RN submarine usually in harbour, when coming alongside or leaving for patrol or exercise.

Tube space As the name suggests, the torpedo room.

Turm Conning tower of U-boat. One important distinction between the British submarine and the U-boat was that a German commander conventionally made a dived attack from the cramped chamber within the conning tower of his boat. British submarine skippers preferred to make their torpedo attacks from the control room.

The design of German conning towers evolved between 1939 and 1945 from the plain cylindrical *Turm 0* to the elaborate *Turm 4* with its dual flak gun platforms known to crews as the *wintergarten*.

Tunis The *Tunis* system of radar detection (a combination of FuMB 24 *Fliege* and FuMB 25 *Mucke*) required two antennae added to the conning tower, firstly a forward-facing *Mucke* cone and secondly the aft-facing parabolic antenna of the *Fliege* system. By late 1944 the bridge of a U-boat was becoming quite crowded with gadgets.

Twill Trunk The favoured British (and German) submarine escape method during the Second World War. Following the Naismith committee recommendations in 1939, escape chambers were removed from submarines as it was felt that their claustrophobic nature had hindered the *Thetis*'s escape.

Instead of a dedicated escape chamber, new submarines were fitted with a Twill Trunk mechanism under designated escape hatches. The Twill Trunk was a rubberised cotton concertina, strengthened with metal hoops. When stored, the Trunk was designed to collapse under the hatch. When required the Trunk could be extended and tethered to the floor of the chamber. In the highest part of the chamber the flood valve was fitted, backed up by a flap valve. These were used to flood the chamber once the skirt was in place and securely tethered. Water entered the chamber via a bore pipe near the floor, thus ensuring that the point of ingress would never be higher than the hatch, so enabling the formation of an air-lock. A guage was fitted near the hatch giving pressure reading both inside and without the submarine. Once pressure had equalised, the escape hatch could be opened. The resultant air lock formed within the Twill Trunk enabled a trapped crew to escape to the surface. This method was successfully used by the crews of *Umpire* and *Truculent* (vol.1) but sadly failed the crew of *Untamed* (vol.4).

U/Dt	Underwater Displacement.
U/Power	Underwater Power.
U-boat	*Unterseeboot.*
Uzo	*Uberwasserzieloptik* – the U-boat torpedo aiming device mounted on front of the conning tower.
W/T	Wireless transmission.
Wabo / Wasserbomb	German term for depth charger.
Wanz	German radar detector set replacement for *Metox*. *Wanz* was considered to be more sensitive than *Metox*. Better still, *Wanz* introduced automatic frequency search but manual fine tuning was possible. The *Wanz* set required a permanent antenna known as the *Runddipol*.
Wintergarten	By mid-1944 most Type VII U-boats were armed with one big 3.7cm AA gun on the lower platform and twin C/38 guns mounted on the upper platform. Heavy armour was applied, ammunition lockers and shelters were installed and the resulting structure reminded some sailors of a green house, hence the name of *wintergarten* for the dual flak platform. In late 1944 this mode was replaced by either a 1–2cm quadruple 38/43U with armoured shield or a 1–3cm twin M42 gun.
Zentrale	German term for the central compartment known as the control room in an Allied submarine.

CHAPTER ONE

THE SOUTH COAST

AN INTRODUCTION

Encompassing Sussex, Hampshire, the Solent, Isle of Wight and Dorset, this region of rolling down-land and sheltered waters has witnessed tides of armies ebb and flow. Throughout the centuries it has played a pivotal role in the defence of Britain. As Britain's premier passenger port, Southampton has provided this coast with a maritime legacy second to none. As if this was not riches enough, we also discover Portsmouth, home of the Royal Navy. Across the harbour, at Gosport, lies Fort Blockhouse, the *alma mater* of the Royal Navy Submarine Service. For both wars, enemy and defender alike appreciated that a successful attack in these waters would, in terms of both *materiel* and morale, constitute a blow struck at the very heart of British naval supremacy.

In the First World War, the U-boats quickly made their presence known, particularly against the vital coal trade (the French economy demanded two million tons of British coal per month). Here the authorities acted decisively and by February 1917 'controlled sailings' were introduced from Weymouth to Cherbourg and Le Havre, with impressive results in reducing U-boat strikes. However the problem could not be totally eradicated. Enterprising U-boat skippers such as Lohs and Stier struck against convoy stragglers or ships sailing independently. As elsewhere, navigational aids on the busy shipping lanes such as the Owers light vessel provided favourite ambush locations. The most spectacular U-boat strike in this sector occurred off Portland on New Year's Day 1915 when *U 24* succeeded in sinking the battleship HMS *Formidable* with the loss of 547 lives.

Anti-submarine minefields offered the most pragmatic solution to the U-boat problem. Between June and November 1917, deep protective minefields were laid off Portland (520 mines) and Portsmouth (510 mines). A more innovative defensive approach was adopted to counter the submarine menace off the key Spithead Roads. Admiralty decided to extend the Folkestone-Griz Nez mine barrage (*see* vol. 1) westwards by means of a curtain of mined boom nets designed to be suspended from six massive lattice steel towers. As initially conceived, 'Project MN' was to extend across the Channel to the French coast. The war ended before this barrier was completed but the surviving Nab tower provides some idea of this ambitious scheme.

A mine destroyed the dashing Reinhold Saltzwedel's *UB 81*. One of the most nerve-shredding escapes in submarine history followed, yet in the harrowing circumstances of Saltzwedel's death, some see evidence of a British atrocity. There was courage as well as controversy. Off this coast, *UB 37* fought an epic duel to the death with the Q-ship HMS *Penshurst*. Here one of the smallest of submarines, *C15*, succeeded in torpedoing the minelayer *UC 65*. A short distance westwards, the British submarine *D4* similarly disposed of *UB 72*.

The Second World War witnessed a variety of convoys picking their way through the Channel and Solent. CW/CE convoys worked between Southend and the Bristol Channel. Atlantic-bound 'Ocean convoys' (OA, OB, OG ON) assembled at Southend, prior to snaking their way slowly westwards along the Channel. WP/PW convoys steamed between the Bristol Channel and Portsmouth. U-boats merely added to the constant menace posed by air and 'E' boat attack. To this day, the Spithead Roads is littered with concrete obstructions, laid to deter marauding U-boats from 'bottoming out' prior to launching an attack. They did not always succeed. Imagine the sight of a U-boat bumping along the bottom with its conning tower fully exposed above the water, surrounded by anchored ships, crammed with military personnel. This actually happened one July evening in 1944 when *U 763* inadvertently strayed into the Spithead Roads. With the trapped U-boat dodging one vessel after another, frantically seeking deeper water, not one person raised the alarm. Eventually *U 763* was able to slip away unchallenged in an incident that could only have emboldened Kriegsmarine planners. Following D-Day, Portsmouth and Southampton became the focus of the mammoth logisti-

Stern compartment of a Type VIIC/41 Kriegsmarine U-boat, showing the electric motors and aft torpedo tube. (Courtesy Kevin Belcher of Swindon: photo taken inside the preserved Second World War U-boat *U 995* at the Marine Memorial (Marine-Ehrenmal) located near Laboe, Germany.

cal supply operation known as 'Operation Neptune'. The tenuous nature of these supply lines offered a major opportunity for the U-boats as Dönitz now prepared to reverse his earlier policy of avoiding the Channel (*see* vol. 1). The submarines destined to bear the brunt of this brief, disastrous campaign were snort-equipped Type VIIC U-boats. As soon as the presence of an invasion fleet was confirmed, the German plan called for every available *Landwirt* boat to sail with dispatch for the Channel ('Group Landwirt' would later be renamed 'Group West'). BdU learned of the invasion early on 6 June:

> 0305hrs report from I. German naval Staff. Large numbers of parachute troops and freight carrying gliders landed west of Trouville and in western Normandy … Therefore at 0310hrs. telephoned F.O.

Submarines West ordering immediate readiness of Group 'Landwirt'. 0532hrs the five schnorchel boats freshly arrived in Atlantic [U 767 −988 −719 −1191 −671] to make for Western France at maximum continuous speed, submerged during day. In the meanwhile news of enemy landing in Seine Bay [Normandy] was broadcast on all frequencies to boats at sea. 0531hrs. Cypher according to key-word order 'Venus' came into force on program Diana [*Landwirt* boats]. Sailing orders are still withheld for boats of Group 'Landwirt' without schnorchel, this time is not being lost as boats will not be ready to put to sea until midday.

BDU DIARY 6 JUNE 1944

British naval intelligence intercepted this somewhat Wagnerian BdU radio message, broadcast to U-boat crews on 9 June 1944:

> Attack the invasion fleet without consideration for anything else whatsoever. Each enemy vessel … is a target demanding maximum U-boat attack. It is to be destroyed even at risk of losing your own U-boat. When it is a matter of destroying the enemy invasion fleets, we must have no regard for shallow water or minefields… the U-boat which cripples the enemy during his landing has fulfilled its supreme task and has justified its existence even if it accomplishes nothing further…

Ranged against the U-boats, in an arc running from Southern Ireland to Ushant, were disposed the ten hunter killer groups of the Royal Navy, arrayed in inner and outer lines of defence. Groups 1, 2, 3, 5, 14 and 15 each consisted of ten British destroyers. The Canadian groups, 11 and 12, were also comprised of destroyers, while nos 6 and 9 were formed from six frigates in each group. These fast, purpose-built anti-submarine groups prowled the Channel with their sole *raison d'etre* being, to hunt any detected U-boat to destruction. And they brought their Hedgehog and Squid mortars with them. Above them flew aircraft from the twenty-five squadrons of 19 Group and US Navy Fleet Air Wing 7. Sea mines completed this defensive ring. Admiralty had responded to the U-boat threat by by laying the 'Brazier' series of deep minefields guarding approaches to Portsmouth and Southampton.

Heavy casualties had been anticipated by German staff and the Royal Navy duly delivered them; U 1191, U 672, U 678, U 212, U 214, U 671 and U 413 were all destroyed during this phase, the Kriegsmarine inflicting only modest damage on the Neptune supply lines. Judging from the unidentified Type V11c wrecks found by Innes McCartney in this sector, it would appear that many more U-boats found their way to Portsmouth roads in the weeks after D-Day than had hitherto been thought. With the passage of so many decades it is very difficult to identify these U-boats using the Lindberg method. The fact that some have been named is due largely to the skill and dedication of three men; Innes McCartney, Dr Axel Niestlé and Bob Coppock of the Royal Naval Historical Branch. Faced with these casualties, Dönitz and his staff made the following telling observation:

> For the submarine men themselves the job of conducting a war for the purpose of tying down the enemy is especially difficult. More so than any other sphere, success, till now, has been the personal reward of the whole crew and has given them the special zest for attack, and vigour and tenaciousness in the teeth of enemy defence. Chances of success are now only slight, and the prospects of not returning from enemy patrol on the other hand very great, in the last few months only 70 per cent of the boats which sailed per month returned from their patrols. That the crews managed at all in this last year of heaviest loss and smallest success to come through untouched in their morale, will to fight and desire for attack is a wonderful proof of courage, a proof of the quality of the human material involved, a reward for the thorough training, and result of the determination of the submarine weapon.

BDU DIARY JUNE 1944 'SUMMARY – GENERAL COURSE OF BATTLE'

Of course Dönitz had no option but to attack the Neptune supply lines. Whether British coastal waters was the most suitable arena for pressing home this attack, is rather more open to question.

The BdU War Diary for the summer of 1944 indicates that the Kriegsmarine greatly underestimated British anti-submarine defences, for example the entry for 16 July states that, '*the route in the north sector of the Channel is better than the south route. Slight anti-submarine activity close to the Isle of Wight. Convoys observed here by their barrage balloons. Use of schnorchel very difficult owing to traffic but in view of the favourable situation close to the Isle of Wight (convoys, little anti-submarine activity), more boats will be directed to this sector.'*

In reality (despite the *U 763* episode) the sea around the Isle of Wight was probably the most guarded stretch of water in the world. The KTBs of surviving U-boats provided more than sufficient evidence to hammer home the point but Dönitz and his staff either would not, or could not, act upon it. The BdU Diary merely bemoans a lack of 'reliable information'. Whatever views they may have held inwardly towards the grotesque regime they served, the morale of the U-boat crews generally held firm. It should never be forgotten that, while they held the moral high ground, the Allies did not have a monopoly of either patriotism or courage.

In the months that followed, the lack of success against the Neptune lines, the St Lo breakout and the weight of casualties forced a change of strategy. On 25 August BdU ordered all U-boats to proceed to Norway as the Biscay ports were no longer tenable against the Allied advance. Dönitz continued to dissipate his U-boat strength against a technologically superior enemy, growing ever more confident, efficient and deadly. EG9 was particularly adept at U-boat hunting. A remarkable (if harrowing) survivor account from this final chapter of the undersea war provides a shuddering insight into the end of *U 1195*. By the end of August BdU turned away from the Channel towards the more promising sea space of the North Channel and the Irish Sea. Courage had not been enough. For Dönitz's young crews, St Catherine's lighthouse on the Isle of Wight had become cockpit, crucible and calvary, all in one.

Of course British submarines were also lost in these waters, notably the historic *Holland 5* and *A1*, the latter falling victim to a collision with a Southampton liner. An element of danger always permeated submarine exercises. All submarine disasters are tragic, but there is something particularly so about the loss of *L24*. The reader should reflect upon the terrific responsibility which burdens the willing shoulders of a submarine skipper. He alone takes the key decisions and, not surprisingly, the 'perisher' is considered to be the most demanding of all military examinations. The success of the

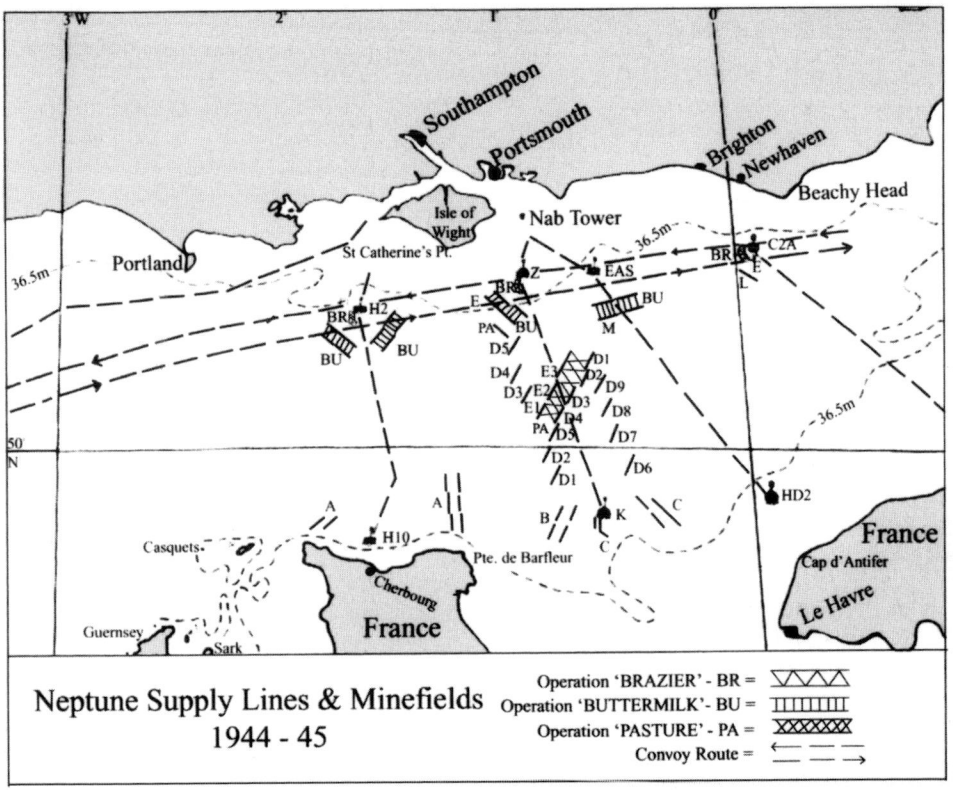

Neptune Supply Lines & Minefields 1944 - 45

Operation 'BRAZIER' - BR =
Operation 'BUTTERMILK'- BU =
Operation 'PASTURE' - PA =
Convoy Route =

mission and the survival of boat and crew depend upon the commanding officer's judgement alone. One miscalculation can bring catastrophe and as the *L24* story warns, even the most experienced and competent of skippers can make mistakes.

M2 started her career as a 'K' boat only to be sacrificed to a combination of service economy and the Washington Naval Treaty. The fitting of a a seaplane hangar and catapult seemed to offer her rebirth as a reconnaissance submarine. Perhaps the enduring mystery of *M2* is not the question over what caused this huge submarine to sink in the course of an exercise, but rather, why was there no evidence of any escape attempts having been made by an experienced crew from a submarine fitted with the latest in DSEA technology? The authors describe how policy change instituted in the aftermath of the *M2* disaster was to govern Admiralty submarine escape policy into the Second World War – and effectively doom the crew of HMS *Thetis* in the process.

Then there is the unutterably sad story of HMS *Swordfish*. For over forty-three years officialdom believed that *Swordfish* and her crew had been lost 'somewhere off Brest'. In reality she lay very much closer to home. The Channel finally unlocked its secret in 1983; *Swordfish* and her crew had been mined off St Catherine's Point on the Isle of Wight.

The Portsmouth naval base has tended to overshadow Portland but the Dorset anchorage deserves a special mention in this account. The Portland anchorage was developed in the mid-nineteenth century to counter the development of Cherbourg. During the First World War, Portland served as both fleet base and as a station for anti-submarine patrols. In the post-war years, HMS *Nettle* (and later HMS *Vulcan*) serviced the RN Periscope School. What is less well known is Portland's link with that device which played a key role in winning the war at sea – ASDIC. Experimentation was carried out in Portland from 1917 under the auspices of HMS *Sarepta*. Meanwhile, a school for hydrophone operators was established around HMS *Gibraltar*. In 1924, following reorganisation ,HMS *Osprey*, the Royal Navy A/S School, was founded at Portland. Apart from training operatives (the course for the much coveted HSD – Higher Submarine Detector status rate was held in Portland) in A/S devices, *Osprey*'s brief was devoted to 'the development of devices to detect, track and kill submarines'. ASDIC (an acronym deriving from the Allied Submarine Detection Investigation Committee) came ino being. The curriculum concentrated upon training surface ship telegraphists in the art of submarine detection, rather than instructing submariners in evasion techniques. Photographs from the 1920s show practice submarines (usually H and L Class) crammed into the destroyer pens. In 1922, *H32* became the first submarine to be fitted with an ASDIC set.

The work carried out at Portland remained, of course, top secret. In 1936 the 6th Submarine Flotilla formed at Portland around the depot ship, HMS *Titania* as the dedicated A/S training unit. The Kriegsmarine would not oblige with the loan of U-boats to practice these techniques upon, so the British 'U' Class of submarine was developed. *Ursula*, *Undine* and *Unity* (see vol. 1) were unofficially referred to as 'the clockwork mice'. The three 'U' Class boats were small, cheap – and totally devoid of armament. The value of the training evolutions was diminished somewhat by the necessity of ending the 'ping running' exercises before darkness fell, not surprising in view of the number of training accidents described in these volumes. In January 1924, the ill-fated *L24* sailed from Portland on her last journey. Later that same year, *K22* misread a light buoy to become hopelessly stranded on the north breakwater. *M2* was attached to the 6th Flotilla at the time of her loss in 1932. A most curious event occurred on 21 July 1937 as the world geared up for war. The British submarine HM S/M *Spearfish* was on exercise with destroyers *Walpole* and *Wolfhound* in British territorial waters off Portland Bill, when a second submarine was detected. Shortly after *Spearfish* surfaced, *U 34* emerged nearby. The crews of both submarines glared at each other as an uncomfortable stand-off developed. As the destroyers approached, *U 34* made off to the eastwards. There is a postscript: on 1 August 1940, HMS/M *Spearfish* was torpedoed and sunk with the loss of all but one of her crew. Her assailant was *U 34*.

The post-war years witnessed the arrival of HMS *Maidstone* and the 7th S/M Flotilla, followed by the 2nd S/M Flotilla in 1946. Torpedo experimentation continued, with tragic results in the case of HM S/M *Sidon*. Like so many submarine stories, it is a tale of heroism and self-sacrifice, only this one took place at a time when submarine disasters were thought to be a thing of the past. The dockyard closed in 1959 but the naval base survived until March 1996. Now the little cemetery below the citadel is the only permanent Royal Naval presence at Portland. Memories and a knot of listed buildings are all that remain of the past glories of Gosport's HMS *Dolphin*, the cradle of the Royal Navy Submarine Service.

Haslar Jetty houses the Royal Navy Submarine Museum, a living memorial to a proud Service that has made a significant contribution to the security of this nation in both peace and war. The centrepiece is the 1947 vintage, HMS *Alliance,* the last remaining Second World War British submarine. Her sleek black streamlined silhouette rears above the yachts in Haslar Creek, an image at once both sinister yet enthralling. It is possible to take a tour in the company of an ex-submariner. Tourists, suitably repelled by the 'hot bunking' method, wonder at the cramped compartments inhabited by her sixty-eight-strong crew but these are luxuriously spacious when compared with conditions endured by submariners in the earlier classes of submarine. Once it is quiet and the last visitor has shuffled off the concrete gangplank, you can almost hear spectral guffaws: 'If you can't take a joke mate, you shouldn't have joined'.

Adjacent to the museum stands the Submarine Memorial, commemorating the 4,334 submariners killed in both world wars. The service suffered a 33 per cent casualty rate in the Second World War and lost a further 739 men in peacetime accidents. Since the memorial was unveiled in 1983, flowers are placed on the anniversary of each submarine's loss. The dignified museum displays add names and faces to the stark statistics. Amid the hardware, the torpedoes, the medals and the Jolly Rogers, we find human pathos in the photographs, the ditty boxes and the last letters home to mum. The highlight for many, the authors concluded, will always be that uncollected bottle of whisky with the faded label, won in a Boxing night pub raffle so many years ago (*see* vol. 1). However, the story of the British Submarine Service began not here, at Haslar Quay but at the other side of the creek in the former Royal Engineers depot occupying the tip of a small peninsula, known as Fort Blockhouse.

Legend has it that general service banished the fledgling Royal Navy Submarine Service, from Portsmouth over to Fareham Creek, out of fear that one of these 'dangerous little craft' might explode and damage anchored warships. What is more certain is that in 1904 the Royal Navy established a 'submarine boat station' on the quay outside Fort Blockhouse, henceforth immortalised as the 'Petrol Quay'. Their Lordships became convinced that submarines offered a better form of harbour defence than mines laid by soldiers. The Royal Engineers moved out and the Submarine Service moved in. A somewhat decrepit accommodation ship, HMS *Dolphin* quickly followed, thus providing the alternative name for Blockhouse (and a constant source of confusion for non-submariners). The Service was designated an independent command on 31 August 1912. For the remainder of the twentieth century, HMS *Dolphin* and Gosport became synonymous with the Royal Navy Submarine Service.

HMS *Dolphin*, petrol quay and boats. (Author's collection)

The little base developed within the embracing fort walls, as the former army buildings were transformed into periscope and torpedo shops, fuel storage, mess halls and accommodation ashore. The 'Periscope School' was founded at Blockhouse in October 1917 (though the Periscope Course, culminating in the 'Perisher', was taught from 1915 under the *aegis* of the 6th Flotilla). At the outbreak of war in 1914, the base housed the 2nd Submarine Flotilla consisting of; *B1, A13, E10, D2, S1, A13* and *A6*. Later in the war, the 6th Submarine Flotilla was formed here. The strength varied from month to month but a pink list snapshot for September 1918 reveals the presence of; *D4, D7, D8, C1, C18, C20, C4, C24, C28* and *C30*.

In the years that followed, the 5th S/M Flotilla, largely concerned with training submariners, moved. Following the introduction of DSEA (*see M2*), the first submarine escape tank was built here in 1933. It was only 15ft deep and could scarcely be said to replicate the realistic conditions of undersea escape. Submarines listed at the outbreak of war, namely; *Oberon, H33, H34, H44, H49, L23, Thames, H43* and *H50*, underline this primary training role. Operational submarines were concentrated here from time to time, notably in the autumn of 1940 when invasion fear was at its height and during the futile 'Ring of Iron' campaign of December 1941 against German capital ships suspected of being on the verge of breaking out of Brest. At this time 'everything that could dive and fire torpedoes' belonging to the 6th, 7th and 9th Flotillas was placed under the control of Captain S/M (5). In recognition of the ever-present danger of air raids, that same month sea training was transferred from Blockhouse to Blyth in Northumberland (*see* vol. 1) but Blockhouse continued as a major administration and specialist training centre throughout the war. The 5th S/M Flotilla remained here until January 1961, thereafter Blockhouse was home to SM 1 until December 1993, when the unit moved to Faslane. By 1997 HMS *Raleigh* had assumed much of the training role and on 30 September 1998, HMS *Dolphin* was finally decommissioned. At the time of writing, the base houses the Defence Medical College but its future is distinctly uncertain. Fort Blockhouse can only be visited by appointment with the Submarine Museum – but it is a visit well worth making.

The base expanded significantly in the decades following the Second World War. Accommodation, mess and office blocks were moved away from the Fort as the base gradually encroached along the neck of the peninsula. These accommodation blocks (named after submarine heroes) and messes date from 1956. The dominating submarine escape tank (SETT) was built in 1953, as a direct result of the Naismith Committee report (*see Thetis*), and the comparatively sedate Atlantis Club has long since taken over from the spit-and-sawdust bar in the (now demolished) Rosario Block, with its memories of Blake's beer and raucous nights spent in the billiard room above. Beyond these post-war buildings, at the end of the spit, the original Fort Blockhouse survives. The historic jetty approach was infilled in 1960. At the same time, a conventional submarine refit facility known as the 'Green Cathedral' was erected on the inner side of the spit, alongside the Petrol Quay. However, sufficient of the old base remains to reward the visitor and virtually every building is listed.

It is possible to mount the ramparts and look out over the infamous 'Blockhouse Corner'. Lest they find their boat aground on the infamous 'Promotion Point', inbound submarine navigators would traditionally memorise the following lines:

First the Nab, then the Warner, Outer Spit, then Blockhouse corner

The actual Fort Blockhouse was originally built in the 1840s. By 1873 it had been taken over by the aforementioned Royal Engineers. The grim utilitarian red brick blocks still cluster around the parade block, their names so evocative of a proud past; Thames Block, the original wardroom, with its panelled mess and seafaring frieze. Here relaxed the British submarine aces of both wars. Vulcan Block, known to inmates, with more than a hint of irony, as the 'grand hotel'. Arrogant Block originally housed ERAs, seamen and stokers; Mercury Block contained the pay office. Alecto Colonnade held the regulating office. However, it should be noted that submariners did not always submit tamely to regulation. At the height of the *Thetis* calamity, a subversive hand was found to have scrawled bitterly obscene comments across the parade ground. For most wartime submariners, the beating heart of the base was the legendary Pactolus Shed, the junior rates mess ('The Stables'). Pactolus Block miraculously survives, tucked in behind the later Onyx Block.

I was dumped in Pactolus Block in early 1940. I was in '32' Mess and each mess had about thirty-five men in, so at a guess up to one thousand or more must have been crammed into that festering hole. This did not include the population of beasties living in the baggage racks above the lockers. Within 24 hours of entering Pactolus Block, I was infested with lice. When you came aboard very late at night and opened the door, the first thing that hit you was the stench and the noise of so many men sweating, scratching, snoring and breaking wind. You could cut the air with a pusser's knife. Then you had to find your hammock in the dark, taking care not to scuff out the chalk marks on the floor, which indicated where the watch keepers were sleeping. It was impossible to find, so it was a case of flop down on the deck as usual. Pactolus Block was a noisome place and its only redeeming aspect was that it made you yearn to be back at sea. Maybe that was the idea.

Frank Palmer

Gus Britton knew the reverse side of Pactolus Block's soul:

…that holy of holies, 'the stables' where thousands of submariners have slept in their hammocks, on tables, on stools, on the deck, have staggered in from runs ashore in Pompey, eaten at wooden tables, written their letters, jumped out of the windows when rounds were piped in the evening as the duty officer, crusher or bootneck approached. Primitive as it was, the stables was our happy home…every brick in the wall holds a story. Countless submariners picked up their steaming bags and strolled through that door, into oblivion.

Perhaps the highlight of any visit is the tiny, evocative Chapel of St Nicholas, high on the South Bastion. It was dedicated in 1917 and has become a shrine. Virtually every object or piece of furniture functions as a memorial (many commemorating people featured in these books). The stained-glass windows dedicated to the crew of HMS *Spearfish* portray haloed saints, only these saints are clad in the muffled garb of the submarine watchkeeper.

If your imagination is sharp enough, at times you can detect an echo from the past – maybe when loitering beneath the massive stones of the Main Gate, strolling along the Petrol Quay or most vividly of all perhaps, at dusk, standing on the ramparts, facing into the Haslar Creek breeze. The water laps beneath you. Dark clouds scurry across the sky. Below the walls, a barrack room door opens and slams with a blink of light and raucous voices sound then laugh then die away. Of course this is just sentimental nonsense. The last boat left years ago. The barracks will inevitably be used for other purposes and soon there will be scarcely a trace to show that submariners were ever there. Perhaps the men of the 'Silent Service' would have had no quarrel with that.

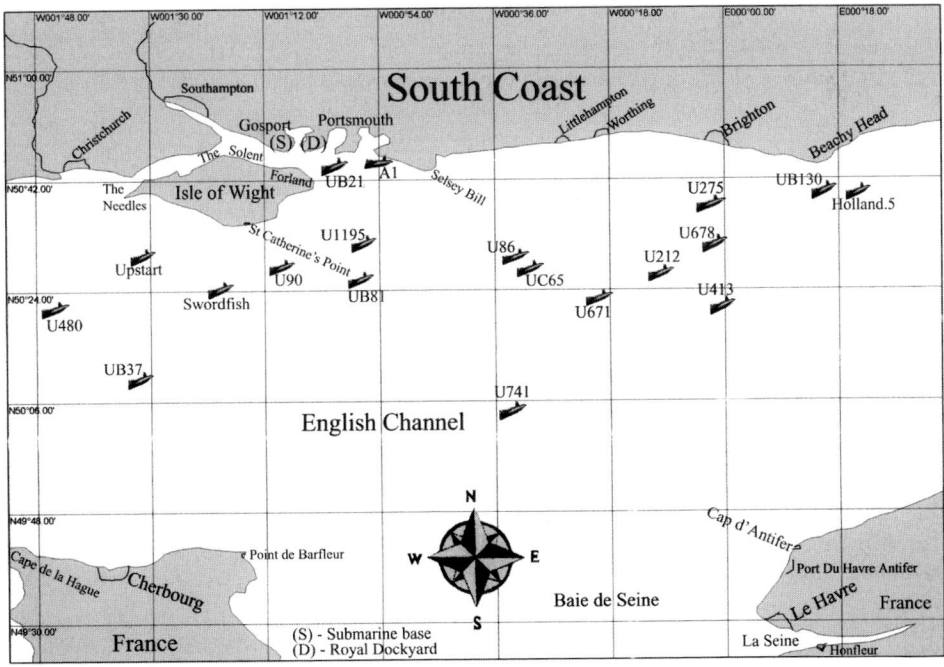

Submarine wrecks along the South Coast.

The following museums all hold submarine material:

Seaford Museum and Heritage Centre
Martello Tower, The Esplanade, Seaford, East Sussex, BN25 1JH
Telephone: 01323 898222

The Newhaven Maritime Museum
Paradise Park, Avis Road, Newhaven, BN9 0DH
Telephone: 01273 612530

The Royal Navy Submarine Museum
Haslar Jetty Road, Gosport, Hampshire, PO12 2AS
Telephone: 023 9252 9217
E-mail: rnsubs@rnsubmus.co.uk

Bembridge Maritime Museum and Shipwreck Centre
Sherbourne, Street Bembridge, Isle of Wight, PO35 5SB
Telephone: 01983 872 223

HOLLAND 5, HM SUBMARINE

DATE OF LOSS: 8 August 1912
DEPTH: 27m
REFERENCE: 50° 39'N 00° 23'E
LOCATION: 7.34 nautical miles SSE of Beachy Head

Type: 'Holland' Class British coastal patrol submarine   *Pendant*: not issued   *Builders*: under licence at Vickers Shipyard, Barrow and Maxim Sons   *Ordered*: for the 1901–1902 programme   *Launched*: on 10 June 1902   *Completed*: on 19 January 1903

TECHNICAL SPECIFICATIONS

Hull: single   *Surface displacement*: 113 tons   *U/Dt*: 122 tons   *LBD*: 19.45m × 3.62m × 3.02m   *Machinery*: 1 × 160hp at 340rpm 4-cylinder petrol engine.   *Props*: 1. *S/Sp*: 8 knots   *Op/R*:   250 nautical miles at 8 knots   *Sub/R*: 25 nautical miles at 7 knots   *U/Power*: 1 × 74hp at 8000rpm electric motors gave 6.8 knots   *Batteries*: 60 cell (of 1,840 AH) with capacity for 75bhp, for 3 hours at 120 volts and 500 amps   *Fuel/Cap*: 685-gallons – 3114 litres   *Armament*: 1 × 45.72cm (18in) torpedo tube positioned 0.61m (2ft) below the 'light' waterline and at the extreme forward end   *Torpedoes*: 5 short, or 3 long ones   *Diving*: max-op-depth 15.25m (50ft) and 5 minutes to submerge. Hull was designed to stand 30.48m (100ft)   *Complement*: 2 officers and 6 ratings

This story is more than just the loss of a submarine; it marks the genesis of Britain's Royal Navy Submarine Service. Ironically the story begins with an Irish nationalist whose hatred of all things British was tempered by inventive genius – allied to an ardent desire to make money.

John Philip Holland was an Irish American who, in 1896, developed a 140-ton submarine in the United States called *Plunger* and he formed the Holland Boat Company. After more modifications to the boat and the use of an Otto petrol engine in lieu of steam, Holland was awarded $120,000 and the US Government then recommended that their Navy should use it. At least two other people offered different designs at the same time as John P. Holland was having financial difficulties. However, investment was forthcoming and he was able to form the Electric Boat Company. In 1900, Holland sold his first submarine to the US Navy for $150,000. (Fifty-five years later, the Electric Boat Company produced the first nuclear-powered submarine for the United States Navy.)

Now for the Admiralty perspective. It is a generally accepted myth that the Royal Navy hierarchy was opposed to developing a submarine fleet of their own. The resultant dichotomy in Admiralty thought is usually expressed by highlighting tensions between modernisers such as Admiral John

'Jacky' Fisher, and the reactionary Admiralty Controller, Sir Arthur Wilson. Fisher prevailed and the design of the new Holland type boat was duly bought from the Americans. This is a gross oversimplification of a far more subtle debate. As we shall see, the fissures that developed in Admiralty policy were concerned not with the question as to whether Britain should have submarines of her own (there was general agreement that she should) but rather, as to just how these submarines should be used. *Holland 5* and her sisters were at the very heart of this argument.

From 1897 onwards successive British Governments realised that war with Germany was likely but in terms of submarine warfare, it was the French who were perceived to be on the brink of possessing a viable submarine weapon with their *Narval* design. British Governments adopted a strategy of *détente*. Officially the Admiralty remained committed to 'do nothing to justify or encourage' rival powers from sponsoring submarine development. Unoffocially Admiralty and their political masters strove to learn as much as possible about the new weapon, while developing defences against it. As early as February 1900 the Naval Intelligence Division became alarmed over French progress in the field of submarine warfare. As a direct response the ban on contact mines was reversed as the commander of the torpedo school, HMS *Vernon*, was ordered to launch an anti-submarine weapon programme. Faced with protestations from the *Vernon* commander that more needed to be known about the capabilities of these vessels, Wilson recommended that the Royal Navy purchase a boat for anti-submarine experimentation. While negotiations carried on for the purchase of five 'Holland' craft from Vickers of Barrow, Admiralty (and Wilson) continued with their official policy of international *détente*. What follows is a revealing extract from Wilson's (often misrepresented) Memorandum of 21 January 1901 entitled 'Submarine Boats':

…The development of submarine warfare must be detrimental to a nation depending on navigation at the surface for its supplies of food…We cannot stop invention in this direction but we can avoid doing anything to encourage it. … Each [submarine] design has been carefully examined and sufficient experiment has been made in each case to ascertain its probable value. It has then been quietly dropped with the result of delaying the development of the submarine boat for about 20 years. Now we cannot delay its introduction any longer but we should still avoid doing anything to assist in its improvement in order that our means of trapping and destroying it may develop at a greater rate than the submarine boats themselves. Politicians should take all favourable opportunities of enlisting the moral sense of nations against this method of warfare, and above all avoid saying anything to prevent the sternest measures being adopted in war against the crews of submarine boats when caught in the act of using them. naval officers should devote their attention to the best means of trapping and destroying them. This necessarily requires as much secrecy as can be maintained without loss of efficiency. In purchasing the Holland boats and directing the attention of the Torpedo Schools to the subject, I think we have done all that is possible at present.

As a reference will have to be made in the First Lord's statement explanatory of the naval estimates, I should propose some such statement as the following;

'Certain foreign nations having devoted considerable sums to the construction of submarine boats and having shown their intention to make use of this underhand method of attack in future wars, it has become necessary to provide the means of training a sufficient number of officers and men in the best methods of trapping and destroying these vessels if they put to sea with hostile intent.'

This paper was written in response to Hugh Arnold Forster MP. As Financial Secretary to the Admiralty, Arnold Forster sought an acceleration of the submarine programme and he used the floor of the House of Commons to make this very public point:

The Admiralty are not prepared to take any steps in regard to submarines because the vessel is only the weapon of the weaker nation. If, however, the weapon can be rendered practical the nations which possess it will cease to be weak and will become powerful. More than any other nation, we should have to fear the attacks submarine.

Admiralty and Government largely shared Wilson's views. On the one hand they felt a very real moral outrage that such a weapon could be developed, but there was general agreement that Admiralty needed to obtain one, if only for experimental purposes. On the other, they questioned how viable these submarines actually were, and if they could be made to work, how should they best be used?

The First World War-vintage American 1,090-ton destroyer USS *Leary* (DD 158), which was sunk by *U 275* resulting in the loss of ninety-seven lives on 24 December 1943 (see page 45). (Author's collection)

Despite the overtly anti-British sentiments of its Fenian founder, the Electrical Boat Co. of America had sold a construction license to Messrs Vickers Sons and Maxim, hence the Admiralty contract (which was later extended to ensure that Vickers had an exclusive contract to build all Royal Navy submarines between 1902 and 1912). Built of a single hull construction, Holland Class submarines were highly experimental craft. They were found to be very poor boats in the open sea with little reserve buoyancy. Once underwater, they were easy to handle and control. The tank system, which encompassed main-ballast tanks (these were split by a longitudinal bulkhead), forward and aft trimming tanks, auxiliary ballast tanks and petrol tanks etc., were arranged within the pressure hull. The boats were fitted with one set of aft-positioned hydroplanes, which meant the boat had to be angled for diving and surfacing, etc. When diving, early boats remained stationary whilst they adjusted trim until a state of positive buoyancy was reached. The diving planes took effect while moving ahead. To navigate, there was a standard compass fitted outside the hull and to read it, the skipper used a primitive optical tube and mirror system. At first the boats were not equipped with a periscope and to see it was necessary to first surface and peer through the 'scuttle-windows' in the small conning tower. These boats were not impressive in performance. It is possible that Admiralty might have rescinded the contract had the dynamic figure of Captain Bacon not bounded on the scene.

In 1901 Wilson was replaced and the new controller made Captain Reginald Bacon his assistant. Bacon was given special responsibility for the five Holland boats under construction at Barrow. Captain Bacon soon discovered the design flaws in the five Holland boats and set about putting them right. Bacon rightly surmised that the low freeboard would render the boats poor sea keepers, if not downright dangerous in operational conditions. Admiralty blocked Bacon's recommendations that production should be halted until these flaws could be revised, after all the boats were not cheap – each one cost the taxpayer £35,000. Their Lordships did however agree to the construction of a sixth submarine to be designed by the visionary Bacon himself. This boat would later be named *A1*. Admiralty agreed to allow Bacon to install a non-extending fixed periscope into each boat, designed by Howard Grubb, an Irish optician. When in use, the periscope was sited in a fixed vertical position. When not in use, it was housed horizontally on the casing. These early periscopes also had the disadvantage that whilst looking aft, the image appeared inverted! In May 1901 Bacon was made 'Inspecting Captain of Submarines' and usefully provided with an office in Whitehall. Bacon's responsibilities included all aspects of organising submarines for the anti-submarine warfare programme. Officers were encouraged to volunteer for the project and by the summer of 1901 the first six lieutenants were selected. Their names were Lts R. Mahon, M. Soutar, H. Sinclair, F. Brooks, H. Richmond, W. Law and F. Arnold Forster (nephew of the aforementioned politician). The first ratings were named as Engineeer Robert Spence, PO William Waller, PO F. Knight, PO J. Knight, PO J. Rees, PO E. Neville, ERAs W. Robinson and W. Muirhead.

It was not until about 1907 that officers began to be assigned specific boats. Until that time a submarine commanding officer would be posted to the depot ship and listed 'For the command of submarine boats'. Even regular commands were not recorded. Crews were often rotated as prolonged exposure to early submarine environments was hazardous to health. This and promotion requisites saw the introduction of the 'general service rule' by which submarine officers and men were only allowed to serve five years before a return to general service was required (*see* Introduction). By August 1902 the first five boats had been launched. As they had been built as experimental craft, there were no launch ceremonies.

Holland 1   launched on 2 October 1901
Holland 2   launched on 21 January 1902
Holland 3   launched on 9 May 1902
Holland 4   launched on 23 May 1902
Holland 5   launched on 10 June 1902

To date, Admiralty had been most generous with the resources provided to its Inspecting Captain of Submarines, Bacon obtaining the cruiser *Latona* to act as depot ship and the cruiser HMS *Hazard* to serve as tender. It should be stressed that these pioneer submarine boats had been built solely to progress the anti-submarine training programme of HMS *Vernon*. Bacon of course recognised the potential of these weapons far beyond the mere guinea pig role envisaged by Admiralty. Indeed, Bacon succeeded in postponing the allotted 'clockwork mouse' function until he had convincing proof of his submarine's capabilities. His disciples were few but they included the influential Fisher and the Prime Minister, Arthur Balfour. The perceptive Bacon offered this outlook in an extract from a performance report written to Sir John Fisher on 31 May 1903:

Control centre of a Second World War Kriegsmarine Type VIIC/41 U-boat (*U 995*). (Courtesy Kevin Belcher of Swindon)

...It is unwise to assume that the strongest power will at all times be able to assume the offensive in all the different theatres of war. Hence torpedo craft for local defence become a wise insurance. But beyond this, the strategic position of Britain gives us two small guts to hold, to prevent the egress of their fleets. Namely the Dover Straits, Channel and the sea between Scotland and Norway. The former might and should easily be held and controlled by torpedo craft without risking large ships at sea, wasting coal and exposed to attack in such narrow waters. Then the only exit for the enemy's fleet will be the more Northern and very circuitous route. In time boats may be built which may control the Northern passage also, but at present a sufficiency of boats would effectually block the Dover passage.

In 1903 Balfour launched a review of imperial defence policy faced with shrinking budgets in the wake of the Boer War. In its subsequent report the Cabinet Defence Committee argued that potential invasion could be prevented by denying an invader any of Britain's deep water ports. The question was how best to do this. Historically these ports had been guarded by the men and mines of the Royal Engineers. Voices within the Royal Navy now argued that this could be done more cheaply and more efficiently by the senior service, in particular by the 'submarine section'. Arnold-Forster, now Secretary of State for War, orchestrated opinion that responsibility for harbour defences should be transferred from the Royal Engineers to the Royal Navy Submarines. In February 1904 the Submarine Service took over Fort Blockhouse. Meanwhile Arthur Balfour discussed submarine warfare with Admiral Fisher, now Commander-in-Chief at Portsmouth. Both were convinced of the key strategic role submarines could play in the future if not in the immediate present.

In October 1904 Fisher became First Sea Lord and one of his first moves was to persuade the Admiralty to endorse the use of the submarine as the primary protection for British naval bases throughout the Empire. This resulted in an immediate expansion in the submarine section and an increase in personnel. Fisher had no intention of using submarines as harbour defences. Rather his enthusiasm for deploying submarines in this role, was actually a ploy to ensure that defence cuts should fall on the Army rather than the Royal Navy. Fisher, like Bacon, was a proponent of 'flotilla defence'. According to this reasoning naval supremacy no longer lay with the country owning the most battleships. Indeed in 1905 Fisher overtly stated that in future no large fleet would dare to sail the narrow European seas because of the danger posed by submarines. Defence strategists should abandon big ships in favour of flotillas of small, cheap vessels such as destroyers, torpedo boats and submarines to deny hostile ships entry to British seaspace. Needless to observe, this was revolutionary thinking. Perhaps it was too revolutionary for the more inelastic service minds.

At any rate from 1904 onwards Fisher commenced redistributing new construction resources away from big ships in favour of flotilla vessels, including submarines (known by his enemies and their press outriders as 'Fisher's toys') with a view to realising his concept of flotilla defence. Of course Fisher made enemies, notably fleet Commander-in-Chief Sir Charles Beresford, who vehemently opposed Fisher's small ship policy. Tensions were such that both men were forced into early retirement by 1910 and Arthur Wilson was again appointed First Sea Lord. The big ship navy was once again secure.

The Holland boats could not be dismissed as mere toys. During trials in the docks at Barrow and the Irish Sea, the boats reached a maximum speed of 8.5 knots at 230rpm average on the surface and 7.2 knots submerged. However they suffered instability. In the manoeuvres of 1904, the Holland Class provided alarming evidence of just what the 'new' weapons could achieve when they managed to 'torpedo' not one but two battleships without being detected. However, as we have seen, their main function was for A/S training purposes and the defence of Portsmouth harbour. All five boats spent their service assigned to these unrewarding duties. One major plus for the Holland Class submarine was that not one single life was lost on them. Interestingly, Holland 2 once dived to 22.86m (75ft) following an accident. Conversely, tests carried out on the salvaged Holland 1 suggest that her pressure hull would have failed below depths of 60ft. Holland 5 famously ran aground outside Fort Blockhouse in 1910. Much to the discomfort of her crew, the stranded hulk was widely photographed.

By 1911–1912 the Holland boats were gradually superceded by the 'A', 'C' and 'D' Class of submarine. It was time to dispose of the Holland boats. As an interesting aside, the hulls of the Holland boats and their 'A' Class successors made useful salvage camels. Following various indignities including tests to guage the abilities of their pressure hulls to withstand depth charges, Nos 2, 3 and 4 were scrapped. Holland 1 followed suit. After she was sold in 1913, she sank near the Eddystone Reef while under tow. In 1981 the boat was raised by Royal Navy divers and, after careful renovation, she has become one of the prize exhibits in the Submarine Museum at Gosport. Ingeniously designed platforms and gantries enable the visitor to enter the boat. Reconstructive imagery and diagrams bring the little submarine to life. It is an experience throughly recommended for all but the seriously claustrophobic.

ADM 1/7515 ADM1/7725

FINAL PATROL

Holland 5 was sold in 1912 and on 8 August she was being towed to Chatham Dockyard when the tow cable broke in inclement weather and she sank in the English Channel.

WRECK SITE

The wreck lies on a seabed of sand and gravel, in a general depth of 27m, being the lowest astronomical depth. It is reported as being upright and intact and in reasonably good condition. The tiny conning tower is closed, with the viewing deadlight in place and even the little boat's single propeller is still attached. The wreck is now deemed an historic wreck site under the 1973 Protection Act and permission to dive the wreck must be granted by the Ministry of Defence and a licence issued.

UB 130, SM IMPERIAL U-BOAT

DATE OF LOSS: Around July 1921
DEPTH: 25m
REFERENCE: 50 40.54 N 00 15.21 E
LOCATION: 3.64 nautical miles S of Beachy Head

Type: UBIII   *Builders*: A.G. Weser, Bremen for Kaiserliche Deutsche Marine   *Ordered*: on 28 February 1917, within the batch of UB 118–UB 132   *Keel laid*: as Yard No.303 on 14 September 1917   *Launched*: on 27 May 1918   *Commissioned*: by Kapitänleutnant Heinrich XXXVII Prinz zu Reuß on 28 June 1918

TECHNICAL SPECIFICATIONS

Hull: double   *Surface displacement*: 512 tons   *U/Dt*: 643 tons   *LBDH*: 55.58m × 5.80m × 3.68m × 8.25m   *Machinery*: 2 × 550ps Benz diesels   *Props*: 2 bronze   *S/Sp*: 13.9 knots   *Op/ R*: 7,280 nautical miles at 6 knots   *Sub/R*: 55 nautical miles at 4 knots   *U/Power*: 2 × 394ps electric motors gave 7.6 knots   *Batteries*: AFA lead/acid   *Fuel/Cap*: 35 + 36 tons   *Armament*: 4 bow and 1 stern 50.04cm torpedo tubes   *Torpedoes*: 10 × 50.04cm (19.7in)   *Guns*: 1 × 105mm (4.13in) forward deck gun   *Ammo*: 160 rounds of 105mm   *Mines*: none   *Diving*: max-op-depth 50m (164ft) and 30 sec to crash-dive   *Complement*: 3 officers and 31 ratings

Heinrich XXXVII Prinz zu Reuß was born on 1 November 1888 and died on 6 September 1970. *UB 130* was originally destined for service in the Mediterranean, but Germany's deteriorating military situation caused the boat to be re-assigned to the German-based I.U-Flottille at Brunsbüttel. With Prinz zu Reuß in command, she made just one patrol into the North Sea from 25 October to 3 November 1918, but no ships were sunk.

FINAL PATROL

At the end of the First World War, *UB 130* sailed to Harwich and surrendered on 26 November 1918. However, other sources contend that she surrendered to the French on that date. Both *UB 130* and *UB 131* were observed awaiting disposal at Harwich in 1919.

On 9 January 1921, *UB 131* was towed from Britain to France by the Government tug *Woonda*, but the tow broke. *UB 131* then drifted ashore near Hastings and a local salvage company broke her up on the beach, in situ. On the other hand, the French Navy at Toulon destined *UB 130* for underwater explosion tests and that was where she was supposed to have been blown up in July 1921. There is more confusion, because a U-boat wreck was located at the position above and identified by the propeller that was stamped *UB 130*. The question remains; did *UB 130* suffer the same fate as *UB 131* and sink before it reached its destination, or was this another U-boat wreck fitted with a spare propeller from *UB 130*?

WRECK SITE

The wreck lies on a seabed of sand and shingle, in a general depth of 25m, being the lowest astronomical depth. It was originally found with the bows pointing southwest; the conning tower hatch was open, but the conning tower was badly damaged with part of the outer skin lying on the seabed. The periscope was in the raised position and the propellers were still in place. Unfortunately, it is now totally collapsed, well broken up and rather dispersed and lying in three separate sections. Only the central section looks anything like that of a submarine. Pieces of the lead/acid batteries and sections of steel hull plate are strewn around the site, but almost all of the interesting parts were heavily salvaged in the early 1980s, including the propellers. One of the propellers (stamped with *UB 130*) is said to be lying in a garden somewhere on the Isle of Wight. The gun now stands outside of the Newhaven Maritime Museum. A number of fish congregate around the highest parts of the wreck and soft corals are reasonably established.

U 275, KRIEGSMARINE U-BOAT

DATE OF LOSS: 10 March 1945
DEPTH: 50m
REFERENCE: 50 36.311N 00 03.049W
LOCATION: 10.33 nautical miles SSW of Beachy Head

Type: VIIC ocean-going attack boat   *Builders*: Vulkan Vegesack Werft, Bremen for Kriegsmarine   *Ordered*: on 10 April 1941, within the batch of *U 274–U 279*   *Keel laid*: as Yard No.40 on 18 January 1942   *Launched*: on 8 October 1942   *Commissioned*: by Oblt.z.S. Helmut Bork on 25 November 1942   *Feldpost No*: M 50 344

TECHNICAL SPECIFICATIONS

See page 342.

Helmut Bork was born on 29 May 1910 in Danzig and commenced his naval career in 1939. He began his submarine service as 2nd Watch Officer on *U 134* between July 1941 and September 1942. Bork was promoted to Oberleutnant zur See (R) on 1 April 1943, but eventually became Kapitänleutnant on Staff, 8th and 7th U-Flotilles until the capitulation.

   U 275 served with 8.U-Flottille at Danzig as *Ausbildungsboot* (training boat) from 25 November 1942 until 31 May 1943.

   (1) On 12 August 1943, *U 275* left Kiel and arrived at Bergen in southwest Norway on the 16th. *U 275* was formally assigned to 3.U-Flottille at La Pallice for frontline service on 1 June 1943. Bork made the following patrols with *U 275*:

   (2) On 4 September 1943 she left Bergen for operations south, southwest of Iceland. A Hudson aircraft of 269 Squadron, piloted by Flying Officer Jones, attacked the boat on 3 October, but she escaped in a rain squall without any damage and arrived at the new base at La Pallice on 28 October.

   (3) On 29 November *U 275* left La Pallice for operations in the North Atlantic and travelled with *U 270* and *U 305* to a waiting area west of the Bay of Biscay. On 20 December 1943 the boats teamed up with *Coronel 3* wolfpack and then formed the larger *Borkum* pack, some 400 miles

northwest of Cape Ortegal. Their objective was to operate against MKS 33/SL 142 and escort the German blockade-runner *Orsono*, which was transporting a cargo of rubber for the Reich.

The 'jeep' escort carrier USS *Card* (CVE-11) CTG 21.14, commanded by Captain A.J. Isbell, escorted by the four First World War-vintage four-funnelled destroyers USS *Leary* (DD158, Cdr James E. Kyes), *Schenck* (DD159, Cdr Earl W. Logsdon), *Decatur* and *Babbitt*, left Casablanca on 17 December 1943, under orders from Washington, and steamed in support of convoy GUS 24; their mission was to track down a U-boat concentration around the area 45°N 22°W. About 695 miles west of St Nazaire at daybreak at around position 47N, 19W, the weather turned for the worse. A Wildcat from *Card* had spotted the *Orsono*, which had refused to acknowledge signals. Around the same time a Luftwaffe pilot out searching for *Orsono* spotted the carrier and radioed to Admiral Dönitz, who ordered *Borkum* group to pursue the warship. With this the tables were turned somewhat and Cdr Isbell had no way of knowing as the ships steamed into the Atlantic, that the wolfpacks had combined and lay in wait for them, 85 miles ahead. Sea conditions became so heavy that a *Wildcat* and her crew were lost overboard from the carrier and a sailor was swept off the deck and drowned. Then *Decatur*'s steering gear room was flooded, causing major problems, leaving just three destroyers to protect the carrier from a wolfpack of thirteen U-boats.

At 2120hrs *Schenck* (pronounced Skeenk) picked up a contact and informed *Card*, then she engaged what was believed to be the lead submarine. *Card*, whose aircraft were not equipped for night flying, and the limping destroyer *Decatur*, made best speed possible and, using evasive action, tried to outrun the pack, but confusion reigned. Cdr Isbell ordered *Schenck* to keep the submarines down during the night and to rendezvous, 40 miles southwest of *Schenck*'s last contact, however *Card* was pursued throughout the night, totally unaware that a torpedo had actually already been fired by *U 275* but had missed its target. By daybreak she launched the aircraft and managed to keep the surrounding U-boats down. At around 0130hrs on 24 December both *Schenck* and *Leary* made three contacts some 5–7 miles north and *Leary* moved to engage the furthest one. *Schenck* made a fourth contact but lost it, however with a series of depth charges she eventually went on to destroy *U 645*; the boat sank at 0229hrs with the loss of fifty-five crewmen, including the *Borkum* group's doctor. At 0158hrs the 1,090-ton USS *Leary* made radar contact and fired star shells to illuminate a target, but this put the warship in full view of the *U 382*, which had been stalking the ship for 10 minutes.

As *Leary* turned at 0210hrs, a well-aimed torpedo struck the stern. Secondary explosions were mistakenly interpreted as more torpedo hits. The ship took on a 25° starboard list, started to break up and settled rapidly. Quick reaction by the torpedo men in making safe the depth charges and by R.T. Butch Hauer, who got the auxiliary generator started and called *Schenck* for help, obviously saved many more lives. *Schenck* was 5 miles distant and collecting oil samples when the call came in, but made flank speed to assist in the rescue. At 0241hrs, while the men were abandoning ship, an explosion occurred in the forward engine compartment. *Leary* then broke up and quickly disappeared beneath the waves in position 45° 15'N 21° 40'W. When *Schenck* reached the scene, she was unable to pick anyone up because of the prowling *Borkum* pack. However, Cdr Logsdon was able to slow the ship down sufficiently to drop a gig and instructed a young lienantnat to 'Save as many as you can. I don't know when we'll be back. Good luck and may God be with you'. *Schenck* then set about chasing the submarines out of the area, before returning 4 hours later. Ninety-seven of *Leary*'s crew were either killed by the explosion or lost, including Cdr Kyes, who bravely gave his lifejacket to one of his crew. The USS *Schenck* rescued fifty-nine hypothermic men and transferred them to the USS *Card*.

On 30 October *U 275* was attacked by frigates, but escaped. Helmut Bork claimed to have sunk two destroyers on 2 January 1944, but this was not so. According to the BdU Diary, the boat left patrol because Bork was suffering from appendicitis.

Allied aircraft attacked *U 275* and *U 541* on 6 January, but *U 275* managed to return to La Pallice on the 11th. *U 275* was then assigned to the anti-invasion group *Landwirt*. Helmut Bork was struck down with appendicitis.

(4) On 23 April 1944 the boat left La Pallice and transferred to Brest, arriving on the 26th.

(5) *U 275* left Brest on 20 May 1944 as part of group Dragoner, but the planned operation in the western exit of the English Channel was abandoned and the boat arrived back at La Pallice on 23 May.

(6) *U 275* departed Brest on 6 June 1944 as part of the *Landwirt* wolfpack, one of eight boats ordered to the area north of Cherbourg, with instructions to attack enemy shipping. Allied aircraft and surface ASW forces leaving base hounded *U 275*. This is an extract from the BdU Diary:

U 275 entered St Peter Port [Guernsey] to recharge battery. Boat sent short signal which shows essentially the great difficulties of operations in the Channel even for boats with schnorchel. Boat left Brest on 6.6. and was shadowed from the start, even in convoy. Enemy aircraft before reaching point 3426, commenced submerged passage. Picked up by anti-submarine unit on 8.6. in BF 2735. One destroyer apparently equipped with noise buoy, a high buzzing tone which drowned engine and propeller noises [Foxer]. Audible over whole boat. Hydrophone and depth charge hunt till 1600. At 0135/9/6 in BF 2576 after 10 minutes sailing on schnorchel, boat was probably located. Gun fire observed. Finally depth charge hunt by four aircraft until 0515hrs. Was not able to execute sailing on schnorchel. In BF 2579 2 destroyers seen making off through periscope. Continuously depth charged again until 1100 – no damage. Retired to south in order to continue passage along coast. On 12.6. sank destroyer in BF 2639 with T 5. Anti-submarine unit in the vicinity commenced strong depth charge hunt after an hour [No destroyer was sunk it this attack]. Boat hunted and forced southwards until 0500/13/6. Was picked up immediately when attempt to schnorchel was made. Entered St Peter Port on account of dead battery. Schnorchel could not be ventilated during day because of the amount of enemy air activity observed through periscope. It is very easy for the enemy to pick up a boat on hydrophones while schnorchelling. Commander considered task of recharging in operational area (BF 32/36) extremely hazardous.

Having recharged the batteries, *U 275* re-sailed on the 14th. The USN Liberator, VP-110 (Lt Cdr J. Munson) attacked *U 275* on 18 June at the western entrance to the Channel, but depth charges caused just minor damage. Bork was given orders to attack the heavy Allied units that were shelling the port, but he was unable to help and arrived back at Brest on 25 June 1944.

(7) Oblt.z.S. Helmut Wehrkamp assumed command of the boat at the beginning of July. (Wehrkamp was born on 29 March 1921 and commenced his naval career in 1939. He was promoted to Oberleutnant zur See on 1 January 1941.) On 16 July 1944 *U 275* left Brest for operations in the English Channel off Plymouth.

16.7. Put out of Brest. Normal passage until 20.7.

20.7. Daily reckoning 50 sea miles. Fast craft with ground trawl apparatus avoided.

21.7. Proceeded to center of operations area Plymouth Bay.

22.7. At 1335hrs position check with Eddystone Lighthouse observed by aircraft, immediate appearance of strong search groups. Intensive search lasting 7 hours. As observed proceeded Seine area.

25.7. Destroyer suddenly sailed at speed over the boat in 3511 at 1600. Well-placed depth charges – action until 0015hrs. Damage: periscope, electrical engines, rudder, 2 battery cells torn. 'Schnorchel' stretched.

27.7. Ten well-placed depth charges at a depth of 50m at 2110.

28.7. Schnorchelling impossible owing to strong and continuous hydrophone bearings, battery practically empty. Boat drifted eastwards with the current

30.7. Depth suddenly 19m. Presume position 3381. Depth charge attack during an attempt to 'schnorchel' to the S.W. at 2333hrs. 2 hours later search group with Asdic and explosive soundings. No success. Drifted N.E.

1.85. Strong hydrophone bearings at 0307hrs. As the battery was quite exhausted and only 180 potassium chlorate cartridges left surfaced and attempted to reach Boulogne. Submerged later as remaining battery current and drifting should bring the boat off Boulogne.

2.8. Tied up in Boulogne at 0045hrs.

During this patrol it was reported that Wehrkamp damaged two naval vessels.

(8) *U 275* left Boulogne on 13 August and resumed operations in the English Channel, but Wehrkamp decided to abort his mission following rumours that six U-boats had been destroyed. Control logged that Wehrkamp had left the area early and without permission to do so.

(9) On 2 September, while off the west of Ireland, Wehrkamp fired a T-5 torpedo at what he thought was a 12,000-ton ocean liner. He claimed that the torpedo detonated and the ship halted twice temporarily, then proceeded towards the coast. *U 275* put into Bergen on 18 September 1944.

On 1 October 1944 *U 275* was formally assigned to the 11.U-Flottille at Bergen for frontline duties. Ob.Fk.Mt. Klaus Frohling, who was born on 6 December 1919, was lost overboard at Bergen on 30 November.

(10) On 2 December 1944 she left Bergen for a patrol, but encountered irreparable damage to her blowers and had to abort; she returned to Bergen on 12 December.

(11) Leaving Bergen on 14 January 1945, *U 275* sailed for operations in the Channel, but *schnorchel* problems in early February forced her into St Nazaire on 10 February 1945.

FINAL PATROL

(12) Following repairs to the *schnorchel*, *U 275* left the French port on 25 February for operations in the eastern part of the Channel, off the south coast of England. At 2041hrs on 16 February, BdU ordered *U 275* 'to patrol further eastwards than her previous patrol', as intelligence indicated heavy traffic steaming to and from Le Havre. Previously *U 275* had patrolled mid-Channel, westwards from Beachy Head. On the morning of 8 March 1945, the combined convoy OS 115/KMS 89 (UK-Freetown) comprising eighteen ships, was located northwest of Fécamp. At 1055hrs (Continental time), Wehrkamp torpedoed and sunk the 4,934-ton British steamer *Lornaston* (1925 – Galbraith, Pembroke & Co. Ltd, London) at position 50° 35'N 00° 30'W; the ship was on passage from Blyth and the Downs for Casablanca with 6,002 tons of coal. The master, Captain David Cownie, forty crewmen and seven gunners were rescued by the frigate HMS *Holmes* (Lt Cdr P.S. Botle) and HM tug *Palencia* and landed at Newhaven.

The *eB-Dienst* (German Navy Signals Intelligence Service) monitored the signals indicating the sinking. *U 275* was expected to have left patrol by the end of March. She failed to return and was stamped 'Verschollen' with effect from 3 April. Some clues to her ultimate fate can be found in British records. On the evening of 10 March, RML 513 was sent to investigate the scene of an explosion off Newhaven, reported by onshore observers. The RML found a slick at 50, 36 N 0004E 'which smelled of diesel oil'. HMS *Baynton*, *Loch Eck* and *Loch Dunvegan* of 10 EG were dispatched to the scene. At 0950hrs the following morning they located a suspected bottomed U-boat. Following the obligatory 'can opener'; a quantity of oil and wreckage bubbled to the surface. Among the debris were scraps of paper bearing German handwriting, fragments of a first aid kit and a pair of leather trousers.

As has already been mentioned in the introduction, the Allies were fully prepared for the expected U-boat onslaught on the Neptune supply lines. Deep anti-submarine minefields had been laid, among them 'Brazier E 2' the deep minefield off Beachy Head, just west of Buoy C2A. Brazier E 2 was one of a necklace of small minefields laid at focal points on the Neptune supply routes, from 5 January to 3 February 1945. It is perfectly feasible that the unsuspecting *U 275* met her end on this field.

NARA T 1022, Roll 3046, PG30360, 30362, 30366 U-Boot-Ehrenmal Möltenort

THE MEN WHO PERISHED IN U 275

Bohn, Herbert Ob.Gfr. (Born: 24-2-192)
Böttcher, Karl-Heinz Ob.Mt. (31-10-1919)
Christoph, Bernhard Ob.Fahnr. (21-5-1908)
Diehl, Fritz Gfr. (22-1-1925)
Frangart, Paul Gfr. (11-1-1926)
Fütscher, Kurt Ob.Gfr. (16-11-1924)
Gabriel, Walter Ob.Gfr. (4-7-1925)
Görner, Horst Ob.Gfr. (10-8-1923)
Greiling, Egon LtIng (1-8-1922)
Hartrumpf, Gerhard Ob.Mt. 16-10-1919)
Hess, Kurt Maat. (30-4-1923)
Heuckeroth, Wilhelm Ob.Gfr. (5-12-1924)
Hochfellner, Eduard Ob.Mt. (6-9-1920)
Höhn, Herbert Ob.Masch. (17-3-1915)
Hufnagel, Hermann Ob.Mt (23-6-1920)
Huth, Wilhelm Maat. (22-1-1923)
Jordan, Hugo Ob.Gfr. (26-1-1923)

Kahmann, Rudolf Ob.Gfr. (2-1-1922)
Kalnischkies, Kurt Ltz.S. (26-10-1921)
Kempermann, Hans-Gerd Lting (20-3-1923)
Klostermann, Albert Ob.Mt. (13-9-1920)
Kochmann, Karl Ob.Masch. (19-11-1916)
Kögel, Erich Ob.Gfr. (10-5-1924)
Lange, Reinhard Ob.Gfr. (7-1-1925)
Leistikow, Karl Ob.Gfr. (5-9-1922)
Leypoldt, Alwin Ob.Gfr. (22-9-1923)
Liebehenschel, Herbert Mtr. (11-3-1926)
Lücking, Heinz Ob.Gfr. (29-1-1923)
Malsch, Max Gfr. (29-10-1924)
Nehring, Heinz Maat. (10-1-1922)
Plötzing, Paul Ob.Gfr. (10-8-1922)
Prochaska, Karl Gfr. (1-2-1925)
Prüssing, Georg Ob.Mt. (27-2-1920)
Raubold, Gerd Maat. (16-4-1923)

Rollwage, Hans-Hermann Ltz.S. (1-5-1923)
Sagelsdorf, Günter Ob.Gfr. (26-2-1924)
Schaipwinkel, Erich Ob.Gfr. (4-6-1923)
Steffen, Rudolf Ob.Gfr. (10-9-1924)
Thamm, Paul Ob.Gfr. (18-3-1925)
Vogel, Andreas Ob.Strm. (7-2-1920)
Wehrkamp, Helmut Oblt.z.S (29-3-1923)

Weiss, Johannes Ob.Gfr. (17-9-1922)
Wiatrak, Josef Ob.Gfr. (13-4-1922)
Winkler, Siegfried Gfr. (23-11-1926)
Wittig, Günter Maat. (20-2-1925)
Wolf, Gerhard Gfr. (4-12-1925)
Wysisk, Edmund Gfr. (21-10-1926)
Zimmermann, Heinrich Ob.Gfr. (14-9-1923)

WRECK SITE

The wreck of what is believed to be *U 275* lies on a seabed of sand, mud and gravel, in a general depth of 50m (164ft), being the lowest astronomical depth. It is upright and intact, but very broken, with the fore deck casing containing a number of large holes. This wreck, which is also a war grave, is covered in soft corals and has lots of fish around it. Using the Lindberg method, a 3–16–2 bow drainage slot pattern would be expected for this submarine.

The next two U-boats were also destroyed while operating against the 'Neptune' supply lines.

U 678, KRIEGSMARINE U-BOAT

DATE OF LOSS: 6 July 1944
DEPTH: 55m
REFERENCE: 50 33.50N 00 04.50W
LOCATION: 12.30 nautical miles SSW of Beachy Head

Type: VIIC ocean-going attack boat *Builders*: Howaldtswerke AG, Hamburg for Kriegsmarine *Ordered*: on 5 June 1941, within the batch of *U 675–U 680* *Keel laid*: as Yard No.827 on 3 September1942 *Launched*: on 18 September 1943 *Commissioned*: Oberleutnant zur See Guido Hyronimus on 25 October 1943 *Feldpost No*: M 52 38

TECHNICAL SPECIFICATIONS

See page 342.

Guido Hyronimus assumed command on 25 October 1943 and was the boat's only commander. He was born in Augsburg on 17 November 1918 and commenced his naval career in 1933; on 1 April 1942 Hyronimus was promoted to Oberleutnant zur See. He had lost his first command, *U 670* just two months earlier, following a collision with the 3,436-ton target ship *Bolkoburg* (1940 – Kriegsmarine – requisition) in the Gulf of Danzig at 2230hrs on 20 August 1943; twenty-two crewmen survived, but twenty-one died.

U 678 was assigned to 5.U-Flottille at Kiel as *Ausbildungsboot* from her commissioning until 31 May 1944.

On 27 May 1944 the boat left Kiel and transferred to Marviken (a place inside Kristiansand harbour, now called Marvika), arriving on 29 May.

U 678 was formally assigned to 7.U-Flottille, St Nazaire for frontline service on 1 June 1944.

FINAL PATROL

(2) *U 678* departed Marviken on 8 June 1944, being one of four *schnorchel*-equipped U-boats sailing for operations in the English Channel. *U 678* had reached her designated area and, on the 5th, made an unsuccessful attack on an ON convoy. With her presence confirmed, the escorts were soon after her scent. The corvette HMS *Statice* (Lt R. Wolfendon) located her at 2200hrs. *Statice* pursued the U-boat, but lost contact in position 230 Beachy Head, 14.7 miles and proceeded to carry out a box-sweep around that position. Meanwhile, the Canadian Escort Group 11 was hunting a contact in company with HMS *Brissenden*. When Commander-in-Chief Portsmouth's report was received,

HMCS *Kootenay*. (Author's collection)

HMCS *Ottawa*. (Author's collection)

Canadian destroyers *Ottawa* and *Kootenay* were detached to join the hunt. At 0715hrs HMS *Statice* was joined by the two Canadian warships, which proceeded to 'box' search outside *Statice*.

At 0930hrs the following morning *Ottawa* (Cdr J. Prentice) obtained an ASDIC contact, so *Kootenay* (Lt Cdr W. Willson) was instructed to gain contact. The wreck-strewn nature of the Channel rendered hunting the U-boat significantly more difficult but the submarine appeared to be altering depth and moving eastwards along the bottom at a speed of 2 knots. At 1017 *Ottawa* decided to attack with Hedgehog. The advantage of Hedgehog was that it fired ahead of the attacking ship (unlike the process of dropping depth charges, where an attacker had to pass over and beyond the target, with the probability of losing contact). An explosion signified a hit but it did not of course guarantee that the Hedeghog had exploded against a U-boat, however in this particular case, a couple of highly effective attacks were executed:

OFFICIAL REPORT – ANTI-U-BOAT OPERATIONS – THE SINKING OF 'U 678'

… 'Ottawa' obtained contact by ASDIC and attacked with Hedgehog, 'Kootenay' dropped a pattern of depth charges and 'Ottawa' then crossed the target and with her echo sounder obtained a very distinct trace of a U-boat at 60ft. Another Hedgehog attack was then made. There was one explosion, some light oil was seen and the U-boat apparently bottomed, but was, however, able to move off across the tide when 'Statice' approached to attack. Defeating the U-boat's manoeuvres she delivered a Hedgehog attack (at 1123hrs) so successfully that one hit was definitely made and a quantity of oil and wood came to the surface. An attack by 'Kootenay' (at 1159hrs) produced not only more wood and oil, but also some clothing and, what is more uncommon, a number of novels. The haul included; 1 tin of German butter, 2 censor stamps, a tin of white powder and a very worn coat of blue serge with three German buttons attached. While these were being collected, 'Ottawa' again crossed the target with her echo sounder and obtained a trace showing the U-boat on the bottom with oil pouring from it. She was, however, dissatisfied at not being able to recover any human remains and decided to batter the U-boat until there could be no doubt as to its destruction. (One account states that an object 'resembling a human lung' was seen floating among the debris.) For about 10 hours the U-boat was therefore attacked, with towed and dropped depth charges and also with Hedgehog. In the course of these attacks 'Ottawa' made another contact two or three thousand yards away from the enemy, but this was probably one of the many wrecks in the area. The U-boat was finally left at daylight on the 8th, having then been giving off oil for over 36 hours. She was later found to be 'U 678'.

The 1123hrs Hedgehog attack probably shattered the pressure hull, killing all on board. For the next two days a series of determined 'can opener' attacks were carried out but the only identifiable wreckage appears to have been a locker door. Indeed the exercise seems only to have elicited the criticism of Commodore (D) Western Approaches who gently rebuked his over-zealous captains for 'pulverising a dead hull without necessity'. Canadian destroyers earned a reputation for ruthless efficiency, not least for their habitual marking of known U-boat wrecks with buoys, thus ensuring that time and effort was not wasted in attacking another 'dead hull'. The BdU Diary contains the following valedictory entry:

U 678 left Kristiansand on 8 June, passage report on 22 June from *AL 66*. 24 June. Ordered to steer for BF 3184. On 2 July. Boat was to break off and put into Brest. She has not arrived so far. According to dead reckoning she must have been in the W. approaches to the Channel on that day. Nothing known of the cause of loss and date. Loss occurred in N. Biscay between *AL 66* and western approach to Channel.

ADM 199/2061 ADM 1/29885 NARA T1022, Rolls 4065–4066, PG 30348–30351 U-Boot-Ehrenmal Möltenort

THE MEN WHO PERISHED IN U 678

Arntzen, Holgar Oblt.z.S. (5-7-22)
Bandemer, Horst Mtr.O.Gfr. (29-10-23)

Baum, Helmut Mtr.O.Gfr. (17-5-24)
Werner Bosse, Werner Bts.Mt. (22-6-24)

Bretthauer, Hermann Ofk.Mt. (4-9-19)
Bütterich, Johann Bts.Mt. (27-10-23)
Dallmann, Friedrich MtrOGfr (26-6-24)
Eckelmann, Günter Masch.H.Gfr. (15-9-20)
Eichholz, Gustav OMaschMt (10-7-19)
Eisenhuth, Ernst Obts.Mt. (8-12-18)
Feil, Albert Mech.O.Gfr. (11-7-23)
Förster, Paul Masch.O.Gfr. (21-01-23)
Frank, Werner Masch.O.Gfr. (20-9-23)
Franke, Helmut LtIng. (16-1-23)
Gernert, Josef Mtr.O.Gfr. (11-10-24)
Giese, Heinz Masch.O.Gfr. (15-9-24)
Göbel, Walter Ltz.S. (05-6-22)
Grimm, Karl Mtr.O.Gfr (25-2-23)
Gröbel, Heinz Mtr.O.Gfr. (21-11-23)
Heimeshoff, Heinrich O.Strm. (24-5-15)
Heinemann, Karl Omasch.Mt. (1-10-19)
Hirschmann, Bruno Masch.O.Gfr. (1-8-23)
Hofmann, Karl-Heinz Mtr.O.Gfr. (17-3-23)
Hyronimus, Guido Oblt.z.S. (17-11-18)
Kaukerat, Fritz Mtr.O.Gfr. (20-4-24)
Koppe, Hans Fk.Gfr. (2-11-24)
Kratzer, Gerhard Mtr.O.Gfr. (25-6-23)
Küchle, Albert Masch.Gfr. (29-9-24)

Küchlin, Gottfried Mtr.O.Gfr. (11-6-22)
Laske, Erich Bts.Mt. (25-2-22)
Lempert, Herbert Ltz.S. (9-10-23)
Lepsy, Willi Masch.Mt. (16-4-20)
Lischewski, Otto Mtr.H.Gfr. (3-11-21)
Löwe, Heinz Masch.Gfr. (19-12-25)
Martin, Viktor Mech.O.Gfr. (29-7-24)
Martini, Wilhelm O.Masch. (13-8-14)
Pertzsch, Walter Masch.Mt. (19-2-23)
Rauchhaus, Wilhelm Mtr.O.Gfr. (24-4-23)
Remesch, Johann Fk.Gfr. (16-12-25)
Scholz, Wolfgang MaschGfr (15-12-25)
Schreiter, Werner Mech.Mt. (10-11-22)
Sonntag, Heinz Masch.O.Gfr. (11-4-24)
Spelleken, Karl Masch.O.Gfr. (30-4-24)
Tanner, Ernst O.San.Mt. (22-9-14)
Teetz, Karl-Heinz Masch.O.Gfr. (23-10-22)
Then, Josef Masch.O.Gfr. (5-11-22)
Weichelt, Rudolf O.Masch. (12-9-20)
Wenzke, Günter Mech.O.Gfr. (7-5-23)
Wetzel, Eduard O.Fk.Mt. (5-1-20)
Willisch, Josef Fk.O.Gfr. (19-3-24)
Wörner, Philipp Masch.Mt. (22-10-20)
Wolf, Karl Masch.H.Gfr. (12-8-20)

WRECK SITE

The somewhat pathetic remains of this boat appear to be well buried by a sand drift. It lies on a seabed of sand and fine shingle, in a general depth of 55m (180ft), being the lowest astronomical depth.

Only the bow emerges from the sand drift and one tube remains visible, the rest of the wreck is completely buried.

U 212, KRIEGSMARINE U-BOAT

DATE OF LOSS: 21 July 1944
DEPTH: 57m
REFERENCE: 50 28'.904 N 000 10'.626 W
LOCATION: 15.38 nautical miles SSW of Beachy Head

Type: VIIC ocean-going attack boat   **Builders**: Krupp Germaniawerft AG, Kiel-Gaarden for Kriegsmarine   **Ordered**: on 16 October 1939, within the batch of U 205–U 212   **Keel laid**: as Yard No.641 on 17 May 1941   **Launched**: on 17 March 1942   **Commissioned**: Kapitänleutnant Helmut Vogler on 25 April 1942.   **Feldpost No**: M 44 245

TECHNICAL SPECIFICATIONS

See page 342.

Helmut Vogler was born on 23 September 1916 at Bad Oldesloe and commenced his naval career in 1935. Vogler began his submarine service as First Watch Officer on U 567 between April 1941 and December 1941. On 1 July 1942 he was promoted to Kapitänleutnant.

Kplt. Vogler, who assumed command from the commissioning, was the boat's only commander.

U 212 was assigned to 8.U-Flottille, Danzig as *Ausbildungsboot* on 25 April 1942.

U 212 left Kiel on 12 September 1941 and sailed to Narvik in northwest Norway, arriving on 26 September 1942. She then formally joined 11.U-Flottille, Bergen on 1 October as a frontline boat.

On 10 October 1942 *U 212* left Narvik for operations in the Norwegian Sea. To assist German destroyers with their mine-laying operations, *U 212* teamed up with *U 586* on the 13th and carried out reconnaissance work near Jan Mayen Island, returning to Narvik on 5 November.

U 212 departed Narvik on 19 November 1942 and patrolled in the Arctic. She arrived back in Narvik on 25 December 1942.

On 28 December 1942 *U 212* and Vogler transferred to Bergen in southwest Norway, arriving on the 31st.

The boat left Bergen for a short patrol in the Arctic on 28 February and returned to base on 1 March 1943.

On 8 March 1943 Vogler left Bergen with *U 212* for a patrol in the Arctic and put into Narvik on 7 April.

On 1 June 1943 *U 212* was formally assigned to 13.U-Flottille, Trondheim, Norway.

(7) *U 212* left Narvik on 3 June 1943 and patrolled in the Arctic. She entered the port of Hammerfest (70° 39 44'N 23° 40 58'E), northern Norway, on 16 May.

(8) Leaving Hammerfest on 3 June 1943, *U 212* transported a number of troops for reconnaissance work on Bear Island, where they destroyed an Allied weather station and, on 12 July, *U 212* arrived back in Narvik.

(9) Having left Narvik on 26 July 1943, Vogler laid mines during the night of the 31st in position 68° 40'N 51° 51'E (centre of the area), near Sengeysky Island and southeast of the island of Kolgujew, in the Peschora Sea. *U 212* returned to Bergen on 10 August.

On 5 August 1943 the little 80-ton Soviet steamboat *Majakovsky* (GUSMP/Archangelskoe Shipping Co.) appears to have detonated one of the mines and sank.

(10) On 11 October 1943 *U 212* departed Bergen and joined up with *Siegfried* group to intercept convoys HX 262 and SC 145, some 500 miles east of Newfoundland. On the 27th the group had been unsuccessful and split into three wolfpacks, with *U 212* joining group 3. On 1 November 1943, *U 212* was formally assigned to 3.U-Flottille, La Pallice, and another change was made. Two larger *Körner* and *Jahn* wolfpacks were formed, with *U 212* joining *Körner*. Later the two packs split into five *Tirpitz* sub-groups, but when the convoys were not found the two wolfpacks were dissolved and the boats sailed eastward. The U-boats all joined up again as *Eisenhart* group, but after a fruitless search for the two convoys, *U 212* joined up with *Schill* 3 group, west of Spain, to wait for the northbound MKS 30/SL 139 convoys. In the evening of 20 November, *Schill* group, including *U 212*, surfaced after failing to find the convoys. *U 212* put into her new base at La Pallice on 2 December.

(11) Kplt. Vogler departed La Pallice with *U 212* on 10 January 1944 and joined *Rügen* wolfpack, to the west of the British Isles. A KMS convoy was sighted on the 26th, west of the North Channel and *U 212* formed a patrol line with six of the most southerly U-boats, called *Hinein* group, west of Ireland. Their intention was to intercept and attack a southbound convoy on the 27th, however the convoy was further west than expected and the mission failed. On the 29th the invasion of Western France was reported. All available boats were sent at full speed to the Bay of Biscay. However after discovering the 'invasion' was nothing more than a grouping of Spanish trawlers, the U-boats returned to their operational areas. *U 212* formed up with *Igel 1* group at the beginning of February and from the 4th operated in an area southwest of Iceland. Three convoys were sighted west of North Channel on the 14th and the two *Igel* packs 1 and 2 made for an assembly area 600 miles southwest of Ireland to intercept, but failed to find them once again. *U 212* sailed south at full speed, but at dawn on the 19th, all they found were destroyers and the operation was cancelled. *U 212* joined *Preussen* group and Control ordered Helmut Vogler to rendezvous with Detlev Krankenhagen in the new Type IXC40 boat, *U 549* and made a transmission using the 'Naxos set'. Then just as the orders were being carried out and the boats were alongside each other, unidentified Allied aircraft attacked *U 212*, first on 25 February and again on the 27th. Following another fruitless operation about 450 miles north of the Azores, *U 212* returned to La Pallice, arriving on 12 March 1944. Ob.Bts.Mt. Willi Rosette was lost overboard on 24 March 1944, the day of his birth in 1921.

(12) Helmut Vogler took *U 212* out of La Pallice on 8 April and sailed to Brest, arriving on 10 April. *Schnorchel* equipment was then fitted while she was in port.

(13) *U 212* departed La Pallice on 6 June, in company with seven other *schnorchel*-equipped boats, to form the *Landwirt* group and proceeded to an area north of Cherbourg. On the 7th, two experienced *Mosquito* crews of 248 Squadron (Flight Officers A.J.L. Bonnet and D.J. Turner) attacked

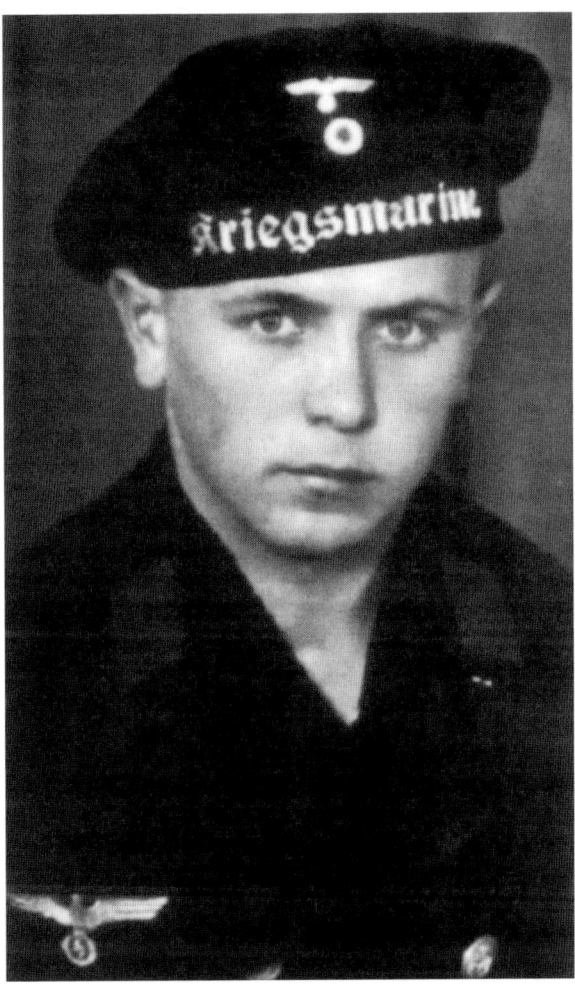

Johan Meyerkia, who had served on *U 212*. (Private collection)

U 212 with 57mm Tsetse cannon fire. (Two days after the attack, pilot Bonnet and his co-pilot-navigator were killed.) After suffering damage to her *schnorchel*, 37mm gun and her port diving and compensating tanks, *U 212* returned to La Pallice on 9 June 1944.

(14) The next patrol, leaving on 12 June was abandoned due to mechanical problems (the boat was beset by malfunctions for much of her career) returning to La Pallice on the 16th.

(15) On 22 June *U 212* left La Pallice on the dangerous mission of transporting machine-gun and anti-tank ammunition to the beleaguered port of Cherbourg, with three other *schnorchel*-equipped boats. The following morning however, Control cancelled the orders because information reached them that the Allies had blocked Cherbourg harbour entrance. *U 212* returned to La Pallice on the 26th, where (the doubtless relieved) Vogler unloaded the deadly cargo.

(16) *U 212* sailed from La Pallice on 28 June 1944 for a torpedo patrol to the Allied landing area in the Bay of the Seine, but the boat was recalled to await orders following the invasion of France. *U 212* put into Brest on 5 July.

FINAL PATROL

(17) That same day, Helmut Vogler departed Brest with *U 212* on his last patrol. It is likely that the boat arrived in her operational area of the English Channel around the 14th. What is known for certain is that on 21 July, the two British frigates, HMS *Curzon* (Lt A.Diggen) and HMS *EKINS* (Lt G. Bonner-Davis) obtained a radar contact 47 miles southeast of Brighton and a frantic chase commenced.

Attacks by *Curzon* and *Ekins* – 21/7/44 50 27 N 00 13 W – Depth 34 fathoms – Time 0111hrs
Escorting Convoy FTM42:

> A radar contact at 3,300 yards was obtained at Green 100 degrees: this was held with difficulty and lost at
> 0114hrs. The contact was at first considered to have been a buoy. HE was then picked up and course was
> altered towards at 0117hrs. Six minutes later radar contact was regained at 2,500 yards bearing 221 but
> was lost after 2 minutes. It was suspected the radar contact might be with a schnorchel.
>
> HE contact was observed to draw left and at 0134hrs schnorchel gear was sighted right ahead at 150
> yards. Altering course to keep the schnorchel in sight on the port quarter, CURZON increased speed.
> The schnorchel then dipped, the U-boat presumably becoming aware of the escort through her increase
> in speed. At 0158hrs CURZON obtained an ASDIC contact bearing red 30 degrees and attacked with
> depth charges at 0214hrs. EKINS joined and gained contact at 0223 at 900 yards range, attacking with a
> five-charge pattern at 0239hrs. At 0248hrs CURZON attacked again and a heavy muffled explosion was
> heard after the last charge had exploded…at 0315hrs and 0349hrs CURZON regained contact carrying
> out a depth charge attack followed by a Hedgehog attack which resulted in large quantities of oil rising
> to the surface.

The attack was not a verified 'kill' and was classified as 'probably sunk'. After the war however, it was
learned that *U 212* failed to return to base, so she was most likely the boat in question. HMS *Ekins*
was herself destroyed by a mine in April 1945.

The BdU Diary contains this entry for 13 August:

> *U 212* and *U 672* must be presumed lost. *U 212* put out of Brest on 5 July and *U 672* on 6 July, for the
> Seine area. There has been no further information since then. *U 212* and *U 672* received instructions to
> return on 27 July and 7 August and should in the meantime have put in.

AUD 1369/44 NARA T 1022, Roll 4066, PG 30202, 30351–30353 U-Boot-Ehrenmal Möltenort

THE MEN WHO DIED IN U 212

Alluskewitz, Alfred Mt. (Born: 4-5-1922)
Apitzsch, Arthur Ob.Gfr. (26-7-1922)
Arm, Werner Lt (18-2-1922)
Bernhardt, Günter Ob.Gfr. (30-5-1923)
Blassing, Erich Ob.Masch. (29-4-1918)
Brieger, Waldemar Matrose. (2-11-1925)
Busch, Herbert Gfr. (26-1-1924)
Czitrich, Heinrich Ob.Mt. (8-7-1919)
Doms, Ludwig Ob.Gfr. (27-3-1925)
Eckhardt, Harry Mtr.Gfr (1-8-1921)
Eichwald, Erwin Ob.Gfr. (17-6-1924)
Ferchland, Werner Ob.Gfr. (6-7-1923)
Fuhrmann, Erhard Ob.Gfr. (3-8-1923)
Gahr, Max Ob.Mt. (18-6-1921)
Groger, Osmar Ob.Mt. (24-7-1921)
Gündel, Gerhard Ob.Gfr. (11-10-1923)
Händel, Heinz Ob.Gfr. (26-6-1924)
Heimes, Günther Oblt.z.S. (14-12-1920)
Heinrichs, Karl-Ferdinand Ob.Mt. (9-7-1921)
Hössinger, Alfred Ob.Gfr. (22-12-1924)
Hübner, Kurt Ob.Gfr. (21-12-1924)
Illek, Josef Oblt.Ing [date unknown]
Jllex, Josef Oblt.Ing (26-7-1921)
Kaupe, Harry Ob.Gfr. (14-08-1923)
Kowoll, Walter Mt. (5-5-1924)

Krämer, Georg Ob.Gfr. (3-11-1924)
Kretschmer, Gerhard Gfr. (20-4-1925)
Lehnoff, Reinhold Ob.Gfr. (31-5-1925)
Maaser, Walter Gfr. (17-6-1924)
Michalowitz, Gerhard Haupt.Gfr. (2-2-1922)
Oschmann. Werner Ob.Gfr. (19-4-1924)
Pagels, Horst Mt. (22-8-1920)
Reichherzer, Xaver Ob.Mt. (28-8-1916)
Reiners, Hans–Günter Ob.Mt. (22-4-1922)
Reinke, Herbert Ob.Gfr. (12-9-1924)
Rüdiger, Alfred Ob.Gfr. (22-11-1923)
Rustenbach, Fritz Mt. (19-3-1921)
Schneider, Karl Mt. (9-11-1920)
Scholten, Gerhard Gfr. (24-8-1923)
Schwarz, Helmut Ob.Gfr. (13-4-1922)
Semrau, Otto Ob.Gfr. (6-1-1924)
Tamm, Anton Ob.Masch. (3-11-1919)
Trutenau, Otto Ob.Strm. (19-12-1915)
Vogler, Helmut Kplt. (Commander)
   (21-7-1944)
Voigtländer, Hans Haupt.Gfr. (2-11-1921)
Wächter, Paul Ob.Gfr. (7-3-1923)
Wirsing, Günter Gfr. (6-5-1921)
Wolff, Horst Mt. (13-1-1920)
Zimmerl, Harald Oblt.z.S. WO. (2-4-1923)

HMS *Ekins*. (Author's collection)

WRECK SITE

The wreck of what is believed to be *U 212* is orientated in an east to west direction, with the bows to the west. It lies on a seabed of sand, shell and pebbles, in a general depth of 45m (147ft), being the lowest astronomical depth. The wreck is upright and standing 5.4m high at the conning tower, but just forward of this point, the casing is shattered on the port side, possibly where one of the depth charges detonated. The stern torpedo tube is positioned some 10-15m away from the stern section which has broken off and collapsed, with no sign of the two bronze propellers. Much of the outer casing is also detached and strewn around the wreck site. A large shoal of bib can usually be found swimming around the conning tower area and a couple of large conger eels have been observed. It should be remembered that this is also a war grave.

U 86, SM IMPERIAL U-BOAT

DATE OF LOSS: 30 June 1921
DEPTH: 53m
REFERENCE: 50 26'.628 N 000 33'.954 W
LOCATION: 18.96 nautical miles SSE of Selsey Bill

Type: Mittel-U (Improved Type U65) ocean torpedo attack boat   *Builders*: Germaniawerft, Kiel for Kaiserliche Deutsche Marine   *Ordered*: on 23 June 1915, within the batch of *U 81–U 86*   *Keel laid*: as Yard No.256 on 5 November 1915   *Launched*: on 7 November 1916   *Commissioned*: by Kapitänleutnant Friedrich Crüseman on 30 November 1916

TECHNICAL SPECIFICATIONS

Hull: double   *Surface displacement*: 808 tons   *U/Dt*: 946 tons   *LBDH*: 70.10m × 6.30m × 4m × 8.70m   *Machinery*: 2 × 1,200ps Maschinefabrik-Augsburg-Nürnberg (MAN) diesels   *Props*: 2 bronze   *S/Sp*: 16.8 knots   *Op/R*: 11,220 nautical miles at 8 knots   *Sub/R*: 56 nautical miles at 5 knots   *U/Power*: 2 × 600ps electric motors gave 9.1 knots   *Batteries*: lead/acid   *Fuel/Cap*: 81 + 83 tons   *Armament*: 2 bow and 2 stern 50.04cm torpedo tubes   *Torpedoes*: 8 × 50.04cm (19.7in)   *Guns*: 1 × 105mm (4.13in) forward deck gun and 1 × 88mm (3.46in) aft off conning tower   *Ammo*: 220 rounds   *Diving*: max-op-depth 50m (164ft) and 45 sec to crash-dive   *Complement*: 35

U 86 was formally assigned to the German-based IV.U-Flottille at Emden on 21 February 1917 with Kplt. Friedrich Crüseman the commander from 30 November 1916 until 22 June 1917.

Crüseman made the following two operational sorties with *U 86*:

U 86 departed Emden on 20 March 1917 for operations in the Atlantic and to the west of Ireland, travelling via the Orkney Isles. The 444-ton Danish sailing vessel *H.B. Linnemann* (1902 – Hans Pedersen, Marstal, Denmark) was on passage from Göteborg to Casablanca when she was left abandoned after being shelled and damaged by SM *U 55* (Wilhelm Werner), however about 25-30 miles off Achille Head on 4 April, Crüseman also hit her with gunfire and four men were killed; the shattered vessel was later towed into Galway, Ireland and repaired. On 14 October 1920 the repairs were completed and she was sold abroad.

On 5 April 1917, three vessels were sunk while bound from Gulfport on the Mississippi for Calais with timber: the 2,968-ton Belgian SS *Siberier* (1907 – Lloyd Royal Belge, S.A., Antwerp) was torpedoed and sunk off Fastnet Rock; she was followed by the 127-ton French sailing vessel *Dunkerquoise*, which was captured and sunk by gunfire, 45 miles west of the Blasket; the 142-ton French sailing boat *Marie Celine* followed her to a watery grave after she was destroyed off southwest Ireland by gunfire and lost with all hands.

Trimmer John Collins (44yrs) and fireman and trimmer William Griffiths (31yrs) were both killed on 6 April when the 6,535-ton steam tanker *Rosalind* (1913 – Oil Tank S.S. Co. Ltd, Liverpool) was sunk in the Atlantic by a torpedo without warning; she was armed for defence and was transporting oil from Port Arthur, Texas and Norfolk, Virginia to Queenstown, Ireland.

On the voyage home via the Isles of Orkney on 18 April, Crüseman found the damaged 1,091-ton Swedish steamer *Atalanta* (1872 – Förnyade Ångfartygs A/B Viking, Göteborg) still afloat in the North Sea, 200 miles off the English coast; the ship was then sunk by torpedo at 56 33'N 04 18'E; the previous day *UC 52* had captured and shelled the vessel, at about 56° 30'N 04° 10'E. Out of her crew of seventeen, only Sven Magnus Ahl survived.

THE MEN WHO DIED

Albert Bengtsson, 34yrs	Nordström, Axel Fritiof, 25yrs
Andreasson, Manne Albin, 36yrs	Norman, Carl Albert, 40yrs, Master
Hansson, Ivar Heribert, 34yrs	Olsson, August Valdemar, 35yrs
Karlsson, Johan Efraim, 35yrs	Olsson, Sven August, 57yrs
Kristoffersson, Axel Bernhard, 26yrs	Rönn, Knut Wilhelm, 18yrs
Larsson, Gustaf Sigfrid born, 28yrs	Svartling, Fritz Leonard, 39yrs
Möberg, Leonard Vallentin, 27yrs	Svensson, Axel Hjalmar, 38yrs
Nordmark, Carl Hjalmar, 30yrs	Svensson, Carl Albanus, 24yrs

U 86 returned to Emden on 19 April 1917.

(2) Leaving Emden on 17 May 1917, *U 86* journeyed round the Orkney Isles to patrol an area in the Atlantic, 200 miles west of the English Channel. During the war cruise *U 86* sank four steamships with torpedoes and without any warning. The defensively armed steamship *Antinoe* (1907 – Egypt & Levant Steam Ship Co. Ltd, London) of 2,396 tons, was sunk on 28 May; she was transporting iron ore from Seville to Newport, Monmouth and all of her crew of twenty-one perished 150 miles off Bishop Rock.

SOME OF THOSE WHO DIED

Aquilena, Emmanuel, 20yrs, Mess Room Steward	De Rouffignac, A. Master
Barnett, K., 31yrs, Sailor	Edwards, Henry James, 21yrs, Sailor
Callega, Alfonso, 52yrs, Donkeyman	Galea, Carmelus Joseph Joannes, 30yrs, Steward
Comerto, James, 42yrs, Fireman	Gauci, George, 42yrs, Fireman
Dallen, William Henry Lance Corporal RMLI	Hamilton, J., 42yrs, Able Seaman
Dawe, William Cephas, 42yrs, Second Engineer	Johnson, W. Able Seaman
	Maginn, J., 53yrs, Sailor

McIntosh, John, 36yrs, 2nd Mate

McNulty, Charles Hugh, 28yrs, Boatswain
(Bosun)

Milne, Fred Joshua, 41yrs, 1st Mate

Minuti, Alexander Francis Paul, 54yrs, Fireman

Mitchley, Matthew Walter, 20yrs, 3rd Engineer

Nelson, M., 30yrs, Ship's Cook

Wilcox, John, 31yrs, 1st Engineer

The *Limerick* (1898 – Union S.S. Co. of New Zealand Ltd, London) a defensively armed 6,827-ton steamer, was sunk on 28 May, 140 miles off Bishop Rock; she was hauling frozen meat and general cargo from Sydney to London.

EIGHT CREWMEN DROWNED

Bjorseth, E., 48yrs, Greaser

Currall, Frederick, 35yrs, Fireman

Harding, Matthew, 33yrs, Donkeyman

Jarvis, George James, 43yrs, Greaser

Maylor, Richard, 47yrs, Fireman and Trimmer

Neild, Roy, 26yrs, 3rd Engineer

Stacey, Frederick Charles, 31yrs, Fireman

Young, George Kinloch, 23yrs, 3rd Engineer (Senior)

The 5,793-ton steamship *Oswego* (1916 – Ellerman.s Wilson Line Ltd, Hull) was defensively armed and carrying a general cargo from New York to Hull when she was sunk, 175 miles from Bishop Rock. The Greek steamer *N. Hadzikyriakos* (1904 – G. Hadzikyriakos, Piraeus) of 3,533 tons was also sunk in the Atlantic, while en-route from Rosario, Argentina to London on 31 May and twenty crewmen died, but three survivors were rescued by the Q-ship *Mavis*.

U 86 returned to Emden on 9 June 1917, via the Orkney Isles.

Oblt.z.S. Alfred Götze assumed command of the boat on 23 June 1917.

(3) On 26 June 1917 *U 86* left Emden for operations in the North Sea against the Shetland/Norway convoys. Götze only managed to sink the 66-ton Swedish fishing smack *Bessie* on 2 July, before returning to Emden on 11 July. On the 9th however, a torpedo actually struck a steamship, but it failed to detonate.

(4) After departing Emden on 4 August 1917, *U 86* travelled around the Isles of Shetland to a patrol area, west of the English Channel. Off Bishop Rock, the 3,929-ton Norwegian SS *Capella I* (1899 – Hvalfanger Aktieselskapet Capella, Sandefjord) was captured, then shelled and sunk, while transporting whale oil from Stromness, South Georgia to Liverpool. The defensively armed 9,920-ton SS *Turakina* (1902 – New Zealand Shipping Co. Ltd, London) was sunk without warning by torpedoes, 120 miles from Bishop Rock; she was carrying general cargo from London to New York and New Zealand and two men, trimmer, C. Barendrecht (19yrs) and the ship's baker, Arthur Cubitt Wenham (29yrs), were both drowned.

U 86 returned to Emden, via Shetland, on 7 September 1917.

(5) *U 86* sailed from Emden on 12 October 1917 via the Kiel Canal, through the Skagerrak and around the Isles of Shetland, to an area off the southwest coast of Ireland. Götze had an uneventful voyage and returned to Emden on 8 November, via the Orkney Isles.

(6) Leaving Emden on 6 December 1917, *U 86* sailed for operations in the Dover Straits and the English Channel, off the French west coast, but Götze took the long route via the Isles of Orkney. Götze torpedoed and sunk the defensively armed 3,146-ton steamer *Polvarth* (1909 – Polvarth S.S. Co. Ltd, Swansea) without warning on 20 December; she was delivering zinc oil, phosphates and naval stores from Gibraltar to Swansea and two men were drowned, including 28-year-old William John Beer, a steward.

The U-boat returned via the Orkney Isles and arrived at Emden on 31 December.

Oblt.z.S. Helmut Brümmer Patzig, who was born in Danzig on 6 October 1890, assumed command of *U 86* on 26 January 1918.

(7) *U 86* departed Emden on 29 January 1918 and took the long route via the North Sea and around the Orkney Isles, along the North Minch and North Channel to reach the Irish Sea.

During the patrol, Patzig sank three steamships and two small vessels. On 14 February, Patzig captured the 119-ton British sailing vessel *Bessie Stephens*, 10 miles off Lundy Island, and sank her with gunfire; she was delivering china clay from Fowey to Preston.

Helmut Brümmer Patzig.
(Author's collection)

Two able seaman, Julian Paimal (32yrs) and James Coombs (58yrs), were killed when the defensively armed SS *Pinewood* (1914 – W. France, Fenwick & Co. Ltd, London) of 2,219 tons, was capured and sunk by gunfire on 17 February, while sailing from Cardiff to Queenstown, Ireland with timber. On the 19th, the ship's cook, Henry Robert Fagrenkrug was killed when the 188-ton steam coaster *Wheatflower* (Spillers, Cardiff) was captured and sunk by gunfire, 10 miles off Tuskar Rock; she was en-route from Cardiff to Dublin with coal.

Captain Ernest Edward Bonner (38yrs) and Robert William Fitzjohn (34yrs), a fireman, were both lost on 20 February when the defensively armed 1,527-ton steamship *Djerv* (1906 – The Shipping Controller, London) was torpedoed and sunk without warning; she was in ballast and en-route from Heysham to Newport, Monmouth.

The steamer *Rio Verde* (1901 – London-American Maritime Trading Co., London), which was 4,025 tons and armed for defence, was on passage from Glasgow for Milford Haven with coal when she was torpedoed and sunk without warning on 21 February, 12 miles off Skerrie Isles. Twenty men died, including three Royal Navy personnel.

THE MEN WHO DIED

Appleyard, William Warson, 26yrs, Carpenter
Arlow, W., Assistant Cook
Blair, Alexander, Leading Seaman RN (DEMS gunner)
Brown, Charlie, 25yrs, Fireman and Trimmer
Buchan, Stewart Able Seaman RN (DEMS gunner)
Buchanan, J.T., 2nd Mate
Bull, John, 29yrs, Fireman and Trimmer
Coker, John, 24yrs, Fireman and Trimmer
Cole, John, 22yrs, Fireman and Trimmer
Davison, George Robertson, 39yrs, 1st Engineer
Estill, W.H., Master

MacDonald, John, 20yrs, Assistant Steward
Marsh, Walter Seaman RNR (DEMS gunner
Martyn, Francis Joseph Leslie, 24yrs, 1st Mate
McClure, Thomas, 31yrs, Boatswain (Bosun)
McInnes, Donald, 32yrs, Able Seaman
Mukro, John, 26yrs, Fireman and Trimmer
Richardson, W., 3rd Engineer
Russell, Alexander, 36yrs, 2nd Engineer
Wallace, G., Donkeyman

U 86 returned to Emden on 3 March 1918, travelling back via the Orkney Isles, through the Skagerrak and along the Kiel Canal.

(8) Leaving Emden on 23 April 1918, Patzig sailed to the south of Ireland, voyaging via the Kiel Canal and Skagerrak to the Orkney Isles, west of the Hebrides, the North Channel and down the Irish Sea. Seven steamships and two sailing vessels were sunk during the month-long voyage.

Richard Edwards, a 19-year-old horseman, was lost, when the 6,044-ton defensively armed steamship *Kafue* (1913 – Bucknall Steamship Lines, Ltd, North Shields), was torpedoed without warning; she was then shelled and sunk off the Mull of Galloway on 30 April; the ship was en-route from Glasgow to Calcutta with general cargo. The 255-ton armed steam coaster *Kempock* (1866 – J.E. Edwards, Glasgow) was bound from Belfast to Manchester with potatoes when she was captured, then shelled and sunk, off Copeland Island light on the 30th. On 2 May, the SS *Medora* (1912 – Canadian Pacific Railway Ocean Lines, Liverpool) of 5,135 tons was armed for defence when she was hit with a torpedo without warning; the ship sank off the Mull of Galloway while transporting general cargo from Liverpool and Lamlash to Montreal; the master, wireless operator and one gunner were taken prisoner. The 4,298-ton steamer *Leeds City* (1908 – St. Just S.S Co. Ltd (1908) was also armed for defence while carrying flour and wheat from Portland, Maine to Manchester; *U 86* torpedoed and sunk her without warning in the North Channel on 6 May.

The Norwegian 1,656-ton steamer *San Andrés* (1911 – D/S A/S Otto Thoresens Linie, Kristiania) was torpedoed and sunk without warning on 11 May 1918 while travelling from Barcelona to Kristiania via Swansea with general cargo. At 1845hrs the master, Captain Georg William Simpson from Sarpsborg, discovered two torpedoes had been fired at the starboard side. The first one missed, but the second one detonated in the aft part of the engine room and the ship sank within 2 minutes, 100 miles west of Lundy, at position 51° 23'N 07° 53'W. Onboard were twenty-five seamen, three from another ship that had also been torpedoed; one was an English signalman. Two of the crew died: 3rd engineer Harald Olausen from Kristiania and Georg Jacobsen, a stoker from Denmark.

On 12 May, the defensively armed 1,412-ton SS *Inniscarra* (1903 – City of Cork Steam Packet Co. Ltd, Cork) was destroyed by a torpedo without warning off Ballycotton Island, while on passage from Fishguard for Cork with a general cargo and twenty-eight crewmen drowned (all hands).

SOME OF THE CREWMEN WHO DIED

Attridge, Arthur, 72yrs, Carpenter
Buckley, F., 27yrs, Trimmer
Clarke, George, 61yrs, Able Seaman
Cox, Patrick, 47yrs, Fireman
Driscoll, Daniel, 39yrs, Able Seaman
Evans, William, 54yrs, 2nd Mate
Forde, Michael, 66yrs, Quartermaster
Geary, Maurice, 42yrs, Fireman
Harrington, John, 48yrs, Fireman
Harris, James, 36yrs, Fireman
Hayes, Robert, 53yrs, Greaser
Mullane, John, 37yrs, Cook

Murphy, Michael, 34yrs, Able Seaman
Neill, William, 60yrs, 1st Engineer
O'Brien, John, 56yrs, Trimmer
O'Connell, John, 27yrs, Fireman
O'Connell, Laurence, 36yrs, Fireman
O'Hare, Michael, 41yrs, Greaser
O'Mahony, Denis, 29yrs, Fireman
O'Shea, Denis, 30yrs, Fireman
O'Sullivan, Matthew, 53yrs, Able Seaman
Peters, Robert James, 32yrs, 2nd Engineer
Ryan, William, 38yrs, Donkeyman

Four days later, and without warning, Patzig sank the defensively armed 4,181-ton SS *Tartary* (1901 – D. MacIver Sons & Co. Ltd, Liverpool) with a torpedo off Skulmartin light vessel, northeast Ireland; she was voyaging from Liverpool to Rio de la Plata, Uruguay with general cargo, but there was no loss of life.

In the Skagerrak off Songvaar, the 656-ton wooden-hulled Norwegian barque *Meran* (1891 – A/S Orion, Holmestrand) was captured on 22 May and set on fire by explosives, after which she sank; the boat was transporting 292 standards of pit props from Holmestrand, Norway to West Hartlepool.

U 86 returned to Emden on 25 May 1918, travelling west of the Hebrides and around the Isles of Shetland, to the Skagerrak and through the Kiel Canal.

(9) On 20 June 1918, *U 86* left Emden and made for a patrol area west of the English Channel, travelling via the North Sea, the Isles of Shetland, west of the Hebrides and the west coast of Ireland and returned via the same route to Heligoland, arriving there on 12 July 1918.

In the North Sea and the same day as leaving port, Patzig attacked the Norwegian barque *Eglantine* (1866 – Aktieselskapet 'Eglantine', Kristiania); the old 339-ton wooden-hulled boat, which was built at Quebec in 1866, had left West Hartlepool at 1150hrs on 18 June, bound for Porsgrunn, Norway. At 1100hrs the following morning a German submarine (*U 86*) fired a shell towards the sailing vessel, but missed. The crew, however, began lowering the lifeboats in anticipation, while the submarine continued firing. One shell hit the davit, leaving the lifeboat badly damaged, but fragments hit most of the crew, killing some and leaving many badly wounded. After a few minutes, those men still able to, managed to lower a small boat and left the ship, which sunk within a matter of minutes. Out of the crew of nine, only one man, Håkon Olsen from Fredrikstad survived.

THE MEN WHO DIED

Andersen, Anders Johan, 27yrs, Sailor
Andersen, Arnt, 18yrs, Sailor
Eliassen, Georg, 40yrs, 1st Mate
Eriksen, Erik E., 19yrs, Sailor

Josefsen, Alexander, 47yrs, Sailor
Ring, C.J., 42yrs, Master
Thoresen, Simon Arthur, 19yrs, Sailor
Woll, Axel, 37yrs, Cook

The 339-ton wooden-hulled Norwegian barque *Eglantine*, which was built at Quebec in 1866. (Author's collection)

Llandovery Castle. (Author's collection)

Torpedoes fired without warning by *U 86* sank the defensively armed 9,399-ton SS *Atlantian* (1900 – Fred. Leyland & Co. Ltd, Liverpool), 110 miles off Eagle Island on the 26th; the chief officer and wireless operator were taken prisoner. The ship was journeying from Galveston, Texas to Liverpool with cotton.

U 86 was attacked by an enemy submarine later that day, but escaped undamaged.

The most controversial sinking was at 2130hrs on 27 June and 116 miles west of the Fastnet Rock, when the 11,423-ton hospital ship *Llandovery Castle* (1914 – Union-Castle Mail Steam Ship Co. Ltd) was torpedoed and sunk by *U 86*. The four-funnelled vessel, which had already made five voyages to Canada and carried 3,223 patients, was travelling independantly and unprotected from Halifax, Nova Scotia to Liverpool. Patzig pursued the liner for almost 4 hours before firing two torpedoes without warning, even though the ship was clearly illuminated and painted with a large Red Cross, the sign of a hospital ship. One of the torpedoes missed its target, but the other struck just abaft the engines at No.4 hold and a second massive internal explosion followed almost immediately. All the lights went out instantly and the after-part of the ship was badly wrecked. The signal was given to stop and reverse engines, but there was no response because all the engine room crew had been either killed or wounded. The big ship just ploughed forward. Lt Col. T.H. MacDonald, the commanding officer, paraded his personnel at the various boat stations and at the same time, the order was given to lower the lifeboats on both sides. However, by this time launching the boats was made extremely difficult due to the steep sloping deck and the ship's continued forward movement. At least two boats were swamped and lost in the operation, but within the 10 minutes it took for the ship to sink, everyone had been taken off, except those killed by the explosion. Major Lyon was the last to leave.

The *Llandovery Castle* had left Halifax on 20 June, under the command of Captain A.E. Sylvester. She was carrying 258 people, including eighty medical officers and fourteen nursing sisters from the Canadian Medical Services, the rest being crewmembers. (As luck would have it, she wasn't carrying any patients at the time.)

Captain E.A. Sylvester later stated in his report:

At 9.30 pm on 27 June, when about 114 miles S. and 74 degrees W (true) from a position 15 miles south (true) from the Fastnet, the ship was torpedoed without warning by an enemy submarine. At the time the vessel was steering a steady N.74 degrees E (true) course at 13.6 knots, and was showing navigation and the usual hospital ship lights.

So far as I am aware, no one saw the wake of the torpedo. About 3 minutes after the explosion, the carpenter reported the ship was hit in No 4 hold, and would not remain afloat. I then gave orders to lower all the boats and sent them away, and on the chief officer coming up to lower the starboard accident boat I ordered the ship to be abandoned. The second officer found a lifeboat with the after end lowered in the water and the fore made fast, the bow hanging in the air by the tackle. With the assistance of a steward, the second officer lowered the boat in the water, and the remainder of those on board went down the ropes into her. I went down a life line into the boat and we pulled off from the ship, pulling away just in time to avoid the suction as she went down stern first. This was not more than 10 minutes from the time she was torpedoed. We pulled over the spot as soon as the turmoil had subsided, and succeeded in picking up eleven men from rafts and wreckage.

We were pulling down to a man who was calling out from the water ahead of the boat when the submarine appeared and ordered the boat alongside. The second officer replied, 'We are picking up a man from the water', as the order was not promptly obeyed, two rifle shots were fired over the boat, and someone on the submarine shouted, 'Come alongside or we will shoot with the big gun'.

The boat accordingly proceeded alongside the submarine. I was taken onboard to the conning tower. An officer, who appeared to be in command, asked me what ship it was. I replied, 'The hospital ship Llandovery Castle'. He said, 'Oh yes but you were carrying eight American flight officers. I answered, 'I beg your pardon; we were not. We have seven Canadian medical officers on board and the ship is chartered by the Canadian government to carry sick and wounded men from England to Halifax'. To this his reply was, 'You have been carrying American flight officers'. I answered, I have been running to Canada for six month with wounded and give you my word of honour that we have carried none except patients, medical staff and crew and sisters'. The officer asked if any Canadian officer was in the boat and on receiving the reply 'yes' ordered him on board. The officer [submarine] said to him, 'You are an American flight officer'. I said, 'No he is not, he is a Canadian medical officer'. The submarine officer then asked the Canadian officer what he was and on receiving a similar reply ordered him back to the boat. I was also ordered back to the boat and warned to get away as soon as possible. The boat was let go, oars got out and we proceeded to pull away from the submarine.

The submarine then circled round through the wreckage at full speed, twice coming close to the boat; the occupants of the boat shouted out 'same boat'. The boat was again ordered alongside the submarine and the second and fourth officers were taken aboard. After a few minutes these two officers returned to the boat and we cast off and proceeded. The submarine after circling round again just missing the boat twice, the last time by about 2ft, went a short distance away and appeared to stop. From this position she opened fire at unseen targets and fired about 12 shells. One shell passed near the boat. We set sail and saw no more of the submarine and were finally picked up by a destroyer [Lysander]. I declare that the German officer's allegations that the Llandovery Castle was being employed contrary to the Hague Convention were utterly false.

Report of Second Officer, Mr L.C. Chapman:

When the explosion took place I was asleep in my cabin but immediately went on deck to superintend the lowering of the starboard boats re the drill. When the last of the boats had been lowered, I myself left in boat No 4…in company with the Fourth Officer I was called onboard the submarine. The German officer asked me who I was and if we were carrying American flight officers. I said 'No' and then he said, 'You had ammunition on board; there was a loud explosion' I explained to him that it was the boilers had burst as the water reached them. He then told us to go back to the boat. We were then ordered to cast off again. After we left the submarine we put up our mast. The submarine came towards us with a high speed and just missed sinking our boat by a few feet. Our captain ordered us to set sail. The submarine again came at us and missed us by 2ft. The wash nearly capsized the boat. Shortly after I heard gun fire and one shell passed over us. I saw a dozen shells burst in different directions. The captain then decided to make for land and try to get help. We sailed and rowed for about seventy miles and then we were picked up.

Major Thomas Lyon:

…when the call came for a Canadian officer to go on board the submarine I responded smartly. I jumped for the submarine and just as I was landing on the deck, a German officer pulled my arm, with the result that I fell heavily, and broke my right leg just above the ankle. I was taken to the conning tower where the commander of the submarine was standing talking to the captain. The commander said to me 'You are an American flight officer'. I said I was not and that was a Canadian medical officer. The German officer asked me whether we carried ammunition. I said 'No' we never carried anything except patients'. We were then told to get back into the boat…

Deposition of Steward T. Burgess:

When I first got on deck, I cut my foot among the mass of broken glass from lamp and windows that was lying about, but I managed to get to my station alongside the oat I was allotted to. As I was going down to the port side, I saw two or three boats hanging up in their davits with nothing but their ropes left – they were just skeleton boats, all the sheafing having been blown away by the explosion. As my boat was being lowered, I jumped into the stern, and somebody who was standing on the ship's deck let go of the fall, causing the boat to drop suddenly into the water. The fastening at one end of the life boat was not loosened and this caused the bows to swing away from the ship, and she filled and broke up, the shop dragging her along. We were all thrown into the water, except for one or two who managed to cling to the life lines hanging from the davits. I got one and had a thirty foot climb back to the ship. The lifeline I was holding swung away from the ship, but a sailor pulled me on board, and I scrambled in. I am afraid most of those who were in that boat were drowned. I went across to the opposite side of the ship, looked over and saw another lifeboat alongside. I went down the rope ladder, and had just set foot on the boat, when she went from under me and filled. I held on to the rope ladder and had just got half way up it when I felt my strength going, but I just managed to get on board the ship, which was then sinking fast and listing to starboard.

After I got on board again, I found that one of the chaps who was in the other boat had escaped too and we were intending to get into the launch but on second thoughts we concluded she would be sucked under when the ship sank and so we changed our minds and got a raft out. There were several of these rafts and each was designed to keep twenty or thirty afloat. We found the second engineer aft in his pyjamas: he had just rushed out of bed; and we helped him on with his lifebelt. He assisted us in getting the raft over but I lost sight of his after that. The sailor who was with me got over the side onto the raft and then a soldier medic turned up and they shoved off. I was standing on the ship up to my knees in water and concluding she would soon go down, I dived over the side and joined them in the raft. We had a difficult job to keep the raft from being sucked under the ship but we managed to clear and we got about a hundred yards astern, when she blew up and sank with her bows upright in the water. There was a terrible roar of things falling as she went.

Well after the ship went down we were busy clinging tight to save ourselves from getting taken off the raft by the wash the ship made but we saw a light in the distance and heard the captain's voice. He was picking up men and we called to him. He said 'All right I will be with you in a minute' and he came alongside in a lifeboat and picked us off the raft. Amongst those our lifeboat picked up, was a fireman who had been in the Canadian nurse's boat and he told us it filled up and they all went under. I saw myself two or three boats go under. That was because the ship's engines could not stop and she dragged them all under. This occurred about 9.30 to 9.45pm and we were out all that night and all Friday and we had two biscuits and about two tablespoons of water; but there was more kept in reserve as there was only twenty-four in the boat and she was provisioned for fifty. We hoisted sail soon after the gun firing and hoped to get out of sight of the submarine before day break. We were all shivering with cold. I had only a vest, a pair of trousers and a thin white coat on. Most of us had been overheard except the captain who had been last off the ship. We were picked up at eight o clock next morning by the destroyer Lysander.

When no proof could be obtained that the ship was carrying Allied airmen, Patzig gave the command: 'Klarmachen zum Tauchen', which means 'clear the decks and prepare to dive'. Only himself, two of the U-boat's officers and the boatswain's mate (bootsmansmaat) stayed on deck. However, U 86 did not dive and instead, it zig-zagged amongst the survivors and debris at a fairly high speed for almost 2 hours, during which time gun-layer Meissner, under the direction of Ltz.S. Ludwig Dithmar and Ltz.S. John Claus Boldt, fired about twelve shells from the deck gun into the darkness. It was later alleged, although there is no proven record of this, that Patzig extracted promises of secrecy from the three crewmen to conceal these atrocious deeds. It was also claimed that Patzig even faked the course of the submarine in the KTB, so that nothing would connect them with the sinking of the Llandovery Castle.

One lifeboat containing twenty-four people – one officer and five other ranks from the Canadian Army Medical Corps and eighteen of the crew – did elude the onslaught, however. They managed to slip away into the night. After 36 hours of being adrift, Patzig's war crimes unfolded, when the torpedo-boat destroyer HMS *Lysander* found them drifting, about 41 miles off the Irish coast. They were landed at Queenstown and arrived at Plymouth on Sunday, 30 June 1918. The British sloop HMS *Snowdrop* and four American destroyers raced to the area where the *Llandovery Castle* had sunk and systematically searched for any more survivors, but found none. However, an undamaged and empty lifeboat was located about 9 miles from where HMS *Lysander* had discovered the captain's boat. The rescued Canadian Medical Corps personnel were: Major T. Lyon, Sergeant A. Knight, Private F.W. Cooper, Private G.R. Hickman, Private S.A. Taylor, and Private W. Pilot.

In a story about the sinking, Sergeant A. Knight later wrote:

> Unflinchingly and calmly, as steady and collected as if on parade, without a complaint or a single sign of emotion, our fourteen devoted nursing sisters faced the terrible ordeal of certain death – only a matter of minutes – as our lifeboat neared that mad whirlpool of waters where all human power was helpless.

The fourteen nurses and eight crewmen were placed in No.5 lifeboat and sergeant Knight took charge. He said they were lowered to the water's surface and found great difficulty in breaking free from the ropes that held them to the ship's side. Two axes were even broken trying to cut them-selves away, without success. All the time the heavy swell and choppy sea pounded the boat against the ship's hull and the oars that they used to fend themselves off with all broke. Sergeant Knight stated that eventually they broke free and commenced to drift away towards the stern of the ship. Nursing Sister M.M. Fraser, the matron, turned to Sergeant Knight and asked: '*Sergeant, do you think there is any hope for us?*' to which he purportedly replied, '*No*'. It was just about then, that the poop deck appeared to break away and the vacuum it caused as it sank pulled the lifeboat into it. The boat tipped over sideways and all the occupants fell into the sea. Knight recalled that everyone was sucked under in seconds, even though they were all wearing lifebelts. That was the last time he saw any of the nursing sisters. Sergeant Knight said that he remembered going down and coming up three times before finding some wreckage to cling onto. Fortunately for him he was eventually picked up by the captain's boat; the only one to escape. Those who perished included twenty Canadian medi-cal staff.

THOSE WHO DIED

Admans, Frederick Charles, Linen Steward
Allan, Thomas, 3rd Engineer
Allen, John, Fireman
Anderson, Allan John, 4th Engineer
Anderson, Thomas, Assistant Cook
Baker, Alfred James, Ward Attendant
Barker, Frederick Victor, Assistant Laundryman
Barton, Andrew, Fireman
Batsford, William Arthur, Assistant Steward
Batsford, William Arthur, Assistant Steward
Beddows, Thomas, Trimmer
Bracken, George, Able Seaman
Bray, Albert, Able Seaman
Brennan, Michael, Trimmer
Broadbent, George, Trimmer
Campbell, Christina Canadian Nursing Sister
Campbell, Harry, Captain's Steward
Carey, George McLacklin, Able Seaman
Clarke, Clifford Hartley, Assistant Steward
Clements, William Joseph, Deck Boy
Cocks, Harry Robert, Assistant Steward
Coe, Ernest P., Chief Steward
Collier, William John, Ordinary Seaman

Cook, Ernest, Able Seaman
Coulson, Robert, 7th Engineer
Crellin, Willie Elliott, Sailor
Cumiskey, John, Trimmer
Curry, William John, Assistant Steward
Curtis, George, Sailor
Davey, William Stephen, Greaser
Davies, Edgar Allan, WO
Davis, Gustave Mitchell, Canadian Major
Douglas, Carola Josephine, Canadian Nursing
   Sister
Doyle, Patrick, Sailor
Dussault, Alexina, Canadian Nursing Sister
Earl, Percy Lionel, Fireman
Edwards, Edward James, Assistant Steward
Enright, William James Canadian Captain
Farley, Algie Victor, Deck Boy
Findlay, William, Watch
Follette, Minnie, Canadian Nursing Sister
Fortesque, Margaret Jane, Canadian Nursing
   Sister
Fox, William John, Sailor
Franklin, George, Fireman

Fraser, Margaret Marjorie, Canadian Acting Matron

Fry, William Richard, Trimmer

Fullbrook, George, Fireman and Trimmer

Fulton, Charles William Allison, Assistant Ship's Cook

Gallaher, Catharine, Canadian Nursing Sister

Gard, Charles Edward, Greaser

Giogis, Gioranni, Chef

Grima, Angelo, Trimmer

Hawker, Albert John, Butcher

Hawkes, George Ernest, WO

Heath, Alfred James, Assistant Butcher

Heath, George, Fireman

Heney, William, Fireman

Hill William Ernest, Able Seaman

Hitchens, John, Quartermaster

Hobbs, Benjamin, Deck Boy

Hodge, Arthur, Greaser

Hogan, Martin, Assistant Baker

Hooper, Frederick, Fireman

Hopley, John Holland, Deck Boy

Johnson, Burton Thomas, Electrician

Johnson, Francis William, Assistant Steward

Jones, Edwin John, Fireman

Jones, John, Able Seaman

Joseph, Harry, Fireman

Justice, James, Fireman

Kadrewell, Martin Alexander Walter, 2nd Cook

Kelly, John Frederick, Sailor

Kelly, William, Fireman

Kentfield, William, Assistant Bed Steward

King, Thomas Inman, Able Seaman

Kinloch, John Frederick, Branch Carpenter's Mate

Lacey, Raymond Edgar, Assistant Steward

Lamb, Henry, Assistant Steward

Lane, B., 2nd Baker

Lee, Lawrence, Fireman

Leighton, William, 2nd Engineer

Lemarechal, Alfred William, 2nd Waiter

Leonard, Arthur Vincent, Canadian Captain

Lodge, Alfred Thomas, Fireman

Long, James Gilbert, Deck Boy

MacDonald, Thomas Howard, Canadian Lt-Col

Mackenzie, John, Able Seaman

MacPhail, Donald G., Honorary Captain Chaplain

Manley, Frederick Leonard, (WC) Kitchen Ptr.

Matthews, Sydney, Pantry Boy

Mayes, T. Able Seaman

Maynard, Samuel John, Head Waiter

McAllen, Sidney, Assistant Steward

McAllister, William, Ship's Cook

McCao (MBE), Charles, Ward Attendant

McDiarmid, Jessie Mabel, Canadian Nursing Sister

McInerny, Edmond, Fireman

McIver, James Murdock, Carpenter

McKenzie, Mary Agnes, Canadian Nursing Sister

McLean, Rena, Canadian Nursing Sister

McMahon, I., Trimmer

Mills, Albert James, Scullion

Moir, William, Greaser

Morey, Herbert Joseph, Baker and Confectionary

Morgan, Francis John, Assistant Cook

Nicholson, James, Quartermaster

Obee, Richard, Able Seaman

Owen, John, Able Seaman

Owens, William, Able Seaman

Paines, Thomas William Job, Able Seaman

Parsons, Walter Henry, Lascelles Attendant

Pay, Leonard John, 1st Assistant Cook

Pearce, Arthur Charles, Ward Attendant

Powell, Edgar Atheling, 2nd Assistant Cook

Purcell, Thomas James, Fireman and Trimmer

RichardsonI, John Henry, Stoker/Kpr

Rolston, Thomas, Fireman Steward

Rowland, Joseph, Chief Mate

Sampson, Maebella, Canadian Nursing Sister

Sare, Gladys Irene, Canadian Nursing Sister

Sharp, Robert, Boatswain

Sharrock, George Francis, Trimmer

Short, Raymond Cyril, Able Seaman

Sills, George Luther, Canadian Captain

Sinden, F., Ward, Attendant

Slater, Harry Glenco, Baker's Boy

Smith, Alfred James, Fireman

Smith, George Henry, 1st Pantrymn

Sneddon, John, Assistant Stoker/Kpr

Stamers, Anna Irene, Canadian Nursing Sister

Starmer, Ernest, Assistant Bath

Start, Reuben Henry, Sailor

Summers, Owen Edward, Assistant Engineer's Steward

Sumner, Harold, 6th Engineer

Sutton, William George, Chief Engineer

Sweet, Thomas, Trimmer

Taylor, Charles, Fireman

Taylor, Murray Christopher, 5th Engineer

Templeton, Jean, Canadian Nursing Sister

Thomas, George, Trimmer

Thomas, Georste, Trimmer

Thomas, Kenneth Albert, Able Seaman

Tunks-Clarke, Victor George, Assistant Steward

Turner, Benjamin Harold, 3rd Mate

Vance, Walter French, Assistant Str/Kpr

Vincent, Walter Henry, Officer's Steward

Walker, Thomas, Trimmer

Walsh, Francis Charles, Trimmer

Watkins, John, Laundryman
Watson, W., Able Seaman
Way, Arthur, Ward Attendant
Weedon, Thomas, Assistant Bed Steward
Weller, Archibald Arthur, 1st Bed Steward

White, Ernest Evelyn, Assistant Cook
Whitty, Percy John, 2nd Steward
Wyatt, James Ward, Attendant
Yeeles, or Yeetes, Frederick, Thomas Fireman
Zahra, Emmanuele, Assistant Steward

On 30 June, Patzig attacked an unknown steamship in a convoy, but it did not sink. In the same convoy and 115 miles off Ushant, Patzig fired three torpedoes without warning at the newly built, defensively armed 3,545-ton steamer *Origen* (1918 – Booth S.S. Co. Ltd, Liverpool) and donkey-man Joseph Cromwell Taylor was killed; the ship, which was bound from London to Oporto and Brazil, finally sunk after the third torpedo exploded. *U 86* was then subjected to an attack with forty-eight depth charges from the escorts. Then, 150 miles southwest of Brest, at position 47° 24'N 07° 44'W, early in the evening of 1 July, Patzig intercepted a westbound US Navy convoy, consisting of eight transports, escorted by seven destroyers, returning to America. The ships were all zig-zagging about in the calm sea, but, because of the deadly U-boat threat, the gunners manned their positions and everyone was on full alert. The threat became reality at 1912hrs, when a torpedo fired by *U 86* slammed into the port side of the 16,339-ton transport USS *Covington* (US Government). She was steaming second from the left in the first row of five ships in the convoy. Her forward boiler-room blew open when the torpedo detonated below the forward funnel and the ship came to a halt.

The other ships in the convoy then immediately split up, but continued on their way, leaving the two destroyers USS *Little* and USS *Smith* with the seriously listing *Covington*. Her crew took to the boats, but six men were killed in the explosion. The two destroyers picked up the surviving crew and then steamed around dropping depth charges in an effort to keep the U-boat at bay. By dawn the next morning the ship was still afloat and two tugs arrived from Brest. They took her in tow, but the list became worse as water gradually filled the compartments. The *Covington* foundered in the afternoon of the 2nd.

THE MEN WHO DIED

Anderson, Ernest C., Fireman from Lynn, Mass.
Seaman Bowden, Joseph P., Seaman from New Jersey
Ford, Ambrose C., Fireman from Somerville, Mass.
Lynch Jr., William Henry, Fireman from New Hampshire
Payne, Alfred S., Seaman 2nd Class of USNRF
Silvernail, Lloyd H., Seaman 2nd Class of US Navy

(Incidentally, the *Covington* was built as the passenger liner *Cincinnati* at Danzig in Germany in 1908. When war was declared in August 1914, being German-flagged, she took refuge in the US and was interned at Boston, Massachusetts. In April 1917 the ship was turned over to the American Navy, commissioned in late July and renamed *Covington*. After refitting, she made five voyages to France and carried 22,000 men to the Western Front before she was lost on the return leg of her sixth troop-carrying voyage.)

On 8 July, *U 86* was badly damaged when she detonated a mine, but boats from the 16th Torpedo Half Flottille helped her to reach Heligoland, where she arrived on the 12th.

(10) Following the repairs from mine damage, Patzig left Heligoland in *U 86* on 26 October 1918. He sailed for operations with the *Hochseeflotte* (High Seas Fleet), planned for 30 and 31 October. The action was expected to take place in the North Sea, northwest of the Dogger Bank and east of Coquet Island, when thirty U-boats, plus large surface warships would search out the British Fleet and provoke them into the ultimate sea-battle. However, there was the beginning of a mutiny on some of the big warships and the action was cancelled. *U 86* developed mechanical problems and returned to Wilhelmshaven via the Skagerrak and the Kiel Canal on 15 November 1918. No ships were sunk on the last patrol.

On 4 February 1915, Chief of the German Naval Staff, V. Pohl, had signed a directive in the *Imperial Gazette* to the effect, '*waters around Great Britain and Ireland are declared in the war zone as from 18 February 1915*'. However on that same day, commanders were also instructed that '*hospital ships are to be spared; they may be only attacked when they are obviously used for the transport of troops from England to France*'. The world was outraged when it was revealed that lifeboats crammed full with innocent victims, including nursing sisters, were deliberately fired on, rammed and sunk by the German U-boat commander.

The following year on 30 June 1916, the Imperial Chancellor informed the Commander of the Fleet, that he was totally against the type of warfare '*which would place the fate of the German Empire in the hands of a U-boat commander*', but the thing he feared most had now come to pass.

At the end of the First World War when war criminals were being sought after, Patzig had fled the country and disappeared into East Prussia, where he changed his family name to Brümmer (his mother's family name before marriage). He was, however, born in Danzig, which had been separated from Germany by the Treaty of Versailles, which meant he was no longer amenable to German jurisdiction, even if he could be found. Both Ludwig Dithmar and John Claus Boldt were arrested by the authorities and put on trial at Leipzig as war criminals, but Mesissner, the gun-layer, had the 'good fortune' to die of influenza before the German authorities felt that justice needed to be done. Amongst the crewmembers of the *U 86* to give evidence as witnesses were: Popitz, Knoche, Ney, Tegtmeier and Kass. The Court declared, '*The act of Patzig is homicide*' and Dithmar and Boldt were sentenced to four years' hard labour for being accessories, however both men were released after a few months due to the political changes in Germany. The men had supposedly promised Patzig that they would not give evidence about the happenings on the 27 June and remained silent throughout.

In an interview in the early 1980s Patzig stated that he and his crew did not make any deliberate attempt to kill the survivors of the *Llandovery Castle*. Patzig died on 11 March 1984.

FINAL VOYAGE

U 86 was handed over to the Allies, with about nineteen other 'U' series and 'UB' boats leaving from various German ports, on 18 November 1918. They collected together near Brunsbüttel first and, escorted by HMS *Sierra Ventura* and HMS *Titania*, preceded to Harwich, where they arrived on 20 November.

U 86, however, was actually then commissioned into the Royal Navy and, from September 1919, she was used by the Admiralty to compare and test the Mittel-U type boat with other later German submarine designs. Experiments were completed by 12 March 1920, but she remained unsold, or wanted. On 30 June 1921, having been stripped of all useful instruments and machinery, the boat was towed out to sea and either dumped or lost, but several miles away from the main disposal area.

Extract taken from *The Union Castle and the War 1914–1919* by E.F. Knight.
The Cross of Sacrifice vols IV,V and II – CWGC
Norwegian Maritime Declarations 1914–1918
Llandovery Castle PRO statements: ADM 137/4018, ADM 137/4150 and ADM137/4149
See Appendix page 344.

WRECK SITE

In 2006, the Wessex Archaeology survey team conducted a detailed ROV investigation of the wreck site and eventually identified it as that of SM *U 86*. The wreck is orientated in a north, northwest to south, southeast (158/338°) direction, with the bows to the south, southeast. It lies on an even keel with a slight list to port, on a rather flat seabed of sand, shell and pebbles, in a general depth of 53m (178ft), being the lowest astronomical depth. The wreck is largely intact, but the stern end is broken off and lies pointing westward, at a 90° angle to the main hull section, while the bow is collapsed and is partially buried. The outer casing has almost diappeared, but the pressure hull is fairly intact. Two deck guns were fitted to these boats, one forward and one aft of the conning tower; the forward one is pointing skywards with fishing gear wrapped around it, however the aft gun, although still attached to its mounting, is lying over the port side. The conning tower is still in place but the protective casing is missing. On the conning tower and forward of the hatch, which is open, there are mountings for three periscopes, but there is no sign of the scopes. Aft and forward of the torpedo rooms, the loading hatches can be seen at the bow and stern; also at the stern, the engine room hatch is open, but the forward escape hatch remains sealed. An anchor can be observed, still secured in the recess at the bows. On top of the pressure hull, a number of what appears to be compressed-air cylinders can be found. The boat's ventilation system is lying across the hull, aft of the conning tower, where it has collapsed. The two bronze propellers are still in place at the stern, but the port one is missing one of its blades.

UC 65, SM IMPERIAL U-BOAT

DATE OF LOSS: **3** November 1917
DEPTH: **35m**
REFERENCE: **50 30.25N 00 28.37E**
LOCATION: **15** nautical miles S of Beachy Head

Type: UCII coastal mine-laying boat   *Builders*: Blohm & Voss in Hamburg for Kaiserliche Deutsche Marine   *Ordered*: on 12 January 1916, within the batch of *UC 65–UC 73*   *Keel laid*: as Yard No.281   *Launched*: on 8 July 1916   *Commissioned*: by Kapitänleutnant Otto Steinbrinck on 7 November 1916

TECHNICAL SPECIFICATIONS

Hull: double   *Surface displacement*: 427 tons   *U/Dt*: 508 tons   *LBDH*: 50.35m × 5.22m × 3.68m × 7.46m   *Machinery*: 2 × 250ps MAN diesels   *Props*: 2 bronze   *S/Sp*: 12 knots   *Op/R*: 10,420 nautical miles at 7 knots   *Sub/R*: 52 nautical miles at 4 knots   *U/Power*: 2 × 230ps electric motors gave 7.4 knot   *Batteries*: lead/acid   *Fuel/Cap*: 41 + 15 tons   *Armament*: 2-external 50.04cm torpedo tubes at the bow, one either side of the mine chutes and 1 stern internal tube   *Torpedoes*: 7 × 50.04cm (19.7in) maximum   *Guns*: 1 × 88mm (3.46in) forward deck gun   *Ammo*: 133 rounds of 88mm   *Mine tubes*: 6   *Mines*: 18 × UC200   *Diving*: max-op-depth 50m (164ft) and 33 sec to crash-dive   *Complement*: 3 officers and 23 ratings

OTHER SPECIFICATIONS

Torpedo load as designed: (4) a torpedo in each tube plus a reload for the stern tube. Storing an additional torpedo in pieces internally for the stern tube later augmented this, although this was optional. Two extra torpedoes (total) for the external bow tubes could be carried as well – these were lashed to the deck. Up to seven torpedoes could potentially be carried.

Otto Steinbrinck, the first CO, was born on 19 December 1888; he assumed command of *UC 65* on 10 November 1916. For his outstanding performance against enemy vessels with *UB 18*, Steinbrinck was awarded the *Pour le Mérite* on 18 December 1916. Steinbrinck was also one of the top submarine commanders of all time, especially of those operating in British waters, forging this reputation while operating in British waters. He died on 16 August 1949.

Steinbrinck made eight patrols with *UC 65*:

(1) *UC 65* left Hamburg on 1 February 1917 and transferred to Zeebrugge, where she arrived on the 3rd and formally joined the Flandern U-Flottille.

(2) On 6 February 1917, *UC 65* left Flanders to patrol and lay mines in the Bristol and St George Channels. Two small vessels were captured and sunk with explosives off the north Cornish coast on 8 February: the 17-ton British fishing smack *Mary Ann*, 18 miles from St Ives Head, and the 148-ton French sailing boat *Guillaume Tell* (1874), 10 miles from Trevose Head. During the night of the 9th, Steinbrinck laid three mine barriers at the northern end of the Bristol Channel around Milford Haven.

On 10 February, the 325-ton steam coaster *Sallagh* (1916 – Howden Bros, Belfast) was on passage from Sydney for Larne with coal when she was shelled and captured off Bardsey Island, the chief engineer, William McKay having been killed; the crew were forced to abandon ship and the vessel was then scuttled with explosives.

Three steamers were sunk on the 11th: the *Lycia* (1896 – Cunard Steam Shipping Co. Ltd, Liverpool), which was 2,715 tons and armed for defence with a light-calibre old Russian field gun, was fired on near the entrance to St George's Channel, after an extended chase she was captured 5.5 miles from Saint David's Head, while bound from Genoa, Italy and Bougie in Algeria to Swansea and Liverpool with general cargo; the crew abandoned ship and the vessel was then scuttled with explosives; two RN minesweepers and the SS *Ireland Moor* rescued all the crew. The 242-ton steam coaster *Olivia* (1883 – Bain Sons, Penzance) was transporting coal from Garston to Portreath when it was captured 21 miles from Bardsey Island and sunk with explosives: the steam coaster *Voltaire* (1890 –Volana Shipping Co. Ltd, Liverpool) of 409 tons, voyaging from Llanelly to Liverpool with general cargo, was also captured and scuttled with explosives, 25 miles from South Bishop. On the 12th, the *Pinna* (1901- Petroleum S.S. Co. Ltd, London), an armed steam tanker of 6,288 tons, sighted the U-boat and tried to escape at full speed, but she stopped after four shells hit the ship. Steinbrinck allowed the crew to abandon her and leave in the boats, before firing two torpedoes into it; however the tanker remained afloat and was later beached at Milford; she was transporting oil from Port Arthur, Texas to Milford Haven. Next day off the Smalls, the 37-ton Brixham fishing smack *Friendship* (1905) was attacked and sunk by gunfire and all four fishermen were killed.

THOSE WHO DIED

Ashton, Thomas, Cook
Rackley, William, Mate
Reid, John McRae, Apprentice
Tucker, Albert Henry, Skipper

The 48-ton fishing smack *Zircon* was going about her normal business on the 13th when she was captured and sunk with explosive charges 25 miles from the Smalls.

On 14 February 1917, four vessels were attacked by *UC 65*: the 791-ton SS *Ferga* (1916 – Michael Murphy Ltd, Cardiff) was bound from Swansea to Liverpool with general cargo when Steinbrinck captured and sunk her with gunfire, 15 miles south of Bardsey Isle. The steamer *Greenland* (1908 – Liverpool & Hamburg S.S. Co. Ltd, Liverpool) of 1,753 tons was also captured 20 miles southwest of Bardsey Isle, while transporting Government stores from Fleetwood to Cherbourg; the crew was forced to abandon ship and it was then scuttled, using explosive charges. The defensively armed 3,050-ton SS *Inishowen Head* (1887 – Ulster S.S. Co. Ltd, Belfast) struck a mine and sank off Skokham Isle, while on passage from Port Talbot to St John, New Brunswick in ballast and sailor John McMaster was drowned; *UC 65* had laid the mine on 9 February.

The 375-ton steam coaster *Margarita* (1902 – Zillah Shipping & Carrying Co. Ltd, Liverpool) was transporting wheat from Liverpool to Swansea when she was captured and sunk with explosives 20 miles from Bardsey Isle.

Explosive charges were also used to sink the 1,156-ton SS *Afton* (1911 –William Sloan & Co., Glasgow) when it was captured 23 miles from Strumble Head on the 15th; the ship was transporting general cargo from Bristol and Belfast to Glasgow.

The SS *Kyanite* (1904 –William Robertson, Glasgow) of 564 tons was travelling from Fleetwood to Bristol when it was captured on the 15th, the crew was forced to abandon ship and it was sunk with explosive charges.

Next day and en-route from Rouen to Port Talbot in ballast, the 2,710-ton steamship *Queenswood* (1897 – Constantine and Pickering Steamship Co., Middlesbrough) was attacked with gunfire at 1130hrs, when *UC 65* was half a mile off the port quarter. Four shells were fired from the U-boat, three of them hitting the steamer and Captain A. Peacock stopped his ship. The crew were ordered to abandon ship at 1150hrs and once they were clear, *UC 65* fired a further sixteen shells into it. However a British patrol vessel was sighted and the U-boat dived and made off. The ship sank 6 miles from Hartland Point. Twenty-one crewmen were picked up by the patrol boat and landed at Milford Haven.

THE THREE MEN WHO WERE KILLED

Cargan, William Henry, Apprentice
Cattermole, Joseph Ernest Wilby, Apprentice
McDougall, Robert, Fireman

While transporting coal from Barry to Bentos, France, the *Ville de Bayonne* (1896 – Faustin & Cie., La Rochelles), a 1,301-ton French steamer, was captured after a gunfire skirmish on 16 February, 6 miles from Hartland Point; the crew was forced to abandon ship and it was sunk, using explosives charges.

On 19 February and on the return journey, Steinbrinck captured and destroyed seven vessels: the 16-ton Belgian cutter *Justine Marie* off Dieppe with explosives; the 18-ton French fishing smack *Alice* (1908) with explosives off Fécamp; the 425-ton British coaster *Brigade* (1914 – Mason Shipping Co. Ltd, Glasgow/Liverpool) by gunfire off Cayeux-sur-Somme while taking flint stones from St Valéry to Weston Point; three French fishing smacks, *Saint Francois*, the 53-ton *Saint Louis de Gonzage* (1905) and 36-ton *Violette* (1902) with explosives, 10 miles off Etaples, and finally, 25 miles off Tréport, the 727-ton Norwegian steamer *Skrim* (1898 – Aktieselskapet Skrim, Skien) was en-route from Tréport to Bordeaux and Cardiff, in ballast, when she was sunk by explosives.

UC 65 returned triumphantly to port on 20 February.

(3) *UC 65* left Flanders on 24 February 1917 for a mine-laying operation in the English Channel. On the 25th, Steinbrinck sank two vessels: north of Dieppe, the 42-ton French smack *Saint Joseph* was fired at with rifle shots before she stopped and was sunk using explosives. The 1,851-ton *Vigda* (1900 – Aktieselskapet Jacob Engers Dampskipsseelskapet, Tønsberg), a Norwegian steamer commanded by Captain Ole Albert Johansen from Nøtterøy, was hauling coal from Hull to Nantes when she was hit by gunfire from *UC 65* at about 1800hrs. The ship stopped and the crew were advised to abandon ship in the two lifeboats within 5 minutes. Kplt. Steinbrinck ordered one of the lifeboats to return with two of the U-boat's crew, who placed two explosive charges onboard, one in the engine room and the other in the aft part of the ship. After a few minutes the steamer exploded and sank, about 5 nautical miles south of Owers Lightship.

On 26 February, three vessels were destroyed by *UC 65*'s actions: the 2,361-ton defensively armed steamer *Algiers* (1882 – Franco British S.S. Co. Ltd, London) was torpedoed and sunk without warning, while voyaging from Calais to Barry Roads in ballast.

THE EIGHT CREWMEN WHO DROWNED

Bing, A., 30yrs, Sailor
Christiansen, O., 29yrs, Sailor
Flynn, John, 36yrs, Fireman and Trimmer
Kenny, Patrick, 37yrs, Sailor
Lewis, Ernest George, 38yrs, Fireman
Llewellyn, James, 40yrs, Fireman and Trimmer
Pilling, William John, 34yrs, Fireman
Williams, Thomas Jones, 43yrs, Donkeyman

The 151-ton British sailing vessel *Hannah Croasdell* detonated a mine and sank off Skokham Island, all four hands were killed.

THOSE WHO DIED

Clarkson. Joseph, Cook
Grenfell, Frederick John, Skipper
Hughes, H., Able Seaman
Sealey, Arthur Henry, Mate

The 134-ton dutch sailing vessel *Alberdina* (1913) was in ballast and en-route from Le Havre to Teignmouth when she was captured 35 miles off Alderney and sunk by explosives.

On the 27th, two more vessels were sunk: the 104-ton French sailing vessel *Brunette* (1899) was captured and sunk off the Needles and the RN trawler *Evadne*, which had been requisitioned in September 1914 and converted to Admiralty minesweeper No.148, sank off the Owers light vessel after detonating a mine.

SOME OF THE MEN WHO DIED

Barron, John, Skipper RNR
Bessey, George Isaac, Deckhand RNR
Conway, George Healas, Engineman RNR
Dick, James, Seaman RNR
Leask, James Alexander, Seaman RNR
Matthews, Martun, Petty Officer RNR
McCallum, James, Trimmer RNR
Rose, Arthur Ernest Benjamin, 2nd Hand RNR
Scutt, George, Trimmer RNR
Sutherland, William, Seaman RNR

On 28 February another two vessels landed on the seabed: the 1,155-ton Norwegian SS *Sjøstad* (1908 – D/S A/S International, Kristiania) was torpedoed and sunk without warning off Cap la Hève, bearing Cap d'Antifer ENE and Le Havre in S ¾ E; she was voyaging from Newport, Monmouth to Fécamp with coal.

THE NINE MEN WHO DIED

Andersen, Arthur – Stoker from Kristiania
Dyhre, August – Steward from Moss
Gjestad, Eugen – Stoker from Kristiania
Johnson, Bernhard – Sailor from Stockholm/Sweden
Larsen, Lars M. – Chief Engineer from Sandefjord
Martiney, Segundo – Stoker from Spain
Siren, Veino – Donkeyman from Åbo/Finland
Smith, Charles – Stoker from USA
Svanstrøm, Hilmer – Sailor from Fredrikstad

The 192-ton French sailing/fishing vessel *Marie Joseph* (1912) was captured and sunk off Le Havre with explosives. That evening, *UC 65* was involved in a gunfight with the 2,933-ton British transport *Huntscape* (1911 – Elder Dempster & Co. Ltd, London (crown nominee), but she escaped at high speed.

On 1 March 1917, Otto Steinbrinck had a field day by sinking thirteen vessels and damaging another: the 11,483-ton liner *Drina* (1913 – Royal Mail Steam Packet Co., Belfast), which was defensively armed and carrying 189 passengers, 145 crew and 4,000 tons of general cargo, including meat and coffee from Buenos Aires to Liverpool, detonated a mine laid by *UC 65*, 2 miles from Skokham Island (some sources, including Lloyd's, claim she was torpedoed, but *UC 65* was on the French side of the English Channel at the time). The ship was making 13 knots when an explosion occurred on the port side level with the engine room, which immediately flooded. The big ship came to a halt and Captain H.W. Stump ordered all the passengers into the boats, followed by the crew. The boats got clear of the ship by 0035hrs the following morning and patrol vessels rendered assistance in picking up survivors, but a second huge explosion occurred at 0045hrs, causing the *Drina* to sink 10 minutes later. The master last saw the ship aground on the seabed with about 40ft of her bow out of the water. Two engineers and eleven firemen as well as two passengers were found to be missing when the muster was made.

SOME OF THOSE WHO WERE LOST

Berry, Edward, 26yrs, Greaser
Briscoe, Robert, 27yrs, Fireman
Donovan, Daniel, 23yrs, Fireman
Doyle, John James, 27yrs, Fireman
England, Thomas, 58yrs, Greaser
Holcs, Norton, 31yrs, 4th Engineer Officer

Jones, Frederico Saldanha, 22yrs, 6th Engineer
Lloyd, Thomas, 39yrs, Greaser
Martin, Thomas Edward, 32yrs, Fireman
Murry, James, 22yrs, Fireman
McTaggart, Edward, 44yrs, Greaser
O'Connor, Patrick, 31yrs, Fireman
Tarpey, Samuel, 22yrs, Trimmer

The 6,824-ton hospital ship HMHS *Glenart Castle* (1900 – Union Castle Mail Steamship Co. Ltd, Southampton) was on Government service when she detonated a mine and was left heavily damaged off Owers/Nab light vessel on 1 March. (On 26 February 1918, she was also serving as a hospital ship when she was torpedoed and sunk by *UC 56*, 10 miles west of Lundy Island, while voyaging fom Newport to Brest, and 168 people, including the master, were lost.)

Off Dieppe, the 29-ton Belgian fishing smack *Diamond Cross* was dispatched with by explosive charges. Then offshore from Boulogne, Steinbrinck disposed of most of a French fishing fleet with gunfire by sinking the 50-ton smack *Elise*, 58-ton *Homocea*, 13-ton *Bout de Zan*, 24-ton *General Radiguet*, 21-ton *Joseph A DolphinE*, 47-ton *N.D. de Lourdes*, 42-ton *Reine des Agnes*, 20-ton *Saint Joseph* and the 25-ton *Sainte Famille*, plus the *Seigneur*, a Belgian smack of 53 tons. Also on 1 March, the 603-ton French steamer *Elorn* (1894 – Chevillotte Frères, Brest), which was probably lost with all hands, was shelled and sunk 6 miles northeast of Le Tréport, near the mouth of the Somme.

Off Boulogne, *UC 65* was involved in a gunfire skirmish with two armed engined schooners, but the U-boat had run out of ammunition and made her escape.

After a successful patrol, *UC 65* returned to port on 2 March 1917.

(4) Steinbrinck made a war cruise to the Irish Sea and laid mines, after departing Flanders on 18 March 1917. She travelled via the Dover Strait and arrived off the River Mersey estuary on 22 March. During the night of the 23, Steinbrinck laid six mines in Liverpool Bay, then in the early hours of the 24th, laid three mines east of the Bar Lightship.

Five vessels were destroyed on the 24th: the 100-ton French sailing vessel *Bruyére* (1902) was demolished with explosives, 10 miles from South Stack Rock, during a passage from Maryport to Blaye with a cargo of creosote.

While in transit with coal from Garston, near Liverpool to Cork, Ireland, the steamship *Fairearn* (1915 – James Inglis & Co., Glasgow) of 592 tons was also captured and scuttled with explosives, 16 miles from South Stack, Holyhead. She was sailing independently at 9 knots when *UC 65* was sighted 3 miles in the distance on the starboard bow, busy sinking the French schooner *Bruyere*. At 0915hrs *UC 65* opened fire with her deck gun at *Fairearn* and the second shell exploded directly overhead, scattering shrapnel. The U-boat was no more than half a mile away by the time the fourth shell was fired and Captain Robinson thought they were in danger of being torpedoed, so the ship was stopped and her crew of thirteen launched the two lifeboats. *UC 65* ceased firing while the men abandoned ship, then it went alongside the boat containing the master and questioned him about the Liverpool and Dublin harbour protection measures. The Germans were predictably given false information. The U-boat crew actually used the master's boat to carry the scuttling charges over; then they were placed in the engine room and then *UC 65* sailed off to the west. The steamer exploded and sank at 1005hrs. The 2,632-ton mail packet steamer *Ulster* (City of Dublin Steam Packet Co., Dublin) found the two boats at 1045hrs, but the men shouted a warning to the ship's crew that there was an enemy submarine lurking in the area and advised them not to stop. The 9,214-ton SS *Custodian* (Charente Steamship Co. Ltd, Liverpool) later picked the men up and took them to Liverpool.

The 689-ton steamer *Ennistown* (1908 – Town Line (London) Ltd, London) was captured 10 miles from South Arklow light vessel and scuttled with explosives, during the voyage from Dublin to Cardiff in ballast. At 1815hrs the ship was steaming at 10 knots when a shell was fired at her from the port quarter, and 5 minutes later a submarine was sighted on the surface about a mile distant. Captain T.R. Tippett altered course to bring the enemy boat astern, however the submarine (*UC 65*) continued to fire until it was about a quarter of a mile astern, during which time two shells had hit their target. The steamer stopped and her crew of fourteen took to the boats at 1850hrs. It was only after the boats were lowered that it was discovered that the mate's boat had been damaged by shrapnel, so all hands had to transfer to the master's boat. *UC 65* went alongside the ship and questioned Captain Tippett as it passed. Submariners boarded the ship and planted explosives, then returned to the submarine after about 10 minutes. The steamer blew up and sank at 1915hrs, while her crew set sail and headed towards the coast, where a trawler picked them all up at 2140hrs and took them to Milford Haven.

The 732-ton Norwegian SS *Korsnæs* (1891 – Dampskipsselskapet Aktieselskapet Korsnæs, Bergen) was in ballast travelling from St Malo to Liverpool when she was captured and sunk with explosives off Bardsey Island.

The *Howe* (1871 – K. Pedersen, Gloucester), a three-masted British sailing vessel of 175 tons, was shipping coal from Garston to Cork when she was captured off South Arklow light vessel; the crew of six were forced to abandon their vessel and explosives were placed on board. After questioning the master, Captain H. Chapple, and his crew, who were all in the lifeboat, the U-boat made off, leaving them to be picked up by a tender from the North Arklow light vessel, which took them to Wicklow.

The 124-ton French sailing vessel *Fringante* (1909) was stopped and sunk off Godling Bank; she was transporting coal from Troon to Tréguier, France.

The defensively armed 3,789-ton SS *Adenwen* (1913 – W. & C. T. Jones S.S. Co. Ltd, Cardiff) was 6 miles off North Arklow light vessel and was bound from Cienfuegos, Cuba via Queenstown, Ireland for Liverpool with sugar when she was torpedoed and sunk without warning at 0415hrs. The *Adenwen* (Captain W.H. Ladd) sank in 5 minutes, but the ship's boats had either been smashed in the explosion or capsized as she sank, so the crew of thirty-three had only floating wreckage to cling onto. While they were struggling in the water, the U-boat had surfaced and one survivor attempted to board it, but was driven off by someone with a revolver. Cdr Steinbrinck demanded to know the ship's name and her cargo and continued to threaten survivors with a pistol until he eventually gave orders to dive and leave the area. At 0715hrs, twenty-three men were picked up from the sea by RN vessels and taken to Milford Haven. A roll call showed that six men were missing and four had died from exposure in the water.

SOME OF THE TEN CREWMEN WHO DIED

Abdu Muha Mmad, Fireman
Ali Darshan, Fireman
Allan, John, 42yrs, Cook
Bowden, Joseph William, 29yrs, 2nd Cook
Burhan Farah, Fireman
Chamberlain, Peter Augustine, 24yrs, 3rd Engineer
Gilchrist, Charles, 43yrs, Steward
Miller, Phillip Harris, 58yrs, Donkeyman
Rashid Ali, Fireman

Also on 25 March, Steinbrinck shelled and sunk the 130-ton British sailing vessel *Brandon* (1862); it was reported missing off Codling Bank and was presumed sunk by *UC 65* with all hands.

SOME OF THOSE LOST

Kanagh, Joseph, Seaman
O'Neil, Michael, Mate
Doyle, Charles, Cook and Ordinary Seaman
Gregory, John, Master

On passage from Les Falaises, Algeria with iron ore for Barrow, the Greek steamship *Poseidon* (1893 – N.P. Roussos & Co., Syra) of 2,589 tons was captured by *UC 65* in the Irish Sea, near Liverpool; the crew were forced to abandon ship after which she was sunk by gunfire

On the 27th one of the mines laid by *UC 65* earlier, accounted for the 3,063-ton SS *Kelvinhead* (1905 – Glasgow Steam Shipping Co. Ltd, Glasgow) off Liverpool Bar light vessel; she was armed for defence and carrying a general cargo from the Clyde and Liverpool to Buenos Aires.

Steinbrinck is credited wih sinking six vessels on 28 March, four of them around South Arklow light vessel: the 778-ton steam coaster *Ardglass* (1914 – Ard Coasters Ltd, Greenock) was transporting steel from Port Talbot to Belfast when she was captured and scuttled with explosives 4 miles east from South Arklow lightship. The vessel was making 9 knots when *UC 65*, which was about 1 mile away on her starboard beam, attacked her with gunfire at 1230hrs. Captain McQuarrie attempted to escape by bringing the enemy boat stern, but the fourth shell hit the ship and the engine was stopped; the twelve crew abandoned ship at 1245hrs. The crew of *UC 65* used one of the lowered boats to scuttle the *Ardglass* with explosives. The master and four crewmen were taken on board the U-boat until their ship sank and then they were returned to the boats; a trawler picked up the survivors at 1535hrs and took them to Wicklow.

While transporting a 6,700-ton cargo consisting of ammunition, wheat, foodstuffs and general cargo, the 4,662-ton defensively armed steamship *Snowdon Range* (1906 – Neptune Steam Navigation Co. Ltd, Liverpool) was voyaging from Philadelphia to Liverpool when crewmen sighted the track of a torpedo heading towards her on the port side. The helm was put hard over to port, but the missile detonated level with the engine room, killing three men there; another man also jumped overboard and drowned. The master sent out a radio distress call and the survivors abandoned ship. *UC 65* then surfaced and went alongside the deserted vessel and some of the German crew went on board and ransacked it for supplies and food, while others placed explosive scuttling charges; after the charges detonated, she was helped on her way with gunfire. The 1,149-ton SS *Somerset Coast* (Powell, Bacon & Hough Lines, Ltd, Liverpool) of 1,149 tons and an RN patrol boat picked up the crew in the boats.

THE MEN WHO DIED

Bowman, James Arthur, 21yrs, 4th Engineer Officer
Keegan, Richard, 29yrs, Fireman and Trimmer
Prentice, Robert Barbour, 19yrs, Fireman and Trimmer
Sawed Husain, Fireman and Trimmer

(One month later on 22 April, the *Somerset Coast* (1911) was also sunk in a collision with the 463-ton steamer *Sound Fisher* (1894 – John Fisher & Co. Ltd, Barrow)

A torpedo fired without warning at 1758hrs on the 28th, sank the SS *Wychwood* (1907 – W. French Fenwick & Co. Ltd, London) of 1,985 tons off South Arklow light vessel; the steamer was transporting coal from Barry to Scapa Flow and sank at 1804hrs, drowning three crewmen; the eighteen survivors having got away in one boat. The U-boat then surfaced and questioned the master, Captain G.D. Fowle, before heading off on the surface. Twelve hours later, the 4,375-ton armed steamer *Potosi* (1905 – Pacific Steam Navigation Co., Liverpool) picked the men up and took them to Wicklow.

THOSE WHO DROWNED

Ciappara, Emanuel, 32yrs, Able Seaman
Palmer, Frederick Charles, 30yrs, 3rd Engineer
Wood, John Harlick, 30yrs, Able Seaman

While in ballast and on passage from Hennebont, France for Glasgow, the 742-ton Norwegian steamer *Dagali* (1909 – Aktieselskapet Ocean, Kristiania) was captured; the crew were forced to abandon ship and then it was shelled and sunk. The 148-ton Russian sailing vessel *Laima* (1902) was on a voyage from Galway to Glasson Dock in ballast when she was stopped 10 miles southeast of Codling lightship on 28 March and sunk by gunfire. The *Harvest Home* (1882 – G. Devereux, Paul Quay, Wexford), a 103-ton wooden British schooner delivering timber from Wexford to Garston, was stopped at 1445hrs when *UC 65* opened fired at her. After the crew had abandoned ship, three shells were fired into the hull and she sank almost at once. The five crewmen rowed towards Aklow and were picked up by a steamer at 1940hrs, about 1.5 miles from the port.

After *UC 65* had arrived back at Flanders on 1 April, three more steamships detonated the mines she had laid. A mine laid on 25 February destroyed the 1,350-ton Norwegian *Thelma* (1906 – D/S

A/S Thelma, Grimstad) off the Owers Lightship on 6 April; the vessel was in transit with coal and carrying a crew of sixteen from the Tyne to Rouen; one man, sailor Petter Gustav Mathisen from Arendal, died.

Two large steamships were damaged near Liverpool Bar light vessel after detonating mines: the 18,565-ton *Lapland* (1908 – International Navigation Co. Ltd, Liverpool) on 7 April, which was transporting general cargo from New York to Liverpool and trimmer Jame O'Connor was killed; the SS *New York* (1888 – International Mercantile Marine Co., New York) of 10,798 tons was on the same voyage when she and struck a mine on 9 April.

(5) Leaving Zeebrugge on 25 April 1917, *UC 65* sailed to the Irish Sea and North Channel for operations against Allied shipping and Steinbrinck had orders to mine the Firth of Clyde. On the outward journey on the 26th, three vessels were destroyed by Steinbrinck: the ketch-rigged motorised barge *Athole* (1892 – Forbes, Abbot & Lennard) of 150 tons, was in ballast and en-route from Le Havre to Shoreham-on-Sea when Steinbrinck attacked her with gunfire 20 miles south of Owers light vessel, at 0815hrs. The five-man crew abandoned the vessel, when shell fragments rained down on it, however *UC 65* continued to shell the barge and one hit the mizzenmast, setting the *Athole* on fire. The U-boat then turned its attention to the ship's boat and fired at it with a machine gun, but the men escaped injury. *UC 65* then approached the lifeboat and Steinbrinck questioned the crew before moving off to the west. A patrol vessel picked the men up and took them to Littlehampton; the last they saw of their vessel was the upturned hull after it capsized at 0830hrs. The 146-ton sailing cutter *Agnes Cairns* (1873) was captured 8 miles off Alderney and sunk with explosives while delivering coal from Portsmouth to Guernsey. The 79-ton French sailing cutter *Bretagne et Vendee* was also destroyed off Alderney by gunfire; it is believed that all her crew were lost. The following day (27th) the 2,902-ton British barque *Burrowa* (1890 – W.H. Potter & Sons) was sailing in ballast from Bordeaux to Newport when she was captured and sunk with explosive charges 60 miles west of the Isles of Scilly.

The Spanish SS *Alu-Mendi* (1907 – Cia. Naviera Sota y Aznar, Bilbao) was captured and scuttled with explosives southeast of Tuskar lighthouse; she was commanded by Captain Medurio and in transit from Sagunto, Spain for Glasgow with iron ore.

On 30 April Steinbrinck waited for darkness in the Firth of Clyde before beginning his mine-laying operations; two barriers at the southern entrance and the next morning, three being deposited in the northern entrance.

Four vessels were sunk on 1 May: the *W.D. Potts* (1874), a 112-ton British sailing vessel, was captured 10 miles off Portpatrick and sunk by gunfire while transporting china clay from Falmouth to Glasgow. The small coaster *Helen* (1904 – R. Neill & Sons, Bangor, County Down) was commanded by Captain J. Cowan and transporting coal from Garston to Bangor, County Down, when she was captured and scuttled with explosives, 11 miles west of the Mull of Galloway; the whole crew took to the boats and survived. The 1,196-ton steel-hulled barque *Ivrig* (1891 – Bulls Seilskibsrederi A/S, Kristiania) was under the command of Captain Martin Howard Johnsen and sailing in ballast from Dublin to Newport News, Virginia when she was captured off Portpatrick and sunk by gunfire; all of her crew survived. The 296-ton steam coaster *Dora* (1900 – Aberdovey & Barmouth S.S. Co. Ltd) was captured 11 miles from Mull of Galloway and was scuttled with explosives while under the command of Captain D. Williams and travelling light from Belfast to Liverpool.

Six more vessels were disposed of on 2 May and as the crews of the different vessels rowed for the mainland, Steinbrinck jokingly explained the bus-times on shore, according to Ian Wilson, author of SUC. The steam coaster *Amber* (1892 – John Henderson, Glasgow (Belfast) of 401 tons was making her way from Troon to Waterford, Ireland with coal, when she was captured, the crew forced to abandon ship and she was scuttled with explosives, about 2 miles from Ballyhalbert. The 402-ton steam coaster *Saint Mungo* (1907 – T. Heiton & Co. Ltd, Dublin) was bound for Dublin from Troon with coal and was captured and scuttled with explosives in Ballyhalbert Bay, County Down. The master of the 485-ton coaster *Derrymore* (1905 – R. McCowen & Sons Ltd, Tralee), Captain J. Mahony, had watched the *Saint Mungo* being sunk and attempted to escape by running for the shore, but *UC 65* commenced firing at her; the engine was then stopped and the eleven-man crew abandoned ship at 0535hrs, scuttled charges were placed on board their vessel and she sank in Ballyhalbert Bay, Co. Down, while in ballast and on passage from Dublin for Troon. The 299-ton steam coaster *Morion* (1894 – William Robertson, Glasgow) was in Ballyhalbert Bay when *UC 65* fired a number of shells at her, before Captain G.N. Wilkinson came to a halt; the eight-man crew then abandoned ship and she was scuttled with explosives; the vessel was travelling light from Dublin to Carnlough, Antrim. The *Earnest* (1884 – Ferguson & McKee) was a 111-ton wooden British schooner and was en-route from Ardrossan to Dublin with coal, when what was believed to be a fishing boat was sighted about four miles away. However as it came closer, the sail was suddenly lowered and a single shell was fired, which went straight through the sail canvas of *Earnest*; the fishing boat turned out to be no other than *UC 65* with a sail hoisted. Otto Steinbrinck gave the four-man crew 5 minutes to clear their vessel and explosive charges sunk it at 1007hrs, 6 miles off Skulmartin light vessel. A patrol vessel picked up the four men at 1035hrs and landed them at Larne.

The Japanese steamer *Taizan Maru* (1895 – Hashimoto Kisen K.K., Dairen) of 3,527 tons was transporting ore from Carthagena to Ardrossan when she was captured and scuttled with explosives, west of Mull of Galloway.

Steinbrinck sank four vessels on 4 May: the 4,136-ton defensively armed SS *Pilar de Larrinaga* (1902 – Miguel de Larrinaga S.S. Co. Ltd, Liverpool) was torpedoed and sunk without warning off Tusker Rock, during the passage from Galveston, Texas for Manchester with wheat and a general cargo. At 2030hrs, a torpedo detonated between holds Nos 1 and 2, with the result that the ship sank very quickly. Unfortunately, the lifeboat containing Captain Charles Thomas Morres and nineteen crewmen capsized as the ship sank and all those men were drowned. The surviving crew of eighteen and one passenger were picked up 1 hour later by an armed drifter and landed at Milford Haven. A patrol vessel later fired on *UC 65*, but she was never seen during the attack.

THE MEN LOST

Airey, John Anthony, 41yrs, 3rd Engineer
Ali Bande, Quartermaster
Connors, William, 26yrs, 2nd Engineer
Featherston, H.J., 22yrs, Trimmer
Ferreno, Francisco, Storekeeper
Forrest, Robert, 30yrs, 2nd Mate
Gibson, James Bell, 54yrs, Chief Engineer
Hall, Charles, 23yrs, Chief Officer
Hasan Bin Yusuf, Sam
Isherwood, Tom Pendlebury, 25yrs, Wireless Operator
Larrinaga, Celestino, 20yrs, 2nd Cook
Madariaga, Sotera, 31yrs, Fireman
Martinez, Jose 38yrs, Fireman
Morres, Charles Thomas, 47yrs, Master
Nabarro, Manuael, 22yrs, Fireman
Patang Hasan, Quartermaster
Sanjurgo, Manuael, 31yrs, Donkeyman
Suarez, Joaquin, 35yrs, Fireman
Wood, John, Leading Seaman RNR (DAMS)

The 66-ton British sailing vessel *New Design No.2* was captured and sunk with explosives, 15 miles off Tuskar Rock, while transporting bricks from Bridgewater to Dublin. Two fishing smacks going about their normal business were both captured off Strumble Head and sunk with explosives: the 45-ton *Strumble* and 39-ton *Victorious*.

On 7 May, the 93-ton sailing vessel *Maude*, en-route from Padstow to Manchester with china clay, was captured and scuttled with explosives about 8 miles off Bardsey Island. The 9,712-ton steam tanker *San Patricio* (1915 – Eagle Oil Transport Co. Ltd, London) was hit with a torpedo off Trevose Head on the 8th, but she reached Avonmouth under her own steam; she was carrying oil-fuel from Puerto Mexico to Sheerness.

UC 65 arrived back at Flanders on 12 May.

Built in 1914 by Duthie Torry, Aberdeen, the 296-ton trawler *Merse* was requisitioned in February 1915 and converted to Admiralty minesweeper No.980, however she detonated a mine off Garrock Head on 22 May and sank with all seventeen hands, including two officers and fifteen ratings.

THOSE WHO DIED

Beckett, Frederick Richard, Temporary Skipper RNR
Corlett, William, Deckhand RNR
Curl, John Clifford, Ordinary Telegraphist RNVR
Dennis, Edgar, Able Seaman RNVR
Flett, Alexander, 2nd Hand RNR
Fox, Robert Edwin Alston, Temporary Lt RNR
Higgins, John, Deckhand RNR
Hulan, John, Deckhand RNR
Jones, John, Deckhand RNR
MacKay, Alexander, Leading Seaman RNR
Owens, Thomas W., Telegraphist RNVR
Price, Cuthbert, Engineman RNR
Roberts, John Deckhand RNR
Roberts, Richard, Trimmer RNR
Ross, David, Engineman RNR
Shoebottom, William Albert, Trimmer/Cook RNR
Stanton, George, Trimmer RNR

(6) The English Channel and Bay of Biscay was the next patrol and mine-laying areas for *UC 65*, after departing base on 15 June 1917. Between 16 and 17 June, Steinbrinck laid barriers off Bologne and Cherbourg. The 310-ton trawler *Fraser* (1907) was requisitioned from Neptune of Hull in April 1915 and converted to Admiralty minesweeper No.1379, but she detonated a mine near Boulogne on 17 June and sank, the mine having been laid earlier that day by *UC 65*.

SOME OF THE MEN WHO DIED

Colvin, Alexander 2nd Hand RNR
Geddes, Alexander Temporary Skipper RNR
Innes, Alexander James Deckhand RNR
Jackson, William John Trimmer RNR
Kennett, George Deckhand RNR
Mitchell, William Seaman RNR
Pitcher, Benjamin Waiter Deckhand RNR
Rae, James Engineman RNR
Weedon, James Taylor Engineman RNR
William, Owen John Telegraphist RNVR
Williams, Francis John Temporary Skipper RNR

Two vessels were sunk on 18 June: the 58-ton sailing vessel *Gauntlet* was in ballast and en-route from St Malo to Par when she was captured by Steinbrinck 30 miles from Hanois lighthouse and sunk with explosives. The SS *Vaering* (1888 – Det Helsingørske Dampskibsselskabet Aktieselskabet), a Danish steamer of 2,157 tons, was bound from Bordeaux to Barry with a 1,000-ton cargo of pit props when *UC 65* hit her with a torpedo off Ushant, however the vessel remained afloat and only sunk after a second torpedo was fired and exploded. Next evening, *UC 65* attacked the 3,804-ton *Morinier* (1901 – Brys & Gylsen Ltd, London), a defensively armed British steamer, with gunfire off Ushant, but through some skilful manoeuvring, the presence of fog and darkness rapidly approaching, the ship made her escape. On 20 June, *UC 65* had a gun skirmish with a three-masted schooner in the Bay of Biscay; eventually the ship appeared to have been abandoned when a boat was launched and the men rowed clear. Fearing it could be a Q-ship trap, Steinbrinck decided to leave the vessel and dived.

Four steamers were sunk on 24 May: the Greek *Aghia Paraskevi* (1890 – Bank of Athens, Syra) of 2,795 tons was torpedoed and sunk in the Bay of Biscay, while voyaging from Bougie, Algeria to Cardiff with ore. The 3,014-ton Greek *Constantinos* (1893 – P. Constantinidis, P. Cavafis & Co., Piraeus) was travelling with a cargo of ore from Bona, France to Glasgow when she was captured, shelled and sunk in the Bay of Biscay. The 2,961-ton Greek *Taigetos* (1903 – A. M. Coulouthros, Andros) was sunk by a torpedo hit 25 miles off Cap Ferret, while travelling from Algiers to Newcastle with ore.

The *Kong Haakon* (1889 – H.M. Wrangell & Co., Aktieselskapet, Haugesund) a steel-hulled Norwegian ship of 2,231 tons on passage from Arguilas, Spain for Ardrossan with ore, was shelled and sunk 23 miles off Cap Ferret; twenty of her crew of twenty-four were drowned.

SOME OF THOSE WHO DIED

Pedersen, Hjalmar – Captain from Koppervik
Johnsen, Julius – 1st Mate from Nøtterøy
Isaksen, Kristian – 2nd Mate from Kragerø
Strand, Rasmus – 1st Engineer from Haugesund
Adolfson, Karl from Sweden
Bjørnsen, Gunlauger – Steward from Haugesund
Knotten, Oskar – Cook from Haugesund
Børresen, Ole – Boy from Stavanger
Johnstad, John – Sailor from Haugesund
Nordby, William – Sailor from Kristiania
Helgesen, Helge – Sailor from Bergen
Hansen, Alf – Sailor from Stavanger
Pedersen, Ole – Sailor from Ålesund?
Milan, Lorenzo – Stoker from Almeria/Spain
Andersen, Kruse – Stoker from Odder/Denmark
Camacho, Juan – Stoker from Spain
Bulder, Constantin – Stoker from Russia
Brahim, Ismail – Stoker from Tunisia
Nilsen, Kristian – Stoker from Skien
Rooyachers, Alphonso Stoker from Hoose Lage/Verde

On the evening of 25 June, *UC 65* attacked a convoy north of Bayonne, that consisted of eleven steamers, one gun boat and one trawler, en-route from St Jean de Luz to La Pallice. At 2000hrs (British time) the 3,693-ton Greek steamer *Petritzis* (1905 – E. Petritzis fils, Syra) was torpedoed and sunk, 14 miles SSW of Contis at position 43° 54'N 01° 30'W. (It was originally believed that the Spanish steamer *Orinon* (Cia.de Nav. Olazarri) had been torpedoed by *UC 65*, while en-route from Bilbao, Spain to Pauillac in the Gironde estuary, France, but in fact she ran aground, 11 miles SSW of Contis and was lost, probably after detonating a mine.)

UC 65 was homeward bound on the 28th, when she encountered the 114-ton British sailing vessel *Lizzie Ellen* (1874), the boat was captured and scuttled with explosives, 46 miles south of Start Point, while delivering scrap iron from Jersey, Channel Islands to Newport, Monmouth.

UC 65 arrived back at Flanders on 30 June.

(7) *UC 65* sailed for a war cruise in the English Channel on 18 July 1917 and laid mines off the Needles and Portland. On the 20th, the defensively armed 3,660-ton steamer *Fluent* (1911 – Westoll Line, Sunderland) was sunk by *UC 65* after a torpedo hit, 16 miles south of Anvil Point, while transporting a 6,100-ton cargo of steel and oats from New York for London. (Lloyd's lists her as having detonating a mine). She was steaming at 8 knots at 2010hrs when an explosion occurred directly under the hull. The master stopped the ship and discovered she was leaking so much, that the crew of twenty-nine abandoned her at 2030hrs; the ship sinking at 2050hrs. Although the ship's cook and chief steward were injured, all the crew was rescued by a steam trawler and taken to Weymouth.

UC 65 arrived back in port on 24 July.

(8) After refuelling and loading torpedoes the legendary skipper left Zeebrugge the very next day (and his last patrol in *UC 65*) and sailed to the English Channel, for 3 days from 25 July 1917. By the afternoon of 26 July, the boat reached the Royal Sovereign Lightship in fog and at 1550hrs Steinbrinck sighted the 11,000-ton protected cruiser HMS *Ariadne* (1898), escorted by three destroyers. The ship was steaming down the Channel with a full load of 400 mines and a crew of thirty-eight when a single torpedo fired from the bow tube of *UC 65*, struck her amidships on the port side, which detonated most of her lethal 'cargo'. The old warship began to sink upright, but

the escorts rescued most of her crew; she was then taken in tow, but soon after, a torpedo fired from the stern tube finished her off; when the old warship fell over on her starboard side and sunk off Beachy Head, thirty-eight officers and ratings were killed or drowned.

SOME OF THE MEN WHO DIED

Allen, Arthur, Leading Seaman RN
Baker, Frank, Stoker 1st Class RN
Battershell, Leonard Stephen, Cook's Mate RN
Carlin, William, Stoker 1st Class RN
Clarke, Alfred, Ship's Cpl 1st Class RN
Dewdney, R., Chief Stoker RN
Donnelly, Michael, Stoker RNR
Griffiths, William George, Stoker Petty Officer
  RN
Hannaford, W., Chief Stoker RN
Hannon, J., Officer's Steward 3rd Class RN
Harrison, Harry, Boy 1st Class RN
Hickson, Samuel, Able Seaman RN
Hill, Isaac, Blacksmith's Mate RN

Hutchins, William George, Officer's Steward
  3rd RN
Jenkins, Stoker lst Class RN
Luke, Thomas Ralph, Carpenter RN
Mounter, Tom, Stoker 2nd Class RN
Munzer, A., Deckhand RNR
Overton, R., Petty Officer RN
Perrin, G., Private RMLI
Vanstone, William John, PO RN
Wainwright, James Stoker RNR
Warren, J., Stoker 2nd Class RN
Watts, William John, Stoker lst Class RN
Whitty, Frank, Stoker RNR
Williams, Thomas Edward, Stoker 1st Class RN

Also on 27 July, a torpedo hit sank the defensively armed 6,482-ton steamer *Candia* (1896 – Peninsular & Oriental Steam Navigation Company, Greeock/London), 8 miles from Owers light vessel; she was en-route from Sydney, Australia and Port Natal, eastern South Africa to London via Falmouth. The ship was carrying a crew of 100 and a general cargo, including 8,000 tons of grain, various foodstuffs, some 1,000 tons of zinc and over 1,025 tons of lead. She was making 12 knots when the torpedo fired without warning, detonated at 0500hrs at the break of the poopdeck on the starboard side. One of the lifeboats was smashed to pieces and Tindal Karim Qasim, the lookout, was killed in the blast. The survivors immediately abandoned ship and were picked up by patrol vessels within 5 minutes and taken to Portsmouth; the ship sinking in 45m at 0535hrs. The defensively armed 3,919-ton SS *Bellagio* (1890 – Forest Shipping Co. Ltd, London) was hit with a torpedo without warning on the 27th, but she was beached and then refloated later; unfortunately, however, the 3th engineer, Percy Knox Brown was killed in the explosion. The ship was in ballast and voyaging from London to Barry.

The newly built French 1,112-ton steamer *Saint Emilion* (1917 – Worms & Cie., Havre) sank off Dungeness, after detonating a mine on the 27th, while bound for Rouen with nitrate ammonia, from Skien in Norway. In the morning, *UC 65* was attacked by a flying-boat, which dropped two bombs very close to her; then in a second attack, the diving tanks and conning tower received several machine-gun hits

UC 65 arrived back at Flanders on 28 July.

The distinguished Kplt Max Viebeg, who was born on 6 April 1887, assumed command of *UC 65* on 1 August 1917. (For outstanding work against enemy shipping in *UB 80*, Max Viebeg won the *Pour le Mérite* on 30 January 1918; he died on 9 November 1961).

(9) Kplt. Viebeg left Flanders on 16 August 1917 and made one patrol with *UC 65* in the English Channel. On 19 August Viebeg laid a mine barrier off Cherbourg and the 585-ton French dredger *General du Temple* (Macadam) detonated one of those mines and sank, with the loss of all hands, some miles to the northwest of the Cape Lévy at: 49° 43.077'N 01° 34.040'W.

On 25 August, the 725-ton Norwegian steamer *Garm* (1916 – Aktieselskapet Garm, Risør) was torpedoed and sunk off Start Point; she was en-route from Garston, Merseyside to Rouen with a cargo of coal and a crew of fourteen; unfortunately the 1st mate, Harald Pedersen from Lavangen near Tromsø was drowned. That same day, a torpedo fired by *UC 65* off Berry Head, sank the 689-ton Danish steamer *Nerma* (1893 – D/S Selsk. A/S Skagerak, Esbjerg/Copenhagen), which was voyaging in ballast from St Malo to Port Talbot.

Viebeg intercepted the 960-ton American schooner *Laura C. Anderson* (1890 – William Anderson, New York) 15 miles east of Barfleur on the 29th; she was carrying general cargo from New Orleans to France and was scuttled using explosive charges.

Off Berry Head on 31 August, the 2,885-ton Greek merchantman *Erissos* (1902 – Ionian S.S. Navigation, Piraeus) was transporting coal, coke and benzol from the Tyne to Savona when a torpedo from *UC 65* struck her; she was beached in Tor Bay, but re-floated after repairs.

On 1 September the French cable ship *Peronne* (1882 – Cie. Francaise de Marine et de Commerse) of 3,342 tons, was torpedoed and sunk 5 miles off Berry Head; she was travelling in ballast from Le Havre to Barry Roads and all her crew of thirty-six were saved.

UC 65 arrived back in port on 3 September 1917. The well connected socialite, Kapitänleutnant Claus Lafrenz, nickname 'Lala' (*see* vol. 1), assumed command on 4 September 1917.

Claus Lafrenz made just two patrols with the boat:

(10) *UC 65* sailed from Flanders on 20 September 1917 for operations in the English Channel and Bay of Biscay. Lafrenz laid three partial mine barriers off Cherbourg on 23 September, then moved west to Ushant in search of Atlantic convoys. Off Ushant on 26 September Lafrenz captured and sunk the 1,337-ton American barque *Paolina* (1900 – The Whitney & Bodden Co., New York) with explosives; she was transporting barbed wire and oil from New York for Le Havre.

On 3 October the SS *Tasmania* (1900 – Soc. Anon. Ilva, Genoa), an Italian steam collier of 3,662 tons, was sunk 8 miles from Prawle Point. She was torpedoed without any warning on the starboard side, while transporting coal from West Hartlepool to Civitavecchia, Italy. The vessel sank very slowly, allowing all of her crew to get away in the boats and a patrol vessel picked them up a short while later and landed them at Plymouth.

UC 65 arrived back at Flanders on 5 October 1917.

After the *UC 65* had returned to port, one of the mines she laid off Cape d'Antifer sank the 63-ton Royal Navy drifter *Comrades* on 18 October.

FINAL PATROL

(11) On 22 October 1917, *UC 65* left her base for a foray along the English Channel to the western exit, with Lafrenz in command. During the night of 23 September, Lafrenz laid eighteen mines in a barrier off Le Havre and then carried on westward. Off Prawle Point on 31 October, the 1,711-ton SS *North Sea* (1899 – James Cormack & Co. Ltd, Leith) was torpedoed and sunk without warning and Able Seaman Gustav Bjorkstrom was drowned; the vessel was in transit with coal from Hartlepool to Pauillac, in the Gironde Estuary.

On 2 November 1917 and without any warning, *UC 65* damaged the 4,262-ton defensively armed steamer *Branksome Hall* (1904 – Ellerman Lines Ltd, Liverpool) with a torpedo off Bolt Head; the steamship was bound from Manchester to Devonport with railway wagons, hay and canteen stores and she beached at Salcombe Bar, but refloated later after repairs. (The same ship, had previously been damaged by a torpedo on 11 April 1917, but then on 14 July 1918, she was torpedoed and sunk without warning by *UB 105*, 68 miles off Marsa Susa in Libya, while on passage from Newport to Port Said with coal.)

Lafrenz then turned his U-boat towards Flanders. The following day (3 November) *UC 65* was 15 nautical miles south of Beachy Head and travelling close to her maximum speed on the surface. The skipper and four other crewmen were in the conning tower and combing the horizon when a periscope was sighted, slightly forward of the beam on the starboard side. The periscope belonged to the British submarine *C15* and both boats spotted one another almost simultaneously.

HM S/M *C15*, commanded by the appropriately named Lt E. Dolphin, dived and flooded both torpedo tubes. Lafrenz, who trusted in his speed and manoeuvrability, continued on the surface. Feeling confident the German commander ordered the helmsman to turn hard to port. *C15* fired a double shot at 400 yards and the watch on *UC 65* stood transfixed at the sight of the first torpedo streaking towards them. The helm of the U-boat was put hard over in an effort to avoid it, but the torpedo struck amidships, however it failed to explode. Seconds later the second torpedo detonated, blowing off U-boat's stern.

Log of HM S/M C15 November 1917:

3 November 1917

2.30pm – Altered course to N12W

2.43 – Sighted enemy submarine on surface bearing 5 points on port bow –

Survivors of *U 1209* in the sea, just before their rescue by the Canadian frigate HMCS *Ribble* on 18 December 1944 (see page 326). (Courtesy Ian Smythe of Edmonton, Canada)

HM SM *C15*. (Author's collection)

Dived and flooded both tubes – Fired double shot at 400 yards. –
One torpedo hit, the other appeared to pass under. – Submarine sank immediately –
Noise of explosion slight
3.17 – Surface. –
Proceeded to pick up survivors. – 6 seen, 5 rescued and these were placed under guard and sent below.

Lt E. Dolphin continued:

He [Lafrenz] told me that *UC 65* had been proceeding on the surface when the periscopes of *C15* were spotted some half an hour prior to our attack. – However, Lafrenz was confident he could deter us by zig zagging. – He confirmed that the first torpedo had passed under, but our second struck aft just as she put her helm over. – Lafrenz considered this a very lucky shot on our part. – According to him *C15* was only 600 yards away. – The submarine sank immediately and of the officers only Lafrenz and Reserve Officer Braune reached the surface. – Captain Lafrenz was blown high into the air by the force of the explosion and came down awkwardly on his chest, which was skinned and very badly bruised. – Lafrenz is of a philosophical turn of mind and highly intelligent. – Reserve Officer Braune and Kplt Lafrenz do not appear to like each other very much. – He showed much interest in our little submarine and we were curious about him – Lafrenz had lost his father and two brothers in the war.

Admiralty interrogation report on the sinking of *UC65*:

The periscope of *C15* had been sighted half an hour previously off the starboard beam but Kplt Lafrenz (who was on the bridge at the time) was confident he could outwit the British submarine. *UC65* turned hard to port and commenced zig zagging. The first torpedo failed to explode but the second blew the stern off … Kplt Lafrenz considered this a very lucky shot under the circumstances. Kplt Lafrenz was blown high into the sky by the force of the explosion. He came down in the water on his chest, which was severely bruised as a result. The only other officer to reach the surface was Reserve Officer Braune…

ADM 137/3898 ADM 137/3994 ADM 137/533 ADM 137/2961 ADM 137/2962 NARA T1022, Roll 109, PG 61986 CWGC U-Boot-Ehrenmal Möltenort The Cross of Sacrifice Vol's IV,V & II Norwegian Maritime Declarations 1914–1918

SOME OF THE MEN WHO PERISHED WITH SM UC 65

Altenberg, Alf, U-Matrose
Apel, Arno, U-Matrose
Basch, Leo, U-Heizer
Dethlefsen, W., U-Obermaschinistenmaat
Drachau, Ernst, U-Maschinistenmaat
Engel, Joh., U-Maschinistenmaat
Fritzsche, E., U-Obermaschinistenmaat d.Res
Grefe, P., U-Steuermann d.Res
Hübner, Albert, U-Heizer
Klar, Wilhelm, U-Heizer
Klinkhardt, Fr., U-Obermatrose
Krohn, Walter, U-Oberbootsmannsmaat

Langner, Karl, U-Maschinist Anw
Mandalka, F., U-F.T.Obergast
Rüterbusch, K., U-Heizer
Röder, Max, U-Oberheizer
Schulz, W., U-Maschinistenmaat
Sommerkamp, K., U-Maschinist Anw
Spekowski, Fr., U-Matrose
Stiefel, J., U-Maschinistenmaat d.Res
Weidner, Karl, U-Heizer
Wüst, Peter, Obermatrose
Zimmermann, W., Marine Ingenieur

WRECK SITE

The wreck of *UC 65* sits on a seabed of sand, in general depth of 35m (115ft), being the lowest astronomical depth. It is now broken into two separate sections that lie about 20m apart. It is possible to view the empty mine chutes, where a few soft corals are established on the casing of the bow. The break in the boat, probably where the torpedo detonated just beyond the engine room bulkhead within the stern, and her two diesel engines are visible. There are no reports of the two bronze screws or periscope still being in place but the 88mm deck gun and a few of its shells are apparently still there.

U 671, KRIEGSMARINE U-BOAT

DATE OF LOSS: 5 August 1944
DEPTH: 40m
REFERENCE: 50 23'.682 N 000 19'.166 W
LOCATION: 20.7 nautical miles S by E of Beachy Head

Type: VIIC ocean-going attack boat   *Builders*: Howaldtswerke AG, Hamburg for Kriegsmarine   *Ordered*: on 20 January 1941, within the batch of *U 669*–*U 674*   *Keel laid*: as Yard No.820 on 2 December 1941   *Launched*: on 15 December 1942   *Commissioned*: by Oberleutnant zur See August-Wilhelm Hewicker on 3 March 1943   *Feldpost No*: M 50 467

TECHNICAL SPECIFICATIONS

See page 342.

August-Wilhelm Hewicker was born in Hamburg on 30 July 1918 and commenced his naval career in 1937; he was promoted to Oberleutnant zur See on 1 September 1941. Hewicker's first command was with 42nd Mine Sweeping Flotilla and he assumed command of *U 671* on 3 March 1943.

U 671 was assigned to 5.U-Flottille, Kiel as *Ausbildungsboot* on 3 March 1943 until 30 April 1944; she then formally transferred to 3.U-Flottille at La Pallice for frontline service on 1 May 1944. On 4 May 1943 August-Wilhelm Hewicker was released from the Officer Corps.

Oblt.z.S. Wolfgang Hegewald assumed command on 7 May. Hegewald was born in Chemnitz on 5 July 1917 and commenced his naval career in 1937. He served as Divisional Officer on board the light cruiser *Königsberg* and was later promoted to Kapitänleutnant on 1 August 1944. Hegewald made two patrols with the boat.

U 671 left Kiel with Hegewald on 13 May 1944 and moved to Marviken (an anchorage within Kristiansand harbour, now called Marvika), where they arrived on 14 May 1944.

On 26 May she left Marviken and arrived at Bergen in southwest Norway the following day.

Leaving Bergen at 1100hrs (Continental time) on 28 May 1944 *U 671* sailed for operations in the North Atlantic. However, following the D-Day landings on 6 June, Hegewald's orders were changed. Along with six other *schnorchel*-equipped boats, *U 671* was re-routed to the English Channel to intercept vessels of the Allied invasion force. With some difficulty, she reached her designated area around 25 June.

U 671 proceeded from the W. entrance to the Channel to her operations area in the N. of the Channel and during this only once sighted a destroyer. Otherwise only frequent, distant, explosive soundings, circular saws, bomb explosions and propeller noises heard. As all the boats proceeding via the southern sector had great difficulty in charging due to interference by searching groups and hydrophone bearings and *U 671* has been able to proceed almost unhindered in the N. Sector, this latter seems the better route for later boats. These experiences were radioed to the boats. Frequent sightings in the operations area, but no chances to fire either because of inclination or range. The boat schnorchelled 3 times by day, once for 20 minutes, and then for 2 hours 20 minutes, and 2 hours 40 minutes, until she had to give the alarm because of destroyers or aircraft. At 1740/30/6, while schnorchelling, 3 destroyers approached at very low speed. No hydrophone bearing at 2000m. Destroyers approached to 500m and circled the boat at very low speed. Two hours after sighting 2 series of depth charges at periscope depth. No damage. T5 fired, gyroscope failed, presumably because of previous depth-charging. On 1.7. boat surfaced to charge, as battery empty. She discharged 30–40 Aphrodite and was able to charge for 2 hours until 2 destroyers were sighted. After alarm one well-placed depth charge, no damage of importance. On 2.7. the boat was depth charged while bottomed by a group of searching destroyers. She was presumably detected by a trace of oil, which may have been due to depth charges on 1.7. In spite of heavy damage, she fired 2 T5 at 20m by hydrophone bearing. Both failed, attributable to depth charges.

HMS *Wensleydale*. (Author's collection)

On 4 July, however, *U 671* was located on the bottom, southwest of Beachy Head and badly damaged by depth charges:

> The boat was bottomed at 62mon 2 July operating in BF 3259 and was surprised and depth charged by a searching group of destroyers. Main periscope top bent, aerial assembly partly smashed, No. 2 inner fuel tank crack to battery compartment, air conduits to No. 4 and 2 diving tanks torn below upper deck. The boat fired 3 T5, but the report does not make it clear whether before or after the depth charge attack. The boat was constantly pursued by the searching group on her way to Boulogne. As Boulogne dockyard can do no work, owing to air attacks, Flag Officer U-boats is sending a detachment of 30 specialist workmen from St Nazaire.
>
> BdU Diary 5/6 July.

FINAL PATROL

(4) Hegewald left Boulogne with *U 671* on 26 July 1944, for more operations in the English Channel, but was twice forced to return, due to a malfunctioning *schnorchel*.

The frigate HMS *Stayner* detected the boat on the evening of 4 August. Force G.D consisting of HMS *Wensleydale*, *Offa* and *Rowley* (in that order), was carrying out a patrol from position 50° 30'N 00° 05'W. Ordered to cut off the U-boat's retreat, the warships were deployed in line abreast, stationed 3 miles apart and steaming towards the contact at 23 knots.

Commanding officer, HMS *Stayner*, Lt Cdr H.J. Hall RNR: Report of U-boat hunt on 4 August 1944:

> While in position 50° 23.6' N; 00° 06.5' E, when ship was on Anti-E-boat patrol with Coastal Forces in company, an ASDIC contact was obtained on the Starboard bow, and Coastal Forces were ordered to proceed clear while 'Stayner' went in to attack. The Hedgehog is not kept loaded when on E-boat patrols, so the first three attacks carried out were Depth Charge attacks. After the second D/C attack, there was little doubt in my mind of the identity of the target – it showed Doppler and movement and carried out violent anti-ASDIC tactics though no H.E. were heard until after the first H/H (Hedgehog) attack, after which a slight whistling effect was heard. (General movement of submarine was towards the S.E.)
>
> The target was difficult to hold, but by carrying out OBSERVANT was regained each time. After the third depth charge attack, the Hedgehog was used and, probably because of the slow speed of the

attack caught the U-boat off his guard and a definite hit was scored, separate explosions being heard and reactions to them seen on the surface. Target was held and attacked intermittently pending the arrival of HMS 'Offa', 'Wensleydale' and 'Rowley' who had been ordered to join. They joined at 0040hrs and 'Wensleydale' gained contact on being given range and bearing by 'Stayner'. 'Offa' also gained contact, but had difficulty in holding it, so cleared the range and carried out OBSERVANT with 'Rowley', while hunt proceeded. 'Wensleydale' picked up one officer and three ratings, one of whom died; 'Stayner' picked up the Engineer officer and one rating from, it was discovered, U.671.

HMS *Wensleydale*: Report of Destruction of *U 671* – Acting Lt Cdr W.P. Goodfellow RNVR:

'Wensleydale' commenced run in at 10 knots in order to ascertain shape of the target by Echo sounder trace and its depth. Survivors were heard and then sighted on both bows in the middle of dispersed oil patch. Way was taken off the ship, the whaler was lowered and the ship manoeuvred as necessary to pick up survivors. Closed position of wreck. Oil was observed to be coming up in large quantities but by moonlight no wreckage was visible. Position 50° 23' 54' N; 00° 18' 18' E. Course as requisite, speed 15 knots to rejoin 'Offa' and resume patrol.

HMS *Wensleydale* picked up Oblt.z.S. Hans Schaefer, Petty Officer Bruno Ehlers and Stoker Petty Officer Ernst Meyer.

HMS *Stayner*, Lt Cdr H.J. Hall RNR – continued:

After picking up survivors, 'Wensleydale' was ordered to drop another pattern on the wreck, after which, 'Stayner' also attacked. All ships returned to their patrols at 04.30.

An S.B.T. was used at about 23.30, and from information gained from the prisoners the submarine was damaged after the third D/C attack, but severely damaged after the fourth attack (H/H), and attempted to surface, but was unable to do so. The submarine showed a very marked (and smelly) oiled track after the first H/H attack. Wreckage was observed while picking up survivors, but could not afterwards be found. In all, six D/C attacks and five H/H attacks were carried out by 'Stayner'. Three depth charge attacks (five-charges) were carried out by 'Wenslydale'. It gives great pleasure to report the destruction of one of the enemy submarines, the wreck of which was accurately fixed in position 50° 23.54'N 00° 18.18'E.

Cdr Hall also reported that gauges in the engine room were damaged and the refrigeration plant put out of action on HMS *Stayner*, due to shock waves from the fierce depth charge attacks. Hall blamed the failure of Hedgehog mortars to expode in the course of the tenth attack on a bad follow-up of gyro repeaters. Admiral Charles Little, Commander-in-Chief, Portsmouth officially credited the sinking of *U 671* to HMS *Stayner* after receiving reports from *Stayner* and *Wensleydale* on 9 August 1944.

The British Interrogation Report:

Survivors intimated that before the last three attacks, they had been underway at slow speed or drifting just clear of the bottom on the tide and that they had taken avoiding action. After the first of these attacks all lights were extinguished and water began to come into the boat. The second attack lifted the submarine and after it she remained heavy and on the bottom. The third attack apparently turned her on her side, but neither of the ratings (Bruno Ehlers and Ernst Meyer) picked up by 'Wensleydale' had a very clear recollection of anything except the water rushing into the boat, and the officer prisoner (Oblt.z.S. Hans Schaefer) refused to discus the matter. The morale of the prisoners was good, but neither rating had any enthusiasm for service in submarines, and Schaefer, while having faith in the cause for which he was fighting, was pessimistic regarding the outcome of the war.

The German perspective – Translated from a letter written by Oblt.z.S. Hans Schäfer:

We left Kiel on 13 May 1944, our destination unknown. Next day we entered Kristiansand, in southern Norway, where we stayed for 14 days. In the last days of May we transferred to Bergen to top up with fuel and provisions. Here, we said our final farewell and left at 1100 on 28 May for our first patrol into the Atlantic. After 8 days, when the invasion took place, we received an order for a new destination, the English Channel being our new operational area. After a nice undisturbed voyage on southerly course, we entered a very difficult operational area between Cherbourg and the British Isle of Wight on 26 June 1944. Our task was to interrupt the enemy transport lines between south-English ports and the Invasion front (Seine Bay). Superiority of the enemy surface ships, especially destroyers, was so great that we could stay there only for a few days. In the early days of July our boat was so seriously damaged after hour-long attacks, that we had great difficulty, using our last air and battery power, to reach Boulogne on 5 July. The repair of the boat lasted three and a half weeks. During this time we recovered pretty well from the strenuous 3½ weeks in the warm French sun. On 1 August we left again to occupy a position even closer to the English coast.

Fate struck on 4 August 1944. After a depth charge hunt by two destroyers lasting 3½ hours, the boat received a direct hit in the fore section at about 0200hrs in the morning of the following day, causing the boat to bottom at once and fill with water, resulting in the instant death of one third of the crew. The rest of the crew from the aft and central sections of the boat gathered at once in the control room and prepared for escape. The boat rested at a depth of 45m. Because of the extremely bad air all except eight men fell unconscious from carbon dioxide poisoning. After a while, following decompression, the conning tower hatch was opened and eight men, including me, were able to escape. I lost consciousness and only came round again when I reached the surface. I saw a few of my comrades around me, all swimming, but lost sight of them soon afterwards when we drifted apart in the strong current. After about half an hour I was picked up by one of the two destroyers, where I rejoined two of my comrades during late afternoon on 5 August. By the evening of the same day the three of us were transferred into a tent camp on land, where two more crewmembers of our boat, which had been picked up by the other destroyer, were waiting for us. In total there were only five survivors, being:

Engineer officer Leutnant (Ing) Robert Schröter
Wachtmeister boatswain Bruno Ehlers
Central room-mate Maschinenmaat Ernst Meyer
Helmsmen Matr. Ob.Gfr. Heinz Pieper
and I (Hans Schäfer).

All research for any further survivors that I carried out at the British department after my capture, were unsuccessful.

Signed Hans Schäfer

The sinking of *U 671* was mentioned in a BBC broadcast intercepted by the Germans as this entry in the BdU War Diary for 22 August 1944 indicates;

In spite of numerous requests to the eight boats (according to dead reckoning in the Seine area) for a situation report, even if this meant leaving the operations area, nothing was received. Apart from this, with the exception of an ASV report there have been no enemy reports of U-boats recently. The report of intensified defences from *U 621* was further strengthened by the news of the loss of *U 671* and *U 741* and by an enemy report of the destruction of a boat which according to English information was attempting to pass through the Pas de Calais. To sum up: Operational possibilities obscure. Uncertainty concerning the whereabouts of the seven boats presumed to be in the Seine area; and existence of very strong defence…

ADM 1/29857 NARA T1022, Rolls 4065-66, PG 30347-53 U-Boot-Ehrenmal Möltenort

THE MEN WHO PERISHED IN U 671

Abenhausen, Albert Mech.O.Gfr. (Born: 27-3-1923)
Berger, Karl-Heinz Masch.O.Gfr. (7-10-1923)
Bönisch, Hellmuth Ob.Strm. (11-4-1915)
Buder, Helmut Masch.O.Gfr. (4-6-1924)

Czipull-Lindenblatt, Klaus-Dieter Fk.O.Gfr. (15-9-1924)
Dittmar, Armin Masch.O.Gfr. (21-1-1924)
Donner, Karl Mtr.O.Gfr. (27-8-1925)
Döring, Johannes Mtr.Gfr. (4-9-1924)

Drescher, Hans Ob.San.Mt. (25-10-1921)
Fänger, Franz Masch.O.Gfr. (26-3-1922)
Friedrichs, Heinz Strm. (15-5-1915)
Fülling, Wilhelm Masch.O.Gfr. (22-7-1922)
Hegewald, Wolfgang Oblt.z.S. (5-7-1917)
Huckwitz, Hermann Masch.O.Gfr. (22-12-1923)
Jahrmarkt, Walter Fk.Mt. (9-1-1922)
Jost, Johannes Mtr.O.Gfr. (23-1-1924)
Krützmann, Fritz Ob.Mech.Mt. (8-1-1916)
Lemke, Kurt St.Ob.Masch. (17-3-1912)
Leonhardt, Gerhard Masch.Mt. (30-3-1922)
Maier, Johannes Ob.Masch.Mt. (5-10-1918)
Maquinion, Johann Masch.O.Gfr. (4-5-1923)
Matthes, Max Fk.Mt. (26-7-1922)
Meyer, Rolf Masch.O.Gfr. (5-4-1908)
Motz, Walter Mech.O.Gfr. (12-11-1922)
Nowak, Waldemar Masch.O.Gfr. (30-3-1921)
Oswald, Kurt Mtr.O.Gfr. (23-7-1924)
Parczyk, Lothar Mtr.O.Gfr. (4-4-1925)

Pecher, Franz Mtr.O.Gfr. (8-12-1924)
Pelz, Oswald Ob.Masch.Mt. (23-1-1921)
Petersen, Ewald Masch.Mt. (22-12-1918)
Petersilka, Johann Mtr.O.Gfr. (4-9-1924)
Peutler, Alfons Mtr.O.Gfr. (22-10-1923)
Pötsch, Georg Mtr.O.Gfr. (24-2-1924)
Rennemeier, Rudolf Bts.Mt. (13-12-1922)
Richter, Helmut Masch.Gfr. (18-10-1924)
Schmidt, Alwin Mtr.O.Gfr. (18-11-1922)
Scholten, Heinrich Bts.Mt. (12-6-1921)
Schwanke, Walter Ob.Masch. (26-5-1916)
Strandt, Siegfried Mtr.O.Gfr. (2-7-1921)
Viel, Ernst Mech.H.Gfr. (18-7-1922)
Vorgang, Karl Masch.O.Gfr. (5-10-1919)
Walter, Ernst Fk.O.Gfr. (15-1-1924)
Weinfurtner, Josef Fk.O.Gfr. (27-3-1925)
Weißkirchner, Josef Mtr.O.Gfr. (19-8-1924)
Westphal, Hartwig Ltz.S. (1-3-1920)
Wieprich, Kurt Masch.O.Gfr. (29-2-1924)
Zinsgrosch, Kurt Masch.O.Gfr. (31-8-1924)

WRECK SITE

The wreck lies on a seabed of sand, shell and gravel, in a general depth of 40m, being the lowest astronomical depth. Local divers report it lying on a 45° angle. The wreck is said to be largely intact with an enormous blast hole in the port side of the forward torpedo room. The conning tower hatch, lower hatch into the control room and the hatch aft of the conning tower are all open, indicating an escape. Much of the pressure hull around the bows has disintegrated, exposing the bronze torpedo tubes, while other sections of the outer casing have broken away. Marine life has established itself all over the upper sections of the wreck and shoals of fish have adopted it as a sanctuary. The wreck, of course, is also a war grave.

U 413, KRIEGSMARINE U-BOAT

DATE OF LOSS: 20 August 1944
DEPTH: 51m
REFERENCE: 50 21.5N 00 00.5W
LOCATION: 24.47 nautical miles SSW of Beachy Head

Type: VIIC ocean-going attack boat **Builders**: Danziger Werft AG, Danzig for Kriegsmarine **Ordered**: on 15 August 1940, in the batch of *U 413–U 416* **Keel laid**: as Yard No.114 on 25 April 1941 **Launched**: on 15 January 1942 **Commissioned**: by Kapitänleutnant Gustav Poel on 3 June 1942 **Feldpost No**: M 40 228

TECHNICAL SPECIFICATIONS

See page 342.

Gustav Poel was born in Hamburg on 2 August 1917 and commenced his naval career in 1936. He began his service as 2nd Watch Officer on *U 27* between April 1939 and May 1939. Poel was awarded the Spanish Cross on 6 June 1939, the Knights Cross, the U-boat Front Clasp, plus of course the Iron Cross 1st and 2nd Class and the U-boat War badge. On 1 February 1943 Poel was promoted to Kapitänleutnant. He served on *U 413* from the commissioning until April 1944.

U 413 served with 8.U-Flottille, Danzig as *Ausbildungsboot* from 3 June to 31 October 1942 and formally transferred to 1.U-Flottille at Brest for frontline duties on 1 November 1942. *U 413* made eight war patrols:

On 22 October 1942 the boat left Kiel and sailed to Marviken where she arrived on 24 October.

U 413 sailed from Marviken on 28 October 1942 for operations in the North Atlantic. On 14 November 1942 *U 413* encountered the northbound Convoy MKF 1 (X) consisting of eleven ships, northwest of Cape Espichal, Portugal. The convoy, which included British troopships and the new 'jeep' carriers HMS *Biter* and HMS *Dasher*, was returning to Glasgow from the Mediterranean via Gibraltar. On his first attack at 0844hrs (Continental time), Poel torpedoed and sank the 20,107-ton troop-transport MV *Warwick Castle* (Union-Castle Mail Steamship Co. Ltd, London) in position 39° 12'N 13° 25'W; she was on Government service and carrying 165 service personnel on passage from Gibraltar to the Clyde. Captain Henry Richard Leepman-Shaw and sixty-one crew were lost.

THOSE WHO DIED

Anderson, John Horne, Assistant Steward
Arch, John Frederick, Able Seaman
Ayles, William BEM, Boatswain (Bosun)
Bicknell, Harry, Steward
Blake, Kenneth Richard Thomas, Baker's Assistant
Bowie, Aubrey Bridge Jackman, 6th Engineer Officer
Brand, Victor Steward
Campbell, William Ross 6th Engineer Officer
Chatfield, William Alfred, Quartermaster
Collins, Bernard, Able Seaman
Colvin. Robert Smeddon, Painter
Conolly, Percy Victor, Quartermaster
Crook, Alfred, Greaser
Cummins, Reginald Oliver, Greaser
Earlie, James, Assistant Pantryman
Emerson, Norman, Ordinary Seaman
Fall, Christopher Alfred, Watchman
Farrell, Frank John Scullion, 17yrs
Finck, Dick Leonard James, Steward
Fulton, Charles James, Boy, 16yrs
Gibson, William Frederick, Assistant Barkeeper
Goodman, Charles Roland, Assistant Purser
Gordon, Denis Michael Hamilton, Cadet
Gordon, James, Assistant Cook
Gurling, Stanley Edward, Deck Boy, 18yrs
Hall, Alfred Henry, Greaser
Hart, Walter, Ordinary Seaman
Heads, Alfred, 2nd Engineer Officer
Hollins, Wrthur William, Boatswain
Hopper, James Edward Charles, Assistant Cook
Houghton, Sidney John, Assistant Steward

Judd, William George, Greaser
Kane, John, Assistant Steward
Kennedy, William Henry, Assistant Steward
Mallam, Thomas William, Cook
Meller, Joseph, Assistant Steward
Mordue, Robert William, Assistant Steward
Muir, Henry Edward, Carpenter's Mate
Mullen, Joseph, Assistant Cook
Murphy, James, Assistant Steward
Murray, Thomas McCall, Electrician
MacArthur, Angus Malcolm Geary, Deck Boy, 16yrs
McBride, Samuel Thomas, Senior 4th Engineer Officer
McIntyre, Alexander, Able Seaman
Orr, George Fulton, Steward
Parry, Alleyne Hughes, Chief Officer
Phillips, John Innes, Assistant Steward
Pratt, William John, Baker
Riley, Fred, Cook
Roberts, John Charles, Boatswain's Mate
Robertson, James, Galley Boy
Rose, Ernest Henry Thomas, Greaser
Savage, Ronald, Assistant Cook
Scott, Andrew, Assistant Steward
Sharpe, Joseph William, Printer
Shaw, Henry Richard Leepman, Master
Summers, Godfrey St. John, Assistant Steward
Taylor, Charles, Pantryman
Tetley, Stanley, Assistant Steward
Walmsley, Gerald Stanley, Assistant Steward
Young, Robert Archibald Edward, Assistant Cook

HM destroyers *Achates* (Lt Cdr A.H.T. Jones), *Vansittart* (Lt Cdr Johnstone) the RCN corvette *Louiseburg* (Lt Cdr W.F.C. Campbell) and the British steamer *Leinster* rescued 201 crewmen, twenty-nine DEMS gunners, five naval and 131 service personnel and landed them at Greenock.

On 19 November Poel was chasing another convoy when a Hudson of 608 Squadron, piloted by Flying Officer A.F. Wilcox, attacked the boat. *U 413* crash-dived, but the plane dropped four depth charges over her, smashing the periscopes to bits, and Poel was forced back into Brest to repair the damage, arriving on 25 November 1942. In harbour, Poel was highly praised for sinking the troopship.

(3) On 27 December *U 413* left Brest for operations northeast of Newfoundland, with the reconstituted *Jaguar* wolfpack. At 2351hrs (Continental time) on 22 January 1943, Poel torpedoed the straggling 3,556-ton Greek steamer *Mount Mycale* (1907 – Atlanticos S.S. Co. Ltd and Giorgilis Bros, Piraeus 888), in the slow Convoy 117, about 200 miles northeast of Cape Race. The ship was enroute from Saint John's, Newfoundland and Halifax, Nova Scotia for Loch Ewe and carrying 4,942 tons of grain and 226 tons of Government stores; all her crew was lost when she sank.

U 413 then refuelled northeast of Newfoundland.

At 1707hrs (Continental time) on 5 February 1943, Poel torpedoed and sank a convoy straggler, the 5,977-ton American merchantman *West Portal* (1920 – Pope & Talbot, Inc., San Francisco) in the area of 53°N 33°W; she was on passage from New York and Halifax, Nova Scotia for Liverpool with army stores and mail. The whole crew perished after taking to the lifeboats.

The U-boat returned to Brest on 17 February, but three of the other U-boats in the pack had been lost in the operation.

(4) On 29 March 1943, *U 413* left Brest again for operations in the North Atlantic and joined *Meise* group off Newfoundland. Weather conditions were very bad south of Greenland and when the group did manage to find a convoy, aircraft drove them away.

At 1345hrs on 21 April 1943, Poel put a torpedo into the British SS *Wanstead* (1928 – British S.S. Co. Ltd, London) at position 55° 46'N 45° 14'W. The vessel was very low in the water because at 0814hrs (Continental time) that same morning, *U 415* (Kurt Neide) had already hit the ship with a torpedo. The 5,486-ton vessel was part of convoy ONS 3, consisting of eighteen ships, and was in ballast, voyaging from the Tyne and Oban for New York. HM's corvette *Poppy* (K.213) (Lt N.K. Boyd DSC) and the 655-ton anti-submarine trawler *Northern Gift* (Lt Cdr A.J. Clemence) had rescued the master, Captain William B. Johnston, forty crewmen and seven DEMS gunners and landed them at St Johns, Newfoundland, but two men were drowned: Greaser Jack Andrews (47yrs) and Greaser Samuel Clarke (50yrs). HMS *Poppy* administered the *coup de grâce* by gunfire.

On 25 April Poel allegedly fired two torpedoes at a steamer, but both missed their targets. The U-boat 'milk cow' *U 461* refuelled *U 413* in mid-Atlantic, sometime around 6 May 1943. Hunting ships was made almost impossible due to constant air attacks and by 20 May, three U-boats had been lost, including *U 954* with Dönitz's second son Peter on board.

U 413 returned to Brest on 13 June 1943.

(5) On 4 September 1943, *U 413* left Brest again for Atlantic operations, but mechanical problems forced her back on 18 September.

(6) On 27 September *U 413* sailed out of Brest, but returned to port the following day.

(7) On 2 October 1943, *U 413* departed Brest and sailed for the North Atlantic to link up with *Schlieffen* group, to the southwest of Iceland. However Allied aircraft harassed the boats and kept them submerged for days on end. By 16 October both *U 844* and *U 964* were lost. *U 413* was carrying special directional finding equipment with an operating team and at one point she reported the outbound north (slow) 20 Convoy to have changed course. That report sent the *Schlieffen* pack in the wrong direction. After changing wolfpacks a few time, *U 413* eventually returned to Brest on 21 November 1943.

(8) On 26 January 1944 the boat sailed out of Brest for North Atlantic operations, but initially off southwest Ireland, where she made several unsuccessful attacks on convoy escort destroyers. Allied Enigma code-breakers were able to read signals of *U 413*, *U 621* and *U 333* and British aircraft and hunter-killer groups set out to look for them. On 10 February Poel reported a convoy, but an unidentified aircraft drove him off. Then on the 20th, after being spotted and reported by a fishing boat off north Cornwall, destroyers began hunting for the U-boat. However, that same day, Poel successfully torpedoed the 1,100-ton British destroyer HMS *Warwick* (D25) (Cdr D.A. Rayner DSC, VD, RNVR) at position 50° 27'N 05° 23'W, west, southwest of Trevose Head. HMS *Warwick* was en-route between Adrossan in Scotland and Plymouth. What follows is an extract from the U-boat KTB:

> fired bow T 5 at destroyer in escort group detonation after 11 minutes 25 seconds. A destroyer firing
> star shells broke off the operations. The boat obtained information from watch on enemy R/T fre
> quency. The same boat sighted 2 destroyers in quarterline formation at 0703hrs and fired the bow T 5.
> Detonation and short crack after 12 minutes 54 seconds. Only one hydrophone bearing after submerg
> ing, no depth charges.

The FaT torpedo detonated against the aft magazine. The ship broke in half. Some of those who took to the water managed to avoid the burning oil, only to be shattered by the concussion from *Saladin* and *Scimitar's* depth charge attacks. In all, three officers and sixty-four ratings were killed. *U 413* managed to slip away. The following day, torpedoes fired by *U 413* also apparently missed both a steamer and a destroyer southwest of Ireland. The U-boat returned to Brest on 27 March 1944.

Oblt.z.S. Dietrich Sachse assumed command on 20 April. Sachse was born in Gipstal on 22 August 1917 and commenced his naval career in 1939. He began his submarine service as watch officer with 27th U-Flottille between March 1942 and April 1942 and on 1 October 1943 was promoted to Oberleutnant zur See.

(9) With seven other non-*schnorchel* boats and under her new commander, *U 413* sailed from Brest on 6 June 1944 for operations against Allied invasion ships, between the Lizard and Hartland Point, but came under heavy aircraft attacks. Using her anti-aircraft guns in the early hours of 8 June, the boat fought a Halifax aircraft of the British 502 Squadron, piloted by J. Spurgeon. The plane was riddled with the heavy Flak fire, but dropped a stick bomb of 600 pounds. Sachse was forced to abort his patrol and put into Brest for repairs on 9 June; the boat's port engine being totally disabled. During her stay in port, *U 413* had a *schnorchel* fitted.

FINAL PATROL

(10) On 2 August 1944, *U 413* left Brest to operate against shipping on the Allied convoy route, between southern England and the Baie de la Seine (Bay of the Seine), after which she was to proceed to Norway. In the evening of 19 August and southeast of St Catherine's Point, Isle of Wight, Sachse found coastal convoy ETC 72 comprised of twenty ships and fired torpedoes at two steamships: the 2,327-ton British *Saint Enogat* (1918 – Ministry of War Transport, Plymouth) and another vessel of 8,000 tons. The *Saint Enogat* (ex-*War Clarion*), which was on passage from London for Juno Beach, Normandy with 1,427 tons of Government stores, sank in position 50° 16'N 00° 50'W, but there was no confirmation of the second, larger one going down. The Landing Ship Infantry *Duke of Argyll* rescued the master Captain Philip Duggan of *Saint Enogat*, thirty crewmen, five DEMS gunners and one army storekeeper, but three crewmen, fireman Patrick Johnson, fireman Arthur William Lehane and George Henry Todd, a donkeyman, were lost, along with one DEMS gunner.

At 0900hrs on 20 August, there were indications that *U 413* was being pursued and she travelled on her motors at 30m depth. *U 413* was located, but managed to escape, though closely trailed by the destroyer HMS *Forester* (Cdr G.W. Gregorie). The following morning other destroyers joined the hunt, including *Wensleydale* (Lt Cdr W.P. Goodfellow), *Vidette* (Lt Cdr G. Woolley) and *Watchman* (Lt Cdr J. Clarke). Between them, the British warships located *U 413* on 20 August 1944 and finished her off with depth charges, which brought various bits and pieces to the surface.

20/8/44 Log of messages between HMS *Watchman, Wensleydale* and *Forester*:

> At 0807hrs on 20 August an ASDIC contact was obtained by HMS *Forester* while on anti-submarine patrol with HMS *Wensleydale* and *Vidette*. At 0915hrs *Forester* attacked with depth charges set to 150ft without result. VIDETTE being the only ship present with any bombs remaining was ordered to close and carry out Hedgehog attack and at 0934hrs she attacked, the bombs being observed to fall on the centre of the target from *Wensleydale*. Bubbles and diesel oil came to the surface and one survivor was picked up by *Wensleydale*. At 0952hrs *Wensleydale* made another depth charge attack, which was considered to have finished off the U-boat. Doubt was expressed by *Forester* as to whether the U-boat was completely destroyed as only a small amount of wreckage had come to the surface.

Message between the ship's captains, reporting on the destruction of *U 143*:

> 12.49 – *Wensleydale* to *Forester* – 'Do you not think there is something wrong here, that all this small wreckage should come from the insides of a U-boat? – This wreckage is small enough to have come from a torpedo tube. – There is something not right here'
>
> 12.51 – *Forester* to *Wensleydale*: 'Agree. – Suggest you drop another pattern to make sure'
>
> 12.52 – *Forester* to *Wensleydale*: 'I now have papers from U413'

12.54 – *Wensleydale* to *Watchman*: 'Do you want any more evidence? – I have just passed a lavatory seat'

13.03 – *Watchman* to *Wensleydale*: 'No, I think its fairly conclusive now

Oblt.z.S. Dietrich Sachse and forty-five crewmen perished with the boat, but the chief engineer managed to escape and was picked up by a destroyer.

HMS *Vidette*. (Author's collection)

HMS *Forester*. (Author's collection)

Survivor account of (Austrian born) Engineer Officer Karl-Hubert Huetterer:

> The first attack was poor but the second was perfect and decisive. – The boat was holed forward and went down by the bows. – They were unable to trim and had to bottom. – By the time of the third accurate attack they were up to their waists in water and decided to abandon ship.

When asked why he was the only survivor, Karl Huetterer, who was described as a 'security risk and confirmed Nazi', replied: 'It is the duty of the Engineer Officer to open the escape hatch. I unscrewed the hatch and the others were behind me, but I do not know what happened to them.

BdU waited for news of *U 413*. It was ultimately provided by the BBC. The War Diary contains this entry for 9 September 1944:

> The loss of *U 413* must now be reckoned with. Boat left Brest on 2.8. for Channel operations. Attack area for *U 413* south of Isle of Wight. On 25.8. boat received orders to make return passage to Norway, but up to date has not yet reported. According to the BBC, engineer officer of *U 413* has been taken prisoner. Cause of loss probably anti-submarine patrols in operational area.

ADM 199/498 NID/1/PW NARA T1022, Rolls 4065-6, PG 30348, 30352-54 U–Boot-Ehrenmal Möltenort

THE MEN WHO PERISHED IN U 413

Altstädt, Werner Ltz.S. (Born: 25-7-1923)
Baake, Kurt Maat. (13-8-1922)
Beckmann, Erwin Mtr. (1-1-1922)
Birnbaum, Freidrich Ob.Gfr. (23-3-1923)
Bohnke, Helmut Ob.Gfr. (29-5-1923)
Brickmann, Gunter Ob.Mt. (18-1-1922)
Dangers, Ewald Ob.Mt. (19-4-1918)
Dembinski, Fritz Ob.Gfr. (7-1-1923)
Externbrink, Heinrich Ob.Gfr. (31-1-1924)
Fiebel, Willi Ob.Gfr. (21.02.1922
Greul, Karl Maat. (9-1-1924)
Hackenbrich, Gottfreid Mt. (30-1-1922)
Hacker, Karl Ob.Gfr. (26-1-1924)
Hafner, Wilhelm Ob.Gfr. (4-1-1925)
Hamann, Ernst (Ob.Mt. (16-9-1917)
Hartwig, Kurt Mt. (29-7-1922)
Heinicke, Werner Ob.Mt. (3-8-1919)
Hellmich, Gerhard Ob.Mt. (23-6-1922)
Hemmen, Johann Ob.Gfr. (31-8-1924)
Horn, Kurt Ob.Gfr. (31-7-1923)
Just, Willibald Gfr. (7-7-1923)
Krischat, Heinz Ob.Gfr. (3-1-1925)
Kröner, Helmut Ob.Gfr. (19-5-1921)

Lorenz, Kurt Ob.Gfr. (1-2-1924)
Malow, Hans Ob.Gfr. (4-2-1924)
Müller, Helmut Ob.Gfr. (23-11-1923)
Musiol, Karl Ob.Masch. (11-8-1917)
Oster, Walter Ob.Mt. (12-1-1914)
Peters, Heinz Ob.Gfr. (10-9-1924)
Pfaffinger, Peter Ob.Gfr. (16-11-1924)
Pfisterer, Erich Ob.Mt. (12-6-1919)
Pölzl, Karl Gfr. (31-8-1925)
Regelin, Karl-Heinz Ob.Gfr. (19-12-1922)
Reinhold, Hermann Gfr. (30-3-1923)
Sachse, Dietrich Oblt.z.S. (22-8-1917)
Bätz, Rolf Ob.Mt. (15-4-1906)
Schmitz, Friedrich Gfr. (26-3-1925)
Schwaiger, Gerhard Ltz.S. (4-11-1922)
Schwarzer, Herbert Ob.Gfr. (21-12-1923)
Serve, Hubert Maat. (8-5-1922)
Sock, Werner Ob.Gfr. (20-3-1924)
Tomalla, Theodor Ob.Strm. (25-4-1917)
Wüst, Hans Ob.Gfr. (7-9-1922)
Zimmermann, Alfons Ob.Masch. (1-12-1913)
Ziwinsky, Christian Gfr. (28-9-1924)

WRECK SITE

The wreck of what is believed to be *U 413* lies on a seabed of sand and gravel, in a general depth of 51m (167ft), being the lowest astronomical depth. It is upright, but broken in two halves just forward of the conning tower and covered in nets. Much of the upper section is also badly holed and broken. This wreck is a war grave.

U 741, KRIEGSMARINE U-BOAT

DATE OF LOSS: 15 August 1944
DEPTH: 52m
REFERENCE: 50 02'.273 N 000 34'.957 W
LOCATION: 42 nautical miles S of Selsey Bill and 42 nautical miles SSE of
St Catherine's Point, Isle of Wight

Type: VIIC ocean-going attack boat   *Builders*: F. Schichau GmbH, Danzig for
Kriegsmarine   *Ordered*: on 5 June 1941, within the batch of *U 741–U 746*   *Keel laid*: as Yard
No.1544 on 30 April 1942   *Launched*: on 4 February 1943   *Commissioned*: by Oberleutnant zur
See Gerhard Palmgren on 10 April 1943   *Feldpost No*: M 41 306

TECHNICAL SPECIFICATIONS

See page 342.

Gerhard Palmgren was born in Kassel on 11 November 1919 and commenced his naval career in
1938. At the beginning of his service he served as watch officer under instruction on the heavy
cruiser *Admiral Hipper* between April and August 1940. Palmgren was promoted to Oberleutnant
zur See (R) on 1 April 1943 and assumed command of *U 741* on 10 April 1943.

U 741 was assigned to 8.U-Flottille, Danzig as *Ausbildungsboot* on 10 April 1943 until
31 October 1943.

On 1 November 1943, *U 741* and Gerhard Palmgren were formally attached to the 1.U-Flottille
at Brest, for frontline service.

U 741 departed Kiel on 25 November 1943 and assembled off the North Channel with other
boats to search for convoys off the west coast of Britain. This wolfpack, consisting of *U 741*, *U 364*,
U 284, *U 471*, *U 981* and *U 976*, was named *Coronel 2*. The packs regrouped again and *U 741*
linked with *Sylt* pack. Off the west of Ireland, the wolfpacks met up and changed into other various
groups. *U 741* sank no ships on the voyage and put into her new base at Brest on 27 January 1944.

U 741 left Brest with *U 526* (Wilhelm Brauel) on 29 February 1944 and headed for operations with
Preussen group in the Atlantic. While crossing the Bay of Biscay *U 741* was twice attacked by Allied aircraft
at night, but sustained very little damage. The two boats were ordered to proceed to the southwest of
Ireland and search for any survivors from *U 625*, which had been badly damaged by six depth charges
from a Sunderland of Canadian 422 Squadron on 10 March. The skipper, Straub, decided to abandon ship
and sent an SOS out to his Control. Straub then scuttled his boat after the men got into dinghies. During
the search for *U 625* on the 11th a Wellington from *407* Squadron of the Royal Canadian Air Force, commanded by Pilot Officer E.M. O'Donnell, attacked the two U-boats. *U 256* sustained serious damage, but
managed to shoot the plane down. Life rafts were found, but no survivors. Later, after surfacing, Palmgren
in *U 741* reported being attacked by four carrier-based planes and three destroyers to the west of the
British Isles, which inflicted slight damage. On 22 March *U 256* reached Brest and *Preussen* group disbanded. *U 741* then patrolled independently between the British Isles and 40°W. After a spell of weather
duty, the boat returned to Brest on 3 May. During her stay in harbour, *schnorchel* equipment was fitted.

Lt Hans Schilling, who left the boat just prior to her loss, recorded that Palmgren took *U 741* out
of Brest on 19 June 1944 and, with another three boats, was ordered to transport machine-gun and
anti-tank ammunition to the beleaguered port of Cherbourg.

On 23 June the four boats were recalled when the submarine command heard that the harbour
was blocked. *U 741* arrived back at Brest on the 29th, unloaded the ammunition and loaded up with
torpedoes.

(4) *U 741* left the port of Brest on 5 July and sailed to the Bay of the Seine. A few hours after leaving port, three Allied destroyers attacked the U-boat and her escorts. *U 741* crash-dived and escaped.
The boat was still able to hug the British coastline and reach the Allied landing area, even though
the A/S measures were intense.

U 741 was moving submerged with electric motors at 131ft (39.9m) on 12 July when sweeping
wires of an Allied minesweeper caught on the conning tower of the U-boat. BdU Diary of 16 July
contains the following entry:

she became entangled in some English minesweeping gear and lost her starboard after and forward jumping wire. The Commanding Officer observed through the periscope that the English minesweeper was trying to haul in the paravanes. During the night the boat surfaced in BF 3185 and threw the gear overboard. At 0126/14/7 she was rammed in BF 3191 while using schnorchel. Main periscope and schnorchel damaged. She put into Le Havre for repairs and made fast there on 16.7.

Clearly an amazing escape but *U 741* had used up her quota of luck.

FINAL PATROL

(5) After the damage was put right, *U 741* departed Le Havre on 3 August, for operations in the English Channel off the Isle of Wight. On 15 August convoy FTM 69 was sighted in the afternoon and two torpedoes were fired at *LST 404*. Miraculously *LST 404* survived a torpedo hit and was towed to Spithead. Having now made his presence known, Palmgren was forced to dive to the bottom at 190ft (57.9m) and remain there. HMS *Orchis* was already on his trail.

HMS *Orchis*, 16 August 1944 Narrative of Events:

At 1435 GMT on 15 August while acting as S.O.Escort to Convoy F.T.C.68, a large explosion was observed close to an L.S.T. in convoy F.T.M.68 fine on Bow some 4 miles distant. HMS 'Orchis' was in position Nan.

(2) At 1451 A/S contact was obtained at 2,800 yards bearing Red 10 on a course 337°. This was considered to be a probable U-boat. [As an aside, in March the corvette HMS *Orchis* had become the first operational warship to be fitted with a Type 271, centimetric radar].

A counter attack was accordingly made and at 1457hrs, one pattern of 5 charges was dropped by bridge hydraulic gear.

(3) Contact was regained astern and at 1508hrs, second counter attack was made and further pattern of depth charges was fired by same means. Contact then classified as submarine and a deliberate attack was made by Hedgehog.

(4) First Hedgehog attack was made at 1525 and shortly afterwards a large patch of light oil was seen to be rising. Second run was carried out but at 600 yards range Recorder paper tore across and attack was broken off.

(5) A third Hedgehog attack was made and at 1544 pattern was fired. Very heavy explosion resulted but contact was still held. Very heavy oil now began to appear. Ship was manoeuvred into position for a fourth Hedgehog attack when loud hissing noises were heard on ASDICs. Two men were seen struggling in the centre of the oil patch and a third man was motionless.

(6) Attack ewas broken off and a boat lowered immediately. Boat proceeded to survivor who appeared to be in the greater difficulty. Balsa life raft was dropped near the other survivor who gained it. Unfortunately the other man sank as the boat reached him. The other survivor was picked up and a search was made for the bodies without success.

(7) The position of the wreck was marked be a Dan-Buoy flying flag 'O' for *Orchis*, in position 50.02'12W 00.36'09W. The position was patrolled until 1730 awaiting instructions after which time vessel proceeded to comply with C in C Portsmouth's 151904. During this time a considerable amount of small wreckage was observed, consisting of small pieces of wood and three objects, which appeared to be mattress covers. It was not advisable to stop and pick up these objects in view of the fact that other U-boats wee possibly in the area, and that one German prisoner was on board in full possession of his faculties.

General. ASDIC conditions were exellent and no none subs were evident. No evidence of anti-ASDIC tactics were observed and it is considered that the U-boat bottomed after second Depth Charge attack. Hunt was abandoned when it was clear U-boat had been destroyed not only from visual findings, but also from prisoner's statement.

U 741 was seriously damaged and holed, and her fore section soon flooded, trapping about eleven men aft. Masch.Mt. (Leading Stoker) Leo Leuwer and another stoker managed to escape via the aft torpedo room hatch. HMS *Orchis* picked Leuwer up alive, but the other man died.

The German perspective account of survivor Leo Leuwer:

We started the last mission on 10 August 1944 from Le Havre and were sunk 15 August 1944 by depth charges in the English Channel. We were lying with flooded fore-ends at 60m depth, with no possibility of resurfacing the submarine. I was with ten more comrades in the stern compartment. This compartment was flooded in order to equalise pressure and facilitiate escape to the surface. Unfortunately the compartment took too long to flood, with the result that the oxygen in my Tauchretter set was virtually exhausted by the time that pressure had equalised and the hatch could be opened. My salvation was only due to the fact that I had a second Tauchretter and thus I had the opportunity to breathe some minutes longer than my comrades. I was able to open the hatch and make my escape to the surface.

ADM1/29878 NARA T1022, Rolls 4065-66, PG 30350, 30352-30353 U-Boot-Ehrenmal Möltenort

The remaining forty-eight crewmen perished.

THE MEN WHO PERISHED IN U 741

Abraham, Wilhelm Masch-Mt- (22-11-1922)
Ahr, Willi Mtr-Gfr- (23-10-1924)
Albrecht, Horst Fk-O-Gfr- (15-11-1924)
Barion, Reiner Mtr-O-Gfr- (15-3-1925)
Berkelmann, Karl-Adolf Ltz.S. (10-2-1924)
Beulecke, Hermann Mtr. (7-7-1917)
Biermaier, Josef Mtr.O.Gfr. (6-4-1920)
Denkl, Siegfried Bts.Mt. (15-8-1923)
Franz, Kurt Masch.Gfr. (16-5-1925)
Geissler, Albert O.Masch. (23-7-1916)
Haldermanns, Heinrich Masch.Mt. (25-10-1921)
Hanak, Werner Mech.Mt. (5-2-1921)
Hartung, Wilhelm Masch.O.Gfr. (16-2-1925)
Heider, Alfred Mtr.O.Gfr. 12-7-1922)
Holzhüter, Oswald Ob.Strm. (7-8-1915)
Hunke, Wilhelm Masch.Mt. 15-11-1919)
Jansen, Werner Masch.Mt. 13-11-1918)
Kleider, Fritz Mtr.O.Gfr. (17-1-1925)
Klingenthal, Heinrich Masch.Mt. (15-7-1923)
Krause, Werner Mtr.Gfr. (22-4-1924)
Küster   Theodor, Mtr.O.Gfr. 30-10-1923)
Lettau, Emil Mtr.O.Gfr. (18-9-1922)
Leubner, Gerhard Masch.O.Gfr. (31-7-1924)
Linder, Hans Oberleutnant zur See (10-3-1919)

Löbel, Franz Masch.O.Gfr. (21-10-1923)
Lötsch, Rudi Masch.O.Gfr. (22-10-1923)
Lülsdorf, Jakob Masch.O.Gfr. (19-3-1923)
Lutz, Heinz Masch.O.Gfr. (6-5-1924)
Maier, Herbert Mech.O.Gfr. (27-5-1923)
Müller, Horst Mtr.O.Gfr. (9-11-1924)
Palmgren, Gerhard Oblt.z.S.d.R. (11-11-1919)
Reiner, Georg O.Masch. (28-12-1915)
Richter, Otto Fk.O.Gfr. (8-4-1922)
Rzepka, Peter Fk.O.Gfr. (24-3-1924)
Schlotterbeck, Günter Masch.Gfr. (1-5-1926)
Schmidt, Erich Mtr.O.Gfr. (18-8-1924)
Scholvien, Karl-Heinz Oblt.Ing. (28-7-1920)
Schubert, Heinz Fk.Mt. (7-2-1920)
Schwarz, Rudolf Oblt.z.S.d.R. (19-7-1914)
Seedig, Curt Bts.Mt. (27-3-1924)
Speckter, Otto Leutnant zur See (3-11-1921)
Stegemann, Herbert Mech.O.Gfr. (11-11-1924)
Stender, Rolf Masch.O.Gfr. (17-6-1924)
Trapp, Werner San.Mt. (11-5-1922)
Tuscher, Franz Masch.O.Gfr. (10-2-1924)
Vogel, Herbert Mtr.O.Gfr. (12-5-1923)
Weichelt, Werner Mech.Gfr. (7-9-1924)
Weitz, Arnold Bts.Mt. (6-3-192)

SURVIVED
Leuwer, Leo Masch.Mt.

WRECK SITE

The wreck lies on a seabed of sand and gravel, in a general depth of 52m (170.60ft), being the lowest astronomical depth. It is reported as being intact and upright and coated in marine growth. A large blast hole penetrates both casing and pressure hull on the port side, just aft of the conning tower. The conning tower is still in place and the hatch is closed, but the aft hatch, where Leo Leuwer made his escape, is open. Some of the casing is showing signs of deterioration. Large shoals of pout whiting (bib) hover over the top of the wreck, close to the conning tower. This wreck is, of course, a war grave.

UB 21, SM IMPERIAL U-BOAT (AND SCOURGE OF THE YORKSHIRE COAST)

DATE OF LOSS: 1920
DEPTH: 2–5m
REFERENCE: 50 44.23 N 01 01.52 W
LOCATION: 3 miles S of Eastney Point, near Portsmouth

Type: UBII coastal torpedo attack boat   *Builders*: Blohm & Voss, Hamburg for Kaiserliche Deutsche Marine   *Ordered*: on 30 April 1915, within the batch of UB 20–UB 23   *Keel laid*: as Yard No.251   *Launched*: on 26 September 1915   *Commissioned*: by Oberleutnant zur See Ernst Hashagen on 18 February 1916   *Combat ready*: on 14 April 1916

SM UB 21, *c.*1916. (Author's collection)

TECHNICAL SPECIFICATIONS

Hull: single, saddle tank design   *Surface displacement*: 263 tons   *U/Dt*: 292 tons   *LBDH*: 36.13m × 4.36m × 3.70m × 7.35m   *Machinery*: 2 × 142ps Körting diesels   *Props*: 2 bronze   *S/Sp*: 9.15 knots   *Op/R*: 6,450 nautical miles at 5 knots   *Sub/R*: 45 nautical miles at 4 knots   *U/Power*: 2 × 140ps electric motors gave 5.81 knots   *Batteries*: lead/acid   *Fuel/Cap*: 22 + 6 tons   *Armament*: 2 bow 50.04cm (19.7in) torpedo tubes   *Guns*: 1 × 88mm (3.46in) forward deck gun   *Torpedoes*: 4 × 50.04cm (19.7in)   *Ammo*: 120 rounds of 88mm   *Mines*: none   *Diving*: max-op-depth 75m and 30 sec to crash-dive   *Complement*: 2 officers and 21 ratings

UB 21 was formally assigned to the I.U-Flottille at Brunsbüttel on 14 April 1916 and remained until 1 February 1917, with Ernst Hashagen the CO from 20 February 1916 to 26 November 1916. Hashagen was born on 24 August 1885 and died 12 June 1947, having also served as commander on *U 62*. He will be remembered as the author of the 1930s classic *U-Boot Westwarts*, which chronicles his adventures as a U-boat commander during the First World War. The book reveals the author to have been a charming, courteous and gifted individual. Ruthless in his advocacy of unrestricted submarine warfare, surviving evidence indicates that Hashagen was nevertheless a humane man, privately repelled by the later Nazi regime. Chapter Six of *U-Boot Westwarts* describes the following frustrating patrols off the east coast of Britain in the autumn of 1916, when U-boat interceptions were fettered by the 'prize regulations'. *UB 21* operated in sea-lanes much frequented by neutral traffic, inbound with pit props, in return for for coal. Having introduced their own blockade of Britain, as far as the Germans were concerned, these Scandinavian vessels were carrying 'contraband'. Hashagen made the first eight patrols with the boat and all from German ports.

  UB 21 sailed from Brunsbüttel on 16 April 1916 to patrol off the Horns Riff, returning to port on the 18th.

On 24 April 1916, *UB 21* sailed to the Firth of Forth for operations against Allied shipping, but found nothing until 5 May, when Hashagen got his first victim in the Nortrh Sea on the journey back to Germany; the 375-ton *Harald* (1902 – Håkon Larsson, Brantevik, Sweden), a Swedish, wooden-hulled, three-masted schooner was captured and sunk with explosives; she was transporting pit props from Gothenburg to the Tyne.

UB 21 arrived back in Germany on 7 May.

(3) Leaving harbour on 21 May 1916, *UB 21* travelled to the Humber estuary to hunt Allied shipping, patrolling from Spurn Point to the Outer Dowsing and Flamborough Head, but the sortie was unsuccessful and she arrived back in port on 3 June 1916.

(4) On 8 July 1916, *UB 21* left from Germany for operations around the Pentland Firth and arrived home on 22 July, but again, no ships were encountered.

(5) *UB 21* sailed from port on 5 September 1916 and travelled back to the Pentland Firth and, after an unsuccessful voyage, returned to Germany on 19 September 1916.

(6) Leaving Germany, *UB 21* headed into the North Sea and west of the Dogger Bank to hunt for ships, but arrived back in port on 11 October, having failed to find any.

(7) Departing Germany on 14 October 1916, *UB 21* made a war cruise along the English and Scottish east coasts, as far as the Pentland Firth. Hashagen finally struck lucky over three days from the 20th, when he sank six Scandinavian vessels and captured one: the 204-ton Swedish sailing vessel *Lekna* (1877 – Otto Boman, Halmstad) was sunk by explosives in the North Sea off Berwick, while travelling from Mandal, Norway to Blyth with pit props. The *Svartvik* (1839 – W.G. Thorburn, Uddevalla), an old Swedish sailing ship of 322 tons, was in transit from Holmstrand for West Hartlepool. The standard procedure was for a U-boat officer to board a vessel and sink her using a bag of grenades (often referred to as bombs or explosives). As this excerpt from *U-Boot Westwarts* demonstrates, things did not always go according to plan. The incident took place off Berwick. Having forced the sailing ship's crew to evacuate the vessel, Hashagen sent young Ltz.S. Illing over alone to the deserted *Svartvik*:

> …after a time Illing appears on deck again and signs to me, 'all clear'. I close the ship and Illing is ready to jump, when a wave throws us apart.
>
> Desperate moments follow. Illing has lit the grenade, which is beginning to take great effect. Fire and smoke mount high in the air. In the uncertain light I see my officer running aft; she's on fire there too. He fights his way through, swings himself over the stern rails and evidently means to lower himself on the empty boat's fall. I catch one glimpse of him on the rails against the flames, and then a dark body vanishes with a loud splash in the sea…it is time for rapid action. I go straight for the stern of the burning vessel, close to the spot where Illing has disappeared. The wood splits open with a crash but by object is attained and the sharp bows of *UB 21* are held firmly for an instant between the splintered planks so that we can rescue Illing…Smoke and flames stream over our heads. Then Illing comes to the surface for a moment, ten yards away from us. A seaman throws him a lifebuoy on a line and we quickly haul him on board.
>
> Luckily, a submarine is not made of wood but men are, after all, combustible, Full speed astern! But our victim will not let us go! In the excitement, no one has observed that one of the dangling falls from the burning sailing ship has hooked itself onto our jumping wire. The flames bite hotly and the smoke is suffocating. The engines tug us back with all their might…A moment later the coxswain reports to me – my own attention had been devoted to the rescue of Illing –
>
> 'Two patrol boats closing fast. Alarm ! …'

UB 21 survived this encounter however.

Her victim was the *Randi* (1888 – A/S Randi, Brevik), a 467-ton wooden-hulled Norwegian barque. The vessel was carrying pit props from Portsgrund to the Tyne on 21 October when *UB 21* captured her off Berwick; it was then set on fire, using explosives. Next came the 667-ton Norwegian steamer *Grønhaug* (1890 – D/S Aktieselskapet Haug, Haugesund), also captured off Berwick on the 21st, then shelled and sunk, while en-route with timber and steel products from Göteborg to Hull. The *London* (1904), a 184-ton Danish schooner, was stopped in the North Sea off Berwick and sunk by gunfire on the 22nd, while en-route from Fönsberg to Hartlepool with eighty-nine standards and props. The 373-ton Norwegian motor-vessel *Thor* (1867 – A/S Thor, Moss) was also destroyed by gunfire off Berwick, while voyaging from Skien for Grimsby, carrying ferro solution (chemicals) and general cargo.

In a celebrated incident, the *Fritzøe* (1909 – Skibs Aktieselskapet Fritzøe, Larvik) was captured at 55° 39'N 0° 57'W and taken back to Germany as a prize-of-war. The *Fritzøe* was on a voyage from Larvik to London, with timber; the ship's voyage and destination was condemned by prize court and in 1918 she was renamed *Munin* by the Imperial German Navy; she was then fitted out as a salvage vessel.

On 30 October *UB 21* arrived back in Germany.

(8) Hashagen took *UB 21* out on patrol on 3 November 1916 and made for the English east coast. They returned to Germany on 14 November, after another successful voyage, having captured the 1,147-ton Norwegian SS *Pluto* (1912 – D/S A/S Pluto, Haugesund) off the Norwegian coast on the 3rd; she was voyaging from Göteborg to Rouen with woodpulp, iron and machines, which were destined for England. The ship was taken back to Germany as a prize-of-war and condemned by a prize court. In May 1917 *Pluto* became German Army transport (Schiffartsabt. beim Chef des Feldeisenbahnwesens). (A French destroyer seized her in the Baltic on 23 February 1919.)

Oblt.z.S. Franz Walther assumed command on 27 November 1916 and Hashagen took over *U 62*. Walther conducted two patrols using German ports.

(9) *UB 21* sailed out from port on 4 December 1916 to make a war cruise off Horns Riff (Horns Reef) against Allied submarines, but no targets were encountered and she returned to port on 16 December.

(10) On 16 January 1917, *UB 21* left Germany and patrolled along the English east coast for operations, but, after an uneventful voyage, returned to port on the 23rd.

On 1 February 1917 *UB 21* formally transferred to II.U-Flottille.

(11) Leaving Heligoland on 1 February 1917, Walther sailed to the English east coast near West Hartlepool for operations, but, following an unproductive patrol, returned to Germany on 7 February.

(12) The boat departed Heligoland on 13 February and sailed to the English east coast around West Hartlepool. The 1,016-ton British steamer *Lady Ann* (1882 – Lambton & Hetton Collieries, Ltd, Newcastle), which was delivering coal from Sunderland for Rochester, was torpedoed and sunk without warning on the 16th. The complete bow section broke off the ship and she rolled over and sank. The master, chief officer, helmsman, chief engineer and two seamen scrambled to launch the port lifeboat, but the ship sank beneath the waves, taking the master and ten crewmen down with her. The helmsman and four seamen clung to floating wreckage and were rescued by a local fishing coble and landed at Scarborough.

THE MEN WHO PERISHED

Chater, Frederick Arthur, 64yrs, 1st Mate
Garrod, Benjamin, 55yrs, 2nd Mate
Gunn, Walter William, 52yrs, Steward
Henderson, Francis, Assistant Engineer
Henderson, James, 51yrs, Fireman (Engr's Steward)
Moon, Thomas, 59yrs, 1st Engineer
Noble, Athony, 62yrs, Fireman
Noble, John, 44yrs, Fireman
Roch, John Alfred ,14yrs, Deck Boy
Sisley, Albert John, 66yrs, Able Seaman and Lamps
Young, Henry, 57yrs, Master

The 157-ton net drifter *Excel* (Pennent No.2300) was captured 53 miles northeast from the Tyne off Longstone and sunk by gunfire the following day.

John Miles (1908 – Stephenson, Clarke & Co., London), a 687-ton British steam coaster, was torpedoed and sunk without warning on the 22nd, 11 miles southeast from Teesmouth; she was hauling coal from the Tyne to Shoreham-on-Sea. The chief engineer, being the senior surviving officer, stated in his report that a violent explosion took place on the port side, abaft of the main hatch, at 1235hrs. The ship sank by the stern in 2 minutes and those of the crew who were on deck at the time were washed overboard. He and four others clung onto floating wreckage for about 30 minutes before they were picked up by a Royal Navy minesweeper and taken to Hartlepool.

Unfortunately, nine men, including the master, died in the sea and one of the five rescued, Robert Slater Wilkinson, the 2nd engineer, died on board the minesweeper.

THE MEN WHO DIED

Atkinson, Andrew, 61yrs, Fireman
Brazier, Thomas Daniel, 50yrs, Chief Mate
Eggen, Magnus, 35yrs Fireman
Johnson, Victor, 51yrs, Able Seaman
Sharman, Henry, 61yrs, 2nd Mate
Tester, Emanuel, 61yrs, Steward
Uwins, George, 35yrs, Able Seaman
Vallint, Thomas, 65yrs, Master
Welfare, Horace George, 65yrs, Lamps
Wilkinson, Robert Slater, 54yrs, 2nd Engineer

UB 21 arrived back in Germany on 24 February 1917.

(13) Departing Heligoland on 25 March 1917, *UB 21* headed to the English east coast for operations off Scarborough. Walther sank the 1,522-ton SS *Bywell* (1913 – Screw Colliers Co. Ltd, Newcastle) with a torpedo on 29 March; she was carrying coal from Shields (the Tyne) to Rouen. Soon after sinking the *Bywell*, *UB 21* was damaged after striking a wreck in 40m and had to abort the patrol. However during the return voyage home, the 776-ton Norwegian steamer *Norden* (1905 – Aktieselskapet Ganger Rolf, Kristiania), which was en-route from Rotterdam to Kristiania with general cargo, was captured off Tersschelling; she was boarded by one officer and two men from *UB 21* and Walther ordered them to take the ship into the port of List on Sylt Island, where she arrived for examination on 2 April 1917. A prize court condemned the *Norden* and in 1919 she became the German Navy transport *Sud*.

UB 21 arrived in port on 1 April.

(14) *UB 21* sailed out of Brugge on 26 April and returned to the east coast of Yorkshire for operations against Allied shipping. Off Scarborough on the 29th, the 1,620-ton steamer *Victoria* (1887 – S.S. Victoria Co. Ltd, Glasgow) was torpedoed and sunk while delivering coal from Jarrow-on-Tyne to Bayonne, and John Kallos, a fireman and trimmer, was killed.

The 1st engineer, Nicolai Corneliussen of Bergen, and the ship's cook, Brunjulf Larsen, also from Bergen, were both killed in their bunks when the 1,123-ton Norwegian steamship *Rikard Nordraak* (1901 – Aktieselskapet D/S Richard Nordraak, Bergen) was torpedoed and sunk, 4.5 miles north, northeast of Scarborough, on the evening of 2 May; the ship was hauling coal from Sunderland to Rouen.

East of Robin Hood's Bay on 5 May, Walther captured the 20-ton British motorised fishing boat *Edith Cavell* (1916), 7.5 miles offshore and scuttled her with explosives. The *Harold* (1878 – Ångfartygs A/B Harold, Göteborg), a 1,563-ton Swedish steamer, was destroyed 80 nautical miles from the Tyne, while en-route from the Tyne for Göteborg with coal. She was attacked with gunfire and the shooting lasted for more than 1 hour. Scuttling charges were then placed on board but the vessel refused to sink even after the charges had detonated and she was eventually sunk by additional gunfire. Out of her crew of twenty, five men were killed.

THE MEN WHO DIED

Wimmerstedt, Anders, 35yrs, Master
Tillman, Oscar Emil, 53yrs
Norling, Carl Oscar Olaus, 27yrs
Persson, Nils Evald, 20yrs
Johansson, Carl Oscar, 17yrs

After leaving the operational area, Walther captured the 157-ton Dutch vessel *Batavier* off the Dogger Bank and returned to Heligoland with her, as a prize-of-war, arriving on 9 May; the prize court however, later released the boat.

(15) Leaving Germany on 29 May 1917, *UB 21* sailed for operations off the Scarborough area of the English coast. On 6 June, the American-built 2,294-ton French steamship *S. N. A. 2* (Le Societé Nationale D'Affetements, Le Havre (1911)) was torpedoed and sunk without warning, 10 miles northeast from Scarborough, during a passage from the Tyne for Dunkerque with coal.

Next day (7 June), the *Sir Francis* (1910 – Cory Colliers Ltd, London), a defensively armed steamer of 1,991 tons, met the same fate, voyaging from London to the Tyne in ballast; out of her crew of twenty-two, ten men, including the master, were lost. She was making 10 knots when the torpedo detonated under No.3 hold and immediately started going down by the stern. As the crew began to lower the ship's boats another torpedo detonated under the bridge causing her to sink almost at once. Survivors were rescued by passing ships and landed at South Shields.

THE CREWMEN WHO PERISHED

De Boer, J., Seaman (from Holland)
Jonsson, John, Seaman (from Japan)
Nishioka, B., Fireman (from Japan)
Kato, I., Fireman
Poulouch, N., Fireman (from Greece)
Sharp, Joseph, 22yrs, Steward
Talbot, Alfred William, 22yrs, Engineer's Steward
Tippet, Albert, 49yrs, 1st Engineer
Van Der Pluym, Johannes Cornelis, Seaman (from Holland)
Wanless, A., Master

Captain C. Jeffers of the 1,833-ton SS *Dryade* (Admiralty requisition (Everett & Newbigin, mgrs.), London *CT-25*), which was in the same vicinity as *Sir Francis*, later reported that he saw the submarine and said the second torpedo was actually fired at his ship.

UB 21 arrived back in Heligoland on 12 June.

(16) On 14 July Walther left port with *UB 21* for operations off Yorkshire. On this voyage however, his orders included the landing of two *maat*: Steuermann d. Res. Gallus and Bootsmannsmaat d. Res. Söhlmann, who were to sabotage an industrial railway by blowing up the rails, a tunnel and a railroad bridge (probably the iron ore line running inland from Port Mulgrave, near Whitby). At 0100hrs on 19 July 1917, the men were towed on a raft to the shore at Hayburn Wyke Bay (south of Robin Hood's Bay). They safely waded ashore at Ness Point, but the mission failed. Both men got lost and were captured soon after. They told their captors that they had been stranded on the conning tower when the U-boat had dived after sighting a patrol boat and they were left in the water to fend for themselves; naval intelligence believed their story. (Of course, if dressed as civilians, they would have been shot.)

UB 21 waited for the two men in vain for three days before commencing her journey.

North of Scarborough on 20 July, the defensively armed SS *Trelyon* (1893 – Hain S.S. Co. Ltd) of 3,099 tons was proceeding from Archangelsk, Russia to Methil and London with timber with a pilot in charge, when a torpedo, which had been fired without any warning, struck the ship's stern at 2230hrs; the engine was stopped and the boats lowered, but the crew of twenty-six and the pilot remained on board until a trawler arrived and took them to Scarborough. Captain Freeman then returned to his ship in the trawler and waited there all night until the following morning when the ship was taken in tow and beached; later she re-floated and then beached at White Nab, Scarborough, but became a total constructive loss.

A torpedo fired without warning at 2130hrs on 22 July, sank the 1,141-ton SS *Glow* (1900 – Gas Light & Coke Co., London) off Robin Hood's Bay; she was armed for defence and voyaging from the Tyne for London with coal. The ship had been making 10 knots when the master noticed a torpedo approaching about 100 yards distant on the starboard side. The missile detonated about 10ft above the sternpost and blew off most of her stern section; the ship then immediately started to sink. The chief gunner was killed in the blast and the ship's steward was injured. The surviving crew of seventeen managed to lower one boat, into which they all scrambled. Three minutes later, the ship capsized and sank at 2140hrs, just as the lifeboat slipped clear. A patrol vessel picked the men up at 2230hrs and took them to Scarborough.

Late in the afternoon of 23 July 1917, *UB 21* began shelling the Swedish 1,285-ton steamer *Vanland* (1893 –Ångfartygs A/B Svithiod, Göteborg) off Runswick Bay, which was en-route from Göteborg to London with a general cargo, including greaseproof paper, boxwood and un-dipped matchsticks. Desperately, Captain Wallin endeavoured to evade further attacks, but his vessel struck Kettleness Point at the same instant as a torpedo from *UB 21* tore into her. The explosion injured five of the crew and caused serious damage to the vessel and then a major fire developed; the surviving crew took to the ship's boat. Runswick lifeboat *Hester Rothschild* was launched at 2030hrs and arrived at the scene just as the enemy submarine surfaced outside of Runswick Bay. Franz Walther made no further attacks and just watched as the eighteen survivors were picked up by the lifeboat and taken back to Runswick. The ship burned for a whole week before she eventually heeled over and settled on the bottom in the shallow water and became a total loss.

THE MEN INJURED IN THE INCIDENT

Osterman, G., 2nd Mate
Gustafsson, G., Able Seaman
Svensson, G., Ordinary Seaman
Landin, V., Stoker
Olausson, J. A., 2nd Engineer

UB 21 then returned to Germany, arriving on 29 July.

(17) *UB 21* departed Heligoland on 21 August 1917 and sailed back to the Yorkshire coast for operations. At 1134hrs on the 24th the defensively armed *Springhill* (1904 – Fisher, Renwick & Co. Ltd, Cardiff/Newcastle), a 1,507-ton British ship, was struck by a torpedo about 6 miles north of Scarborough. The steamer, which was hit without warning, was transporting 2,200 tons of coal from West Hartlepool to London. The explosion ripped a huge hole in her side amidships, instantly killing the chief engineer and a fireman, who were both in the engine room. The vessel went down in less than 4 minutes, drowning the second steward and an able seaman, while a fifth man later died of his injuries.

FOUR OF THE MEN WHO DIED

Ahmad Masil, Fireman
Shepherd, George William, 42yrs, Able Seaman
Welch, George Albert, 28yrs, Steward
Young, Christopher James, 54yrs, Chief Engineer

The 1,446-ton British steamer *EDEN* picked up most of the surviving crew and HM drifter *White Rose II* rescued one other man.

On 4 September, in an eloquent gesture of defiance towards perceived British naval supremacy, *UB 21* fired thirty shells into Scarborough town, killing three people and wounding five others.

UB 21 sailed to Heligoland, where she arrived on 6 September 1917.

Oblt.z.S. Franz Walther stepped down as commander on 9 September 1917 and Oblt.z.S. Walter Scheffler assumed command on 10 September. *UB 21* was then formally transferred to V.U-Flottille and operated once again out of the German ports of Emden, Heligoland and Brunsbüttel with Oblt.z.S. Walter Scheffler the CO. Scheffler made five patrols with the boat:

(18) *UB 21* left Emden on 15 October and sailed to the Flamborough Head area, where two ships were sunk. On 18 October 1917, the *Amsteldam* (1907 – South Metropoitan Gas Co., Cardiff/London), which was a 1,233-ton steamship armed for defence, was carrying a crew of twenty and transporting 1,900 tons of coal from Shields (the Tyne) to London when a torpedo struck her without warning in the boiler-room on the port side. The ship was about 6 miles off Flamborough Head and making 8 knots when the missile detonated, killing four men, either in the engine room and/or on deck, while Capt. Letonge was blown clear overboard, into the sea. Within 5 minutes, the crew had abandoned ship at 1635hrs, some in the lifeboat, while others, including the injured chief officer, took to a life raft. The ship's boat picked up the master and an RN warship picked up all the survivors and landed them at Grimsby.

THE MEN WHO DROWNED

Butchart, James, 33yrs, 1st Engineer
Charlton, Frank, 45yrs, Donkeyman
Green, John Thomas, 46yrs, Fireman
Ovenden, Frank, 56yrs, Able Seaman

At 1630hrs on 19 October 1917, the 1,385-ton, defensively armed, ex-German steamer *Gemma* (1904 – The Admiralty, London), was hit by a torpedo without warning, 5 miles from Flamborough Head, while transporting 2,100 tons of coal from Blyth for London. The explosion tore a gaping hole in her side and killed a DEMS gunner, a fireman, the second engineer and the second mate. The ship went down in 5 minutes and the seventeen survivors went into the sea. A Royal Navy motor-launch rescued twelve of the men, picked up the body of the second mate and landed them at Bridlington. The 556-ton steamship *Tay & Tyne* (Dundee, Perth & London Shipping Co. Ltd, Dundee) rescued the captain and three crewmen and took them to Grimsby, while two others, one of whom died later, were plucked out of the sea by the 634-ton SS *General Havelock* (1884 – Tyne-Tees Steam Shipping Co. Ltd, Newcastle) and taken to London.

THREE OF THE MEN WHO DIED WERE

Cardona, Milchor, 44yrs, Fireman
Findlay, James, 52yrs, 2nd Mate
Raffell, Joseph Sanderson, 32yrs, 2nd Engineer

UB 21 returned to port on 22 October.

(19) *UB 21* headed out of Emden on 17 November 1917 and sailed to the River Tyne and Tees estuaries for operations. On the 23rd, Scheffler hit the 1,442-ton defensively armed SS *Ocean* (1894 – Cory Colliers Ltd, London) with an underwater torpedo shot in Tees Bay, causing the steamer to sink, but the crew abandoned ship safely; she was voyaging from Granton to London with coal.

UB 21 arrived back in Germany on 28 November.

(20) On 26 December 1917, *UB 21* left Heligoland and once again sailed for the English east coast. The *Patria* (1882 – Wasa Nordsjo Angf. Aktieb, Wasa), a Russian steamer of 838 tons, was travelling from Newcastle to Archangelsk, Russia with coal, when a torpedo struck her without warning on the 29th; the vessel ploughed on for a further 20 miles before rolling over to one side and, within 3 minutes, she sank, about 5 miles from the mouth of the River Tees.

North of the River Tees, Scheffler fired a torpedo without warning and damaged the turret-hulled steamer *Inverness* (1902 – Sutherland SS. Co. Ltd, Newcastle) on 29 December, the ship was armed for defence and on passage from the Tyne for Genoa, but put into Middlesborough for repairs. The 1,295-ton SS *Hercules* (1881 – The Shipping Controller, London), which was armed for defence, was torpedoed and sunk without warning on 30 December; she was en-route from the Tyne to Newhaven with coal. The torpedo detonated amidships on the port side at 1550hrs and panic broke out amongst the crew; the master and nine men were drowned when their lifeboat capsized and the second officer took charge of lowering the dinghy. The ten remaining survivors clambered into the little boat, but two of them died of exposure before being rescued by a fishing vessel and landed at Whitby.

THE MEN WHO DIED

Abdul, Ali, Fireman	Longstaff, Alfred, 50yrs, Master
Battye, Joseph Ingham, Leading Seaman RNVR	Richardson, Albert, 23yrs, 2nd Engineer
	Said, M., Fireman
Griffiths, Charles, 47yrs, Steward	Salim, A., Fireman
Hamid, S., Fireman	Stevenson, Hector MacDonald, 17yrs, Mess
Kayopolos, J., Able Seaman	Room Boy
Kylimbas, C., Able Seaman	Symon, William Pyper, 68yrs, 1st Mate

UB 21 arrived back in Germany on 1 January 1918.

(21) Leaving Heligoland on 30 January 1918, Scheffler sailed with *UB 21* to the Yorkshire coast for operations, travelling through the Skagerrak, but the patrol was uneventful and they returned to port on 19 February 1918.

(22) On his last patrol with *UB 21*, Scheffler left Germany on 14 March 1918 and headed back to the Yorkshire coast, via the Skagerrak. On 25 March 1918, the defensively armed 1,095-ton SS *Hercules* (1881 – The Shipping Controller, London) was torpedoed without warning at 0830hrs off Flamborough Head; she was voyaging from London to the Tyne in ballast. The torpedo detonated on her starboard side, abreast of the mainmast, and killed one DEMS gunner, but the remainder of her crew of twenty managed to abandon ship in the boats and were eventually picked up by a Royal Navy minesweeper and landed safely at Scarborough.

UB 21 arrived back in Germany on 1 April.

On 29 April 1918, *UB 21* was formally transferred to I.U-Bootflottille, Brunsbüttel and Oblt. z.S. Bruno Mahn assumed command. Bruno Mahn was born in Dorfilm/kreis Lautenberg on 3 December 1887 and died on 6 February 1961. Mahn took the boat on four patrols:

(23) Leaving Brunsbüttel on 1 May 1918, *UB 21* sailed for a successful operation off the North Yorkshire coast, where four steamers were sunk. At 0500hrs on 8 May and without any warning, Mahn torpedoed the 772-ton British SS *Constantia* (1890 – The Shipping Controller, London), 2 miles off South Cheek, Robin Hood's Bay; it was en-route from the Tyne for Rouen, carrying a cargo of coal and crew of twenty. The explosion blew the entire forecastle away, instantly killing two firemen who were sleeping on the starboard side. The ship went down by the head in just 3 minutes. A trawler picked up the survivors, including Captain O. Janssen, and landed them at Whitby, however, 20 minutes after being rescued from the sea, boatswain Evans died.

THE MEN WHO DIED

Evans, Jenkin, Boatswain (Bosun) & Lamps
Macaulay, Thomas, Fireman and Trimmer
Power, James, Fireman and Trimmer

The 2,114-ton Spanish steamship *Anboto Mendi* (1907 – Cia. Euskalduna de Const., Bilbao) was on passage from Sagunto, Spain for Middlesborough with iron ore, when Mahn sunk her with a torpedo on 10 May, 7 miles off Runswick village.

The *Gothia* (1883 – R. Göhle, Norrköping), a 1,826-ton Swedish steamer, was torpedoed on the 11th; she was 10 miles northeast of Hartlepool and in ballast, on passage from Hull for Blyth. The messroom boy, Birger Mauritz Eriksson, had, at the moment of explosion, arrived on the bridge with coffee for the second mate and was injured in the face and shoulder by flying debris, but he managed to get himself into one of the lifeboats. Since his injuries were not serious, he soon fully recovered.

Eleven crewmen, including the master, perished when Mahn torpedoed the 1,934-ton steamship *Haslingden* (1895 – F. Yeoman & Sons, West Hartlepool) at 0524hrs on 12 May; she was in ballast on passage from Rouen for Newcastle-upon-Tyne. A crewman spotted the torpedo's track and the master attempted evasive action, but the missile slammed into the vessel amidships on the port side. The explosion destroyed the wireless room, bridge and wheelhouse; even the funnel was blasted up in the air and thrown into the sea. The master, Captain H. Johns, died instantly, along with the wireless-operator, the second officer and the helmsman, and the steamer heeled over and sank almost immediately. Seven other crewmen were also lost, but a patrol vessel rescued fifteen men and landed them at the Tyne.

NINE OF THE ELEVEN MEN WHO DIED

Bell, John Lenney, 17yrs, Sailor
Carroll, Edward, 28yrs, 2 Engineer
Crawshaw, James, 17yrs, Wireless Operator
Heugh, Robert, 26yrs, Fireman and Trimmer
Hunt, Cyril Reynolds, 22yrs, Cook

The wrecked *UB 21* alongside the wreck of SS *Oushla*. (Courtesy Newhaven Museum)

Johns, H. (DSC), 60yrs, Master
Whitehurst, 19yrs, Mess Room Steward
Whitfield, William, 17yrs, Sailor
Wiles, William Thomas, 65yrs, 1st Mate

UB 21 returned to Germany on 18 May.

(24) Mahn left Heligoland with *UB 21* on 29 June 1918 and sailed to the River Tyne estuary, travelling via the Skagerrak. Mahn attacked a well protected convoy off Whitby on 3 July, but no ships were sunk. Next day, the 539-ton wooden-hulled Norwegian barque, *Mentor* (1880 – A/S Mentor, Kristiania) was badly damaged by a torpedo, fired from *UB 21* without warning, about 12 miles east of Hartlepool; she was sailing from Svelvik, Norway to West Harlepool with pit props and was towed into Hartlepool, unloaded and then broken up. *UB 21* was then subjected to a 3-hour depth charge attack by a British warship. Many of the submariners were left injured in the ordeal, so Mahn decided to abort the patrol, however on the voyage back to Germany, *UB 21* encountered a British submarine, which fired a torpedo; luckily the crew spotted the track of the torpedo and the boat escaped unharmed.

On 14 July, *UB 21* put into the port of Brunsbüttel.

(25) On 3 August 1918, *UB 21* left Brunsbüttel and proceeded to the English east coast, off Yorkshire. On 16 August, Mahn attacked a steamer, but was subjected to an intensive depth charge attack and *UB 21* retreated back to port, arriving at Brunsbüttel on the 28th.

The wrecked *UB 21* on the beach. (Courtesy Newhaven Museum)

Inside the engine room of the wrecked SM *UB 21*. (Courtesy Newhaven Museum)

(26) On her final sortie, Oblt.z.S. Mahn sailed from Brunsbüttel with *UB 21* on 14 September 1918 and headed for operations around the estuary of the River Tyne.

The boat's last victim was the 659-ton Belgian steamer *Paul* (1880 – L. Hermans, Brugge), on 26 September; the ship was torpedoed and sunk without warning in Robin Hood's Bay, while bound from Caen for the Tyne in ballast. *UB 21* steered a course for Zeebrugge the following day, but a radio instruction informed Hahn to put into Heliogland, where they arrived on 3 October.

On 7 October 1918, *UB 21* transferred to the training U-Flottille and remained there until the end of the war.

FINAL PATROL

Following the Armistice, the boat was surrendered to the French and was put up for sale. Early in 1920 she was sold for scrap and was under-tow to Cherbourg when her lines slipped and she collided with *Oushla*, a steamer that had previously run aground under the Seven Sisters. How ironic that this little submarine, so often in the thick of action, should have survived the war unscathed, and that even in an unmanned state, it had nevertheless managed to wreck *Oushla*, a far larger vessel. Had he been aware of the circumstances surrounding the demise of his boat, Ernst Hashagen would have doubtless allowed himself a wry smile.

Office of naval Intelligence: Roll Number TA-12-D – Record I: PG 61764 <u>ADM 137/2961 ADM 137/2962 ADM 137/2963 ADM 137/2964</u> CWGC

WRECK SITE

The wreck of *UB 21* was partially salvaged where it lay after the collision, however the basic hull of the submarine was re-floated. The salvage team made an attempt to tow it to another scrap yard, but once again it foundered. The remains lay in the Solent until 1921 and, being a navigation hazard, were demolished with explosives (achieving something the Royal Navy had never been able to do in five years). Around 1970, the wreck, which was lying in two halves, was sold to new owners and was dived for quite some time. Recent reports, however, suggest that the remains have now finally disappeared under the silt and mud of the Solent.

U 1195, KRIEGSMARINE U-BOAT

DATE OF LOSS: 6 April 1945
DEPTH: 26m
REFERENCE: 50 33'.351 N 00 56'.280 W
LOCATION: 9.34 nautical miles SSE from Foreland, Bembridge, Isle of Wight

Type:VII C ocean-going attack boat   ***Builders***:F. Schichau GmbH, Danzig for Kriegsmarine   ***Ordered***: on 25 August 1941, within the batch of *U 1191–U 1198*   ***Keel laid***: on 6 February 1943 as Yard No.1565   ***Launched***: on 2 September 1943   ***Commissioned***: by Oberleutnant zur See Karl-Heinz Schröter on 4 November 1943   ***Badge***: Unicorn   ***Feldpost No***: M 54 254

TECHNICAL SPECIFICATIONS

See page 342-343.

Karl-Heinz Schröter was born in Apolda on 13 March 1921 and commenced his naval career in 1939. He first served as Watch Officer on *U 603* and was promoted to Oberleutnant zur See on 1 October 1943. Oblt.z.S. Schröter was CO from the commissioning until 31 October 1944.

 U 1195 was allocated to 21.U-Flottille Schulboot (training/school boat) at Pillau on 4 November 1943 until 31 December 1943. She was then assigned to 24.U-Flottille, Memel as *Schulboot* (training boat) on 1 January 1944 until 31 October 1944.

 Kapitänleutnant Ernst Cordes assumed command when the boat transferred to 5.U-Flottille at Kiel as *Ausbildungsboot* on 1 November 1944. (Cordes was born in Hagen-Haspe on 28 June 1913 and commenced his naval career in 1934. He first served as 2nd watch officer on *U 123* between May 1940 and April 1941; he was promoted to Kapitänleutnant on 1 September 1943. Cordes also commanded *U 763* and during *Landwirt* operations, drifted his boat into the Spithead Roads, astonishingly surviving to tell the tale. The log of *U 763* contains the following, almost surreal, entry for 7 July 1944:

> Spotted land. Boat had drifted into Spithead roads. No minefields or patrols noticed. Everything nice and peaceful. Noted ships at anchor in St Helen's Roads. Spent 24 hours NW of Nab Tower (12 of them N of the Warner Shoal) made off without being noticed or fired upon among the peaceful traffic riding at

anchor. In spite of most exciting circumstances, such as diving in front of an approaching ship when the boat touched bottom at 9m leaving the conning tower sticking high out of the water, boat still managed to reach the open Channel. In so doing boat had to pass by a number of ships at the closest range.

Rear Admiral Godt was impressed with this patrol and added a comment in his diary appendix of 14 July 1944, '*Patrol carried out with perseverance and determination...commanding officer will receive the German Cross in gold'*. Cordes was not decorated, however his experiences were recorded by BdU and codified into the classic instructions issued to U-boat captains for avoiding detection while operating in British coastal waters at this stage in the war:

> Bottoming out was found to be very successful when being hunted. To change position, leave bottom silently without using engines and drift in the current. By this means boats have avoided close depth charge attacks during a hunt lasting 30 hours. When the schnorchel was extended 3–4m, accurately-placed depth charges followed, but once the schnorchel is extended to just the normal height, the numerous runs-in by aircraft have resulted in inaccurately-placed bombs and no searchlights.
> BdU Diary 16-30 July 1944

U 1195 with Cordes was formally assigned to 11.U-Flottille, Bergen in southern Norway, on 1 January 1945, for frontline service.

U 1195 sailed from Kiel on 4 February 1945 and with two other VIIC Class boats, *U 913* and *U 1021*, arrived in Horton on the morning of 8 February, *U 953* leaving again the same day and *U 1195* remaining until 12 February to carry out *schnorchel* and deep diving trials, after which she proceeded alone on the surface to Kristiansand in southern Norway, arriving on the 13th. In Kristiansand, one of the forward torpedoes was found to be defective and exchanged for a new one; sabotage was suspected.

On 15 February, *U 1195* left Kristiansand for her first patrol, in company with two other VIIC boats. She proceeded submerged, on motors by day at *kleine Fahrt* (dead slow), and on *schnorchel* from midnight to dawn at *langsame Fahrt* (slow). Following the discovery of magnification defects in the attack periscope, the patrol was abandoned and the boat entered Bergen alone, on the evening of 22 February. She was berthed for two days at the pier in the Marineholm, where the problematic periscope was changed. (On her last patrol *U 1195* was to have carried T11 acoustic homing torpedoes, but they did not arrive in time.)

FINAL PATROL

(4) Cordes set course for the Channel area on 24 February 1945, his orders being to operate at his own discretion in English waters. On 10 March Cordes transmitted his *Passiermeldung* from AM 0296. On 13 March *U 1195* was ordered to the Channel where she was given freedom of movement. While it would be reasonable to expect the boat to have arrived off the western entrance to the Channel by 18 March, the crew later maintained this had taken some twenty-seven days and that she had arrived as late as the 23 March.

Lt Heinz Schick gave this account following the end of hostilities:

> On the evening of 24 February the boat left Bergen in company with another VIIC boat bound for the Channel. We dived soon after leaving the coast and proceeded seperately, *U 1195* passing through the Rosengarten and along the West coast of Ireland. She took 27 days to reach the entrance to the Channel, surfacing three or four times during this stage. We surfaced twice, once to dump refuse and the other for transmission of the 'Passiermeldung'. Each time positions were checked astronomically. On our first day in the Channel we surfaced at 2200 to dispose of refuse. There was a surprising amount of navigational lights around. I recall thinking, 'There'll be plenty to get our teeth into round here – if they don't get theirs into us first'. We dived to 50-–60m and proceeded dead slow on our motors, taking periscope bearings at night. When the current was too strong to aid us, the captain ordered *U 1195* to bottom out.

While in St George's Channel on 21 March 1945, Cordes stalked convoy TBC 103.

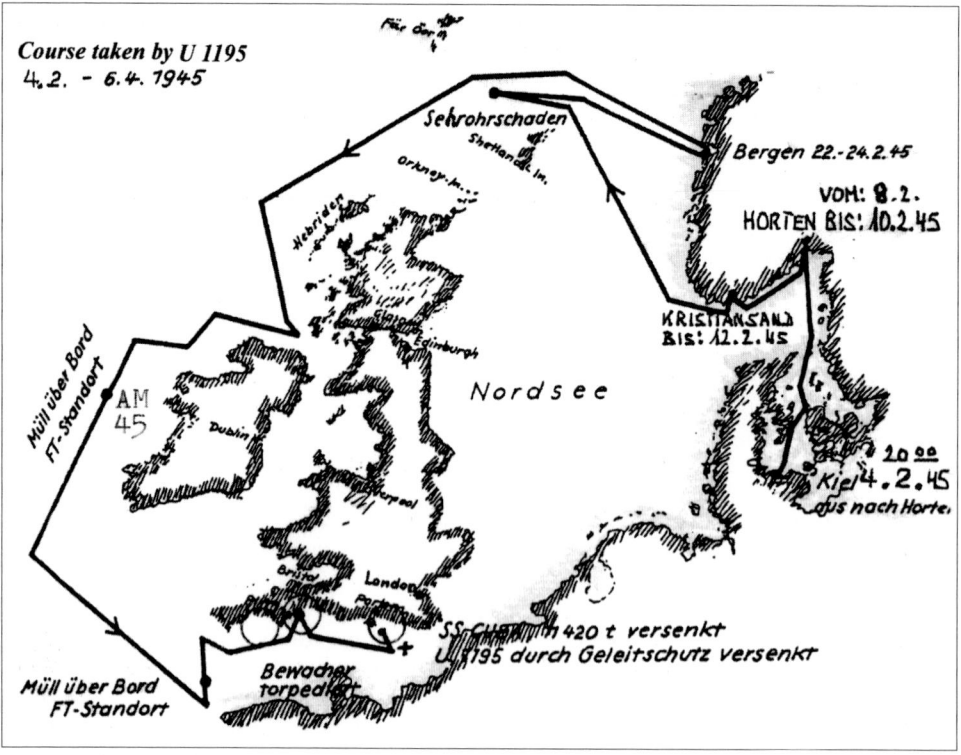

The voyage and course taken by *U 1195*. (Coutesy Rudolph Wieser, 2004)

Lt Schick again:

> Off Plymouth HE was detected while we were lying on the bottom. On coming to periscope depth the captain saw two ships in convoy, one a tanker. A spread of two Lut torpedoes was fired at one ship and a single T5 at the other. We did hear an explosion after the last torpedo was fired, but the Captain put it down to the' fish' striking the seabed.

Some authorities claimed that at 1540hrs (Continental time) Cordes had torpedoed the 7,194-ton American steamer *John R. Park* at position 49° 56'N 05° 26'W; she was voyaging from Southampton for Mumbles and the USA, in ballast, and all the crew were saved. An analysis carried out in the post-war years by Mr Coppock of the Royal Naval Historical Branch, firmly disputes that *U 1195* was responsible for sinking this vessel. Two weeks later, while south, southwest of Selsey Bill on 6 April, Cordes approached Convoy VWP16 at periscope depth.

Schick again:

> During the night of 4 April *U 1195* schnorchelled for 3 hours in order to charge batteries and again on the night of the 5th and again when she entered the sector where her next attack was made. This was close to a harbour (Portsmouth or Southampton south, southwest of Selsey Bill). The boat remained bottomed in 35–39m for 2 or 3 hours. Then screw noises were heard and we rose to periscope depth, proceeding at slow speed on motors. A couple of T5s were fired at two big vessels, range 1,640 yards. Detonation noises were heard at about 0715hrs, but we did not think we had got anything.

Cordes had approached Convoy VWP16. Most impressive of the two ships hit was the 11,420-ton steamship *CUBA*, a troop-transport and the largest victim of a U-boat during 1945. (Originally, the vessel was a British-built French passenger liner owned by Cie. Générale Transatlantique, however a British warship intercepted her on 31 October 1940. She was then placed under the Ministry of

War Transport, London, with Cunard White Star managing her. She was on passage from Le Havre for Southampton and in position 50° 36'N 00° 57'W when the torpedo detonated at 0613hrs (Continental time) on 6 April 1945. Crewman Jean Leroy, a Greaser was lost, but the master, Captain J. Cailloce, 221 crew, twenty-nine gunners, ten army staff and three signallers were rescued by HMS frigate *NENE* (Lt Cdr R.F.J. Maberley) and landed at Portsmouth.

Immediately after firing the boat dived to 25m just above bottom. At one point she had to dive to avoid being struck by one of the T5s, which had circled back. This was at a time when the captain was about to torpedo a closing destroyer. The escorts approached and foxer was heard. The boat continued under way at about 90rpm on both motors. Silent routine was observed. The first depth charge exploded some distance away, there was a pause enabling the boat to bottom out for 30 minutes. The Telegraphist reminded the Captain that it was 15 minutes before W/T Programme time, and the Captain decided to surface. Lt Gmoeling had just started up the pumps when a pattern of depth charges exploded very close. Once again the boat resorted to silent routine. ASDIC transmissions were heard getting ever closer.

The British view: Lt-Cdr J.R. Clarke, commanding officer HMS *Watchman* E.G.9 – 6 April 1945:

At 0703hrs, VWP 16, consisting of 6 ships in single line, was about to turn to the northward round F Buoy, HMS 'Watchman' was in position F, when an explosion close under the counter of SS 'CUBA' (Pts 11) was observed. The explosion was violent and threw up a column of water approximately 100ft high.

The Senior Officer, H.M.C.S. 'Loch Alvie' who was in position A turned to port to sweep astern of the convoy and ordered F.S. 'L'escarmouche' in position N to join him. HMCS 'Nene' was ordered to close the wreck, as rescue ship. H.M.C.S. 'MONNOW' in position D and HMS 'Watchman' were ordered to screen convoy into harbour.

HMS 'Watchman' turned 180° with the intention of sweeping down the starboard side of the convoy, round the stern and up to a position on the port bow. Sweep was commenced at 8 knots – at 0720hrs, speed was increased to 15 knots.

The convoy had been ordered to make best speed into harbour and HMS 'Watchman' maintained position on the port flank until the last ship had passed the NAB, then turned 180° to a course of 167° as ordered by HMCS 'Monnow' maintain station at 1½ miles on her starboard beam at a speed of 7 knots.

At 0740hrs, HMCS 'Monnow' turned to investigate a contact. HMS 'Watchman' continued on a course of 167 and at 0810hrs, obtained a contact at Red 50, Range 2400.

The H.S.D. [Higher Submarine Detector, i.e., senior Telegraphist] at first classified the contact as non-sub, but the A/S Control Officer reported it as being well worth attacking and it was decided to carry out a Hedgehog attack. At 1,900 yards, the range recorder was marking with firm contact. – Target was moving slowly right, which was at first thought to be due to tide, but later, realised to be actual movement of target. Recorder was switched into scale 10 at 1,000 yards and 'action Hedgehog' ordered at 800 yards. Stand-by was given at 400 yards and Hedgehog fired at 0815hrs.

Twenty-three bombs fired and exploded on the bottom. – Oil, stale in appearance, bubbles and a large steel cylindrical object appeared, this sank almost immediately, also the usual scum, which follows the bursting of a pattern on the bottom. Engines were stopped after firing and ship carried on through the disturbed water, trying for an Echo Sounder Trace. Only a slight trace appeared as Echo Sounder oscillators were masked by rising bubbles, Echo was picked up again astern at Red 150, range 350 yards, and moving very slowly left. Noises were heard which the H.S.D. thought to be breaking up noises, but the A/S Control Officer thought them to be caused by tide. The Echo Sounder Trace shows echo at 6 fathoms and bottom of 15 fathoms.

The German view – Lt Schick continued:

Suddenly a depth charge fell on the fore ends. The impact sounded like a violent hammer blow on a piece of iron. The depth charge rolled over onto the starboard hydroplane and a few seconds later it exploded. This produced a major leak in the fore-ends and within 2 minutes the men were up to their knees in water. There was no option but to evacuate the torpedo space and close the bulkhead door. Unfortunately, this door had been blown off its seating by the explosion and water continued to leak through. By this stage the boat was so bow-heavy that the motors were unable to power her to the surface, even though tanks were blown. The bow lifted a little, then fell back. *U 1195* now took on a

45-50 degree angle. The after part of the boat was closed off from the control room, but messages were passed by tapping on the bulkhead door. Flooding drill was carried out simultaneously in control and engine rooms. Pressure was equalised and the men began to escape.

Telegraphist Franz Selinger later wrote a more dramatic account of this terrifying experience:

U 1195 was hit of one of the Hedgehogs on the starbord side, forward… The crew was shaken out of their bunks as the sub plunged bows first into the deep.

The depth gauge in the control room showed 38m. The Matrosenobergefreite Wieser and Heller were trying to fix the leak (in the bow section near the starboard torpedo-tubes) but their efforts failed. Within a short period of time the water level in the sub rose over the floor plates, the forward section had to be evacuated. Wieser collected all the escape sets before closing the fore ends bulkhead door but due to the damage, he was unable to seal it totally. Kapitänleutnant Cordes ordered the crew to evacuate the whole forward part of the sub, petty officers mess included. Telegraphists Lämmle and Brockel were ordered to destroy all important documents, then the men from the ore ends gathered in the control room as U 1195 was prepared for destruction. The chief engineer Gmöhling tried to get the submarine off the sea bed, using compressed air to blow all tanks and setting both motors to reverse full. This too failed.

While the submariners fought for their very lives, their adversaries fretted over losing contact with their prey.

The British view: HMS *Watchman* – 6 April 1945 – Lt Cdr J.R. Clarke:

After the attack, the echo diminished in sharpness and no very definite cut-ons could be obtained, echo showing non-sub qualities. Ship ran out for an Echo Sounder run, which did not mark and ran out again for another Echo Sounder run on a different approach course. The echo was fading and difficult to hold, S.T.U. (short transmission unit) used off and on. On this third run, a dan buoy was dropped over bubbles, as it was felt that the position could be marked and examined again later. It was felt certain that the target was hit. It was not, however, thought to be a submarine, although it was considered that, if it was, it would have been destroyed. – ASDIC conditions were good, but considerable interference was experienced from other ships transmissions. At 0900hrs, HMS *Watchman* proceeded to take up position on the Western flank of the line abreast sweep, which had been ordered by Escort Group 9.

(Some reports maintain that HMCS *Monnow* first detected the submarine, but her captain was ordered to keep his ship back, while *Watchman* made the attacks herself. If so, there is no mention of this in the official report of the action, merely that '*ASDIC conditions were good, but considerable interference was experienced from other ship's transmissions*'. It may be than an element of Canadian nationalism has clouded interpretation.

For Telegraphist Selinger and his crewmates, the ordeal was just beginning:

The commander ordered the crew to abandon ship through the control room hatch and the hatch in the rear part of the boat. He himself took charge of the escape operation in the control room. In the the galley, the escape bid was overseen by the 3rd officer, Leutnant Schick. Obermaschinist Dernkorn took command of the escape bid in the E-Motor-Room. In the control room all men, save Wieser, had an escape set. Wieser swopped his escape gear with Sanitätsobermaat (NCO medical orderly) Clement. Clement climbed up, together with Gmöhling, Obermaschinist Nordmann, Bootsmann Siebenbrodt, Maschinenmaat Ickenstein, Maschinenobergefreiter Uhlin and Heine, into the tower. Next the control room escape trunk was lowered. The outboard valves were opened and seawater poured into the submarine. When it levelled with the lower part of the flap the tower hatch was opened. A wire from a hand lamp lead from the inside of the control room to the tower hatch because the sub was lying in the dark with a heavy list and the emergency lights were not glowing any more. Wieser was sitting on the chart table and waiting for the opening of the tower hatch together with his comrades. Suddenly he felt sick and smelled chlorine gas. Now he exited the submarine together with Obergefreiter Hellier. On the surface there were other comrades, others were popping out of the sea. Altogether nine men from the control room were saved this way, including the chief engineer. They were fished out by the corvette *L'escarmouche*.

The men in the galley followed the same escape procedure with the lowered flap and the opening of the galley hatch. Because men here lacked drager sets, the first one without a set – Maschinenobergefreiter Waskowitz – was ordered to exit in the air bubble. Unfortunately he ascended too early and became entangled in the twill trunk flap, which was dangling as a result of the list taken on by the boat. He drowned. Maschinenmaat Schwandt wanted to help but both got stuck in the hatch. He was freed from this position by three comrades with escape gear but was found to be dead. This led to some men losing their nerve, but Schick managed to calm them again. All six men were now herded out by Schick. All this without him having a drager set himself! The last one to exit from there was Schick. Together with his six surviving comrades he was fished out by HMS *Watchman*. Out of the E-Motor-hatch only two were able to safely reach the surface to be picked up by the British.

(Kindly provided and translated by Mr Oliver Meise of www.taucher.net.)

In December 2004 Rudolph Wieser gave the authors the following account, which was kindly translated by Juergen Meyer-Brenkhof (Fregattenkapitän D):

U 1195 was dived when we were hit by HMS *Watchman*'s Hedgehogs and the crew was catapulted out of their bunks; the boat went down and hit the bottom. The depth gauge showed 38m. Heller and I tried to close a hole in the front torpedo room, but to no avail and the water rushed in. I gathered all Tauchretter escape sets and left the bow torpedo chamber. I tried to close the bulkhead behind me, but could no more. Lt Cdr Cordes gave order to leave the front of the ship. The radio operators destroyed all secret equipment and documents. The crew now huddled together in the control room. The LI tried to surface the boat with air pressure, but it didn't work. The CO now ordered the crew to prepare to escape via the control room hatch. A second group gathered around Lt Schick in the galley and a third in the electrical engine room under PO Derkorn.

All men except me had escape sets. I had given mine to the Medical Orderly, Clement. In the meantime the conning tower hatch was opened and the outboard valves opened to flood the chamber. The chamber was plunged into darkness and in order to find our way to the hatch, a cable was attached. I sat on the chart table and waited for the hatch to open, dived and went back to the chart table, when all of a sudden I felt sick from the chlorine gas that was escaping and said to my comrades 'I'm getting out'. Fireman Heller heard that and also swam to the hatch and swam to the surface. When we arrived at the surface we found nine comrades from the central and among them was the chief engineer. We were eventually rescued and very unfairly treated by the crew of the French ship, *L'Escaramouche* and later transferred to HMS *Hoste* (Lt P.J.H. Hoare). From the galley, five men surfaced and from the aft hatch only two survived. On the British ships we were treated very well and got back to Germany in 1947

(Sadly Rudi passed away in 2007.)

U 1195 had bottomed out at an angle of 40°. The implications were that once pressure had equalised and the hatches were opened; the men could not ascend up through the twill trunk as per the drill. Instead they had to scramble up the tunnel-like trunks. The men began to panic so Lt Schick had to manhandle them through the trunks. Schick had to hold his breath as he pushed and cajoled each man through the trunking. After each man went out, between each escape, Schick returned to the foul compartment to snatch a breath of what passed for air.

There is no evidence that he ever received any award for his courage and endurance.

Eighteen men survived, but Ernst Cordes, Oblt.z.S. Fulda and Mayer-Claas were not amongst them. At 0947hrs, F.S. *L'Escarmouche* reported that she was proceeding to pick up men in the water. One of the survivors was actually clinging to the dan buoy dropped by *WATCHMAN*. It was appreciated in HMS *Watchman* that F.S. *L'Escarmouche*'s position was near that of the Hedgehog attack and a signal was made to Escort Group 9, T.O.O. at 0953hrs, claiming a successful attack. Three months later *Watchman* suffered severe damage following a collision with LST 367 with the result that she was written off.

Above left: Survivor of *U 1195*, Matr. Ob. Gfr. Rudolph Wieser, who also kindly gave an account of the sinking to the authors.

Above right: Matr. Ob. Gfr. Rudolph Wieser in happier days. (Courtesy Rudi Wieser)

HMS *Watchman.* (Author's collection)

ADM 1/30296 CB04051(103) NARA T1022, Roll 3900, PG 31752 RNHB (FDS 476/97)
U-Boot-Ehrenmal Möltenort

THE MEN WHO DIED IN U 1195

Barthold, Kurt Matr.Ob.Gfr. (13.9.1924)
Beermann, Horst Matr.Ob.Gfr. (9.2.1924)
Brockel, Manfred Ft.Ob.Gft. (20.4.1923)
Cordes, Ernst Kplt.z.S. (26.6.1913)
Derkom, Erwin Ob.Masch. (28.3.1919)
Dorner, Roland Bts.Mt. (25.6.1922)
Dunkmann, Rudolf Mech.Ob.Gfr.
  (18.11.1923)
Etschel, Alfred Masch.Ob.Gfr (30.11.1923)
Fledler, Masch.Ob.Gfr.
Franke, Heinrich Matr.Ob.Gft. (23.3.1925)
Fulda, Eberhard Oblt.z.S. (2.6.1923)
Gaisser, Willi Masch.Ob.Gfr. (18.3.1923)
Gebhardt, Hermann Masch.Mt. (3.9.1920)
Günther, Karl.Heinz Matr.Ob.Gfr. (24.7.1922)
Happ, Emil Mech.Ob.Gfr. (8.1.1924)

Heblik, Aribert Mech.Ob.Mt. (21.10.1919)
Hoffmann, Donatus Masch.Ob.Gfr. (9.8.1922)
Jurek, Walter Masch.Ob.Gfr. (4.1.1926)
Knipp, Frierich Ob.Strm. (23.12.1919)
Lämmle, Helmut Fk.Ob.Gfr. (4.1.1925)
Mayer.Claas, Eberhard Oblt.z. S. (11.1.1921)
Nogay, Josef Matr.Ob.Gfr. (29.12.1923)
Paar, Richard Fk.Ob.Mt. (30.11.1922)
Preußer, Otto Matr.Hpt.Gfr. (12.4.1923)
Schröder, Otto Masch.Hpt.Gfr. (5.10.1922)
Schröder, Walter San.Mt. (20.4.1921)
Schwandt, Gerhard Masch.Mt. (5.6.1920)
Schwed, Konrad Matr.Hpt.Gfr. (21.11.1923)
Sladek, Gerhard Matr.Gfr. (17.7.1926)
Waskewitz, Günter Matr.Ob.Gfr. (11.20.1920)
Wösten, Wilhelm Matr.Ob.Gfr. (15.1.1922)

THOSE WHO SURVIVED

Adam, Gunther Masch.Ob.Gfr. (26.10.1923)
Bantje, Friedle Masch.Ob.Gfr. (16.11.1923)
Bonk, Georg Masch.Ob.Gfr. (2.10.1926)
Clement, Erhardt Ob.Bts.Mt. (11.12.1918)
Frühwald, Ernst Ob.Masch.Mt.12.9.1919)
Gmöhling, Walter LtIng. (30.11.1922)
Harnisch, Otto Masch.Mt. (16.10.1919)
Heine, Norbert Masch.Ob.Gfr. (23.6.1923)
Hellier, Richard Mech.Ob.Gfr. (27.9.1924)

Ickenstein, Hugo Masch.Mt. (5.6.1920)
Niederhausen, Walter Masch.Ob.Gfr. (9.6.1922)
Nordmann, Heinz Ob.Masch. (2.10.1919)
Schick, Hermann Leutnant zur See (2.9.1923)
Schmitt, Walter Fk.Mt. (20.10.1923)
Selinger, Herbert Fk.Ob.Gfr. (26.6.1924)
Siebenbrodt, Bernhard Btsm. (15.8.1918)
Ühlin, Ernst Masch.Ob.Gfr. (25.1.1922)
Wieser, Rudolph Matr.Ob.Gfr. (10.7.1924)

WRECK SITE

The wreck is orientated in a south, southeast to north, northwest (160/340°) direction, with the bows to the north, northwest. It lies on a reasonably firm seabed of coarse sand and shingle, in a general depth of 26m, being the lowest astronomical depth. The wreck is intact and upright, with a 45° list to starboard and stands 5.4m high around the conning tower. The outer casing and deck casing are badly corroded in a number of areas and, although the conning tower is intact, there is a clear vertical break right through the hull and a gaping hole 2-3m forward of the conning tower. The *schnorchel* has snapped off and lies close-by on the seabed. One of the boat's propellers and the port shaft was also visible at the end of November 2003.

UB 81, SM IMPERIAL U-BOAT

DATE OF LOSS: 2 December 1917
DEPTH: 27m
REFERENCE: 50 29'.442 N 000 58'.351 W
LOCATION: 10.50 nautical miles SE of Dunnose Head and 15.78 nautical miles
SSW of Selsey Bill

Dunraven with her decks awash. (Author's collection)

Type: UBIII coastal torpedo attack boat **Builders**: A.G. Weser, Bremen for Kaiserliche Deutsche Marine **Ordered**: on 23 September 1916, within the batch UB 80–UB 87 **Keel laid**: as Yard No.281 on 5 January 1917 **Launched**: on 4 August 1917 **Commissioned**: by Oberleutnant zur See Reinhold Saltzwedel on 18 September 1917

TECHNICAL SPECIFICATIONS

Hull: double **Surface displacement**: 516 tons **U/Dt**: 647 tons **LBDH**: 55.85m × 5.80m × 3.6m × 8.25m **Machinery**: 2 × 550ps Körting diesels **Props**: 2 bronze **S/Sp**: 13.3 knots **Op/R**: 8,180 nautical miles at 6 knots **Sub/R**: 50 nautical miles at 4 knots **U/Power**: 2 × 394ps electric motors gave 7.5 knots **Batteries**: lead/acid/accumulators **Armament**: 4 bow and 1 stern 50.04cm torpedo tubes **Torpedoes**: 10 × 50.04cm (19.7in) **Guns**: 1 × 105mm (4.13in) forward deck gun **Ammo**: 160 rounds 105mm **Mines**: none **Diving**: max-op-depth 50m (164ft) and 30 sec to crash-dive **Complement**: 3 officers and 31 ratings

Respected by his opponents and adored by his crews, the charming, sophisticated Iron Cross holder, Reinhold Saltzwedel, was as far removed from the British propagandist image of a 'heel clicking Hun' as could be imagined. The escape of some of his crew is one of the most nerve-shredding accounts related in this book, but the ultimate fate of Saltzwedel and the rest of his men remains one of the most tragic and controversial of wartime episodes.

UB 81 was formally allocated to Flandern I.U-Flottille on 11 November 1917 with Reinhold Saltzwedel the CO from 18 September 1917. Saltzwedel was born on 23 November 1889 and commanded six boats during his illustrious career: *UB 10*, *UC 10*, *UC 11*, *UC 21*, *UC 71* and finally *UB 81*, in which he was lost. Credited with being the eleventh most successful U-boat commander of the First World War, Reinhold Saltzwedel sank 150,000 tons of Allied shipping, which he achieved in just twelve war patrols with *UC 71*. For outstanding duty against enemy shipping, he was awarded the *Orden Pour Le Mérite* (Order of the Blue Max) on 20 August 1917, Germany's highest military honour. Saltzwedel was well known to naval intelligence because of his epic duel with Campbell's Q-ship *Dunraven* on 8 August 1918.

On 9 November 1917, *UB 81* departed Bremen and transferred to Flanders, where she arrived on 11 November.

FINAL PATROL

(2) *UB 81* sailed from Zeebrugge on 28 November 1917 for operations in the English Channel. Survivors later maintained that the boat had crossed through the mine barrage close to the Folkestone gate, making use of the tide to cross the nets (*see* vol. 1). Some 9 miles southwest by west of Beachy Head, the British steamer *Molesey* (1912 – Britain S.S. Co. Ltd, London) was torpedoed and sunk without warning by Saltzwedel at 0015hrs on 1 December; she was defensively armed and transporting phosphate rock from Sfax, Tunisia to The Downs. The thirty-four crew and one passenger abandoned ship in three boats and, three quarters of an hour later, *UB 81* surfaced and went alongside the master's boat and the Germans questioned him. Using the master's boat, explosive charges were then placed on the *Molesey*, causing her to sink in 45m, with the masts showing above the surface. The ship proved to be Saltzwedel's last victim, but the German commander allowed the crew to abandon ship and take to their boats before delivering the *coup de grâce* on 1 December.

A violent storm forced *UB 81* to take refuge at periscope depth. Unknown to Saltzwedel and his crew, *UB 81* was heading directly into the Portsmouth minefield laid by HMS *Angora* and *Wahine* between 26 June and 1 July 1917. At 1745hrs on 2 December, the boat was dived at 20m, 2 miles south of Owers Lightship:

Marine Ingenieur Hans Denker witnessed events in the control room:

> Lieutenant Freudendal was on periscope watch. As I recall the captain and I were drinking coffee when Freudendal called out 'There's a steamer on a converging course'. The captain observed: 'Well we'd better go see then'. I took over in the control room and the captain and the navigator went into the conning tower. A torpedo shot missed probably due to heavy seas. The time was 1620. Suddenly order screamed out: 'Go to twenty metres!'. A heavy explosion aft followed and all the lights went out. Bulkhead doors were shut and fastened. Reports from the individual compartments indicated that we were watertight for'rard but the after torpedo room was flooding through the torpedo tube. This compartment was abandoned and the watertight door closed. We sank down to 35m. I entered the engine room and to my dismay I discovered that the so-called watertight door to the torpedo room was leaking badly, gradually flooding the engine room and shorting fuses – all very frightening. All our efforts to seal it failed. I reported to the captain that the boat must surface before she became too heavy ever to surface again.

Matrose Carl-Detlef Blunck:

> When we were at about 15 to 12m, the boat was suddenly shaken by a violent explosion. All the glass was broken, but as that always happens when depth charges are exploded, we who were in the torpedo compartment forward did not pay any particular attention and went on making jokes about the British. I had just been relieved at the helm in the conning tower and had gone forward. Suddenly I saw Torpedoman Köhler lying unconscious and wet through in the Warrant Officer's quarters. Still we did not realize the situation. When he came to, however, he said: 'The stern compartment is full of water'. Then for the first time we began to realize that there would be no homeward voyage for us. The boat had of course quickly sunk to the bottom again. Attempts were now made to bring the boat to the surface by every available means. Eight o'clock came, and still no change in the situation. Our good Commanding Officer gave the boat up. The rivets had sprung, and water was pouring into the engine room in a thin, but steady stream. It was high time to act. The bow was raised by compressed air, in the hope of raising the boat far enough to enable us to get out through a hatch or torpedo tube.

(Translation of a letter from Karl to his mother living in Bergdorf, near Hamburg, passed on via the Red Cross.)

Hans Denker:

The captain ordered that all tanks be blown but a ruptured pipe prevented us from forcing air into tank No. 1. Tank 2 was successfully blown but the steering rudder and aft dive planes refused to answer. The net results of our efforts were that the boat took on a pronounced 20-degree stern-down angle. We tried again with the motors but she refused to budge. Next I ordered the crew out of the engine room (which was flooding fast in any case by this time) and into the fore-ends. Maschinistenmaat Redlin remained in the engine room to pull the electric motor fuses. I pulled all the control room fuses except those for the emergency lighting system. The watertight door to the engine room was closed, and the entire crew, except for the telegraphist, gathered in the forward torpedo room. The bows jerked upwards on a steep angle. The time was 1730. The captain called me over. He reckoned that the forward hatch must now be out of the water. I was ordered to go forward and try to unclip it in the hope that we could use it as a means of escape. I was unable to open the hatch which, as matters transpired, was well underwater. Now we were left in little doubt as to our predicament. All that was left was an escape via the bow tubes. With terrific effort for cold and frightened men, one of the 'fish' was pulled out of its tube then lashed down but this took hours to accomplish. The remaining tanks were blown using what little was left of our compressed air. The air pressure was intolerable. So intense were the headaches that it was impossible to think clearly. When the forward depth guage showed 9m we stopped. Air pressure was gradually dispersed through the torpedo tube outer door.

Matrose Carl-Detlef Blunck:

Removing the torpedo was a hard and nerve-racking job. We rigged a tackle to the after end of the torpedo and lowered it from the tube and attached it to the overhead track. Everyone had to lend a hand. The track gear kept jamming because of the uneven load imposed by the up angle. Torpedoheizersmaat Tiedt used a hammer to free the jams. The hard work quickly used up the air and we were all breathing very hard. With the torpedo removed, the captain used up our remaining compressed air to blow the forward ballast tanks again. We still did not know if the outer door was above the water or not. The outer door was opened slowly and there was a tremor as the air pressure inside the boat rushed out. We again

Matrose Carl-Detlef Blunck of SM *UB 81*.
(Author's collection)

had fresh air, and no water came down the tube. It seemed our way out was clear. Now imagine this, the boat was almost upright. It was a case of getting to the surface through the smooth, greasy, steep tube, about 7 to 8m in length. The cap was opened and the sea was 0.5m below it. The way to the surface was clear. The captain called for volunteers to go through the tube and Wagner stepped forward. We shoved him up the tube, but he said that he could not reach the outer lip because the angle was too steep. Kohler went into the tube so that Wagner was standing on his shoulders and we shoved them both up the tube. When that did not work, Schroder went in and we shoved all three up the tube. Wagner still could not reach the top, so we placed a block between Schroder's legs and used a gun staff to push them higher. Finally Wagner said that he was outside and the opening was a half metre above the water, and the bow was only fractionally above the surface. The other two went out and rigged a tackle so that we could hoist the rest of the men up the tube. Water cascaded down the tube from time to time and anyone below the tube was wringing wet.

Miraculously four men had managed to claw their way out of the slippery torpedo tube, raised precariously 1m above the sea. The time was 2100hrs and all the time the sea was rising, ominously. Saltzwedel realised that the only hope for his crew lay in a British rescue. A pragmatist, he must also have recognised that only the slimmer members of his crew would ever be able to escape from the tube and that as their commander, his duty must lie with the men who remained behind. Leutnant Freudendal, Steuermann Bathge, matrosen Blunck, Sell, Kirschbaum, and Heizer Meyer clambered up the slippery tube, while out on the casing Bootsmannsmaat Wagner fired flares.

Hans Denker watched events unfolding within the boat:

Most of the men inside the boat had donned life jackets. Unfortunately, the strain had taken a toll on many of the men. Someone had broken open the provisions and many men sat around eating and taking no part in the continuing rescue operation. After the first four men were out, the watch officer called down that everyone should remain below because it was too cold outside. Shortly Wagner came back inside to obtain more flares, but they were all in the flooded after torpedo room. Shortly after that Schroder and Sell came back inside. Both were half frozen and kept saying that they would rather drown than freeze to death. Right behind them were Kohler and Meyer. There were now four people outside. Following a short discussion with the captain it was decided that everyone should go outside because there was a strong possibility that chlorine gas would soon develop. There was also the risk that the heavy seas would pour enough water down the open tube to sink the boat. That fear increased as the tide rose and the boat turned, bringing the open tube to the windward side. The captain ordered me to lead the way out. I took the portable searchlight with me and behind me came Maschinistenmaat Redlin. The order was passed below for everyone to come out. It was terribly cold and the waves were now breaking over the bow.

The time was now 2200hrs. Those doubting the ferocity of the Channel in winter should consider that, having inched their way out of the torpedo tubes to face conditions outside, several submariners now decided to slide down back inside the boat.

Carl-Detlef Blunck again:

Owing to the icy cold and their wet clothes, the others, even the courageous pioneers, were obliged to return to the boat. They said they would rather die down below than up above. I fired some star shells, and after 3 hours they were seen. There were seven of us up there.

Outside it was pitch black and the light at Beachy Head was only faintly visible. The bow stuck up out of the water like a lone rock pinnacle. The watch officer and the navigator were sitting on it, but I did not see anyone else. The sea was breaking over the bow. I found a spot on the net cutter and sat down to wait. It was terribly cold and I was soon sorry that I had shed my oil skins. In a short time my feet were numb. Shortly the chief engineer came out and brought with him more flares. He asked me if I wanted to go back inside and I said no. While we were sending SOS against the clouds, more men came up. I do not know in what order they arrived, but they were Kirschbaum, Redlin, and Bories. After a long while a ship appeared headed toward us. We soon recognized it as a British patrol boat, and we did not know if we were all going to be shot or rescued.

At 2216hrs, the flares had been spotted and destroyer HMS *P32* had been quickly dispatched to investigate. It would be pleasing to be able to record that salvation was at hand for the German sailors but what happened next remains shocking to this day:

Matrose Blunck:

> Just before midnight two destroyers came along and illuminated us with searchlights. The ship moved in close, in fact so close that Redlin and Kirchbaum were able to jump aboard. The seas were so heavy that one minute the deck was above us and the next it was below us. Then there was a crash as the patrol boat rammed the *UB 81*. I tried to jump but found myself under water. When I regained the surface our boat was gone. All of us were picked up, but Bories was dead of a heart attack brought on by exposure by the time the British fished him out of the water.

Of the seven men who were outside when *UB 81* sank, six were picked up. The British destroyers remained in the area for an hour but there were no more men to rescue. Some of the German survivors claimed that the ramming had been deliberate and therefore an atrocity. Indeed newspaper reports in the days that followed indicated that a patrol boat had deliberately rammed an enemy submarine. The source of this information remains unclear, as no official British source makes reference to a deliberate ramming. What were the views of the survivors? Maschinistenmaat Paul Redlin: '*P32 arrived, came along the starboard side and rammed us. The blow drove the bow under and our boat disappeared with the torpedo bow cap open.*' When first discovered, the wreck of *UB 81* revealed a deep bow incision, suggesting that *P32* may have been under significant engine power at the time of impact. However the 'P' Class were noted for their sharp bows and survivor Lt Hermann Freudendal thought a combination of heavy seas and bad seamanship was to blame: '*...we fired red flares and attracted the attention of four patrol boats. P32 came alongside to take us off and in manoeuvring she rammed the ballast tank. The boat sank instantly.*' Hans Denker was also inclined to believe the ramming had been an accident: '*The destroyer approached cautiously to windward but was unable to lower a boat due to the high seas. Instead the crew threw life rings and lines over the side. The destroyer came so close to our bow that Kirchbaum was able to leap aboard. Moments later the destroyer rammed UB81 sinking it instantly*'.

HMS *Wild Goose* attaching a U-boat with Hedgehogs. (Private collection)

HMS *P28*, a similar ship to HMS *P32*. (Author's collection)

This is the log of the Portsmouth-based *P32* for 2 December 1917:

2216hrs Investigated rockets 7 miles SSE
2245hrs Picked up survivors – 2 officers and 5 men from mined submarine UB81
Survivors placed under arrest and isolated. Personal papers confiscated and personal property removed
Handed over to C in C on arrival in harbour
Lost overboard whilst saving men from German submarine – 16 life buoys and 1 oar from skiff

Some idea of the prevailing conditions can be found in the log: '*8 p.m.: wind direction: WSW, wind force 4, weather: be state of the sea: 4, height of barometer: 30.34, air temp.: 56 deg.F, sea temp.: 50 deg.F (appr. 10 deg. C).*'

What follows is an extract from a letter written by Carl-Detlef Blunck to his parents from a Scottish PoW camp. Obviously it was written in the knowledge that the British censor was hovering, pen at the ready, nevertheless it is worth repeating here: '*The British sailors really made the most self-sacrificing and zealous efforts to save us. – No trouble was spared. In spite of the heavy seas, two of them lowered a boat and rescued Seaman Kirschbaum. The highest praise is due on this occasion to all the rescuers…*'

Hardly the words of a man who has just witnessed an atrocity.

While the British were certainly not immune from individual acts of brutality in the extreme heat and tension of battle (*see* vol. 1), having examined the available evidence, the authors conclude that the deaths of Reinhold Saltzwedel and his men resulted from a botched rescue attempt rather than cold-blooded murder. Such are the fortunes of war.

ADM 53/56393 ADM 137/3060 U-Boot-Ehrenmal Möltenort CWGC *The Cross of Sacrifice* Vol. II

THE MEN WHO DIED IN UB 81

Adomeit, Paul U-Matrose
Bergner, Kurt U-Oberheizer
Borries, Heinrich U.Maschinistenmaat
Brosig, Richard U-Obermaschinistenmaat

Cornely, Philipp U-Oberheizer
Hülfert, Hugo U-Oberheizer
Haase, Willy U-Maschinistenmaat
Kleuser, Friedrich U-Heizer

Kniepkamp, W. U-Matrose
Köhler, Oswald U-Heizer
Lettermann, Heinrich U-F.T.Obergast
Meyer, Hermann U-Heizer
Nehl, Emil U-Oberheizer
Otto, Julius U-Heizer
Palm, Alfred U-Maschinistenmaat
Peters, Henry U-Oberheizer
Pringnitz, W. U-Matrose
Reinhold, Walter U-Matrose
Roskam, Bernhard U-Maschinistenmaat

Räubert, Otto U-Heizer
Sadowski, O. U-Matrose
Saltzwedel, Reinhold Oberleutnant zur See
Schleh, Friedrich U-Maschinist
Schröder, Heinrich U-Oberheizer der Reserve
Sell, Fritz U-Matrose
Staabs, Oskar Leutnant zur See
Tiedt, August U-Maschinistenmaat
Wagner, Franz U-Bootsmannsmaat
Westaedt, Paul U-F.T.Gast

WRECK SITE

The wreck is orientated in an almost east to west direction (083/263°) with its bows to the east. It lies on a hard flat seabed of sand and rock, in a general depth of 27m (89ft), being the lowest astronomical depth. *UB 81* is broken in two, with the other half lying some distance away. The wreck was salvaged in the mid-1970s and the bow section, conning tower and stern end have all been blown off. The conning tower can be seen lying on the seabed on the starboard side. Amidships, she is reasonably intact. The holes and cracks in the casing are home to several very large conger eels and crabs. The stern torpedo tubes are now exposed and it is possible to see inside. On the port side, sections of the outer casing have collapsed and the wreck is fast deteriorating. The bow torpedo tubes, propellers and the bridge telegraph have all disappeared in recent years and the deck gun, which had fallen off the wreck in recent years, appears to be missing too. Ammunition used to be scattered around the seabed, but even much of this has been removed/stolen. Items including the lamps and horn are on display in the Bembridge Shipwreck Museum.

RAMBLING WRECK?

It is known that Commander Damant first visited the wreck on 10 December 1917. The intention to raise the boat was prevented by bad weather. The wreck was then 'lost'. Legend has it that *UB 81* has travelled nearly 20 miles over the years. Divers have apparently discovered the same submarine in two different locations. Indeed, artic les have been written about *UB 81*'s tendency to wander along the seabed. Here is the mystery: *UB 81* is recorded as having been sunk 2 miles south of the Owers light vessel. In 1961 the RN commenced a sonar search and could not find her. In 1970 divers found the boat at 50° 27.00'N 00° 51.00'W, a position some 12 miles away from where she allegedly sank. Even if allowance is made for the location of the Owers light vessel having shifted half a mile to the northeast in the intervening years, we are still faced with an anomaly. The current position of the wreck is about 5 miles to the west of the 1970 location.

The authors decided to investigate the subject and approached experts in submarine construction and hydrodynamics. Dr Pieter Van Deulen of Smit Tak International confirmed that if four or more ballast tanks are intact, it is true that a 'dead' submarine may roll; it can change orientation, but only for a short period after it has been sunk. However, even if we remove potential undersea barriers such as sandbanks, gullies, debris fields, rocks and wrecks from the equation, a sunken submarine nevertheless cannot move very far. The thin membrane surrounding the ballast tanks is usually the first part of the submarine to erode and it will corrode very quickly. The condition of the submarine at the time of its loss is a major factor. In this particular case we know that the boat had been dived for some time when the mine detonated. We also can be sure that the impact with the bows of *P32* against the ballast tank, coupled with the open torpedo tube, would have caused the entire fore ends of *UB 81* to flood. In other words, we can be certain that, because of the time spent dived, only a relatively small amount of air would have been trapped within her flasks and the resultant flooding would have been sufficient to keep *UB 81* anchored for eternity, in the location where she first sank.

Next the authors turned to contemporary records. Interrogation of German survivors offered a position some 2 miles south of the Owers Lightship. We examined the log of *P32*. No precise location was given, merely the information given above, namely, '*2216 Investigated rockets 7 miles*

SSE…'. The little-known *Leith Lockhart Mining History* written in the 1920s, utilised the records of HMS *Vernon* to faithfully record First World War minefields and described the fate of those submarines believed to have been destroyed by them. Leith Lockhart describes the position of *UB 81* as being 50° 27'N 00° 53'W. If we compare this position with the 1970 location of 50° 27.00'N 00° 51.00'W and make allowance for 'rounding off', we have a mystery solved. Well, maybe…

A1, HM SUBMARINE

DATE OF LOSS: August 1911
DEPTH: 7m
REFERENCE: withheld
LOCATION: WNW from Selsey Bill

Type: 'A1' Class coastal patrol submarine of Group I   *Ordered*: 1902 and 1903 programme   *Keel laid*: on 19 February 1902 as No.6 (of the 'HOLLAND' Class), changed to Yard No.285   *Pendant*: not issued   *Builders*: Vickers, Barrow-in-Furness for Royal Navy   *Launched*: on 9 July 1902   *Completed*: on 23 July 1903. (Commanding officers were not nominated for individual boats, only to a depot ship 'for command of submarine attached')

TECHNICAL SPECIFICATIONS

Hull: single   *Surface displacement*: 165 tons   *U/Dt*: 180 tons   *LBD*: 31.47m × 3.62m × 3.53m   *Machinery*: 1 × 450bhp, vertical 12-cylinder Wolsey petrol engine.   *Props*: 1 × 3-blade of 1.70m (5ft 7in) (bronze)   *S/Sp*: 11.5 knots   *Op/R*: 310 nautical miles at 10 knots   *Sub/R*: 20 nautical miles at 5 knots   *U/Power*: 1 × 80bhp at electric motor gave 7 knots   *Batteries*: Exide lead/acid   *Fuel/Cap*: 7 tons   *Armament*: 1 bow 45.72cm (18in) torpedo tube.   *Torpedoes*: 1 × 45.72cm (18in)   *Guns*: none   *Diving*: max-op-depth 15.25m (50ft) and 5 minutes to submerge   *Complement*: 2 officers and 9 ratings

A1 (ex-Holland 6) was the fruit of Captain Reginald Bacon's fertile mind, the direct result of his studies of, and experimentation with, the Holland Class. *A1* was 40ft longer than the Holland boats with a much greater displacement. She was narrower in the beam than her predecessors and was shaped differently forward of the conning tower because Bacon had made solving the freeboard problem his priority (*see* Holland 5). Among the innovations was a proper conning tower which prevented the submarine being swamped when running on the surface. There were quite a few internal differences too. The petrol engines were of a similar design to the Wolseley car engines (and were just as unreliable). *A1* was built at a cost of around £41,000 but the price seemed to rise with each submarine ordered. The 'A' Class of submarine was the Royal Navy's first attempt at an all-British submarine. She was the only boat in the 'A' Class to be fitted with a single torpedo tube. The submariners were very proud of *A1* but there must have been some negative comment in Admiralty circles when Captain Bacon earnestly proposed to call her HMS *Icthyosaurus*. The numbering system was retained, perhaps wisely (Memorandum from Bacon to Admiralty Controller Sir William May, 3 July 1902 ADM 1/7522).

Vickers of Barrow were exclusively contracted to build the fourteen 'A' Class, though *A14* would ultimately be designated *B1*. Four distinct classes can be discerned, each a slight improvement on the last; *A1*, *A2* to *A4*, *A5* to *A12* and *A13*. Captain Bacon, the Vickers designers and the submariners were pioneers on a learning curve. At times this learning curve could be dangerous. These new submarines retained the Holland's worst defect – a pitifully small reserve of buoyancy. The 'A' Class were disconcertingly prone to killing their crews. Even before she was delivered from the yard, a pocket of hydrogen gas caused a small explosion inside the boat. The submariners were not dismayed and A1 sailed from Barrow to Gosport. Off Land's End, a heavy sea swamped the casing. Salt water entered the batteries producing a small amount of chlorine gas. The boat was temporarily evacuated but an examination of Captain Bacon's report indicates that the incident was not a serious one. The boat duly arrived at Fort Blockhouse and Lt Mansergh took command.

HM SM *A2*. (Author's collection)

HM SM *A12* ashore on Promotion Point. (Private collection)

HM SM *A12*, *c.*1910. (Author's collection)

Lieutenant Loftus Charles Ogilvy Mansergh was born in Bridgetown, County Cork on 2 March 1873 and assumed command of *A1* at the age of 31. Mansergh was the son of an army officer and entered the navy as a cadet. In 1893 he had beeb promoted to sub-lieutenant then to lieutenant in 1895. Mansergh had volunteered for the new Submarine Service, two years from its very beginning. The boat's second commissioned officer was 21-year-old Sub-Lieutenant John Preston Churchill. He was promoted to sub-lieutenant in September 1902 and commenced submarine training on HMS *Thames*, on 1 January 1904.

Debate as to how best to use these submarines sharpened in the years between 1903 and 1905. At one extreme lay the argument expounded by Arthur Wilson, namely that submarines were a modern evil, required only for the purposes of experimentation – in order to find more efficient means of destroying them. Britain's naval supremacy was unquestioned. Vast sums had been poured into developing battleships and cruisers. The prospect of submarine warfare had the potential to unravel British dominance of the seas. It could not be allowed to continue unchecked. This view was not merely the preserve of the blinkered big ship 'salt horse'. Many of the more cerebral politi-cal and service minds recognised that Britain was now dependant upon imports from the Americas. The prospect of some future submarine war against Britain's supply lines filled them with horror. In effect proponents of this view were making Fisher's point in reverse. Their response to German mil-itarism was not to flood the North Sea with torpedo craft but rather to pursue a policy of détente while simulataneously encouraging all methods of exorcising the submarine spectre.

At the other extreme stood Fisher and Bacon, the champions of the submarine. Visionaries ahead of their time, they passionately argued the case for the offensive as well as defensive capabili-ties of the submarine. Advocates of this view called for nothing less than a revolution in British naval strategic thought. The submarine advocates saw beyond the present shortcomings of the 'A' Class. Providing there was a steady flow of investment, superior designs would be forthcoming. Fisher and his acolytes wanted patrol submarines – boats capable of taking the fight to the enemy, whether by enforcing a maritime blockade or lying in wait within the Heligoland Bight. Above all, Fisher was driven by the belief that if Britain did not invest in submarine technology, German militarists undoubtedly would.

Fisher and friends faced an uphill task. For the most part, Britain's decision makers were content to keep faith with the big ship navy. Submarines were a somewhat distasteful symbol of the new zeitgeist. Nevertheless, most in positions of responsibility would concede that subma-rines had a strong deterrent value if stationed in key naval anchorages such as Portsmouth and Portland. It was generally accepted that no invading warships would dare penetrate within 10 miles of an anchorage guarded by submarines. Technology was rapidly improving the endurance, propulsion, armament, habitability and sea-keeping qualities of these submarines, but the submarine remained an unreliable craft of limited endurance. Until these essential flaws had been ironed out, Admiralty could only conceive of a defensive role for their small submarine fleet. Interestingly, the records of Vickers indicate that viable designs for patrol submarines existed on paper as early as 1904 but as far as Admiralty was concerned, any offensive role constituted a potentially expensive gamble. It was a gamble that would have to wait. In short between 1904 and 1906, Admiralty was content to provide funding for the 'B' and 'C' coastal (defensive) class submarines but development of the first patrol ('D' Class) submarines was delayed until the 1907/1908 naval estimates. In the meantime the Royal Engineers were moved on and the 'A' boats took up station at Fort Blockhouse.

This minute is dated 14 December 1903:

> …the Admiralty is prepared to substitute submarines for existing minefields at the following places and dates
>
> At Portsmouth   1 February 1904
> At Devonport   1 October 1904
> At Sheerness   1 October 1904
>
> If Mr Arnold Forster agrees, it is proposed that the Royal Engineer mining establishments at Block House Fort, Portsmouth, Cattewater (Plymouth) and Sheerness, be handed over to the Admiralty on the dates named.

There was a widespread belief in Admiralty circles that submarines still had much to prove. In March 1904 Captain Bacon responded by organising showcase manoeuvres for his submarines. Commencing on 8 March in the Solent close to the Nab, this ten-day-long exercise would involve the *Hollands* and 'A' Class making dummy attacks on surface ships under the gaze of an impressive array of gold braid and suitably influential politicians. From Bacon's point of view, the exercises proceeded well. The Inspector of Submarines could do little about the civilian maritime traffic steaming close to the exercise zone. Friday 18 March was the final day of manoeuvres. The cruiser *Juno* was to steam towards Portsmouth while *A1* and the *Hollands* attempted to take up firing positions. Shortly before 1400 *Holland 2* fired a torpedo which missed its target. *Holland 3* fared much better and her dummy torpedo struck home.

Next, Lt Mansergh in *A1* got his chance to attack following a signal from Captain Bacon on HMS *Hazard*. Lt Mansergh was determined to make an impression and was probably so absorbed in the task of lining up for the attack that he failed to notice the liner SS *Berwick Castle* (Union-Castle Mail Steamship Co. Ltd, London – Capt Henry Cruise) steaming towards *A1* on a collision path. The liner's duty watch officers were too absorbed in these fascinating evolutions to observe how close they were to *A1*. After all, very few people had ever seen a submarine. At the last moment the steamer's crew sighted 'something' ahead, although the object was not identified as a submarine. What follows is an extract from the log of *Berwick Castle*:

14.11   Felt double concussion under port bow as if struck by torpedo
14.12   Stopped, turned round and reported occurence to Nab guardship

The ship's starboard helm was applied instantaneously and she was put full astern. *A1* however was struck a fatal blow and must have then gone to the bottom in seconds. The liner carried on with her voyage between Southampton and Hamburg. When *A1* did not return after several hours, Captain Bacon became concerned and set out in *Hazard* to search for her. Look-outs spotted a patch of white water, created by air bubbling up to the surface. HMS *Seagull* was summoned to the scene and the two ships kept a silent vigil throughout the night. *Seagull's* powerful searchlights constantly swept the area, hoping upon hope that at least some of the men would escape. There was simply nothing anyone could do. That night Fisher (Commander-in-Chief, Portsmouth), sent the following terse telegram to Admiralty:

HM SM *A1*. (Private collection)

HM SM *A1* being inspected by the King, the Prince of Wales and the Duke of Connaught. (Private collection)

Regret to report loss with all hands of A1 submarine boat which was run down by a Castle Line steamer off the Nab about three o' clock this afternoon. Lt Mansergh and Sub Lt Churchill were on board. Names of men will follow when verified.

Divers were sent down to examine the wreck the following morning, Saturday 19th. *A1* was lying on her port side with damage on the starboard side of the conning tower, clearly where the liner had struck her. Attempts to raise her that day failed when the lifting hawsers snapped under the weight. Salvage proved a difficult venture. First the damaged hull was repaired by divers, then the boat was

A Class submarine. (Private collection)

pumped full of air. Stronger wire hawsers were placed under the hull fore and aft and the lift began at 1100hrs on the morning of Monday 18 April. Strong suction on the seabed had also caused some problems, before she was pulled free. The salvage vessel *Belos*, owned by Swedish Neptune Co. of Stockholm, towed *A1* semi-submerged back towards 'D' Dock, Portsmouth. During this dismal voyage, a flotilla of private boats belonging to curious onlookers followed the tow. Naturally the newspaper reporters were on the scene, reporting every last nuance. The bodies of the crew were removed overnight and in secrecy. Sub Lt Churchill's father, also a serving naval officer, was allowed to attend the 'evacuation', the first of many in the Royal Navy Submarine Service.

Lt Mansergh was found slumped at the foot of the conning tower. He had suffered serious head injuries, although death was actually caused by drowning. Captain Bacon concluded that Loftus Mansergh had been observing through the periscope at the time of the collision. There are clear parallels with the later loss of *L24*. Bacon noted the following in his report:

> Although the conning tower had suffered damage the leak was so small that it could easily have been stopped from inside if the crew had not been stunned. It appeared that no attempt had been made to blow any of the ballast tanks.

In other words, the evidence pointed to the crew having been knocked out by the impact, then drowned as the water poured into the little boat. The funerals took place on 18 April in Haslar Cemetery, off Clayhall Road in Gosport.

THE MEN WHO DIED IN A1

Baker, George Gibson, Petty Officer.1st
Baly, Clinton Parker, Engine Room Artificer.4th
Churchill, John Preston, Sub-Lieutenant RN
Dudgeon, William, Petty Officer.1st
Ellis, Albert Benjamin, Stoker.1st
Fleming, Albert Bertram, Chief Stoker

King, Charles William, Able Seaman
Mansergh, Loftus Charles Ogilvy, Lieutenant RN CO
Parkinson, William Joseph, Engine Room Artificer. 3rd
Roberts, Vivian William Lake, Petty Officer. 1st
Wallace, Peter Scott, Able Seaman

In the years that followed, a memorial obelisk to these men was erected in Haslar Cemetery in Gosport. The names of others men who died in 'A' boat accidents were steadily added. The limestone memorial also commemorates the crews of *A3, A5* and *A8*. There was one other legacy of the *A1* disaster worth mentioning; as an additional safety measure, a second watertight hatch was fitted at the foot of the conning towers of newer submarine designs.

The disaster had been played out under critical public gaze. The incident provided welcome ammunition to those who wished to maintain the submarine boat merely as an experimental craft.

The accident overshadowed the exercises which had otherwise been an unqualified success for the submarines. Captain Robert Arbuthnott, the senior umpire (who would later die at Jutland), was not reknowed as a 'progressive' within naval circles. His report on the exercises must have made chilling reading for many in Admiralty:

> In conclusion we consider that the submarine, used as either an offensive or defensive weapon, has achieved a sense of completion and perfection which must render it in naval warfare a continual danger and menace to an enemy in enclosed waters or in any position within its radius of action. Its capabilities in the hands of a well trained and experienced officers are very great and fear of what it can do renders its strength yet greater…Finally it may be considered as most conclusively proved by these manoeuvres that submarines are a powerful and deadly addition to any port, fortified or mercantile…if we are effectively to deny the waters of these ports to our future enemies and moreover, to make invasion impossible.

Fisher also knew the submarine was here to stay. Despite the accident, his enthusiasm for the craft was undimmed as this letter written to the Admiral of the Fleet, Sir William May, on 20 April 1904, theatrically reveals:

> I have not disguised my opinion…as to the essential, imperative, immediate, vital, pressing, urgent (I can't think of any more adjectives) necessity for more submarines at once, at the very least twenty-five in addition to those now ordered and building and a hundred more as soon as practicable – or we shall be caught with our breeches down just as the Russians have been. I don't blackguard you personally. It's the damned cautious old age spirit which actuates and always has actuated the Board of Admiralty… In all seriousness I don't think it is even FAINTLY REALISED, the immense, impending revolution which the submarine will effect as an offensive weapon of war.

The Germans understood Fisher's point, even if the Admiralty failed to fully grasp it. Ten years after these prophetic words were written, HMS *Pathfinder* was torpedoed and sunk off St Abbs Head (*see* vol. 3).

Once the grief and controversy had subsided, HMS *A1* was repaired and returned to service, for harbour defence and training purposes. Problems with the boat continued however. On 6 August 1910, *A1* was under the command of Lt Regnart. The boat lay in Haslar Creek under preparation for a diving exercise when a spark ignited petrol fumes which had built up within the boat. Two officers and five ratings were injured in the resulting explosion. Petty Officer Blunsdon was blown out of the conning tower, breaking both legs. All present suffered severe burns and shock.

ADM 1/7718 ADM 1/7717 ADM 1/7795 ADM 116/942

CASUALTIES NAMED BY THE PRESS

Officers:
Regnart, Cornelius Octavius, Lieutenant RN CO
Stopford, Robert Neville, Sub-Lieutenant RN

Ratings:
Blunsdon, Frederick D., Petty Officer
Cook, Arthur J., Able Seaman
Bell, Stephen T., Engine Room Artificer 2nd Class
Bullen, Walter C., Engine Room Artificer 2nd Class
Higgins, George, Leading Stoker

FINAL PATROL

HM S/M *A1* was not repaired this time and in August 1911 she was set up as a target, suspended in shallow water off Selsey Bill. She was then used for testing experimental explosives devices, fired from varying distances. Later that month she sank to the bottom after the pressure hull collapsed during a test.

WRECK SITE

Willie Pledger, a local trawlerman, located the little submarine in 1988, when he accidentally snagged the wreck. It lies on a seabed of mud and sand, in a general depth of around 7m. The wreck was also reported to be upright and fully intact, with some damage to the hull. After being invited by the divers who first located her, Martin Woodward helped to identify the wreck and then eventually bought it. HM S/M *A1* is now designated as an historical wreck site and buoyed as such. It is illegal to dive the site without the prior permission of Martin and the DCMS.

U 90, SM IMPERIAL U-BOAT

DATE OF LOSS: 1921?
DEPTH: 31m
REFERENCE: 50 30'.656 N 001 09'.051 W
LOCATION: 6.81 nautical miles SE from St Catherine's Point, Isle of Wight

Type: Mittel-U (UI Project No.25, improved Type U50) torpedo attack boat   *Builders*: Kaiserliche Werft, Danzig for Kaiserliche Deutsche Marine   *Ordered*: on 23 June 1915, within the batch of *U 87–U 92*   *Keel laid*: as Yard No.34 on 29 December 1915   *Launched*: on 12 January 1917   *Commissioned*: by Kapitänleutnant Walter Remy on 2 August 1917

TECHNICAL SPECIFICATIONS

Hull: double   *Surface displacement*: 757 tons   *U/Dt*: 998 tons   *LBDH*: 65.80m × 6.19m × 3.9m × 8.70m   *Machinery*: 2 × 1,200ps Maschinefabrik-Augsburg-Nürnberg (MAN) diesels   *Props*: 2 bronze   *S/Sp*: 15.6 knots   *Op/R*: 11,380 nautical miles at 8 knots   *Sub/R*: 56 nautical miles at 5 knots   *U/Power*: 2 × 600ps electric motors gave 8.6 knots   *Batteries*: lead/acid/accumulators   *Fuel/Cap*: 54 + 79 tons   *Armament*: 4 bow and 2 stern 50.04cm torpedo tubes   *Torpedoes*: 12 × 50.04cm (19.7in).   *Guns*: 2 = 1 × 105mm (4.13in) forward facing and 1 × 88mm – 5m aft of conning tower   *Ammo*: 220 rounds   *Mines*: none   *Diving*: max-op-depth 50m (164ft) and 45 sec to crash-dive   *Complement*: 36

After her initial trials and training period, *U 90* was formally assigned to III-U-Flottille, Wilhelmshaven on 10 September 1917, with Kplt. Walter Remy the CO from 2 August 1917.

On 16 September 1917, *U 90* departed Wilhelmshaven and sailed around the Isles of Orkney for a war tour in an area, west of the western entrance to the English Channel and the west coast of France. *U 90* patrolled in that vicinity between 24 September and 12 October.

On the 25th Remy destroyed the unarmed 45-ton French fishing smack *Union Republicaine* (M. Bihan, Tudy) off Ushant. The smack had left the fishing grounds with 450 'thons' of fish worth 17,000 francs. At 0700hrs *U 90* fired five shells at the vessel which was abandoned, then another fourteen rounds were fired, of which three or four scored direct hits and she sank at position 47° 56'N 07° 13'W. The crew of seven all survived, including the skipper, Benjamin Yvon.

U 90 in port. (Author's collection)

[Author's note: A. Fischdick's book on *U 90* (published between the wars), gives the time of the attack as 0845hrs and twenty-one shells were expended. Also, according to Arno Spindler the vessel was 'stopped and bombed', but bombs are not mentioned in the book.]

On 27 September, three French tuna boats were captured and sunk off Ushant: the 49-ton *Liberte*, the 41-ton *Peuples Freres* and the 58-ton *Deux Jeannes* (No. G.1137). The tuna boats sighted *U 90* at 0800hrs and she fired at them from a distance of about 5–6,000m at 0830hrs at `05° 52'W. Altogether, *U 90* fired 140 shells, but only hit the *Peuples Freres*, which sank at 0930hrs, 4 miles to the east of the original position and 30 nautical miles west of Ile de Sein (48° 20'N 05° 52'W).

The *Deux Jeannes* (M.M. Etesse, Kerzaho, Baron et Mme. Yves Baron, Groix) was armed with a 5.7cm American gun and had left Sables d'Olonne on 25 September for the tuna fishing grounds under the command of her skipper, Joseph Baron. The tuna boat's gunners: Francois le Floch, Tudy Nero and Pierre Noel, fired about 45 shells against *U 90*, but with no effect. The crew of six finally abandoned their boat, which was sunk with explosives. The crew reached *Ushant* in their boat the next day, but the skipper was taken prisoner. (On 16 September, the *Deux Jeannes* was out fishing for tuna from Sables d'Olonne with a crew of seven when *UC 31* was sighted at 0800hrs, 300 miles N70°W Ushant. The tuna boat fired twenty-eight rounds at the U-boat, which fired twenty-five to thirty rounds back; *UC 31* was last seen at 0930hrs, 4 miles further to the east after she dived. That same day *UC 31* sank the fishing smack *Quatre Freres* at 0700hrs.)

The *Liberté* (M. Callot, Croix), which was armed with a 5.7cm American gun and commanded by Captain Armand Stephan, had left Ile de Croix for the fishing grounds on 25 September; *Liberté* fired at *U 90*, but eventually surrendered and the skipper was taken prisoner, the fishing boat being sunk with explosives after her crew had abandoned ship. The four remaining crewmen in their boat reached the island of Ushant off Brittany, the next day. The Groix registered *Peuples Frères* was also armed with a 5.7cm gun and had left Ile de Croix on 25 September for the fishing grounds under the command of Captain Alphonse Burgod. The gunfight against the little boats lasted from 0900hrs to 1030hrs, each smack firing about 45 rounds at *U 90*; however *Liberté* reported 70–75 rounds alone. The three fishing boat skippers were held on board *U 90* until the steamer *Drake* (General Steam Navigation Co. Ltd) was captured, shelled and sunk on the 30th, then Remy handed the men over to the *Drake's* lifeboats; she was a 2,267-ton steamer, armed for defence and en-route from London to Genoa with general cargo, including explosives/ammunition, the master was taken prisoner.

The defensively armed SS *Heron* (1889 – General Steam Navigation Co. Ltd, London) of 879 tons was torpedoed and sunk without warning on the 30th, 500 miles west of Belle Ile; she was voyaging from the Tyne to Oporto with coal and twenty-two crewmen (all hands), including the master were lost.

THOSE WHO DIED

Adkin, William James, 27yrs, Able Seaman
Akigama, F. 37yrs, Fireman and Trimmer
Bristow, R.S., Master
Davey, Charles William, 42yrs, 1st Engineer
Davis, James Robert, 29yrs, Able Seaman
Eagles, Percy Allen Frederick, 22yrs, 3rd Engineer
Fernandes, B., 19yrs, Assistant Steward
Fletcher, Bernard Cyril Wallis, 16yrs, Ordinary Seaman
Gomes, J., 47yrs, Fireman and Trimmer
Hidaka, S., 24yrs, Fireman and Trimmer
Jamieson, Harry Lionel, 21yrs, Seaman
Kerr, William, 39yrs, Mate
MacKenzie, John Alexander, 28yrs, Ship's Cook
Meechan, Thomas Jeffreys, 28yrs, 2nd Engineer
Nye, Robert, 57yrs, Steward
Oberg, C., 38yrs, Able Seaman and Lamps
Paterson, Walter H., 33yrs, 2nd Mate
Periera, J., 56yrs, Fireman and Trimmer
Sanada, S., 24yrs, Fireman and Trimmer
Vinton. J., 56yrs, Carpenter

The *Neuilly* (Societé Général d'Armement, Nantes) was a 2,300-ton unarmed, three-masted French barque. On 9 June 1917 she left Geelong in southeast Australia for Pauillac, Bordeaux with 3,000 tons of wheat for Ministère des Travaux Publics, but at 0818hrs on 1 October, *U 90* fired eight shells at her. The vessel stopped at 0823hrs, then another five or six shots were made after she was abandoned; the *Neuilly* (Captain Emilien Louis Léon Brignaudy) was first looted, with the Germans taking stores, cabin fittings, tools etc., in fact removing everything of value they could find, including the chronometers and even the crew's personal effects and after two explosives were placed on board with 5-minute fuses, she finally sank at 1130hrs, in position 46° 27'N 15° 07'W. The lifeboats, containing the crew of twenty-two, included twenty-one Frenchmen and one Australian, plus one Japanese donkeyman from the steamer *Heron*, who had been handed over by *U 90*; they were picked up by HMS *Camellia* at 0400hrs on 3 October 1917 and she reached Queenstown, Ireland on the 7th. When asked about the Germans, the barque's master said:

> The captain and two other officers were seen, the captain was tall and strong looking with red hair, blue eyes and a full beard, which was very crisp and curly, he was about thirty years old ... the U-boat had on board and lashed down on the port side of the conning tower, a 75mm gun taken from a French fishing vessel they had sunk off Ushant on the 30th.

The crew of SM *U 90*. (Author's collection)

He also said the bombs used to sink his vessel in a few seconds were of a very large size.

Two days later, the 228-ton *Jeannette* (M. Tremaudan et Cie., St Malo), a wooden, three-masted French barquentine, was captured off the Bay of Biscay. Commanded by Captain Marie-Baptiste Commereux, she had left Newfoundland Banks with 2,000 'quintaux' (200 tons) of salted cod on 17 September 1917 and reached position 46°40'N-14°34'W, west of the Bay of Biscay, on 2 October, where she was attacked with gunfire. The French fishermen thought *U 90* had raised a small sail becuase to Captain Commereux the U-boat resembled a small sailing vessel in the distance, but he quickly realised what it was after a few moments, when a shell, fired at 1915hrs from 2,700m, passed over the mast between the mainmast and the foremast. Soon after, a second shell crashed a few metres in front of the sailing ship. (The evening was clear and *Jeannette* was unarmed.) The master immediately brought down the sails, lowered the six small dories into the sea and abandonsed ship in them, then they quickly rowed clear from the vessel. The U-boat did not approach the *Jeannette* immediately, because Kplt. Remy was suspicious of it, thinking it may have been a Q-ship; then slowly and cautiously, *U 90* moved towards the barquentine and in doing so, *U 90* ran into the group of dories that were unseen in the falling darkness.

Remy spoke in both French and English and asked who the master was and which of the boats carried him. Captain Commereux and the 1st officer François Leroux were then taken on board the submarine and questioned about their destination and port for unloading. Remy ordered the master to evacuate one of their dories and the men in it had to be divided amongst the other five; the dory was then confiscated. Captain Commereux informed the U-boat commander that they would not have enough food in the boats to make the 400-mile perilous crossing to shore and suggested they go back on board to collect some, but Remy said: '*IMPOSSIBLE*'. The two men were then instructed to return to the dories and Remy said to them: '*I will sink your sailing boat tomorrow morning, leave and good voyage*'. At 2100hrs, the five little boats got under way for their dangerous crossing and all that night they sailed together.

A typical French fishing dory in which the crew from *Jeanette* were forced to abandon ship in the Atlantic. (Author's collection)

Meanwhile, next morning of 3 October, after the scuttling charges placed onboard the *Jeannette* failed to detonate and, given the worsening sea conditions, *U 90* fired some sixteen rounds into the barquentine before it sank.

After rowing and sailing all night, the dories had lost sight of each other by the next day.

The full-rigged three-masted sailing vessel, *Buffon*, picked up one of the dories. Report of L. Cloatre, Captain of the *Buffon*:

Friday 5 October 1917, by Lat. 46°10' North – Long. 9°50' West with heavy weather of NNW and travelling for Melbourne, Australia, I collected five shipwrecked men from the schooner *Jeanette* under Captain Commereux, coming from the Newfoundland Banks, was bound for Bordeaux with the Dinan registered seamen: ordinary seaman Jules Lucas, ordinary seaman Louis Ricordel, ordinary seaman Henri Levacher, ordinary seaman Joseph Le Mee and Jean Menard, an appentice. From their statements, these men were given orders to evacuate their vessel as soon as possible at about 1900hrs on 2 October 1917 and U-boat commander said he had intentions of sinking their ship at daybreak on the 3rd; he also told them that they were 390 miles from land. The men were very exhausted and four of them could hardly stand up, even being unable to climb on board. We gave them the necessary care and comfort and also saved their dory. The fishermen informed me that the remaining crew of eighteen were in four other boats, so we probed the horizon, but we did not see any sign of them. That evening we called by the wireless to see whether there were any other vessels or a warship in the vicinity that could have taken them home. Not having received any answer, we carried on our voyage with the intention of handing them over to the first ship we met travelling towards Europe.

Signed: L. Cloatre, captain of the 3-masted vessel *Buffon*, Société Générale d'Armement, Nantes – 14 November.

Captain Cloatre asserted in a letter dated 14 November:

A sister ship of the 228-ton French barquentine *Jeanette*. (Author's collection)

In port at St Malo and the French fishing fleet. (Author's collection)

I met an English cruiser at 2° 23.3'N 4° 29.0'W and the commander accepted the five shipwrecked men who were taken aboard in order to repatriate them within the shortest times.

On 17 January 1918, the Minister of the Navy was informed by the French Foreign Office that the French Consul in Rio de Janeiro repatriated five survivors from the crew of barquentine *Jeannette* registered at Saint Servan, who were cast adrift on 2 October 1917, some 500 miles off (the) Belle-Isle en Mer. These shipwrecked men were landed in Rio de Janeiro, Brazil by the cruiser HMS *Glasgow*, which had picked them up in the open sea from the sailing ship *Buffon*. After a few days in Rio, the men were placed on board the barque *Dupleix* for their return voyage to France; they landed at Brest at the beginning of February 1918.

Five survivors in another dory – ordinary seaman François Huet, ordinary seaman Georges Bertrand, ordinary seaman Joseph Connan, apprentice Albert Colas and ordinary seaman Louis Tachot – were picked up by the schooner *Gardenia* at 0845hrs on 7 October and taken to the port of La Pallice, out of La Rochelle.

Four of the other men in one boat – the master, Captain Marie-Baptiste Commereux, ordinary seaman Auguste Blais, ordinary seaman François Lemasson and ordinary seaman François Michel – landed at St Jean de Monts on 10 October 1917 after sailing and rowing for ten days; these men, who were very tired but healthy, were soon directed on to Nantes for cross-examination.

On 7 October and about 2–3 miles south of Penmarc'h, the fishing cutter *ROSSIGNOL* rescued another boat containing the 1st officer and master of fishing François Leroux, ordinary seaman Edouard Perrot, ordinary seaman Pierre Saiget and Alfred Duval, the ship's boy. They were landed at Lorient that same day.

The fifth dory, occupied by the 2nd Officer Marie-Ange Chéhu, the salter Jacques Martel, apprentice Severe Duguily, pilotin and future young officer Mr Gautier and three ordinary seamen: Edouard Perrot, François Lebret, François Hamon, was never seen again, the men probably all drowned in rough seas, encountered the following days.

Incidentally, 2nd officer Marie-Ange Chéhu was the grandfather of Daniele Chéhu (a friend of Yves Dufeil who is a friend of the authors and who still keep in touch with her). Yves made this investigation into the loss of the *JEANNETTE* on Daniele's behalf and he said it has been a fascinating experience to bring back to the surface this history which had been completely altered in the family's memory over the years. Moreover, producing documents such as a photo of Kplt Remy and an excerpt of his KTB were very impressive to the Chéhu family. (Courtesy of Yves Dufeil in France)

U 90 returned to Germany on 16 October 1917, travelling back via the dangerous Dover Strait.

(2) *U 90* left Wilhelmshaven for a war cruise on 15 November 1917 and travelled via Borkum through the Dover Straits to the area about 200–250 miles southwest of the Isles of Scilly and west of the western entrance to the English Channel. Remy captured the 146-ton British sailing vessel *Robert Morris* on 20 November, 155 miles from Bishop Rock, and sank her with explosive charges. The *Aros Castle* (1901 – Union Castle Mail Steamship Co. Ltd, London) a defensively armed British steamer of 4,459 tons, was torpedoed and sunk without warning on 21 November, 300 miles from Bishop Rock; she was in ballast, steaming from London to Baltimore, Maryland and two fireman and trimmers were killed: James Maloney (42yrs) and Richard Herbert Spindler (42yrs).

On 6 December, *U 90* began her return voyage home, going through the Irish Sea and North Channel, then around the Hebrides, the Isles of Orkney and across the North Sea to Wilhelmshaven, where she arrived on 10 December.

(3) On 16 January 1918 *U 90* sailed from Heligoland for operations off the Western Channel, with Remy in command. She travelled past the Hoofden and through the Dover Strait to reach her destination and returned to Germany the same route, on 7 February 1918.

The 6,565-ton *Admiral Cochrane* (1917 – Byron S.S. Co. Ltd, London) was a steamship that was armed for defence, but on the 22nd *U 90* damaged her with a torpedo 3 miles from Berry Head; the vessel was en-route from Le Havre to Portland and Plymouth in ballast and was towed into Dartmouth for repairs. The next day (23rd), the defensively armed SS *Corton* (1913 – William Cory & Son Ltd, London) of 3,405 tons, was voyaging from Le Havre to Portsmouth, when she was damaged by a torpedo fired from *U 90*, south of Dunose Head; however she arrived at Stokes Bay later that day; but a foreign fireman named Ali was killed. On 24 January, the 78-ton British sailing vessel

Full-rigged sailing ship *Buffon*. (Author's collection)

Second officer Marie-Ange Chéhu of the *Jeanette* and his wife. (Courtesy Danielle Chéhu)

Oblt Vater, Kplt Remy and Oblt Kurtz. (Author's collection)

Charles was captured 16 miles southwest of the Casquets and sunk by gunfire, while transporting iron ore from Granville to Swansea.

While transporting a general cargo and mail from Southampton to Cherbourg, the 618-ton defensively armed steam coaster *Normandy* (1910 – London & South Western Railway Co., Southampton) was hit with a torpedo without warning off Cape la Hague; she sank with the loss of all fourteen hands on the 25th.

SOME OF THOSE WHO DIED

Battrick, P. (22yrs), Able Seaman MM
Budden, Frederick John (40yrs), Chief Engineer MM
Glow, William Ernest (26yrs), Able Seaman MM
Glouskofsky, Alexander (49yrs), Able Seaman MM
Holloway, Bertie John (35yrs), Fireman MM
Ingram, J. S. (33yrs), Able Seaman MM
Mulgrave, E. (16yrs), Assistant Steward MM
Oliver, Thomas (56yrs), Fireman MM
Page, Sidney Leopold (36yrs), Fireman MM
Pleace, Thomas Edward (48yrs), Chief Officer MM
Stevens, Josiah Henry Temp/Assistant Paymaster RN
Waugh, Wallace Helier (45yrs), Steward MM
Young, Walter Henry (44yrs), Fireman MM

While in transit from Newport to Bordeaux with 1,390 tons of coal, the 1,254-ton Danish steamer *Lindeskov* (1883 – Dampskibsselskabet Storebaelt, Copenhagen) was captured and sunk by gunfire off Ushant on 30 January. The 248-ton, three-masted, wooden-hulled Russian barque *Martin Gust* (1901 – M. Brunsleep, Wandsen, POR (Riga) was captured off Ushant and sunk with explosives on the 31st; she was carrying rum and cocoa from Fort de France in Martinique to Bordeaux. The

Arrino (1906 – Australind S.S. Co. Ltd, London), a 4,484-ton defensively armed cargo ship, was torpedoed and sunk without warning on 1 February, 14 miles from Ile de Vierge; she was travelling in ballast from Brest to an unknown destination.

(4) *U 90* left Wilhelmshaven on 11 March 1918 for a war patrol off the west coast of Ireland. To reach the designated area, Remy took the boat via the Kiel Canal, through the Kattegat and Skagerrak, then across the North Sea and around the Isles of Orkney, to the west of the Hebrides. Northwest of Cape Wrath on 16 March, Remy, without warning, torpedoed and damaged the 4,005-ton steam tanker *Oilfield* (1896 – Hunting S.S. Co. Ltd, Newcastle). She was armed for defence and in ballast, on passage from Grangemouth and Methil for New York and was beached near Stornoway, however the ship was a constructive total loss; the after part was later salved and towed into the Clyde for scrapping. Unfortunately, three crewmen were killed when the torpedo exploded.

THE THREE CREWMEN WHO DIED

Hung Liang, Fireman and Trimmer
Kong Wong, W. Quartermaster
Tam Li, 2nd Steward

On 28 March 1918, the *City of Winchester*, a 114-ton British sailing vessel, was travelling in ballast from St Malo to Cardiff when she was stopped, 10 miles from Les Hanois lighthouse, and sunk by gunfire. The 489-ton wooden-hulled Norwegian schooner *Superb* (1882 – A/S Tunøy, Sarpsborg) was also captured and sunk by gunfire, 40 miles south of Lindernaes, while transporting pit props from Porsgrund, Norway to West Hartlepool.

U 90 returned to base on 11 April, taking the same route home.

(5) Leaving Heligoland on 10 May 1918, *U 90* sailed for operations off the south and southwest coasts of Ireland. Remy chose the long route across the North Sea, by going around the Orkney

The conning tower of *U 90*. (Courtesy Mark Gilmore)

Typical French fishing schooner. (Author's collection)

Isles and keeping west of the Hebrides, then travelled down the west coast of Ireland. The patrol was a big success with three large steamships being sunk. On the 29 May, the 4,646-ton defensively armed steamer *BEGUM* (1907 – Asiatic Steam Navigation Co., Liverpool) was torpedoed without warning and sent to a watery grave, 270 miles from Bishop Rock; she was on passage from Cardiff to Santiago de Cuba in ballast and sixteen crewmen were drowned.

THOSE CREWMEN WHO DIED

Ale Ali, Fireman
Allah Rakhkha, Frireman
Aman Ali, Oilman
Amin Sharif, Secunny
Basu, Fireman
Dias, D., 5th Engineer
Faizu Miyan, Secunny
Faizu Miyan, Fireman
Fazlur Hasan Ali Rahman, Fireman
Fazlur Muha Mmad Ali Rahman, Fireman
Firoz Ali, 1st Tindall
Habibullah, Trimmer
Kalamiyan, Oilmn
Nawab Ali, Fireman
Taja Mmul Husain, Bhandary
Wakefield, Wilmont E. 4th Engineer

The next ship to founder was the *Carlton* (1905 – Carlton S.S. Co. Ltd, Newcastle), a 5,265-ton defensively armed steamer; she was torpedoed and sunk without warning in the same area, while in ballast and en-route from Cardiff and Milford Haven to Chile. At 1040hrs on Friday, 31 May, Remy got a bonus when his torpedoes slammed into the 18,168-ton American liner *President Lincoln* (US Navy transport – Cruiser-Transport Force). Under the US Government control, she was being used as a troop transport and was returning to the US from Brest after delivering a contingent of troops to Europe. The liner sank about 600 miles off the French coast at approximate position of 47° 57'N 15° 11'W. (Originally she was launched by Harland & Wolff Ltd of Belfast on 8 October 1907 as the *Servian* for Wilson's & Furness Leyland, however the ship was laid up in the yard unfinished; she was completed May 1907 and taken over by Hamburg-Amerika Linie, Hamburg, who initially proposed to rename her *Berlin*, but she was then laid up again in New York during August 1914. In April 1917 the vessel was seized as a prize-of-war after America entered the First World War.)

U 90 returned to Germany on 11 June, travelling via the Isles of Shetland, across the North Sea, through the Skagerrak and Kattegat and along the Kiel Canal, to reach the German, North Sea port of Wilhelmshaven.

U-Obermatrose Tippmann, a crewman on *U 90*, died on 2 August 1918, for reasons unknown.

Oblt.z.S. Helmut Patzig took over the command on 1 August 1918, Remy having been stricken by a viral infection.

(6) With her new temporary commander, *U 90* departed Heligoland on 5 August 1918 and sailed to an operational area west of the western entrance to the Channel and some 500 miles into the Atlantic Ocean. Patzig took the long, but safer route across the North Sea, around the Isles of Orkney, keeping west of the Hebrides and Irish coast. Three vessels were sunk on 15 August: the 7,117-ton American steamer *Cubore* (1917 – Ore Steamship Corp., New York), bound from St Nazaire to New York, was suspected of being torpedoed and sunk by *U 90* 250 miles from Cape Finisterre, however later evidence shows that *U 107* sank her. The 6,659-ton US liner SS *Montanan* (1913 – American-Hawaiian Steamship Co. Inc., New York) was torpedoed and sunk without any warning at 46° 47'N 13° 42'W; she was on passage from New York for St Nazaire; the crew took to the boats, but some were taken prisoner. The 24-ton French smack *J.M.J.* (captain and owner Joseph Jaffres, La Rochelle) departed Concarneau on 3 August 1918 with a fishing-convoy heading for the fishing grounds, escorted by the 302-ton French Navy trawler *Rosemonde* (1911 – V. Fourny, Bologne), but due to defects she fell behind and lost touch with the convoy; two other smacks also fell behind and she met up with them. On 15 August and 300 miles N80°W of Ushant (48°40'N–11°30'W), *U 90* fired ten to twelve shells at *J.M.J.*, which was immediately abandoned, the seven men taking to the dinghy. *U 90* then fired about another thirty rounds at the smack, of which seven or eight scored direct hits and she sank at 0900hrs (A. Fischdick's book on *U 90* asserts 0600hrs).

The seven men in the lifeboat were not questioned and *U 90* just passed by them at about 50-60m distance. The 742-ton US destroyer *Burrows* (1911) picked the men up at 1700hrs on the 16th; also onboard *Burrows* were survivors from two American steamers: *Montanan* and the newly built 5,799-ton *West Bridge* (1918 – U. S. Shipping Board, Seattle) The *West Bridge* was in an inward-bound convoy and on passage from Seattle and New York for Bordeaux when she suffered engine trouble and fell behind; however on 16 August *U 90* located and torpedoed her in the Bay of Biscay. Although heavily damaged, the ship reached Brest under her own steam later that day. Also on 16 August, Patzig sank the defensively armed 4,251-ton steamer *Escrick* (1910 – St Just S.S. Co. Ltd, London/Bideford) was 360 miles off Cape Finisterre when she succumbed to a torpedo, fired without warning. The ship was on passage from La Rochelle for Montreal in ballast; the 22-year-old 4th engineer officer, Ernest Arthur Frank from West Hartlepool, was drowned and the master was taken prisoner.

The 3,302-ton *Joseph Cudahy* (1917 – American-Italian Commercial Corp., New York), an American steam tanker, was torpedoed and sunk without warning on the 17th, about 700 miles from the English coast and casualties are unknown; this turbine-powered ship was in ballast and on passage from Bordeaux for New York.

U 90 jubilantly returned to Wilhelmshaven on 29 August 1918, travelling via the Orkney Isles, through the Skagerrak and Kattegat and along the Kiel Canal.

Kplt. Heinrich Jeß assumed command of the boat on 1 September 1918.

(7) On 29 September 1918, *U 90* left Kiel for operations off Southern Ireland. The outward voyage was via the Skagerrak, Orkney Isles, west of the Outer Hebrides and then down through the North Channel and Irish Sea. On 14 October, Jeß is suspected of sinking the 863-ton defensively armed British steamer *Dundalk* (1899 – Dundalk & Newry Steam Packet Co. Ltd, Dundalk), 5 miles from the Skerries, off Anglesey with a torpedo; she was carrying a crew of twenty-seven plus five

Sketch of *U 90* wreck by Pam Armstrong.

passengers and was delivering a 150-ton general cargo from Liverpool to Dundalk when a torpedo struck her without warning. The missile detonated the port side amidships at 2300hrs and she sank almost immediately. The mate and one other crewman managed to get away in one of the boats and they picked up five survivors from the sea; the survivors observed the submarine about 10 yards away from their boat before it quickly made off and was never seen again. The esort vessel *Stormcock* picked up the men in the boat, while two men, the 2nd engineer and a fireman, who floated off the sinking vessel on a raft, were rescued by the SS *Douglas* (Lancashire & Yorkshire Railway Co., Goole) and landed at Douglas, Isle of Man. Unfortunately, twenty-one crewmen, four cattlemen and one passenger were lost.

SOME OF THE MEN WHO DIED

Bennett, Edward, 38yrs, Fireman
Creegan, Margaret, 38yrs, Stewardess
Fox. Joseph, 27yrs, Cattleman
Halfpenny, Joseph, 38yrs, Fireman
Hernon, James, 40yrs, Fireman
Hughes, Patrick, 41yrs, Trimmer
Johnston, Edward, 41yrs, Chief Engineer
Kieran, Francis John, 20yrs, Able Seaman
Matthews, Peter, 46yrs, Steward
McKeown, William, 55yrs, Fireman
Melia, Patrick, 50yrs, 2nd Mate
Morgan, Vincent, 25yrs, Greaser
Muckean, John Michael, 47yrs, Fireman
O'Neill, Hugh, Master
Sloane, Peter Valentine, 17yrs, Ordinary Seaman
Stack, John, 33yrs, Fireman
Stowell, Daniel, 33yrs, Quartermaster
Tuite, Thomas, 21yrs, Donkeyman
Grey, Harold, Ordinary Seaman RNVR

On the 16th the 3,587-ton armed steamer *Pentwyn* (1910 – Pentwyn S.S. Co. Ltd, Cardiff) was also torpedoed and sunk without warning in St George's Channel; one crewman was lost on the ship, which was delivering African produce from Lagos, Nigeria to Liverpool. On 20 October 1918, the *Emily Millington*, a British sailing vessel of 111 tons, was captured and sunk by gunfire, 13 miles NNE from South Bishop.

U 90 returned to Kiel via the west coast of Ireland and the Hebrides, around the Orkney Isles, across the North Sea and through the Skagerrak and Kattegat, arriving at Kiel on 31 October 1918.

Heinrich Jeß officially stayed with the boat until 11 November and *U 90* was surrendered to the British in December 1918.

ADM 137/4002 ADM 137/2964 ADM 137/4019 CWGC

FINAL PATROL

U 90 is listed as being in Pembroke during February 1919. It would appear that *U 90* sank in the English Channel after her tow broke sometime in 1921, but other sources contend she was broken up at Bo'ness, sometime in 1919–1920. It follows that there is something of a question mark over the identity of the wreck, but her good condition points to a salvage rather than a war loss.

WRECK SITE

The wreck is orientated in an east to west direction and lies on a seabed of hard sand and rock, in a general depth of 31m, being the lowest astronomical depth. She is reported as fairly intact and leaning to starboard at an angle of about 45°. The wooden decking can be clearly seen and there are quite a few holes in the outer casing; the bow section is also missing, possibly marking where the boat hit the seabed. Between casing and pressure hull, pipe work, etc., can be seen. The two large intact deck guns, one positioned just forward of the conning tower and the other just aft of it, are both pointing skyward. The conning tower and one periscope are present (the other is in the Bembridge Museum). Lots of large conger eels inhabit nearly all of the crevices and holes in the wreck, as well as some large crabs. The diving planes, rudders and propellers are all there to view. *U 90* is not a war grave, but local diver/historian Mr Martin Woodward owns it. Anyone damaging or pilfering the wreck will undoubtedly be prosecuted.

UB 37, SM IMPERIAL U-BOAT

DATE OF LOSS: 14 January 1917
DEPTH: 58m
REFERENCE: 50 10.20N 01 38.40W
LOCATION: 27.6 nautical miles SW of St Catherine's Point, Isle of Wight

Type: UBII coastal torpedo attack boat **Builders**: Blohm & Voss, Hamburg for Kaiserliche Deutsche Marine **Ordered**: on 22 July 1915, within the batch of UB 30–UB 41 **Keel laid**: as Yard No.261 **Launched**: on 28 December 1915 **Commissioned**: by Oberleutnant zur See Hans Valentiner on 10 June 1916

TECHNICAL SPECIFICATIONS

Hull: single, saddle tank design **Surface displacement**: 274 tons **U/Dt**: 303 tons **LBDH**: 36.90m × 4.37m × 3.70m × 7.35m **Machinery**: 2 × 135ps Benz diesels **Props**: 2 bronze **S/Sp**: 9.06 knots **Op/R**: 7,030 nautical miles at 5 knots **Sub/R**: 45 nautical miles at 4 knots **U/Power**: 2 × 140ps electric motors gave 5.71 knots **Batteries**: lead/acid/accumulators. **Fuel/Cap**: 21 + 7 tons **Armament**: 2 bow 50.04cm (19.7in) torpedo tubes **Torpedoes**: 4 ×50.04cm (19.7in) **Guns**: 1 × 88mm (3.46in) forward facing **Ammo**: 120 rounds of 88mm **Mines**: none **Diving**: max-op-depth 50m and 30 sec to crash-dive **Complement**: 2 officers and 21 ratings

UB 37 was formally assigned to the Flandern U-Flottille on 5 July 1916, with Oblt.z.S. Hans Valentiner the commander from 17 May 1916 until 6 November 1916. Valentiner made seven patrols with the boat:

On 2 July 1916 *UB 37* departed Hamburg and transferred to Flanders, where she arrived on 5 July.

(2) *UB 37* sailed from Zeebrugge on 15 July 1916 and patrolled off the Tyne Roads to search for British warships, but having found none, Valentiner decided to wage war on merchant vessels instead. Off the River Tyne on 21 July 1916 the 191-ton Swedish freighter *ALF* was stopped and Valentiner made her crew dump its cargo overboard. Also on 21 July, the 388-ton Dutch motorised schooner *SAMSÖ* (1876 – Aktieselskabet Dansk Gemyse- & Kartoffeleksport, Copenhagen) was attacked with gunfire, 30 miles east, northeast from the Tyne, but she remained afloat and was towed into the Tyne on the 22nd; she was delivering timber from Halmstad, Sweden to Hull.

Four Scandanavian sailing vessels were captured and sunk offshore from Hartlepool on the 22nd, all carrying pit props: the 579-ton wooden-hulled Norwegian barque *Subra* (1875 – A/S Juno, Skien) was sailing from Drammen in Norway to West Hartlepool and was set on fire with explosives; the 222-ton wooden-hulled Swedish brigantine *Preference* (1861 – J. A. Samuelson, Mollosünd), which was voyaging from Göteborg to West Hartlepool, was stopped and set on fire; the 308-ton wooden-hulled Norwegian schooner *Bams* (1872 – A/S Bams, Sandefjord), en-route from Sandrfjord to West Hartlepool, was captured and set alight with explosives. The 302-ton wooden-hulled Swedish barque *IDA* (1870 – Carl Johannson, Kakmar), travelling from Kristiania to the Tyne, sank after being set on fire. On the 23rd, the 355-ton wooden-hulled Norwegian brig *Juno* (1850 – A/S Juno, Skien) was also captured and sunk after being set ablaze, some miles out off Hartlepool, while transporting pit props from Drammen to West Hartlepool.

UB 37 then returned to Flanders, arriving on the 24th.

(3) Leaving Zeebrugge on 5 August, *UB 37* went back to the Tyne Roads and captured and sunk the 1,246-ton Danish SS *Danevang* (1901 – Dampskibsselsk af 1915, Copenhagen) with gunfire on 9 August 1916, she was transporting deals from Karlsborg, Sweden to Hull. On 12 August, while voyaging from Fredrikshald to Sunderland with pit props, the 202-ton wooden-hulled Norwegian brig *Rufus* (1871 – A/S Rufus, Fredrikshald) was captured and sunk after being set alight, about 60 miles off Sunderland. Next day (13th), the 261-ton, wooden-hulled, three-masted Swedish barkentine *Pepita* (1869 – Chr Pettersson, Nyhamsläge) was sunk after being captured and set on fire, 25 miles off Longstone, in the Outer Farne Islands, while voyaging from Göteborg to Sunderland with railway sleepers. Later that day the 473-ton wooden-hulled Norwegian barque *Respit* (1877 – A/S Respet, Kristiania) was captured and set ablaze in the North Sea with explosives, at about 54° 48'N 01° 15'E; she was transporting pit props from Brevik, Norway to Hull. While bound from Filtvedt near Kristiania, Norway to Hartlepool with pit props, the 104-ton wooden-hulled Norwegian schooner *Fremad* (1870 – A/S Fremad, Fredrikshald) was sunk after being captured and set on fire, 50 miles north of Hartlepool.

UB 37 returned to Flanders on 15 August 1916.

(4) Valentiner left Flanders with the boat on 18 August 1916 and patrolled in support of a German High Fleet sortie off Terschelling Bank along with *UB 5, UB 12, UB 16* and *UB 19*, then returned to port on the 25th.

(5) Leaving Zeebrugge on 8 September 1916, *UB 37* patrolled off the Hook of Holland. The 400-ton Dutch motor vessel *Zeemeeuw* (1911 – N.V. tot Exploit. van de Dubbelschroef Motorb. Zeemeeuw, Rotterdam) was loaded with food for England when it was captured in the North Sea and taken into Zeebrugge; a prize court then condemned it. While in tow of the SS *Batavier II* to Hamburg, the vessel went adrift when the *Batavier II* was attacked and sunk off Texel by HM S/M *E55* on 27 July 1917; Dutch fishermen and tugs retrieved the *Zeemeeuw* and took it into Den Helder, where it was returned to the owners.

UC 37 returned to Flanders on 13 September 1916.

(6) *UB 37* sailed from Zeebrugge on 21 September 1916 and patrolled the English Channel, where Valentiner sank three steamers and a fishing boat. The old 805-ton coastal steamer *Dresden* (1865 – Leith, Hull & Hamburg Steam Packet Co.) was voyaging from the Tyne to Rouen with coke when it was captured by *UB 37* and sunk by explosive charges. The steam coaster *Pearl* (1904 – Wetherall S.S. Co. Ltd, Goole) of 613 tons was also captured and sunk by explosives that same day, while on passage from Llanelly for Tréport with coal. The 60-ton French fishing smack *Oceanien* was

captured and sunk off Start Point, on 24 September. Valentiner also captured and sunk the 1,743-ton French SS *Afrique* (1886 – Soc. Commerciale & Maritime, Oran) with explosives on the 25th; she was in transit with pit props from Bayonne for Barry.

UB 37 returned to Zeebrugge on 28 September.

(7) Valentiner's last patrol with *UB 37* was to the English Channel, leaving port on 22 October 1916. Just one small schooner, the 128-ton British *TWIG* (1875), en-route from Guernsey to Southampton with stone, was captured and sunk by explosives, 15 miles off Alderney on 24 October.

UB 37 arrived back at Flanders on 1 November.

Oblt.z.S. Paul Günther assumed command of the boat on 7 November 1916 and Hans Valentiner took over the command of the new *UC 71*. He was later killed on *UB 56* (*see* vol. 1). Günther had previously served as commander of *UC 6*, for about two months.

(8) *UB 37* departed Flanders with her new CO on 12 November 1916 and operated around the Hoofden area of the North Sea. Two small British fishing smacks were captured off Smiths Knoll Spar Buoy and sunk by gunfire on the 13th, the 63-ton cutter *Our Boys* (1885) and the 50-ton Lowestoft cutter *Superb* (1902). On the 15th, Günther stopped a Dutch ship and then a Swedish one, but after checking their papers and cargoes, allowed both to continue on their way. Early on the 16th, the boat was involved in a gun skirmish with a trawler, but both vessels escaped unharmed. Later that day, *UB 37* arrived back in port on the 16th.

(9) On 26 November 1916, *UB 37* left Flanders for operations in the English Channel and out as far as Ushant, where Günther sank nine vessels, including three steamers. On the 28th, *UB 37* tried to halt the 2,286-ton defensively armed steamship *Ballater* (1894 – Underwood Shipping Co. Ltd, Liverpool), but she had more fire-power and made off at high speed. Also on the 28th, three fishing smacks *Amphitrite* of 44 tons, the 36-ton cutter *Catena* and the 38-ton *Provident*, were captured off Portland Bill; the first two were sunk by gunfire, but the latter one by explosive charges (no lives were lost). The 42-ton fishing smack *Sea Lark* was also captured on the 28th, but off Berry Head, and sunk by gunfire. *UB 37* then found the 4,941-ton steam tanker *Swazi* (1901 – Ellerman & Bucknall Steamship Co. Ltd, London), but it immediately opened fire on the U-boat and Günther had to dive to escape. Two days later Günther captured the 42-ton smack *Concord* off Start Point and sunk it with explosives. While en-route from Glasgow to Gibraltar with coal on 1 December 1916, the Norwegian steamship *Erich Lindøe* (1912 – Peder Lindøe, Haugesund) was captured in the Atlantic and scuttled wih explosives. The SS *Fofo* (1892 – P. Macris & E. D. Hadjiconstantis, Syra), a Greek ship of 2,615 tons, was on a voyage from the Tyne for St Vincent, when she was captured and scuttled with explosives 100 miles off the Isles of Scilly. The *Halfdan* (1906 – Aktieselskab D/S Selsk. Skjold, Copenhagen), a 1,305-ton Danish steamer, was captured and then torpedoed and sunk off the Eddystone at 50° 00'N 04° 20'W; she was transporting coke from Newcastle to Livorno, in north-west Italy. On 7 December, Günther captured and sunk the 1,948-ton French barque *Marguerite Dollfus* (1898 – Société des Voiliers Français), 35 miles northwest of Guernsey at 49° 45'N 03° 40'W; it was in ballast and en-route from Le Havre to Port de France, Martinique in the West Indies.

UB 37 returned to Zeebrugge on 9 December.

FINAL PATROL

(10) On 2 January 1917 Günther took *UB 37* out of Zeebrugge for a sortie along the French coast in the English Channel. The 573-ton Norwegian steam coaster *Asta* (1891 – Rafens Rederi Aktieselskapet, Holmestrand) was captured and sunk with explosives off the Casquets on the 5th; she was in ballast travelling from Duclais to Barry Roads. Two days later the Norwegian steamer *Hansi* (1914 – A/S D/S Hansi, Bergen) of 1,142 tons was captured off the Ile Vierge and scuttled with explosives; she was en-route from Newport, Monmouth to Gibraltar with coal. Günther then sank two Danish steamships: the 2,043-ton *Tuborg* (1915 – Aktieselskab Dampskibsselskab. Selsk af 1896, Copenhagen) was captured and scuttled with explosive charges on the 10th, while en-route from Sunderland to Lisbon with coal; the 1,993-ton *Norma* (1884 – Dampskibsselskabet Orion, Copenhagen), on passage from Gandia, Spain for London with fruit and general cargo, on 14 January.

However in the western Channel, Nemesis was fast approaching in the unlikely form of a battered old tramp steamer. *Manford*, alias HMS *Penshurst* (Cdr F. Grenfell R.N. Rtd), was actually

An unidentified Q-ship, *c.* 1917 (c/f Keble Chatterton, *The Q-Ships.*) Above: gun ready for action. Below: Gun swung in and hidden from view.

a Q-ship, designated Q7. She appeared to be a 1,191-ton cargo ship with funnel aft and bridge amidships but appearances were deceptive. She also carried two concealed 6-pounder guns, a couple of 3-pounders housed within her after deckhouse and a mighty 12-pounder gun disguised inside a dummy boat just forward of the funnel. She was well supplied with depth charges and, should the need apply, could change her appearance by means of altering masts and funnel banding. Her crew was drawn largely from Wales. Despite the un-heroic lines, *Penshurst* had already accounted for *UB 19* in November 1916. When Q7 left left Devonport, Grenfell and his crew could not have guessed that fate had placed *UB 37* on a converging course. The dry language of the log can only hint at the epic confrontation which ensued:

Log of Q7 – 14 January 1917 – Cdr F Grenfell:

15.50 Submarine sighted on port beam, distance about 3,000 yards
15.52 Action Stations

A rather poor-quality photograph of HMS *Penshurst*. (Author's collection)

15.55 Submarine opened fire. Submarine firing at frequent intervals and closing rapidly
      [At this point Penshurst stopped engines and the 'panic party' went into action. Lifeboats were
      lowered. The submarine, *UB 37* closed rapidly off Penshurst's starboard bow. She was firing at
      intervals and when range closed to 700 yards the shelling began to tell. One German shell struck
      an awning pole on the bridge but another killed two of the gunners at the hidden 6-pounder gun,
      wounding two other men. The engine room telegraph was also shattered.]
16.21 Enemy shell struck fore bridge
16.22 Enemy shell struck fore lower bridge killing two ratings and wounding two others
16.24 Opened fire
      [Two lyddite shells from the 12-pounder gun fired in quick succession struck the base of the sub-
      marine's conning tower, which disintegrated. Three shells from Penshurst's starboard 3-pounder
      crashed into the conning tower and ruptured *UB 37*'s pressure hull]
16.26 Submarine sank
16.30 Dropped depth charges
20.40 Returned Portland

Grenfell noted the following casualties in his log: G.F. Burrens, Able Seaman of the Royal Fleet
Reserve aged 32 years and J. E. Garret, Signalman of the RNVR aged 21 years. There were no
survivors from the submarine crew.

Now under the command of Lt Cde Naylor DSO★, *Penshurst*'s incredible luck finally ran out on
Christmas Eve 1917 when she was torpedoed by *U 110* in the western approaches. Fortunately all
of her crew survived. She had been scarred by war and she ultimately paid the price for her audacity,
but *Penshurst* was credited with sinking two U-boats. Not a bad score for a dirty old collier.

ADM 53/56985 NARA T1022, Roll 61,71, PG61795, PG61934 U-Boot-Ehrenmal Möltenort
CWGC

THE MEN WHO DIED IN UB 37

Bergerhausen, M. U-Obermatrose
Bihr, Thomas U-Heizer

Brall, Christof U-Heizer
Burghardt, W. U-Maschinistenmaat
Ernst, Erhard U-F.T.Gast
Günther, Paul Oberleutnant zur See
Hanisch, W. U-Obermaschinistenmaat
Holzhüter, W. Leutnant zur See d.Res
Kamm, W. U-Heizer
Kotzem, Walter U-Bootsmannsmaat d.Res
Lepold, W. U-Matrose
Lorenzen, Th. U-Oberbootsmannsmaat de.Res
Ludwinsky, O. U-Maschinist Anw
Lüder, Wilhelm U-Heizer
Mattern, B. Marine Ingenieur Ober.Asp
Naumann, Arthur U-Heizer
Rother, Kurt U-Matrose
Schlothauer, H. U-Maschinistenmaat
Torreck, Paul U-Maschinistenmaat
Tüting, A. U-Maschinistenmaat
Ziesel, Albert U-Matrose

WRECK SITE

Diver/historian Innes McCartney discovered the wreck of *UB 37* in 1999. It lies with a list to starboard, on a seabed of gravel and pebbles, in a general depth of 60m, being the lowest astronomical
depth. It is said to be completely intact and covered in soft corals, with one of the propellers visible.
The deck gun is still in position and both torpedo bow caps are open, suggesting, as Innes observes,
that 'HMS *Penhurst* might well have been about to receive a torpedo'. The wreck will also be classed
as a war grave.

For over forty-three years officialdom believed that *Swordfish* and her crew had been lost
'somewhere off Brest'. In reality she lay very much closer to home…

SWORDFISH, HM SUBMARINE

DATE OF LOSS: 7 November 1940
DEPTH: 40m
REFERENCE: 50 28'.783 N 001 21'.950 W
LOCATION: 10 miles SSW of St Catherine's Point, Isle of Wight

Type: Swordfish Class, medium patrol submarine 1929 Programme 'S' Class Group-I type   *Pennant*:
No-61.S   *Ordered*: postponed until 2 July 1930, because of the London Naval Treaty   *Builders*:
HM Dockyard at Chatham   *Keel laid*: on 1 December 1930   *Launched*: on 10 November
1931   *Completed*: 24 November 1932   *Commissioned*: 16 September 1932 '*With Sword and With
Courage*' – the motto of HM S/M *Swordfish*

TECHNICAL SPECIFICATIONS

Hull: Admiralty saddle-tank type with main ballast tanks arranged outside the pressure hull   *Surface
displacement*: 640 tons   *U/Dt*: 927 tons   *LBD*: 61.72m × 7.31m × 3.63m   *Machinery*: 2 × 6-cyl-
inder Admiralty pattern diesels of 1,550bhp   *Props*: 2 bronze   *S/Sp*: 13.75 knots   *Op/R*: 3,700
nautical miles at 10 knots   *Sub/R*: 106 nautical miles at 4 knots   *U/Power*: 2 × 650hp General
Electric motors gave 10 knots   *Batteries*: Exide 224 cells lead/acid each weighing 95.9 tons   *Fuel/
Cap*: 38 tons   *Armament*: 6 × forward 53.34cm (21in) torpedo tubes (no stern)   *Torpedoes*: 12 ×
53.34cm (210in).   *Guns*: 1 × 76.20mm (3-in/45) Quick-Firing Mk-I deck gun and 1 × 7.696mm
(0.303in) Lewis machine-gun   *Ammo*: 160 rounds of 76.20mm   *Mines*: none   *Diving*: max-op-

The 11,420-ton liner *Cuba*, which was sunk by Kapitänleutnant Ernst Cordes in the Kriegsmarine U-boat *U 1195* (see page 108). (Author's collection)

Type VIIC/41 U-boat (*U 995*) conning tower and wintergarten. (Courtesy Kevin Belcher of Swindon)

depth 91.44m (300ft) and 60.96m (200ft) test-depth   ***Complement***: peacetime – 4 officers and 23 ratings, wartime: 4 officers and 34 ratings

The six tubes were arranged internally in the bows, resulting in a pronounced oval bow section. Six reload torpedoes were stored in the stowage compartment. *Swordfish* originally carried one 76.20mm (3-in/45) Quick-Firing H.A. Mk-X deck gun on a disappearing mounting placed forward of the conning tower. This boat was the third RN vessel of the name *Swordfish*, the first being in 1895.

The 'S' Class underwent gradual improvements and in time went on to become the most numerous single type submarine ever built for the Royal Navy (sixty-two in all between 1931 and 1945). *Swordfish* was, however, one of the first of the class.

Between 1932 and 1935 the boat alternated between Portsmouth and Portland, operating with the 6th Flotilla from 1935 to 1939. Lt Cecil Crouch took command of the boat on 24 July 1939 (*see Thetis/Thunderbolt*, vol. 3). In the high summer of 1939 the 'S' boats took up war stations at Dundee, patrolling the Obrestad line. In November the boat joined the 3rd Submarine Flotilla, formed at Harwich on 17 November 1939 (*see* vol. 1).

Swordfish left Harwich with Lt Crouch on 1 September 1939 and proceeded to 'Position -5'. On the 14th an unknown submarine attacked the boat, but luckily the torpedo missed. She returned home that same day, having suffered no damage. It was revealed later that HM S/M *Sturgeon* had made the attack in error, in what would have been a repeat of the *Oxley* incident.

With Crouch in command, *Swordfish* departed Harwich on 20 September and sailed to 'Zone E', before returning on 3 October 1939. Later that day she left Harwich for Dundee, arriving the next day. A refit was carried out on the boat at Rosyth from 13 February 1940 prior to the boat sailing to Scapa Flow for a working-up exercise, arriving on 16 February 1940. *Swordfish* sailed to Blyth on 12 March and arrived the next day. She passed to the administration control of 6th Submarine Flotilla and Lt P.J. Cowell assumed command of the boat. Lt Cowell took her on the following patrols:

On 22 March 1940 she left Blyth and sailed to 'Zone A1', before returning to Blyth on 9 April. Departing Blyth on 16 April, she sailed to Arendal in Norway, in the course of which, she was bombed and depth charged. Cowell returned to Blyth on 28 April.

At a time when the 6th Flotilla was suffering grievous losses, *Swordfish* was considered a lucky boat. This is borne out by events surrounding her 16 April patrol when the Germans were intensifying their stranglehold on Scandinavian waters. Lt Cowell's report reads like a microcosm of all the perils facing British submarines operating during this period. She suffered a near-miss bomb attack by aircraft on the 19th. On the 26th she actually struck a mine on reaching periscope depth! What follows is just one extract from her patrol report:

Saturday 20 April
10.20 Bombed at periscope depth by aircraft
10.25 Heard HE. Came up to investigate and found Swordfish surrounded by five German destroyers and one large escort vessel. Depth charged until 1230 causing leak in 'Z' tank Stopped all machinery
1300 Sighted smoke of convoy to the SE. Had to go deep again…

(5) Leaving Blyth on 10 May *Swordfish* proceeded to 'Zone A3', returning to Blyth on the 25th.

(6) On 6 June 1940 she left Blyth and sailed to 'Zone H2' where she was bombed by 'friendly' aircraft, before returning to Blyth on 12 July 1940.

(7) She sailed from Blyth on 7 July and patrolled 'Zone H2', returning to Blyth on the 12th.

(8) After leaving base on 27 July she sailed to 'Zone E1' and rescued the crew of the Norwegian yacht *Marski*, before arriving at Blyth on 8 August.

(9) Three weeks later on the 27th, *Swordfish* sailed to 'Zone J' for a patrol and returned to Blyth on 13 September. Following this patrol the boat was attached to the 5th Submarine Flotilla at Blockhouse. *Swordfish* was certainly regarded as a happy boat with an efficient veteran crew, many drawn from the northeast of England. Just before the move to Blockhouse, at least one of the submariners suffered a premonition of disaster. Petty Officer Trevor Dando gave AB 'Shorty' Cranmer of *H31* (*see* vol. 3) his much-prized scouting wristwatch. Bernard Cranmer treasured it for the rest of his life.

(10) On 26 September 1940, *Swordfish* departed Blockhouse for 'Zone W2' and attacked a German MTB boat with a torpedo during the voyage. Following an abortive attack on the E-boats *Falke* and *Kondor* off Cap de la Hogue, she returned to Blockhouse on 5 October.

Lt M. Langley (29yrs) assumed command of *Swordfish* on 14 October 1940. Lt Langley was a rising young star within the Submarine Service constellation of new battle-hardened skippers. Langley fast gained a reputation for daring and 'offensive spirit'.

(11) Leaving Blockhouse on 21 October, *Swordfish* sailed for a patrol at 'Zone W2', where Langley attacked an unknown 5,000-ton motor vessel amid a convoy of eight vessels. Langley heard one explosion and saw black smoke. The boat returned to Blockhouse on the 30th.

FINAL PATROL

(12) *Swordfish* sailed from Blockhouse on 7 November 1940 to relieve *USK* off Brest, in an area where enemy invasion vessels were suspected of concentrating. Nothing more was heard from her. In March 1941 the Admiralty confirmed the boat's loss with all hands to next of kin. On 10 June 1941, the family of Lt Langley were presented with a posthumous DSC for the 21 October attack. For decades the families of all concerned believed that the boat lay somewhere in her billet off Ushant. However on 17 July 1983 celebrated Diver/Historian Mr Martin Woodward of Bembridge Maritime Museum discovered the last resting place of Lt Langley and his crew. A few hours after sailing, the submarine had detonated a mine, while diving to catch a trim off St Catherine's Point on the Isle of Wight. This mine had probably been laid by an E-boat the day previously. At any rate, one of our submarines is no longer missing.

REMEMBERED ON THE PLYMOUTH, CHATHAM AND PORTSMOUTH NAVAL MEMORIALS

Apps, David C/JX 141903 Able Seaman
Blackmore, William George D/SSX 17741 Able Seaman
Bush, Roland William C/J 109431 (MiD) Chief P.O.
Buttress, Harry D/KX 81751 Leading Stoker
Cox, James Frank P/J 60278 Leading Seaman
Crean, W. Leading Seaman (Torpedo-Branch)
Dando, Trevor John Bladon C/J 105215 PO
Davies, Harold P/JX 127080 (MiD) Leading Signalman
Fry, Alexander Frederick Lieutenant RNR
Gratton, Francis Arthur John D/JX 126186 Able Seaman
Hollingworth, Arthur Charles D/JX 151882 L/Seaman
Jarret, Thomas John Charles C/KX 92020 Stoker
Jones, Edward Lewington P/JX 127991 Able Seaman
Kellet, Oswald D/J 98620 Petty Officer
Kennard, Victor Albert C/K 59839 Petty Officer Stoker
Langley, Michael Armitage (DSC) Lieutenant
Lee, William Thomas D/MX 45635 (MiD) E.R.A.2nd
Loines, Charles Walter Leonard C/JX 179106 Ord Seaman
McMann, Thomas D/JX 134363 Leading Telegraphist
Millerick, Frank Frederick C/KX 79882 Stoker
Morrison, Charles Archibald C/KX 84966 L/Seaman

Nichols, Richard Thomas P/J 58636 Able Seaman
Northwood, Arthur D/JX 135376 P.O. Telegraphist
O'Neill, Joseph Patrick D/KX 84929 Stoker.1st
Owen, Amos John D/MX 52169 E.R.Artificer.3rd
Plested, Edward D/KX 86488 Stoker.1st
Preddy, Leonard John D/KX 83716 Leading Stoker
Ratcliffe, Michael Eric Price Lieutenant
Selway, Harry Thomas Warrant Engineer
Shipley, James Henry Newton P/JX 145303 Able Seaman
Souris, Edward George C/KX 83535 Stoker.1st
Sproat, David Jameson C/KX 83324 Stoker.1st
Spurgeon, Harold Vincent D/MX 46961 E.R. Artificer.2nd
Stacey, Harry Arthur Lieutenant (Bronze Medal)
Stapley, Ernest William P/MX 56585 E.R.Artificer.4th
Tonks, Leonard D/J 112969 Leading Telegraphist
Ward, Frederick C/MX 46205 (MiD) ERA
Williams, Norman Charles D/JX 142211 Telegraphist
Williams, Reginald Herbert C/JX 148322 Able Seaman
Wood, John Hardy D/JX 134058 Telegraphist
Young, Jack C/JX 144322 Leading Seaman

ADM 173/14433-16568

WRECK SITE

The wreck lies with its bows to the west, on a seabed of shingle, sand and gravel, in a general depth of 40m (131ft), being the lowest astronomical depth. It is broken into two sections, just forward of the gun mounting, with the stern standing upright. However the bow section, including the forward hydroplanes, has fallen over onto its port side. The hydroplanes are deployed and the bridge telegraphs are set at 'slow-ahead'. This evidence confirms that the boat was mined while dived and steering due west at the time. It seems likely that the men in the fore ends and control room died in the explosion and subsequent flooding. An official naval communiqué of 10 August 1983, states that the after-escape hatch is open. This seems to suggest that an escape using DSEA was mounted. The reader has only to recall the *Umpire* and *Truculent* cases (vol. 1) to understand the small chances of survival, without assistance standing by. There are no British reports of bodies being washed ashore during this period and we can only assume that the tide carried them into the Channel. Driven by an all-too-real fear that sports divers will violate the sanctity of this war grave, Mr Woodward has never disclosed the position of the wreck; and nor will the authors. Together, the crew of *Swordfish* had braved the worst of the North Sea war and together as a crew, on patrol for eternity, they remain.

(Mr Woodward has a permanent display with photographs of and artefacts from *Swordfish* in the Bembridge Maritime and Shipwreck Museum. There is also material on *A1* and *UB 81* on show. The Submarine Museum also has *Swordfish* relics including her battery plate and the medals of Tel Williams.)

UPSTART, HM SUBMARINE

DATE SUNK: 9 July 1957
DEPTH: 31m
REFERENCE: 50 30.37N 01 32.75W
LOCATION: 10.30 nautical miles SW from St Catherine's Point, Isle of Wight

Type: 'U' Class British small patrol submarine of Group II series   *Pennant*: No P.65.
Ordered: for 1941 War Emergency Programme   *Builders*: Vickers-Armstrong, Barrow-in-Furness for Royal Navy   *Keel laid*: as Yard No.838 on 17 March 1942   *Launched*: on 24 November 1942   *Completed*: on 3 April 1943   *Name*: In February 1943 her name was changed to *Upstart*, first boat of that name

TECHNICAL SPECIFICATIONS

Hull: Admiralty saddle-tank type with main ballast tanks arranged outside the pressure hull   *Surface displacement*: 545 tons   *U/Dt*: 740 tons   *LBD*: 59.99m × 4.87m × 4.41m   *Machinery*: 2 × Davey-Paxman 6RXS diesels, each rated at 400bhp, coupled to a 275kw generator (diesel-electric-drive).   *Props*: 2 bronze   *S/Sp*: 11.25 knots   *Op/R*: 5,000 nautical miles at 10 knots   *Sub/R*: 120 nautical miles at 2 knots   *U/Power*: 2 × Metro-Vickers electric motors rated at 412bhp gave 9 knots   *Batteries*: Exide lead/acid   *Fuel/Cap*: 55 tons   *Armament*: 4 × 53.34cm (21in) bow torpedo tubes   *Torpedoes*: 8 × 53.34cm (21in) (**or**) *Mines*: 6 M.Mk II   *Guns*: 1 × 76.20mm (3in/45) Quick Firing Mk I deck gun mounted just in front of conning tower and 3 × 0.303in Lewis or Vickers machine guns   *Ammo*: 160 rounds of 76.20mm   *Diving*: max-op-depth 60.96m (200ft)   *Complement*: 33 (wartime)

On completion, *Upstart* joined the 3rd Flotilla (HMS *Forth* at Holy Loch). Lt Paul Charles Chapman DSO, DSC★ (formerly of *Torbay*), CO from 29 December 1942 to January 1945, was her only RN wartime commander.

On 11 September 1943 *Upstart* sailed for the Mediterranean.

She was one of the last boats to use Algiers (HMS *Maidstone*, 8th Flotilla). From November *Upstart* joined the 10th Flotilla (HMS *Talbot*) at Malta. Although a late starter with the 10th Flotilla, Chapman and his crew set a blistering pace. As Paul Chapman later observed: '*We had been given an expensive piece of kit by His Majesty. We must do the best we could with it*'.

Crest of HM SM *Upstart*.
(Author's collection)

On 14 September 1943, crews were taken off before the fishing boats *Grotte de Bethlehem* and *Torpille* were sunk by gunfire. Both vessels had been acting suspiciously in a forbidden zone. On 2 November 1943 *Upstart* attacked a 3,000-ton vessel off Cap Sicie. The three torpedoes exploded harmlessly on the shore. However, another attack was carried out on this same patrol on 6 November 1943 when *Upstart* missed a 5,000-ton merchantman off Cap Cepet with three torpedoes. During late December 1943, generator problems delayed her joining the rest of the flotilla, which had moved to Maddalena (HMS *Talbot II*). When the repairs were complete she joined them, staying with the 10th Flotilla until it was disbanded on 12 September 1944. *Upstart* proceeded to menace Axis supply lines off the French Riviera ports. On 14 January 1944 the boat left Malta for La Maddelana.

On 21 January 1944 *Upstart* missed a large tanker with a torpedo off Cape Camarat, near Saint Tropez.

Sharing Ben Bryant's 'gun fever', Lt Chapman responded with a couple of fierce shore bombardments. On 23 January he surfaced the boat close inshore to shell a suspected seaplane base in the Gulf of Napoule. On 27 January, a second seaplane base at St Raphael received the same treatment.

Upstart torpedoed and sunk the 1,794-ton auxiliary minelayer *Niedersachsen* (Kriegsmarine) off Toulon, in position 43° 02'N 06° 01'E on 15 February 1944. (As the Italian *ACQUI*, the ship was requisitioned by the Royal Italian Navy in July 1943 and converted to an auxiliary convoy escort, but was scuttled by her crew at La Spezia on 9 September 1943. German salvors refloated the vessel and then re-built it as minelayer *Niedersachsen* in December 1943.) On 2 May 1944 she attempted to torpedo a ship behind the breakwater in Nice harbour, but missed. It has been claimed that on 21 May 1944, *Upstart* torpedoed and sank the 2,955-ton *Saumur* (German Government), half a mile east of Port Vendres. (The wreck was refloated in 1950 and scrapped.) We can state with more certainty that *Upstart* hit the 2,939-ton Italian steamship *Pascoli* ('Tirrenia' Società Anonima di Navigazoione, Fiume) off Cap Cepet on 28 July 1944, but the torpedoes turned out to be duds. (On 3 August 1944, a torpedo fired by the French submarine *Curie* damaged the *Pascoli*.)

The crew adopted a Sardinian billy goat called 'Percy'. This was not unusual in itself, but in order to differentiate him from 'common' army mascots, the crew of *Upstart* painted their 'boat goat' blue. (As an aside, many submarine crews kept animal mascots ranging from the more predictable cats, ducks, dogs, hawks and budgies to a couple of baby reindeer, 'Pollyanna' and 'Minnie', thrust upon the bemused crews of *Trident* and *Tigris* as gifts from their Russian hosts in 1942. Pollyanna survived the long journey from Polyarnoe to Blyth to end up in the London Zoo. Minnie, alas, died on arrival at Holy Loch and was served up to the crew with chips.)

On 18 September 1944 *Upstart* left Malta for a brief stint in the Aegean, before arriving back on 10 October following an uneventful patrol.

Upstart left Gibraltar for home in convoy MKS.67 on 17 November 1944, arriving at Portland on 25 November 1944. At this stage her operational life was effectively over. From June to January 1945 she is listed as a training boat at Blyth, after which she was transferred to the Royal Hellenic Navy (Greek Navy) and renamed *Amfitrite*. In 1952 she was repatriated to serve as a Blockhouse training boat from 1953 to 1955.

ADM 199/1814 ADM173/18372-20206
With additional information kindly supplied by Andy Mair.

FINAL PATROL

On 29 July 1957 the boat was sunk as A/S target off the Isle of Wight.

WRECK SITE

The wreck lies on a seabed of gravel and shingle, in a general depth of 31m, being the lowest astronomical depth. Divers located the wreck in 1975 at which time it was intact and complete. However, since that date, commercial salvage has taken place and the brass/bronze conning tower has been removed. It is still reasonably intact, with the inner conning tower hatch visible. The casing is coated in anemones and large shoals of fish have adopted the wreck as a sanctuary. Some years ago the Brewers Arms Sub Aqua Club detached a piece of wood from the wreck. They had it carved in the shape of a submarine and presented it to Commander Chapman as a souvenir.

Note: an area to the south of the Isle of Wight was designated as a disposal ground for U-boats from 28 June to 1 July 1921: *U 122*, *U 123* (28 June), *U 152* (30 June) *U 153*, *UB 122* (30 June) and *UC 110* (1 July).

U 480, KRIEGSMARINE U-BOAT

DATE OF LOSS: between 29 January and 20 February 1945
DEPTH: 55m
REFERENCE: 50 22'.139 N 001 44'.243 W
LOCATION: 16 nautical miles SSE of Anvil Point, Swanage

Type: VIIC ocean-going attack boat   **Builders**: Deutsche Werke AG, Kiel-Gaarden for Kriegsmarine   **Ordered**: on 10 April 1941, within the batch of *U 475–U 480*   **Keel laid**: as Yard No.311 on 8 December 1942   **Launched**: on 14 August 1943   **Commissioned**: by Oberleutnant zur See Hans-Joachim Förster on 6 October 1943   **Feldpost No**: M 53 621

TECHNICAL SPECIFICATIONS

See page 342.

OTHER TECHNICAL FITTINGS

U 480 was fitted with *schnorchel*. She was also one of nine boats covered in two 2mm layers of a black rubbery anti-ASDIC coating called *Alberich* (*see* Glossary). It was actually a success, but worked best at 150m. Following June 1944 when U-boats were operating in shallow British coastal waters, the value of *Alberich* was questionable.

Hans-Joachim Förster was born in Gross-Köris, Teltow, south of Berlin on 20 February 1920 and commenced his naval career in 1938. He began his service on a mine-clearance ship working in the Baltic and North Sea and was eventually promoted to Oberleutnant zur See on 1 April 1943.

U 480 was assigned to 5.U-Flottille at Kiel as *Ausbildungsboot* with Oblt. Hans-Joachim Förster the commander from 6 October 1943.

On 18 May 1944, *U 480* departed Kiel and sailed to Arendal, near Kristiansand, where she arrived on 19th. (During May the uncoated *U 247* and *U 999* took part in sea-trials off Norway for comparisons against *U 480*.)

Following a change of a propeller at Bergen, *U 480* departed that port on 10 June for operations in the English Channel. On the 13th a Canso aircraft of 162 Canadian Squadron, piloted by Flight-Lieutenant Laurence Sherman attacked the boat. The Type VII U-boat had sharp teeth. *U 480*'s Flak gunners riddled the plane with holes and Sherman was forced to ditch. (Five out of the eight of the plane's crew clambered into a rubber dinghy, but Sherman and two others were killed. Four of the men eventually died in the dinghy but on 22 June and ten days after the crash, J.E. Roberts, the lone survivor, was picked up by a Norwegian whaler. Roberts was turned over to the Germans north of the Shetlands on 11 June. It is worth noting that Lt Laurence Sherman had earlier attacked and sunk the new VIIC boat *U 980*, commanded by 28-year-old Herman Dahmns. The plane dropped four depth charges on the U-boat. Sherman reported debris and about thirty-five men on the surface, but none survived.

Owing to lack of information on the operational situation in the Channel, BdU ordered Förster to abort his voyage to the invasion area and put into Brest, where he arrived on 7 July. This was a sensible move when one considers that two boats which had attempted to operate in the Western Channel, *U 243* and *U 678*, were both lost.

(3) *U 480* left Brest on 3 August 1944 and set course for operations in the English Channel. Her billet was BF32, between Cherbourg and the Isle of Wight. On the 18th Förster made an unsuccessful attack on a convoy, northeast of Barfleur. However, three days later at 1140hrs (Continental time) on 21st, Förster torpedoed the 925-ton Canadian corvette HMCS *Alberni*. The ship sank within minutes in position 50° 18'N 00° 51'W. Fifty-nine men were killed, but British MTBs rescued thirty-one survivors. The following day at 1606hrs (Continental time) Förster torpedoed and sank the 850-ton RN fleet minesweeper *Loyalty* (ex-*Rattler*) in position 50° 09'N 00° 41'W and twenty men were killed.

On 8 August, the 7,134-ton British Liberty ship OHMS *Fort Yale* (Ministry of War Transport, London) was sailing with convoy ETC 72 when she detonated a mine near L8 Buoy, at position 49° 25.24'N 0° 27.30'W; the 294-ton RN tug *Hudson* and the 1,117-ton American steamer *Farallon* was in the process of towing her from Juno Beach, Normandy towards Portsmouth, when Förster hit her with a torpedo on 23 August. The ship sank at position 50° 23'N 00° 55'W and a naval signalman was lost, but the master, Captain George William Mortimer, fifty-seven crewmen and eight DEMS gunners were rescued by Landing Craft and taken to Portsmouth.

> *U 480*, whose fate was beginning to cause anxiety, reported situation from operations area in Channel. Traffic in BF 3270 as before. Steamer convoys loaded only at night, empty during the day. Always a number of landing craft, heavy patrol, anti-submarine units. Location by explosive soundings. Five metres over bottom during depth charge attack. 'Alberich' best method. Boat lay in operational area 17 days and sank 14,000 GRT and 2 frigates. Also explosion heard after 9 minutes 20 seconds after firing LUT 3-spread. Remained submerged for 40 days.

BdU War Diary, 11 September

In the afternoon of 25 August, coastal convoy FTM 1774 over-ran the U-boat as she travelled submerged, but Förster still managed to torpedo the straggling 5,712-ton SS *Orminster* (South American Saint Line, Cardiff) at 1443hrs (Continental time), 35 miles northwest of Cap d'Antifer; she was on passage from Juno Beach, Normandy for the Isle of Wight (Convoy FTM 74) and sank at position 50° 09'N 00° 44'W. The corvette HMS *Pennyworte* (K.111) (Lt W.P. Hart) and HM trawler *Damsay* (T.208) rescued the master, Captain Harold Gittens, forty-three crewmen, twelve DEMS gunners and an army storekeeper and landed them at Portsmouth, but one crewman and five gunners were lost.

THE SIX MEN WHO DIED

Heward, Edward William Henry P/JX 33812,6 Able Seaman HMS President III (22yrs)
Howard, Albert D/JX 391830 ,Able Seaman HMS President III (21yrs)
Toby, Thomas, Fireman and Trimmer (42yrs)
Wagstaffe, Ronald P/JX 444873, Able Seaman HMS President III (19yrs)

U 480 proceeded to Norway and on 4 October 1944 arrived at Trondheim on the Atlantic coast, to a hero's welcome. Admiral Dönitz presented Förster with a *Ritterkreuz* (Knight's Cross) on the 18 October 1944. Forster's second patrol had been a triumph. He was highly praised by BdU for his '*skilled, precise navigation under most trying circumstances, smooth snorchel deployment, zeal, panache and strictly-led internal operations*'. The KTB entry for 6 September 1944 reveals something of the latter in Forster's concern with hygiene. He describes how his boat '*stinks devilishly of decay and putrefaction*'; he suspects who the culprits are and '*is resolved to take action against them*'. It is unlikely he got the chance.

On 29 December 1944, Admiralty decided to introduce a system of evasive routing and simultaneously to lay a necklace of deep minefields around Channel buoys. On 6 January, the very day *U 480* set out on her final patrol, MTBs *724*, *728* and *787* left HMS *Vernon* to lay minefield Brazier D2 (part 2) clustered around the H2 Buoy.

Grossadmiral Karl Dönitz.

FINAL PATROL

(4) *U 480* and her crew of forty-seven departed Trondheim on 6 January 1945 and sailed for the English Channel. The boat was expected to arrive in its billet on or about 30 January. On 24 February a U-boat torpedoed and sank the 1,644-ton British steamer *Oriskany* (Ministry of War Transport, London), between Land's End and the Scilly Isles, at position 50° 05'N 05° 51'W, in coastal convoy BTC 78, comprising nine ships; she was en-route from Newport, Monmouth to London with coal. The two frigates and convoy escorts, HMS *Duckworth* (Cdr R.G. Mills) and HMS *Rowley* (Lt Cdr F.G.J. Jones), set about hunting for the U-boat. Depth charges were dropped over the target, bringing debris and oil to the surface including fragments of a rubbery/plastic substance, later believed to be fragments of the *Alberich*. The Admiralty assessed that the submarine was *U 480*, but it was later discovered to have been *U 1208*. It seems likely that *U 480* and her crew were already dead, having run into one of the Brazier D2 mines sometime around 24 February 1945. These mines were laid at 80ft along a line extending eight cables, in a direction 225° from 50° 24.8'N to 01° 44.0'W. Whatever its other qualities, *Alberich* provided no protection against sea mines.

THE MEN WHO DIED IN U 480

Blume, Karl Masch.O.Gfr. (19-3-1924)
Burghardt, Hans Fk.O.Gfr. (12-5-1923)
Eckleben, Karl Mtr.H.Gfr. (3-6-1921)
Eichner, Konrad Mtr.O.Gfr. (5.02.1925)
Faust, Richard Mtr.O.Gfr. (13-3-1923)
Förster, Hans-Joachim Oblt.z.S. (20-2-1920)
Gerhardter, Johann Mtr.H.Gfr. (25-5-1923)
Haas, Hans-Rudolf Mech.O.Gfr. (30-9-1924)
Haltner, Erich O.Ltz.S. (20-10-1922)
Haring, Jörg Bts.Mt. (18-6-1921)
Heuser, Anton O.Masch.Mt. (3-6-1923)
Hollube, Otto Fk.Gfr. (23-7-1925)
Imhof, Hans Masch.O.Gfr. (23-2-1925)
Körber, Hans Masch.Mt. (8-6-1921)
Krause, Kurt Masch.Gfr. (1-11-1925)
Kuhn, Hermann San.Mt. (21-4-1923)
Küppers, Wilhelm Masch.O.Gfr. (6-12-1923)
Lange, Karl-Heinz Bts.Mt. (4-8-1923)
Laurenz, Herbert Mech.Gfr. (6-9-1925)
Lösken, Horst Mech.Mt. (13-10-1922)
Mittendorf, Hermann Masch.O.Gfr. (2-10-1924)
Morgner, Hans Masch.Mt. (16-6-1921)
Müller, Helmut Fk.Mt. (3-5-1921)
Müller, Karl-Heinz Oblt.Ing. (17-1-1923)

Neumann, Friedhelm Mtr. (13.03.1926)
Oppermann, Walter Masch.Mt. (31-12-1919)
Ortseifen, Georg Masch.Mt. (10-11-1920)
Otto, Heinz Mtr. (7-9-1926)
Parzmair, Josef Fk.Mt. (24-7-1924)
Ripke, Peter Ltz.S. (8-4-1923)
Scheidemantel, Heinz.O.Strm. (16-8-1918)
Schmidt, Johann Mtr.O.Gfr. (27-4-1923)
Schmied, Alois Mtr.O.Gfr. (23-7-1923)
Schmitt, Heinz Mtr.O.Gfr. (26-7-1922)
Schulz, Gerhard O.Masch. (23-2-1917)
Schwab, Theodor Masch.O.Gfr. (23-7-1924)
Spalt, Alfred O.Masch. (11-5-1916)
Steffens, Heinz Mtr.O.Gfr. (16-1-1925)
Steichele, Reinhold Mtr.Gfr. (17-8-1926)
Steldermann, Herbert Mtr.O.Gfr. (18-12-1924)
Thiel, Rudolf Masch.O.Gfr. (1-3-1923)
Thiemke, Fritz Mtr.O.Gfr. (2-9-1921)
Wesener, Hermann Bts.Mt. (14-1-1924)
Wiedemann, Xaver Masch.O.Gfr. (18-9-1924)
Wirth, Friedrich Masch.O.Gfr. (7-5-1924)
Wolfrum, Oskar Masch.O.Gfr. (17-4-1924)
Zeischka, Herbert Fk.O.Gfr. (12-5-1924)
Zollt, Josef Mtr.O.Gfr. (8-4-1924)

In October 1992 a Type VIIC U-boat was located some 16 nautical miles from Anvil Point at Swanage. Since the wreck was found, numerous dive-teams have visited the site, including John, Steve and Mike Ballett of Poole and divers from a French Telecom vessel. The Ballett family apparently located the wreck while potting and exploring the area in 1994. Then during the summer of 1998, author and maritime historian Innes McCartney took a dive team to the site and later, with help from the Naval Historical Branch, identified the wreck as that of *U 480*. The swastika-incised range finder (UZO) from the conning tower is now on display in the Blue Boar Inn at Poole.

NARA T1022, Roll 4066, PG30529, 30362 CWGC U-Boot-Ehrenmal Möltenort

WRECK SITE

The wreck, probably that of *U 480*, is orientated in a north to south direction. It sits in a 1m scour and lies on an undulating seabed of sand and gravel, in a general depth of 55m (180ft), being the lowest astronomical tide. When first discovered, the wreck was intact, upright and sitting level on the seabed, with both propellers in place. There was also some slight damage at the stern and one of the rudders was broken off, but the rubbery coating of *Alberich* could be seen on the decking. The Flak guns, although damaged, were in place aft of the conning tower. All the hatches were sealed and the interior appeared to be airtight. In 1994 a section of the stern was reported as lying near to, and forward of the conning tower; a large fissure was visible along the pressure hull. A circular hatch was also partly open, almost certainly an engine room exhaust cover. In common with the other snort boats, *U 480* was equipped with two such vents on the conning tower with a further three on the flak platforms. Following recent visits, divers have maintained that the wreck changes orientation, adding to the speculation that air is still trapped inside, making it buoyant. It has been suggested that the submarine rolls back and forth. Some people have witnessed the conning tower standing upright and others have seen it close to the seabed. However, salvage experts regard this as unlikely following the passing of so many years. The bow casing is reported to show signs of severe damage, suggesting that *U 480* plummeted into the seabed at a fair rate of knots, after detonating a mine. Tidal streams are very brisk and the surface of the sea close to the wreck site is prone to over-falls, due to the undulating seabed and varying depths.

A3, HM SUBMARINE

DATE OF LOSS: 15 May 1912
DEPTH: 35m
REFERENCE: 50 31'.460 N 002 11'.318 W
Also suggested: 50 31.41N 02 11.25W
LOCATION: 5.95 nautical miles SW of St Alban's Head

Type: 'A1' Class coastal patrol submarine of the Group I   *Ordered*: 1902 and 1903 programme   *Keel laid*: as Yard No.295 on 6 November 1902   *Pendant*: not issued   *Builders*: Vickers Yard, Barrow-in-Furness for Royal Navy   *Ordered*: for 1901–1902 programme   *Launched*: on 9 May 1903   *Completed*: on 13 July 1904 (Commanding officers were not nominated for individual boats, only to a Depot Ship 'for command of submarine attached')

TECHNICAL SPECIFICATIONS

Hull: single   *Surface displacement*: 165 tons   *U/Dt*: 180 tons   *LBD*: (A2 – A3 boats) 32.05m × 3.89m × 3.53m   *Machinery*: 1 × vertical 12-cylinder 450bhp Wolsey petrol engine   *Props*: 1 bronze × 3 blade of 1.70m (5ft 7in).   *S/Sp*: 11.5 knots   *Op/R*: 310 nautical miles at 10 knots   *Sub/R*: 20 nautical miles at 5 knots   *U/Power*: 1 × 80bhp at electric motor gave 7 knots   *Batteries*: Exide lead/acid.   *Fuel/Cap*: 7 tons   *Armament*: 1 × 45.72cm (18in) bow torpedo tube.   *Torpedoes*: 1 × 45.72cm (18in)   *Diving*: max-op-depth 15.25m (50ft) and 5 minutes to submerge   *Complement*: 2 officers and 9 ratings

Following her launch on 9 May 1903, HM S/M *A3* was damaged in a collision with the steamship *PRINCE OF WALES* on 31 December 1903. Repairs followed, then the boat was allocated a training role.

THE OFFICERS WHO COMMANDED A3

Lt Francis Newton Allen Cromie from 5 February 1906
Lt Andrew Francis Gordon Tracy from 1 January 1909
Lt Athelstan Alfred Lennox Fenner from 1 November 1909 (*see* vol. 4)
Lt Charles Worthington Craven from 1 March 1910

HM SM *A3*. (Author's collection)

HM SM *A3* afloat again, 3 May. (Private collection)

HM SM *A3*. (Author's collection)

The regular skipper of *A3*, Lt Charles W. Craven, was not on duty due to illness when *A3* sailed for an exercise off Portsmouth on 6 February. Lt Francis Thompson Ormand assumed temporary command of the boat.

FINAL PATROL

At 0930hrs on 6 February 1912, *A3* left the Petrol Jetty, Fort Blockhouse and sailed for an exercise on the eastern side of the Isle of Wight, near Bembridge, with several other 'A' and 'C' Class submarines. The weather was inclement, with a blustery wind and heavy snow showers. The incident took place about noon, some 2 miles southwest of East Princess Buoy. The submerged *A3* blew tanks to surface. Whether due to poor visibility or bad periscope drill, we will never know. What is certain is that Lt Ormand failed to see the bows of the tender HMS *Hazard* heading straight for his craft. The initial impact was not fatal. *A3* was struck a glancing blow and passed down the port side of *Hazard* until the ship's rudder and port propeller ripped a large hole in her ballast tank. The little submarine plummeted to the seabed, out of control. Examination of *Hazard* confirmed damage to her rudder and propellers.

The boat was located the following day, but bad weather prevented any serious rescue operation. Five weeks later, on Sunday 8 March, salvage operations commenced in earnest. Divers from HMS *Liverpool* worked throughout that day and managed to place a sling under the boat. Eventually, suspended between two lighters, *A3* was towed to a sheltered area of shallow water in St Helen's Bay, opposite Ryde on the Isle of Wight. On Thursday 12th she was towed across the Solent to Portsmouth, the tug *Seahorse*, her White Ensign flying at half-mast, leading the poignant 'procession'. Following her were two tugs, one towing the lighter and the other lashed to it, while two destroyers with their flags also at half-mast, brought up the rear. The sad flotilla slowly steamed towards the south lock, passing Fort Blockhouse, to the salute of bugles and dipped ensigns. After berthing in the south lock, the boat was pumped out and the bodies of the fourteen submariners were transferred to Haslar Hospital mortuary, to await burial. Thirteen of the men were ceremoniously laid to rest at the Royal Navy Cemetery, close to the crew of HM S/M *A1*, which had been lost eight years earlier. Mention has already been made of the memorial obelisk commemorating the deaths of the 'A' boat crews. Lt Donald Campbell was buried in his native Oban, where there is a memorial in the cathedral.

THE MEN WHO DIED IN A3

Armstrong, Charles Elliott /EA 2277 E.R. Artificer
Barden, William Thomas P/ 206027 Able Seaman
Campbell, Donald Patrick Colin Lieutenant
Compton, Edwin Frederick 238021 Able Seaman
Farr, Charles P/193220 Leading Seaman
Fowler, George Herbert P/ 302987 Stoker
Gent, Alfred William P/ 295847 Leading Stoker
Good, Arthur Ernest P/ 269500 Chief E.R. Artificer
Kelly, Parker P/ 205230 Able Seaman
Ormand, Frank Thompson Lieutenant
Page, Charles George P/ 219768 Able Seaman
Richardson, Leonard Faler Lieutenant
Thornton, Ernest Jones Vernon Lieutenant
Wilder, George P/ 166859 Petty Officer. 1st

Given that *A3* was damaged beyond reasonable repair, Admiralty decided to make the best of a bad job by disposing of her as a gunnery target. On 17 May 1912, *Seahorse* towed *A3* back out to sea on her final patrol. A number of experiments were carried out before the 4in guns of HMS *St Vincent*, one of Britain's giant dreadnoughts, opened fire at a range of 2,000 yards. Three shells were fired and the third one slammed into *A3*, sending her down to a watery grave. As a postscript, HMS *Hazard* did not long survive her little victim. On 28 January 1918 she was rammed and sunk by the hospital ship *Western Australia*. Four lives were lost. The forlorn wreck of HMS *Hazard* lies upside down in Solent mud at 50° 43.75'N 01° 03.23'W.

Until 1907 the only way of even hoping to save a crew was to locate and salvage the submarine in time. It can only be observed that submarine salvage did not have a very impressive history to date. Considerable international thought had been invested in attempts to find some means of enabling the crew of a stricken submarine to escape themselves. In 1907 Cdr R. Hall, Inspecting Captain of Submarines, encouraged Admiralty to take out a patent on the Rees-Hall escape suits. Admiralty additionally invested the generous sum of £27,000 in developing a viable submarine escape set. Sadly, the sheer bulk of these suits rendered them hopelessly impractical for stowage aboard cramped British submarines. It is interesting to note that while the KDM placed its first order for the Drager

The funeral procession of the crew of HM SM *A3*, 13 March 1912; sold as a postcard to raise money for the widows and families left behind. (Private collection)

HMS *Hazard*. (Private collection)

lung as early as 1912 (and used it throughout the First World War), DSEA set did not become standard submarine equipment until 1932 (*see M2*).

WRECK SITE

Simon Bird, the skipper of diving vessel *Trio*, discovered the wreck fairly close to a reef during
the summer of 1989. After consultation with the late Gus Britton, of the Royal Navy Submarine
Museum, the wreck was confirmed as *A3*. The wreck, which stands around 3.5m high for most of its
length, is rather difficult to locate. It lies just to the south of a sloping reef. The surrounding seabed
is undulating, but firm and consists mostly of gravel and rock, in a general depth of 35m, being the
lowest astronomical depth. The submarine stands upright and is reasonably intact, although the brass
conning tower hatch and porthole-window have been removed. The hatch is now displayed at the
Deep Sea Adventure Centre in Weymouth. Tidal streams can be quite severe during spring tides.
Nor should it be forgotten that this is the resting place of some brave pioneers.

SAFARI, HM SUBMARINE

DATE OF LOSS: 8 January 1946
DEPTH: 38m
REFERENCE: 50 25'.330 N 02 02'.560 W
LOCATION: 9.26 nautical miles S of St Alban's Head and 16.65 nautical miles
ESE of Portland Bill

Type: 'S' Class medium to short-range patrol submarine of Group-III   *Pennant*: No. P.211   *Builders*:
Cammell Laird, Birkenhead for Royal Navy   *Keel laid*: on 5 June 1940 as P61; renumbered P211
in July 1941   *Launched*: on 18 November 1941   *Completed*: with Cdr B. Bryant as commanding
officer on 14 March 1942   *Motto*: 'HOT ON THE TRAIL'

TECHNICAL SPECIFICATIONS

Hull: partly welded construction   *Surface displacement*: 814 tons   *U/Dt*: 990 tons   *LBD*:
61.14m × 7.24m × 4.m   *Machinery*: 2 × 8-cylinder Admiralty pattern 950bhp diesels   *Props*:

2 bronze   **S/Sp**: 14 knots   **Op/R**: 4,000 nautical miles at 10 knots   **Sub/R**: 106 nautical miles at 4 knots   **U/Power**: 2 × Admiralty pattern 650bhp electric motors gave 9 knots   **Batteries**: 2-Exide lead/acid of 112 cells each   **Fuel/Cap**: 44 tons   **Armament**: 6 × 53.34cm (21in torpedo tubes   **Torpedoes**: 12 × 53.34cm (21in).   **Guns**: 1 × 76.20mm (3in) Quick-Firing Mk-I deck gun, barrel length of 3.35m (11ft), plus 2 × 7.696mm (0.303in) Lewis machine-guns   **Ammo**: 100 rounds of 76.20mm (3in)   **Mines**: (sometimes) 12 × Mk. II magnetic ground-mine type with 453.60 kilo (1,000 pound) charge. These were half the length of a torpedo and were laid through the torpedo tubes   **Diving**: max-op-depth 106.68m (350ft)   **Complement**: 5 officers and 43 ratings

In January 1943, the boat was renamed *SAFARI*. The 'S' Class of submarine was a very successful marque, in production for over fifteen years and was also the largest single group of submarines built for the Royal Navy.

COMMANDERS

Cdr Ben Bryant from October 1941
Lt R. B. Lakin from April 1943
Lt Cdr D. A. B. Abdy from December 1943
Lt Cdr J. R. G. Harvey from March 1944

'HOT ON THE TRAIL' – ON SAFARI WITH BEN BRYANT

The Submarine Museum displays *Safari*'s fearsome Jolly Roger – a black flag with skull and cross-bones in centre with five daggers underneath. To the right are fourteen white stars and two red stars. To the left are thirteen white bars, one broken white bar and one broken red bar. The story behind this trophy is an epic of the Second World War.

Under the legendary Ben Bryant, one of the rare survivors from the North Sea campaigns of 1939–1941, the boat enjoyed a charmed existence. Bryant's magic (he always wore an array of religious amulets) rubbed off on his crew and the boat was something of a hothouse taltented submarine commanders. Amongst the officers who served on *SAFARI* we find (later rank) Lt Cdr

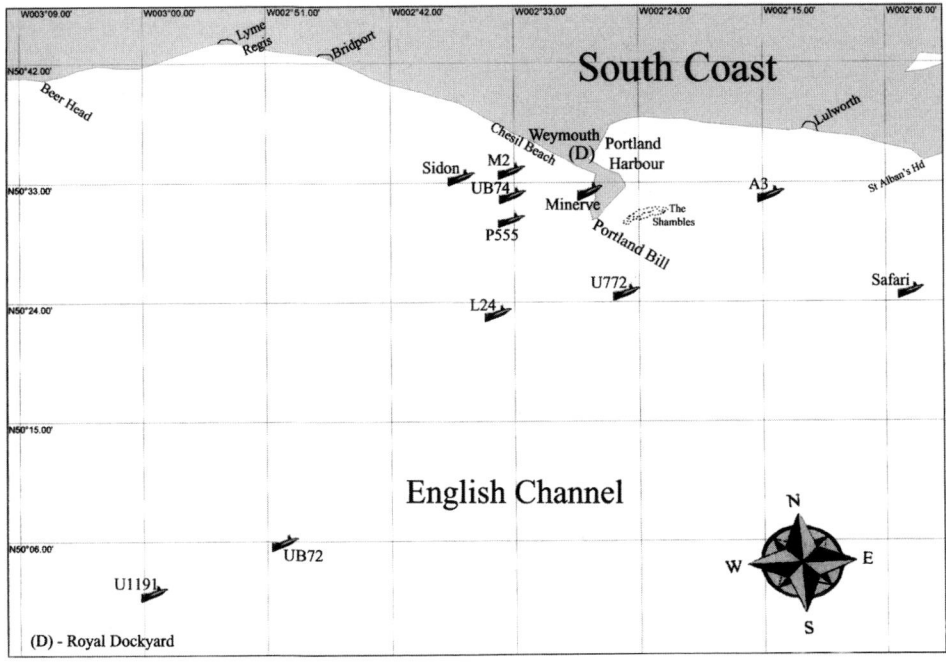

Submarine wrecks off Portland, South Coast. (Produced by Ron Young)

Frederick Henry Sherwood DSC★ RCNVR (Canada's most highly decorated Second World War submarine commander), Lt Cdr Ronald A.A.C. (Sharky) Ward DSO DSC, who went on to command *Umbra, Uther, Storm* and *Token*. To this list we must add the promising Lt John Blackburn, protégé of Ben Bryant, who commanded *AFFRAY* and died with her on 15 April 1951. (John Blackburn's father was also a submariner and won the DSC in the First World War as an RNR and later transferred to the Royal Navy. John's son is now actually a Vice Admiral.)

With his combination of pugnacity, animal cunning and ruthless addiction to gun action, Ben Bryant was the epitome of an Elizabethan buccaneer. Operations in the Norwegian leads had given Bryant a taste for gun action indeed and this became his favourite mode of attack. *Safari's* main sphere of operations was to be the Mediterranean.

Following a short working-up phase with the 5th Flotilla, in late May 1942, *Safari* arrived at Gibraltar to join HMS *Maidstone* and the 8th Flotilla. However the boat was destined to spend most of this critical phase of the war on loan to the famous 'Fighting Tenth' Flotilla, based at the Malta Lazzareto (and later Algiers). Along with other boats attached to the 10th Submarine Flotilla, *SAFARI* was to play a significant role in disrupting Rommel's critical supply route to North Africa. Bryant and Lakin's tallies speak for themselves. The following information has been extracted from patrol reports by Andy Mair:

On 5 June 1942, *Safari* left Gibraltar under Cdr Bryant for a patrol southeast of Sardinia. During the patrol, two Condotierri Class cruisers were identified and a U-boat was sighted at extreme periscope, but no vessels were attacked. *Safari* arrived back at Gibraltar on 23 June.

On 4 July 1942, *Safari* left Gibraltar to patrol off Sardinia and by the 11th was in the Gulf of Orosei. At 1325hrs on 12 July, the 792-ton *Adda* (1905 – Gestione Armamento Piroscafo 'Adda', Genoa), which was transporting 700 tons of cargo from Savona to Cagliari, was sighted. *Safari* surfaced 2,200 yards on port quarter of the target at 1405hrs and opened fire with the gun. The second shot, and nearly every one of the twenty-four shells fired, hit the engine room before the gun jammed, however the crew of *Adda* abandoned ship. Four elderly men, hanging onto some wreckage, were picked up and the *Adda* sank 3,000 yards offshore, 5 miles northwest of Cape Monte Santo. At 2045hrs on 15 July, smoke was sighted to the north, northeast. *Safari* ran eastward to intercept, but her bearing indicated that the 1,302-ton Italian steamer *Tigrai* (1918 – Elia Bibolini, Genoa) was hugging the coast. *Safari* turned back and carried out an advancing attack in rapidly failing light.

At 2127hrs the boat surfaced; the ship stopped approximately 3,000 yards away and Bryant decided to disable her with the gun, opening fire at 2135hrs from 1,000 yards range. Unfortunately owing to failure of the gun layer and trainer to use their open sights, Bryant testily recorded that the shooting was appalling and only 18 of the 35 rounds hit their target. Men began to abandon ship, but several remained onboard and the steamer made for the cliffs and opened fire; some light-calibre shore guns also opened up. *Safari* returned seawards for 3 miles and then turned in to attack by torpedo. A torpedo fired from 5,000 yards into Gonome Cove, ran a little to starboard, but went up the landing and would have undoubtedly finished off the ship had it struck its target. At 2130hrs *Safari* surfaced and proceeded to Cagliari. On 18 July, between 0507hrs and 0705hrs and 9 miles from Cape Spartivento, Bryant attempted to torpedo a schooner, but was unable to get in a shot.

Safari arrived at Gibraltar on 24 July 1942.

On 4 August 1942, the boat left Gibraltar for Operation Pedestal. At 1722hrs on the 6th, a U-boat was sighted on her quarter at position 37° 70'N 03° 21'E, some 6 miles green on opposite course; this was possibly *U 205*. At 1030hrs on the 10th, a 3,000-ton Armed Merchant Cruiser was observed, but Bryant refrained from attacking so as not to compromise his position.

On 16 August *Safari* made landfall on Cape Bella Vista at dawn and at 1103hrs a sailing vessel was spotted to the north. At 1200hrs the submarine surfaced and engaged the 158-ton Italian *Giovannino* with the gun at 2,000 yards, which left it damaged in this attack. At 1145hrs on the 17th, the large 218-ton schooner *Ausonia* was sighted and at 1223hrs Bryant opened fire on it at 1,000 yards. The crew abandoned ship quickly and luckily so, because the sixth round hit the cargo and she blew up with the most monumental explosion. (Had *Safari* been closer Bryant said she could have been sunk, or badly damaged.) At 0843hrs on the 18th the empty and unescorted 4,857-ton Italian tanker *Perseo* (1921 – Società Ligure di Armamento, Genoa) was torpedoed and sunk off Capo Carbonara, Sardinia; it was en-route from Naples to Bone. At 0856hrs, an Italian submarine was also observed, crossing astern, but well out of range.

A salvo of three torpedoes was fired at *Perseo* and it stopped after two hits, 8 miles SSW of Cavoli Island; the fourth torpedo fired almost certainly ran under the ship. The vessel was abandoned and began to settle by the stern. At 2000hrs, the Italian submarine *Bronzo* was spotted 24 miles from Cavoli Island and at 2031hrs Bryant fired six torpedoes at a range of 3,500 yards. Unfortunately *SAFARI* broke the surface disappointingly on firing and one torpedo suffered a premature detonation, 29 seconds after firing the first; the Italian submarine then took the necessary avoiding action and departed.

Safari arrived back at Gibraltar on 24 August 1942.

Safari left Gibraltar with Bryant on 9 September and arrived at Malta on the 19th. Leaving Malta in the evening of 26 September 1942, *Safari* set course for the Straits of Otranto.

On 1 October, she dived and approached Dubrovnik and spent the day investigating traffic in the approaches to Gruz harbour and by passing between Gabini and Kolocep Islands.

At 0945hrs on the 2nd, a northbound vessel was sighted and at 1007hrs *Safari* surfaced and attacked with the deck gun at a range of 3,000 yards; fifteen out of thirty-five were hits and the enemy was forced ashore at Podobuce. The boat dived and at 1028hrs put a torpedo into it amidships. The ship was the 896-ton Italian steamer *Veglia* (1909 – Italian Government, ex-*Kosovo*), which was left on fire, however she was beached and salvaged on 12 October 1942.

That night *Safari* crossed the Adriatic to the Italian coast, establishing a patrol in the Gulf of Manfredonia.

On 4 October at 0637hrs, the heavily laden 4,553-ton Italian freighter *Valentino Coda* (1924 – 'Corrado' Società Anonima di Navigazione, Genoa) was sighted in mist under Gargano Head. At 0644hrs, Bryant fired four torpedoes at a running range of 5,000 yards, but all torpedoes missed the target. At 0650hrs the boat surfaced for gun action, however the ship opened fire on *Safari* before Bryant could get onto the bridge. Fifty-six rounds were fired by *Safari*, securing one hit at over 5,000 yards. *Valentino Coda* (Captain Arnaldo La Rovere) gave a spirited defence by replying with thirty-two shells. *Safari* broke off the attack at 0700hrs and submerged 8 minutes later. The Italian torpedo boat *Mosto* was immediately sent to hunt for the submarine, but without success. (On 14 June 1943, HM S/M *Unruly* torpedoed and sank the *Valentino Coda*, 19 miles from Cape Vaticano.) During the night of 5 October, *Safari* crossed the Adriatic to the Yugoslav shore and was approaching the coast south of Komorica Island, when a 6,000-ton ship was sighted at 0940hrs. It appeared to be carrying troops and was in fact the 545-ton Italian steamer *Eneo* (1907 – Italian Government).

At 1021hrs *Safari* surfaced and, at 1,000 yards, secured twenty hits with her gun; the vessel beached on Trara Island. During this action *Safari* was under fire from shore batteries, but fired one torpedo from 1,000 yards at 1049hrs; gyro failure, however, made it strike the island. (*Eneo* was left badly damaged and was towed to Split, but it was scuttled on 8 October, and then after the war the ship was raised and repaired.) Shore batteries continuously fired at the submarine's periscope, so at 1050hrs Bryant ran *Safari* out seaward to 180ft, while air and surface patrols continued to hunt for the boat. At 1945hrs the *Safari* surfaced and proceeded for Promontore.

On 8 October, an escorted convoy was sighted at 0840hrs, with probably four ships, but mist and mirage prevented accurate observation and attack. Surface patrol activity increased and was joined by aircraft in the late afternoon, but despite glassy calm conditions and a torpedo boat only two cables from the submarine, an attack was made on a '1,500-ton' deep-laden ship at 1629hrs. Three torpedoes were fired and the second torpedo hit, then the boat dived to 280ft and altered away from the land (position 1 mile south of Ploca Point). The attack was made on the 935-ton Italian steamer *Giuseppe Magliulo* (1917 – Giuseppe Magliulo, Torre del Greco), at 43° 30'N 15° 58'E, south of Sebenik, Croatia. A torpedo boat attacked *Safari* with nine depth charges. At 1930hrs, she surfaced and proceeded for the coast, southeast of Dubrovnik.

At 2118hrs, while passing the island of Sueti Andrya, *Safari* was sighted by a lookout, who fired a flare, and then a torpedo boat immediately closed and commenced a hunt, but *Safari* slipped away.

On the 9th, off Gruz, two large empty lighters were sighted at 1400hrs and two tugs, towing a dredger with two more empty lighters behind the dredger. Gun action was not taken because there was a shore battery within 8 cables and not enough ammunition left, plus it was too rough for accurate shooting.

At 0920hrs on 10 October south of Dubrovnik, a northbound convoy was observed, consisting of one medium-sized and two small vessels, escorted by two torpedo boats. At 1000hrs, Bryant

HM SM *Safari*. (Author's collection)

Crew of HM SM *Safari*. (By kind permission of CERA Roy McCurrach)

fired three torpedoes at a range of 2,000 yards and claimed two hits, but in fact all missed. (What is known now is that the convoy consisted of the 854-ton Italian steamer *Carlo Margottini* (1893 – ex-Yugoslavian *Bled*, Società Jugoslava Jadranska, the Plovidba), the requisitioned 4,438-ton SS *Goffredo Mameli* (1909 – Società Anonima Cooperativa di Navigazione Garibaldi, Genova) and the requisitioned 840-ton SS *Enrico Baroni* (1902 – ex-Yugoslav *Zagreb*, Compartimento Marittimo di Fiume); escorting them was the 338-ton torpedo boat *T.7* (ex-torpedo boat *96F* of the Austrian/Hungarian Empire and ex-*T.7* of the Yugoslav Navy). (HM S/M *Unbending* eventually sank *Carlo Margottini* on 2 February 1943.)

A hunt for *Safari* began at 1007hrs and lasted for 45 minutes, the thirteen depth charges causing no damage, with the boat diving to 390ft with no adverse effects.

At 1930hrs *Safari* surfaced and proceeded to Malta, where she arrived on 14 October 1942.

At 1710hrs on 18 October 1942, *Safari* left Malta and proceeded for patrol billet 36° 18'N 11° 53'E. At 0845hrs on the 19th, a Climene Class torpedo boat, accompanied by flying boat, passed by at 5,000 yards range.

At 0042hrs on the 20th and at position 35° 14'N 12° 52'E, a submarine was sighted, then at 0510hrs *Safari* surfaced. The 5,397-ton Italian motor vessel *Titania* (Società Anonima Cooperativa di Navigazione 'Garibaldi', Genoa) was sighted and it was stopped in position 158° Lampion 70 miles; closed with two destroyers also in company. (On 19 October 1942, the *Titania* was voyaging from Naples to Tripoli when it was torpedoed and damaged by HM S/M *Unbroken*, and the ship was taken in tow.) At 0529hrs Bryant fired the first torpedo at a range of 6,000 yards, but it missed. *Safari* dived and approached the target submerged. At 0618hrs and 1,800 yards and closing, at a moment when both destroyers were about 1 mile away, a detonation occurred after 77 seconds. One destroyer attacked *Safari* with a three-charge pattern and the boat was hunted for 20 minutes before both destroyers made off. The back of *Titania*, with a deck cargo of motor transport, was broken abaft the funnel; at 0833hrs, small explosions followed the rapid sinking of the ship.

Safari arrived back at Malta on 22 October.

On 3 November 1942, *Safari* left Malta in company with HM S/M *Sahib* and *Saracen*, sailing for the opening phase of Operation Torch. Shortly after leaving harbour *Safari* was attacked by a Messerschmitt, but evaded damage. At 1331hrs on 13 November, *Safari* surfaced 6 miles east of Sousa and engaged the 269-ton Italian auxiliary brigantine *Bice* (Michele Barrera & C. di Napoli) with the deck gun at a range of 1,000 yards. Fifty-two rounds were fired with forty hits and the ship sank; her master, Captain Tandurella, was taken onboard. The *Bice* was carrying oil and barley from Trapani to Tripoli.

On 16 November 1942, a large darkened ship that anchored close inshore was sighted at 2120hrs and a torpedo was fired at 2200hrs. This was the 2,646-ton Kriesmarine transport *Hans Arp* (1926 – Heinrich F. C. Arp Dampfschiffs-Reederei, Hamburg), which went up in a sheet of flames and sank off Ras el Hilal, Benghazi, at position 30° 28'N 18° 48'E.

At dawn on the 17th, one torpedo was fired from 4,500 yards into a collection of TLCs and lighters, at a landing place near Ras Ali; satisfactory fire and explosion were heard (the torpedo sank the 155-ton German lighter *F.346*). At 2024hrs another torpedo was fired at a 300-ton schooner anchored in Mersa el Brega, but it missed and probably hit the bottom.

At 0910hrs on 18 November *Safari* engaged a TLC, some 10 miles off Ras Ali and damaged her with gunfire before breaking off owing to the nearness of shoals and enemy aerodromes.

On the 21st at 0830hrs, one torpedo was fired at a large TLC at 3,500 yards range, but it missed.

On the 22nd a TLC with a lighter in tow, was engaged at 1015hrs; the lighter contained a lorry and a number of petrol drums. A patrolling *JU88* prevented the boat from surfacing. (Bryant thought he had obtained two hits, but there is no record of this.)

Safari arrived back at Malta on 24 November for short refit and docking.

Safari departed Malta on 16 December 1942 and proceeded to the Gulf of Hammamet with two SBS (Special Boat Service) personnel onboard.

At 1448hrs on the 18th, Bryant sank the 49-ton Italian motor/sailing schooner *Eufrasia* (Vittorio Isidoro Meli di Palermo) with gunfire in the Gulf of Hammamet at 600 yards range; it was transporting petrol.

On 20 December, 18 miles north of Susa (Sousse, northeast Tunisia), *Safari* surfaced at 1116hrs and engaged the 349-ton Italian *Costantina* (1895 – Italian Regia Marina, requisitioned as *F.139*) with gunfire at 2,000 yards range; the steamer was hit with the fourth round and turned to beach herself, while the crew abandoned ship. More hits were obtained before aircraft forced Bryant to dive. (The *Costantina F.139* later became a total loss following the Italian evacuation on 10 April 1943.)

At 1814hrs on the 22nd, *Safari* attacked a southbound schooner with the gun at a range of 500 yards; forty-one hits were observed, but the ship, the 299-ton Italian auxiliary minesweeper *ROSINA S* (Catello Sorrentino & C. di Torre del Greco), which was strongly built of wood, would not sink. One torpedo was fired and the ship blew up in position 36° 18'N 10° 37'E. Twelve persons, including the captain, were taken prisoner. (The Regia Marina had requisitioned her on 3 November 1940 as auxiliary minesweeper *DM23*.)

Safari arrived at Malta at 1400hrs on 23 December and disembarked the prisoners before departing at 1700hrs for a patrol off the Tripolitanian coast.

At 0652hrs on the 27th, *Safari* attacked the 54-ton Italian motor/sailing schooner *Elonora Rosa* (Rocco Ferrigno di Gela) with gunfire and four or five shells hit the boat; a fire broke out and the vessel burnt out. It was transporting 100 tons of petrol to Tripoli and two prisoners were taken. (The Regia Marina had requisitioned the boat on 18 November 1942.)

A course was set to intercept a vessel between Djerba and Sfax and at 0420hrs on 29 December the 1,012-ton Italian MV *Torquato Gennari* (1890 – Ubaldo Gennari fu Torquato, Rimini) was sighted in the moonlight with two *JU88*'s always in sight. At 0801hrs three torpedoes were fired and one hit the ship, which sank in position 34° 20'N 10° 49'E. Enemy aircraft accurately dropped nine bombs immediately after the torpedoes were fired.

Safari arrived back at Malta on 30 December 1942.

On 2 January 1943, *Safari* left Malta and arrived at Algiers on the 6th.

The boat left Algiers on 20 January 1943 for a patrol off Naples.

At 0226hrs the following morning, a Wellington mistakenly dropped four bombs over the submarine, 95 miles northeast of Algiers; fortunately no damage was done.

On the 24th an enemy destroyer was sighted at 0520hrs and *Safari* dived; the warship passed *Safari* at 60ft and, 15 minutes later, dropped fifteen depth charges. Five more were dropped at 0546hrs, but *Safari* dived to 400ft; more sporadic charges were also dropped

On the 26th *Safari* was submerged 12 miles south of Bocca Piccola and at 0637hrs identified two large ships, escorted by two destroyers. Four torpedoes were fired at 0648hrs in an inverted arrowhead formation, but all missed, due to speed error.

At 0820hrs on 30 January, Bryant sighted the masts of two small schooners running down the east shore of the Gulf of Policastro. *Safari* closed on them while submerged and at 0944hrs surfaced 1,000 yards on the starboard quarter of the rear boat, the 67-ton Italian motor sailing boat *Gemma* (Alberto Zolesi & C., Porto Santo Stefano), the other being some 3,000 yards ahead of it. All but one of the crew abandoned ship and after it was hit twelve times in the waterline with shells, Bryant went after the other one, which had already been abandoned. The second schooner, the 73-ton Italian motor sailing boat *Sant'aniello* (Maurizio Scotto, Procida), was soon ablaze and quickly sank. The first schooner did not appear to be sinking so Bryant returned to it, opened fire and it sank soon after. Its cargo included drums, which did not catch fire, was presumed to be lubricating oil, as the vessel was deep laden.

Two vessels were sighted leaving Bocca Piccola at 1347hrs on 2 February. At 1438hrs three torpedoes were fired at a range of 1,000 yards at the leading ship, the 5,733-ton Italian steamer *Valsavoia*; two of the missiles hit the ship, which sank, but the second ship, the 1,176-ton Italian freighter *Salemi* (Italian Government (ex-French *Pontet Canet*), which was voyaging from Naples to Messina, turned back for Naples. At 1442hrs, *Safari* surfaced and engaged this smaller steamer with gunfire at a range of 2,000 yards. The first shell scored a direct hit, as did most of the twenty-six others, before enemy aircraft forced *Safari* to dive; the steamer was lying on beam ends and sank shortly after. The action took place off Galli Island, near Capri.

Safari arrived at Algiers on 8 February 1943.

At 1800hrs on 22 February, the boat left Algiers for Sicily with a folbot (portable folding kayaks) party in a special operation between 27 February and 9 March, which precluded Bryant from attacking enemy shipping. Having completed the special operation on the 9th, Bryant sighted a deep-laden schooner westbound at 1017hrs. *Safari* surfaced at 1110hrs, halfway between Raisi Point and St Vito and fired twenty-three rounds at the 69-ton Italian motor/sailing schooner *Stefano M* (Nicola Santiago & C. di Torino) at a range of 1,000 yards and, at 1129hrs, it sank. (The Regia Marina had requisitioned the boat on 9 December 1942.) On 12 March *Safari* arrived back at Algiers.

On 27 March *Safari* departed Algiers for a patrol off southeast Sardinia.

On 3 April, the 314-ton Italian steamer *Nasello* (Italian Regia Marina requisition −*F.67*) was sunk by gunfire off Cala Lula in the Gulf of Orsini, while en-route from Olbia, on the Tyrrhenhenian Sea side of Sardinia to Cagliari. Soon after, the 102-ton Italian motor/sailing fishing boat *S. Francesco di Paula* (built 1909) was sunk by gunfire off Gonome, in the Gulf of Orosei.

On 6 April, a deeply laden motor vessel of 4,000 tons, with a smaller ship in ballast, astern and with one destroyer and one aircraft escort, was sighted well inshore, west of Cavoli. Bryant fired three torpedoes at 600 yards, but only one torpedo hit; the target appeared to limp into Cagliari harbour. The resulting counter-attack was 'painfully inefficient' (according to the log).

On 9 April, the 117-ton brigantine (sailing vessel) *V295 Bella* (Italian auxiliary minesweeper No. 295) was engaged by gunfire west of Cavoli, and despite an escort, it was sunk. Shore guns opened fire and *Safari* dived.

On the 10th Bryant fired four torpedoes against a three-ship convoy at 1711hrs; two vessels were each hit by two torpedoes and sank, 12 miles from Punta Elia (Cagliari): the 1,357-ton Italian steamer *Loredan* (Italian Regia Marina requisition – convoy escort *D.19*) was en-route from Cagliari to La Maddalena (a Sardinian town in the Straits of Bonifacio); the second ship, was the 3,363-ton Italian naval oil tanker *Isonzo* (Italian Regia Marina). In all the confusion the third vessel beached itself. Escorting the convoy were numerous aircraft, minesweepers, E-boats and assorted small craft. *Safari* found herself in the uncomfortable position of being grounded at 210ft, only 1 mile from the shore and twenty-four depth charges were counted until darkness fell and the hunt was called off.

On 11 April, Bryant fired two torpedoes at 1,000 yards at the third ship of the convoy, which had beached itself near Torre Finocchio; this was the 2,691-ton Italian steamer *Entella* (L. Mangiarotti & E. Ravano, Genoa), which was on passage from Cagliari to La Maddalena.

After evading an E-boat CA in which twenty-one depth charges were dropped, *Safari* made a return passage to Algiers, where she arrived on 14 April 1943.

Between March 1942 and September 1943, *Safari* completed over twenty war patrols recording fifty-eight actions against Axis shipping. *Safari* also took part in special operation and beach reconnaissance for the Sicily landings. Promoted to captain, in the latter part of the war, Bryant was given command of the 7th, 3rd and 4th Submarine Flotillas in turn.

Lt R.B. Lakin took over the command of *Safari* from Bryant in April 1943.

With Lakin in command, *Safari* departed Algiers on 29 April 1943 to patrol off northwest Sardinia and by 2 May was close inshore, west of Asinara Island. At 0800hrs, the unescorted 307-ton trawler *Sogliola* (Societa'Anonima Pesca Atlantica Di Trieste) was sighted close to the shore and northbound. At 0837hrs *SAFARI* surfaced and opened fire at a range of 500 yards; twenty-six shells were fired and twenty-five hits obtained. The crew of thirty-five abandoned ship and she sank 1½ hours later, 1 mile west of Monte Ruda (Isola dell'Asinara). The *Sogliola*, which had been requisitioned as pilot boat *F.111* by the Italian Regia Marina, was en-route from Carloforte to Northern Sardinia.

On entering the Gulf of Asinara on 6 May, smoke was sighted in the direction of Porto Torres at 0655hrs. *Safari* surfaced at 0922hrs and Lakin fired forty-six rounds at the Italian fishing boat *Onda* (Armatore Nicola Delfino Di Porto, Torres) at a range of 600 yards; after forty hits, the 98-ton *Onda* sank at 0933hrs. (The Italian Regia Marina had requisitioned the vessel as Auxiliary minesweeper *R106 Onda* on 12 May 1940.)

Safari sheltered in the Gulf of Asinara during a northwest gale on the 8th and at 1928hrs one torpedo was fired at a merchant ship through the breakwater end in Porto Torres harbour, Sardinia, however it exploded against the breakwater. Taking up a new point of aim, Lt Lakin fired another torpedo, which hit the 3,070-ton steamship *Liv* (Italian Government) and it sunk alongside the jetty in 20ft of water. The ex-Norwegian *Liv* had previously been sunk following an air attack on 18 April 1943, but the ship was raised soon after; only to be sunk by *Safari* three weeks later. (After the Second World War the ship was re-floated and was broken up at La Spezia in January 1948.)

Safari was also alleged to have torpedoed and sunk the 2,034-ton Italian SS *Peppino Palomba* (Armatore Giuseppe D'Amico Di Roma) on 8 May 1943, while the ship was voyaging from Patras to Italy, however Ultra decrypt mentions this vessel being sunk at 2220hrs on 7 May 1943 near Niticha, off the Greek island of Santa Maura Island (now Lefkadas).

Safari departed Algiers at 1830hrs on 26 May for Operation Marigold. On 7 June, a fast vessel attacked *Safari* with small automatic gunfire from a range of about 2,000 yards and tracer passed 50ft over bridge.

At 1219hrs and 600 yards range on 10 June, Lt Lakin fired three torpedoes at the deep-laden 834-ton Kriegsmarine transport *KT-12*, in position 40° 21'N 09° 45'E; the centre torpedo exploded after 25 seconds, just aft the mainmast. The vessel was carrying a large number of brown containers on the upper deck that were thought to be cased petrol. The engine room and after part of ship were burning furiously and the remainder of the ship was awash when Lakin observed it through the periscope at 1226hrs. What was thought to be an E-boat rescuing grimy survivors, turned out to be a grey rescue launch, unarmed except for two machine guns; Lakin therefore decided to leave them to their humanitarian occupation and turned away to seaward.

Safari left Algiers on 30 June 1943

HMS *Cyclops*. (Author's collection)

On 1 July the boat arrived at Bizerta and along with *Seraph* and *Shakespeare* was to act as a beacon submarine for the landings in Sicily (Operation Husky).

At 0410hrs on 10 July, there was indiscriminate dive-bombing by JU88s. Two sticks fell near *Safari*, but at 0452hrs a bomb exploded on the quarterdeck of the USS destroyer *Maddox* and she sank in 3 minutes. *SAFARI* searched for survivors, but none were found.

Later she arrived at Malta.

On 15 July *Safari* departed Malta and proceeded to the northeast coast of Sardinia.

On 18 July the 101-ton Italian motor/sailing minesweeper *Amalia* (Armatore Nicola Marchigiani Di San Benedetto Del Tronto) felt her wrath and was sunk by gunfire off Cape Comino; a seaplane picked up *Amalia*'s master. Off Favone Cove on the afternoon of the 19th, two 200-ton German barges, the *Maria* and *Paula*, were despatched by gunfire and the 88-ton Italian schooner and naval auxiliary *Margherita* was left damaged after one torpedo had passed under one of the barges.

While patrolling north of Boca Grande on 20 July, the 208-ton Italian auxiliary patrol yacht *Silvia Onorato* (Armatore Achille Onorato, or Silvio Colonna Di Napoli) was sunk at 1640hrs. Two torpedoes, which were individually aimed, detonated just abaft the stem and below the stern and the ship disintegrated, its mainmast almost striking *Safari*. (The Regia Marina had requisitioned the vessel as pilot boat (pilotina) *F50* on 31 May 1940.)

On the morning of 22 July, the 610-ton Buccari-type minelayer *Durazzo* was engaged by gunfire off Chiappri Point and was driven ashore, *Safari* then finished it off with one torpedo (During this action, *Safari* fired her one thousandth 3in shell at the enemy warship.)

During the morning of the 25th, *Safari* got mixed up in a real fracas, being engaged by the 120-ton Italian Navy minesweeping trawler *FR 70* (ex-French *LA Coubre*), plus three Tank Landing Craft and some shore batteries. The trawler had been previously mistaken for a vessel of around 600 tons, and two torpedoes were fired at it, but both missed. The *FR.70* was finally sunk by gunfire, however a large liner that had rounded Cape Enfoli unfortunately escaped.

On 26 July, *Safari* dived southeast and close to Elba and examined Porto Vecchio, but the vessels inside the harbour were inaccessible. In the Piombino Channel that evening, a 5000-ton motor vessel, escorted by three destroyers was sighted and attacked. Three torpedoes were fired at a range of 750 yards, but all missed their target. The cargo ship and one destroyer turned back to Porto Vecchio, while the other two destroyers searched for *Safari*. Fifteen minutes later two other large vessels were sighted against the land; the largest of which resembled the ex-French tanker *Champagne*, while the

HM SM *Sealion* and HM SM *Shark* in port, *c.*1938. (Private collection)

smallest looked like a 5,000-ton cargo ship. At 1918hrs *Safari* fired her last torpedoes at the tanker at a range of about 1,500 yards, but all three missed again.

Safari arrived back at Algiers on 30 July 1943.

On 15 August the boat left Algiers and arrived at Gibraltar on 19 August 1943. *Safari* departed Gibraltar on 19 August 1943 and after a patrol in Bay of Biscay returned to the UK for a much-needed refit, arriving at Portland on 7 September 1943. The refit was completed by late February 1944. *Safari* made one more war patrol to Norwegian waters under Lt Cdr John Robert Garstin Harvey, from 18–23 March 1944, but it was uneventful.

With Lt Cdr Harvey as commander, *Safari* joined the 7th Flotilla at Rothesay attached to HMS *Cyclops*, mainly for submarine training duties in home waters, until being paid off in July 1945. Being of an earlier design, partly riveted and having seen much war service, *Safari* was decommissioned on 7 January 1946 and sold to the ship-breakers J. Cashmore.

(In 1951 Ben Bryant retired from the Royal Navy to Storrington in West Sussex, where he wrote his memoir *One Man Band*. Most of this book, written in Ben Bryant's inimitable style, is devoted to his most famous commands, *Sealion* and *Safari*. Rear Admiral Ben Bryant CB, DSO★★, DSC, died in November 1994, aged 89 years. Though frequently arrogant, ruthless and intolerant, Ben Bryant's indomitable spirit mesmerised all who sailed with him. He was an indisputable master of the undersea war and one of the greatest sailors this country has produced. Other 'Safaris' have written of their experiences on this action-prone boat, including *Crash Dive* by Telegraphist Arthur Dickison and ERA Rob Roy McCurrach's *In Fear and Affection*. Both provide a rare glimpse of submarine life from the lower-deck perspective.

FINAL PATROL

On 8 January 1946, the submarine was in tow of *Empire Susan*, from Gosport (Blockhouse) to Newport, where she was to be scrapped, when events took an unexpected turn.

H. Griffiths, the master of *Empire Susan*, contributed this to the enquiry:

> We proceeded at 7 knots. At 22.05 there was a slight underwater concussion forcing the navigation lights on Safari to go out. We put the searchlights on the submarine but everything looked normal. Then Safari took a big shear to port. The tow rope lookout reported a tremendous strain, then the tow rope broke and Safari sank.

The inquiry concluded: 'Safari *had suffered a battery explosion because the fans had stopped'*. The batteries had overheated, *'the preparations for towing were lax'* but, as Ben Bryant could have reminded the inquiry, 'a *submarine is a wilful lady'*. At any rate it was a more fitting end for this proud boat than a cutter's blowtorch.

ADM 199/1888 ADM 199/1226 ADM 199/1345 ADM 199/1839

WRECK SITE

The wreck lies on a firm seabed of sand and gravel, dotted with small boulders, in a general depth of 38m (125ft), being the lowest astronomical depth. It is intact, lying 40° over to port and its bows aligned south, southeast. The submarine wreck is reportedly intact with hatches open and a large net is/was caught midships, although the conning tower itself is missing. Most, if not all of its fittings were removed before the boat sank, but the submarine is still an interesting one to visit. It is, of course not a war grave, but divers should beware of the conger eels that have taken up residence in the control room area.

U 322, KRIEGSMARINE U-BOAT

DATE OF LOSS: 29 December 1944
DEPTH: 48m
REFERENCE: 50 24'.773 N 002 26'.134 W
Also suggested: 50 24.87N 002 26.20W
LOCATION: 6.18 nautical miles SSE of Portland Bill

Type: VIIC/41 ocean-going attack boat   *Builders*: Flender Werke AG, Lübeck-Siems for Kriegsmarine   *Ordered*: on 14 October 1941, within the batch of *U 317–U 322*   *Keel laid*: as Works No.322 on 13 February 1943   *Launched*: on 18 December 1943   *Commissioned*: by Oberleutnant zur See Gerhard Wysk on 5 February 1944   *Feldpost No*: M 49 889

TECHNICAL SPECIFICATIONS

See page 342-343.

U 322 was assigned to 4.U-Flottille at Stettin as Ausbildungsboot from 5 February 1944 to 31 October 1944, with Gerhard Wysk the boat's only CO. Wysk was born in Weilburg, Lahn on 2 May 1920 and commenced his naval service in 1938; he served as First Watch Officer with the 38th, 7th and 5th Minesweeping Flotillas, between July 1940 and March 1943. Wysk was promoted to Oberleutnant zur See on 1 April 1943.

On 1 November 1944 *U 322* was formally assigned to 11.U-Flottille at Bergen, Norway for frontline duties.

U 322 left Kiel on 2 November 1944 and transferred to Horten near Oslo, where she arrived on 6 November.

FINAL PATROL

(2) *U 322* left Kristiansand South on 16 November 1944 for her first war patrol. There is no record of any signals having been received from *U 322* after the boat had left port. On 28 November 1944, U-boat Command advised the boat to proceed to naval grid square AM 70 as a provisional steering area. Six days later *U 322* was ordered to operate in the English Channel between the meridians of BF 2630 and BF 3620, using squares BF 3520, 3530 and 3610, off the French port of Cherbourg.

However, U-boat Command was still uncertain about the feasibility of operations in the English Channel, the reason being, there was a lack of reports from the first batch of U-boats sent from Norway to this area. In case the condition of the boat or its crew excluded operations in the Channel, Oblt.z.S. Wysk was given the freedom to choose alternative billets; the area off Milford, or the costal waters northeast of Land's End.

On 18 January 1945 *U 322* was routinely allocated Bergen as its port of destination. When the boat thereafter failed to return to port, it was posted as missing in late January 1945 (with effect from 3 January 1945). No information about the cause of its loss was then available to U-boat Command.

After the war the Allied U-boat Assessment Committee attributed the loss of *U 322* to an attack by the frigate HMS *Ascension* on 25 November 1944 in position 60° 18'N 04° 52'W after a sighting report of Sunderland 'G' of 330 Squadron RAF. At 2257hrs on 24 November 1944, flying at 1,500ft, the aircraft had obtained a radar contact at 6 miles in position 60° 26'N 04° 55'W, but heavy fog reduced visibility and nothing could be seen in spite of flying several times over the contact. Eventually, the nearby 17th Escort Group was contacted on VHF and the Sunderland led the frigates *Ascension* and *Moorsom* to the scene. After gaining a firm ASDIC contact running on course 210° at 0155hrs on 25 November 1944, *Ascension* carried out a Hedgehog attack at 0247hrs. Two of the projectiles appeared to have hit the target 19½ seconds after firing, with the remainder of the pattern exploding on the sea bottom at approximately 500 plus fathoms, several minutes later. Contact then became woolly and faded completely after 10 minutes. On passing over the position of attack after daylight, a large patch of oil and a strong odour of diesel oil were observed. Oil was still rising 10 hours after the attack and stretched for some 10 miles down wind. Samples could not be collected, as the oil slick was beginning to break up in heavy seas. Initially assessed as 'B – believed sunk', the attack was eventually credited on 26 September 1945 with the destruction of *U 322*, when details about its loss had become known from German records.

U 772 (Kapitänleutnant Alfred Rademacher) left Trondheim on 19 November 1944 for its second war patrol. There is likewise no record of any signals having been received from *U 772* after the boat had left port. In the following weeks *U 772* received the same operational orders as *U 322*. When *U 772* also failed to return to Trondheim as its port of destination at the end of the patrol, it was posted as missing in late January 1945, with effect from 8 January 1945. No information about the cause of its loss was then available to U-boat Command.

After the war the Allied U-boat Assessment Committee (AUD) attributed the loss of *U 772* to a depth charge attack by the Wellington 'L' of 407 Squadron RCAF at 0313hrs on the 30 December 1944 in position 50° 05'N 02° 31'W. Homing on a radar contact obtained at a range of 7 miles, both captain and second pilot sighted a very pronounced wake and then a *schnorchel* on course 300° true, clearly visible under the prevailing full moon and smooth sea conditions. Being too high to attack during the first run, the aircraft dropped six Mk XI Torpex depth charges spaced to 60ft with the *schnorchel* still visible on the second pass. After the depth charge explosions the *schnorchel* disappeared immediately. The aircraft remained a further 47 minutes in the vicinity but despite the clear moonlight no wreckage or oil was observed. Although the rear gunner stated that the *schnorchel* wake was straddled by charges Nos 2 and 3, some 30 yards astern of it, post-attack calculation revealed that they were at best across the extreme tip of the U-boat's tail, inflicting some damage. Consequently, the attack was initially graded as 'H – insufficient evidence of damage' on 29 January 1945. However, probably based on tracking evidence drawn from 'Ultra' signal intelligence, indicating the loss of at least one U-boat in the Channel at the end of December 1944, the attack was up-graded to 'B – believed sunk' less than a month later. On 26 September 1945 the AUD Committee eventually attributed the loss of *U 772* to the aircraft when details regarding its loss had become known from German records.

After the war, *U 772* was attributed with the torpedoing of no less than five merchant vessels between 23 and 29 December 1944, which were left unaccounted for by the other boats that were then known to have operated in the Channel. One of the largest was the 5,149-ton *Dumfries* (Gdynia America Shipping Lines, London). She was part of convoy MKS 71 comprising twenty-four ships when she was attacked at 1150hrs (Continental time), south of St Catherine's Point, off the Isle of Wight, at position 50° 23'N 01° 43'W. She was carrying 8,258 tons of iron ore and two passengers, on a voyage from Bona for the Tyne. The master, Captain Robert Blackey, forty-eight crewmen, two passengers and eight gunners were rescued; the corvette HMS *Balsam* (K.72) (Lt Cdr Sir J.H.S. Fayer DSC) picked up the master and seven crew and landed at Portsmouth, while forty-one crew, eight gunners and passengers were taken on board the trawler HMT *Pearl* (T.22) and landed at Southampton.

During the early afternoon of 29 December 1944, the two corvettes HMCS *Calgary* and HMS *Dahlia* were accompanying convoy TBC 21 when two US merchant ships in the convoy were torpedoed in quick succession. *Arthur Sewall*, a 7,176-ton steamship, was off Portland Bill, en-route from the Seine Estuary to Mumbles in ballast when she was hit by a torpedo; she was carrying twenty-nine armed guards and a crew of forty; two crewmen, Junior Engineer Joseph Alfred Gauvin and Irving Gilbert Harrington, a Fireman/Wiper, were both killed. The vessel was towed to Portland harbour and, after temporary repairs, arrived at Falmouth in tow on 1 March 1945. (In May 1946 *Arthur Sewall* was towed to Bremerhaven, loaded with poison gas bombs and sunk.)

The 7,192-ton New Orleans-registered steamship *Black Hawk* was en-route from Cherbourg to Fowey in ballast, when a torpedo exploded opposite No.5 hold on the port side and the entire stern disintegrated; at the same instant, the after magazine blew up. A large crack then appeared on the starboard side at No.3 hold, which continued from the deck to the waterline. As the ship flooded immediately at the after-end, putting her in astern-down position, the crew abandoned ship, but the Chief Cook, Ho Leung was drowned. The surviving crew of forty, twenty-seven armed guard and one US Army officer left in four boats and two life rafts and HMS *Dahlia* picked them up an hour later and landed them at Brixham at 1830hrs. The ship was taken in tow and beached in Worbarrow Bay, Weymouth in position 50° 36.45'N 02° 12.21'W, but was written off as a total loss.

Five minutes after the last torpedo detonated, HMCS *Calgary* turned in to make an attack of her own.

AUD 50/45 – Report HMCS *Calgary* – 50° 26'N 02° 28'W – 29/12/44

Two ships had been torpedoed so *Calgary* took up 'observant':

> At 1329 an ASDIC contact was obtained bearing 160 at 2000 yards. This was classified as 'doubtful', but attacked with a 10 charge pattern of dcs…A good contact was obtained bearing 045 at 1700 yards and an attack delivered, which produced an oil slick, but caused damage to *Calgary*'s ASDIC. During the run in, a torpedo was reported approaching from Green 20 and on altering course hard to starboard and steadying on that course, loud HE was heard to starboard. A further 10 charge pattern was dropped near the marker at 1359 after which *Calgary* rejoined the convoy.

In spite of the oil slick, this attack was initially assessed, 'insufficient evidence of damage'. However we now know that a late-war Type VIIC U-boat wreck lies at 50° 24' 87N 02° 26' 20W, which is close to the position of the attack on the SS *Arthur Sewall* and SS *Black Hawk I* in July 1999. The Naval Historical Branch (FDS) concluded that *U 772* had been sunk by HMCS *Calgary* on 29 December 1944, in position 50° 26'N 02° 28'W. However, the identity of the boat in question remains a mystery. According to the BdU Diary *U 322* was expected to be in this sector, square BF 31 on 19 December, having been allocated a patrol billet in BF 35. *U 772* was expected to remain in BF 35, moving to BF 26 on 31 December. Was the target of *Calgary*'s onslaught *U 322* or *U 772*?

Dr Axel Niestlé has assembled the pieces of this intriguing mystery to produce the convincing analysis outlined below:

U 322 or U 772? – An Analysis by Dr Axel Niestle

Although no direct information on the identity of the U-boat attacked by Wellington 'L' of 407 Squadron RCAF could be found in German records, it was probably directed against *U 486*. No war diary of its patrol in the Channel has survived, but from its situation report radioed to U-boat Command on 7 January 1945 it is known that the boat had stayed in its operational area off Cherbourg from 21 to 29 December 1944. Thus the boat is to be expected to have passed through the area of the attack at exactly the same time, although the attack is not mentioned in radio report. Of the other two boats previously ordered to patrol off Cherbourg, *U 680* had turned back to Norway already on 23 December 1944 and *U 485* is known from its war diary to have stayed about 25 miles east of the attack position. In addition, in U-boat Commands message of experience No. 217 radioed to all boats on 31 January 1945, it is mentioned that U-boats having returned recently from patrol had twice experienced air attacks while schnorchelling at full moon in a calm sea. This description fits perfectly with the attack report of Wellington L/407 and the full moon phase on 29 December 1944.

Diving exploration carried out since 1996 on the U-boat wreck found close to *Calgary*'s recorded attack position produced information on numerous details of the wreck. One of the prominent features was the presence of four pressure-proof rubber boat containers fitted on the forward upper-deck. From the war diary, *U 322* is known to have been fitted with the containers in October 1944, while it is most unlikely that *U 772*, then based at Trondheim, ever carried them. In addition, from comparison with the outbound routes of other boats departing from Trondheim at the end of 1944, it appears very probable that *U 772* took the route via the Iceland-Færoe gap into the Atlantic. Instead, *U 322* is likely to have used the shorter way through the Shetland-Færoe gap, thus saving several days on its passage to the allocated operational area. According to the daily plot maintained by U-boat Command, *U 322* is expected to have arrived off Cherbourg around 16 December 1944. The delay by using the northerly outbound route may have caused the commander of *U 772* to use the option given by U-boat Command to occupy the alternative operational area off Milford, in order to lengthen the stay in the operational area. In this case *U 772* can be expected to have passed to the south of Ireland around 17 December 1944. In the light of the details presented above there can be little doubt that the boat sunk by the *Calgary* was in fact *U 322*, while *U 772* fell victim to the *Nyasaland*.

From the reports covering the loss or damage of the five merchant ships previously credited to U 772 and comparison of the individual positions given for the actions, it is also obvious that two losses: SS *Slemish* and Landing Craft Infantry *Empire Javelin*, can no longer be attributed to *U 322*, because the distances to later attacks are unlikely to have been covered by a submerged U-boat in the time remaining. Instead, both ships were probably lost after detonating mines. Thus, *U 322* should now be credited with the sinking of the British SS *Dumfries* on 23 December 1944 and the torpedoing of the American Liberty-ships SS *Arthur Sewall* and SS *Black Hawk*, which were both damaged beyond repair, 6 days later.

The authors wish to thank Dr Axel Niestlé for his kind permission to reproduce the information on the last voyages and the final fate of *U 322* and *U 772* from his report on the loss of the two U-boats. All copyrights remain with the author.

NARA T1022, Roll 3900, PG30401, 31752 U-Boot-Ehrenmal Möltenort

THE MEN LOST WITH U 322

Bauer, Ernst Ob.Mt. (25-4-1921)
Becker, Alois Maat. (29-11-1920)
Bettzüge, Karl-Ludwig Ob.Gfr. (4-1-1924)
Blank, Walter Ob.Gfr. (16-05-1924)
Bohlemann, Werner Maat. (18-09-1922)
Bräunsdorf, Gerhard Mt. (20-1-1922)
Burchardt, Dieter Ob.Gfr. (10-12-1925)
Casper, Johann Ob.Gfr. (29-12-1924)
Chromback, Guido Ob.Gfr. (18-11-1924)
Coeler, Werner Maat. (28-10-1922)
Dankworth, Walter Mtr. (12-9-1924)
Ebner, Josef Gfr. (13-2-1924)
Geuther, Heinz Maat. 24-1-1922)
Goltz, Alfred Ob.Gfr. (7-1-1925)
Hartlieb, Herbert Ob.Gfr. (26-2-1925)
Heinzmann, Werner Ob.Gfr. (15-5-1925)
Kapell, Rolf Maat. (13-4-1922)
Katzer, Gerhard-Fritz Ob.Gfr. (12-5-1924)
Kramer, Meinolf Mtr. (20-2-1925)
Kramer, Wilhelm Maat. (2-3-1925)
Kremer, Oskar Ob.Gfr. (30-6-1921)
Krempel, Erich O.Strm. (22-6-1920)
Krüger, Hans Ob.Gfr. (1-3-1924)
Kuchenreiter, Albert Maat. (22-8-1920)
Lausch, Heinrich Ob.Gfr. (10-7-1921)
Lazarowitz, Fritz Gfr. (26-6-1925)

Lohaus, Paul Ob.Gfr. (18-6-1925)
Lutz, Franz Ob.Gfr. (10-3-1925)
Mayr, Franz Ob.Gfr. (13-3-1925)
Michler, Herbert Maat. (21-3-1923)
Mothes, Johannes Ob.Gfr. (6-1-1925)
Müller, Karl O.Masch. (6-3-1919)
Polomski, Erich Ob.Gfr. (21-4-1924)
Prokscha, Josef Maat. (10-7-1921)
Rehdner, Helmut Ob.Gfr. (16-3-1925)
Reusch, Ludwig Oblt.Ing. 26-8-1915)
Richter, Heinz Gfr. (9-5-1925)
Ries, Heinrich Maat. (6-6-1922)
Ruppert, Wilhelm O.Strm. (30-9-1919)
Schiffmann, Johannes Gfr. (18-4-1924)
Schrenk, Heinz Ob.Gfr. (13-5-1924)
Schulz, Helmuth Maat. (29-9-1920)
Seifart, Wilhelm O.Masch. (9-1-1918)
Steinbrecher, Alfred Ob.Gfr. (14-11-1923)
Strack, Ernst-Jürgen Ltz.S. (28-12-1923)
Twardzik, Walter Ob.Gfr. (21-12-1924)
Walter, Franz Ob.Gfr. (30-1-1924)
Weisskopf, Hans-Joachim Ob.Gfr. (13-3-1924)
Wiemann, Gerhard H.Gfr. (24-2-1923)
Wysk, Gerhard Oblt.z.S. (2-5-1920)
Zeisbrich, Walter Maat. (27-11-1920)
Zimmer, Josef Ob.Gfr. (9-5-192)

WRECK SITE

This wreck lies on a seabed of gravel and shingle, in a general depth of 40m, being the lowest astronomical depth. It is upright, with the complete stern section broken off, possibly as a result of salvage, or trawler damage. The casing is now also badly broken and only the resident anemones and shoal of bib keep the wreck alive.

Using the *Lindberg* identification method, we would expect to find a bow slot pattern of 3-14-4 for *U 322*. Whatever its identity, the wreck is a war grave and should be respected as such.

L24, HM SUBMARINE

DATE OF LOSS: 10 January 1924
DEPTH: 54m
REFERENCE: 50 22'.536 N 002 37'.894 W
LOCATION: 10.63 miles SSW of Portland Bill

All submarine disasters are tragic, but there is something particularly so about the loss of *L24*. The reader should reflect that a terrific responsibility burdens the willing shoulders of a submarine skipper. He alone takes the key decisions and, not surprisingly, the 'perisher' is considered to be the most demanding of all military examinations. The success of the mission and the survival of boat and crew depend upon the commanding officer's judgement alone. One miscalculation can bring catastrophe, but even the most experienced and competent of skippers can make mistakes.

Type: L9 Class Group-II overseas mine-laying patrol boat   *Pennant*: No.L24   *Builders*: Vickers-Armstrongs at Barrow-in-Furness for the Royal Navy   *Keel laid*: on 25 February 1918   *Launched*: on 19 February 1919   *Commissioned*: by Lt Cdr Phillip Esmond Phillips DSO★ on 24 February 1920

TECHNICAL SPECIFICATIONS

Hull: Admiralty saddle tank design   *Surface displacement*: 911 tons   *U/Dt*: 1,068 tons   *LBD*: 72.72m × 7.02m × 4.03m   *Machinery*: 2 × 12-cylinder solid injection Vickers diesels   *Props*: 2 bronze   *S/Sp*: 17 knots   *Op/R*: 24 days and 3,800 nautical miles at 10.5 knots   *Sub/R*: 65 nautical miles at 5 knots   *U/Power*: 2 × 2,400bhp General Electric motors gave 9 knots   *Batteries*: 3 × 112 cell Exide-lead/acid   *Fuel/Cap*: 51 tons normal and 71 tons max   *Armament*: 4 × 53.34cm (21in) bow torpedo tubes   *Torpedoes*: 8 × 53.34cm (21in)   *Guns*: none   *Mine chutes*: 76.20cm (30in)   *Mines*: type 'S Mk. IV' and 52.96cm (20.85in) in diameter; weighed 244.94 kilos (540 pounds), with 95.26 kilos (210 pounds) of Amatol and activated 4 × Herz horns, mounted uppermost; suitable for 55–61m depth   *Diving*: max-op-depth 45.72m (150ft) (L.2 once survived a 300ft uncontrolled dive)   *Complement*: 5 officers and 34 ratings.

Group-II were built with the same general armament as Group-1, but were modified. Mine-laying boats, including *L24*, were not fitted with beam torpedo tubes because of the mine-chutes. *L24* was attached to HMS *Dolphin* submarine school flotilla from her commissioning to being lost.

There were twenty-seven boats in Group II, of which six were completed as minelayers, along the lines of the 'E' Class, with vertical mine-chutes in the saddle tanks. *L14, L17, L.26* and *L.27* had 16 mine-tubes and carried 16 mines, but *L24* and *L.25* had only 14-tubes. There were many variations of design in the 'L' Class. From *L12* onwards, the 4-inch (101.60mm) gun was raised to the bridge-deck level, where an enclosed revolving access trunk served it. However *L24* and *L.25* differed from the rest of the group, by having a different conning tower and no gun-mount. (It was said the raised gun was intended to enable the engagement of targets when trimmed down, but this is a very debatable point.) This class was also fitted with an additional watertight bulkhead abaft the torpedo tubes, to separate the torpedo-tube compartment from the torpedo-room. The boats in Group II were built under the 1916 Emergency War Programme, while Group III were

HM SM L24. (Author's collection)

from the 1917–1918 Emergency War Programme, of which seven were completed: *L52* to *L56* and *L69* and *L71*.

Lt Cdr Phillip Esmond Phillips RN DSO★ was her first commanding officer and served with *L24* from 24 February 1920 until 11 December 1920. (He was also one of only two submarine commanders to sink two U-boats.)

Lt Cdr Anthony Bevis Lockhart RN DSC assumed command of the boat from 11 December 1920 until 30 August 1923, when Lt Cdr Paul Leathley Eddis took over. Eddis served from 30 August 1923 until her loss on 10 January 1924. He joined submarines on 1 May 1913 for his submarine training at HMS *Dolphin*. On 25 August 1913, Sub-Lt Paul Eddis (Seniority 15 December 1911) was appointed to HMS *Vulcan*, the Depot Ship of the 7th Submarine Flotilla, at Dundee 'for submarines'. No submarine was specified in the 'Navy List' of December 1913, but it is probable that it was submarine *C23* – of which Geoffrey Layton was the commanding officer. Promotion to lieutenant followed on 15 December 1913 and, on 12 October 1914 he was appointed to HMS *Maidstone*, the Depot Ship of the 8th Submarine Flotilla at Harwich 'for submarines – for *E13*'.

(Note: Lt Cdr Layton and 1st Lt Eddis both took part in the disastrous attempt to try and enter the Baltic with *E13* through the narrow waters of the Sound between Denmark and Sweden, during the night of 19 August 1915. The boat unfortunately grounded in Danish territorial waters where she was attacked by two German torpedo-boat destroyers and fifteen men were killed. Fourteen men, including Lt Cdr Layton and Lt Eddis, escaped and returned home.)

Lt Eddis was appointed to HMS *Dolphin* on 30 September 1917, but one month later was relocated to HMAS *Platypus* on 27 October 1917, 'for command of submarine *E38*'. His next assignment was to the Depot Ship HMS *Bonaventure* 'for Submarine *E32* in Command'. He was further assigned to the battle cruiser HMS *Lion* on 25 May 1919 and then to the battle cruiser HMS *Hood* in March 1920. On returning to submarines he was appointed to *HMS Dolphin* 'for Command of Submarine *H 32*', to date 15 April 1921. He was also the senior submarine officer of the 3rd Submarine Flotilla. His next appointment was to HMS *Lucia* 'for Submarine *L71* in Command', to date 11 December 1921. Paul Eddis was promoted to lieutenant commander on 15 December 1921 and, on 30 August 1923, he took over the command of HM S/M *L24*.

FINAL PATROL

The submarine was taking part in fleet exercise, operation 'GA' off Portland. The fleet consisting of submarines, battleships and destroyers were divided into two sections, Red and Blue. *L24* (Lt-Cdr Eddis) was assigned to Blue Force and leader of submarines *H23* and *H48*. Blue Force also consisted of submarines attached to HMS *Dolphin* and *Maidstone* and aircraft from 10th Group RAF. One of the aims of this major exercise was to provide submarines with the rare experience of attacking a battle-fleet. Red Force was to sail down the Channel from Portland on the 10th. Conversely, Blue Force submarines would seize any opportunity to attack. The Blue Force submarines weighed anchor in Weymouth Bay and headed out to sea at 0345hrs. By 0810hrs the submarines were in position and by 0920hrs they could detect the screws of Red Force on their hydrophones.

The battleships of the 1st Division of the First Battle Squadron had been assigned to Red Force. Now they were thundering down the Channel with the battleship *Resolution* (fourth ship) following astern of *Revenge*.

Captain G. Stephenson, in command of *Revenge,* viewed proceedings from the bridge:

> Shortly after 11.00 I head the chief yeoman report a submarine on the port beam. I observed a large swirl of discoloured water about 300 yards distant. Red 100. I imagined this was a submarine about to break surface after a dummy attack. Almost immediately afterwards I observed a periscope in the patch coming towards the battleship line. The periscope was well out the water, about 4ft and the submarine seemed to be travelling fast and was endeavouring to pass between *Revenge* and *Resolution*. I followed the movement of the periscope and feared that the submarine must be rammed. As the periscope moved across *Revenge*'s wake and arrived at a certain distance across the starboard bow of *Resolution* I had a feeling of great relief, as I then believed she had just cleared the *Resolution*. I estimated that the periscope was in sight about 50 seconds. A minute or two after this *Resolution*'s signal was received reporting a heavy bump felt and my attention was called to *Resolution*'s starboard paravane chain, having been carried away.

Leading Seaman Horace Samson was on the Admiral's Bridge of *Revenge* during the mock attack:

> I was on the admiral's bridge and sighted a periscope brown in colour endeavouring to get between two ships, speed 10 knots. I watched the periscope until it got nearly ahead of *Resolution* 50 yards distant. When the periscope suddenly dipped as if to do a crash dive, I turned to the Flag Officer and said, 'Oh God Sir, she'll ram her'.

Commander Frank Elliott on the fore-bridge of *Revenge*, recollected climbing onto the port 6in director tower and seeing 6-8ft of periscope above the surface on his port quarter and moving to cross at right angles from port to starboard across the bows of *Resolution*. Commander Elliott then looked across to starboard and seeing nothing break the surface, breathed a sigh of relief in the thought that she had cleared the bows in time.

Gunner S.H Vennard on *Revenge* also reported that he had witnessed the periscope about 1ft from the surface and approximately 800 yards (731.52m) on the port beam. He said it rose up to about 3ft, stopped rising momentarily and then rapidly began to disappear down, close to the port bow of *Resolution*. Gunner Vennard said that he was concerned for the boat and waited to see if the battleship showed any signs of a collision, but then her bows lifted to the sea just at that precise moment and he expected the submarine would have been struck. He concluded that within the next 5 minutes there was also no sign of the submarine surfacing on the starboard side, either.

Minutes later the Blue Force submarines *H23* and *H48* surfaced and passed down between the lines on completion of their attacks. However there was no sign of *L24*. The search was on for the missing submarine as salvage vessels headed for the scene. At 1640hrs *Resolution* docked and divers immediately examined her bow for damage but the search proved fruitless because of the silt stirred up by the screws. The starboard paravane chain showed certain collision damage and as the chain had been at 32ft, this damage was almost certainly caused by striking a submarine hard enough to fracture a link at the lowest point of the stem. And an impact capable of fracturing a thick chain link would most certainly rip through a pressure hull. On the 11th Admiralty personnel were privately briefing journalists that the crew of *L24* were probably already dead.

The Daily Sketch reported that *'the damage to* Resolution *makes it clear that the submarine was badly holed by the collision'.* It was also reported that *L24* had suffered a near miss a few weeks earlier when she had been 'skimmed' by a battleship on similar exercises. With rescue apparently out of the question, the media turned to human-interest stories.

Paul Eddis was a highly respected officer who helped organise and teach the 'Perisher' course. Likewise a hard core of his crew were veterans of the First World War. Tel Parkhurst and L/S Dempsey DSM had earlier served in *E7* and had both been prisoners of the Turks. The wife of CERA Andrew Wallace had lost her first husband in *A3*. It did not take the media long to find the inevitable premonition tale and it found its way into most of the tabloids. It surfaced in the form of Mrs Matthews of Southsea, who related how her husband, ERA Charlie Matthews had been much troubled by nightmares and a sense of an overwhelming disaster in the offering. *'I know what will happen. The boat will come up, take her distance, go down and when we come up again, we will be struck by something.'* At 1600hrs on the day of the accident, Mrs Matthews heard Charlie call her name. So vivid was the experience that she called out, *'Charlie, is that you?'* At the same time, her lodger Mrs Dicks heard the voice of Charlie Matthews clearly say, *'You look after her now'.*

The salvage vessels could have done with some of Mrs Dicks' clairvoyant skills in the days that followed because they were not having much luck with science. According to the logs of the vessels involved in the search, an obstruction thought to be *L24* was located on the morning following the accident. However the position could not be buoyed and the ships were unable to relocate it.

On the 11th the weather was so bad and the seas so rough, currents so treacherous, that divers could not be used. By the 12th, all but one of the salvage vessels returned to harbour. All attempts at salvage were abandoned. *L24* joined the sad litany of inter-war submarines lost to accidents. She was forgotten for nearly sixty years until one day a diver from Guildford BSAC chanced upon her. (Note: this was not the SS *VIDAR* that sank *M1*.)

THE MEN WHO WERE LOST WITH THE BOAT

Arnold, Able Seaman

Backhurst, Petty officer Telegraphist

Ballard, Sidney Roland K.22780 Stoker.1st

Barton, Donald Howell, 1st Lieutenant

Bennett, Sidney Frank J.15947 Petty Officer

Buck, Elijah Frederick 224883 Chief Petty Officer

Bulbeck, Harold John J.27703 Leading Seaman

Byron, John Warrant Engineering Officer

Cann, Hedley Acting K.16998 Leading Stoker

Chevis, Harry Fielder J.13882 Leading Signalman

Crumbie, David William K.55839 Stoker.1st

Dempsey, William George (DSM) 215684 L/Seaman

Donald, Hugh Lamberton 228142 Able Seaman

Eddis, Paul Leathley Lieutenant Commander – CO.

Flanagan, Bertie Wannell K.61053 Stoker.1st

Fletcher, David Kerwin M24883 E.R.Artificer.4th

France, Alfred John Mead J.20742 Able Seaman

Garrish, William John J.16122 Able Seaman

Gray, Donald Nixon (MBE) Lieutenant 3rd Officer

Green, George William Frederick K.59790 Stoker 1st

Gregory, Leslie Leading Aircraftsman RAF

Grigg, Alfred John K.60726 Stoker.1st

Harman, A. Leading Aircraftsman RAF

Hillman, Edward Jame K.15258 Stoker Petty Officer

Johnson, Edwin George K.20107 Act Leading Stoker

Lane, Percy M.3721 Engine Room Artificer.1st

Lawley, Arthur Reginald J.226961 Able Seaman

Lough, Frederick Albert Ignatius J.11342 Leading Seaman

Lyon, Edmond K.17360 Stoker.1st

Matthew, Charles M.6689 E.R.Artificer.2nd

Mitchell, James J.92053 Telegraphist

Parkhurst, Thomas Milner James J.8151 P.O. Tele

Phillips, Sydney Frank K.60396 Stoker.1st

Pound, Ernest Percy Victor K.24137 Stoker.1st

Quantock, Thomas Henry J.42358 Able Seaman

Smith, Allan J.86413 Signalman

Stapleton, Joseph Benjamin J.2681 Leading Seaman

Stendall, Eric Sub Lieutenant

Stewart, George William K.56820 Stoker.1st

Tippen, George James Niven K.16549 L. Seaman

Toppin H. Lt (Pilot RAF)

Walker, William K.22942 Stoker.1st

Wallace, Wallace Andrew Chalmers M1390
CERA
Waterfield, George Harry J.32831 Able Seaman
Watkinson, Donald William Grange Lieutenant
Navig/Of.

Wilson, John J.71669 Petty Officer
Wise, William John 239452 Petty Officer

The crew of *L24* are remembered on a memorial plaque in St Ann's Church, Portsmouth, there are further memorials to Lt Cdr Eddis in Bisham Abbey and in Holy Trinity Church, Ryde.

ADM 1/8660/85 ADM 173/9754-9800

WRECK SITE

In 1981 diver Andy Smith found the wreck in 55m (180ft) with a deep scour at bow and stern. The submarine was upright and apparently intact. Close inspection revealed a deep 'V'-shaped cleft just aft of the conning tower on the starboard side. It was noted that the edges of this gash turned inwards. The cleft was 2ft at its widest, narrowing to a mere groove over the top of the hull. It seems highly likely that as Lt Cdr Eddis made his attack on HMS *Revenge*, the sheer noise generated by the battleships may have baffled the hydrophone operators. Likewise Lt Cdr Eddis may not have made a full periscope sweep, believing *Revenge* to be the last ship in the line. Once committed to the attack, there was no going back. Lt Cdr Eddis spotted the bows of HMS *Resolution* too late. Had the boat been a mere 6ft deeper it is feasible she may have survived the encounter. The hydroplanes remain for eternity at hard a dive – eloquent testimony that Lt Cdr Eddis attempted to take avoiding action. As the bows dived, *L24*'s stern naturally tilted upwards – directly into the path of *Resolution*. The bows are starting to deteriorate now but it is apparent that the upper port side torpedo tube is open and the remaining three are closed. There is a postscript: the torpedo-loading hatch was found to be open – evidence of an escape attempt. The control room would have flooded on impact with the battleship but perhaps survivors in the fore ends were able to close the watertight doors and mount an escape. DSEA sets were not yet standard issue. If any of these unfortunate men did make an escape bid, no trace of them was ever found.

Memorial tablet in St Anne's Church, Portsmouth Dockyard. (Private collection)

P555, HM SUBMARINE

DATE SUNK: **25 August 1957**
DEPTH: 36m
REFERENCE: 50 30'.902 N 002 33'.680 W
LOCATION: 3.80 nautical miles W of Portland Bill

Type: P551 Type, ex-US – 'S' Class submarine   *Pennant*: No.P555   *Builders*: Fore River Shipbuilding Co., Bethlehem shipyard, Quincy, MA, USA   *Keel laid*: on 1 November 1918   *Launched*: as S.24 (Pendent No.SS-129) on 27 June 1922   *Commissioned*: by Lt Cdr Louis E. Denfield on 24 August 1923

TECHNICAL SPECIFICATIONS

Hull: single   *Type*: American 'S' Class lend-lease, non-Government-designed submarine of the EBCo type, sponsored by Mrs Herbert B. Loper   *Surface displacement*: 854 tons   *U/Dt*: 1,062 tons   *LBD*: 66.87m × 6.29m × 4.80m   *Machinery*: 2 × 600hp 8cyl 'NELSECO' diesels   *Props*: 2 bronze   *S/Sp*: 13 knots   *Op/R*: 8,000 nautical miles at 10 knots   *Sub/R*: 150 sea miles at 5 knots   *U/Power*: 2 × 750bhp 'Ridgeway Dynamo and Electrical' electric motors gave 11 knots   *Batteries*: lead/acid   *Fuel/Cap*: 168 tons   *Armament*: 4 × 53.34cm (21in) bow torpedo tubes   *Torpedoes*: 12 × 53.34cm (21in)   *Guns*: 1 × 101.6mm (4in /50) Quick Firing (QF) deck gun   *Ammo*: 90 rounds 101mm   *Mines*: none   *Diving*: maximum diving depth 60.96m (200ft)   *Complement*: 42 (originally 4 officers and 28 ratings)

The USS *S.24* operated from New London and Connecticut during 1923 and 1924, but in February 1924, also served at the islands of St Thomas and US Virgin Island. From 6-13 March 1924 she made a visit to Trinidad, then to the Panama Canal area during April 1924. From 27 April to May 1925 she across the Pacific and visited Hawaii. Additional service was seen around the Panama Canal area between February and March 1926 and yet again in February 1929. *S.24* made more visits to Hawaii during 1927 and 1928, but twice the following year, 1929.

The next principal ports *S.24* was to serve in, up until early 1930, was San Diego, San Pedro and Mare Island. On 1 December 1930, she sailed from San Diego and on the 12th, reached Pearl Harbour. This remained her base until 15 October 1938 when she left and returned to New London, arriving on 4 January 1939. New London became her new base, but the boat was just partially crewed from 1 April until 1 July 1940, when she resumed full duties. The Panama Canal area was cruised from late December 1941 and up to May 1942 and she sailed back to New London on the 21st. *S.24* was decommissioned at New London on 10 August 1942 and struck from the US Navy list on 11 September 1942. In October 1942, now commissioned into the Royal Navy as HM S/M *P555*, she was transferred under the Lend-lease agreement to Britain, along with five other American 'S' Class submarines.

P555 spent most of her Royal Navy time in home waters attached to HMS *Cyclops*, 7th Flotilla, at Rothesay, after initially being posted to Freetown Sierra Leone for ASW training. She was used for ASW training and usually under the command of a new submarine CO, to give them experience before going on to the real thing. She had the nickname of 'State Express' after the famous American cigarette brand of the time 'State Express 555'. The commanding officers changed about every six to eight weeks and Lt Edward Young RNVR took command of *P555* on 26 March 1943. (The first Volunteer Reserve Officer to take command of a Royal Navy submarine was Lt Frederick Henry Sherwood RCNVR who assumed command of *P556* on 15 March 1943.)

P555 was the only submarine out of the six 'S' Class lend-lease boats to serve on frontline duties. In 1944, *P555* was slightly damaged in a collision in the Clyde and she was found to be too uneconomic to remain in service. She was 'paid off' for return to the USN administration on 20 December 1944, but the US Navy had no further use for such an aging submarine, so she was struck from their list.

FINAL PATROL

On 25 August 1947, *P555* was towed out and intentionally sunk as ASDIC target by the Royal Navy, off Portland Bill.

WRECK SITE

The wreck of *P555* is orientated in a northwest to southeast direction and lies on a seabed of sand and shingle, in a general depth of 36m, being the lowest astronomical depth. It is upright and intact, except for the deck gun and propellers, which were removed prior to the boat being sunk. Due to the fact that the wreck lies along the tidal flow, it is rather a difficult target to get a shot/anchor into. The wooden decking on the casing has decomposed, but almost everything else is just as it was when it sank, including the intact hatches, conning tower and the periscope housing. At the stern, the empty prop shafts protrude. The rudder and hydroplanes are undamaged. On the bow, a section shaped like a wedge is visible, probably marking the position of a fitting that was removed prior to disposal. On the starboard side of the bow, a small anchor had been folded into purpose-built alcove. The hydroplanes and four torpedo tubes, two on each side, can also be seen at the bow. The wreck has its own resident fish swimming around, as well as some very big congers that have been reported. Well-established colonies of hydroids and anemones have also inhabited the submarine's hull, especially around the upper bow and stern sections.

UB 74, SM IMPERIAL U-BOAT

DATE OF LOSS: 26 May 1918
DEPTH: 32m
REFERENCE: 50 31.48N 02 33.34W
LOCATION: 3.86 nautical miles WNW from Portland Bill

Type: UBIII coastal torpedo attack boat   *Builders*: AG Vulcan, Hamburg for Kaiserliche Deutsche Marine   *Ordered*: on 23 September 1916, within the batch UB 72–UB 74   *Keel laid*: as Yard No.98   *Launched*: on 12 September 1917   *Commissioned*: by Oberleutnant zur See Karl Neureuther on 24 October 1917

TECHNICAL SPECIFICATIONS

Hull: double   *Surface displacement*: 508 tons   *U/Dt*: 639 tons   *LBDH*: 55.52m × 5.76m × 3.68m × 8.25m   *Machinery*: 2 × 550ps Körting diesels   *Props*: 2 bronze   *S/Sp*: 13.4 knots   *Op/R*: 8,420 nautical miles at 6 knots   *Sub/R*: 55 nautical miles at 4 knots   *U/Power*: 2 × 394ps electric motors gave 7.5 knots   *Batteries*: lead/acid/accumulators   *Fuel/Cap*: 37 + 78 tons   *Armament*: 4 bow and 1 stern 50.04cm torpedo tubes   *Torpedoes*: 10 × 50.04cm (19.7in)   *Guns*: 1 × 105mm (4.13in) forward deck gun   *Ammo*: 160 rounds of 105mm   *Mines*: none   *Diving*: max-op-depth 50m (164ft) and 30 sec to crash-dive   *Complement*: 3 officers and 31 ratings

UB 74 was assigned to the German-based V. Flottille at Bremerhaven on 6 January 1918 until 25 January 1918. Karl Neureuther was commander from 24 October 1917 and made one operational patrol with the boat:

On 16 January 1918, *UB 74* departed Bremerhaven and sailed around the Shetland Isles for operations, before putting into the Zeebrugge on 25 January 1918; no ships were sunk.

Upon arrival at Zeebrugge, the boat formally transferred to the Flandern.I U-Flottille and Oblt. z.S. Ernst Steindorff assumed command on 31 January.

(2) *UB 74* left Flanders on 21 February and sailed to the western end of the English Channel. Steindorff torpedoed and sank the 1,263-ton SS *Greavesash* (1917 – Newbigin Steam Shipping Co. Ltd, Newcastle), 10 miles northeast of Cape Barfleur without warning on the 26th; she was defensively armed and in ballast, en-route from Le Havre for Barry Roads; eight crewmen were lost

SOME OF THE CREW WHO DIED

Ali Ahmad, Fireman
Blurton, J.H., Second Mate

Davies, David Jones, 44yrs, Boatswain (Bosun)
Gunther, Robert Henry, 40yrs, Donkeyman
Heslop, George, 52yrs, Steward
Horn, James Frederick, 58yrs, Able Seaman
Richards, William Warren, 33yrs, Able Seaman

That same day, the steamer *Romny* (1893 – The Shipping Controller, London) of 1,024 tons and armed for defence, was torpedoed and sunk without warning, 10 miles off Cape Barfleur, while travelling in ballast from Rouen to Swansea; nine crewmen were lost.

SOME OF THE MEN WHO DIED ON ROMNY

De Waard, William, 33yrs, Able Seaman
Corkish, William Henry, Leading Seaman RNR
Firoz Ali, Fireman and Trimmer
Jensen, Ernst, 25yrs, Sailor
Pappas, John, 24yrs, Fireman
Polfliet, Isidoor, 56yrs, Donkeyman
Smith, A., 40yrs, Boatswain (Bosun)
Snowley, Arthur, 48yrs, Able Seaman

Steindorff allegedly made a number of torpedo attacks on other steamships, but no vessels were sunk; by 3 March he was of the opinion that the weapons were faulty and decided to abort the patrol.

UB 74 arrived back at Flanders on 6 March.

(3) Departing Flanders on 31 March 1918, *UB 74* operated at the western end of the English Channel, travelling via the Dover Strait. Off Beachy Head, Steindorff fired a torpedo at a ship and an explosion was heard after 90 seconds, but there is no confirmation of a hit. On 7 April the 986-ton *Rye* (1914 – Lancashire & Yorkshire Railway Co., Goole), which was a defensively armed steamer, was transporting military supplies from Newhaven for Rouen, when she was torpedoed and sank without warning, 19 miles off Cape Antifer; four of her crew were drowned.

THREE OF THE MEN WHO WERE KILLED

Chilvers, Joseph, 56yrs, Cook and Steward
Combs, William, 34yrs, Fireman
Pettinger, Thomas William, 28yrs, Fireman

On 10 April the 4,196-ton steam tanker *Paul Paix* (1908 – Lennard's Carrying Co. Ltd, Middlesbrough) was empty and on passage from Rouen for Plymouth when it was left damaged by a torpedo, however the ship managed to reach its destination. (*Paul Paix* was the first ship to employ the Isherwood Longtitudinal framing system.) The 3,603-ton Spanish SS *Luisa* (1897 – Hijos de José Taya, S. en C., Barcelona) was torpedoed and sunk without warning on 12 April, while voyaging from Barcelona to Liverpool with general cargo. On 14 April, Steindorff fired a torpedo without warning at the 2,694-ton *Boma* (1889 – British & African Steam Navigation Co. Ltd, Glasgow) a defensively armed British steamer, but it was a dud and failed to explode. (She was later torpedoed and sunk by *UB 80* on 11 June 1918, 10 miles off Beer Head, while en-route from Belfast to St Helen's, Isle of Wight with a general cargo.)

The French steamer *Maroc* (1897 – Delmas frères, La Rochelle) of 2,898 tons also sank in the Channel following a torpedo hit on 24 April, while on passage from Port Talbot for La Rochelle. The 4,538-ton defensively armed SS *Tanfield* (1916 – British India Steam Navigation Co. Ltd, Glasgow), which was carrying a general cargo from London and Plymouth to Bombay, was attacked without warning and left damaged, but she was towed into Plymouth.

UB 74 returned to Flanders on 18 April 1918.

FINAL PATROL

(4) With Ernst Steindorff in command, *UB 74* left Zeebrugge on 11 May 1918 with the purpose of attacking the escorted American transports off St Nazaire. On the 18th, Steindorff torpedoed the 1,985-ton US steamer *John G. Mccullough* (1890 – United States S.S. Co., Inc., New York), which sank in the Bay of Biscay, 8 miles south of Ile d'Yeu; she was on passage from London for Rochefort, France. About 80 miles southwest of Ushant on the 25th, Steindorff exchanged information with Carl-Siegfried Ritter von Georg, in *U 101*, but *UB 74* never returned to port and was posted as missing. On the evening of 26 May 1918, HM steam-yacht *Lorna* (Lt C. Tottenham RNR) was busy escorting a convoy at the eastern end of Lyme Bay, having been forewarned that a U-boat was operating in the vicinity. Lookouts on *Lorna* suddenly sighted a periscope, just 50 yards away, and the U-boat was totally oblivious of the warship. *Lorna* approached to within 10ft (3.05m) before *UB 74* began to dive and the patrol yacht scraped the conning tower side as it passed over the U-boat. A depth charge set at 50ft was immediately dropped along with a marker-buoy and then another depth charge was dropped after 50 yards, also set at the same depth. There were loud explosions as *Lorna* circled around for another attack and masses of oil, debris and huge bubbles of air rose to the surface. The patrol boat was determined to finish her off and dropped a further depth charge, despite the presence of what appeared to be four men who were clearly heard amongst the debris. This did not dissuade *Lorna* from dropping another depth charge in their midst. Three of the German sailors were killed outright but one oil soaked, shattered wretch who was heard calling, 'Kamerad…. HELP' lived long enough to be picked up by *Lorna*. The submariner confirmed that his boat was that of *UB 74* and she was one week out of port, during which time she sank three ships. Unfortunately the man died of his injuries 3 hours after being rescued. A cap was also fished out bearing the words, 'Unterseeboots Abteilung'.

Lt Tottenham was awarded a DSO for his role in the sinking of *UB 74*.

CWGC U-Boot-Ehrenmal Möltenort NARA T1022, Roll58, PG61834

THE MEN WHO PERISHED WITH UB 74

Bolutus, Ernst U-Maschinistenmaat
Bulling, Eugen U-Heizer
Burghof, Hg. U-Obermatrose
Bülow, Karl U-Maschinistenmaat
Depkat, Hermann U-Matrose
Forthmann, J. U-Maschinist der Reserve
Frevert, Karl U-Heizer
Gichtenberg, T.J. U-Maschinistenmaat
Gleim, Heinrich U-Oberheizer
Godegast, Johann U-Maschinistenmaat
Habel, Paul U-Heizer
Hattwig, Georg U-Maschinistenmaat
Horstmann, J. U-Oberbootsmannsmaat
Hördt, Philipp U-Obermatrose
Ihrig, Johann U-Heizer
Jürgens, Gerhard U-Steuermann der Reserve
Laffrentz, H. U-Matrose
Lang, Franz U-Bootsmannsmaat

Ludolph, Johann U-F.T.Gast
Lumpp, Julius U-Heizer
Mades, Heinrich U-Heizer
Müller, Friedrich Marine Ingenieur der Reserve
Möller, Karl U-Heizer
Pfeil, Rudolf U-F.T.Maat der Reserve
Puls, Richard U-Maschinistenmaat
Rostock, Otto U-Matrose
Seyfried, Otto U-Maschinistenmaat
Speer, Paul U-Oberheizer
Steindorff, Ernst Oberleutnant zur See
Sturm, Heinrich U-Heizer
Stöver, Theodor U-Obermatrose
Tewes, Josef U-Obermatrose
Wendland, W. Oberleutnant zur See
Weniger, Gustav U-Matrose

Royal Navy divers found the wreck sitting upright in 21 fathoms (38.40m), early in June 1918. The conning tower upper lid was open and aft of the torpedo tube on the port side the blast from depth charges had ripped a 7.62cm by 12.19m (3in by 40ft) long tear in the casing. On 6 June the divers were instructed to blast open the forward hatch to get access to the officers' quarters, but all they

Crewman from *UB 74*.

found were corpses, signal cartridges and two small tin boxes. Nothing else was recovered of any importance and at the end of May the conning tower was demolished, however the periscope with the eyepiece missing and a few small items were sent to London.

Post-war, Warrant Shipwright Ernest Charles Miller RN MBE of HMRFA (His Majesty's Royal Fleet Auxiliary) salvage vessel *Corycia* and Naval Intelligence Division was awarded the DSC on 10 July 1919 for operations carried out on *UB 74*, for over three months. He worked at depths up to 21 fathoms and in very unfavourable weather. An entry was forced into the control room by means of explosives, but the floor set up was found to be blocking the objective. The gun was recovered by divers, along with other fittings of war, which resulted in the '*acquisition of information of inestimable value to the successful prosecution of the war*', according to Admiralty. Cdr Guybon Chesney Castell Damant OBE (M) also took part in the operations.

WRECK SITE

The wreck lies on a seabed of sand, gravel and shell, in a general depth of 32m, being the lowest astronomical depth. It is well broken up and has been heavily salvaged, its hull was blasted down to the keel in two places and the bow, stern, and conning tower were removed. The deck gun also could not be located. The conning tower sits some distance from the main wreck – modern salvagers are not to blame for that though, because it was the handiwork of the Royal Navy in 1918, when they entered the wreck to search for documents.

SIDON, HM SUBMARINE

DATE SUNK: 16 June 1955
DEPTH: 32m
REFERENCE: 50 32'.986 N 02 38'.487 W
LOCATION: 7.33 nautical miles WNW of Portland Bill

HMS *Lorna*. (Author's collection)

Type: British 'S' Class medium-range patrol submarine of Group III ***Pennant***: No. P.259 ***Builders***: Cammell Laird, Birkenhead for Royal Navy ***Ordered***: for 1942 War Emergency Programme ***Keel laid***: on 7 July 1943 ***Launched***: on 4 September 1944

Sidon was the chief city of ancient Phoenicia and this boat was the second of that name, the first being an RN sailing ship in 1846.

TECHNICAL SPECIFICATIONS

Hull: partly welded construction. ***Surface displacement***: 814 tons ***U/Dt***: 990 tons ***LBD***: 61.14m × 7.24m × 4.11m ***Machinery***: 2 × 8-cylinder Admiralty pattern 950bhp diesels. ***Props***: 2 bronze
S/Sp: 14.75 knots ***Op/R***: 4,000 nautical miles at 10 knots ***Sub/R***: 106 nautical miles at 4 knots ***U/Power***: 2-Admiralty pattern 650bhp electric motors gave 9 knots ***Batteries***: 2-Exide lead/acid of 112 cells each ***Fuel/Cap***: 44 tons standard, 63 tons max. ***Armament***: 6 × 53.34cm (21in torpedo tubes (no stern tube) ***Torpedoes***: 12 × 53.34cm (21in) ***Guns***: 1 × 101.6mm (4in) Quick-Firing Mk XII deck gun, a 20mm (0.78in) Oerlikon mount, two-0.303in-machine guns. ***Ammo***: 100 rounds of 101.6mm (4in). ***Mines***: (sometimes) 12 × Mk. II magnetic-ground-mine type with 453.60 kilo (1,000 pound) charge. These were half the length of a torpedo and were laid through the torpedo tubes ***Diving***: max-op-depth 106.68m (350ft) ***Complement***: 5 officers and 43 ratings

After an initial work up period with the 3rd Flotilla, attached to HMS *Forth* at Holy Loch and a short patrol off Norway, being her only war patrol. In early April 1945, *Sidon* was dispatched to the Far East under the command of Lt Henry Carty Gowan, but before she could actively participate in any patrols, the war ended.

Lt Cdr Hugh Verry, who was 30 years old, entered the Royal Navy as a midshipman in 1944. Lt Cdr Verry also served on X-craft at one stage of his career. He assumed command of *Sidon* on 30 March 1954.

See Appendix, page 344.

HM SM *Sidon*. (Private collection)

FINAL JOURNEY

'*Greater love hath no man than this, that he lay down his life for his friends*' – inscription on Surgeon Rhodes' grave, Portland RN Cemetery.

In the early hours of Monday morning the boat arrived alongside her 'mum' HMS *Maidstone* at Portland, depot ship of the 2nd Submarine Flotilla, at the end of a twenty-eight-day-long exercise. *Sidon* was scheduled to take part in experiments with staff from the Admiralty Underwater Establishment. *Maidstone* was anchored a short distance to the east of the big coaling pier, her bows pointing to the west. *Sidon* was one of five submarines moored alongside the depot ship HMS *Maidstone* on the morning of 16 June 1955. *Sidon* was moored on her port side. The next two days were spent 'de-storing' the boat as eight weeks' stores had been stowed prior to sailing on exercise. Some of the boats, including HMS *Springer* (which was moored on *Sidon*'s starboard side, next to *Maidstone*), were to take part in a torpedo-firing exercise and were preparing to cast off. With the sun just breaking through to brighten up the day, *Springer* departed at 0820hrs.
ERA Trevor Shaw takes up the story:

> During the late afternoon (Tuesday) the experimental HTP torpedo was loaded into the boat's tube, with the intention of a practice firing out at sea on the Wednesday. This programme was then put back 24 hours and an Ordnance Artificer of the Experimental Group came onboard to do hourly checks on the highly volatile fuel contained in the 'fish'. The revised programme was for us to go out on Thursday with 'harbour stations' at 0800hrs. As Weapons ERA I had a permanent 'harbour stations' in the fore ends of the boat with forendsman Alfie Mullet.

Sidon was one of five submarines moored alongside the depot ship HMS *Maidstone* on the morning of 16 June 1955. Some the of the boats, including HMS *Springer*, which was moored on *Sidon*'s starboard side, were to take part in a torpedo firing exercise and were preparing to cast off. With the sun just breaking through to brighten up the day, *Springer* departed at 0820hrs.

Trevor Shaw again:

> With all the activity taking place in the fore ends and the presence of Lt Cdr Needham (Experimental Group CO) and our 'nav' Lt Rycroft, it was obvious that something was not quite right. I was chatting to CERA Geordie Pearson when ERA Geoff Hopkins requested an urgent visit to a dentist. The Chief

agreed but turning to me, said my presence would be required in the engine room instead of the fore ends, especially as the fore ends seemed rather overcrowded. I made my way to the engine room. A terrific explosion ripped through the boat, the tower being the only hatch open. Those in the control room in the path of the blast suffered severe blast burns. I was struck in the face by a flying object then thrown over onto the starboard engine. I eventually made my escape from the after hatch in the stoker's mess deck, then splashed out onto *Maidstone*'s gang plank as the for'rard casing was now awash, the bows sinking.

On *Maidstone*, Surgeon-Lt Rhodes was having breakfast in the wardroom when an awful muffled thump – thump was heard, followed by alarm bells sounding, within minutes of the boats leaving. Rhodes leapt to his feet and raced up on deck to find smoke pouring from the conning tower of *Sidon*. An eyewitness described how a sheet of flame shot up through the conning tower hatch, followed by lots of smoke and more flames. Even broken bits of furniture, various items of clothing and clouds of paper, blew up into the air. *Sidon* sank by the bow soon after the unfamiliar thudding sound rang out, and the visiting Danish submarine *Saelen*, which was moored on the port side of *Sidon*, was quickly towed clear.

ERA Peter Leech described how he was talking with PO William 'Happy' Day at the control panel when the explosion occurred and a burst of orange flame shot out. He said they were about 100ft from the torpedo compartment, but he was flung about 10ft through the radio room door. Leech maintained that he had an idea what had happened as yellowish and green-coloured smoke began to thicken, then somebody shouted 'Everybody out of the boat'. PO Day said he remembered a dull type of thump and was also lifted off his feet by some kind of blast, then woke up in hospital. Surgeon-Lt Rhodes realised what had taken place. He calmly removed his spectacles, donned some breathing apparatus and jumped down onto *Sidon*'s deck, according to Derek Jones, a steward on *Maidstone*. Rhodes then disappeared down the hatch and began half carrying and half dragging out injured sailors. Jones watched Rhodes clamber down into the smoke-filled boat four times to rescue crewmen, but the fifth time he saw him go, the doctor was having breathing problems and the boat was starting to sink. The doctor did not emerge from the boat.

Engineer Officer Roy Hawkins witnessed what took place within the boat. Lt Hawkins had been on the bridge when the explosion happened. Hawkins observed a blast of air shoot up from the hatch after the explosion and then stunned and dazed men started to emerge. He went down into the boat, but couldn't see anything for the smoke, even though the lights were on. He found 'Geordie' Pearson and the two men got a blower going and attempted to get rid of the smoke with some difficulty. By that time they were unable to breath and had to go topside to get breathing gear. Unaware that the boat was sinking, Hawkins, accompanied by the captain, Surgeon Rhodes and 1st Lieutenant Puxley, then went down below again to help the get the other men out. They struggled forward through broken equipment until a pile of metal blocked the gangway. Roy Hawkins described how they had to tunnel a 2ft hole through the debris but a blocked bulkhead prevented further progress. His nose-clip then came away and he began to suffocate. Surgeon Rhodes managed to drag Hawkins back just before he became unconscious. A 23-year-old engineer off *Maidstone*, Jack Gill, was probably the last man to emerge from *Sidon*. Jack recalled that he went down to help and through the choking smoke he saw Surgeon Rhodes at the bottom of the conning tower, attempting to work levers that controlled the oxygen flow. However he was also struggling with his breathing equipment and gasping. Someone shouted a warning and Jack scrambled clear just as *Sidon* sank by the bows.

During the rescue, the 767-ton mooring vessel *Mooardale* had moved in and attached a wire rope to the stern of *Sidon*, but as the submarine sank, it became too heavy for the ship and the wire was drawn down too. Divers from *Maidstone* went over to the submarine in launches and then swam along the submerged hull. Looking for any signs of life, a message was tapped out in Morse, but there was no reply. However one of the torpedoes was seen protruding out of a tube. On 18 June work commenced on lifting the stricken vessel and two 'camels' (large buoyancy cylinders) were secured to the boat. She was raised slightly off the bottom and another two were attached, after wire hawsers were slipped beneath the hull. The stern then rose to the surface and the conning tower became visible. After further lifting, the after-hatch was clear, but *Sidon* was left listing to port. She was lowered down again after 20 minutes in an attempt to correct the angle and work continued until the 23rd. Working by powerful searchlights from *Maidstone* and salvage vessels, the submarine

Navigator's station on a Kriegsmarine Type VIIC/41 U-boat (*U 995*). (Courtesy Kevin Belcher of Swindon)

Depth and hydroplane control in Kriegmarine Type VIIC/41 U-boat (*U 995*). (Courtesy Kevin Belcher of Swindon)

was once again raised to the surface. Her periscope and bridge first appeared at 0210hrs and at 0430hrs she was finally secured. With two fishing vessels towing and two lifting craft at her stern, she was beached near the oil tanks on the western side of the harbour at noon on the 24th.

Official Report of Loss of HM Submarine *Sidon* at Portland – 16 June 1955:

> At 0825hrs a severe explosion took place in the torpedo compartment of HMS *Sidon* who was berthed second submarine out alongside HMS *Maidstone* in Portland Harbour, and preparing to slip and proceed for exercises. All hatches except the conning tower hatch were shut. Injured personnel and survivors immediately started coming up the conning tower hatch.
>
> 2. Rescue and. medical parties from the Depot ship rushed onboard equipped with Salvus breathing sets Capt. (SM), the Commanding Officer, First Lieutenant, Engineer Officer and Depot ship Surgeon Lieutenant went below, but it was evident that the blast had reached as far aft as the control room, lighting was extinguished, the submarine full of smoke and a lot of debris in the control room Furniture and loose fittings jammed the forward bulkhead doors and it was impossible for any personnel left alive forward to get aft or for the rescue personnel to get forward.
>
> 3. It very soon became obvious that the submarine was making water forward and. was sinking by the bows. An effort to hold her stern above water by the mooring vessel that had quickly arrived was unsuccessful and personnel below were ordered out. At 0845hrs the submarine sank.
>
> 4. One casualty was in the conning tower and delayed escape by that route, personnel therefore escaped through the engine room and after DSEA hatches.
>
> 5. Three officers and nine ratings are known to have been killed either in the initial explosion or, by failing to escape before the submarine sank. One rating is still unaccounted for.
>
> 6. The names of the officers are:
> Lieutenant Commander J.K. Needham, Squadron Armament Officer, Lieutenant J.M.W. Rycroft, Torpedo Officer of The submarine and Surgeon Lieutenant C.E. Rhodes R.N.V.R. of *Maidstone*
>
> 7. One officer and seven ratings injured in R.N.H. Portland and two ratings in Sick Bay *Maidstone*, none believed serious.
>
> 8. Divers are confirming that there are no signs of life in submarine, which is resting on the bottom in 36ft, flooded throughout, with a 40-degree list to starboard. Portion of burst torpedo protruding three foot from No.3 bow V cap orifice.
>
> The explosion took place at 0834A.
>
> Number three and four tubes contained fancy S.R. torpedoes. From evidence to date (16 June 1955) it is thought that when loading torpedo the top stop was not down, possibly having been lifted by mistake for the tripper, thus the torpedo was launched too far. The air lever went aft allowing air pressure to go to H.T.P. containers resulting in a burst in the H.T.P. line. Further evidence will not be available until after salvage.

What had caused the explosion? *Sidon* was lost due to the torpedo having been confined in the tube and the missile's hydrogen peroxide propellant beginning to expand. With both ends of the tube sealed shut, a massive pressure built up and the intense heat that developed caused an explosion, blowing the tube door and bow cap open, similar to what is believed to have happened on the Russian submarine *Kursk*. Most of the explosion's force dispersed through the tube door and into the boat's interior. Then, with the bow cap open, seawater flooded straight inside the boat.

THE MEN WHO DIED ON SIDON

Needham, Gerald Keith – Lieutenant Commander RN of Preston, Dorset
Rhodes, Charles Eric – Surgeon Lt R.N.V.R. (National Service) of Southwell Farm Portland
Rycroft, Julian – Lieutenant RN of Weymouth
Clayton, C. D. P/SSX 871290 – Telegraphist of Ferndown, Dorset
Davies, D. G. S/SSX 835908 – Acting Leading Seaman of Weston-super-Mare
Dorey, P. R .A. C/JX 819932 – Leading Seaman of Belting, Kent
Ford, J. R. P/SSX 898366 – Able Seaman of Bognor Regis, Sussex
Peake, R. H. P/SKY 880828 – Marine Engineering Mechanic of N. Kensington
Rice, P. J. W. P/MX 807734 – Acting Leading Cook of Southwick, Sussex

Smith, Colin P/MX 912901 – Leading Cook of 18, East Boldon Road Cleadon, near Sunderland (20yrs – born 15 April 1935)

Sunderland, J. R. P/SLX 901679 – Steward of Reading, Berks.

Waite, D. P. P/SSX 835715 – Able Seaman of Boscombe, Bournemouth

McLeod, 'Verne' L.D., Petty Officer, Royal Canadian Navy 10242H P2TD of Dartmouth, Nova Scotia

Surgeon-Lt Rhodes had completed sixteen months of his National Service. He was from Manchester and a doctor in civilian life, having done part of his training at Harold Wood Hospital in Essex where he met his wife. Rhodes also left a wife and daughter. Surgeon Lt Rhodes was posthumously awarded the Geoge Cross.

Colin Smith had just recently volunteered for duty on submarines. His service record must be among the shortest in Submarine Service history. Colin, 20 years old, had just been drafted to *Sidon* and was a submariner for barely 20 minutes before he was killed. The inscription on his grave reads 'Love of the sea, *Submariner brave, in Portland's Bay his life he gave'*.

'Verne' McLeod was a native of Goderich, Ontario and joined the RCN in 1949. In September 1998, a memorial was unveiled in Halifax to honour the 'Canadian Submarine Volunteer' and it is dedicated to the memory of PO2TD L.D. McLeod.

All but one of the men who died on *Sidon*, including the heroic Surgeon Rhodes, were buried together on 28 June in the steep little Royal Naval cemetery at Portland, on the cliff edge overlooking the anchorage (just below the Verne Prison, Fortuneswell). Most of the naval personnel buried here lost their lives in accidents in and around the anchorage (including sixteen Libertymen from carrier HMS *Illustrious*, who drowned when their pinnace overturned on 16 October 1948). Nearby lies L/S Jack Mantle VC who heroically died defending HMS *Foylebank* from air attack. The *Sidon's* men are in good company.

Above left: Grave of Surgeon Lt C.E. Rhodes RNVR. (Courtesy Ray Smith)

Above right: CWGE grave of Colin Smith. (Courtesy Ray Smith)

Sidon as an ASDIC target just before she was sunk. (Author's collection)

Salvage crews recovering *Sidon*. (Private collection)

There is a postscript. On 16 June 2005 a memorial stone was unveiled in commanding position, a short distance from the Portland Heights Hotel. Although it does not overlook the site of the tragedy, it is in an easily accessible location and the views are awesome. Those present at the unveiling on this 50th anniversary included *Sidon* survivors and Surgeon-Lt Rhodes' daughter.

ADM1/25919 – CWGC

FINAL VOYAGE

The career of *Sidon* was brief; after the accident, she was stripped and on 14 June 1957 she was deliberately sunk as an ASDIC target.

WRECK SITE

The wreck of *Sidon* is orientated in a northwest to southeast direction ands lies on a seabed of sand and shingle, in a general depth of 32m, being the lowest astronomical depth. At the time of writing (2005), the wreck is upright, with anemones beginning to establish themselves on the casing. It is virtually intact, with no holes or splits, so it is not possible to get access to the inside of the boat, unlike many other submarine wrecks. Large shoals of fish can usually be found swarming over and around it.

M2, HM SUBMARINE

DATE OF LOSS: 26 January 1932
DEPTH: 28m
REFERENCE: 50 34'.587 N 002 33'.998 W
Also: 50 34.60N 02 33.93W
LOCATION: 5.63 nautical miles NW of Portland Bill and 2.45 nautical miles SE of Chesil Beach

Type: British 'M' Class Monitor submarine   *Pennant*: No. P.259   *Builders*: Vickers Yard, Barrow-in-Furness for Royal Navy   *Ordered*: in May 1916 for Emergency war programme   *Keel laid*: as Yard No.494 on 13 July 1916   *Launched*: on 15 April 1919   *Completed*: on 14 February 1920

TECHNICAL SPECIFICATIONS

Hull: double, 11 × watertight bulkheads and 12 × main compartments   *Surface displacement*: 1,650 tons   *U/Dt*: 1,950 tons   *LBD*: 90.14m (88.39m LPP) × 7.46m × 4.87m   *Machinery*: 2 × 12-cylinder, Vickers-Admiralty single-acting, 4-stroke, solid injection 1,200bhp diesels   *Props*: 2 bronze × 3-blade (1.57m). An auxiliary 20bhp propelling motor was also fitted to the starboard shaft   *S/Sp*: 15.5 knots   *Op/R*: 3,600 nautical miles at full power, or 5,500 nautical miles   *Sub/R*: 10 miles at 9.5 knots or 80 nautical miles at 2 knots   *U/Power*: 4 × double-armature-type Admiralty pattern 400bhp electric motors gave 8–9 knots   *Batteries*: 3 battery tanks containing 336 Exide lead/acid cells of 137 tons   *Fuel/Cap*: 110 tons fuel in external tanks   *Armament*: 4 × 45.72cm (18in) bow torpedo tubes   *Torpedoes*: 10 × 45.72cm (18in)   *Guns*: 1 × 30.48cm (12in) Mk IX 50-ton BL deck gun forward of conning tower, plus 1 × 76.2mm (3in) Quick-Firing HA Mk II anti-aircraft gun fitted on after casing, on disappearing mount   *Ammo*: 40 rounds of 76.2mm and 72 rounds of AA   *Mines*: none   *Diving*: max-op-depth 60.96m (200ft)   *Complement*: 60–70

In February 1915 Churchill had ordered the building of twenty 'K' Class submarines (originally designed in 1913). Powered by steam turbines and capable of speeds of up to 24 knots, these craft were designed to function as fleet submarines, able to keep pace with the fastest cruiser. However, due to the passing of the Conscription Act in 1916 and the resultant dilution of skilled shipyard labour, only a handful of these vessels were available in the last year of the war. There were four 'K' Class submarines, *K18*, *K19*, *K20* and *K21*, from Armstrong Whitworth and *K18* to *K19* from

Vickers. (*M4* was cancelled prior to completion and sold back to Armstrong Whitworth as scrap.) After the orders were received, Vickers were given instructions to build a new design of boat, in effect an anti-submarine submarine armed with a 1in gun. *K18* and *K19* were remodelled to become *M1* and *M2* respectively.

In the late 1890s, Vickers originally designed the Mk IX 12in gun, which had a theoretical range of 11.9 miles. The 12in guns fitted to the 'M' Class were the same as those used by the Majestic Class battleships. They weighed about 120 tons and the shells weighed in at 850 pounds (383.55 kilos) each while the total weight of the forty shells carried was 29 tons.

Only *M1* was completed by the end of hostilities and did not see action

M2 went straight from the builders yard to Fort Blockhouse reserve boat. The early history of *M2* is rather complicated by virtue of long refits and the 'ready reserve' crewing method. The ready reserve system required several boats to have but one crew, the boats being used on a rotational basis. The Navy List merely names one officer in charge of a 'reserve group' of other officers, some of them qualified as commanders. Determining just who served on *M2* and when they served is therefore a tortuous business.

Lt Cdr Frederick Henry Taylor DSC served as officer in reserve for both *M1* and *M2* from 17 August 1920 to 10 December 1920.

Cdr Hubert Vaughan-Jones commanded *M2* in reserve from 10 December 1920.

From 1921 to 1924 *M2* was assigned to the Atlantic Fleet.

Lt Cdr Henry Francis Morton Peto was CO on 15 August 1922.

Lt Cdr Jermyn Rushbrooke was CO on 1 September 1924 to 25 November 1924, for *M1* and *M2* (both in reserve).

Lt Cdr James Lawrence Boyd DSC assumed command on 13 January 1926 to 3 December 1926.

Lt Cdr Colin Mayer was CO from 21 October 1926 for *M2* in reserve.

Lt Cdr John Domville Auchmuty Musters assumed command on 22 January 1927.

April 1928 conversion at Chatham.

The Washington Disarmament Treaty required that signatories reduce the calibre of armament fitted to warships. In April 1928 HMS *M2* went into Chatham for conversion work. The guns were removed from both *M2* and *M3*. *M2* was further converted to carry a small Parnall Peto seaplane. A hangar was fitted forward of the conning tower where formerly the gun tower had been situated, and she was equipped with a catapult for launching the plane (*M3* meanwhile was transformed into a minelayer). Her surface speed reduced to 14.1 knots, submerged speed to 6.4 knots *M2*'s surface operational range was now 2,350 nautical miles at 14 knots, 3,700 nautical miles at 10 knots. Submerged range was then 1.7 hours at 6 knots, 6 hours at 4 knots, 12 hours at 1.9 knots and the fuel bunkers held 97.5 tons. Following this conversion, Lt Cdr Alexander Scrope Hutchinson took over as commanding officer from 14 May 1929 to 17 November 1930. Lt Cdr John Duncan de Mussenden Leathes, who was her last CO, assumed command on 17 November 1930. 'Snakey' Leathes was Ben Bryant's mentor during his early years in *L52*:

> Snakey Leathes was a man from whom I learned much. He could and did sleep at any time, anywhere, at a moment's notice – a most valuable quality in a submariner. He was long and thin, liked his quiet glass of gin and never took any exericise. Once ashore, Snakey hated sunshine and never went out. He darted around the control room like a reptile but Snakey was an artist in attack, a gimlet-eyed killer.

FINAL PATROL

At 0900hrs on 26 January 1932 *M2* left Portland harbour for a series of manoeuvres in West Bay, off Portland Bill. These lone exercises were scheduled to involve an aircraft launch as well as gun and torpedo practice. These lone exercises would involve an aircraft launch as well as gun and torpedo practice. During this time *M2* was to maintain radio contact with the depot ship HMS *Titania*. At the conclusion of these evolutions, *M2* was to join submarines *L67* and *L71* in combined training operations.

The sea was calm but there were intermittent fog banks. At 1011hrs *M2*'s captain, Lt Cdr J. de M. Leathes sent the customary diving signal, '*About to commence exercises*', to HMS *Titania* at Portland.

Port and starboard telegraph in the control centre of a Kriegsmarine Type VIIC/41 U-boat (*U 995*). (Courtesy Kevin Belcher of Swindon)

However the boat failed to send a message informing the depot ship that she had safely surfaced. *M2* did not go on to join the two 'L' boats, nor did she return to Portland harbour at the appointed time of 1615hrs. To add to the general state of alarm it was learned that there had been no radio contact with the submarine since her dive that morning. By early evening of 26 January, it was apparent to all concerned that *M2* must be in serious trouble. The survival of her sixty-man crew was now at stake and depended upon locating *M2* without further delay. In theory, the submariners should have had a fighting chance. The submarine had 48-hours' worth of air and the overwhelming majority of the crew were highly experienced submariners who had demonstrated their capacity to cope in earlier emergencies. There were reasonable grounds for confidence, after all, the crew of *M2* were trained in, and equipped with the new DSEA escape sets, of the kind used in the recent *Poseidon* escape. Indeed, AB Morris, one of the crew of *M2*, had been an escapee.

The Davis Submerged Escape Apparatus became standard issue for the Submarine Service from late 1929 and *M2* was the first submarine to be fully equipped with the sets. Each DSEA set contained a high-pressure cylinder with sufficient oxygen to support the user for 30 minutes. Carbon dioxide exhaled through the mouthpiece was directed into a canister containing purifying salts before being cycled back to the breathing bag. The apparatus incorporated a buoyancy bag and a drogue apron designed to significantly slow ascent to the surface. The cash-strapped Admiralty installed a 15ft-deep training escape tank at Blockhouse. Modifications were made to submarines in the form of the introduction of pull-down twill trunks. In the later thirties, rescue chambers situated directly under the escape hatches replaced these collapsible trunks. Nevertheless the Admiralty was faced with a desperate race against time. Supposing the crew did reach the surface, how could they survive in a January sea?

At 1730hrs the Portland destroyers *Rowena*, *Torrid*, *Salmon* and *Thruster* put to sea in a desperate search of West Bay. Meanwhile in Portland and Weymouth sailors were recalled back to their ships. Coaches were sent around the Portland area to round up any sailors who could be found. Billets, pubs and brothels were all combed. Contemporary newspapers relate how cinema performances were interrupted by police and military. Officers and men abandoned a charity show at Weymouth Pavilion to return to Portland harbour still dressed in their Pierrot costumes. The submarines *H44* and *H49* sailed at 1900hrs, followed at 2107 by launches, tenders, trawlers and anything else the Navy could scrape together to search for *M2*. Just after midnight the Admiralty made the following announcement:

> An object, presumed to be submarine *M2*, has been found 3 miles west of Portland Bill, in a depth of 17 fath-
> oms… Salvage craft and divers have been sent from Portsmouth to this position with the utmost despatch.

HMS *Sabre*, a destroyer carrying divers trained for submarine salvage work, left Portsmouth and
headed for the spot where the contact had been made. Meanwhile scores of metropolitan journalists
headed for the south coast. Obsessed with BBC bulletins, seeking every last driblet of news, it
seemed as if the whole nation was wracked with anxiety. Prayers were also said. Unfortunately,
divers confirmed that the contact, which had been the source of so much optimism the previous
day, was in fact just the wreck of an old steamer. Time, too much time, had been frittered away. The
press noted that the next Admiralty statement was not as upbeat as the first:

> The following information was received tonight from the Rear-Admiral of Submarines who is con-
> ducting search operations to the westward of Portland Bill for Submarine *M2*: Two objects have been
> located by sweep-wires, but, owing to the strong tide, divers have had difficulty in reaching the bottom to
> investigate. Diving is being continued when possible throughout the night.

The search continued at a frantic pace, coordinated by Admiral (S) on *Alecto*. Unfortunately the
divers were exhausted and the currents worked against the sweeping mechanisms, time and time
again. There were simply too many wrecks in West Bay. There was a brief flurry of excitement on
the 28th when the hydrophone operator of HMS *Thruster* picked up a sound:

> '…at 1058 on the 28 *Thruster* reported that at the position where the destroyer, *Salmon* had found her
> lead bent and marked with paint, *Thruster* had made contact with something on the bottom with her
> sweeping wire. Sounds resembling tapping have been heard…

So the press reported. The origins of the sound could not be located but it is unlikely they emanated
from the stricken submarine. Meanwhile the media had discovered a couple of potential witnesses,
but their accounts gave little comfort to Admiralty. Captain Hunt of *Crown of Denmark* had been on
passage to Portland, 16 miles southeast of Lyme Regis, when at 1840hrs he observed:

> …a very sudden bright light of about three seconds on my port beam. It lasted for about three seconds,
> dimmed then reappeared very bright again before disappearing altogether. The light was followed 10
> minutes later by two loud explosions, which echoed over the water. It occurred to me at the time that
> it might be a submarine, and as soon as I heard that the *M2* was missing I put into Portland and made a
> statement to the authorities.

The master of the steamer *Tynesider*, Captain Arthur Howard, also had a tale to tell:

> The submarine I saw yesterday morning is the same which disappeared off Portland. I was coming from
> Charleston, Cornwall, with a cargo of china clay yesterday at 11.30. – As I was getting near Portland I saw
> the submarine. I could read quite clearly her mark 'M'. She was on top of the water, but I soon noticed
> that her head was getting right out of the water. I saw her sink rather suddenly, her stern first. At first I
> thought it was a bit queer, but as I had never seen a submarine dive I thought well this might be normal
> after all. However, I called at Portland at 2.30 p.m. and on leaving the harbour I met a submarine going
> in and I thought that it was the one I had seen earlier and that everything was all right. Of course I was
> sorry to learn this evening on the wireless that *M2* was lost. But the position the Admiralty gave is not
> a good one. When I saw the *M2* she was approximately 8 miles NW by N. from Portland Bill, 2½ miles
> from shore. I am afraid they are searching in the wrong place.

Off the record, Admiralty might have agreed with Captain Howard. In fact the Royal Navy had
given up all hope by this time. Now it was a time for telegrams and the drawing down of blinds. As
the sixty ominous buff telegrams were despatched, sailor-towns all over Britain were plunged into
mourning. On the evening of the 29th the BBC solemnly broadcast the following communiqué:
'The Secretary of the Admiralty regrets to announce that in view of a report now received from
Rear-Admiral Submarines, who has been attempting to salve the sunken submarine *M2*, it is no
longer possible to hope for the rescue of any of the officers and men on board.'

The newspapermen returned to London. On 3/4 February *M2* was found.

There had been clues that the search was nearing its climax. In February a fishermen sighted, but failed to recover, a decomposing body, dressed in a standard issue submariner's jumper. Nearby a canvas bag was found to contain a cap bearing the name of *M2*'s coxswain, James King. A sweep at this spot brought to the surface the collar of a CPO, known to have been onboard *M2*. The ASDIC-equipped HMS *Torrid* identified a stationary submarine on 3 February. Sweep wires from *Pangbourne* and *Dunoon* snagged the wreck. Divers from HMS *Albury* read the letters 'M2' on the conning tower and the search was over. Although over 3 miles from the position given by Captain Howard of *Tynesider*, the wreck was very close to that offered by Captain Hunt of *Crown of Denmark*. Some contemporary experts maintained that the partially flooded submarine crept ahead on her motors in a desperate attempt to find water shallow enough for a DSEA escape to be attempted, hence the distance from Captain Howard's position. Yet others claimed that Arthur Howard had simply been wrong. A memorial service was held over the spot on 5 February. The singing died away and the story moved on to pose the question 'what had sunk *M2*?'

Salvage operations began on the 7th. The *Albury* divers found *M2* in 18-fathoms. Her stern was partially buried in sand and shingle and her bow was raised sufficiently off the seabed enabling divers to walk underneath. Impact marks on the seabed at the stern did point to a stern-first dive as described by Captain Howard, but there were no obvious signs of damage to the pressure hull. Both the hangar door and the upper conning tower hatch were open, but the forward hatch and engine room hatch were closed. This is consistent with an aeroplane launch having been underway at the time of the catastrophe.

(In a *Daily Mail* article dated 1 February 1932, Cdr H. Daniel suggested a premature opening of the hangar doors, while the bows were still awash might be a possible cause of the sinking.) Indeed a famous photograph exists of the crew launching the Parnall Peto seaplane with the bows danger-ously awash. A sudden overwhelming catastrophe of this nature would certainly explain much of the mystery away. However, the hangar was situated forward of the conning tower. If the hangar was to flood (and with it via the small access hatch, the fore ends) surely the submarine should have sunk bows first and, it follows, would have struck the seabed bows-on rather than stern first. Experienced mariners opined that a hydroplane mechanism failure combined with the premature opening of the hangar doors was the likely cause of the sinking. A letter from ex-Lt Freegard in the Submarine Museum describes these 3-minute aircraft launches. Only the bow tanks would be blown. The bow would be kept on the surface using the motors with the boat still in a state of negative buoy-ancy. An aircraft launching, following submersion, was known to place significant strain upon the hydroplanes because it was essential to keep the fore ends above water. A failure in the hydroplane mechanism would have resulted in the bows plunging without warning. The force of water entering the boat through the open hangar and conning tower hatches would have been immense. A third theory contends that ballast vent valves may not have been properly shut prior to surfacing. The tanks would have started to refill as soon as *M2* neared the surface and the sheer volume of water combined to the ballast already in the tanks could have forced her stern down to the seabed.

This was, of course, all speculation. Only salvage could reveal the truth.

In the course of salvage attempts two bodies were found. The first, Leading Seaman Jacobson, was discovered in the hangar. On the seabed, divers by complete chance also found the remains of RAF Leading Aircraftsman Leslie Gregory, still in a full flying suit, lying 15ft away from the portside of *M2* and in line with the rudder. The body was positively identified by the name in the waders. As Jacobson regularly assisted in aircraft launches, this is strong evidence that a launch was underway at the time *M2* was lost. Crucially, the tiny access hatch between the open hangar and the fore ends was found to be open. The aircraft was salvaged leading to the discovery of the pilot's gold watch in the cockpit. The watch had stopped forever at 0845hrs.

Strong currents, difficult conditions and waning official interest hampered the salvage operation. Twice the stern broke surface, twice it slipped back beneath the surface. On 8 December the salvage operation was finally called off.

HM Submarine *M2* – Reports of the Incidents Connected to Her Loss:

> It is feasible that the sudden flooding of the hanger to a depth of feet or more above the floor boards, pre-
> vented the crew from either closing down the Access Hatch or shutting the Hanger Door; moreover the

latter operation might not have been feasible due to the water going down the Access Hatch falling on the electric motor of its telemotor unit and putting the motor out of action. It was not practical to close the Access Hatch from below and therefore the water would continue to enter the Pressure Hull until it filled the compartment in which the Hatch was situated. This weight of water, even if the Watertight Doors to other compartments were closed in time, to prevent their flooding, would combine with the weight of water, which had entered the hanger – estimated to be 55 tons if flooded to 4ft above the floor boards – to be more than sufficient to destroy the positive buoyancy that had been maintained by blowing the Main Tanks and '*M2*' would founder.

The question remains as to whether the crew could have been saved by external intervention; the answer must be, probably not. The reader delving into contemporary newspaper accounts cannot be in any doubt as to the effort expended on the search at all levels. It could be argued that, had a few more ASDIC-equipped destroyers been sent to West Bay, *M2* might have been found earlier. However, available evidence points to a rapid and overwhelming ingress of water, one that led to the immediate flooding of the control room and paralysis of systems.

By the time the alarm was raised in *Titania*, the crew of *M2* were probably mostly dead. It is feasible to suggest that some men in the fore-ends or stern did survive the initial flooding. It appears from official papers that Admiralty did not dwell on the taxing question as to why there had been no evidence of DSEA escape attempts – unless the body was an escapee rather than one of the aircraft/bridge party. Depth had not been a factor but the acute angle of the boat may have frustrated flooding-up attempts to equalise pressure. The fact remained that for some unknown reason, not one man was known to have escaped from *M2* using DSEA, yet Admiralty's faith in the apparatus remained undimmed. Much time and effort had been spent on salvage but *M2* marked a watershed in Admiralty rescue strategy.

THE LEGACY OF M2

On 17 February 1932 a conference was held at Admiralty into submarine rescue procedures '*to examine what steps could be taken to ensure that DSEA could be used to the best advantage and the question of escaping from submarines was therefore examined at great length*'. This was followed by a second discussion on 1 June 1933. In the intervening months, salvage operations on *M2* had commenced. In the words of the resulting statement, '*these proved unsuccessful and were abandoned in December of 1932 after ten months of tedious work during which time the whole operation was carefully planned and undertaken by naval personnel, assisted and advised by the most experienced salvage men in the country*'.

The June conference sought to clarify procedures and formulate such recommendations as they thought necessary in the light of experience.

Volume 3 contains an extract from the agenda and the conclusions arrived at. The procedures which emerged were codified in AFO 568/34 and AFO 569/34 which appear in Appendix 2.

The 1932 conference made the following recommendations:

Bulkheads to be strengthened to withstand pressure equivalent to a depth of 200ft
Special escape hatches to be fitted as near the ends of the submarine as possible
Conning tower and gun tower to be fitted as escape hatches as far as practicable
Design of watertight doors to be improved and tested
Accessibilty of bulkhead valves to be investigated with a view to rapid closing
Telephones to be introduced instead of voice pipes, to reduce holes in bulkhead
The question of special escape chambers to be investigated.

These recommendations were adopted as far as possible. All submarines were duly fitted with special escape hatches and new construction boats were equipped wth special escape chambers. Procedures were tightened up significantly with a view to ensuring a rapid response to a submarine facing an emergency. A submarine on exercises was required to radio its position prior to diving and indicate the length of the proposed dive time. In the event of a submarine failing to surface, Blockhouse would transmit code '*Subsmash*' throughout the Royal Navy. Emergency action would then be co-ordinated from the base nearest to the last known position of the submarine. *Subsmash* was founded on the assumption that a submarine crew could now save itself without outside help. A trapped submarine crew should revert to DSEA as soon as rescue craft were at hand, '*and not wait for outside salvage*'. *Subsmash* laid down no provision for salvage, as this Memo written by Rear Admiral (S) Bertram Watson on 13 June 1939, demonstrates:

> …in view of the approval of this policy [568/34], it was apparent that the air connections fitted to each compartment in existing submarines as possible aids to rapid salvage could now be dispensed with in the interests of fighting efficiency, as the more the pressure hull is pierced by such fittings, the greater becomes the vulnerability of the submarine to depth charges. Such connections were therefore discontinued in new construction submarines…

In effect, a trapped crew was primarily responsible for saving itself. Salvage was no longer an option. The policy did not factor in the implications should DSEA escape be delayed or prevented. Was AFO 568/34 a pragmatic response to the realities of submarine warfare or was it, rather, an example of general service institutional myopia? The *Thetis* affair of June 1939 would deliver a comprehensive verdict.

As far as *M2* is concerned, it is difficult to argue with the statement that everything that could have been done by outside forces had been done. In common with so many submariners before and since, the crew of *M2* had simply run out of luck. Perhaps we should not be surprised, after all, *M2* had started off life as a 'K' boat.

ADM 116/2909 Papers D.3475/32, MF.10379/33. AFO 568/34 ADM 116/1404

THE MEN WHO PERISHED IN M2

Arbuthnott, Crofton, Lieutenant Commander
Back, Leonard, Engine Room Artificer
Banks, Sid, Petty Officer LTO
Blake, Fred, Petty Officer (TGM)
Brown, Dougal, Leading Seaman
Burridge, Jack, Leading Telegraphist
Butcher, Harold, Able Seaman
Chapman, Cecil, Able Seaman
Clark, Allan, Petty Officer
Coleshill, Charle,s Able Seaman
Drummond, James, Stoker
Edwards, John, Able Seaman
Ellis, Stanley, Petty Officer Telegraphist
England, George, Able Seaman
Estcourt, George, Stoker
Ferguson, Dougla,s Stoker
Gregory, Leslie, Leading Aircraftsman RAF
Harding, Charles, Engine Room Artificer
Harman, A., Leading Aircraftsman RAF
Hayes W., CERA
Head, C., Lieutenant
Hill, T., Sub-Lieutenant RNR
Horne, Stanley, Engine Room Artificer
Jackson, Victor, Engine Room Artificer
Jacob, Albert, Leading Seaman
Jarret, Sidney, Able Seaman
King, James, Petty Officer (Coxwain)
Lakin, John, Leading Stoker
Leathes, John, Lieutenant Commander
Leavey, Frederick, Signalman
Lewis, John, Stoker

Macdonald, Louis, Stoker Petty Officer
Matthews, Edward, Stoker
McDonald, Sub-Lieutenant.
Morris, Thomas, Able Seaman
O'Dwyer, Anthony, Able Seaman
Oliver, Frank, Leading Steward
Peplow, William, Able Seaman
Powell, Henry, Stoker
Rawlings, William, Able Seaman
Ready, Frank, Able Seaman
Sharp, George, Leading Stoker
Sims, John, Engine Room Artificer
Smales, Frederick, Yeoman of Signals
Smith, Reginald, Able Seaman
Sweetland, Cecil, Stoker
Thomas, Ernest, Telegraphist
Thornton, Tom, Able Seaman
Threlfall, Charles, Stoker
Toppin H., Lt (Pilot RAF)
Totterdell, James, Stoker
Townsend, C., Lieutenant (Observer)
Treacy, Phillip, Leading Seaman
Vincent, Athur, Able Seaman
W Hayes, W., Warrant Engineer
Walker, Ralph, Stoker
Watson, William, Stoker
Whiting, Francis, Able Seaman
Williams, Leonard, Engine Room Artificer
Winfield, Harold, Able Seaman
Woodhouse, Frank, Stoker
Wrathnell, Charles, Able Seaman

Sketch of *M2* wreck by Pam Armstrong.

The ditty box of George Estcourt is on display within the Submarine Museum. Its contents throw a fascinating light upon the life of the ordinary inter-war submariner.

WRECK SITE

The wreck lies on a seabed of shingle, gravel and sand, in a general depth of 28m (92ft), being the lowest astronomical tide. It is completely intact and upright, but the jib of the recovery crane is now collapsed. The hangar door is open and the little aircraft was removed during salvage. All the hatches are sealed with steel and concrete, except for the conning tower outer hatch, which is open, however the inner hatch is sealed like all others. The straight upright edge of the bow is covered in colourful anemones, as are the two propeller shafts, rudder and keel at the stern end, where sizeable shoals of pout whiting and other fish often hover. A carpet of hydroids and clusters of soft corals also cover the entire hull.

The wreck is said to be a very interesting one to visit, but visit with respect.

UC 49, SM IMPERIAL U-BOAT

DATE OF LOSS: 8 August 1918
DEPTH: 40m
REFERENCE: 50 10.90N 03 30.00W
LOCATION: 4.10 nautical miles S of Berry Head and 2 nautical miles ESE from River Dart Estuary

Type: UCII coastal mine-laying boat   *Builders*: Germaniawerft, Kiel for Kaiserliche Deutsche Marine   *Ordered*: on 12 January 1916, within the batch of *UC 49–UC 54*   *Keel laid*: as Yard No.265   *Launched*: on 12 November 1916   *Commissioned*: by Kapitänleutnant Karl Petri on 2 December 1916

TECHNICAL SPECIFICATIONS

Hull: double **Surface displacement**: 434 tons **U/Dt**: 511 tons **LBDH**: 52.69m × 5.22m × 3.68m × 7.46m **Machinery**: 2 × 250ps Körting diesels **Props**: 2 bronze **S/Sp**: 11.8 knots **Op/R**: 8,820 nautical miles at 7.2 knots **Sub/R**: 55 nautical miles at 4 knots **U/Power**: 2 × 230ps electric motors gave 7.2 knots **Batteries**: lead/acid/accumulators **Fuel/Cap**: 41 + 15 tons **Armament**: 2-external 50.04cm torpedo tubes at the bow, one either side of the mine chutes and 1 stern internal tube **Torpedoes**: 7 × 50.04cm (19.7in) maximum **Guns**: 1 × 88mm (3.46in) forward deck gun **Ammo**: 133 rounds of 88mm **Mine tubes**: 6 **Mines**: 18 × UC200. **Diving**: max-op-depth 50m (164ft) and 33 sec to crash-dive **Complement**: 3 officers and 23 ratings

Torpedo load as designed: (4) a torpedo in each tube plus a reload for the stern tube. Storing an additional torpedo in pieces internally for the stern tube later augmented this, although this was optional. Two extra torpedoes (total) for the external bow tubes could be carried as well – these were lashed to the deck. So up to seven total torpedoes carried, although not all boats sailed with that many.

UC 49 began her career based in German ports and was assigned to the I.U-Bootflottille at Brunsbüttel on 1 March 1917, with Kplt. Petri the commander from 2 December 1916 until 21 April 1917. Petri made one war patrol with the boat:

UC 49 sailed from Germany on 25 March 1917 for a sortie off the Scottish east coast, where mines were laid in the Cromarty Firth and northern entrance to the Moray Firth. The patrol was cut short through problems and *UB 49* returned to Heligoland on 5 April 1917.

Oblt.z.S. Alfred Arnold assumed command on 22 April 1917.

(2) *UC 49* left port on 2 May 1917 and sailed to the Scottish east coast and the Isles of Orkney. Arnold captured and sunk the 162-ton Danish sailing vessel *Helge* (1893) on his outbound voyage with explosives on the 3rd, 140 miles off Horns Riff; she was transporting 253 tons of coal from Newcastle to Nakskow in Denmark. On the 5th, Arnold laid a mine barrier off Peterhead. The 1,256-ton Norwegian steamship *Tore Jarl* (1903 – Det Nordenfjeldske Dampskibsselskab, Trondheim) was torpedoed and sunk on 7 May, approximately 109 miles from Sumburgh Head, Shetland; she was transporting mail, a cargo of coal and coke and twenty-five passengers from Newcastle-upon-Tyne to Trondheim; one passenger, Olaf Johansen Berklund from Tønsberg, died.

Two trawlers detonated mines and sank off Peterhead, Scotland: the 226-ton Hull-registered (H.692) *Windward Ho* (1902) went down with all eight hands on 9 May.

THE EIGHT MEN WHO DIED

Burnham, George, 45yrs, Cook
Eddom, George William, Skipper
Foot, William, 25yrs, Extra Hand
Matson, William Josephus, 21yrs, Trimmer
Stones, Albert, 27yrs, 2nd Engineer
Watts, William, 45yrs, Extra Hand
Wilson, William Henry, 37yrs, Boatswain (Bosun)
Wright, Joseph Alfred, 43yrs, Chief Engineer

The 168-ton Grimsby trawler (GY168) *BEL LILY* (1899) sank with all ten hands on the 14th.

THE TEN MEN WHO DIED

Atkinson, Fred, 4th Hand
Barnett, Thomas, 3rd Hand
Ellis, John Robert, 4th Hand
George, Walter Robert, 2nd Hand
Gibson, Frank, 2nd Engineer
Harvey, Harry, Cook

Meeds, Thomas, Trimmer
Smith, Amos, Skipper
Smith, Charles Thomas Lewis, 4th Hand
Smith, James (30yrs) 1st Engineer

UC 49 returned to port on 17 May 1917 and Arnold stood down as CO.

Kplt. Karl Petri resumed command again on 17 May 1917 and made four patrols:

(3) Departing Brunsbüttel on 6 June 1917, *UC 49* operated off the Isles of Orkney and Shetland. The *Tosto* (1904 – A/S D/S Tosto (B. Stolt-Nielsen), Haugesund), a 1,234-ton Norwegian steamer, detonated a mine and sunk on 17 June, 3.5 miles SSW of Noup Head, Isle of Westray, Orkney; commanded by Captain T. Matland, she was voyaging from Methil to Haugesund with coal and all the crew survived; the mine was by *UC 49* on 9 June 1917. On 12 June, mines were laid at the entrance to Kirkwall.

UC 49 returned to Germany on 19 June.

(4) Petri took *UC 49* to the Isles of Orkney and Shetland, then on to the Outer Hebrides to lay mines and attack Allied shipping, leaving port on 15 July 1917. During the voyage, four vessels were destroyed: a contact mine laid on 19 July demolished the 4,020-ton defensively armed SS *Cotovia* (1911 – Frumentum S.S. Co. Ltd, London) off Auskerry, Orkney Isles on the 22nd; she was carrying flax from Arkhangelsk, Russia to Dundee. The mine was laid on 19 July. (One month earlier, the ship had been heavily shelled by a U-boat in the Arctic, but managed to escape.) Under the command of Captain Philip H. Colomb, the 12,077-ton Armed Merchant Cruiser *Otway* (1909 – The Admiralty, London) succumbed to a torpedo on 23 July; the missile detonated in the engine room aft and she sank in 20 minutes near Rona in the North Minch, while serving as a unit of the Northern Patrol; ten ratings were killed.

TWO OF THE MEN WHO DIED

Campbell, Donald, Seaman RNR
Carter, Ephraim, Petty Officer RN

On 24 July, a torpedo sunk the 3,740-ton turret-hulled steamship *Blake* (1906 – Zodiac Shipping Co. Ltd, London) without warning, while part of a convoy off Cape Wrath, she was armed for defence and sailing from Penarth to Archangelsk, Russia with coal and five crewmen were lost.

FOUR OF THOSE WHO DIED

Lloyd, David Albert, 3rd Engineer
Nazlrullah, 2nd Tindal
Siddiq Myan, Trimmer
Sikandar Myan, Fireman

Off the Butt of Lewis on the 25th, the 1,094-ton steel-hulled Norwegian barque *Dea* (1890 – Skibs-A/S Dea, Farsund) was sailing in ballast from Stavanger to Halifax, Nova Scotia when she was stopped and sunk by explosive charges at: 60° 20'N 04° 01'W.

UC 49 arrived back at port on 2 August.

(5) Petri sailed from Germany with *UC 49* on 20 August 1917 and patrolled off the Irish south coast. Close to 27 miles from Bishop Rock, the defensively armed 4,969-ton SS *Nascent* (1915 – Westoll Line, Sunderland) was sunk without warning by a torpedo on the 25th; the ship was journeying from Tegal, Java and Dakar, Senegal to Hull with a general cargo and six men were drowned.

THOSE WHO DIED

Adramitrianos, F., Fireman and Trimmer
Bowen, William, Chief Boatswain
Dimitriades, Marcus, Fireman

Edwards, Hywel Oscar, 3rd Engineer
Thomson, Thomas, Able Seaman
Thulin, Carl Ludwig, Steward

Petri laid mine barriers in Bantry Bay and off Bull Rock around 28 July 1917.

The Auxiliary Merchant Cruiser *Dundee* (1911 – The Admiralty, London) of 2,187 tons was employed as an Armed Boarding Steamer when, on 2 September, two torpedoes sunk her without warning, southwest of the Scilly Isles.

AMONG THOSE WHO DIED

Arthur, William, Petty Officer RNR
Brodie, Thomas Patterson, Temp. Engineer Sub-Lt RNR
Chapman, Frank, Greaser MMR
Fenwick, Andrew Small, Stoker MMR
George, William Robert, Leading Fireman MMR
Lavery, James, Stoker MMR
Lawson, Frederick Herman, Acting Temporary Lt RNR
Thorne, Percy Charles, Greaser MMR
Tye, Patsy, Stoker MMR

UC 49 arrived at Heligoland on 14 September.

(6) Leaving Heligoland on 15 October 1917, *UB 49* sailed through the Skaggerak to operate against Allied shipping off the Yorkshire coast. On 21 September Petri laid nine mines in the area north of Whitby and a further nine mines were deposited in the entrance of Tees Bay. The 73-ton tug *BUNTY* (1914) was carrying coal from Hull to Rosyth when she detonated one of the mines and sank off Whitby on the 21st and all four hands, including a pilot, were killed.

THE MEN WHO DIED

Batty, Robert Edward, Master
Clark, Herbert, 29yrs, Fireman
Eales, William Charles, Pilot
Lee, William, 26yrs, Mate
Speck, Henry William, 49yrs, Engineer

UC 49 returned to Germany on 29 October.

Oblt.z.S. Hans Kükenthal assumed command on 3 November 1917.

(7) *UC 49* sailed from Germany with her new commander on 28 November 1917 and operated off the English and Scottish east coasts. Two barriers of six mines were deposited in the entrance to the Firth of Forth on 4 December. The SS *Maindy Bridge* (1899 – Maindy Bridge Shipping Co. Ltd, North Shields/Cardiff) of 3,653 tons was torpedoed and sunk 4 miles east, northeast of Sunderland, on 8 December, while on a voyage from Middlesbrough to the Tyne in ballast, and two men were drowned, one being the mess steward, John Perry. Destroyers immediately attacked the U-boat with five depth charges; Kükenthal then left the area and headed north to the Firth of Forth, where he laid the remaining six mines on 10 December, in the northern entrance near Fifeness.

Kükenthal arrived back in port with *UC 49* on 15 December.

On 3 January 1918, one of the mines sank the 237-ton Whaler 'Z' Class patrol boat *Blackwhale* (Z.5) (1915) off Fife Ness.

AMONG THOSE WHO DIED

Albert, Thomas James, Leading Trimmer RNR
Beresford, Alfred, Chief ERA RNR
Dalton, Henry, Leading Trimmer RNR
Dungey, Samuel Henry, Trimmer RNR

Enright, James Francis, Trimmer RNR
Gage, G.W., Ord Seaman RNCVR
Kirk, Tom, Deckhand RNR
Larvin, Henry, Trimmer RNR
Morris, James Stanley, Trimmer RNR
Newman, Herbert James, Stoker RNR
Toulson, Harry Percy, Trimmer RN

(8) Departing Brunsbüttel on 15 January 1918, Kükenthal travelled to the Scottish east coast for operations; on the 20th, mines were dropped in the Firth of Forth and more places north of Bell Rock on the 25th. Two Swedish steamers were sunk with torpedoes on 24 January: the *Fylgia* (1889 – Rederi A/B Svenska Lloyd, Göteborg) of 1,738 tons sank off Bell Rock, at position 56° 23.00'N 02° 15.00'W, while on passage from Göteborg for Rouen with general cargo, which included iron and steel and wood pulp. From her crew of twenty-one, three men were killed.

THE MEN WHO DIED

Schagerström, Gustaf Adolf Nikolaus (32yrs)
Holmer, Carl William (25yrs)
Kjellstrand, Sven Olof Wilhelm (18yrs)

The 1,274-ton *Jönköping II* (1888 – Rederi A/B Nordstjernan, Stockholm) was also sunk, 3 miles east, northeast of Bell Rock, while transporting a general cargo, including wood and paper from Göteborg to Hull. She carried a crew of nineteen, and one man, stoker Gustaf Erik Benjamin Krusell (23yrs), was killed.

UC 49 arrived at Heligoland on 30 January 1918.

At 0600hrs on 9 February 1918, two fishing boats reported being fired on 3 miles north of Bell Rock and a submarine was observed submerging directly after, then about the same time a loud explosion was heard and a huge volume of water was seen; wreckage was also found soon after; this was presumed to have been from the 24-ton motor fishing boat *Maggie Smith* (AH 158); which had blown to pieces and sunk with all three hands, because she never returned to port. An extensive sweep was made, but no mines were found.

THE CREWMEN LOST

Beattie, James Deckhand
Cargill, David Skipper
Spink, John Deckhand

(9) Leaving his German port on 17 February 1918, Kükenthal revisited the English east coast, where two mine barriers were deposited off Tynemouth on the 20th. Next day, the 91-ton North Shields-based drifter *Reaper* detonated one of the mines and sank, 2 miles off the Tyne, with the loss of all eight hands.

SOME OF THE MEN WHO DIED

Appleby, Thomas, Cook
Blackman, Henry, 1st Engineer
Blythe, James, 2nd Engineman
Fyall, Thomas Andrew, Deckhand
Gibbons, Martin, Fireman
Pye, Alfred, 3rd Hand
Sparks, Walter, 2nd Hand

(Most records and reference books contend that *UC 49* laid the mine that damaged the 3,752-ton SS *Berwen* (1903 – W.&C.T. Jones Steamship Co. Ltd, Sunderland/Cardiff) off the Shipwash light vessel, but the U-boat did not lay any mines in that location, according to her KTB.)

The Norwegian steamship *Bør* (1914 – Aktieselskapet Bonheur, Kristiania) commanded by Captain John Sundby, was torpedoed off the River Coquet on 21 February and sank after 45 minutes, while sailing from the Tyne to Kristiania with coal and aluminium powder; out of the crew of eighteen, Leif F. Dæhlin, the first engineer from Kristiania, was lost.

Hans Kükenthal's KTB for the 24 February 1918, states:

> …convoy steering south, in sight consists of six steamers and is protected by destroyer and fishing boat
> Convoy steering zig zag course
> Fired from first tube
> Hit on laden steamer of 2,500 tons
> Loud explosion – since destroyer is close behind stern of boat went to 40m quickly

That 2,500-ton steamer was the 806-ton SS *Amsterdam* (ex-Avon 1877 – Rankine Line Ltd, Glasgow) which he torpedoed and sank without warning, 6 miles from Coquet lighthouse; the ship was on a voyage from Leith to Rotterdam, carrying eighty-seven passengers and a general cargo, including coal, but just four of the crew was lost.

THE MEN WHO DIED

Craig, Norman Scott, 24yrs, Wireless Operator
Daly, Peter, 18yrs, Cabin Boy
McGregor, David Arthur, 26yrs, Second Engineer
McMillan, Alexander, 34yrs, Mate

UC 49 arrived back in port on 14 March 1918. On 1 May however, the Danish motor-schooner *SAMSÖ* (1876 – Aktieselskapet Dansk Kartoffel-og Gemyseeksport, Kalundborg, Denmark) of 324 tons, detonated one of the mines laid earlier and sank with nine hands off Sunderland. The *SAMSÖ* (Captain Marius Niels Svarre) had been in the Tyne waiting to join a convoy. The master had asked for a pilot and one was agreed, but he didn't show up for convoy's departure time of 0215hrs. At around 1600hrs the ship steamed out of the Tyne and the convoy started heading south, but at about 1700hrs there was a massive explosion and by the time the third engineer had rushed up from the engineroom aft, the stern-end was the only part of the ship above water. Captain Svarre, who was born on 10 June 1878 (two years after the ship was built), later explained in court that his vessel was in a great convoy and that those on the bridge had been speaking about a big ship outside of the convoy, giving several warning blasts with its whistle.

In response, three or four aeroplanes were directed towards that ship, but in the same moment the explosion occurred. Only three men were rescued by a patrolboat, which arived shortly after: the captain, the third engineer, K. Billing and E. Rasmussen, an ordinary seaman. The crew consisted of twelve men when they left Aarhus via the Tyne for London, with about 180 tons of machinery-parts. The captain explained in court that the ship didn't have the word 'Danmark' and the Danish national flag painted on her sides, because they had been to France on their last voyage; the French authorities, for some unknown reason, wouldn't allow those to be painted on the ship's hull. Also, no one remembered to paint them on afterwards, either.

The above is extracted from the official Court of Inquiry at Newcastle-upon-Tyne and Copenhagen in 1918.

(The ex-paddle steamer *SAMSÖ* did not have much luck, because on 21 July 1916 she was damaged by gunfire from *UB 37*, 30 miles off the Tyne.)

On 22 May 1918 *UC 49* was formally assigned to the U-Flottille Flandern II.

(10) On 22 May 1918 Kükenthal left Germany with *UC 49* and transferred the boat to Flanders, where she arrived on the 25th and joined U-Flottille Flandern II at Zeebrugge.

(11) Departing Zeebrugge on 2 June 1918, *UC 49* travelled to the English and Bristol Channels, where a barrier of nine mines were placed at the entrance to Etaples, northern France on 5 June. Kükenthal torpedoed and sank the *Mountby* (1898 – Sir R. Ropner & Co. Ltd, West Hartlepool),

8 miles off the Lizard on 19 June; she was armed for defence and was torpedoed without warning, while transporting Admiralty stores from London to Swansea.

The requisitioned Elders & Fyffes steamer *Patia* (1916 – The Admiralty, London) was torpedoed and sunk 25 miles off Hartland Point on 13 June, while on Government service employed as an Armed Merchant Cruiser and sixteen people died on her, including one officer and eight of her mercantile crew.

AMONGST THOSE WHO DIED

Atwell, Leslie Victor, 209524 Able Seaman RN
Blair, Hugh, Ship's Cook MM
Bowren, Harold, Assistant Steward MM
Brown, William Richard (DSM), 203661 Able Seaman RN
Chetwood, George Albert, Chief Gunner RN
Cook, Percy, Ordinary Seaman RNVR
Getgood, Francis Harold, Wine Steward MM
Matthews, Joseph, Assistant Steward MM
McDonald, John Edward, Steward MM
Richards, William, Private RMLI
Roe, William Harold, Beebee Signalman RNVR
Stewart, Claud Lapsley (MiD), Engineer Cmdr RNR
Taylor, James Harold, Assistant Steward MM

For the assault on *Patia*, *UC 49* was subjected to an attack with twenty depth charges, which damaged her fuel bunkers. Kükenthal then travelled to the Isle of Wight, where the remaining nine mines were placed off the Needles.

Mines laid off Etables by *UC 49* on 5 June also sunk the 1,308-ton defensively armed SS *RHEA* (1917 – The Shipping Controller, London) on the 22nd, voyaging from the Newcastle to Rouen with coke.

The U-boat arrived back at Zeebrugge on 21 June 1918.

(12) *UC 49* cruised along the English Channel from 8–20 July 1918, but no ships were sunk.

FINAL PATROL

(13) With Kükenthal in command, *UC 49* left Zeebrugge on 1 August 1918 with a mission to attack Allied shipping and lay mines in the Plymouth and Falmouth areas.

Probably the most notable ship that Kükenthal sunk was the defensively armed 7,713-ton *Warilda* (1912 – Adelaide S.S. Co. Ltd, Port Adelaide), an ambulance transport under escort and torpedoed without warning on 3 August; she was returning to Southampton from Le Havre with 614 wounded troops, plus 117 crew and 70 medical staff on board. *UC 49* had been sighted on the surface and the steamer tried to ram her, but failed. A torpedo then detonated level with the bulkhead between the engine room and No.4 hold at 0130hrs. One hundred and one patients were killed in the explosion in No.1 ward, which was positioned in the No.4 hold, while in the engine room the third engineer, John Milne, and greaser, George Frederick Maidment, were killed outright. The ship remained afloat for 2 hours before sinking at 0410hrs, but during the time she was being abandoned, two boats capsized and drowned a number of patients, staff and crew. Altogether 123 people were lost, including seven crew, two military officers, 112 British troops, one American soldier and one Queen Mary's AAC. Escort vessels picked up the survivors and the master, Captain J. Sim, managed to save the War-Time codebooks and confidential papers. (King George V later decorated Captain J. Sim with the OBE.)

THE MERCHANT MARINE CREWMEN WHO PERISHED

Courtney, Alfred Henry, Steward
Harris, Victor, Troop Deck Steward
Jordan, Edward, Fireman

Maidment, Frederick George, Greaser
Milne, John, 3rd Engineer
Newnham, Bernard George, Saloon Steward
Phillips, Douglas William, 3rd Cook

Two days later, a torpedo damaged the 5,275-ton defensively armed SS *Tuscan Prince* (1913 – Prince Line, Ltd, Newcastle), sailing in ballast from Hull to New York; she was towed to Dover, but two crewmen, fourth engineer James Huddleston and John William McKenzie, a donkeyman, were killed.

The 2,241-ton Admiralty Collier Transport No.28, *Portwood* (1913 – Wm France Fenwick & Co. Ltd, London (manager)), which was armed for defence with one stern-mounted 12-pounder, had sailed in ballast from Sheerness at 0900hrs on 8 August, bound for Barry Roads, via Weymouth. The *Portwood* (Captain George Henry Lawson) was travelling independently on a zigzag course at 10 knots, with one man in the crow's nest as lookout, two on the bridge and one gunner aft, on the platform. By 1140hrs she was off Dartmouth at position 50° 13.30'N 3° 35.45'W and within sight of Start Point Lighthouse when a torpedo was sighted about 50 yards from the ship. At 1143hrs the torpedo detonated in the engine room on the port side and three of her crew of twenty-one were killed: the chief engineer, a donkeyman and fireman, Abdullah Mubarak. As soon as the missile exploded the ship went out of control, but the crew kept calm. The U-boat was never seen, however Captain Lawson reported that patrol vessels were sighted to the eastward, plus one steamer was on the starboard beam and two or three other steamers were observed to the south. (Visiblity was good, the sea was calm although slightly disturbed and the wind force-3.) Eventually the ship was taken in tow and arrived at Dartmouth at 1500hrs. (There was a note written by RN staff indicating that there was a submarine in the vicinity, which would be an apparent reference to *UC 49*.)

At 0751hrs (British time) on the morning of 8 August 1918, a loud detonation off Start Point attracted the attention of HMS *Opossum*, which was in the vicinity and on a routine A/S patrol. The destroyer's crew observed a huge column of water thrown into the air by an underwater explosion. At about that same time, *UC 49* was laying her mines in that area; it was also later thought possible, that the U-boat had possibly detonated one of her own mines and had been damaged. The Torbay-based *Opossum* (1895) was operating as part of one of the hunter patrols instituted in the spring of 1918. The Torbay unit consisted of *Opossum* and seven MLs. All vessels were equipped with Mk II hydrophones.

At 1505hrs a lookout on *ML 191* spotted an oil slick approximately where the explosion had occurred earlier and immediately dropped a depth charge, realising immediately that oil was probably emanating from a U-boat. *Opossum* and her consorts began a search with hydrophones and sweeps. Almost immediately submarine motors were detected. *Opossum* left three MLs in the area of the slick before moving off to a point close to where the noises were coming from, about 3 miles away (identified as position 'one') *Opossum* dropped ten depth charges on position 'one' and commenced listening after the last explosion had subsided. Kükenthal would have been aware of the surface vessels and probably decided to order 'silent routine', i.e., to carefully lay the U-boat stationary on the seabed. This technique generally worked providing there were no tell-tale air bubbles, or oil slicks. However in July that year, the Admiralty had acquired a copy of the German U-boat manual, which recommended 'silent routine' as an evasion technique. British Naval Intelligence wasted no time in briefing destroyer captains that a hunted U-boat might well 'bottom' out in the hope that the danger might pass. During this time, *Opossum* ordered the three MLs disposed around the slick to noisily move away.

At 1520hrs the U-boat's motors were started, but within minutes, depth charges exploded close to the boat. Like Kükenthal, the British warships had also been playing a 'cat and mouse game'. The warship's log is notably undramatic!

The log of HMS *Opossum* reads:

Morning 8 August 1918:
7.51 – Loud explosion heard abeam.
8.30 – Out hydrophones.

9.45 – Quarters. – Clear guns for action. –Patrol sweep for enemy submarine.
18.17 – Sighted submarine on surface. – Action stations. – Dropped depth charges.

For the next hour *Opossum* and her three motor launches dropped more depth charges over the spot where the U-boat had dived and then, at 1917hrs, *ML 465* dropped more depth charges and a large quantity of oil and air came bubbling to the surface. Further hydrophone sweeps revealed nothing. To obtain proof of a 'kill', the following day *Opossum* returned to drop more depth charges over the doomed submarine. The location was methodically dragged. At 2120hrs there was a sudden gush of oil and air. Oil and air was still rising on 10 August when one of the sweeps fouled an obstruction. *Opossum* dropped four more depth charges. Finally a light bulb bobbed to the surface, bearing the stamp of a Viennese munitions plant. This was satisfactory evidence that the submarine's pressure hull must have broken open and the boat was lost, along with her crew of thirty-one. The hunter patrol group buoyed the position and returned triumphantly to Devonport.

AUTHORS' NOTE

The explosion could very possibly have just been the detonation of a mine laid some time earlier. This leaves a scenario of *Opossum* and the MLs opportunistically encountering *UC 49* after she torpedoed *Portwood*. In the absence of further evidence, all is speculation.

THE MEN WHO PERISHED IN UC 49

Bey, Wilhelm U-Oberheizer	Lepis, Georg U-Matrose
Boller, Jacob U-Oberheizer	Meerjanssen, U-Obermatrose
Czecziwodda, Kriegslotse	Mohrmann, H. U-F.T.Maat
Dennhardt, R. U-Matrose	Pfefferkorn, A. U-Obermaschinistenmaat
Dürow, Wilhelm U-Heizer	Retzlaff, Herbert U-Obermatrose
Festor, Tranz U-Maschinistenmaat	Rieke, Heinrich U-Matrose
Fikus, Ludwig U-Obermatrose	Roggenbau, B. U-Obermatrose
Finster, Paul U-Heizer	Schubert, W. U-Maschinistenmaat
Gans, Hans U-Heizer	Steinbusch, J. U-Maschinistenmaat
Griebsch, Walter U-Maschinistenmaat	Stuhlmacher, U-Matrose
Jenniges, Jonas U-Heizer	Suppke, Hans U-Oberbootsmannsmaat
Kretschmar, F. U-Maschinistenmaat	Tatoy, Anton U-Oberheizer
Kükenthal, Hans Oberleutnant zur See	Wackernagel, Leutnant zur See der Reserve
König, Hermann U-Obermaschinistenmaat	Wagner, Alfred U-Matrose
Lackert, Willi U-F.T.Gast	Wegner, Otto Marine Ingenieur As
Laslowski, J. U-Matrose	

(*UC 49* was the first U-boat to be destroyed following a sustained hunt using hydrophones. All previous U-boats sunk were by mining, ramming, or a combination of ramming followed by a few depth charges dropped on the still shallow U-boat. *UC 49* was also the last U-boat sunk in the Channel by surface vessels.)

NARA T1022, Roll 48, PG 61962 Technical History No 7 Board of Trade Return: M.37827 N.I.D. 10937 ADM 137/2964 CWGC U-Boot-Ehrenmal Möltenort ADM 53/53412 Norwegian Maritime Declarations 1914–1918

WRECK SITE

The wreck, possibly that of SM *UC 49*, lies on a seabed of sand and shingle, in a general depth of 40m (131ft), being the lowest astronomical depth. It is upright, but very badly damaged at the bows, around amidships and the conning tower. The upper sections have an assortment of soft corals attached and tidal streams around the area are quite brisk.

UC 68, SM IMPERIAL U-BOAT

DATE OF LOSS: 13 March 1917
DEPTH: Unknown
REFERENCE: possibly around 50° 17'N 03° 31'5'W
LOCATION: approximately 6 nautical miles NE of Start Point

Type: UCII coastal mine-laying boat **Builders**: Blohm & Voss, Hamburg for Kaiserliche Deutsche Marine **Ordered**: on 12 January 1916, within the batch of *UC 65–UC 73* **Keel laid**: as Yard No.284 **Launched**: on 12 August 1916 **Commissioned**: by Oberleutnant zur See Hans Degetau on 17 December 1916

TECHNICAL SPECIFICATIONS

Hull: double **Surface displacement**: 427 tons **U/Dt**: 508 tons **LBDH**: 50.35m × 5.22m × 3.68m × 7.46m **Machinery**: 2 × 250ps MAN diesels. **Props**: 2 bronze **S/Sp**: 12 knots **Op/R**: 10,420 nautical miles at 7 knots **Sub/R**: 52 nautical miles at 4 knots **U/Power**: 2 × 230ps electric motors gave 7.4 knots **Batteries**: lead/acid **Fuel/Cap**: 41 + 15 tons **Armament**: 2-external 50.04cm torpedo tubes at the bow, one either side of the mine chutes and 1 stern internal tube **Torpedoes**: 7 × 50.04cm (19.7in) maximum **Guns**: 1 × 88mm (3.46in) forward deck gun **Ammo**: 133 rounds of 88mm **Mine tubes**: 6 **Mines**: 18 × UC200 **Diving**: max-op-depth 50m (164ft) and 33 sec to crash-dive **Complement**: 3 officers and 23 ratings

Torpedo load as designed: (4) a torpedo in each tube plus a reload for the stern tube. Storing an additional torpedo in pieces internally for the stern tube later augmented this, although this was optional. Two extra torpedoes (total) for the external bow tubes could be carried in addition, lashed to the deck. Up to seven total torpedoes could be carried, although not all boats sailed with this number.

On 16 February 1916, *UC 68* was formally assigned to the Flandern U-Flottille with Oblt.z.S. Hans Degetau the commander from 17 December 1916. Degetau made two patrols and was lost on the second:

On 14 February 1917, *UC 68* left Hamburg for her transfer to Flanders, arriving at Zeebrugge on the 17th.

FINAL PATROL

(2) Degetau left Zeebrugge with *UC 68* on 10 March 1917 and sailed to the English south coast, where mines were to be laid off Dartmouth and Plymouth. On the 13th, British patrols observed a massive underwater explosion 6 nautical miles northeast of Start Point. Four German mines were later discovered in the area by British minesweepers, which lead the Germans to believe that their U-boat, *UC 68*, had accidentally detonated one of her own mines. However on 5 April, off the Dutch coast the British submarine *C7* fired a torpedo at what the Admiralty reckoned could have been *UC 68*. HM S/M *C7* claimed a 'hit' although the British boat was never credited with the sinking, possibly because no evidence was ever produced.

Mines laid by *UC 68* badly damaged the 12,036-ton British hospital ship HMHS *Orsova*, 3 miles off the Eddystone Lighthouse, on 14 March 1917; she was on passage from London for Devonport with Government stores and on the 17th she was beached at Cawsand Bay; the ship refloated later, but nine crewmen had been killed in the explosion.

THE MEN WHO DIED

Edwards, W., Greaser MM
Edwards, William John Thomas, Greaser MM
Fleming, Andrew, 2nd Engineer MM
Goodrum, W., Stoker/kpr MM
Hirst, Arthur, 5th Engineer MM
Norris, W. G., Greaser MM

Smith, Thomas James, Greaser MM
Sparrow, William Ernest, Trimmer MM
Thomson, W. J., 9th Engineer MM

On 15 March 1917, the 550-ton two-funnelled British 'E' Class destroyer HMS *Foyle* (1903) detonated one of *UC 68*'s mines at 50° 11'N 03° 58'W and her bow was blown off; *Foyle* was taken in tow, but sank offshore from Dover, at position 50° 16'N 04° 10'W, and twenty-nine of the seventy people on board were killed.

SOME OF THOSE WHO DIED

Allison, James Steele, Signalman RNVR
Archer, Ernest, Petty Officer RN
Arnold, James, Stoker 2nd Class RN
Bennett, John William, Signalman RN
Butler, Arthur William, Stoker
Coates, Frederick Jame,s Able Seaman RN
Cole, Harold George, Stoker 1st Class
Crittenden, Howard George, Stoker 2nd Class
Danes, Albert Victor, Leading Stoker RN
Davis, Alexander, Stoker 1st Class
Davis, John Hughes, Stoker 1st Class
Gander, George Arthur, Able Seaman RN
Goatham, Augustus, Leading Stoker RN
Harris, Bert, Leading Stoker RN

Hatfield, John Isaiah, Boy Tel RN
McDonnel, George Frederick, Fireman MMR
McKeown.G., ERA 4th Class RN
Middleton, James William, Stoker 1C RN
Pearson, John Arthur, AB RN
Peek, Samuel, Stoker lst Class RN
Rickarby, Arthur John, Able Seaman RN
Roake, Arthur, DSM, MiD, Able Seaman RN
Russell, Alfred, ERA4C1 RN
Smith, Henry George, Able Seaman RN
Stearn, Sydney James, Leading Signalman
Woodley, Edward Arthur, Ordinary Seaman
   RNCVR

It still remains a mystery as to what actually happened to *UC 68* and she may have been lost for other reasons, and at another location.

THE MEN WHO PERISHED IN UC 68

Becker, Gustav Kriegslotse
Degetau, Hans Oberleutnant zur See
Dietzel, Franz U–Heizer
Donnerstag, W. U–Maschinistenmaat
Feilcke, Karl Marine Ingenieur Ober Asp
Fischer, Karl U–Obermaschinistenmaat
Fricke, O. U–Matrose
Gläser, Albert U–Oberbootsmannsmaat der
   Reserve
Hallsen, Karl Genannt Hansen U–
   Maschinistenmaat
Hartmann, E. U–Matrose
Hildebrandt, G. U–Obermatrose
Haag, Johann U–Oberheizer
Kleine-Bley, W. U–Heizer

Knechtel, Max U–Heizer
Liebelt, Oswald U–F.T.Gast
Martin, Franz U–Obermaschinistenmaat
Michnikowski, U–Heizer
Nicolay, Albert U–Maschinistenmaat
Petereit, Karl U–Matrose
Peters, Oskar U–Maschinistenmaat
Pfister, August U–Heizer
Poppen, Peter U–Matrose
Reichelt, Georg Leutnant zur See der Reserve
Schreck, W. U–Bootsmannsmaat der Reserve
Schwanbeck, R. U–Heizer
Schütte, Friedrich U–Matrose
Winkler, Georg U–Maschinist Anw

CWGC U-Boot-Ehrenmal Möltenort NARA T-1022, Roll 109, PG61989

WRECK SITE

The wreck of *UC 68* has never been located to date (March 2007).

MINERVE, FREE FRENCH SUBMARINE

DATE OF LOSS: 19 September 1945
DEPTH: 5m
REFERENCE: 50° 31.01'N 02° 27.06'W
LOCATION: Off Chesil Beach, west side of Portland Bill

Type: Free-French 'MINERVE' Class submarine   *Builders*: Admiralty design by Arsenal de Cherbourg for Free French Navy   *Ordered*: for 1930 programme   *Keel laid*: in 1931.   *Launched*: on 23 September 1934   *Commissioned*: in 1935

TECHNICAL SPECIFICATIONS

Surface displacement: 662 tons   *U/Dt*: 856 tons   *LBD*: 68.1m × 5.62m × 4.03m   *Machinery*: 2 × 900ihp Normand-Vickers diesels   *Props*: 2 bronze   *S/Sp*: 14.5 knots   *Op/R*: 4,000 nautical miles at 10 knots   *Sub/R*: 85 nautical miles at 5 knots   *U/Power*: 2 × 615shp electric motors gave 9 knots   *Batteries*: 2 × lead/acid   *Fuel/Cap*: 60 tons   *Armament*: 6 × 551.17mm (21.7in) torpedo tubes (4 bow and 2 stern) plus 3 × 400mm (15.75in) in triple traversing mount (not used once stocks ran out)   *Torpedoes*: 9 × 551cm (21.7in).   *Guns*: 1 ×76.2mm (3in/35) model deck gun and 2 × 13.2mm machine guns   *Mines*: none   *Diving*: max-op-depth 106.68m (350ft)   *Complement*: 42

Lt De Vasseau P.M. Sonneville is the only commander known for *Minerve*.

The boat arrived at Harwich along with *Junon*, *Ondine*, *Orion* and *Creole* belonging to the French 10th Submarine Flotilla. While the British were delighted to see these submarines 'come over' they nevertheless posed serious logistical problems. They were under-manned as many of the crews had decided to remain in occupied France. The tubes were incompatible with the British Whitehead torpedoes, while only submarines equipped with Vickers Normand engines could be maintained in British yards. Only *Minerve* and *Junon* were classified as operational and joined the heroic *Rubis*. The others were paid off into reserve at Blockhouse. Ultimately they would be cannibalised to keep the operational submarines in action.

Armed with modified torpedo tubes, *Minerve* served alongside British forces as early as 1941 and enjoyed an honourable and eventful career. The boat operated from Rosyth and later from Dundee or Lerwick (*see* vol. 3). Most of her operational patrols were spent patrolling Scandinavian waters. In February 1941 the boat joined *Sealion* and *Sunfish* in operations against the German iron ore trade. On 19 April 1941 the boat attacked, but missed, the large tanker *TIGER* off Jaederens, Norway. The submarine was depth-charged and machine-gunned by an escort Arado seaplane when she broke surface. Lt Sonneville urged permission to enter the Norwegian Fjords in search of prey but this was refused. By 18 May she was off Stattlandet in Norway hunting for *Bismarck* and *Prinz Eugen*. In June 1941 the boat was engaged in A/S missions off the Færoe Islands.

On 21 September 1941 the boat attacked but missed a heavily escorted vessel in Bue Fjord. In Frosjoen Fjord on the 28th she sighted three U-boats but the conditions made attack impossible. On her next patrol off Obrestadt the submarine again missed a tanker on 29 October but by this stage the boat was in urgent need of a refit. In early 1942 the boat was engaged in shadowing *Tirpitz* off Grip and Stattlandet and covering convoys PQ 16 and PQ 17.

On 10 October 1943, the Free French submarine, with a Royal Navy liaison officer on board, was just surfacing to take a sighting and repair a diesel motor, about 300 miles west of Brest; the boat was also in an area where it had not been reported to be in.

F/O Mick Ensor, a Coastal Command Liberator pilot, was on his 76th operation and one that had lasted for 15 hours; at the time, F/O Ensor's squadron had been experimenting with new rocket projectiles.

F/O Ensor had picked up a convoy northeast of the Azores and escorted the ships for 1½ hours, towards the British coast. F/O Ensor sighted the submarine and, suspecting it to be a German U-boat, attacked it, firing eight 5in rockets carried on little winglets below the cockpit, on either side. One of the 25lb solid-shot rockets struck *Minerve* at an angle of 20° from right astern on

Free French submarine *Minerve*. (Author's collection)

the starboard side. The missile didn't detonate, but penetrated one-eighth vertical plate at the side, damaging some pipework just below the starboard external torpedo tubes. It then penetrated two plates, each 13mm thick, at the junction of the pressure hull. The hole was about 6 x 5in. The rocket continued to gouge its way through the port switchboard of the main motors, going through three strong 1in fibre panels and intervening switchgear. It was being gradually deflected to starboard and finally cracked the main engine room bulkhead at the level of the footplates, before falling into the bilge. The switchboard was set on fire, which the crew extinguished in 30 seconds, or less. However, in the course of its passage across the electric motor compartment, two French mechanics were killed, one by the rocket's head and the other by a fragment of the boat's pressure hull.

The hole in the pressure hull was below the normal waterline and the submarine was hit just as she was surfacing, so the aft section of the boat was still submerged and the boat sloping. Water poured in at a great rate and the main motors were completely flooded before the leak could be stopped. Water aft also got under the controls.

The boat's officers were highly impressed with the performance of the shot and considered themselves lucky that it had not struck them at an angle more on the beam, because it would have also penetrated the other side of the pressure hull too, which could have had a disastrous effect.

After the attack, the captain was on the bridge and intended to dive, but he was informed that damage was too great, so he gave the order to surface and quickly to fire off a recognition flare, because the aircraft was on the point of coming in for a second attack. Had the pilot done so, *Minerve* was at the mercy of shallow depth charge and gunfire attack, but he had suddenly realised the mistake.

It was later revealed that F/O Ensor had seen large white letters painted on the conning tower that looked like P.26 and he thought they read P.35, however no French submarine bore the number P.35. Mick Ensor had turned and was going in to depth charge the boat when he saw the letters at the last minute, but then realised that it could not be a U-boat because they were never marked in that style. The recognition flare set off in the conning tower had been taken by the pilot as a fire and he had just seen smoke, but no actual colour.

The almost undamaged rocket, which was deemed to be dangerous and likely to explode, was thrown overboard. The tail tube of the rocket must have been ripped off as it went through the steel plates, because there was no sign of it in the boat.

Squadron aircraft spent almost a week escorting *Minerve* back to Falmouth. The bodies of the two dead submariners were still on board and it was stated that the stench was unbelievable by the time the boat docked. F/O Mick Ensor and Arthur Clouston, who published his memoirs *Dangerous Skies* in 1954, made the journey to Falmouth to visit the French crew. However, the two men were ordered by their group commander to wear civilian clothes, because the Frenchmen were feeling very hostile towards the RAF. Mick apologised, but the hostility was so great that they both left the boat in a hurry. Captain Sonneville admitted he was to blame for disobeying orders and surfacing where he did and F/O Mick Ensor was completely exonerated of any blame.

(In 1954, when the memoirs were published, Mick Ensor was still serving in the RAF.)
D.I.N.O. 11549/43
Anti-Submarine Warfare Division 13 October 1943

FINAL PATROL

On 19 September 1945, the Free French submarine was under tow to a breaker's yard when the cable parted and she ran into shallow water off Chesil Beach, on the west side of Portland Bill. The wreck was then broken up where she lay.

WRECK SITE

The wreck lies on a seabed of gravel and pebbles, in a general depth of 5m, being the lowest astronomical depth. She is now badly broken up, with just the skeletal remains to be found.

UB 72, SM IMPERIAL U-BOAT

DATE OF LOSS: 12 May 1918
DEPTH: 66m
REFERENCE: 50 06' 58 N 002 50' 58 W
LOCATION: Midway between Guernsey and Portland Bill

Type: UBIII coastal torpedo attack boat   *Builders*: AG Vulcan, Hamburg for Kaiserliche Deutsche Marine   *Ordered*: on 23 September 1916, within the batch of UB 72–UB 74   *Keel laid*: as Yard No.96 on 30 July 1917   *Launched*: on 30 July 1917   *Commissioned*: by Kapitänleutnant Walter Hildebrand Creutzfeldt on 9 September 1917

TECHNICAL SPECIFICATIONS

Hull: double   *Surface displacement*: 508 tons   *U/Dt*: 639 tons   *LBDH*: 55.52m × 5.76m × 3.68m × 8.25m   *Machinery*: 2 × 550ps MAN diesels   *Props*: 2 bronze   *S/Sp*: 13.4 knots   *Op/R*: 8,420 nautical miles at 6 knots   *Sub/R*: 55 nautical miles at 4 knots   *U/Power*: 2 × 394ps electric motors gave 7.5 knots   *Batteries*: lead/acid/accumulators   *Fuel/Cap*: 37 + 78 tons   *Armament*: 4 bow and 1 stern 50.04cm torpedo tubes   *Torpedoes*: 10 × 50.04cm (19.7in)   *Guns*: 1 × 105mm (4.13in) forward deck gun   *Ammo*: 160 rounds of 105mm   *Mines*: none   *Diving*: max-op-depth 50m (164ft) and 30 sec to crash-dive   *Complement*: 3 officers and 31 ratings

UB 72 was formally assigned to the German-based V.U-Flottille at Bremerhaven on 28 October 1917, with Walter Hildebrand Creutzfeld the commander from 9 September 1917 until 9 February 1918. Creutzfeld made the following patrols with the boat:

(1) On 11 November 1917, *UB 72* left Germany and made an uneventful patrol in the North Sea before returning to port on the 17th.

(2) *UB 72* sailed from Bremerhaven on 4 December 1917 for operations along the English east coast as far as Longstone in the Outer Farne Islands, where Creutzfeld may have hit an unidentified Danish steamer of around 1,500 tons.

UB 72 returned to Germany on the 18th.

(3) Leaving Bremerhaven on 12 January 1918, *UB 72* sailed to the Irish Sea for operations, taking the long route via the Isles of Orkney and North Channel. Creutzfeld captured, shelled and sunk the 896-ton Norwegian steamer *SVANFOS* (1905 – Aktieselskapet Manchester, Kristiania), at the approximate position of 59° 12'N 03° 55'W, at 1120hrs on 3 February; the ship was en-route from Liverpool for Skien with soda ash and iron; the whole crew of fifteen, plus one passanger, took to the boats and survived.

UB 72 returned to Germany on 9 February.

Oberleutnant zur See Friedrich Traeger assumed command of the boat on 2 March 1918.

(4) Traeger left harbour on 16 March 1918 and took *UB 72* into the northern section of the North Sea, for operations against Scotland – Norway convoys, where Traeger sunk two ships. The 3,643-ton steamer *Tithonus* (1908 – The Admiralty, London) was escorting a convoy for Norway when Traeger sunk her with torpedoes on 28 March, 50 miles east of Aberdeen at 57° 04'N 00° 33'W. (The ship was originally named SS *Titania* (Finska Ångfartygs A/B, Helsingfors), but was requisitioned in March 1916 and commissioned as an Armed Boarding Steamer).

THE FOLLOWING MEN DIED

Hamilton, Edward Robert, Key Telelegraphist RN
Harris, John Sword, Ordinary Seaman RNVR
Morley, Austin Clement, Stoker 1st Class RN
Walton, Tom Westmoreland, Junior Engineer MMR

On the 30th, the 1,322-ton Norwegian SS *Vafos* (1906 – Aktieselskapet Manchester, Kristiania) was voyaging from Hull to Skien with a general cargo when she was sunk. According to the 'Declaration hearing', the master was not sure how, but he suspected a torpedo, due to the nature of the explosion; records later showed this to be correct. Four men were killed and another four wounded when the ship sank, at approximately, 35 nautical miles southwest to west of Marstein lighthouse, off the west coast of Norway.

THE MEN WHO DIED

Steen, Einar Donkeyman from Kristiania
Friling, Thoralf Stoker from Kristiania
Klausen, Kristian Sailor from Florø
Andreassen, Elias Sailor from Bergen

UB 72 returned to base on 4 April 1918.

On 25 April 1918, *UB 72* transferred from V.U-Flottille, which was being disbanded and moved to II.U-Flottille at Heligoland.

FINAL PATROL

(5) Friedrich Traeger's second war patrol and the boat's fifth, was to be around the western end of the English Channel and the Scilly Isles, but it was delayed, because of the presence of a number of minefields. To reach his destination and avoid the dangerous Dover Strait entailed SM *UB 72* making the long voyage up the North Sea, around the Isles of Orkney and Scotland, via the Fair Isle Channel, then through the Minch and down the North Channel and the Irish Sea.

UB 72 sailed from Kiel through the Skaggarak on 1 May 1918 (other sources allege 27 April) carrying three officers and thirty-one men. However before the boat could venture cross the North Sea, five minesweeping boats had to escort her through the danger areas. Without warning, on 6 May, Traeger torpedoed and sunk the defensively armed steamship *SANDHURST* (1897 – Britain S.S. Co.Ltd, London) of 3,034 tons, 6 miles from Corsewall Point; she was travelling from Bilbao to Ardrossan with iron ore; twenty crewmen and one Royal Marine DEMS gunner were drowned.

SOME OF THE MEN WHO DIED

Abdullah Hamid, Fireman and Trimmer
Ahmad Saleh, Fireman and Trimmer
Ahmad Salim, Fireman and Trimmer
Barrick, Frank Addison, 19yrs, Able Seaman
Bullen, Victor Albert, 39yrs, 1st Engineer
Cox, Edwin, 15yrs, Cooks Boy
Dowdall, William Robert, 17yrs, Engineers' Boy
Evans, Frederick John, 17yrs, Steward's Boy
Goldsmith, Alexander Nobel, 40yrs, 2nd Engineer
Hardey, Albert, 43yrs, 2nd Mate
Heard, Frederick Ernest, Private RMLI (DAMS)
Higgs, William, 33yrs, Fireman
Hirst, Frank Russell, 17yrs, Apprentice
Ismail Hasan, Donkeyman
Jones, William Morris, 43yrs, Mate
Metcalfe, George, 18yrs, Sailor
Russum, George Edward, 17yrs, Apprentice
Trubshaw, Ronald Howard, 15yrs, Apprentice
Webber, Richard Arthur, 47yrs, Steward
Williams, Arthur Mafeking, 18yrs, Apprentice

The 3,358-ton defensively armed SS *Quito* (1900 – Ocean Navigation Co. Ltd, Glasgow), on passage from Barrow to Barry Roads, was torpedoed without warning by *UB 72* and left damaged; she was beached at Salt Head Point, Holyhead but refloated later.

By 9 May the U-boat had reached the Scilly Isles and, without warning, torpedoed the 1,836-ton steamer *Baron Ailsa* (1912 – Kelvin Shipping Co. Ltd, Ardrossan); the ship was defensively armed and transporting Government stores from Queenstown, Ireland to Barry; ten men drowned, including two DEMS gunners.

THE MEN WHO DIED

Ali Hasan, Fireman and Trimmer
Black, Daniel, 58yrs, Steward
McIntosh, Leonard Victor, LdgSmn RNVR (DAMS)
Mouat, Thomas, 53yrs, Boatswain (Bosun)
Oliver, Walter Herbert, 18yrs, Wireless Operator
Osborne, Percy, AB RNVR (DAMS)
Qaid Said, Fireman and Trimmer
Robertson, James, 27yrs, Mess Room Steward
Routledge, Colin Easton, 18yrs, Sailor
Somerville, William, 24yrs, 3rd Engineer

Apart from attacking some Allied vessels during the voyage, *UB 72* had a very eventful patrol in other ways, because destroyers and patrol boats had attacked her for much of the voyage. During the passage through St George's Channel, a Royal Navy destroyer dropped twenty-three depth charges over the boat, which resulted in a leaking port ballast tank. Two further attacks were made with twenty depth charges, then five more, leaving the U-boat with broken lightbulbs and damage to a forward starboard oil tank, even before she had reached the patrol area near the Scilly Isles. By this time, *UB 72* was leaving a long trail of oil astern. Träger crossed over to the approaches to Brest and was on the surface, sailing midway between Guernsey and Portland Bill in the English Channel. His quarry was to be a convoy that included one of the largest passenger liners in the world, the White Star Line's 46,359-ton troopship *Olympic* (1911), which was packed with American troops. The U-boats *U 103, U 46, U 55, U 70* and *U 94* were also waiting for the convoy, but were positioned further down Channel. German information about the convoys had been gathered from documents collected from a captured American merchantman. They indicated that troopships only remained with the convoy as far as Fastnet Rock and from that point, they travelled independently.

Unknown to the commander of *UB 72*, His Majesty's Submarine *D4*, under the command of Lieutenant Claude Barry B. 83P294 RN, had been ordered to intercept the U-boat. The British information regarding the concentration of U-boats actually came about following the interception of German signals. At 0430hrs on 12 May 1918, Lieutenant Claude Barry in HM S/M *D4* was travelling submerged when he sighted *UB 72*, some 2 miles distant and on a southerly heading. At 0435hrs, the surfaced *UB 72* unwittingly altered course towards the British submarine. Lt Barry decided to lower his periscope, so as to not attract the U-boat's attention. Barry raised the periscope again at 0443hrs and found *UB 72* on his port side about 1,200 yards (1,097m) away. She was now steering an easterly course, while the U-boat men on watch, were eagerly (and conveniently) gazing westwards, away from *D4*. It was rather unfortunate for the crew of *UB 72* that *D4* had an 'IS-WAS' installed. This was a calculator devised by Captain Martin Naismith VC designed to compute the target solution for small, distant targets (after the war it was superceded by the Torpedo Data Computer, irreverently known as 'the fruit machine').

Lieutenant Barry waited until the U-boat was lined up in his sights, then at 0450hrs, with the enemy submarine a mere 600 yards (548m) away, he fired one torpedo, lowered the scope for a few moments, before firing a second one. Just ten seconds later, a huge explosion was heard and *D4* shuddered under the shockwaves. *D4* then surfaced and headed to the spot where the boat had been, but all that was left were three bedraggled sailors floundering in the sea and a large patch of oil. The only three men to suvive and on their first war-patrol in a U-boat were picked up by *D4*. At 520hrs *D4* dived again to 20ft (6.10m) and on periscope watch altered course to 270°. They indicated that troopships only remained with the convoy as far as Fastnet and from that point onwards they travelled independently.

Log of *D4*:

Sunday 12 May 1918
5.30am – Sighted enemy submarine at 50.08'N 2.41'W – enemy bearing 20 green approx speed 6 knots – distance 1200 yards
5.50 – Fired 2 bow torpedoes heard explosion
5.53 – Surfaced rescued 3 seamen no others of crew or wreckage afloat.

One of the survivors said that just before the torpedo struck, Petty Officer Heroch was on the conning tower, as Officer of the Watch. A/S Diers and PO Laabs were acting as the lookouts when Stoker Gabriel (who had just arrived on the bridge) spotted the track of the approaching torpedo. He immediately dived overboard and seconds later the warhead detonated against *UB 72*. Stoker Gabriel watched the boat sink stern first, just like a 'stone'. The other three men on the conning tower were carried below, but as the boat went down, a rush of air from inside pushed them back up to the surface. Dragged down by the vortex, Petty Officer Heroch unfortunately sank before the crew of *D4* could reach him. HM S/M *D4* landed at Plymouth, where the three survivors were made prisoners-of-war.

Petty Officer James Hollier Hague of *D4* was awarded the DSM, while Lieutenant Claude Barry was awarded the DSO for their actions in sinking SM *UB 72*. (In the award it read: 'Their Lordships consider that this attack was carried out with great skill and gallantry.')

ADM 173/1069 NARA T1022, Roll 58, PG 61832 CWGC U-Boot-Ehrenmal Möltenort
Norwegian Maritime Declarations 1914–1918

HM SM *D4*. (Author's collection)

HM SM *D4*. (Author's collection)

THE MEN WHO DIED IN SM UB 72

Bille, Rudolf U-Maschinistenmaat
Bilot, Josef U-Matrose
Breiter, Friedrich U-Maschinistenmaat
Delion, Joh. U-Obermaschinistenmaat
Döring, Karl U-Heizer
Engelmann, H. U-Matrose
Fischer, Alwin U-Matrose
Fuchs, Richard U-Heizer
Fürst, Wilhelm U-Matrose
Gurlt, W. U-Obermatrose
Hagemeister, E. U-Maschinistenmaat der Reserve
Hennemann, W. U-Maschinistenmaat
Herok, Franz U-Oberbootsmannsmaat
Kochan, Gustav U-Maschinistenmaat
Kolp, Friedrich U-F.T.Maat
Köllisch, Philipp U-Heizer

Langbauer, J. U-F.T.Gast
Lichtenberg, J. U-Heizer
Liebetrau, K. U-Matrose
Neuschmelting, U-Heizer
Rieck, Fritz Oberleutnant zur See der Reserve
Ropenus, Karl U-F.T.Gast
Schlosser, Friedrich U-Heizer
Schmidt, Adam U-Bootsmannsmaat
Schmidt, Franz U-Maschinistenmaat
Schmidt, Bruno U-Matrose
Schuhmacher, A. U-Heizer
Schär, Gottfried U-Matrose
Steinfeld, J. U-Maschinistenmaat
Strothenke, W. U-Oberheizer
Träger, Friedrich Oberleutnant zur See
Weiß, Max Marine Ingenieur

WRECK SITE

The wreck was first dived in 1997, the author Innes McCartney being one of the diving team. It lies on a seabed of sand and gravel, in a general depth of 66m (216ft), being the lowest astronomical depth. The bows and stern of the boat are rather collapsed and there is other damage to the outer hull. The conning tower hatch is still tightly sealed and on the port side of the conning tower rests the muzzle of the deck gun, the gun having swung round after it went down and struck the seabed. Aft of the conning tower and towards the stern end, two large trawl nets are now entangled with her remains, one of which floats upover. Tidal streams are quite brisk. This wreck site is a war grave.

U 1191, KRIEGSMARINE U-BOAT

DATE OF LOSS: 25 June 1944
DEPTH: 60m
REFERENCE: 50 01'.291 N 002 59'.772 W
LOCATION: 27.82 nautical miles SE of Start Point

Type: VIIC ocean-going boat   *Builders*: F. Schichau GmbH, Danzig for Kriegsmarine   *Ordered*: on 25 August 1941, within the batch of *U 1191–U 1198*   **Keel laid**: as Yard No.1561 on 4 November 1942   *Launched*: on 6 July 1943   *Commissioned*: by Oberleutnant zur See Peter Grau on 9 September 1943   *Feldpost No*: M 52 991

TECHNICAL SPECIFICATIONS

See page 342.

Oblt.z.S. Peter Grau was born in Elmshorn on 8 March 1920 and commenced his naval career in 1939. His first posting was on board the destroyer *Karl Galster* (Z 20), serving as secretarial officer and 3rd watch officer between October 1940 and June 1942. On 1 April 1943 Grau was promoted to Oberleutnant zur See.

From her commissioning *U 1191* was assigned to 8.U-Flottille at Danzig as Ausbildungsboot (training boat) until 30 April 1944, with Peter Grau the boat's only commander. On 1 May 1944, *U 1191* formally transferred to 7.U-Flottille at St Nazaire in France for frontline service.

On 9 May 1944, *U 1191* departed Kiel and sailed to Stavanger (58° 57.52'N 5° 43.36'E) in southwest Norway, where she arrived on the 15th.

FINAL PATROL

(2) Leaving Stavanger on 22 May 1944, *U 1191* put out into the North Atlantic on her first, and final, war patrol. Along this stretch of Norwegian coast, aircraft of Coastal Command now plagued the U-boats. Following the D-Day landings on 6 June, *U 1191* was ordered to proceed towards western France. On 8 June this order was made more specific when *U 1191* was directed to the Channel via BE 15. Oblt.z.S. Grau received orders on 9 June, instructing him to proceed to the English Channel. This day, Grau transmitted a *Passiermeldung* from *AL 27*. At 0430hrs west of Achill Head off Ireland, Grau reported to U-boat Command and sent a weather report on the 12th, at position 54°N, 18°W. This was followed on 14 June by orders to enter BF 2752 then proceed to within 15 miles of the French coast (as far as 3° west). Thereafter, all boats were to head for the area of BF 3180. At 2340hrs on the 20 June, *U 1191* was directed to BF 3610. On 3 July the boat was ordered back to base, but of course she never returned and was presumed lost by 17 July. To determine what fate befell her, we must turn to British records.

We know that at 2257hrs on 18 June, north, northeast of Plouguerneau (49° 03'N 04° 48'W), Wellington bomber 'A' of 304 (Polish) Squadron dropped a stick of six depth charges over a U-boat, believed at the time to be *U 1191*. The depth charges straddled the target while the conning tower was still visible. Oil and wreckage was spotted by the rear gunner. The contemporary assessment was that the 'U-boat probably sunk'. *U 1191* should have been nearby at this time, but the assessment verdict is questionable. Certainly the RNHB concluded that the Polish Wellington had destroyed *U 1191*.

There is another claim. At 2129hrs on 26 June HMS *Balfour* obtained an ASDIC contact in the English Channel, southeast of Torquay, which was also thought to be *U 1191*. *U 269* had already been apparently sunk by HMS *Bickerton* earlier that morning and Escort Group-5 was continuing with their operations, until *U 984* hit HMS *Goodson* with a torpedo at 1514hrs. The other warships in EG-5 had to be escorted her back to port. Escort Group-1 then took over the pursuit for this other submarine, to the west of the search area. *Balfour* found a contact at 175ft (53m) and HMS *Affleck* attacked it with Hedgehogs, which detonated nine seconds later. *Affleck* turned to make another run with depth charges and found herself ploughing through a welling oil slick. There was some concern that the target the ships were attacking might just be the wreck of *U 269*. However confirmation was quickly received that *U 269* had been destroyed some 3 miles distant. The two Captain Class frigates, *Balfour* and *Affleck*, then destroyed the submarine.

OFFICIAL REPORT OF EG5 BALFOUR AND AFFLECK

At 2129hrs on 26 June *Balfour* 1½ miles on *Affleck*'s starboard beam reported a submarine contact. *Affleck* turned towards…gained contact and confirming the classification as 'submarine' attacked with Hedgehog. Contact was held right in and bombs detonated after 9 seconds sinking time seeming to indicate an explosion on or near the bottom. This was exceptionally violent…As we ran on, thin wisps of oil coloured water were observed here and there and a slight oily smell was noticeable. It occurred to me that we were attacking a bottomed U-boat who had left slight oils streaks from a recently used schnorchel exhaust so I turned to go in with depth charges. At this moment a rapidly widening oil patch of very thick oil was easily seen. I then asked *Keats* if we were clear of *Bickerton*'s successful attack of 16 hours earlier and when he replied that we were, I was confident we were in contact with a fresh-bottomed U-boat.

As the enemy made no move, but continued to gush oil, I decided to keep *Balfour* with me and send the others off of my previously arranged sweep…at this time we obtained an echo sounding trace outline of a U-boat on the bottom. My trace was so graphic that it might have been taken from a book of silhouettes. The stern appeared first, followed by a clear outline of the conning tower, foredeck and bow. Even the bulges of the saddle tanks could be seen abreast the conning tower…By 0410hrs I was convinced that the U-boat was destroyed and most probably by my first Hedgehog attack.

Awards were duly presented to twelve officers and men of HM Ships *Affleck* and *Balfour* for sinking *U 1191* south of Torquay on 25 June 1944. However as the RNHB pointed out, this is all rather too neat. *U 1191 had been expected to pass through this area 2 days earlier by BdU. On the date of this attack,*

U 1191 should have been on the verge of entering BF 361, some 80 miles to the east of the attack position. The Assessment Committee credited the two warships with sinking a U-boat. The assessment was given as a 'B' grade though, because, due generally to the dense fog that prevailed, there was no positive proof. The BdU Diary contains the following pithy entry for the 17 July: 22 May left Stavanger, passage report 9 June from AL27. 6 June, 8 June, 14 June. and 21 June orders as for U 767. July ordered to return, has not arrived so far. No clue as to cause, date or place of loss; presumably in the Channel.

Divers, including Innes McCartney, visited the wreck site in the summer of 1999. Using the *Lindberg* method, it was possible to conclude that the wreck was most likely that of *U 1191*.

ADM 1/29746 ADM 1/29746 NARA T1022, Roll 4065-4066, PG30347-30351 U-Boot-Ehrenmal Möltenort

THE MEN WHO PERISHED IN U 1191

Allgaier, Ernst Mech.Gfr. (born: 5-7-1923)
Baranowski, Kurt Mtr.O.Gfr. (7-1-1925)
Bode, Ernst Masch.O.Gfr. (23-8-1922)
Böttcher, Gerhard Ob.San.Mt. (2-9-1920)
Britzke, Werner Ob.Masch.Mt. (21-6-1921)
Brüggemann, Hubert Bts.Mt. (8-1-1921)
Bühler, Heinrich Mtr. (7-12-1924)
Colmann, Wldemar Mech.Gfr. (21-4-1922)
Erler, Walter Mech.O.Gfr. (4-5-1925)
Esch, Walter Fk.Mt. (26-11-1921)
Frick, Arno Masch.Gfr. (3-11-1924)
Grau, Peter Oberleutnant zur See (8-3-1920)
Grimmeis, August Masch.Gfr. (18-7-1924)
Gschössl, Franz Masch.Ob.Gfr. (22-6-1922)
Hambauer, Josef Mtr.Ob.Gfr. (16-3-1924)
Hänisch, Walter Mtr.Ob.Gfr. (24-11-1922)
Heinrich, Hans Masch.Ob.gfr. (6-12-1923)
Helfenstein, Jabob Ob.Masch. (24-2-1915)
Hütter, Emmerich Masch.Gfr. (13-6-1924)
Kessel, Karl Fk.Mt. (13-12-1922)
Knödler, Erwin Fk.Ob.Gfr. (25-11-1923)
Koch, Heinrich Masch.Gfr. (4-1-1924)
Kochendörfer, Willi Fk.Ob.Gfr. (14-3-1923)
Kollenberg, Albert Ob.Masch.Mt. (21-11-1920)
Kraus, Johann Bts.Mt. (8-10-1919)
Kunze, Hanns-Dieter Leutnant zur See (29-7-1921)

Kurras, Herbert Bts.Mt. (29-3-1918)
Kutschmann, Franz Masch.Mt. (21-1-1921)
Lehmann, Karl-Heinz Fk.Ob.Gfr. (21-12-1924)
Lilienthal, Wilhelm Masch.Ob.gfr. (26-1-1924)
Lipinski, Paul Mtr.Ob.Gfr. (23-9-1924)
Lohrer, Karl Masch.Ob.gfr. (3-11-1924)
Lorenz, Kurt Mtr.Ob.Gfr. (26-5-1922)
Mettler, Hermann Masch.Ob.Gfr. (6-6-1923)
Oltermann, Hans Mtr.Gfr. (10-1-1924)
Pinschke, Willibald Masch.Mt. (4-5-1919)
Pokoyski, Alex Ob.Strm. (4-11-1914)
Rausch, Ernst Masch.Ob.Gfr. (16-3-1925)
Reinicke, Ekkehard Leutnant zur See (5-8-1924)
Rühle, Konrad Ob.Mech.Mt. (18-6-1921)
Schäfer, Klaus Ob.Masch. (3-3-1917)
Schauenburg, Heinz Masch.Og.Fr. (6-6-1925)
Scheler, Heinz Masch.Mt. (7-1-1922)
Schmidt, Fritz Mtr.Ob.Gfr. (6-4-1924)
Schwab, Willi Mtr.Gfr. (15-3-1925)
Stuhldreher, Ernst-Heinrich Mtr.Ob.Gfr. (26-8-1924)
Uelner, Eberhard Leutnant Ingenieur (19-4-1923)
Wegener, Willi Mtr.Ob.Gfr. (17-6-1923)
Werner, Heinz Mtr.Ob.Gfr. (5-12-1923)
Zehnsdorf, Werner Mtr.Ob.Gfr. (12-6-1925)

WRECK SITE

The wreck lies on a seabed of sand and shingle, in a general depth of 60m (196ft), being the lowest astronomical tide. It is upright and completely intact with the anti-aircraft platform in place and the inner and outer conning tower hatches both open. The propellers are just visible, but mostly buried. The outer casing also shows signs of savage depth charging, with a fair amount of damage. This wreck will be classed as a war grave.

U 672, KRIEGSMARINE U-BOAT

DATE OF LOSS: 18 July 1944
DEPTH: around 60m
REFERENCE: 50° 03'N 03° 25'W (approximate)
LOCATION: approximately 14 nautical miles SW of Start Point

Type: VIIC ocean-going attack boat   *Builders*: Howaldts Werke AG, Hamburg for Kriegsmarine
Ordered: on 20 January 1941, within the batch of *U 669–U 674*   *Keel laid*: as Yard No.821 on 24
December 1941   *Launched*: on 27 February 1943   *Commissioned*: by Oberleutnant zur See Ulf
Lawaetz on 6 April 1943   *Feldpost No*: M 51 135

TECHNICAL SPECIFICATIONS

See page 342.

OTHER EQUIPMENT FITTED

Armament consisted of one 37mm (1.46in) and two twin 20mm (0.79in) Flak guns, plus 220
rounds of ammunition, five torpedo tubes (one stern and four at the bow) and she carried 'Lut'
and T5 torpedoes with bakelite caps. The T5 were loaded in Tubes II, III and V and there was one
spare aft. Pi.2 pistols were carried for 'Lut', and Pi4B for the T5 torpedoes. (The loading rail was
fitted during final adjustments.) She could also carry mines or a combination of torpedoes and
mines. *U 672* was fitted with a 'Presskohle Grenzwellen' receiver for 'Y' work. (Although no special
operator was carried, the commander was an excellent W/T operator and had a good knowledge
of English.) The boat was also equipped with standard 'Gema' radar, which could pick up an aircraft
at 26km.

Ulf Lawaetz was born in Copenhagen on 5 November 1916 and commenced his naval career
in 1937. He began his service as No.2 Gunnery Officer aboard the destroyer *Z 18 Hans Lüdemann*
between November 1939 and April 1940. On 1 April 1942 Lawaetz was promoted to Oberleutnant
zur See.

U 672 was assigned to 5.U-Flottille at Kiel as Ausbildungsboot (under training boat) from the
commissioning with Oblt.z.S Lawaetz the CO until 30 September 1943. The boat and skipper then
formally transferred to 6.U-Flottille at St Nazaire on 1 October 1943, for frontline service.

At 0800hrs (Continental time) on 13 November 1943, *U 672* departed Kiel alone and transferred
to Bergen (60° 23.17'N 5° 19.54'E) in southwest Norway. From the Kiel lightship, an 'M' Class
minesweeper escorted her to Kristiansand and then she proceeded via Haugsund, arriving at her
destination on 16 November.

U 672 left Bergen the next day for operations in the North Atlantic. After passing between Færoe
and the Isles of Shetland, *U 672* operated in the North Atlantic, where she teamed up with a
number of other U-boats west of the North Channel in early December to form *Coronel* group.
The wolfpack searched unsuccessfully for westbound convoys *ONS 24*, the convoy having passed
by to the north. By mid-December more boats joined up and *Coronel* group split into two smaller
sub groups, awaiting *ON 214*, but the mission failed again as the convoy passed by to the south.
On 19 December *U 672* became part of *Föhr* group and over the next month, formed up with the
Amrum, *Sylt*, and *Rügen-5* wolfpacks to the west of Ireland. In mid-December she was ordered to
join various patrol sweeps in succession, but never sighted anything. Three convoys were sighted, but
no attacks made due to efficient escorts.

At the end of December she set course for St Nazaire, arriving on 13 January 1944, her group
having disbanded on the 5th. During the next six weeks, a 37mm gun was fitted on the lower bandstand, instead of the quadruple 20mm version.

(2) *U 672* departed St Nazaire on 26 February 1944 and sailed for operations in the North
Atlantic, to the west of the British Isles, where she teamed up with *Preußen* wolfpack. The pack
disbanded on 23 March and *U 672* patrolled independently, between 40°W and the British Isles.
Lawaetz carried out weather duties during the best part of April.

Just after midnight on 24 April, *U 672* was on the surface in the Bay of Biscay and the crew was busy depositing *Thetis* radar decoys, when a Leigh Light-equipped *B-24* of British Squadron 120 discovered the boat. Pilot L.T.Taylor found the U-boat by radar using the light and attacked her with six depth charges, but all fell wide of their marks. At 1230hrs, later that day, in position 46° 55'N 10° 40'W, a Sunderland flying-boat, piloted by Flight-Lieutenant F.G. Fellows of 423 Squadron Royal Canadian Air force, also caught *U 672* on the surface and dropped six depth charges over her. Lawaetz's gun crew immediately retaliated with heavy flak, but one of the boat's batteries was severely damaged and a fuel tank ruptured, when a depth charge detonated prematurely. The plane however, was also badly damaged, either from the exploding depth charge or the flak and abandoned making any more attacks; Flight-Lieutenant Fellows managed to return to base.

U 672 dived and remained submerged for a while before surfacing, then continued planting *Thetis*. On 12 May 1944 Lawaetz put into St Nazaire for damage repair and provisions. During her stay in port, *schnorchel* was fitted and 'Lut' setting gear supplied, Lawaetz having earlier taken a 'Lut' course at the Torpedo Arsenal West, in Paris.

(3) *U 672* left port on 28 June for deep diving test and returned three days later on 1 July, having any problems checked before the next long patrol.

FINAL PATROL

(4) At 2130hrs on 6 July 1944, *U 672* and 27-year-old Ulf Lawaetz, headed out from St Nazaire, escorted by five minesweepers. Her destination was the Allied convoy route in the Bay of the Seine at position 50° 20'N 01° 50'W. Lawaetz was ordered to proceed via the swept channel to the northward, then leave the swept channel and make his way to the designated patrol zone. At the 25-fathom (45m) line at 0230hrs (Continental time) on the 7th the escorts parted company and from there *U 672* had to dodge her way through heavy anti-submarine patrols. She used her *schnorchel* almost continuously at night, travelling at a speed of 5 knots. Through the day, Lawaetz took the boat to between 40m and 50m (131ft and 164ft) and moved slowly along at 2 knots.

U 672 left the swept channel on 10 July and made a 360° heading. At position 49° 15'N 06°W on the 13th she was ventilating the boat using the *schnorchel* when she was located by an Allied aircraft, which dropped four depth charges over her at 1200hrs. The U-boat was undamaged, but the pilot informed Allied surface vessels of her whereabouts. Later that afternoon at 1500hrs, four destroyers and a light cruiser were sighted at 2,000 yards (1,828m). Lawaetz believed these ships were part of an American hunter-killer group. Opportunistically, as the force was altering course from 270° to 180°, Lawaetz fired two T5 torpedoes, one at the cruiser and the other at a destroyer. *U 672* then dived to within 10m of the seabed, stopped motors and lay motionless in a stopped trim. Both warheads failed to make contact or detonate. The U-boat rose to periscope depth and, with nothing in sight, continued on course 360°. She later altered course to 70° and continued for a few days, running submerged at depths between 30m and 50m during daylight hours and breathing via her *schnorchel* by night.

Following instructions from U-boat Command, *U 672* sailed for an area immediately south of the Isle of Wight. Arriving on the 18th at approximately 50° 03'N 03° 25'W, Lawaetz bottomed out at 1100hrs and lay motionless awaiting the tide to change. Lawaetz ordered his crew to take to their bunks, with the exception of the watch. However, HMS *Balfour* (Lt Cdr C.D.B. Coventry) detected the U-boat at 15.42hrs.

ACCOUNT OF HMS *Balfour* – 18/7/44 (*U 672*). Attack carried out at 50° 03'N 02° 30'W:

> EG1 was sweeping in shallow waters in good sub ASDIC conditions in spite of the prevalence of 'non subs'. At 15.42 *Balfour* gained ASDIC contact at 2,000 yards bearing red 85. This was classified as 'submarine', which was estimated to be at 26 fathoms. A deliberate attack was delivered with Hedgehog and three explosions were heard seconds after firing…six seconds after firing the rest of the pattern exploded on the bottom. The recorder trace before the attack shows a possible U-boat contact. There is evidence that the projectiles hit a solid object some 50ft from the bottom.

(Note: not in agreement with *U 672* having bottomed at that time. Note also the difference in position.)

Icy water flooded through the stern glands of *U 672* and further explosions caused more leakages, swamping the battery panels. In an attempt to correct trim, water was pumped out, but the air inside the boat was becoming stale and poisonous. Realising the boat was finished, in the early hours of the 19th, Lawaetz ordered his crew to prepare for scuttling. The Enigma machine and secret papers were destroyed first and then Lawaetz surfaced the boat, ascending at an angle of 70° due to the flooding. Once on the surface the saturated diesel engines refused to start. The crew were ordered to abandon ship in individual rubber dinghies, while the skipper and Georg Käseberg, his chief engineer, set scuttling charges before leaving. The crew bobbed around in the freezing water for almost 12 hours after their boat sank. At 1330hrs two Spitfires spotted them at position as 50° 03'N 03° 25'W and 17 miles southeast of Start Point. First, a Walrus seaplane of the Fleet Air Arm seized Lawaetz as a 'sample' and then Air-Sea Rescue and PT boats picked up the remaining crewmen.

Official report – Anti-U-boat Operations – The Sinking of '*U 672*':

> On the night of 18/19 July '*U 672*' ended her career by being scuttled off Start Point she had been damaged by depth charge attacks made by HMS '*Balfour*' during the previous afternoon. The outstanding feature of the information obtained from survivors is the extreme slowness of the boat's progress. Making apparently 2 knots by day, when she proceeded on her motors submerged to between 30–50m, and at 5 knots by night, when she used schnorchel almost uninterruptedly, she took from 2130hrs on 6 July, to about noon on the 18th to get from St Nazaire to Start Point. After leaving her base she steered first to the southwest, then to the northwest and finally altered to 360° on reaching the meridian of 6° W., while still southwest of Ushant.
>
> On the 13th, when she was about 40 miles south by east of the Scilly Isles, she altered course to 070° and began to creep up the Channel, making about 35 miles each day. Whenever the tide was unfavourable to her course the U-boat lay on the bottom until it had changed. By her amended orders she was to operate against cross-Channel shipping, in an area due south of the Isle of Wight.
>
> There were few incidents in the course of the passage. On the 13th, shortly before the U-boat altered course to enter the Channel, an aircraft made an ineffective attack and on the same day the U-boat fired two Gnats at some warships which do not seem to have been aware of her presence. When in the Channel, Leigh-light aircraft were sighted from time to time, the U-boat diving from schnorchel depth to avoid them.
>
> At about noon on the 18th the U-boat bottomed off Start Point to await the change of an unfavourable tide. A few hours later hydrophone effect was heard and then a pattern of depth charges was dropped close to the boat, others being heard later soiree distance away. The U-boat was badly damaged, both diesel and electric motors being made unserviceable and a battery wrecked. High-pressure air bottles began to leak and water to enter both forward and aft. The pumps kept it in check but the atmosphere grew very bad and at about midnight on the 18th/ 19th the Captain gave the order to destroy all papers and prepare to abandon the boat. Owing to the loss of high-pressure air and the weight of the water aft, he had some difficulty in surfacing.
>
> The U-boat was abandoned and scuttled without haste about 0330hrs on the 19th. There was a flat calm and the crew were got safely into their dinghies, which they had taken care to stock with ample provisions. In due course they were sighted by aircraft and picked up by Air/Sea Rescue launches.

ADM 199/2061 NARA T1022 Rolls 4065–4066, PG 30350 – 30353

U 672 sank no Allied vessels.

BdU Diary for 10 August 1944 contains this entry: '*The loss of U 672 has been made known. According to information received from the Red Cross, 26 of the crew are in English, 26 in American, prison camps*'.

One of these men, Ob.Strm. Horst Hofmann, Obersteurmann of *U 672* (and former crewman of *U 48*) held the prestigious Knight's Cross; an honour rarely bestowed on a rating.

WRECK SITE

The wreck of *U 672* has never been located to date (2007). The position offered for the wreck is that suggested by the crew of *U 672*, but this would have been a rough estimate and may have been made to confuse the interrogators.

U 214, KRIEGSMARINE U-BOAT

DATE OF LOSS: 26 July 1944
DEPTH: 60m plus
REFERENCE: 49° 55'N 03° 31'W (estimate)
LOCATION: approximately 19 nautical miles SSE of Start Point and S of Eddystone

Type: VIID ocean-going mine-laying boat   *Builders*: F. Krupp Germaniawerft AG, Kiel-Gaarden, Kiel for Kriegsmarine   *Ordered*: on 16 February 1940, within the batch of *U 213–U 218*   *Keel laid*: as Yard No.646 on 5 October 1940   *Launched*: on 18 September 1941   *Commissioned*: by Oberleutnant zur See Günther Reeder on 1 November 1941   *Feldpost No*: M 31 973

TECHNICAL SPECIFICTIONS

Hull: single, saddle tank design   *Surface displacement*: 965 tons   *U/Dt*: 1,080 tons.   **LBDH**: 76.9m × 6,38m × 5.01m × 9.70m   *Machinery*: 2 × Germaniawerft (GW) diesels fitted with *Gebläse* (super-chargers). The diesels developed 1400ps each at 475 revolutions per minute continuous power, or 495 revolutions maximum power for 30 minutes developed 1600ps   *Propellers*: 2.   *S/Sp*: 16 knots   *Op/R*: 8,100 nautical miles at 12 knots or or 13,000 nautical miles at 10 knots   *Sub/R*: 69 nautical miles at 4 knots   *U/Power*: 2 × 375ps electric motors gave 7.3 knots   *Batteries*: 2 × AFA 62 cell lead/acid   *Fuel/Cap*: 169 tons   *Armament*: 4 bow and 1 stern torpedo tubes   *Guns*: 1 × 88mm (3.46in) forward deck gun and 1 × 20mm Flak.   *Ammo*: 220 rounds of 88mm 3.46in) and 4,380 rounds of 20mm (0.79in)   *Torpedoes*: 14, or   *Mines*: 15 SMA mines, or a combination of torpedoes and mines   *Diving*: max-op-depth 100m (328ft), max-depth 165m (541.33ft), crush-depth 200m (656ft) and crash-dive to 20m took 30 seconds on average   *Complement*: 44–52

OTHER EQUIPMENT FITTED

From October 1943, the gun arrangement was changed to one 37mm (1.46in) plus 1,195 rounds of 37mm and two twin 20mm (0.79in) Flak guns with 4,380 rounds (no machine guns).

Fourteen torpedoes were carried until the summer of 1943, with two of them in the upper-deck reserve containers. These were later removed and in 1944 the number was reduced to ten.

From Autumn 1944 onward, on boats operating in the Atlantic, or British coastal waters, the ten torpedoes usually consisted of five T5 and 5 Lut, often stowed as follows: T5 one in forward tube, three in forward bilges and one in aft tube. Five Lut stowed: three in forward tube, one in forward bilges and one in the aft bilges.

The VIID was similar to the VIIC boat, but a longer version, with additional SMA main shafts just aft of the conning tower. Out of the six in this class built, only one survived, with the other five being lost with all of their 241 crewmen.

Günther Reeder was born in Berlin-Karlshorst on 2 November 1915 and commenced his naval career in 1935. He began his submarine service as 1st Watch Officer on *U 58* between February 1939 and September 1940. On 1 June 1942 Reeder was promoted to Kapitänleutnant.

U 214 was assigned to 5.U-Flottille at Kiel, as Ausbildungsboot (training boat) on 1 November 1941 until 30 April 1942 with Reeder the CO from 1 November 1941. On 1 May 1942, *U 214* was formally assigned to 9.U-Flottille at Brest in western France, as a frontline boat.

U 214 sailed from Kiel on 18 May 1942 for her transfer to Brest, arriving on 4 June.

The boat moved out of Brest on 13 June and proceeded to the Bay of Biscay on temporary torpedo operations; however she sustained heavy damage from an attack by British aircraft in Biscay. Reeder was forced to abort the mission and returned to Brest for repairs on 18 June.

On 9 August 1942, Reeder left Brest with *U 214* for operations in the Freetown area off West Africa. Southeast of the Azores on the 13th the *U 214* teamed up with three of the boats of *Blücher* wolfpack. Other boats had not arrived to join the pack by the 14th, when *U 653* sighted the north-bound convoy SL 118. The four boats available shadowed the ships, but escorts kept them at bay until the 17th, then during the daylight hours and the afternoon of the 18th, while east, northeast of the Azores, *U 214* broke through and fired a full bow salvo of four torpedoes into the convoy formation. Reeder claimed four ships sunk for 20,000 tons, but actually sank two and damaged another. The Dutch 6,318-ton steamer *Balingkar* (1921 – N.V. Nederland Indische Mij. tot Zeevaart, Batavia) was sunk at 1852hrs (Continental time), with the loss of two crewmen, in position 41° 34'N 19° 49'W; she was on passage from Lourenço Marques, Mozambique via Freetown, Sierra Leone for Liverpool with rubber, seed, tea, copper and cotton. A torpedo also fatally damaged the 7,522-ton British SS *Hatarana* (1917 – British India Steam Navigation Co. Ltd), which was voyaging from Calcutta, Karachi and Cape Town, South Africa for Glasgow, via Freetown with an 8,300-ton general cargo. The master, Captain Percival Arthur Clifton James, ninety-seven crewmen and ten gunners were all rescued; the corvette HMS *Penstemon* (Lt Cdr J. Byron) rescued twenty survivors and the 5,682-ton British steamship *Corabella* (1937 – Saguenay Terminals, Ltd, London) picked up eighty-eight. HMS *Penstemon* later sunk the *Hatarana* with gunfire.

The 10,552-ton Armed Merchant Cruiser HMS *Cheshire* was also torpedoed and damaged in position 41° 30'N 19° 49'W at 1852hrs (Continental time). The ship was later repaired and put back into service.

Operations against the ships ceased on the 20th, chiefly due to increased Allied land-based air cover, according to Reeder's report.

After taking aboard surplus fuel and extra supplies from the homebound *U 505*, Oblt.z.S Reeder joined up with the *Iltis* (Pole Cat) group, northeast of the Azores and sailed south. West of Lisbon on the 26th, Reeder sighted the northbound convoy *Sierra Leone 119* midway between the Canaries and the Azores, but escorts drove *U 214* down and away. Both *Iltis* and *Eisbär* wolfpacks then united to attack this convoy and three ships were sunk. Reeder in *U 214* later reported that radar-equipped planes had kept him down for a whole night, which resulted in him falling behind the rest of the pack. Due to heavy air cover, Dönitz ceased the operation on the 29th and on that same day Reeder's boat rescued a survivor from one of the ships. *U 214* then sailed south with two other boats and waited, west of Lisbon, where *U 89*, *U 333* and *U 590* joined them. The reformed pack of *Iltis* then cruised south, around the north side of Cape Verde Islands first and over towards Freetown, but the pack disbanded on 24 September. *U 214* and *U 404* sailed back to France, *U 214* arriving at Brest on 9 October.

(4) After a general overhaul and renewing supplies, etc., *U 214* left Brest on 30 November 1942 for operations to the east of the Caribbean. At 0819hrs (Continental time) on 30 December, Reeder was patrolling 100 miles east of Galera Point, Trinidad, when he torpedoed the 4,426-ton Polish steamship *Paderewski* (1941 – Gydnia-America Shipping Lines, Ltd, Gdynia) and finished it off with gunfire in position 10° 52'N 60° 25'W; the steamer was on passage from Para and Salinas, Brazil for Trinidad and New York with 4,100 tons of general cargo, including rubber, nuts, mahogany and oil in drums; three of her crew were killed. On 3 January 1943, Reeder took the boat into the Caribbean and almost immediately incurred problems with his gyrocompass. He had to arrange a meeting with Jürgen Nissen in *U 105*, who had a number of spare compass parts. Reeder then cruised around Curacao and Aruba, before going back into the Atlantic on the 23rd. After cruising about 500 miles northeast of the Caribbean for about a week, *U 214* sailed east to rendezvous with *U 118* for refuelling, southeast of the Azores. The boat arrived at Brest on 24 February 1943.

(5) On 4 May 1943, *U 214* left Brest for Atlantic operations, but two days out in the Bay of Biscay, she was depth charged by a Whitley bomber of 10 OUT, piloted by Sergeant S.J. Barnett. The plane's machine gun from the front turret also caused mayhem on the U-boat. Oblt.z.S. Reeder was seriously wounded and injuries were inflicted on other crewmen. Leutnant zur See Rupprecht Fischler Graf von Treuberg took temporary command of *U 214* and returned her to Brest on 10 May.

(6) *U 214* left Brest on 18 May 1943 for mine-laying operations off the North African coast near Dakar, with Lt Graf von Treuberg in command. One of the SMA mines laid by *U 214* on 4 June at position 14° 34'N 17° 28'W damaged the 6,507-ton American steamer *Santa Maria I* (1942 – Grace Line Inc., New York) on 20 June 1943 and one of her crew was lost; the ship was carrying a cargo of sisal and a crew of eighty-one, including armed guards, and was on passage from Dakar for New York; the ship was towed into Dakar for temporary repairs that same day.

U 214 returned to Brest on the 26th.

Kplt Rupprecht Stock assumed command of *U 214* on 29 July 1943. Rupprecht Stock was born on 16 February 1916 in Frankfurt/Main and commenced his naval career in 1937. However Stock was seconded to the Luftwaffe between September 1939 and February 1942 and then began U-boat training. On 1 June 1944 he was promoted to Kapitänleutnant.

(7) *U 214* sailed out of Brest on 22 August 1943 for operations in the Caribbean. Stock took the boat via the Azores but, sailing on the surface 90 miles south, southwest of the islands, she was caught-out by an Avenger aircraft from the USS escort-carrier *Croatan*. The pilot, Lt J.W. Steere did not wait for help arriving and attacked *U 214* with depth charges. *U 214* hit back with heavy flak and badly damaged the aircraft, before diving deep. Nine carrier-based planes then arrived and searched unsuccessfully for the U-boat until it got dark. On 14 September, Stock rendezvoused with *U 198*, commanded by Werner Hartmann. Stock transferred an engineer to the homeward-bound U-cruiser and acquired some extra fuel, before going on his way.

Off Colón, Panama *U 214* laid fifteen SMA mines on 10 October. In the very early hours of the 13th, *U 214* was caught on the surface and attacked by a Mariner from the Guantanamo-base, but the plane was driven off with gunfire.

Kplt. R. Stock claimed to have fired a torpedo and sunk the '7,000-ton' American steamer *Cape Douglas*, northeast of the Leeward Islands at 2210hrs (Continental time) on 22 October, but the vessel was not hit.

U 214 returned home via the Azores and Stock was advised to use one of the two XIV U-tankers to refuel. *U 214* was busy filling from *U 488*, but an American 'jeep' carrier interrupted them. Eventually the IXC40 boat *U 193* refuelled her on 7 November, before sailing for Brest, where she arrived on the 30th.

(8) Leaving Brest on 19 February, *U 214* made a patrol off the Atlantic coast of Morocco. SMA mines were laid off Casablanca on 3 April and Allied ships detonated four of them on 3 and 12 April, but very little damage was caused.

On 8 April, *U 214* attacked one of the destroyer escorts protecting the escort-carrier USS *Guadalcanal* with a torpedo, but the missile ran wide. The boat returned back to Brest on 29 April. While in Brest, *U 214* was equipped with *schnorchel* equipment.

(9) *U 214* left port on 11 June to lay fifteen SMA mines off Plymouth in the western Channel, but a *schnorchel* defect forced her to return to Brest on the 14th.

(10) On 16 June, *U 214* sailed again and proceeded into the English Channel for the aborted mine-laying operation. Having laid thirteen SMA mines off Plymouth on the 26th, she returned to Brest on 2 July 1944; no vessels were reported lost or even damaged by those mines.

At the beginning of July, 23-year-old Oblt.z.S. Gerhard Conrad assumed command of the boat and Kplt. Stock took over the command of *U 218*. Gerhard Conrad was born on 18 August 1922 in Berlin/Karlshorst and commenced his naval career in 1939. After U-boat training Conrad was 2nd Watch Officer on *U 260* between March 1942 and November 1943. He was promoted to Oberleutnant zur See on 1 December 1943.

FINAL PATROL

(11) *U 214* left Brest on 22 July and proceeded to Start Point to plant a field of fifteen SMA mines. Just four days later, on 26 July, the British frigate HMS *Cooke*, commanded by Lt Cdr L.C. Hill, attacked the boat with depth charges. Nothing more was ever seen of *U 214* or her crew of forty-eight, and it was assessed at the time that HMS *Cooke* had carried out a successful attack.

Narrative of the attack by HMS *Cooke* A.M. 26 July 1944:

> While proceeding on a line abreast patrol with other ships of the Third Escort Group, AS contact was picked up ahead, bearing about 298°, range 1700 yards. Speed was reduced immediately to 6 knots to classify, and to plot the contact, which was closed, passed to starboard and held astern as we opened up the range. At this stage the plot reported movement not attributable to tide and on the run in echo pitch was reported as low. It was then decided to attack with depth charges, speed 18 knots, setting 'F'. Setting was chosen as it was appreciated that the target was moving slowly away and close to the bottom (38 fathoms) and we wanted the charges to explode both above and below the submarine. The first ten charges pattern was dropped at 0703hrs and, as on the way back to the swirl it was noticed that oil was bubbling up in the explosion area, it was decided to run out and repeat the performance. This second ten charges pattern was dropped at 0719hrs after which it was immediately clear from the wreckage and the vast quantity of oil, that we had severely damaged or sunk the submarine.

HMS *Berry* briefly joined in to assist with a Hedgehog attack, but after the second depth charge pattern the contact becoming weaker, and Berry was forced to break off the attack; therefore it was decided to pick up wreckage.

All the wreckage revealed the German origin of the contact and the signal pads and other books recovered had clearly been immersed for a very short time. This was also true of the plywood wreckage and other trophies of the kill, while the broken mess deck locker indicated that the crew numbered 30 at least. Oil and wreckage continued to rise throughout our search until eventually the area was literally stinking with fresh diesel oil, which gradually spread over an area of 3 square miles. By about 0825hrs it was thought that sufficient evidence had been obtained and it was decided to regain contact if possible to make doubly certain of a kill; acccordingly *Cooke* carried out a Hedgehog attack at 0845hrs, and a further depth charge s attack at 0906hrs a Dan buoy was dropped at 0927hrs to mark the spot while once again the hunt for wreckage was resumed.

The Dan buoy was recovered at 1145hrs after *Berry* had delivered one final depth charge attack. We left to resume patrol at 1215hrs after deciding that any further expenditure of charges was unnecessary.

ASDIC conditions were good and no anti-ASDIC tactics were noticed possibly because the first attack crippled him.

ITEMS RECOVERED

(1) One German text book.
(2) One signal pad (Schlusselzettel). Numbered Forms.
(3) Two serial numbered legs.
(4) One form marked Antwerp Funksperch. Interrogative telegrapg form.
(5) Two bottles of oil samples.
(6) Shaving brush.
(7) Horse hair padding.
(8) Envelope containing a) Pencil b) Top of ointment tin.
(9) Large sheet of crumpled metal with wood attached.
(10) Portion of blue woollen jersey.
(11) Portion of copper strip with electric leads attached.
(12) Black leather glove.
(13) Splintered leather with plywood with leather, key hole, and tally No.30 attached.
(14) Coat hangers, wooden.
(15) Portion of imitation leather wallet.
(16) Cleaning tissues.
(17) Portions of wood.
(18) Portions of cardboard and material.
(19) Portions of seat with green leather and horsehair padding.
(20) Plywood with green covering (oilcloth).

Six officers and men of HMS *Cooke* were given awards. Meanwhile the BdU Diary contains the following entry for 26 August 1944:

The boat put out of Brest on 22.7. for mining operations south of the Lizard, and has not since reported. It received orders to return on 16.8. and should have put in by now. Place of loss presumably west Channel. No information as to possible cause… As five boats in succession have not returned from the Channel it must be presumed that the enemy has considerably intensified his defences. Whether by means of minefields flanking the convoy routes, or by the use of new anti-U-boat measures or only by massing his anti- submarine groups – is not known. For this reason, the boats last reckoned to be in the Channel (*U 92*, *U 989*, *U 275*) received orders to return and proceed to Norway.

ADM 1/29947 NARA T1022, Roll 4066, PG 30351-30353 U–Boot-Ehrenmal Möltenort

The 'happy time' was well and truly over.

THE MEN WHO PERISHED IN U 214

Anter, Egon Leutnant zur See. (born: 12-12-1923)

Aspern, von Heinrich Mtr. (25-3-1923)

Auth., Willibald Ob.Masch.Gfr. (15-7-1922)

Bahr, Karl-Heinz Ob.Mech.Mt. (14-9-1918)

Becker, Friedrich Mtr.O.Gfr. (5-12-1922)

Bersin, Albert Mtr.O.Gfr. (25-4-1922)

Bollermann, Gisbert Mtr.O.Gfr. (19-5-1922)

Brandt, Johannes O.Fk.Mt. (1-10-1918)

Carlssen, Einar Mtr.Gfr. (31-1-1924)

Conrad, Gerhard Oberleutnant zur See (18-8-1922)

Czempiel, Joseph Ob.Bts.Mt. (19-11-1920)

Döhler, Arthur O.Masch.Mt. (18-10-1917)

During, Johannes Masch.Mt. (8-5-1922)

Erstling, Erich Bts.Mt. (23-8-1921)

Fiedler, Horst Mech.O.Gfr. (4-10-1924)

Freund, Hubert Masch.Gfr. (30-4-1923)

Friedel, Heinz Mtr.O.Gfr. (30-12-1920)

Gierl, Johann Mtr.O.Gfr. (2-7-1923)

Gottwald, Dieter-Hans Masch.O.Gfr. (8-5-1924)

Hallenberger, Walter Bts.Mt. (13-12-1919)

Heim, Konrad Fk.Gfr. (6-2-1924)

Heinemann, Heinrich O.Masch.Mt. (30-12-1916)

Hell, Kurt Mtr.O.Gfr. (5-11-1923)

Herzog, Fritz O.Masch. (10-11-1914)

Hildebrand, Karl Masch.Mt. (11-11-1921)

Jarius, Paul Mtr.Gfr. (27-9-1921)

Kraitzek, Johannes Masch.O.Gfr. (3-5-1923)

Niemann, Ulrich Oberleutnant Ingenieur (23-2-1921)

Pietsch, Hans Masch.O.Gfr. (19-10-1923)

Raths, Erich Masch.O.Gfr. 24-4-1923)

Roggatz, Werner Masch.O.Gfr. (29-11-1922)

Römermann, Hans-Wilhelm Mtr. (27-5-1922)

Schallenmüller, Karl Mech.Gfr. (4-6-1924)

Schicha, Erich Masch.O.Gfr. (17-3-1922)

Schlaugat, Helmut Leutnant zur See (22-4-1923)

Schmidt, Günter Bts.Mt. (14-8-1922)

Schmied, Kurt Fk.O.Gfr. (18-3-1925)

Schulz, Reinhold Mtr.O.Gfr. (21-7-1922)

Schwarz, Roland Fk.Gfr. (1-11-1925)

Schwindt, Hans Mtr.O.Gfr. (2-4-1925)

Sehring, Heinz Masch.O.Gfr. (19-2-1925)

Siegert, Friedrich San.O.Mt. (3-10-1919)

Sikora, Karl Mtr.O.Gfr. (5-6-1924)

Straube, Werner Masch.O.Gfr. (29-10-1922)

Vogt, Heinrich Masch.Mt. (4-12-1921)

Völker, Johann Ob.Masch. (28-7-1917)

Winkler, Wilhelm Mech.O.Gfr. (2-1-1924)

Zschaller, Johannes-Heinz Ob.Masch.Mt. (20-6-1918)

WRECK SITE

To date (September 2007), the wreck of *U 214* has not been located.

Above: Prisoners of *U 1209*
onboard HMCS *Ribble*
(see page 326). (Courtesy
Ian Smythe of Edmonton,

Right: U 1209 prisoners
peeling potatoes onboard
HMCS *Ribble* (see page 326).
(Courtesy Ian Smythe of
Edmonton, Canada)

CHAPTER TWO

THE SOUTH WEST

AN INTRODUCTION

This chapter covers the archetypal shipwreck coast. This western end of the Channel provided access to rich hunting grounds of the southwestern approaches, which is the very portal to the Atlantic and beyond; these waters were liberally mined by HMS *Wahine* and *Angora* in the autumn of 1917. Records indicate that a total of 340 mines were sown off Mounts Bay, 300 off the Lizard, and a further 680 off Prawle Point. Clouded by a combination of indifferent record keeping and shattered wrecks of doubtful identity, confusion surrounds the destruction of a number of U-boats believed to have been mined in this sector. The reality is that we can use circumstantial evidence to reinforce the case for a certain U-boat identity, but it is becoming increasingly difficult to prove the point, particularly when the numbered propellers are invariably removed following discovery. Michael Lowrey has pieced together an illuminating analysis regarding the loss of four boats in January 1918, an analysis which runs counter to officially accepted accounts.

This sector witnessed some of the fiercest Q-ship versus U-boat encounters in 1917.

U 85 fought a duel with HMS *Privet*, while the epic story of the fight between the Q-ship HMS *Prize* and *U 93* has passed into legend. Using recent research, Michael Lowrey casts doubt on some of the traditionally accepted aspects of these accounts. While heroic duels between Q-ships and U-boats stirred the public imagination, they equally distracted attention from the ever-increasing shipping losses and in so doing, delayed the only real answer to the U-boat menace, the introduction of the convoy system.

Prior to the adoption of the convoy system in 1917, maritime traffic was relayed along a selected shipping route, known as the 'safe route system' (which was anything but). The most frequented sea lanes converged into a heavily patrolled apex as they approached the British coast. Colliers, steaming independently between Cardiff and Brest were a favourite U-boat prey in this sector. The resultant dilution of anti-submarine patrols (patrolling vessels only being able to patrol the very tip of the apex in sufficient numbers), allowed the U-boats to operate with ease outside these zones. From mid-1917, the 'safe route' system was abandoned. Atlantic convoys now sailed from Falmouth (OF) and Devonport (OD) every few days under escorts provided by the 4th Flotilla at Devonport. As has been noted in Volume 1, the adoption of the convoy system wrenched the initiative from the U-boats and handed it to the Allies.

Denied easy pickings, the boats were now forced to attack unescorted vessels attempting to join, or disperse from convoys. As the designated dispersal zone for Atlantic convoys using the Bristol Channel was just a few miles off Land's End, the U-boats were forced to operate inshore with all the related hazards. The U-boats responded to the convoy system by altering their own tactics. For instance in 1917/18 there was a tendency to attack on the surface and under cover of darkness – a pattern developed to perfection in the Second World War. From time to time there was the chance to bag a real prize. One day the majestic SS *Olympic* sailed into the sights of *U 103*. As the U-boat crew were to discover, not only was there plenty of fight in the liner turned troopship, she also had very sharp bows.

In an effort to bar the U-boats, the Royal Navy laid small minefields around the fierce headlands but in the main the U-boats tended to avoid the area until the summer of 1944. Following their ill-fated attempt to attack the Neptune lines, the U-boats were largely driven out of the English Channel:

> After 28 August 44 …no further boats were sent to the Channel, and instead boats sailing from Biscay were detailed to the west coast of England (Bristol and North Channel) in the expectation that these

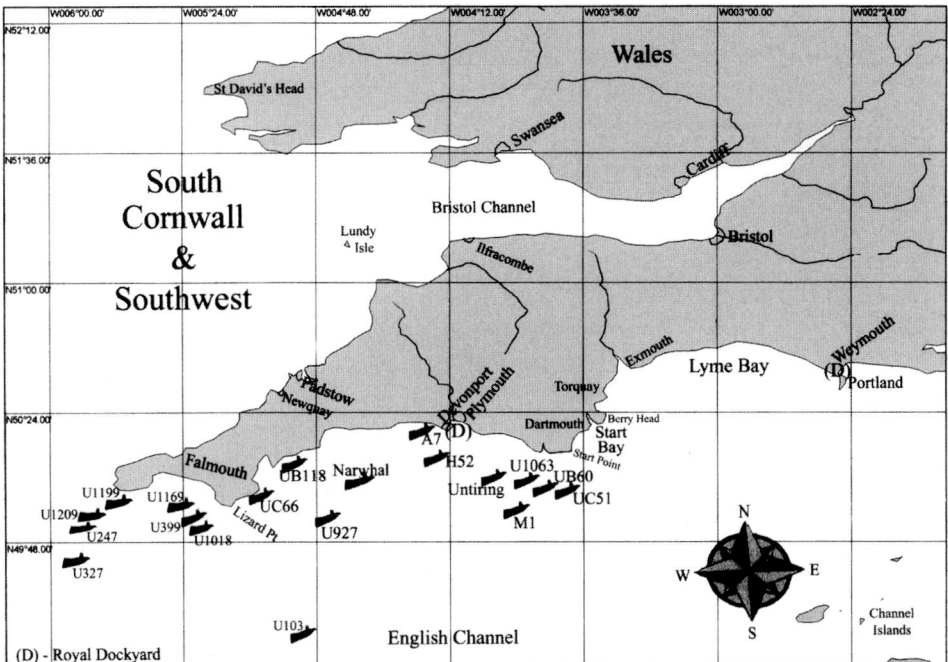

Chart showing submarine wrecks in south Cornwall and Devon and the South West. (Produced by Ron Young)

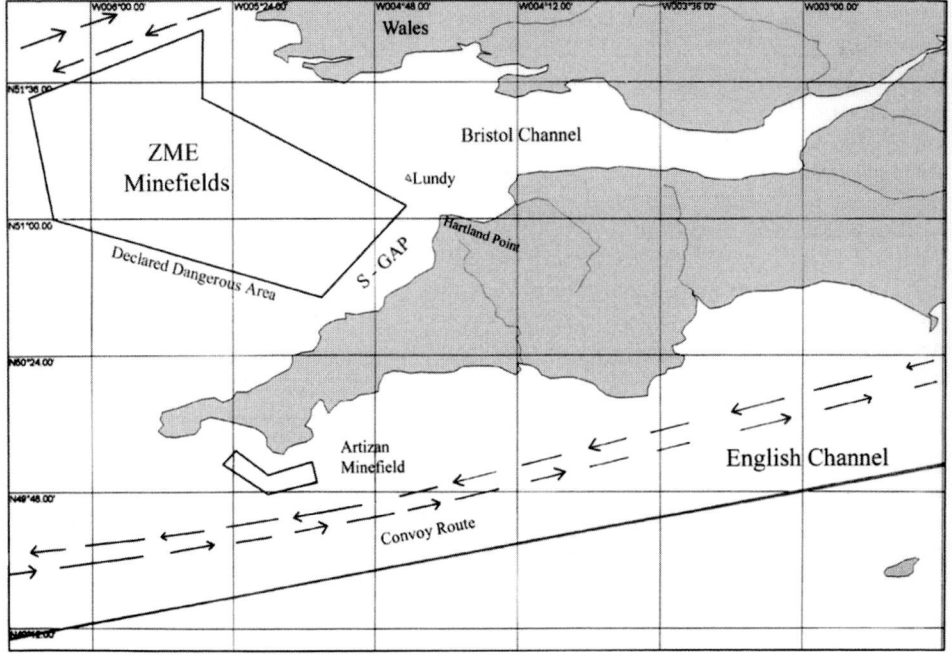

Chart showing convoy routes and minefields in 1944. (Produced by Ron Young)

Officers' quarters in a Kreigsmarine-type VIIC/41 U-boat (*U 995*). (Courtesy Kevin Belcher of Swindon)

areas would be less heavily defended. The traffic situation according to the small amount of available data should be favourable.

BdU Diary October 1944

Dönitz had correctly deduced from a combination of radio decryptions and observations that convoy sailings through the Bristol Channel would be resumed following the Normandy landings. Between 18 November 1944 and the end of the war, twenty-one sorties were made to the south western approaches involving an estimated twenty U-boats. All the Second World War U-boats featured in this chapter were destroyed in this great endgame. Dönitz promoted the view that his U-boat crews were engaged in a holding campaign designed to tie down Allied warships until the war-winning *Elektro* boats became available in large enough numbers. Acutely aware of stuttering production figures from German shipyards reeling under Allied bombs, Dönitz, Godt and Hessler were rewarding the loyalty of their crews by peddling a lie designed to keep them fighting for a doomed cause.

Warships of the 2nd, 3rd, 6th and 9th Escort Groups accounted for most of the U-boats featured in this chapter; *U 1208, U 1199* and *U 247* were detected by ASDIC. The snort mast of *U 1063* was located by radar. *U 327* was sighted at periscope depth by an aircraft (which guided surface forces to the scene); *U 927* was similarly spotted by a radar-equipped aircraft. The majority of these U-boats were destroyed following attacks on convoys or while manoeuvring to make an attack. Deadly new minefields merely added to the plight of the U-boat crews. An air of unreality pervades the BdU Diary in this late stage of the war. The multitude of KTB reports, warning of '*ominipresent circular saw noise* [Foxer]' and increased anti-submarine patrols in coastal waters, are simply ignored. BdU increasingly saw only what BdU wanted to see. Evidence as to just how divorced from reality the German staff had become can be found in Appendix 3 of the BdU Diary dated 1 January 1945:

> …As, however, in all coastal areas, these strong defences were not nearly as powerful as they seemed when it came to the point, as submarines are particularly difficult to detect by hydrophone gear and asdic, owing to currents and density layers. Only rarely did depth charge hunts 'on the old scale' take place in coastal areas, during which three or more destroyers would hunt a submarine for hours at a stretch. Mines

HMS *Onyx* and 'A' boats at Devonport. (Author's collection)

> are only considered to be dangerous on the outward routes and are not taken much into consideration in the attacking areas or in the areas through which enemy traffic proceeds on a large scale.

In the final analysis, the unprecedented concentration of the Second World War U-boat wrecks in the deep waters off Land's End demonstrates the near impossible odds confronting the Kriegsmarine in the closing stages of the war. An estimated 33 per cent of U-boat casualties during this phase were lost on their first patrols, most without inflicting any material damage on the Allies. To paraphrase Nicholas Monsarrat, for all the good they did, the U-boats might as well have stayed in port and saved many good ships and fine men. By colluding in the madness of Hitler, Dönitz and his staff had simultaneously prolonged the war and thrown away the lives of their men with profligate abandon. BdU had drawn deep from the well of human courage – but so often had its waters been poured wastefully away.

Finally, as any West Country sailor will confirm, this coast is savage enough without modern warfare adding to its terrors. The survivors of *U 681* and *U 1209* discovered the natural perils of this coast for themselves when both U-boats ran aground in the Scillies, thus adding a new chapter to the long litany of shipwrecks in this region.

History relates that a Mr John Day may have become the first British submarine casualty when his experimental submarine the *Maria* failed to surface following a dive off Drake's Island, Plymouth Sound in 1774. What is certain is that submarine pioneers paid a high price for their efforts. As the Haslar Obelisk testifies, the crews of British 'A' Class boats paid more than most. In 1904 'Section VI' consisting of seven 'A' Class boats was based at Devonport around HMS *Onyx*, its function being to take over harbour defence from the Royal Engineers. In June 1905 *A8* was rocked by an explosion on exercise, which killed most of her crew. In January 1914, *A7* was lost following a collision with her tender HMS *Pygmy* again while on exercise off Plymouth.

Devonport has been a Royal Dockyard since 1693 and, as we have seen, its association with submarines dates from before the First World War. By December 1914 the Devonport unit had been renamed the 1st Submarine Flotilla with a strength of four 'B' and five 'C' Class submarines. On Churchill's orders, Devonport became a centre for submarine building. Dock No. 5 at Keyham, became known as the 'Submarine Dock'. Among the submarines featuring in these volumes, *J6, K6* and *K7* were all built at Devonport. K6 exhibited the wayward tendencies of her class from the very start, when she made a trial dive in the North Dock and failed to surface for 2 hours. Tragedy was averted thanks to the skills of the civilian dockyard staff. Tragedy struck in No. 2 Basin on 9 August

1926, when *H29* (Lt Fred Skyrme) sank while surface trimming during the closing stages of a refit. The boat had been returning to her moorings when the aft hatch was forced under, owing to the precipitate flooding of No. 3 ballast tank. *H29* heeled over, taking CERA Dalton and five civilian workers with her to the bottom. When the boat was brought to the surface four days later, the bodies of the six unfortunate men were found huddled under the fore hatch.

M1 sailed from Devonport on her last, fateful exercise in 1925. Lost with all hands she was forgotten for decades until the recent discovery of her wreck (in itself an epic of undersea research) awoke interest in her story. Using the evidence of the wreck combined with the expertise of marine accident investigators, the authors reconstruct the last journey of HMS *M1*. One irony is that the gun, which made her such a deterrent, appears to have played a significant role in her loss.

An equally sad and confused incident took place on 3 July 1940 when a group of British sailors attempted to take over the monster French submarine *Surcouf* in Devonport. One of the German terms of armistice following the fall of France was that all French warships were to be handed over to occupying forces. The British had other ideas. L/S Webb and Cdr Sprague were shot dead in the *melee*. The incensed French sailors killed the British liaison officer Lt Pat Griffiths of *Rorqual*. The casualties of this little-known episode were buried in the nearby Weston Mill Cemetery. *Surcouf* was handed over to what was thought to be a more reliable Free French crew, but the rest of her career was marred by mystery and controversy.

In the post-war years the 2nd Submarine Flotilla was based at Devonport until its disbandment in 1966. Covering 650ha 'Guz' remains one of the largest naval bases in Europe. Much of the former Royal Dockyard has been leased out to the private sector, but Devonport now houses the Submarine Refit Centre. At the time of writing there are seven SSN Trafalgar Class nuclear submarines based here under the *aegis* of COMDEV. The south west coast of England remains a major submarine exercise zone, making it one of the few places where operational submarines, including visiting NATO boats, may be glimpsed.

Happily, not all of the British submarines in this section are graves; *H52* was sunk to make a movie, while *Untiring* and the cold war boat *Narwhal* were sunk as ASDIC targets. All are said to make exhilarating dives.

UC 51, SM IMPERIAL U-BOAT

DATE OF LOSS: 17 November 1917
DEPTH: 66m
REFERENCE: 50 08'.386 N 03 41'.571 W
LOCATION: 3.89 nautical miles SSE of Prawle Point

Type: UCII coastal mine-laying boat　*Builders*: Germaniawerft, Kiel for Kaiserliche Deutsche Marine　*Ordered*: on 12 January 1916, within the batch of *UC 49–UC 54*　*Keel laid*: as Yard No.267　*Launched*: on 5 December 1916　*Commissioned*: by Kapitänleutnant Wilhelm Schröder on 6 January 1917　*Combat ready*: on 8 April 1917

TECHNICAL SPECIFICATIONS

Hull: double　*Surface displacement*: 434 tons　*U/Dt*: 511 tons　*LBDH*: 52.69m × 5.22m × 3.68m × 7.46m　*Machinery*: 2 × 250ps Daimler diesels.　*Props*: 2 bronze　*S/Sp*: 11.8 knots　*Op/R*: 8,820 nautical miles at 7 knots　*Sub/R*: 54 nautical miles at 4 knots　*U/Power*: 2 × 230ps electric motors gave 7.2 knots　*Batteries*: lead/acid/accumulators　*Fuel/Cap*: 41 + 15 tons　*Armament*: 2 external 50.04cm torpedo tubes at the bow, one either side of the mine chutes and 1 stern internal tube　*Torpedoes*: 7 × 50.04cm (19.7in) maximum　*Guns*: 1 × 88mm (3.46in) forward deck gun　*Ammo*: 133 rounds of 88mm　*Mine tubes*: 6　*Mines*: 18 × UC200　*Diving*: max-op-depth 50m (164ft) and 33 sec to crash-dive　*Complement*: 3 officers and 23 ratings

Torpedo load as designed: (4) a torpedo in each tube plus a reload for the stern tube. One further option was to dismantle an additional stern torpedo and keep it stored within until required. Two extra external bow tube torpedoes could be lashed to the deck.

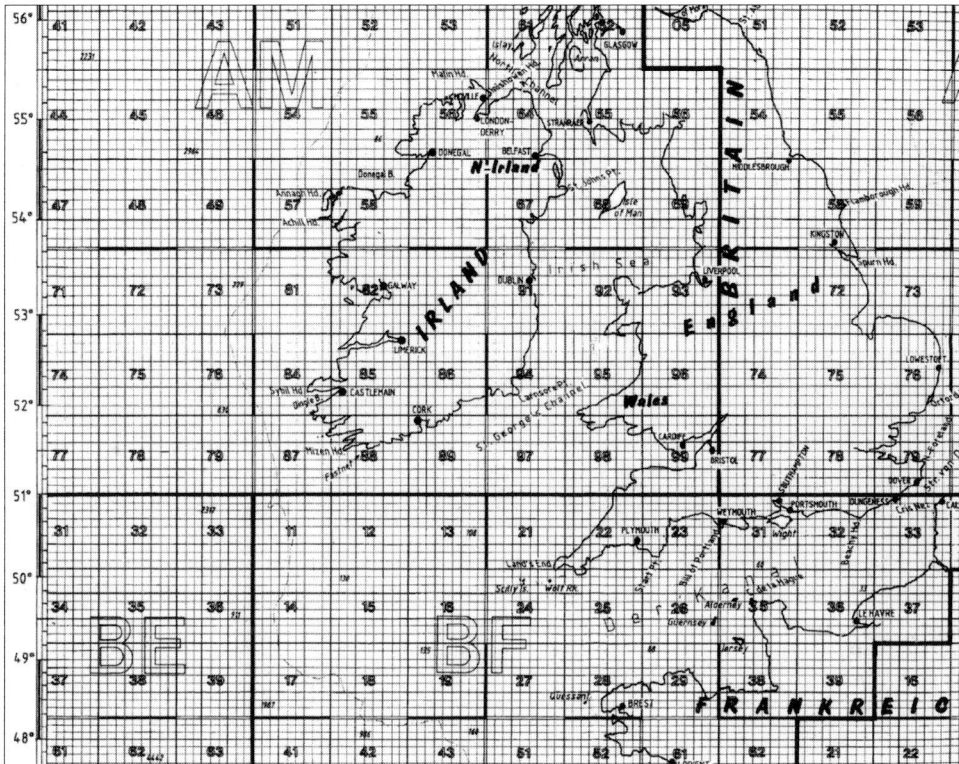

Kriegsmarine Grid Quadrant of UK and Ireland.

The boat was originally assigned to the German-based I.U-Bootflottille at Brunsbüttel from 8 April 1917 until 20 August 1917 when she transferred and arrived at U-Flottille Flandern at Zeebrugge, with Kplt. Schröder the CO from 6 January 1917 to 28 April 1917.

Schröder made one patrol in the boat.

UC 51 left port on 14 April 1917. Schröder proceeded to capture and sink two Scandinavian sailing vessels in the North Sea with gunfire on the 16th: the 509-ton wooden-hulled Norwegian barque *Polykarp* (1880 – A/S Polykarp, Porsgrund) was north of the Dogger Bank and voyaging from West Hartlepool to Kristiania with coal. The Swedish *Amanda* (1872 – Anders Bernhard Tolle, Göteborg), a wooden-hulled schooner of 232 tons commanded by Captain J. A. Gustavsson, was transporting pit props to West Hartlepool from Frederikshald, Norway.

On 17 April, Schröder captured and shelled the 1,164-ton Swedish steamer *Atalanta* (1883 – Förnyade Ångfartygs A/B Viking, Göteborg) at about 56° 30'N 04° 10'E; she was voyaging from Göteborg to Hull with iron and general cargo, but the sea was rough and Schröder did not hang around to see it sink. However, Kplt. Crüsemann in *U 86* found the vessel still afloat the following day and sank her at position 56° 33'N 04° 18'E. *U 86* picked up one man from the sea, Sven Magnus Ahl, however she was carrying a crew of seventeen and from those, sixteen men died.

THE SIXTEEN MEN WHO DIED

Andreasson, Manne Albin, born 5/12-1881
Bengtsson, Albert, born 13/3-1883
Hansson, Ivar Heribert, born 25/8-1883
Karlsson, Johan Efraim, born 1892
Kristoffersson, Axel Bernhard, born 1891
Larsson, Gustaf Sigfrid, born 20/12-1889
Möberg, Leonard Vallentin, born 1890

Nordmark, Carl Hjalmar, born 3/1-1886
Nordström, Axel Fritiof, born 17/6-1891
Norrman, Carl Albert (Captain), born 24/11-1876
Olsson, August Valdemar, born 1882
Olsson, Sven August, born 1859
Rönn, Knut Wilhelm, born 5/7-1898
Svartling, Fritz Leonard, born 23/6-1877
Svensson, Axel Hjalmar, born 19/12-1887
Svensson, Carl Albanus, born 9/5-1892

UC 51 returned to port on the 18th.

Oblt.z.S. Hans Galster, who was born on 4 March 1890, assumed command of the boat on 29 April 1917 and made six patrols.

(2) On 2 May 1917, *UC 51* departed Germany for operations off the Scottish east coast and Isles of Shetland. The *Marie* (1910 – A/S D/S Selsk., Vesterhavet, Esbjerg), a 772-ton Danish steamer, was transporting 250 tons of wood pulp and 279 standards of timber from Fredriksstad to Hull when she was torpedoed and sunk in the North Sea at 58° 30'N 1° 4'W, on 4 May 1917.

Whilst voyaging from Newcastle-upon-Tyne to Gibraltar with coal, the 1,394-ton Norwegian steamer *Segovia* (1903 – D/S A/S Otto Thoresen's Linie, Kristiania) was captured off the Auskerry Islands on 5 May; she was then shelled and sunk. On 6 May, mines were laid in the Moray Firth, before *UC 51* moved to Lerwick to lay mines and Tarbet Ness in the morning, followed by the Moray Firth, where the last mines were placed.

UC 51 returned to Heligoland on 15 May.

(3) After leaving port on 10 June 1917, *UC 51* made a war cruise along the Irish south coast and laid mines during the evening of 16 June; two mine barriers of six mines each were laid to the south and southeast of Galley Head. On 18 June, Galster captured and sunk two British sailing vessels with gunfire: the 158-ton *Violet* (1874) was sunk 10 miles from Coningbeg light vessel, while delivering pitwood from Waterford, Ireland to Cardiff. The 76-ton *Kangaroo* was destroyed 20 miles off Tuskar Rock, while hauling coal from Cardiff to Ballyhack in Ireland and four men, including the master, were lost (all hands).

THE MEN WHO DIED

Adams, John, Mate
Carr, Luke, Able Seaman
Mansfield, James, Master
Ryan, John, Able Seaman

The 3,762-ton defensively armed *Miami* (1904 – Elders & Fyffes Ltd, Glasgow) was torpedoed and sunk without warning on 22 June, 11 miles off Fastnet Rock, while en-route from New York to Manchester with general cargo.

The 1,505-ton *Hilversum* (1883 – Stoom Maats. Oostzee, Amsterdam), a Dutch steamer, was torpedoed and sunk about 5 to 6 miles off Lundy Island on 22 June; she was travelling from Rouen to Barry in ballast and six crewmen were lost (names unknown).

UC 51 returned to port on 30 June.

One month later, on 26 July, the *Ludgate* (1906 – Carrington S.S. Co. Ltd, London (Cardiff)) detonated at least one of the contact mines laid on 16 June. The 3,708-ton steamer was carrying a crew of thirty and a cargo of 5,600 tons of copper material, including bar and sheet copper and cast-iron pigs/ingots from Huelva, Spain to Garston, Liverpool. The explosion took place on the starboard side of the engine room at 0430hrs and then a few seconds later another explosion occurred on the port side level with the No.3 hold; the ship went down off Galley Head in just 2 minutes. About twelve people were left clinging to floating wreckage, but strong winds and tides pushed them all apart; by the time a patrol vessel arrived, only five survivors were found and those men were landed at Berehaven, Ireland. In total, twenty-four crewmen were lost.

The 1,505-ton SS *Hilversum*. (Author's collection)

SOME OF THE MEN WHO DIED

Cameron, Frederick Whitelaw, 19yrs, Wireless Operator
Carr, Gladstone, Able Seaman RNVR (DAMS gunner)
Evans, David John, 25yrs, 4th Engineer Officer
Foley, Daniel, 36yrs, Steward
Fullarton, Lewis William, 3rd Engineer
Hansen, A., 33yrs, Able Seaman
Helsen, G., 45yrs, Fireman
Kitamuree, S., 28yrs, Sailor
McDonald, C., 41yrs. Sailor
Merrix, J.H., Master
Mikelson, C., 27yrs, Sailor
Nettleton, Benjamin, 29yrs, Fireman
Nilsson, W., 38yrs, Donkeyman
Palsson, Karl Messen, 27yrs, Fireman and Trimmer
Rothwell, William Henry, 33yrs, Able Seaman
Sheel, William, 32yrs, 2nd Engineer
Stephenson, Arthur Ernest, 36yrs, 1st Mate
Stringer, George Harry, 26yrs, Fireman
Suton, H., 31yrs, Carpenter
Thompson, Harold Edwin, 16yrs, Ordinary Seaman
Vitue, Oliver, 31yrs, 1st Engineer
Wallington, George Henry, 47yrs, Boatswain (Bosun)
White, John Henry, 26yrs, Fireman
York, Thomas, 51yrs, Ship's Cook

(4) *UC 51* sailed from Heligoland on 4 August 1917 for a mining patrol in the Bristol Channel. The British had liberally sown mines, forcing *UC 51* to thread her way through the West Hinder Bank (where numerous mines were visible on the surface). On 11 August *UC 51* began laying mines near the Helwick lightship, on the north coast of the Bristol Channel, prior to fouling the fairways, east of Bull Point.

On the 11th and 12 miles off Caldy Island, the 23-ton British fishing cutter *Gloriosa* was going about her normal business when Galster captured and sank her with explosives; during that night however, *UC 51* had a short inconclusive gunfire duel with the armed 356-ton French schooner,

Antoine de Padoue (1895). Later that day, the 111-ton British trawler *Eleazar* (1895) was captured 25 miles off St Ann's Head and sunk with gunfire. On 14 August, two steamers were sunk: the French *N. Verberckmoes* (1890 – Cie. des Bateaux à Vapeur du Nord, Dunkerque) of 1,353 tons was torpedoed off Lundy Island while on passage from Swansea for Dunkerque with coal. That was followed by the defensively armed 1,282-ton *Wisbech* (1901 – Wisbech S.S. Co. Ltd, Newcastle), which was torpedoed without warning off Trevose Head while carrying patent fuel and tyres and manufactured steel items from Cardiff to St Malo; the torpedo detonated in the engine room at 1635hrs, killing Mark Warren Stephens, a fireman and donkeyman. The surviving crew of nineteen took to the boats and a patrol vessel rescued them. The track of the torpedo was observed, but the submarine, which was submerged, was not seen until the ship had been actually abandoned.

UC 51 then proceeded to Zeebrugge, where she arrived on 20 August and formally transferred to the Flandern U-Flottille.

(5) *UC 51* left Flanders on 7 September 1917 and returned to its former hunting ground off the south coast of Ireland and Bristol Channel. Galster sank two vessels on the 8th: the 163-ton sailing vessel *Ezel* (1873) was captured and sunk with gunfire 20 miles from St Valéry-en-Caux; she was en-route from Teignmouth to Tréport with china clay. Soon after and 25 miles off Fécamp, the 104-ton sailing vessel *Laura* was captured and scuttled with explosives while transporting china clay from Par to Rouen.

Galster sank five sailing vessels on 10 September: the 91-ton *Mary Orr* (1868), en-route from Runcorn to Dieppe with coal, was captured 8 miles off Pendeen Lighthouse and sunk with explosives. The 161-ton *Moss Rose* (built 1888) was captured off Pendeen Lighthouse and sunk by gunfire; she was on passage from Ellesmere Port for Cherbourg with coal. *Mary Seymour* (1865) of 150 tons was also captured close by and sunk by gunfire while travelling on the same voyage. The 197-ton *Jane Williamson* (1870), which was hauling coal from Liverpool to Cherboug, was captured 20 miles off St Ives and sunk with gunfire and sadly the crew of four, including the skipper, were killed.

THE MEN WHO DIED

Cassidy, J., Ordinary Seaman
Deacon, J., Ordinary Seaman
Kearon, Robert Valentine, Master
Keegan, James, Able Seaman

The 111-ton *Water Lily* met the same fate; she was also on the same journey and was captured close by, however the crew survived.

On 11 September another three vessels were sunk: the defensively armed 1,417-ton steamer *Luxembourg* (1910 – Leith, Hull & Hamburg Steam Packet Co. Leith) sank, while transporting 700 tons of Government stores from Le Havre to Newport, Monmouth; the vessel had detonated a mine laid by *UC 51* the previous day. At 0650hrs the lookouts observed a floating mine, which they exploded with rifle fire, but minutes later, the ship was forced to manoeuvre quickly to avoid a second mine, then immediately afterwards a huge explosion occurred, forward and under the ship. The crew safely abandoned ship in the boats and were rescued by the 954-ton French steamer *Celte* (Chevillotte Frères, Brest) and landed at Barry.

The 60-ton sailing vessel *William* was voyaging from Cardiff to Saint Brieue with coal when it was captured off Crackington Haven, Cornwall and sunk with explosive scuttling charges.

Explosive charges were used to sink the *Rosy Cross*, a 25-ton British fishing cutter, which was captured in the same area.

On 14 September, the *Zeta* (1888 – Turner, Brightman Co., London), a defensively armed steamer of 2,343 tons, commanded by Captain G.H. Gregory, sank from a torpedo hit off Mine Head and no warning was given; she was transporting coal, coke and cast-iron ingots from Barry to Zarate, Argentina.

A torpedo destroyed the 2,459-ton French steamer *Saint Jacques* (1909 – Société Navele de l'Ouest, Le Havre) on the 15th off St Ann's Point in the Bristol Channel; it was transporting coal from Barry to Bizerta, Tunisia.

UC 51 returned to the Flanders port on 19 September.

(6) Leaving from Zeebrugge on 10 October 1917, *UC 51* returned to the Irish south coast and Bristol Channel areas, where, on the 14th, mines were laid off St Govan's lightship and Milford Haven. Galster returned to Flanders with *UC 51* on 26 October, without realising just how destructive his sortie would be. Three steamers and one drifter were lost to *UC 51*'s mines.

The first sinking occurred on 9 October when the defensively armed *Poldown* (1904 – The Shipping Controller, London) of 1,370 tons, which was armed for defence, detonated a mine at 1350hrs off Trevose Head, the mine having been laid on 10 September. The ship, commanded by Captain J.K. Watson, was on passage from Penarth for Boulogne with 1,700 tons of coal. The mine exploded under the forefoot, blowing the bows completely off and leaving no time to lower the boats. Just as the ship sank, some of the men cut through the falls of the starboard boat. The suction of the ship going down dragged the second officer under water, but he managed to reach the surface again and climbed on to the boat, which by then had turned upside down; four others then scrambled onto it. Another man had climbed onto a hatch cover and floated past those in the boat, however at 1530hrs a fishing boat recued all six men and took them to Padstow. Unfortunately the *Poldown*, ex-German *Pellworm* (Hamburg-Manchester Dampfer Linie, Hamburg), sank with the loss of the master and seventeen men, including two DAMS gunners.

THE MEN WHO DIED

Fenech, Antonio, 53yrs, Donkeyman
Fromut, Karl, 39yrs, Boatswain (Bosun)
George, Walter John, 38yrs, Mate
Griffith, Walter, 42yrs, Fireman
Harman, J., 21yrs, Fireman
Lynch, Julian Oscar, E. 23yrs, Fireman
McDonald, Charles James Lionel, 24yrs, Fireman
Morgan, Charles Bernard Francis, 18yrs, Wireless Operator
Murphy, Richard, 23yrs, 3rd Engineer
Ryan, Edward, 23yrs, Sailor
Smith, Thomas, 17yrs, Mess Room Steward
Spank, John, 18yrs, Sailor
Thompson, Thomas Rowland, 60yrs, 2nd Engineer
Watson, J.K., Master
Williams, T., Fireman
Yak, Nicholas, 39yrs, Sailor
Abbott, Joseph Johnson, Able Seaman RNVR (DAMS)
Wilson, Arthur Naylor, Ldg Seaman RNVR (DAMS)

The 81-ton net drifter *Active III* was hired by the Admiralty in 1915 and converted to Armed Patrol Vessel No.2486, but she sank off Milford Haven on 15 October after detonating a mine laid by *UC 51*. All hands were lost including one officer and nine ratings.

THEN MEN WHO DIED

Bruce, Thomas Arthur, Trimmer RNR
MacLeod, William, Deckhand RNR
Mathias, Frederick James, 2nd Hand RNR
Picton, William Richard, Deckhand RNR
Slater, John, Engineman RNR
Smith, Alexander, Temporary Skipper RNR
Smith, James, Deckhand RNR
Tibble, Joseph Thomas Ward, Seaman RNR
Turpin, Alfred Charles, Deckhand RNR

On 20 October, the armed 8,268-ton steamer *Ionian* (1901 – Allan Line Steamships Co. Ltd, Glasgow) detonated a mine that had been laid on 14 October. The vessel had been under the command of Captain I. Williams and travelling between Liverpool and Plymouth in ballast; the following seven men were drowned.

THE MEN WHO DIED

Brown, J., Waiter
Doyle, D., Trimmer
Keenan, Charles, 50yrs, Fireman
Maguire, J., Assistant Cook
Monjou, P., Steward
Shallow, J., 36yrs, Seaman
Simmons, Francis Daniel, 17yrs, Waiter

The 2,601-ton Italian steamship *Madalena* (1891 – Gaetano Maggiolo fu A., Genoa), disappeared with all hands after passing St Ann's Head on 25 August, most probably after detonating a mine laid by *UC 51*; she was sailing from the Clyde and Milford Haven to Bagnoli, Italy.

Galster returned to Flanders with *UC 51* on 26 October.

FINAL PATROL

(7) Oblt.z.S. Galster left port on 15 November 1917; once again *UC 51* set course for a mining operation off the Irish coast and Bristol Channel areas. Two days later the Admiralty trawler *Lois* (No.961) was suddenly rocked by a massive underwater explosion south of Start Point. *Lois* was engaged on an anti-submarine patrol around the British minefield detailed below. (*Lois* was a 310-ton Fleetwood (*FD113*) hired trawler built in 1910 and requisitioned in January 1915. She was normally employed as an auxiliary minesweeper and was armed with a single 12-pounder, Quick Firing gun.) Startled by the sudden deluge of water, the crew of *Lois* were transfixed by the sudden appearance of a U-boat breaking surface. The U-boat half submerged again, then rolled over and sank. Almost immediately, a mine bobbed to the surface close to where the U-boat had disappeared. The trawler's crew detonated the mine with gunfire. All around, streams of oil, bits of wreckage, wood, various pieces of debris and even human remains were rising to the surface. Amongst the flotsam was a submariner's sea-boot, which apparently belonged to Heizer Ewald Metzger of *UC 51*; all hands, including Oblt.z.S. Hans Galster had perished. Between 5 and 11 November the British had set a U-boat trap placing 680 deep-laid mines in the Start Point sector.

The co-ordinates for the minefield laid on 5 November 1917:
Line A from 50° 10.00N 03° 40.30W to 50° 10.24N 03° 37.18W
Line B from 50° 09.50N 03° 39.48W to 50° 10.10N 03° 37.05W
Line C from 50° 09.20N 03° 38.50W to 50° 09.20N 03° 36.38W
Line D from 50° 09.05N 03° 39.40W to 50° 09.05N 03° 36.40W

This Admiralty minefield was laid on 11 November 1917:
Line E from 50° 09.35N 03° 43.00W to 50° 08.30N 03° 40.25W
Line F from 50° 09.15N 03° 43.00W to 50° 08.20N 03° 40.38W
Line G from 50° 0.54N 03° 47.10W to 50° 09.27N 03° 44.10W
Line H from 50° 08.38N 03° 46.45W to 50° 09.12N 03° 44.05W

Line A, D, E and G were laid by the *ANGORA*, lines B, C, F, and H by the *Wahine*. *UC 51* was listed as sunk on 17 November 1917 by a mine at 50° 08'N 03° 42'W, which would correspond to line E or F. Of course given the history of the class it is possible that *UC 51* may have been destroyed by one of her own mines.

NARA T-1022 ,Roll 73, PG61965 ADM 137/2962 U-Boot-Ehrenmal Möltenort

THE MEN WHO PERISHED IN SM UC 51

Aurich, Clet. U-Maschinistenmaat
Baden, Wilhelm U-Matrose
Beuter, Paul U-Bootsmannsmaat
Brandt, Fritz U-Matrose
Burmeister, H. U-Matrose
Dittmann, E. U-Oberheizer
Frank, Georg U-F.T.Obergast
Galster, Hans Oberleutnant zur See
Gumprecht, M. U-Heizer
Hammje, G. U-Oberbootsmannsmaat der Reserve
Hansen, A. U-Maschinistenmaat
Harrich, Kurt U-Obermatrose
Heegewaldt, A. Leutnant zur See der Reserve
Jendryssek, J. U-Heizer
Kemena, F. U-Maschinistenmaat
Kultermann, H. U-Maschinistenmaat
Mennicken, K. U-F.T.Gast
Merkt, Johann U-Maschinist Anw
Metzger, Ewald U-Heizer
Ranke, K. U-Maschinistenmaat
Renkel, Otto U-Oberbootsmannsmaat
Riffelmacher, E. U-Matrose
Rüger, Bruno U-Matrose
Salzmann, Fr. U-Obermaschinistenmaat
Schumacher, P. U-Bootsmannsmaat
Sieffert, Edgar Marine Ingenieur Asp
Sprenger, Ernst U-Heizer
Tielke, Adolf U-Heizer
Weber, Freidrich U-Maschinistenmaat

WRECK SITE

The wreck, possibly that of *UC 51*, is orientated in a northeast to southwest (045/225°) direction. It lies on a firm seabed of shingle, sand and stone, in a general depth of 66m (217ft), being the lowest astronomical depth. The wreck is reported as being upright and almost intact, except for a 12m long section blown off the stern. A pronounced debris field lies·at the stern. The mine-chutes appear to be still full and the net-cutter is firmly bolted to the bows, wreathed in a large billowing trawl net which floats up, over the wreck. The casing is showing signs of deterioration but colourful anemones have become established. Tidal streams are very severe all around this area.

UB 60, SM IMPERIAL U-BOAT

DATE OF LOSS: 12 June 1919
DEPTH: 60m
REFERENCE: 50 08'.011 N 03 47'.734 E
LOCATION: 4.96 nautical miles SSW of Prawle Point

Type: UBIII coastal torpedo attack boat   **Builders**: AG Vulcan, Hamburg for the Kaiserliche Deutsche Marine   **Ordered**: on 20 May 1916, within the batch of UB 60–UB 65   **Keel laid**: as Yard No.85   **Launched**: on 14 April 1917   **Commissioned**: by Oberleutnant zur See Peter Ernest Eiffe on 6 June 1919

TECHNICAL SPECIFICATIONS

Hull: double   ***Surface displacement***: 508 tons   ***U/Dt***: 639 tons   ***LBDH***: 55.52m × 5.75m × 3.68m × 8.25m   ***Machinery***: 2 × 550ps MAN diesels.   ***Props***: 2 bronze   ***S/Sp***: 13.3 knots   ***Op/R***: 8,420 nautical miles at 6 knots   ***Sub/R***: 55 nautical miles at 4 knots   ***U/Power***: 2 × 394ps electric motors gave 8 knots   ***Batteries***: lead/acid/accumulators by Accumulatoren-Fabrik-Aktiengesellschaft   ***Fuel/Cap***: 32 + 36 tons   ***Armament***: 4 bow and 1 stern 50.04cm torpedo tubes   ***Torpedoes***: 10 × 50.04cm (19.7in)   ***Guns***: 1 × 105mm (4.13in) forward deck gun   ***Ammo***: 160 rounds of 105mm   ***Mines***: none   ***Diving***: max-op-depth 50m (164ft) and 30 sec to crash-dive   ***Complement***: 3 officers and 31 ratings

On completion, *UB 60* was kept exclusively as a training boat and Peter Ernest Eiffe served with her from the commissioning until 1 July 1917.

FINAL PATROL

On 26 November 1818, *UB 60* was surrendered to the Allies and ran aground on the English east coast. The boat was recovered and taken to Harwich where she was put up for sale, however on 12 June 1919, while being transferred to a breakers yard, she sank off Start Point, for reasons unknown.

NARA T-1022, Rolls 68, 69, PG 61819

WRECK SITE

There is an unknown U-boat wreck at the position offered above, which could very possibly be that of *UB 60*, but to date, August 2007, the wreck has not been positively identified.

U 1063, KRIEGSMARINE U-BOAT

DATE OF LOSS: 16 April 1945
DEPTH: 56m
REFERENCE: 50 08'.943 N, 03 53'.462W
LOCATION: 5.44 nautical miles SW of Bolt Head

Type: VIIC/41 ocean-going boat   ***Builders***: F. Krupp Germaniawerft AG, Kiel-Gaarden for Kriegsmarine   ***Ordered***: on 14 October 1941, within the batch of *U 1063–U 1065*   ***Keel laid***: as Yard No. 700 on 7 September 1943   ***Launched***: on 8 June 1944   ***Commissioned***: by Kapitänleutnant Karl-Heinz Stephan on 8 July 1944   ***Feldpost No***: M 40 438   ***Badge***: Galleon in a shield

TECHNICAL SPECIFICATIONS

See page 342.

Karl-Heinz Stephan was born in Posen on 18 September 1915 and commenced his naval career in 1936. He began his service as Garrison Officer Naval Flak Detachment 262, between September 1939 and July 1940 and was promoted to Kapitänleutnant (R) on 1 April 1943.

After the commissioning, *U 1063* spent about four days carrying out acceptance trials in Kiel, prior to proceeded to Danzig, for ten to fourteen days further acceptance trials. After this she did silent running trials for about four days in Rönnc and from there docked in Konigsberg for about eight days to repair one of the diving tanks, which had been slightly damaged in an air raid on Kiel. Eight days were then spent in Pillau, doing preliminary training, followed by ten days *Agrufront* at Hel.

U 1063 was then detailed about 7 September 1944 to go to Aarhus, in Denmark, for depth charge trials. This novel exercise required the U-boat to lie submerged, while depth charges were exploded from floats at pre-determined depths and distances and the effects of the explosions assessed.

Subsequent prisoner interrogations provided valuable information regarding the robust construction of the Type VII C. One prisoner stated that nineteen to twenty depth charges were detonated in this way, none nearer than 33 yards from the U-boat, which was never submerged below periscope depth. The trials were apparently supervised by civilians, and lasted about three weeks. The explosions caused heavy shaking and slight leakages through glands in the pressure hull to GSR and D/F aerials; air bottles and battery coils were shattered, and the main motors thrown out of alignment. One further indignity awaited *U 1063*. While on passage from Aarhus, the boat grounded and damaged her diesels. She was towed away then sailed to Lübeck for repairs at the Flenderwerke.

From Lübeck the boat returned to Hel to complete her interrupted *Agrufront* trials and subsequently carried out pro-tactical exercises and torpedo firing at Pillau and tactical exercises at Gdynia. *U 1063* returned to Germania yard at Kiel, early January 1945, remaining there until February for final adjustments, fitting out and anti-aircraft practice.

Kplt. Karl-Heinz Stephan was the CO from 8 July, 1944 until 28 February 1945. Stephen took the boat on two patrols, the transfer and one war patrol. From 8 July 1944 to 28 February 1945 *U 1063* was assigned to 5.U-Flottille at Kiel as *Ausbildungsboot*.

U 1063 and Kplt. Stephan were then formally assigned to 11.U-Flottille at Bergen, southwest Norway on 1 March 1945, for frontline service.

U 1063 left Kiel at 1900hrs (CT) on 4 March 1945, with a crew of forty-six and in company with two or three other VIIC boats, carrying about 98 tons of fuel. On passage to Horten, while passing through the Great Belt, the minesweeping gear of one of the escorts became defective, forcing the boats to put into Korsö (Denmark) while this defect was repaired. Later in the Skagerrak, there was an attack by a single aircraft, but all the bombs fell at a safe distance. The U-boats arrived at Horten, near Oslo in Norway on 9 March 1945.

U 1063 carried out *schnorchel* trials and sailed independently on the evening of 10 March for Kristiansand in southern Norway.

FINAL PATROL

(2) On 12 March, *U 1063* left Kristiansand, escorted for 50 miles along the Norwegian coast, remaining surfaced until the escort parted company. She then proceeded submerged into the North Atlantic adopting the *Nordweg* route between the Færoe and Shetland Isles. About ten days out, she surfaced and proceeded on both diesels for about an hour, in order to make better speed. Only a single aircraft was sighted, although there had been no GSR or radar contacts. The boat crash-dived, but no attack developed. About fourteen days out, she surfaced to report her position. She then proceeded down the west coast of Ireland and entered the operational area approximately between Land's End and Brest.

U 1063 was travelling submerged and navigating by means of an experimental *Elektra-Sonne* antenna, positioned on the snort (which proved rather unpredictable). At around 2345hrs (CT) on 15 April Stephan came to periscope depth off Land's End to take bearings. The boat was manoeuvring to attack convoy TBC 128, with the snort raised. Stephan was dismissive of the sound of loud screw noises from three ships, believing them to be from three fishing vessels he had sighted the previous day. Owing to a mistake in the trimming of the boat, the *schnorchel* emerged too far, resulting in detection.

The German perspective – Lt Hecker (post-war account):

> As you are aware, we left Kristiansund on the 12 March under escort for 50 miles along the Norwegian coast. We remained surfaced until the escort parted from us. Our route took the boat into the North Atlantic, passing roughly halfway between the Færoes and the Shetlands. We followed routine diving procedures until 10 days out it was felt we had fallen behind schedule. The captain decided we should proceed surfaced in daylight hours for an hour each day until we had caught up again. We used our Hohentwiel radar [GSR removed] about four or five times during this period, each time for one revolution only. We first became aware of problems when a single aircraft was sighted and of course we crash dived but there had been no GSR or radar contacts. 14 days out of harbour we surfaced to report in. We used Hohentwiel again but our suspicions were aroused that there was a serious problem. We proceeded submerged down the west coast of Ireland, eventually reaching our billet.

We simply could not obtain a fix. We were forced to resort to Elektra-Sonne but transmissions were being interfered with by English land stations. We surfaced to obtain an astronomical fix on 12 April. We realised we were close to the Scilly Islands. Would you believe the sextant was faulty! The Elektra-Sonne was being jammed and next the Goliath gave up on us. Abandoning the patrol was never even mentioned. We reverted to Runndipol and used Nauen for the long wave. The trouble was, we now had to keep the Schnochel aerial dry. Schnorchelling usually commenced shortly before 2200hrs, so that the last rotation of messages in the programme time was received. We generally kept it going for 3 hours. Foxer was detected from time to time but to the best of my knowledge nothing was ever sighted apart from fishing boats.

As Stephan came to periscope depth off Land's End to take bearings, the three 'fishing vessels' stood by, observing the periscope with interest. Frigates HMS *Loch Killin* (Lt Cdr Darling), HMS *Cranstoun* (Lt Cdr E.W. Rainey) and HMS *Burges*, of British Escort Group 17, which had been engaged in trailing the convoy, now moved in for the kill.

U1063 – Lt Hecker continued:

We were going down to 20m when the first depth charge pattern went off. Close all right. We went a bit deeper after that. Two more patterns went off and the boat sustained serious damage but I don't think the pressure hull was seriously breached but there was a bad leak aft. I do know that some of the tanks were damaged. The motors were functioning but the diesel frames had cracked. The third pattern was not so severe as the earlier ones.

The British view – HMS *Loch Killin* – Lt Cdr Darling:

Before the third attack a small underwater explosion was heard (probably Burges and Cranstoun's Hedgehog attacks) and immediately after the attack delivered on the bottom, loud blowing of tanks was heard. The ship was stopped short of the pattern on firing and the 10in projector was trained on the disturbance in case the U-boat should surface, which it did 2 minutes later in the centre of the pattern, stern first with an angle of 40°.

U 1063 – Lt Hecker – continued:

Next thing I knew was that the captain was giving conflicting instructions. He certainly shouted 'Abandon Ship' – which was in my view, unnecessary. We were going ahead on our motors with our bow swinging up because of the leak in the stern.

HMS *Loch Killin* – Lt Cdr Darling:

The U-boat surfaced fully, bows to the right and was engaged by the 4in and bridge oerlikons. It got under way but altered course to starboard and steamed around us…During this time she was also engaged and illuminated by Cranstoun.

We were unable to keep pointed at it but engaged it with twin oerlikons and pom pom. When it passed close to our port quarter in a sinking condition, the port thrower was fired which exploded close to the conning tower. The U-boat had taken a trim forward and sank almost vertically. Apparently 750 ton painted light grey, one 3in gun before the conning tower, two close range HA mountings. Schnorchel in raised position.

Lt Hecker continued:

The captain himself was the first out through the conning tower. When I emerged, he was preparing the big dinghy for launch. Not an act to fill you with confidence. Some men had manned the guns, but this made the English fire on us and of course our guns were no match. One English shell passed inches away from me. It made a big hole in the conning tower but fortunately for the rest of us it did not explode. Messerschmidt was blown up by a second shell though.

Post-war interview with Lt Hecker reproduced by kind permission of Peter Hampe.

Lt Cdr Darling continued:

Observed further hits and a number of survivors recovered which included 3 officers, the captain having been lost in the water. More survivors might have been recovered had the boats been lowered earlier instead of wasting time manoeuvring the ship.

In 2007, Franz Neumayr kindly offered the authors this personal account. (The following statement also remains the copyright of Mr Franz Neumayr):

I arrived on *U 1063* in July 1944 and, except for the odd weeks when I had additional training on new radar and radar-detector, was one of the radio operators on the boat.

After the order 'ABANDON SHIP' was given, I queued to ascend the conning tower and, spotting the tracers of gunfire from one or more of the attacking ships, quickly descended onto the deck and around the conning tower to avoid getting hit and I jumped into the sea; the boat was still under power and moving away from me. Later I heard and felt more depth charges.

After about half an hour, I noticed by the lights of the attacking ships, that they were moving away. I met up with two other swimmers and after quite some time met one of our inflatables occupied by four or five others. We took hold of the ropes around the inflatable and sort of pulled it as we were swimming. I remember vividly loosing one slipper and then the other and feeling very cold on my feet. After what seemed well over an hour, we spotted lights in the distance and realised they were coming closer. HMS *Loch Killin* returned to look for survivors. It took, what seemed to me, an awful long time before we were spotted and picked up. I attribute our survival to swimming and pulling the inflatable, which must have kept us from getting too cold. All three of us needed help from the British sailors to get on board *Loch Killin*. I have no idea what happened to the four or five men in the inflatable.

Onboard *Loch Killin* we were treated very well. We received dry clothing, and one of our survivors, who spoke some English, was asked to go with a sailor from *Loch Killin* to collect some food and hot tea. He asked him why, being their enemies, we were treated so well, with food, drink and cigarettes being offered. He said, 'We treat you just as WE would expect to be treated..

Left: Franz Neymayr during the Second World War.

Below: Franz Neumayr in 2008.

It took some hours before we docked at Plymouth, where we were taken for the rest of the night and locked up in what seemed an old castle. The next morning we were moved by train to Kempton Park PoW interrogation camp.

Later, I heard from two of our other survivors, that during the last minutes we were aboard *U 1063*, one diesel engine was leaning toward the other and, that the electric motors could not be switched off. Another survivor said that the 'Abandon Ship' command was given when a damage report from the forward torpedo room, mentioned heavy flooding.

After Kempton Park PoW camp, I also spent some time at Leicester, Doncaster, Tupsley (Hereford) and Ledbury PoW camps.

Franz Neumayr was born in August 1925 in Beckstetten, near Buchloe, Schwaben, in Germany. He applied to join the Kriegsmarine U-boats in early 1942 and after completing infantry and radio operator training, served for a few months on *U 678*. He then carried out radio operator duties on a torpedo target ship in the Baltic before becoming a radio operator on *U 1063* in July 1944.

After his capture in April 1945, Franz was held in PoW camps at Kempton Park – Leicester – Doncaster – Tupsley (Hereford) and Ledbury, being released in late 1948. Franz was then given a paid holiday to his home in Germany, on the promise that he would return to England to do agricultural work for the next five years, which he did and later became a steel erector. From 1955, Franz worked his way up through the ranks of a Birmingham steel fabrication company, becoming Managing Director in 1972. He retired in 1992 and still lives in his adopted Worcestershire.

Franz is the elder brother of Lorenz Neumayr, reportedly the youngest person to be awarded the Knight's Cross.

The frigates rescued seventeen men, including one officer, two senior ratings and six injured. Twenty-nine men were lost or drowned, including Kplt. Stephan, Ob. Messerschmidt and Lt Hampe. Among the officers, only Leutnant Helmut Hecker survived.

THE MEN WHO DIED IN U 1063

Adam, Ludwig Mtr.Ob.Gfr.	Klonn, Gustav Mtr.Gfr.
Engel, Horst Masch.Gfr.	Kraft, Willy Msch.Gfr.
Feldewert, Werner Mtr.Ob.Gfr.	Meder, Jacob Masch.Mt.
Folz, Walter Masch.Gfr.	Messerschmidt, Ernst Oblt.Iing
Forderer, Hans Masch Og.Fr	Pehl, Arthur Mtr.Gfr.
Frohlich, Herbert Ob.Ts.Mt.	Pens, Arnold Masch.Gfr.
Grasse, Eberhard Masch.Mt.	Pfitzner, Willi Fk Ob.Gfr.
Grondilzilewski, Gerhard Masch. Mt	Riegeler, Walter Masch.Gfr.
Hamerl Walter Fk.Mt.	Schenk, Paul Masch.Gfr.
Hampe, Klaus Lt	Schiedl, Martin Bts.Mt.
Hauptig, Erwin Masch.Gfr.	Schimmel, Paul Ob.Masch.
Heimerl, Adolf Masch.Ogfr.	Schweiger, Mattias Ob.Masch.
Klein, Hugo Masch.Gfr.	Stephan, Kapitänleutnant

THE CREWMEN TAKEN PRISONER

Böckels, Herbert Mech.Mt.	Peters, Masch.Ob.Gfr.
Grimm, Lorenz Masch.Mt.	Proft, Masch.Mt.
Hauschild, Masch.Mt.	Reitzner, Ernst Bt.Smt.
Hecker, Helmut Ltz.S.	Rennbaum, Johann Ob.Masch.
Kattner, Robert Masch.Mt.	Rosorius, Masch.Ob.Gfr.
Kopf, Heinz Matr.VII	Simon, Matr.Gfr.
Maleika, Georg Fk.Gfr.	Stephan San.Ob.Mt.
Müller, Matr.Ob.Gfr.	Woithe, Heinz Fk.Mt.
Neumayr, Franz Fk.Gfr.	

ADM 1/30419 CB 04051 (103) NID 1/PW/REP/1-19 NND 873041 <u>U-Boot-Ehrenmal Möltenort</u>
<u>NARA Series T-1022 ,Roll 3900, PG 30849, 31752</u>

German survivors would later accuse the dead commander of *U 1063* of having issued the abandon ship order prematurely. However, this order undoubtedly saved the lives of seventeen crewmen, in what had become a distinctly one-sided contest in the closing stages of the war.

WRECK SITE

The wreck lies on a seabed of sand, pebbles and shell, in a general depth of 56m (184ft), being the lowest astronomical depth. It is mostly intact, with most of the damage at the bows, where a large hole penetrates through the forward torpedo room. This damage was possibly caused by the Squid attack. The wreck lies with a 45° list over to its starboard side. The conning tower is in place, as are the periscope and *schnorchel* (both said to be in the raised position) and the hatches are open, just as the escapees left them. The wreck is a profusion of soft corals, thronged by shoals of fish; large conger eels can also be found at the bows.

UNTIRING, HM SUBMARINE

DATE OF LOSS: 29 July 1957
DEPTH: 50m
REFERENCE: 50 12'.750 N 004 00'.600 W
Also: 50 12'.802 N 004 00'.669 W
LOCATION: 5.66 nautical miles WSW of Bolt Tail

Type: 'U' Class British small-patrol submarine of Group II   *Pennant No*: P.59   *Builders*: Vickers-Armstrongs Naval Yard, High-Walker, Newcastle-on-Tyne for Royal Navy   *Ordered*: for 1941 War Emergency Programme   *Keel laid*: on 23 December 1941   *Launched*: on 20 January 1943. *Completed*: on 9 June 1943

TECHNICAL SPECIFICATIONS

Hull: Admiralty saddle-tank and riveted steel construction   *Surface displacement*: 545 tons   *Full/ L*: 658 tons   *U/Dt*: 740 tons   *LBD*: 59.99m (196ft/10in) × 4.87m (16ft) × 4.41m (14.5ft)   *Machinery*: 2 × Davey-Paxman 6RXS diesels, each rated at 400bhp, coupled to a 275kw generator (diesel-electric-drive)   *Props*: 2 bronze   *S/Sp*: 11.25 knots   *Op/R*: 5,000 nautical miles at 10 knots   *Sub/R*: 120 nautical miles at 2 knots   *U/Power*: 2 × Metro-Vickers electric motors rated at 412bhp gave 9 knots *Batteries*: Exide lead/acid   *Fuel/Cap*: 55 tons   *Armament*: 4 bow 53.34cm torpedo tubes (no external tubes   *Torpedoes*: 8 × 53.34cm (21in) (**or**) *Mines*: 6.M.Mk II.   *Guns*: 1 × 76.2mm (3in/45) QF Mk I deck gun mounted just in front of conning tower and 3 × 0.303in Lewis, or Vickers machine guns   *Ammo*: 160 rounds 76.2mm   *Diving*: max-op-depth 60.96m (200ft)   *Complement*: 33   *Name*: UNTAMED was the first of the name

The engines had a fabricated steel frame and were specially designed for service in submarines. Coupled to a 275kw generator, it powered the later British 'U' Class and all the 'V' Class submarines built during the Second World War. RXS engines were made in pairs, left and right handed, so that all the controls were between the two engines. The Bosch fuel pump fed fuel through an injector with a pintle-type nozzle with an injection pressure of 1,800psi. The compression pressure was 530psi and the maximum firing pressure at full load 760psi. The governor ran at half engine speed and the over-speed-governor was set to cut off fuel at engine speeds above 950rpm. Bore and Stroke was: 9½in by 12in. Cylinder configurations were: 4, 5, 6, 7 and 8. Power output (per cylinder): 56/70bhp at 600/750rpm (naturally aspirated); 75/93.3bhp at 600/750rpm (supercharged).

Other features were: wet cylinder liners; Ricardo 'Comet' head and CAV-Bosch-type fuel pump; a cylinder block supported on 'A' frames and secured by long high-tensile through-bolts to the

HM SM *Untiring*. (Private collection)

bedplate, which carried the main bearings. (This arrangement permitted large inspection doors for removing connecting rods and pistons, etc. Where weight or shock-resistance justified the cost, a fabricated welded steel frame was also available.)

Boats were often commissioned before completion in order to run acceptance trials with a navy crew.

In 1943, following the losses of *Vandal* and *Untamed* (*see* vol. 4), Admiralty harboured a genuine fear that sabateurs were at work in British shipyards. Vickers Armstrong's yards at Barrow and the Tyne were thought to have been infiltrated. It is known that a certain amount of low-level 'interference', such as the placing of foreign bodies in submarine lubricating oil tanks, had occurred while boats were under repair in various yards. Communist sympathisers had long been under suspicion but following the invasion of Russia in 1941, the threat from hard left agitators was believed to have diminished. While completing at High Walker on 23 April 1943, *Untiring* suffered a battery explosion, which delayed the boat's sailing date for one month. One day earlier HMS *Unswerving*, also under construction at High Walker, had also suffered a mysterious accident, all of which provoked Rear Admiral (S) to lend his account of these events in a letter to the Admiralty:

> I feel this run of accidents is somewhat suspicious and request that the possibility of malicious intent or even sabotage may be rigorously investigated and a close watch kept on the activities of sabateurs in these yards.

There is absolutely no hard evidence of sabotage, but rather, of human error. Faced with the *Vandal* and *Untamed* disasters, some senior officers merely felt that these incidents demonstrated that the men of the High Walker Yard lacked the submarine expertise of their Barrow counterparts, Captain S (1) observing that, ' *a more intimate liaison between the experienced Barrow Yard and the Tyne Yard…might well have lessened these early troubles…*'

The reality was that submarine construction programmes were being rushed through *all* participating yards by a diluted and inexperienced labour force. The records of Vickers in Barrow, Scotts on the Clyde and Tyne Wear Archive, reflect forced circumstances in which human error was inevitable. The reader should bear in mind that systems and equipment installed within these submarines was, in theory at least, checked and rechecked first by shipyard specialist technicians, followed by Admiralty overseers prior to 'signing off'. It is also worth pointing out that in the pre-war years, a certain royal dockyard had poor reputation among submariners. However, submarines built in this yard had a proven track record of standing up to sustained depth charge attack, much in the same way as boats built at Walker and Barrow later proved their resilience in the Mediterranean theatre.

Untiring's commanding officers during the Second World War were: Lieutenant Robert Boyd, DSO★, DSC, a laid-back, quiet, fair-haired Ulsterman (known as 'the man who nearly sunk the bank at Monte Carlo'.) served from February 1943; Lieutenant Charles Barry, DSC, served from January 1944; Lieutenant George E.L.F. Edsell was CO from December 1944. Now for a summary of her career.

Untiring carried out a total of fourteen operational patrols. Her first was a working up patrol off the Faeroes and North Cape. Off the Faeroes on 27 August 1943, *Untiring* sank the fishing boat *Havbris I*, having first removed the Norwegian crew. Now Lieutenant Boyd took the boat to the Mediterranean. *Untiring* was based at Algiers for a short time, but the best part of her time was attached to the 10th Flotilla, patrolling first from Malta then from Maddalena.

On 15 October 1943 the British submarine missed *U 616* with a torpedo off Toulon.

On 14 December 1943 *Untiring* encountered the German minelayer SS *Netzender* in the Monaco Roads and responded by chasing her back inside the harbour. *Untiring* fired a torpedo at an acute angle *through the harbour gates*. The secondary mine explosions which followed, virtually blew out every window in Monte Carlo – hence Lieutenant Boyd's sobriquet. On 17 December, *Untiring* narrowly escaped the torpedoes of a German destroyer while travelling on the surface off Cape Moli. Later that day the British submarine sank the tug *Faron* off Toulon. It appears the tug's helm jammed because she accidently rammed one of her charges, *Faron* was subsequently beached. Lieutenant Boyd managed to mount a second attack and his torpedo detonated against the side of the beached vessel. The ship was carrying ammunition and the explosion which followed was immense. *Untiring* dived deep to avoid enemy detection, however when she surfaced to periscope depth half an hour later, the escorts were still waiting for her. The boat dived immediately, but was subjected to a barrage of 300 depth charges. Extensive damage was caused to the boat, however she managed to escape detection beneath a thermal layer. Following this patrol, *Untiring* returned to the new 10th Flotilla base at Maddelana. Don Wilson, first lieutenant of *Untiring*, was awarded the DSC for 'his courage, skill and devotion to duty'. (Lieutenant Wilson went on to command HM S/M *Voracious* in May 1945.)

Untiring sank an 'F' boat near Rapallo on 6 January 1944. On 31 January 1944, the two coast-ers *Jean Suzan* and *St Antoine* were sunk, despite a heavy escort, southeast of Drammont. On 11 April 1944, the *Enseigne* was torpedoed and sunk off Cannes. The tanker SS *Cerere* was sunk on 12 April 1944; also torpedoed and sunk that afternoon, was the 1,190-ton SS *Diana* off Oneglia. *Untiring* torpedoed and sank the SS (UJ6705) *Clairevoyant* on 27 April 1944. On 1 May 1944, the SS *Astree* was sent to the bottom with a torpedo off Port Vendres. Off Ciatot on 10 June 1944 she also sank *UJ6078 (ex-SS la Havraise)*. Lieutenant 'Johnnie' Coote, who was third hand on *Untiring* during this period, has written an opinionated, racy (but always entertaining) account of these patrols entitled *Submariner*. This book introduces us to the characters among the crew, including such immortals as Coxswain 'Guts' Willoughby who rounded off the mess tables to enable him to manoeuvre his monstrous bulk around them. Then there was the amorous teleg-raphist 'Dickie' Bird, whose Algerian girlfriend had a son old enough to have fought in the First World War.

At long last, on 25 November 1944, *Untiring* returned to the UK. The boat arrived at Rothesay on 5 December. A long refit followed. The war ended and *Untiring* was surplus to requirements. Instead of being broken up, the boat was loaned to the Royal Hellenic Navy (Greece). She was transferred in June 1945 and was renamed *Xifias* (the Greek name for swordfish) on 25 July 1945. Obsolete and worn out, the boat returned to Britain in 1952, suitable only for training duties. Amongst her commanders during this latter phase were Lieutenant C.A.J. French from December 1953 and Lieutenant M.L.P. Badham from December 1954.

ADM 173/18434-20173 ADM 199/1818 ADM 199/1818 ADM 1/15478
With additional information kindly supplied by Andy Mair.

FINAL PATROL

On 25 July 1957 the Admiralty scuttled the submarine off the 'East Rutts', sending the old warhorse to join her sister *Upstart* on the seabed as a useful ASDIC target.

WRECK SITE

The wreck is orientated in an east to west direction (080/260°). She lies on a firm seabed of sand, gravel and silt, in a general depth of 50m (164ft), being the lowest astronomical depth. The wreck was reported as intact, but sonar shows her to be only 40m in length. Divers confirmed that she is standing upright with a slight list to starboard and still in very good condition and showing little sign of collapse. The conning tower stands 10m high. It is possible to have a good look around this area, but divers are strongly advised not to enter the hull. At the stern, her two phosphor-bronze propellers are still firmly secured attached. The hull of the submarine is carpeted with plumose anemones and numerous species of fish have adopted the wreck as their home. The torpedo tubes are the most recognisable feature at the bow section and all the hatches/doors are closed. Underwater visibility is usually in the region of 5-8m.

M1, HM SUBMARINE

DATE OF LOSS: 12 November 1925
DEPTH: 75m
REFERENCE: position withheld on request
LOCATION: 20 nautical miles SW from Prawle Point

The dismal end of *M2* was described in the last chapter. Some distance off Start Bay, her sister, the equally monstrous MI, also came to grief. Ironically the very gun which made her such a deterrent may well have led to her destruction.

Type: 'M' Class British Monitor submarine   *Builders*: Vickers, Barrow-in-Furness for Royal Navy   *Ordered*: in February for 1916 Emergency War Program. In February 1916 four 'K' Class submarines *K18*, *K19*, *K20* and *K21*, had been ordered, *K20* and *K21* (*M3* and *M4*) from Armstrong Whitworth and *K18* to *K19* from Vickers. (*M4* was cancelled prior to completion and sold back to Armstrong Whitworth as scrap.) After the orders were received, Vickers were given instructions to build a new design of boat, so *K18* and *K19* were remodelled to become *M1* and *M2* respectively   *Keel laid*: as Yard No-491 in July 1916   *Launched*: on 9 July 1917   *Completed*: on 17 April 1918 with Cdr Max Horton as CO

TECHNICAL SPECIFICATIONS

Hull: partially double. Surface displacement: 1,650 tons   *U/Dt*: 1,940 tons   *LBD*: overall length 90.14m (88.39m LPP) × 7.46m × 4.87m, 11 × watertight bulkheads and 12 × main compartments   *Props*: 2 bronze   *Machinery*: 2 × 12-cylinder Vickers-Admiralty single-acting, four-stroke, solid injection 1,200bhp diesels   *Props*: 2 bronze × 3-blade, 1.57m diameter, with an auxiliary 20bhp propelling motor also fitted to starboard shaft   *S/Sp*: max 15.5 knots   *Op/R*: 3,600 nautical miles at full power, or 5,500 nautical miles aat 10 knots   *Sub/R*: 10 nautical miles at 9.5 knots, or 80 nautical miles at 2 knots   *U/Power*: 4 × double-armature-type Admiralty pattern 400bhp electric motors driving two shafts, gave 8–9 knots and 1½-hours at full power   *Batteries*: 3 battery tanks containing 336 Exide lead/acid cells of 137 tons   *Fuel/Cap*: 110 tons external tanks   *Armament*: 4 × 45.72cm (18in) bow torpedo tubes   *Torpedoes*: 10 × 45.72cm (18in)   *Guns*: 1 × 0.48cm (12in) Mk IX 50-ton BL deck gun forward of conning tower, plus 1 × 7.62cm (3in QF) Quick-Firing HA Mk II anti-aircraft gun fitted on the after casing on a disappearing mounting. (In the late 1890s, Vickers originally designed the Mk IX 12-inch gun, which had a theoretical range of 11.9 miles) *Ammo*: 40 for large gun and 72 for AA   *Diving*: max-op-depth 60.96m (200ft)   *Complement*: 6 officers and 62 ratings

M1 firing her gun. (Author's collection)

M1 was the only 'M' Class boat to be completed before the end of the First World War. The 'M' boat project was kept highly confidential The 12in guns fitted to the 'M' Class were identical to those installed on Majestic Class battleships. They weighed about 120 tons and the shells weighed in at 850 pounds (383.55 kilos) each; while the total weight of the forty shells carried was 29 tons.

M1 did not see action, some maintain because Admiralty feared that if the Germans replicated adding massive guns to submarines, German gunnery skills would prove superior to those of their British counterparts. The recommended gun attack procedure was to cruise at periscope depth. When the target was properly lined-up and within range, the boat would rise until the gun barrel was about 6ft out of the water. The shell would be fired, the boat would then dive quickly. The fact that the huge gun could only be loaded on the surface, in favourable sea conditions, was one of the major drawbacks of the marque. Much has been written concerning the impractical nature of *M1*'s gun, however it should be pointed out that surviving patrol and technical reports all praise the boat's handling both surfaced and submerged.

On 25 June 1918 the boat left Portsmouth on patrol. During a practice firing on 1 July, the gun was fired by accident. The resultant damage forced the boat to return to base next day. On 19 October the boat left to join the 11th Flotilla at Blyth as an additional boat. Following a refit, the boat returned to Devonport, sailing to Malta in early November 1918. Some in Admiralty evidently regarded *M1* as a white elephant, moreover, as we shall see, the boat had inherited the curse of the 'K' Class. *M1*'s deterrent status is debatable, yet she looked a highly potent symbol of Britain's naval power, the boat spending much of the post-war years in Mediterranean waters. Her Mediterranean commission ended in 1920 when the boat returned to Britain, operating largely in the Channel between Blockhouse and Devonport.

Commander Max Horton was the boat's first commanding officer and served with *M1* during building, from 4 December 1917 to 12 October 1918.

Cdr Robert Bertram Ramsey took over as CO from 12 October 1918 to 1 August 1919.

Cdr Charles Gordon Brodie assumed command on 20 March 1921 to 10 July 1922.

Lt Cdr Edward Geldard Stanley was commander from 10 July 1922 to 1 September 1924.

Lt Cdr Jermyn Rushbrooke was CO from 1 September 1924 to 25 November 1924, for *M1* and *M2*, both in reserve.

Lt Cdr Alec Murray Carrie became commander and served from 24 November 1924 to loss.

FINAL PATROL

On 9 November 1925, *M1*, commanded by Lt Cdr Alec Carrie, left her base for exercises in the western Channel. The submarine had recently been painted a shade of green for aerial recognition purposes (other 'M' boats were painted shades of blue). The exercise would simulate a troop convoy moving up Channel while *M1* and a selection of other submarines would take up assigned escort positions. At 0030hrs on Thursday 12 November, *M1* and *M3* (Lt Cdr C. Mayers) left Plymouth in line-ahead formation. The exercise began at 0707hrs and both submarines dived. At 0726hrs *M3* surfaced to engage a motley array of surface ships in simulated 'gun action'. Lt Cdr Mayers sighted *M1* on the surface heading in a westerly direction about 3 miles away. The 'enemy' mine-sweeper *Newark* also spotted *M1* and exchanged signals at 0736hrs. Apart from the minesweeper, the nearest ship was the 2,045-ton Swedish steamer *Vidar* (1907 – Stockholms Rederi A/B Svea (Hj. Blomberg), Stockholm) an estimated 1 mile to the northwest. At 0737hrs *Newark* watched *M1* dive for the last time. The SS *VIDAR*, which was pitching sharply in a heavy sea, was on her way from Cardiff to Stockholm with a cargo of coal. At 0745hrs, the crew of *Vidar* (Captain Anell) felt a heavy blow forward and far heavier than the pitching experienced earlier.

Extract from log of *VIDAR* – 12 November 1925:

> 07.45 – Heavy breaking sea…Shipping water over…Two severe shakings were felt as if vessel had struck something hard below water. As some English warships were exercising in the area it was supposed that they had fired some depth charges as our ship after sounding, was found perfectly right.

When *M1* failed to report in, a hydrophone search by minesweepers was ordered. It produced nothing. No immediate full-scale search was ordered and the following message was sent from Commander in Chief Atlantic Fleet to the Admiralty:

'..IT IS FEARED THAT THE SUBMARINE *M1* HAS BEEN LOST WITH ALL HANDS'.

On the slightest of evidence it was being assumed in Admiralty circles that the entire crew of *M1* had died on the very day she went missing. At 1945, Admiralty released the following statement to the media:

DURING EXERCISES EARLY THIS MORNING THE SUBMARINE *M1* WAS SEEN TO DIVE IN A POSITION FIFTEEN MILES SOUTH OF START POINT. EVERY EFFORT IS BEING MADE TO LOCATE HER AND ESTABLISH COMMUNICATION.

That evening a full-scale search was organised using the most up-to-date equipment including magnetometers and the chernikeef log used for obtaining fixes. Although the search continued for two days no trace of *M1* or her sixty-nine crew was discovered. Sadly it now appears from the search chart track that *M1* had actually been located by magnetometer but the searchers were unable to differentiate the submarine from an older wreck. It is doubly sad to realise that we now know that *M1* was leaking oil. The searchers actually found the oil slick but assumed it was issuing forth from a wartime wreck. More disturbing still was the detection of fragmentary W/T transmissions suggesting that some of the crew were still alive and attempting to communicate using Fessenden equipment. This information was not made public for understandable reasons. It should be noted that DSEA was still in the development stage when *M1* sank.

If rescue was not on the horizon, at least the media had plenty of human-interest stories, to relay to the public. The press found Able Seaman Sales, who had gone ashore on learning of the death of his mother just hours before the boat sailed:

> When I last saw my mates they were in the best of spirits. They laughed and chatted at harbour stations. You could not have had a jollier bunch of messmates…most are married men with families…we all have the utmost confidence in Commander Carrie. He is simply splendid.

There was more to print. Carrie had just become a father; Petty Officer Bell had suffered a premonition. Photographs of the smiling crew taken in earlier times occupied pages of the *Daily Mirror*. On 13 November Rear Admiral Haggard released this depressing communiqué to the newsmen:

THE ADMIRALTY DEEPLY REGRET THEY CAN NO LONGER HOLD OUT ANY HOPE
THAT THE CREW OF *M1* STILL SURVIVE.

What else could the Admiralty have said?

Could it have disclosed that identifying the boat amid the litter of wrecks off Start Point was beyond the Royal Navy's technical capability?

Could Admiralty have revealed that even the event of *M1* being located, the depth involved would have been too deep for the operating range of its rescue divers?

Above all, how could Admiralty have admitted to dependents that there was no chance whatsoever of those trapped men surviving the ascent to the surface?

Some drew wider conclusions about the tragedy. The Chairman of Lloyds turned to the letters page of the *Times* to denounce the submarine as a '*deadly machine, which treacherously destroys those in charge of it and, it is feared, inflicts slow torture as well as death*'. The public and many politicians might have been forgiven for thinking that perhaps he had a valid point.

On 16 November as SS *Vidar* was steaming through the Kiel Canal, Captain Anell learned of the loss of *M1* from a German newspaper. The conscientious Swedish captain informed his employers, who in turn advised the Swedish Defence authorities. When *Vidar* arrived at Varta on 18 November, a diver found her bow buckled and bent to port. Traces of paint found on the crumpled stem matched that recently applied to *M1*. The Admiralty now had the probable cause of loss and they had a clear idea of the position, but where precisely was *M1*? The search continued for a further month, then the following announcement was issued on 2 December:

DIVING OPERATIONS IN CONNECTION WITH THE SUBMARINE *M1* HAVE BEEN DISCONTINUED AS NO POSITIVE RESULTS HAVE BEEN OBTAINED. IT IS NOT CONSIDERED NECESSARY TO PROLONG THE SEARCH AS THE CAUSE OF HER LOSS HAS BEEN FULLY ESTABLISHED.

And that was that. During the years that followed, the Admiralty did invest in new technologies and equipment, with a view to at least providing trapped submarine crews with a chance of escape. DSEA sets became standard submarine issue from 1932 and purpose-designed (if complicated) escape chambers were introduced to new boats. Fleet Order 971/35 *Subsmash* entered the Naval lexicon as the designated general mobilisation signal in the event of a serious submarine accident. However, events surrounding the loss of *Thetis* (*see* vol. 3) were to demonstrate that a misguided reliance upon DSEA to the exclusion of salvage was a dangerously complacent strategy.

Memorial plaques to the sixty-nine crew of *M1* and an individual plaque to Lt Cdr Carrie can be found in St Ann's Church, Naval Dockyard at Portsmouth. There is a wall plaque to L/S Herbert Neighbour in his parish church at Turville in Buckinghamshire. There is also a memorial to Lt Robert Thorp in Ryton Church, Tyne and Wear. ERA Harding was the youngest of five brothers, three of whom died in the First World War.

THE MEN WHO PERISHED IN M1

Adams, Cecil Passey P/J 52992 Leading Seaman

Alexander, Arthur Horace C/J 14439 Petty Officer

Allen, William Charles C/J 51725 Able Seaman

Andrews, Enoch James P/J 89562 Able Seaman

Baby, Ernest Arthur C/J 71374 Able Seaman

Baker, Edward Charles Goodchild C/K 12595 Stoker P.O.

Ball, Harold C/J 39475 Able Seaman

Ball, John Samuel D/K 35977 Leading Stoker

Bell, William Macdonald P/M 7020 E.R. Artificer

Bicker, Rowland P/ 223812 Chief Petty Officer

Buttle, James Fry D/J 22045 Able Seaman

Carrie, Alec Murray RN Lieutenant Commander

Casey, Robert Cameron Royal Australian Navy★ Lieutenant

Clark, Walter Thomas C/J 98756 Able Seaman

Cleaver, Edward George C/K 58802 Stoker

Clough, Nelson Orlando C/J 39878 Signalman

Cowling, Albert George P/K 18120 Leading Stoker

Dearing, Leonard Andree Percy C/J 78620 Able Seaman

Dennis, Dennis Francis C/M 12651 Engine Room Artificer

Dixon, Reginald Charles P/ 231628 Petty Officer

Duggan, Albert Frederick Harvey C/J 62085 L/Seaman

Edden, Thomas Henry D/M 14577 Engine Room Artificer

Erskine, William P/K 63811 Leading Stoker

Evans, Albert D/J 96697 Able Seaman

Feltham, Frank C/K 57863 Stoker

Foley, John Frederick C/J 48119 Able Seaman

Gardner, Charles C/ 233422 Chief Stoker

Gay, Albert Arthur P/J 62961 Telegraphist

Good, Cyril Sidney RN Warrant Engineer

Gore, Sydney John Ethelbert C/M 4730 E.R. Artificer

Harding, Gordon George D/M 10953 E.R. Artificer

Hewson, Philip P/M 8641 Engine Room Artificer

Hobday, Albert Edmond C/ 236378 Petty Officer

Huckin, Reginald Augustus P/J 9676 Able Seaman

Jewell, Henry George P/J 48749 Able Seaman

Jones, Bertie William C/J 20035 Petty Officer

Kemble, George P/K 10187 Leading Stoker

Kent, Arthur William P/J 15182 Leading Seaman

Kidney, James D/J 53085 Leading Seaman

Law, John William D/J 65730 Able Seaman

Littell, Robert Charles C/M 35596 Engine Room Artificer

Lovering, Ernest Thomas C/J 24897 Able Seaman

Manning, John D/J 103109 Able Seaman

Mansell, Cecil George Cobden C/K 600530 Stoker

Martin, Charles James D/J 90561 Able Seaman

Millard, Harold P/K 62220 Stoker

Morgan, George Petvin D/ 239799 Petty Officer

Moyse, Victor Charles P/J 23751 Able Seaman

Neighbour, Herbert Edwards C/J 89917 Able Seaman

Nichols, David Richard D/K 57987 Stoker

Nicholson, William Frederick P/J 19870 Leading Seaman

Pearson, William Adolphus P/J 42467 Able Seaman

Philpott, Thomas Walter 1st Lieutenant – Gunnery Officer

Price, William Frederick P/J 25784 Leading Seaman

Sayers, Charles Alfred C/J 31401 Able Seaman

Smith, Frederick William P/J 9944 P.O. Telegraphist

Spratley, Percival C/J 69385 Telegraphist

Storey, Charles Clarence P/K 58715 Stoker

Tamblin, William John D/J 94557 Leading Seaman

Taylor, Robert C/J 41914 Able Seaman

Thorpe, Charles Arthur Robert RN★ Lieutenant

Turner, Walter Isaac P/J 36092 Leading Signalman

Vaughan, William Charles Albert D/J 32281 L/Seaman

Washington, Sidney William C/J 24170 Leading Seaman

Webster, Albert Ernest C/J 92635 Leading Seaman

Williams, Henry Richard P/K 56132 Stoker

Wright, Charles Edwin C/L 12944 Officer Steward

Wright, Frederick George P/J 99863 Able Seaman

ADM 1/8679/85 ADM 116/2922 ADM 173/11205-11289

(The Swedish SS *VIDAR* was mined off Terschelling on 19 July 1943, while on a voyage from Rotterdam to Trelleborg with coal and coke; she ran ashore, but became a constructive total loss. Coincidentally, after HM S/M *E13* sank in August 1915, it was a steamer named *VIDAR*, albeit a Danish vessel, that transported the bodies of the fifteen dead crewmen back to England for burial.

WRECK SITE

As for *M1,* it withheld its mysteries for decades, forgotten by all except a dwindling number of relatives and a handful of skilled and determined divers, such as eminent maritime historians Richard Larn and Innes McCartney, who regarded *M1* as *the* missing Channel wreck. Thanks to years of dedicated research, Innes McCartney discovered her sitting upright, but leaning slightly over to port, in a depth of 75m (246ft), being the lowest astronomical depth. The wreck is deteriorating and heavily netted. It was identified by the distinctive foot-holes in the conning tower. The most distinctive feature, the huge gun, was missing, lying on the sand, off the port beam of the wreck.

One plausible theory advanced by marine accident investigator Keith Dixon (and subject of a BBC documentary in the *Journeys to the Bottom of the Sea* series (2000), suggested that *M1* had blown tanks in order to gain periscope depth following her dive. The boat rose blindly towards the surface. While we can never know for certain what transpired, there may have been a failure in hydrophone drill. Certainly Carrie appears to have been totally unaware that *Vidar* was bearing down fast. According to Mr Dixon's scenario, two collisions occurred. The first was serious but not fatal. Impact damage in the form of a 'V'-shaped cleft can still be inspected in the casing just forward of the gun mounting. This impact whipped the stern around, causing a second, heavier collision between the gun mounting and the ship's bows, snapping the gun barrel. Immediately after the second impact with *Vidar* the submarine lost trim as the weight of her 17-ton gun destabilised the boat. It must be assumed that *M1* had already expended her supply of compressed air, for Carrie was unable to arrest the descent. As the boat careered to the bottom, the gun sheered off, pulling away the turret superstructure. The king pin was wrenched out of its mounting ring. Unfortunately the size of the gun was so great that this pin had been designed to project down through the casing and into the pressure hull. Mr Dixon was able to deduce that water would have flooded in via the king pin socket, swamping first the magazine or 'shell room', then, crucially, the control room. This is informed speculation as to what transpired, what actually happened is a mystery sealed for eternity within *M1* at the bottom of the Channel.

There is evidence that some men survived the initial flooding. The forward torpedo-loading hatch is open. The gloomy innards of the submarine reveal a fan and plates protruding from the silt. Not surprising when one considers that the officers' mess lay aft of this point. A second hatch is open just aft of the conning tower. This heavy hatch mechanism could only have been opened by survivors within having first flooded the compartment to equalize pressure. No bodies were ever discovered. In the course of the BBC documentary, one interviewee asserted that the crew of *M1* had been issued with 'suicide pills'. This emphatically was not, nor ever has been, the policy of the Royal Navy Submarine Service.

Records reveal that many of the crew had survived the First World War only to die in this freak accident. As experienced submariners, the survivors must have realised that escape from this depth was impossible. All told, the inherent dangers were merely an accepted risk of the 'trade' – reflected in the higher wages paid to submariners in comparison to general service sailors.

Before Kevin Gurr and his team left the wreck, they placed a small plaque on the hull. The words are partly a play on the RN Submarine Service motto – 'We come unseen':

THEY DIED UNSEEN – BUT NOT FORGOTTEN

It could be said of these career submariners of 1925, that they died for king, country – and two shillings per day.

U 85, SM IMPERIAL U-BOAT

DATE OF LOSS: 12 March 1917
DEPTH: 69m
REFERENCE: 50 02'.469N 04 04'.851W
LOCATION: 16.80 nautical miles SSE of Rame Head

During the First World War and beyond, the British public were thrilled by the exploits of the mysterious Q-ships. One epic confrontation took place off Rame Head. However failure to find a wreck to date, coupled with doubts over the identity of the U-boat concerned, has resulted in significant question marks hanging over the episode.

Type: Mittel-U (Improved Type U65) ocean torpedo attack boat   ***Builders***: Germaniawerft, Kiel for Kaiserliche Deutsche Marine   ***Ordered***: on 23 June 1915, within the batch *U 81–U 86*   **Keel laid**: as Yard No.255 on 29 November 1915   ***Launched***: on 22 August 1916   ***Commissioned***: by Kapitänleutnant Willy Petz on 23 October 1916

TECHNICAL SPECIFICATIONS

Hull: double   **Surface displacement**: 808 tons   **U/Dt**: 946 tons   **LBDH**: 70.10m × 6.30m × 4.0m × 8.70m   **Machinery**: 2 × 1,200ps Maschinefabrik-Augsburg-Nürnberg (MAN) diesels. **Props**: 2 bronze   **S/Sp**: 16.8 knots   **Op/R**: 11,220 nautical miles at 8 knots   **Sub/R**: 56 nautical miles at 5 knots   **U/Power**: 2 × 600ps electric motors gave 9.1 knots   **Batteries**: AFA lead/acid/accumulators   **Fuel/Cap**: 81 + 83 tons   **Armament**: 2 bow and 2 stern 50.04cm torpedo tubes   **Torpedoes**: 8 × 50.04cm (19.7in).   **Guns**: 1 × 105mm (4.13in) forward facing deck gun and 1 × 88mm (3.46in) aft 5m of conning tower.   **Ammo**: 276 rounds   **Diving**: max-op-depth 50m (164ft) and 45 sec to crash-dive   **Complement**: 35

U 85 was assigned to the German-based IV.U-Bootflottille at Emden on 15 January 1917 with Kplt. Willy Petz the commander from 23 October 1916. Petz made three patrols with the boat:

(1) On 22 January 1917, *U 85* departed Ems and sailed into the North Sea to hunt Allied shipping. On the 26th, Petz captured the 923-ton Norwegian SS *Dicax* (1916 - Fredrikstad Shipping Co. Aktieselskapet, Fredrikstad).

The *Dicax* had left Fredrikstad at 2230hrs on 25 January with a cargo consisting of case-boards, planed boards and 150 tons of feldspar, for Garston. At 0300hrs on the 26th, the ship had been steering well away from the coast due to the heavy ice and was approximately 69 miles west from Ryvingen lighthouse, being the southernmost lighthouse in Norway. At 0830hrs, E. Nilsen, the first mate, who was on watch, observed a German submarine (SM *U 85*) on the port bow and a warning-shot was fired. The steamer's engine was immediately stopped and the captain went on deck and ordered the starboard lifeboat launched. The first mate and four men then rowed over to the submarine with ship's papers. Two minutes later, after reading the papers, the submarine commander, Kapitänleutnant Petz, ordered the steamer to be sunk. The lifeboat was taken in tow and when they were a little closer to the *Dicax*, an 'AB' (abandon ship) signal was hoisted.

The ten men onboard launched the port lifeboat and rowed over to the starboard one; then, in rough seas, the men were evenly distributed between the boats. The U-boat then began firing grenades at the ship; about thirteen to fifteen were fired all told, but she would not sink; a torpedo was then fired into the engine room and the *Dicax* sank almost immediately.

Meanwhile, as this event was taking place, a steamship was lying to the leeward side of *DICAX* and for a while steered towards the lifeboats, but it suddenly changed course and made off. The U-boat then took the crew onboard and set course for Bovbjerg (Jutland, Denmark) in order to land them there. The crew of the U-boat stated that the other steamer was one of the Swedish Svea Company ships of the Fredrikstad type.

At 1630hrs on 26 January, *U 85* came across the Danish sailing vessel *Fuglen*, but as she did not have provisions for so many people, the east-going Danish steamer *Express* of Copenhagen was approached and it took the crew of *Dicax* onboard. At noon on Sunday the 28th the crew was landed in Copenhagen and the men were sent home, through the Norwegian Consulate.

Witnesses later explained that the sea was dangerously high when they boarded the lifeboats, and because of the high sea, the lifeboats could not be taken in tow by the U-boat. The commander had hoped to come across a fishing boat in order to send over the crew of *Dicax*.

U 85 arrived back in port on the 27th.

(2) *U 85* sailed from Emden on 1 February 1917 for a war patrol around the British Isles, going through the Dover Straits on the outbound journey. On 5 February, Kplt. Petz damaged the 7,608-ton SS *Explorer* (1910 – Charente SS. Co. Ltd, Liverpool) with a torpedo; the steamer was travelling to Calcutta from Liverpool and put back into Queenstown, Ireland on 7 February.

At 1100hrs on 6 February and without any warning, Petz torpedoed and the *Cliftonian* (1911 – Cambrian Steam Navigation Co. Ltd, London), a 4,303-ton defensively armed steamship, off Galley Head; she was voyaging from Cardiff to Marseilles with a crew of thirty-four and a 6,000-ton cargo of coal. The crew abandoned the ship immediately, except for Captain Owen, the chief engineer and second officer, who attempted to beach her near Galley Head, but she sank before reaching the coast. Armed Patrol Vessels rescued all of the men and took them to Queenstown, Ireland.

At 0910hrs on 7 February, Petz torpedoed the 8,669-ton defensively armed steamship *California* (1907 – Anchor Line Ltd, Glasgow) without warning, 38 miles off Fastnet Rock; she was on passage from New York for the Clyde with 205 passengers and crew and a general cargo, including nickel ingots. The torpedo struck the vessel aft at 0920hrs and many of the forty-three people, who died, were actually killed in the explosion. The boats were launched quickly, but one of them capsized and several people were drowned. The master, Captain John Henderson, went down a considerable depth with his ship, but struggled back to the surface and one of the boats picked him up. A British warship picked up the survivors and landed them at Queenstown. Of the thirteen passengers lost, there were seven women and four children. Nine merchant crewmembers were injured, but thirty-nine were killed or drowned.

SOME OF THOSE WHO DIED

Alexander, George Smith, 17yrs, Assistant
  Steward
Algeo, William Frederick, 32yrs, Surgeon
Bell, Joshua, 38yrs, 2nd Engineer
Breslin, Patrick, 34yrs, Fireman
Burns, John, 22yrs, Fireman
Campbell, John, 17yrs, Sailor
Chainey, George, 45yrs, Fireman
Coyle, John, 41yrs, Fireman
Cunningham, William Millar, 35yrs, 2nd
  Engineer
Darcy, Michael, 17yrs, Fireman
Doolan, James, 31yrs, trimmer
Eadie, William, 22yrs, Assistant Purser
Etherington, James Bannerman McDonald,
  32yrs, Purser
Evans, John Mather, 35yrs, Mess Room Steward
Gillespie, George, 29yrs, Trimmer
Halbert, Peter, 45yrs, Leading Stoker

Kelway, Ernest, Sailor
Lees, William Pettie, 27yrs, Assistant Steward
Lemon, Nickolas, 65yrs, Able Seaman
Midgley, Thomas Jackson, 14yrs, Deck Boy
Millar, Daniel, 60yrs, Trimmer
Monaghan, James, 19yrs, Trimmer
Moore, John, 41yrs, Hospital Steward
Murray, John Joseph, 59yrs, Greaser
McAllister, Archibald, 34yrs, 2nd Cook
McCann, Matthew, 55yrs, Fireman
McGarvey, Alexander, 41yrs, Barber
McQueen, John, 31yrs, Fireman and Trimmer
O'Donnell, James, 22yrs, Sailor
Pollock, David, 38yrs, Carpenter's Mate
Rigney, Francis, 18yrs, 3rd Cook
Simpson, John, 59yrs, 3rd Mate
Smith, Donald, 45yrs, 1st Engineer
Steel, George Grant, 44yrs, Assistant Steward
Williamson, Charles, 41yrs, 1st Bed Steward

THE CREWMEN INJURED

Davidson, John – Greaser (crushed fingers)
Griffin, Peter – Fireman (crushed)
Hay, John – Engineer (head injury)
Kesson, ? – Chief Officer (broken arm)
McDonald, ? – Assistant Steward (shock/strain)
McDonald, Peter – Printer (crushed ribs)
McGarth, Joseph – Greaser (dislocated shoulder)
McKay, Archibald – ? (shock)
Neill, John – Greaser (crushed legs)
Proctor, Harry – Quartermaster (strained arm)

At 0600hrs that same day (7th), the defensively armed 6,330-ton SS *Vedamore* (1896 – Johnston Line Ltd) was also torpedoed and sunk without warning, 20 miles west of Fastnet Rock (51° 17'N 10° 03'W), Ireland; she was carrying three passengers, a crew of fifty-seven and a general cargo, including 2,000 tons of copper from Baltimore, Maryland to Liverpool. The ship, which was abandoned immediately in bitterly cold weather, went down in just 6 minutes. Thirty-six men, including the passengers, got away in the boats, but most of the rest were either drowned or killed in the explosion. After 10 hours, the 3,158-ton SS *Wyvisbrook* (1912 – Brook S.S. Co. Ltd, Glasgow) picked up the survivors and later transferred them to an Armed Patrol Vessel, which landed them at Berehaven, on the southwest coast of Ireland.

THE MEN WHO DIED

Adamson, Samuael Joseph, 48yrs, 2nd Officer
Browitt, Harold Charles Reginald, 19yrs, 3rd Officer
Conception, Santiago, 24yrs, Trimmer
Connorton, W., 32yrs, Trimmer
De La Cruz, Floentino, 44yrs, Seaman
Dongug, Thomas, 25yrs, Fireman and Trimmer
Entillan, Marian, 35yrs, Fireman
Fell, James Forsyth, 18yrs, Apprentice
Gentry, Amos Harry, 21yrs, 2nd Cook
Gomez, Urbano, 29yrs, Fireman
Hagan, Thoma,s 59yrs, Assistant Steward
Knox, John, 43yrs, 2nd Engineer
MacKay. Alex, 48yrs, Seaman RNR DAMS Gunner
Paradis, Max, 31yrs, Fireman
Shepherd, Edward, Fireman
Slavin, James, 43yrs, Able Seaman
Sterling, James, Fireman
Topas, T.S., 24yrs, Fireman
Toriello, P., 26yrs, Greaser
Walker, Albert Edward, 40yrs, Boatswain (Bosun)
Wiley, Basiloc C., 27yrs, Fireman

U 85 put into Heligoland on 16 February.

FINAL PATROL

(3) On their last war cruise, *U 85* and *U 81* left Heligoland at 1400hrs on 6 March 1917 and soon after they sailed they encountered heavy weather. Both boats intended to sail through the Dover Strait and return via the north of Scotland; they gradually became separated and *U 81* last saw *U 85* just before midnight.

Twenty miles from Portland on the 12th, the SS *Tandil* (1900 – Buenos Ayres & Great Southern Railway Co. Ltd, London) of 2,897 tons was torpedoed and sunk without warning; the British vessel was commanded by Captain W.L. Chambers and was transporting coal from Barry to Portland and four of her crewmen were drowned.

THE MEN WHO DIED

Daly, Thomas (30yrs), 3rd Engineer
Lawrence, Bert (30yrs), Fireman
Montrose, Henry (36yrs), Fireman and Trimmer
Pocock, Frederick Redvers (16yrs), Cabin Boy

Later that same day (12 March), Petz attacked what appeared to be an insignificant 803-ton steamship with a torpedo, 20 nautical miles south of Start Point. The innocent 'steamship' was none other than the Q-ship *Privet* (*Q19*) (Lt Cdr G. Matheson RNR) with orders to hunt for U-boats between Alderney and Land's End. Just before 1500hrs and 24 miles south by east of Start Point, a torpedo narrowly missed *Privet*, but the U-boat then surfaced on the starboard side aft, about 2,400 yards distant and began shelling the Q-ship. German shellfire was accurate, with five direct hits and *Privet* stopped after the second round, but the shelling continued. The steering gear on *Privet* was completely wrecked and a number of holes were blasted through the hull. One lifeboat was destroyed and the falls of the other shot away, causing a number of casualties amongst the 'panic party' when the shell exploded in their midst. Matheson had little option but to transmit an SOS radio signal. Assessing the damage inflicted, the U-boat confidently closed in for the kill. However, *Privet*'s gun crews were already in place and lying low and as soon as the submarine was within range, at 2,000 yards, down fell the shutters. Both port side 12-pounders opened fire at 1525hrs, which must have given the U-boat's crew the shock of their lives. At least three and probably four British shells detonated around the conning tower, probably killing some of the gun crew. The submarine fired only one more round before attempting to crash-dive, but she was apparently fatally damaged. The boat appeared to rise up at a steep angle then slid stern-first under the surface and disappeared. Nothing more was ever seen of that U-boat but we should not automatically assume that the submarine had been sunk.

Privet meanwhile was also seriously damaged in this encounter. Although taken in tow by the destroyers *Christopher* and *Orestes*, she sank in Cawsands Bay, en-route to Plymouth. The crew of *Privet* received a bounty of £1,000 for sinking a U-boat (deemed to be *U 85*) and the following awards were made:

Matheson, Charles G N/E Lt Cdr RNR was awarded the DSO: *'for the gallant manner in which he fought and handled his ship under great difficulties was most praiseworthy. The action reflected great credit on every one concerned. Their Lordships' appreciation expressed to Lt Commander Matheson, officers and men for the manner in which they carried out their duties.'*

Sells, John W N/E Assistant Paymaster RNR was awarded the DSC: *'he remained on the bridge throughout the action carrying out orders promptly and with exceptional coolness and made arrangements for the care of the wounded'.*

Lyons, David N/E Lt (E) RNR was Mentioned in Despatches: *'he did excellent work in keeping his engines running as long as possible seeing to his boilers when the engine room was filling with water'.*

Smithard, Edmund G N/E S/Lt RNR was awarded the DSC: *'he was stationed in the engaged battery throughout and kept his guns crews steady when balking was struck by a shell. The excellent firing was largely due to his spotting and coolness'.*

FOOD-FOR-THOUGHT? – MICHAEL LOWREY

An examination of German source material calls into question the official attribution that *PRIVET* sank *U 85*. *U 85* ordinarily should have been well beyond the Start Point area by the time she was listed as being sunk, the afternoon of her sixth day at sea. On her previous patrol, *U 85* sailed on 1 February, was off Bishop Rock by the 4th and was home on the 16th, having sailed around the British Isles.

The KTB of *U 81*, which was the boat that sailed with *U 85*, provides a possible answer for this delay – but also strongly suggests that *U 85* never even entered the Channel on her final patrol. On 7 March, *U 81* encountered very heavy seas. Operating with diesels proved impossible as water was coming in through the induction and conning tower hatch. *U 81* also developed an oil leak and was not handling the weather well; with fuel in the reserve tanks for extra range, the U 81/86 series boats were low in the water and did not enjoy the good sea-keeping qualities they experienced with lighter fuel loads. Kplt. Weisbach decided to abandon the attempt to go through Dover (he was only off the Dutch coast at the time) and turned to the north and went around Scotland.

On 28 March 1917, the day after *U 81* returned home, and with *U 85* listed at least among the semi-missing (not quite overdue, but not heard from in some time), Weisbach wrote up his experiences from his patrol. He opens by talking about *U 85*:

> Aus der Meldung *U 85*, daß das Boot eine stärke Ölspure hätte, und der Angabe *U 81*, da ß*U 85* von Terschelling aus einen nördlichen Kurs genommen habe, ist es zu entnehmen da ß*U 85* den Nordweg eingeschlagen hat. Diese wurde auch der Anweisung der Flottille entsprechen.
>
> From the message of *U 85* that she had a larger oil leak, and the report from *U 81* that *U 85* from Terschelling took a northern course, it is to infer that *U 85* took the Nordweg (went around Scotland). This would also correspond with the Flotilla's instructions.

The observations Kplt. Willy Petz of *U 85* made after his previous patrol make quite clear that he had no liking for taking his big U-boat through Dover.

While *U 85* was not likely to be in the Plymouth area on 12 March 1917, a different U-boat most definitely was; it was *UC 68*. The Flanders-based minelayer sailed on 10 March. The German official history credits her with laying two minefields off Plymouth on the 12th. She then supposedly sailed for the Start Point area, where she supposedly blew up while laying the last of her mines. This loss attribution comes from Spindler; it is a case of a big underwater explosion being noted and four (German) mines later being swept up. Debris was not associated with the explosion nor was a wreck discovered. Random mine explosions were, however, not uncommon and are not necessarily associated with a U-boat going down. In three other cases of U-boat losses being associated with large minefield explosions, the submarine supposedly sunk has been located elsewhere.

A likely scenario would be that *UC 68* torpedoed the *Tandil* while en-route to lay mines off Start Point. She then continued on, toward Plymouth to deploy the rest of her mines. One of the Plymouth-area fields was actually nearer to Eddystone – the British steamer *Orsova* would hit one of *UC 68*'s mines, 3 miles east by south, half south of Eddystone. This location is less than 10 miles from where *Privet* engaged her submarine that very afternoon! After laying her mines, *UC 68* encounters *Privet* and was presumably sunk.

UC 68 was assigned to patrol in the English Channel during March 1917, but there are no unexplained sinkings in that area. Given that the convoy system had not yet been introduced and U-boats were extremely effective, there is a strong case for asserting that *UC 68* was lost on or shortly after 12 March.

Again we face the question of how did the Royal Navy know they had sunk a specific U-boat? It is clear from material within the National Archive that by 1918 British Naval Intelligence had identified the *Privet* 'victim' as *U 85*, though the reasoning behind this attribution is not provided. Without the Royal Navy attribution, we would easily conclude that *Privet* sank *UC 68*. What made the Royal Navy then think the submarine that *Privet* attacked was *U 85* and not *UC 68*? (The RN thought during the war that the submarine HM S/M *C7* sank *UC 68* on 5 April 1917 in the North Sea. The Germans rejected this as requiring an excessive patrol length. One possibility is that the Royal Navy decided that *C7* sank *UC 68* and then credited *Privet* with sinking the other missing U-boat, *U 85*.) The Naval Historical Branch failed to answer this question, leaving the authors to conclude that (not for the first time) loose ends have been conveniently tied off without due reference to German records.

NARA Series T-1022 Rolls 8, 37, PG61667 ADM 137/2961 U-Boot-Ehrenmal Möltenort

THE MEN WHO PERISHED IN U 85

Barner, Friedrich U-Matrose	Kratje, Hermann U-Maschinistenmaat
Bartelsen, H. U-Bootsmannsmaat	Krüger, Paul U-Obermatrose
Becker, Christ U-Oberbootsmannsmaat	Kühn, Johannes U-Heizer
Bergmann, J. Heizer	Köhler, Reinhard Bootsmannsmaat d.S.II
Bock, Georg Heizer	Langfeldt, U-Heizer
Damm, Ernst Steuermann	Link, Michael U-Heizer
Dilfer, Adam U-Bootsmannsmaat	Matthes, Siegfried Leutnant zur See
Eickhoff, Wilhelm U-Heizer	Maxeiner, Friedrich U-Obermaschinistenmaat
Endress, Karl U-Oberheizer	Müller, E. U-Maschinist
Fatthauer, E. U-Maschinistenmaat	Pennig, Jakob Oberheizer
Flessner, Johann U-Matrose	Petz, Willy Kapitänleutnant
Fox, Theophil U-Matrose	Pollmer, Paul U-Steuermann
Frischmuth, Otto U-Maschinistenmaat	Richert, Alfred U-Obermatrose
Grabowski, P. U-Heizer	Rüdiger, Herm U-F.T.Obergast
Heineke, G. U-Obermaschinistenmaat	Schulz, E. Steuermannsmaat
Heller, Walter Marine Ober Ingenieur	Starckloff, Fritz Oberleutnant zur See
Henne, August U-Obermaschinistenmaat	Stoll, Lorenz U-Heizer
Hennig, H. U-Obermatrose	Szdzuy, Joseph U-F.T.Gast
Hintz, Friedrich U-Maschinistenmaat	Wilkens, Hermann U-Matrose

Not far from fearsome Eddystone lies a British submarine with a unique claim to fame – she was deliberately sunk in the interests of making a film.

H52, HM SUBMARINE

DATE OF LOSS: 3 January 1928
DEPTH: 55m
REFERENCE: 50 11'.552 N 004 17'.251 W
LOCATION: 1 nautical mile NW of the Eddystone Rocks and 7.58 nautical miles SSW of Rame Head

Type:'H.21' Class coastal defence submarine of the Group III (*H47* and *H.50*) **Builders**: one of two (*H.51* and *H52*) at HM Dockyard, Pembroke Dock for Royal Navy **Ordered**: for 1917 Emergency War Programme **Keel laid**: on 16 January 1918 **Launched**: on 31 March 1919 **Completed**: on 16 December 1919

TECHNICAL SPECIFICATIONS

Hull: single **Surface displacement**: 410 tons **Full/L**: 440 tons **U/Dt**: 500 tons **LBD**: 52.35m (171.9ft) × 4.67m (15ft-4in) × 3.42m (11ft-3in) **Props**: 2 bronze **Machinery**: 2 × 4-stroke 8-cylinder, air-injection NELSECO (New London Ship and Engine Co. of Groton, Connecticut, USA.) diesels 240bhp at 375rpm each continuous, with 480hp max. (Diesels were licensed from MAN & Vickers) **Props**: 2 bronze **S/Sp**: max 13 knots as designed, but sea-speed of 11.5knots **Op/R**: 1,375 nautical miles at 10 knots, 2,985 nautical miles at 7.5 knots or 1,100 nautical miles at full power **Sub/R**: 10 nautical miles at 9 knots, or 130 nautical miles at 2 knots **U/Power**: 2 × Electric Dynamic Co. (Bayonne, New Jersey, USA) electric motors rated 320bhp continuous or 620bhp maximum (for less than 1 hour) gave 9 knots max **Batteries**: Exide batteries of 120 cells. **Fuel/Cap**: 16 tons **Armament**: 4 × bow 53.34cm torpedo tubes **Torpedoes**: 8 × 53.34cm (21in) **Guns**: 1 × 7.62cm (3in) deck gun **Diving**: max depth 54.86m (180ft) **Complement**: 22

H52 was equipped with a new 3kW arc transmitter, enabling her to report to shore stations.

The Group III series of 'H' Class had the canvas conning tower weather-protection system of the class predecessors Group I and II replaced with a more permanent structure and they were fitted with 21in torpedo tubes instead of the 18in ones, otherwise they differed very little. Some of the class, notably *H31* and *H32*, served as training boats in the Second World War.

Following the signing of a contract between Admiralty and the Bethlehem Steel Corporation. It had been planned to build the first 'H' Class boats in the United States. However, trade limitations frustrated the deal and eventually production was switched to the Canadian Vickers shipyard. When the United States entered the war, production of the 'H' Class moved to British shipyards. The 'H' Class proved to be very popular, of good design, quite fast and ideal boats for patrolling shallow waters. The armament of four bow torpedo tubes made them among the best armed small European submarine at the time. The Group III marque was of a single hull construction. The hull was divided into five watertight compartments, providing a margin of safety greater than previous British submarine designs. Torpedoman Bernard Cranmer remembered his days in *H 31* with stoicism:

> You could say the old dear was unpredictable – like a dotty old aunt. She would roll and buck and occasionally slam us bow first into the Dogger Bank. The fact that all 'H' boats were lousy sea keepers only added to the discomfort. You had to be particularly careful while passing between light and heavy water densities. I mean it would not take much to swamp an 'H' boat. We had one or two dirty hammocks infested with lice but most preferred to sleep on tarpaulins spread over the lockers (about a foot wide) or drape ourselves over tables. Unlike other British submarines, the senior rates (ERAs and LTOs together) monopolised the roomy tube space waited on by a messman. They slept on the fish. As I later discovered, torpedoes can make reasonably comfortable beds. Nobody liked sleeping on the control room floor as you were liable to be stood on by someone wearing seaboots or freeze to death because the conning tower hatch was open. We junior rates did our cooking on a smelly old cooker heated by four elements. Bear in mind we could never spare water for hand washing. Scrambled egg, cheese oosh, trainsmash and potmess with babies heads were our staple diet. They all looked alike on the plate. If the sea didn't make you sick, the oily greased-up offerings produced on that box were guaranteed to have you hurling your guts out. If we were really lucky

HM SM *H51*. (Private collection)

a passing trawler would take pity on us and offer some fresh fish. As regards ablutions, there was a heads in the control room for the officers and senior rates. Unfortunately it leaked – another reason to avoid sleeping on the control room floor. For the most part we had to make do with a a trumpet-shaped fitting in the tube space discharging into the bilges. There you sat in full view of everyone – until the boat rolled and you fell off. Mind you, two weeks on patrol in an 'H' boat and you were beyond caring.

Incidentally Bernard's skipper was none other than the future ace Malcolm Wanklyn, *H31* being his first command.

The commanding officers of *H52* included:

Lt Charles Gordon Norrie Graham from 8 September 1920 to 9 August 1922.
Lt Maurice Blood served from 9 August 1922 to 7 February 1923.
Lt Harold Edward Spragge commanded from 7 February 1923 to 15 February 1924.
Lt Sidney Moffatt Raw assumed command on 15 February 1924 until 14 June 1924.
Lt John Reginald Hughes D'Aeth took command on 14 June 1924 until 14 October 1926.

With hostilities having ceased the year before she was completed, *H52* spent most of the next seven years being used for training purposes at Fort Blockhouse. During a training exercise in the late 1920s, the boat was running submerged when a surface vessel struck her conning tower, causing widespread damage to the bridge and periscope. *H52* was paid off into dockyard control on 31 March 1927.

FINAL PATROL

On 9 November 1927, the boat was sold to the film company New Era Productions, who were making a film called *The Q-Ships*. Having been disguised to look like a First World War Imperial German submarine, she was sunk by gunfire 1 nautical mile northwest of the Eddystone Lighthouse on 3 January 1928. (Another vessel called *Amy*, also used in the production, was sunk near Weymouth.)

WRECK SITE

The wreck is orientated in a west to south by east to north direction (100/280°). It lies on a firm seabed of sand, shell and gravel, in a general depth of 55m (180ft), being the lowest astronomical depth. The wreck is intact and upright, with a 45° list, but the casing is rather battered and is deteriorating rapidly; the bows are also badly damaged, probably caused by the boat careering into the seabed. However, a significant amount of salvage work has also taken place, because the two bronze propellers are missing. There was no mention in the report whether the brass conning tower was still in place, either. This is not a war grave, but tidal streams are very brisk.

In 1774 the intrepid Mr John Day, may or may not have died when his experimental submarine, the red-painted *Maria*, is said to have dived off Drake's Island in Plymouth Sound. What is certain is that submarine pioneers paid a predictably high price for their efforts. As the Haslar Obelisk testifies, the crews of British 'A' Class boats paid more than most.

A7, HM SUBMARINE

DATE OF LOSS: 16 January 1914
DEPTH: 33m
REFERENCE: 50 18'.504 N 004 17.994 W
LOCATION: 2.85 nautical miles WSW of Rame Head, Whitsands Bay

Type: 'A' Class British coastal patrol submarine of Group II **Builders**: Vickers Yard, Barrow-in-Furness for Royal Navy **Pendant No**: I-17 **Ordered**: for 1903 and 1904, programme (*A5* to *A13*) **Keel laid**: as Yard No-305 on 1 September 1903 **Launched**: on 23 January 1905 **Completed**: on 13 April 1905. (Commanding officers not nominated for individual boats, only to Depot Ship 'for command of submarine attached'.)

TECHNICAL SPECIFICATIONS

Hull: single **Surface displacement**: 180 tons **U/Dt**: 207 tons **LBD**: 32.0m × 3.81m × 3.50m **Machinery**: 1 × vertical 16-cylinder 550bhp Wolsey petrol engine **Props**: 1 bronze × 3 blade of 1.70m (5ft 7in). *S/Sp*: 11.5 knots **Op/R**: 490 nautical miles at 10 knots **Sub/R**: 20 nautical miles at 5 knots **U/Power**: 1 × 150bhp at electric motors gave 7 knots **Batteries**: Exide lead/acid/accumulators **Fuel/Cap**: 7 tons **Armament**: 2 bow 45.72cm torpedo tubes **Torpedoes**: 2 × 45.72cm (18in) **Diving**: max-op-depth 30.48m (100ft) **Complement**: 2 officers and 12 ratings

As has already been mentioned, the 'A' Class boats were were stationed at Portsmouth and Devonport. During her career, HM S/M *A7* was commanded by the following officers:

Lt Charles James Colbrooke Little, is recorded as CO in April 1905
Lt Claude Congreve Dobson – 1 May 1909 to 10 March 1910
Lt Roland Aubin Vavasor Durrell – 8 August 1910 to 24 May 1911
Lt Rowland Kerie Cecil Pope – 24 May 1911 to 8 November 1911
Lt Henry Phillip Hughes – 8 November 1911 to 15 August 1912
Lt Geoffrey Warburton – 15 August 1912 to 13 May 1913
Lt Gilbert Molesworth Welman – 15 November 1913 until loss

Gilbert Molesworth Welman had previously been attached to the depot ship *FORTH* in the China Station prior to taking command of *A7*.

FINAL PATROL

On 16 January 1914, the 3rd Flotilla of six submarines, including *A7*, left Devonport for simulated torpedo attack exercises in Whitsand Bay, led by the two depot ships *Pygmy* and *Onyx*. *A7* (Lt G.M. Welman) and *A9* were to concentrate their mock attacks on *Pygmy*. The boats took up their designated positions with *A9* at a point some 2½ miles west, northwest of Rame Head with *A7* about 2 miles distant (but on the same bearing). The first boat, *A9*, carried out two mock attacks on *Pygmy* and on completion the vessel recovered her spent dummy torpedo. *Pygmy* then sighted *A7* about 2 miles to the southeast of her original position. She appeared to be trimmed down and awaiting the gunboat to make her run. At 1110hrs *A7* was already submerged and *Pygmy* was making her first run, but just as the gunboat moved, her crew spotted the submarine on the surface prior to diving. *Pygmy* continued to the end of the designated course. No attack was made. Either *A7*'s first attack had failed miserably or else had never been made in the first place. The question was answered when the submarine failed to surface. *Pygmy* began an immediate search for the boat in the direction of Rame Head.

Account of CO of HMS *Pygmy*:

> It was obvious that *A7* had failed in her attack. The red flag and 'A' flag were dipped and a course shaped S63E for Rame Head in search for A7. The blackball was hoisted at 11.55 as a signal for *A7* to come to the surface…my attention was called by the crew to a disturbance. This personally I could not see but shaped course for it. At 12.18 a second disturbance showed itself on the surface and this I did see.

The second disturbance was about 3 miles west-by-north of Rame Head and the ship steamed towards this position. Cross bearings were taken and the position marked by a buoy. *Pygmy* sailed for the harbour and a report was made to C-in-C Forth. A small convoy of tugs and ships was dispatched from Devonport and an aircraft took part in the search. Tugs arrived with sweeping gear to hunt for the missing boat, but in the end, after five days of continuously dragging the seabed, it was HMS *Pygmy* that found her on the 22nd. The gunboat crew sighted a large patch of oil on the surface and when divers went down, they confirmed it was *A7*. The stern of the boat, and up to about 22ft forward of her hydroplanes, was found to be buried in mud and clay. She was also lying at an angle of 39° to 40°, with her bow about 30ft off the seabed. The people of Plymouth and Devonport were shocked and dismayed. It was time to carve another set of names on the Gosport memorial.

On Friday the 23rd, the same salvage vessel that had earlier raised *C14* arrived at the scene and commenced operations. The weather conditions were deplorable at the time, as it was extremely cold and visibility was very hazy. Hawsers were attached to the boat and a tug unsuccessfully tried to pull the submarine clear of the mud. Another attempt was then planned for the following day. Meanwhile, both press and public rounded on the Navy for its perceived incompetence. At a time when war with Germany seemed inevitable, such criticism was scarcely what the Royal Navy needed. Nor was it deserved. On Saturday the 24th, a big swell had developed and conditions were so bad that divers were unable to attach the big shackles to the stricken boat. All further attempts were cancelled until the 28th, when the wind and swell had moderated. A 5½in steel-hawser was then rigged up to an eye-plate at the bow section and the other end was attached to the *Exmouth*, but still the boat remained fast in the mud. To cut a long story short, salvage efforts were abandoned. When the sea calmed down, the Admiralty held a memorial service over the wreck site and wreaths were thrown onto the silent waters as a Royal Marine fired a salute.

THE MEN WHO DIED IN A7

Crowley, Joseph Francis 353697 Petty Officer
Dyer, Ernest Frederick C/ 239725 Able Seaman
Harris, Frank Charles D/ 234433 Able Seaman
Jewell, Frederick D/ 238164 Able Seaman
Morrison, Robert Herman Grant Sub-Lieutenant
Nagle, Robert William D/ 270745 Engine Room Artificer
Northam, John D/ 304857 Leading Stoker
Russell, Charles Edward James D/ 233337 Able Seaman
Venning, Richard 269321 Engine Room Artificer
Wagstaff, Lancelot D/K 13882 Leading Stoker
Welman, Gilbert Molesworth Lieutenant

WRECK SITE

The wreck was forgotten until 1999 when a local diver removed the compass binnacle from the boat, earning a deserved police caution in the process. The binnacle was confiscated. Experienced diver (and ex-serviceman) Peter Washburn discovered a large hole in the wreck that had been systematically enlarged to permit access to the interior. On 12 August 1999, the Plymouth *Evening Herald* published an article about *A7*, asking divers not to desecrate the sunken submarine, on behalf of a Plymouth lady, whose grandfather John Northam, had been lost on the boat. Following the newspaper article, local police assured that any divers caught damaging the wreck will be prosecuted.

The wreck of HM S/M *A7* has now been listed under the 1986 Protection of Military Remains Act. The safeguarding of this wreck is now rigorously enforced by civil and military authority alike. Anyone wishing to dive her must first obtain a licence from the Ministry of Defence.

The wreck site lies within a present-day submarine exercise area. It rests on a seabed of muddy clay, in a general depth of 33m, being the lowest astronomical depth. *A7* is upright and largely intact, with the quaint little conning tower, hatches and periscope still in place. However most of the interesting items can still be seen. Shoals of small pollack and bib have now adopted top of the wreck. Eleven brave men rest within her for eternity – and respect is surely due.

This exercise zone was also the scene of an earlier tragedy involving one of *A7*'s sister boats

A8, HM SUBMARINE

DATE OF LOSS: 8 June 1905
DEPTH: Salvaged
REFERENCE: Devonport
LOCATION: Plymouth Sound

Type: 'A' Class British coastal patrol submarine of Group II   *Builders*: Vickers Yard, Barrow-in-Furness for Royal Navy   *Pendant No*: I.18   *Ordered*: for 1903 and 1904, programme (*A5* to *A13*)   *Keel laid*: as Yard No-306 on 1 September 1903   *Launched*: on 23 January 1905   *Completed*: on 13 April 1905. (Commanding officers not nominated for individual boats, only to Depot Ship 'for command of submarine attached')

TECHNICAL SPECIFICATIONS

Hull: single   *Surface displacement*: 180 tons   *U/Dt*: 207 tons   *LBD*: 32.0m × 3.81m × 3.50m.   *Machinery*: 1 × vertical 550bhp 16-cylinder Wolsey petrol engine.   *Props*: 1 bronze × 3 blade of 1.70m (5ft 7in)   *S/Sp*: 11.5 knots   *Op/R*: 490 nautical miles at 10 knots   *Sub/R*: 20 nautical miles at 5 knots   *U/Power*: 1 × 150bhp at electric motors gave 7 knots   *Batteries*: Exide lead/acid/accumulators   *Fuel/Cap*: 7 tons   *Armament*: 2 × 45.72cm bow torpedo tubes   *Torpedoes*: 2 × 45.72cm (18in)   *Diving*: max-op-depth 30.48m (100ft)   *Complement*: 2 officers and 12 ratings

It was not until 1908 that Admiralty commenced officially appointing commanders to a specific submarine. During her career, HM s/m *A8* had the following commanding officers:

Lt Algernon Henry Chester Candy – record of him as a CO in June 1905
Lt Hubert Vaughan-Jones – 18 May 1908 to 15 February 1909
Lt Gilbert Esdaile Venning – 15 February 1909 to 4 January 1910
Lt Charles Lester Kerr – 8 August 1910 to 22 February 1911
Lt Herbert William Shove – 22 February 1911 to 1 December 1911
Lt Francis Thomas Hewson – 1 December 1911 no leaving date, but he went to General Service on 1 August 1913
Lt Robert Neville Stopford – 30 October 1913 to 16 May 1915
Lt Richard Ivor Pulleyne – 16 May 1915 to 10 February 1916
CB1815 (notice of disposal) issued 1 June 1916

Commander Robert Turner DSO was a lieutenant attached to *A6*. His memoirs, held in the Royal Navy Submarine Museum, conjure up the stoicism of these submarine pioneers.

> …trimming the submarine in those early years was about a day's work. We did a standing trim as it was called. Having got to the diving area off Sandown Bay [Isle of Wight] the petrol engine was stopped and the crew went to diving stations, being very confined, the crew sat alongside the valves etc. The conning tower hatch was closed and the captain stood on a moveable shelp hooked onto the conning tower ladder with his head in a sort of dome like a diver's helmet in the top of the hatch. The dome had glass

scuttles fixed round and water was admitted to the ballast tanks of the submarine until the buoyancy was so far reduced that the surface of the sea came up to the level of these scuttles. The submarine then had a few lbs of buoyancy and by going ahead with the main motors, was forced underwater by the after dive planes at an angle of five degrees down by the buoy. The whole procedure of trimming was most tricky as when buoyancy was reduced, the submarine became more and more horizontally unstable and would take up most alarming angles unless anticipated. Water could be blown from forward or aft but this was often too slow to correct the sudden desire of the boat to stand on her head or stern, so we generally had the fattest member of the crew available to dash forward or aft as necessary. In this way, water passing from one trimming tank to the next could correct the angle and release the human ballast for his next dash!

Sometimes when nearing the trim, when a little buoyancy was left, a wave bigger than the rest would plop on top of the conning tower and down the boat would sink, so water would have to be blown out of the tanks to keep her level and a new start made. We didn't realise in those days that by going ahead we could gain control of the boat. It was all rather like someone learning to swim but afraid of putting their head under.

Submarine exercises were always accompanied by a tender which flew a large red flag to indicate to shipping that submarines were nearby. Periscopes in those days were very primitive, the eye piece being in the conning tower so that the captain had to sit on a stool perched on the ladder, in a most cramped position. To train the periscope a motor was provided with the switch by the captain's right hand. As water frequently came down the conning tower when on the surface, the switch was generally damp and an electric shock was a common happening, generally upsetting the captain in the middle of his attack. We had a submarine alphabet – two lines come to mind –

'P is the periscope used by the captain

M is the perpetual mist it is wrapped in'

That pretty well describes the periscopes of those early days. On one occasion Tom Triggs mistook a large red beach umbrella for the target red flag and fired his torpedo, much to the astonishment of an old lady who was sitting peacefully under the umbrella on Sandown Bay beach !

…in the early days the two main causes of danger from accident other than the diving risk, were the petrol engine and the battery. Batteries were enclosed and ventilated by fans. Electric cells gave off hydrogen when charged or discharged. Should a concentration of gas occur, a highly volatile mixture could result in a violent explosion if sparked off…. Exhaust leaks from the engine inside the submarine gave off carbon monoxide which on several occasions gassed all the crew not on deck. As a warning on the presence of CO gas, white mice were carried as they were supposed to be more susceptible to the presence of gas than human beings. On one occasion when I and all the other ratings were laid out, our mice were full of beans! As the design of engines improved, this risk lessened. Leakage of petrol was an ever present risk, especially when refuelling with all the electric equipment around. An explosion of gas could be caused by a spark from a motor with very serious results to personnel. The danger of petrol gas on the personnel was that it caused a similar condition to drunkenness. In such a state a man would be liable t switch on electric motors and thus ignite the petrol vapour. On one occasion I entered a refuelling submarine to find Commodore Hall [Sydney Hall, Inspector of Submarines] overcome by petrol gas arguing about who was the drunkest and refusing to leave the submarine until forcibly removed…

Reproduced by kind permission of the RN Submarine Museum.

FINAL PATROL

HMS *A8* was under the command of Lieutenant Algernon Candy on the morning of 8 June 1905. Lieutenant Algernon Candy, who entered the Royal Navy in 1892, had spent more than four years in submarines at the time of the accident. The boat was in Plymouth Sound carrying out a series of exercises in company with *A7* (Lt G. Welman) and torpedo boat No.80. The skipper, Sub-Lt Hugh Murdoch, Petty Officer William Waller and Acting L/Stoker George Watt were all on the bridge of *A8*, with the submarines trotting off the breakwater. At 1030hrs *A8* was overwhelmed by an explosion. Unfortunately, at the time of the explosion, diving stations had just been called and *A8* was running at about 10 knots with her conning tower hatch open. The stern lifted out of the water and she drove under instantaneously, leaving the four men from the bridge floundering in the sea.

HM SM *A5*. (Author's collection)

Although quite close, the other two vessels were totally oblivious of the tragedy. An out-bound trawler, the *Chanticleer*, commanded by a Mr Johns, just happened to be steaming past when the explosion occurred and the crew saw what had happened. Mr Johns immediately veered round towards *A8*, stopped his vessel and quickly lowered the boat to help the survivors. As the four men struggled in the sea, Lieutenant Candy became aware that PO Waller was having difficulty in staying afloat. The Petty Officer was kitted out in typical seaman's gear, consisting of heavy sea-boots, thick sweater and oilskin and in a waterlogged state. they were dragging him under. Lieutenant Candy kept Waller afloat until the *Chanticleer's* boat arrived and picked them up. Petty Officer Waller was a Submarine Service legend. Among the very first intake of men for submarines, Waller had been cox-swain of *Holland No. 1* and was therefore the Royal Navy's first submarine coxswain. Petty Officer Waller had led a charmed life, having earlier survived the sinking of HMS *Victoria* in 1893 and the explosion on *A5* at Queenstown. The tugs *Assurance* and *Perseverance* were rushed to the scene with divers and equipment and rescue operations commenced. Divers from the King Edward Class bat-tleship *Commonwealth* and the 10,850-ton cruiser *Carnarvon* were also ordered to assist. In reality there was nothing for them to do.

All hope for the men trapped in *A8* was dashed when a huge underwater explosion racked the boat. Observers watched in horror as the explosion sent a huge plume of water 10ft into the air, flinging sundry wreckage in all directions. This was followed very quickly by a smaller and quieter detonation, surely the *coup de grâce*.

The battered *A8* was brought to the surface in four days and at 1040hrs on 12 June, the tugs *Assurance*, *Trusty* and *Industrious* began a 2-hour tow back to Devonport Dockyard, with *Assurance* at the head and the others on each flank. A hole was made in the hull by removing a metal plate and one by one the bodies were brought out. The same metal plate was used later to make a cross for the funeral procession.

On Tuesday the 20th, an inquiry was held on board the battleship *Empress of India* and the four survivors attended. Captain Bacon, who had examined the wreck in minute detail, was called as a witness. Reginald Bacon described how a rivet was missing from the foremost petrol tank, resulting in a hole large enough to allow a ton of water to enter the submarine in 10 minutes. However, as Bacon poined out, it was impossible to prove whether or not this rivet had been missing when the accident occurred. Witnesses added that *A8* was going down by the bow as she was steaming along the surface. Salvagers confirmed she had settled on the bottom with between 20 to 30 tons of water inside. This was the strongest evidence that the boat had suffered a major leak. Next it was time to analyse the explosion. Volatile petrol fumes were ruled out in favour of a chemical reaction caused by salt water lapping over the batteries – quite a common problem in early submarines. There was supporting forensic evidence for this scenario. Some of the bodies bore evidence of burns inflicted before death. Most of the crew must have still been alive at the time of the explosions but had been rendered unconsciousness for some considerable time before they died. The verdict was not in doubt:

> The court finds that A8 was lost outside Plymouth Breakwater about 1030 on 8 June through founding from water getting into the conning tower.

Many thousands of people thronged the 2-mile funeral route from the Dockyard chapel to Plymouth and Devonport cemetery, with the half-mile-long funeral cortege taking 1½ hours to reach their final resting place. The dead submariners were transported on gun carriages, drawn by naval ratings, while various army regiments and the crews from all ships moored in Plymouth Sound lined the procession route. A military band, sombrely playing Chopin's Funeral March, accompanied the procession. The firing party discharged three volleys over the gravesite at 1630hrs after the final blessing had been said, and four buglers sounded the Last Post. King Edward VII even sent a personal message to all relatives. At the family's request, Sub-Lieutenant Fletcher was interred near his family home at Mallingford, Norwich, while Leading Seaman John Kerswell was buried at Crediton. ERA Vickers lies in Southsea cemetery.

The submarine *A8* was completely overhauled and put back into service and in fact was ready in time for the naval manoeuvres in 1906. She remained in service until the war ended, then on 8 October 1920 she was sold to the firm of Philip of Dartmouth, for scrap. As for Lieutenant Candy, he remained in submarines until 1911, spent a short time in general service, before returning to submarines again from 1913 until 1916. Candy retired from the Navy in 1927, but was recalled at the outbreak of the First World War. He died in April 1959 at the age of eighty-one, having reached the rank of Rear Admiral.

THE CREWMEN WHO DIED IN A8

Ayloff, William George, Petty Officer
Bauckland, William George, Engine Room Artificer
Beedham, George, Engine Room Artificer
Birch, Stephen, Able Seaman
Bunn Crew, Arthur, Petty Officer
Cusick ?, Leading Stoker
Fletcher, E.T., Sub-Lieutenant
Green, Edmond, Stoker
Kerswell, J., Leading Seaman
McKnight, John, Able Seaman
Reeves, T.G., Stoker
Rylands, Arthur, Able Seaman
Simpson, W., James Leading Seaman
Thomas, J., Leading Seaman
Vickers, F., Engine Room Artificer

UB 118, SM IMPERIAL U-BOAT

DATE OF LOSS: 21 November 1920
DEPTH: 60m
REFERENCE: 50 09'.905 N 04 43'.145 W
LOCATION: 4 miles S by E of Dodman Point

Type: UBIII coastal torpedo attack boat **Builders**: AG Weser, Bremen for Kaiserliche Deutsche Marine **Ordered**: on 8 February 1917, within the batch of UB 118–UB 132 **Keel laid**: as Yard No-291 on 4 April 1917 **Launched**: on 13 December 1917 **Commissioned**: by Kapitänleutnant Hermann Arthur Krauß on 22 January 1918

TECHNICAL SPECIFICATIONS

Hull: double **Surface displacement**: 512 tons **U/Dt**: 643 tons **LBDH**: 55.85m × 5.79m × 3.7m × 8.25m **Machinery**: 2 × 550ps Daimler diesels **Props**: 2 bronze **S/Sp**: 13.9 knots **Op/R**: 7,280 nautical miles at 6 knots **Sub/R**: 55 nautical miles at 4 knots **U/Power**: 2 × 394ps electric motors gave 7.5 knots **Batteries**: lead/acid/accumulators **Fuel/Cap**: 35 + 36 tons **Armament**: 4 bow and 1 stern 50.04cm torpedo tubes **Torpedoes**: 10 × 50.04cm (19.7in) **Guns**: 1 × 105mm (4.13in) forward deck gun **Ammo**: 160 rounds of 105mm **Mines**: none **Diving**: max-op-depth 50m (164ft) and 30 sec crash dive **Complement**: 3 officers and 31 ratings

UB 118 was formally assigned to the German-based III.U-Bootflottille at Wilhelmshaven on 26 March 1918 with Kplt. Hermann Arthur Krauß the boat's commander from 22 January 1918. Krauß made the following five patrols:

On 1 April 1918, *UB 118* left Heligoland for an uneventful patrol off the English east coast and returned on the 14th.

Departing Kiel on 5 May 1918, *UB 118* made a sortie in St George's Channel, travelling via the Isles of Orkney and the west coast of Ireland. Krauß captured the old 582-ton Spanish steam coaster *Yturri Bide* (1877 – Compania Naviera Iturri) northeast of Tuskar Rock on 16 May; the crew were forced to abandon ship and she was sunk by gunfire; she was transporting pitch from Maryport to Aviles in Spain.

UB 118 arrived back in Germany on 28 May 1918.

(3) Having left Heligoland on 20 June, *UB 118* crossed the North Sea and travelled around the Isles of Sheland to reach the operational area in the English Channel. On 7 July, Arthur Krauß made a torpedo attack on a 4,000-ton British ship in a convoy off the Irish south coast, but the torpedo was a dud; there was also no official confirmation of any ship sinking.

UB 118 returned to Germany on 16 July, having sunk no ships.

(4) On 14 August 1918, *UB 118* left Heligoland and sailed to St George's Channel for operations. During the voyage Krauß sank three British steamships: in the morning of 27 August, the 3,544-ton

Deck gun of *UB 131*, similar to *UB 118*, on display outside the Newhaven Museum. (Author's collection)

The 6,833-ton liner *Mesaba* at anchor. (Author's collection)

defensively armed *Ant Cassar* (1902 – Cassar Ltd, London/Malta) was torpedoed without warning in the Irish Sea while on passage from Glasgow for Milford Haven with coal. Twenty crewmen, including the master, were drowned when the 6,833-ton *MESABA* (1897 – Atlantic Transport Co. Ltd, Liverpool), a defensively armed steamship, was torpedoed and sunk without warning in St George's Channel on 1 September; the ship was in ballast and travelling in convoy from Liverpool to Philadelphia; the convoy being escorted by two USN destroyers.

SOME OF THE MEN WHO DIED

Bush, James Albert, 17yrs, Sculleryman
Chaloner, Edgar Stanley, 19yrs, Able Seaman
Clarke, Owen Percy, 52yrs, Master
Clifton, Robert Joseph, 32yrs, Fireman
Foster, Frank 16yrs, Assistant Steward
Glover, William Stanmore, 39yrs, Chief Officer
Hampton, Adam Stanley, 26yrs, Junior 4th Engineer Officer
Kennedy, John, 41yrs, Greaser
Kerr, William Edward, 25yrs, Fireman
Land, G.W., Carpenter's Mate
MacClure, John, 48yrs, Chief Steward
McNeil, H.Y., 19yrs, Assistant Steward
Mills, Leonard Charles, 27yrs, Purser
Rehill, William George, 54yrs, Able Seaman
Riding, Thomas, 37yrs, Fireman
Stewart, Donald, 64yrs, Trimmer
Tineich, Dominik, 35yrs, Fireman
Wilson, Alexander, 39yrs, Donkeyman
Francis, James, Leading Seaman RNR

The *City Of Glasgow* (1906 – Ellerman Lines Ltd, Glasgow) was a 6,545-ton passenger/cargo ship that had been taken over by the Government as a British Expeditionary Force troopship in 1914. She was armed for defence and travelling in the same convoy as the SS *Meseba*, but was voyaging from Manchester to Montreal in ballast, when she too was torpedoed and sunk without warning on 1 September, 21 miles from Tuskar Rock; twelve men were lost.

SOME OF THE MEN WHO DIED

Hoag, Alexander Mathieson 59yrs, Troop Baker
McCurdie, Archibald 26yrs, 3rd Engineer Officer
Thomson, John Young 25yrs, 4th Engineer
Ikramullah Zahirulla, Trimmer
Imanullah Tausanullah, Greaser

Jamalullah Amanullah, Fireman
Kamalmyan Nur Miyan, Greaser
Mirza NazirI, Fireman
Shafaatullah Yusufullah, Fireman
Amjadullah Kalimullah, Greaser
Azim Bakhsh Karim Bakhsh, Pantiymn 2nd Class

Being low on fuel, *UB 118* was forced to end its patrol, travelling back to Germany via the Irish Sea and North Channel. On 4 September a British submarine made a surprise torpedo attack on *UB 118*. The fish, which struck *UB 118*'s portside, turned out to be a dud. *UB 118* arrived back in Germany on 10 September.

(5) On her last war patrol, *UB 118* sailed from Heligoland on 27 October 1918 in support of the German High Seas Fleet in the North Sea, but Krauß attacked no vessels.

On 28 October *UB 118* was in a collision with *UB 98* and was left damaged; she was then transferred to Wilhelmshaven for repairs, but by the time the war ended, the damage had never been completed. *UB 118*, surrendered to the French on 20 November 1918 and was sent to Harwich under Royal Navy escort. On 19 February 1919, the U-boat was moored up alongside other German submarines in the harbour at Harwich; later she was transferred to Devonport docks.

FINAL PATROL

On 21 November 1920, *UB 118* was towed from Devonport to a breakers yard at Falmouth, but it was alleged that valves in the fore-ends failed to work, which made her impossible to handle in the choppy seas. Eventually the sloop HMS *Kennet* sank her with gunfire, after she became a danger to navigation.

CWGC

WRECK SITE

The wreck is orientated in a northeast to southwest direction and lies on a seabed of mud, sand, gravel and broken shells, in a general depth of 60m (197ft), being the lowest astronomical depth. She is reported as being intact, but partially salvaged, with considerable deterioration and damage to the outer casing, especially the upper sections. Shoals of fish and numerous crustaceans have now also adopted the wreck.

NARWHAL, HM SUBMARINE

DATE OF LOSS: 3 August 1983
DEPTH: 78m
REFERENCE: 50 00'.781 N 004 41'.360 W
LOCATION: 15 miles S of Falmouth

Type: Second Porpoise Class British Fleet submarine   *Builders*: Vickers-Armstrong, Barrow-in-Furness for Royal Navy   *Keel laid*: as Yard No.1031   *Launched*: on 25 October 1957   *Commissioned*: in 1959

TECHNICAL SPECIFICATIONS

Hull: partly welded construction   *Surface displacement*: 2,030 tons   *U/Dt*: 2,410 tons   *LBD*: 89.99m-length (295ft-3in) × 8.07m-beam (26ft-6in) × 5.48m-draught (18ft).   *Machinery*: 2 × Admiralty Standard Range 116VMS (16-cylinder) diesels, delivering 3,300hp (2745kW)   *Props*: 2 bronze   *S/Sp*: 12 knots   *Op/R*: 10,352 nautical miles at 10 knots   *Sub/R*: 106 nautical miles at 4 knots   *U/Power*: 2 × electric motors delivering 5,000hp (4475kW) gave 17 knots   *Batteries*: 2 × huge main batteries   *Fuel/Cap*: 44 tons   *Armament*: 6 × 53.34cm (21in) bow torpedo tubes   **Torpedoes**: 20 × Mk 24.   **Mines**: (sometimes) 12 × Mk. II magnetic–ground-mine type with 453.60 kilo (1,000 pound) charge. These were half the length of a torpedo and were laid through the torpedo tubes   **Diving**: max–diving depth 339.85m (1,115ft)   **Complement**: 69

To help with the long operation range, the boats were designed with maximum snort facilities (long *schnorchels*), which allowed them to operate in rough sea anywhere in the world. They were also able to remain submerged for several days without snorting, due to the oxygen replenishment and carbon dioxide and hydrogen eliminators. Using the snorting equipment also allowed the boats to remain submerged for as long as six weeks at a time. Another innovation was the apparatus fitted to distil freshwater from seawater for drinking purposes and the stowage capacity for large quantities of provisions and stores that allowed the submarine to stay operational at sea for months.

Narwhal was one of three built by Vickers-Armstrong in 1956 and 1957; the three boats in 'first-of-class', *Porpoise*, *Rorqual* and *Narwhal*, were designed over a few years in the early 1950s.

Narwhal travelled extensively all over the world during her fifteen years service. In March 1963 she became famous for remaining beneath the Arctic ice cap for a whole month. Then during the first four months of 1969, *Narwhal* circumnavigated the entire coast of South America, taking part in exercises with the Peruvian, Argentinean and Chilean navies. In April 1974, her starboard external tanks were damaged in an incident and she was taken out of service, but remained in reserve until 1980. The once proud *Narwhal* was then used in a submarine salvage exercise and sunk deliberately in Weymouth Bay, however she was raised again later that year. Three years later, on 3 August 1983, the boat was sunk as a sonar training target, some 15 miles south of Falmouth.

WRECK SITE

The wreck is orientated in a northwest to southeast direction and lies on a firm seabed of sand and shingle, in a general depth of 78m (256ft), being the lowest astronomical depth. It is upright and intact, with very little obvious damage, but the whole wreck is covered in an ASDIC-baffling rubbery coating.

U 927, KRIEGSMARINE U-BOAT

DATE OF LOSS: 24 February 1945
DEPTH: 80m
REFERENCE: 49° 54'N 04° 45'W (approximate)
LOCATION: 18 nautical miles SE of The Lizard (estimate distance)

Type: VIIC ocean-going attack boat   **Builders**: Neptun Schiffswerft und Maschinenfabrik AG, Rostock for Kriegsmarine   **Ordered**: on 25 August 1941, within the batch of *U 925–U 928*   **Keel laid**: as Yard No.514 on 1 December 1942   **Launched**: on 3 May 1944   **Commissioned**: by Oblt. z.S. Jürgen Ebert on 27 June 1944   **Feldpost No**: M 21755   **Badge**: Cockerel in a shield

TECHNICAL SPECIFICATIONS

See page 342.

Jürgen Ebert was born on 25 September 1918 at Osterburg, Altmark and commenced his naval career in 1937. Ebert was seconded to the Luftwaffe between September 1939 and June 1943 before undertaking U-boat training. He was promoted to Kapitänleutnant on 1 October 1945.

U 927 was assigned to 4.U-Flottille at Stettin as *Ausbildungsboot* from the commissioning until 31 January 1945 with Oblt.z.S. Ebert the CO from 27 June 1944.

On 11 January 1945, *U 927* left Kiel with Oblt. Jürgen Ebert and sailed to Horten (59° 24.45'N 10° 29 08'E) near Oslo, Norway, where she arrived on the 15th.

U 927 left Horten with on 23 January 1945 and arrived at Kristiansand in southern Norway (58° 08.41'N 7° 59.54'E), on the following day of the 24th.

On 1 February 1945 both *U 927* and her CO formally transferred to 11.U-Flottille at Bergen in southwest Norway for frontline service.

Above: U 927 emblem.

Left: Kplt Jürgen Ebert of *U 927*.
(Author's collection)

FINAL PATROL

(3) On the last day of January 1945, *U 927* sailed from Kristiansand for operations in the English Channel. The boat transmitted a *Passiermeldung* on 8 February from *AM3426*. On 16 February the boat was ordered to a patrol zone between Land's End and Portland Bill. BdU predicted she would arrive in position on or about 20 February and return to base during the third week of March. She failed to return and was presumed lost with effect from 25 March. Now we must examine British records to find a potential cause of destruction.

Mining must always remain a possibility. *U 927* may have blundered into the minefields guarding Portland and therefore be one of the unidentified boats found by Innes McCartney. The authors could not find any escort group encounter along the U-boat's projected track. RAF records may provide a solution. Southeast of the Lizard on 24 February, 179 Squadron Warwick 'K' picked up a suspicious radar trace. It was evening but the Leigh-Light illuminated 4ft of snort mast in its glare. Flight-Lieutenant Anthony Brownhill banked away, turned then made his attack. Brownhill dropped six depth charges in position 49° 45'N 04° 45'W from an altitude of 70ft, straddling the target. Oil and wreckage were observed. Flight-Lieutenant Brownhill was awarded the DFC for the sinking, but the 'kill' was later allocated a 'B' grading because of the lack of supporting evidence. Incidentally the Warwick was designed to replace the Wellington. If indeed the attack had been successful, this was the Warwick's only kill. The area where Lt Brownhill made his attack has since been surveyed, but no U-boat wreck has yet been found. *U 927* remains elusively '*verschollen*'.

NARA T-1022 Roll 4066 PG30362, Roll 3900, PG 31752 U-Boot-Ehrenmal Möltenort

THE MEN WHO PERISHED WITH U 927

Andrag, Siegfried Ob.Mt. (7-3-1922)
Arnold, Georg Gfr. (14-3-1925)
Arnold, Hans Gfr. (3-8-1925)
Behrens, Walter Ob.Mt. (25-5-1921)
Bink, Kurt Maat. (17-4-1921)
Bleick, Hans Maat. (14-12-1921)
Brender, Leonhard Ob.Gfr. (10-10-1923)
Brucker, Friedrich-August Ltz.S. (28-2-1924)

Claude, Josef Gfr. (3-12-1921)
Dolensky, Alois Ob.Gfr. (22-6-1925)
Doss, Dietmar Ob.Gfr. (4-7-1925)
Dunkelmann, Willi Ob.Gfr. (23-8-1925)
Ebert, Jürgen Kplt. (25-9-1916)
Fischer, Gustav Maat. (1-10-1921)
Fischer, Hermann Ob.Gfr. (23-4-1925)
Fischer, Karl Ob.Gfr. (13-7-1921)

Friedrich, Hans Ob.Gfr. (3-12-1922)
Fuchs, Max Ob.Gfr. (16-11-1925)
Gabrisch, Leo Maat. (9-11-1920)
Halm, Werner Ob.Masch. (18-4-1914)
Heimann, Karl Gfr. (7-5-1924)
Herrig, Gerhard Gfr. (17-12-1926)
Hofen, Hans von Ob.Gfr. (1-11-1924)
Hoffknecht, Adale Ob.Gfr. (29-10-1925)
Holziegel, Rolf Ob.Gfr. (16-6-1923)
Hotze, Harry Gfr. (3-10-1925)
Klemm, Otto Ob.Mt. (26-7.1920)
Krause, Harry Maat. (16-06-1921)
Kreimeier, Wilhelm Maat. (31-5-1923)
Marten, Heinz Ob.Gfr. (4-12-1922)
Meyer, Helmut ObGfr. (25-4-1925)
Mucha, Manfred Ob.Mt. (16-7-1919)

Pobanz, Günter Ob.Gfr. (6-1-1924)
Przewalla, Günter Mtr. (19-4-1921)
Reifenberg, H Ob.Masch. (3-4-1918)
Rölleke, Fritz Ostrm. (18-10-1915)
Salg, Otto Maat. (16-3-1922)
Schmücking, Hans Gfr. (6-1-1925)
Sodann, Werner Ob.Gfr. (12-10-1924)
Sparwel, Walter Ob.Gfr. (1-3-1925)
Tiersch, Dietrich Ltz-S. (21-7-1924)
Uhlig, Horst Maat. (21-9-1921)
Wachsmuth, Rudi Gfr. (9-2-1925)
Waschhofer, Karl Gfr. (18-9-1925)
Wikelski, Hans Ob.Gfr. (28-12-1923)
Woelke, Gerhard Oblt-Ing (22-7-1921)
Wörner, Willi H.Gfr. (11-9-1923)

WRECK SITE

To date (September 2007), the position of the wreck remains unknown.

UC 66, SM IMPERIAL U-BOAT

DATE OF LOSS: 12 June 1917
DEPTH: 69m approximate
REFERENCE: 49° 56'N 05° 10'W
LOCATION: approximately 2 nautical miles SSE from the Lizard

Type: UCII coastal mine-laying boat   *Builders*: Blohm & Voss, Hamburg for Kaiserliche Deutsche Marine *Ordered*: on 12 January 1916, within the batch of *UC 65–UC 73*   **Keel laid**: as Yard No.282   *Launched*: on 15 July 1916   *Delivered*: on 14 November 1916   *Commissioned*: by Oberleutnant zur See Herbert Pustkuchen on 18 November 1916

TECHNICAL SPECIFICATIONS

Hull: double   *Surface displacement*: 427 tons   *U/Dt*: 508 tons   *LBDH*: 50.35m × 5.22m × 3.68m × 7.46m   *Machinery*: 2 × 250ps MAN diesels   *Props*: 2 bronze   *S/Sp*: 12 knots   *Op/R*: 10,420 nautical miles at 7 knots   *Sub/R*: 52 nautical miles at 4 knots   *U/Power*: 2 × 230ps electric motors gave 7.4 knots   *Batteries*: AFA lead/acid/accumulators   *Fuel/Cap*: 40 + 15 tons   *Armament*: 2-external 50.04cm torpedo tubes at the bow, one either side of the mine chutes and 1 stern internal tube   *Torpedoes*: 7 × 50.04cm (19.7in) maximum   *Guns*: 1 × 88mm (3.46in) forward deck gun.   *Ammo*: 133 rounds of 88mm   *Mine tubes*: 6   *Mines*: 18 × UC200.   *Diving*: max-op-depth 50m (164ft) and 33 sec to crash-dive   *Complement*: 3 officers and 23 ratings

Torpedo load as designed: (4) a torpedo in each tube plus a reload for the stern tube. Storing an additional torpedo in pieces internally for the stern tube later augmented this, although this was optional. Two extra torpedoes (total) for the external bow tubes could be carried as well – these were lashed to the deck. So up to seven total torpedoes carried, although not all boats sailed with that many.

UC 66 was formally assigned to the Flandern U-Flottille on 3 February 1917 with Oblt.z.S. Pustkuchen the CO from 14 November 1916.

On 1 February 1917, *UC 66* sailed from Hamburg for the transfer to Flanders, where she arrived on 3 February.

The boat departed Zeebrugge on 10 February 1917 and sailed for operations along the French coast of the Channel, as far as the Bay of Biscay. Pustkuchen attacked three vessels on 11 February:

the 1,400-ton Greek steamer *Vasilissa Olga* (1869 – Stakos & Nanopoulos, Volos), which was in transit with coal from Port Talbot to Dunkerque, was torpedoed and sunk without warning off Beachy Head. The *ADA* (1872), a 187-ton British sailing boat, was captured and sunk by gunfire off Anvil Point, while en-route from London to Landermeau, Brittany with manure. A torpedo fired without warning damaged the 4,300-ton defensively armed steamship *Woodfield* (1917 – Woodfield S.S. Co. Ltd, London), 3 miles from Royal Sovereign light vessel; she was in ballast travelling from North Shields to Newport, Monmouth; the ship was beached east of Newhaven pier and re-floated later.

Pustkuchen sank two ships on 12 February: without any warning, the defensively armed 11,948-ton steamer *AFRIC* (1899 – Oceanic Steam Navigation Co. Ltd, Liverpool) was torpedoed, 12 miles from the Eddystone. The liner was carrying a crew of 167 and a general cargo, on passage from Liverpool and Devonport for Sydney, Australia; five people were killed in the explosion and seventeen others drowned, but 145 people survived, including the master, Captain V.W. Hickson.

FOUR OF THE MEN WHO DIED

Lawes, William Cooban, 24yrs, Assistant Cook
Miller, Edison Gordon, 7th Engineer
Ryan, Alfred William, 40yrs, 2nd Engineer
Stanley, John, 45yrs, Greaser

Later that day, the 1,409-ton steamer *Lucent* (1879 – Westoll Line, Sunderland), commanded by Captain R.M. Rendall, was captured and sunk by gunfire 20 miles from the Lizard, while transporting coal from Cardiff to St Malo.

On 15 February Pustkuchen captured and destroyed three Gironde-based fishing cutters in the Bay of Biscay: the 31-ton *Desire Louise*, the 33-ton *Alma Jeanne* and the 27-ton *ARGOS*.

Ninety miles off Ushant, on 17 February, the *Driebergen* (1910 – N.V. Stoomv. Mij. Hollandia, Rotterdam), a Dutch steamer of 1,884 tons, was transporting coal from Port Talbot to Huelva, Spain, when Pustkuchen captured and scuttled it with explosives. The following day, two more Dutch steamers were sent to the bottom: the 2,313-ton *Ootmarsum* (1900 – N.V. Stoomv. Mij. Oostzee, Amsterdam), voyaging from Penarth to Las Palmas was also captured and scuttled with explosives and the 1,608-ton *Trompenberg* (1906 – N.V. Stoomboot Mij. 'Hillegersberg', Amsterdam), on the same voyage, was torpedoed and sunk, 65 miles from Quessant.

UC 66 then began her journey home, but about 30 nautical miles south from Wolf Rock Pustkuchen encountered a 'tanker' that stopped after a short chase; the crew then seemed to have abandoned ship in two boats. However, Pustkuchen became suspicious and took the boat down as a precaution. He began manouvring *UC 66* for an attack on the 'tanker' and came to the surface at conning tower level. Suddenly, a grenade hit the U-boat and the tanker tried, unsuccessfully, to ram the boat. *UC 66* crash-dived and a depth charge followed her down, but it missed.

The 'tanker' was in fact the 1,191-ton Q-ship HMS *Penshurst*, which operated as Q7 and *Manford*, which had previously sunk *UB 19* and *UB 37*.

On the 21st, three British fishing smacks were captured and destroyed off the Eddystone: the 35-ton *Monarch* (1903) by explosives, the 25-ton *Energy* (1915) by gunfire and the *K.L.M.* (1914) also sunk by gunfire. On 22 February, the 3,598-ton *Ambon* (1901), another Dutch steamship owned by N.V. Stoomv. Mij. 'Nederland', Amsterdam, was damaged by a torpedo off the Isles of Scilly; she was transporting loden from Amsterdam to Java, but was towed safely into Plymouth.

UC 66 returned to her Flanders base on 23 February.

(3) On 10 March 1917, *UC 66* departed Zeebrugge and laid mines off the south coast of Ireland. This was another successful patrol for Pustkuchen, with five vessels sunk on 12 March: second engineer Robert James Stote (51yrs) was lost, presumed drowned when the 1,394-ton SS *Glynymel* (1890 – Harris Bros & Co., Swansea) was captured, then torpedoed and sunk, 23 miles off St Catherine's Point, while in ballast and en-route from Le Havre and Rouen to Swansea. At 0330hrs and without warning, *UC 66* fired a shell which exploded on the bridge and wounded the first mate, followed by a second shell, which passed through the charthouse. By that time, Captain Nicolas had reached the bridge and ordered the engine stopped and the crew to abandon ship. *UC 66* continued the gunfire, even as the boats were being lowered, and the second engineer was

killed during that time. The fourteen survivors rowed clear of the ship while the U-boat kept up a continuous bombardment. At 0415hrs the master heard a loud thud and suspected the ship had been torpedoed, although he did not witness it. The 1,226-ton SS *Farraline* (1903 – London & Edinburgh Shipping Co., Leith) picked up the survivors at 0530hrs and landed them at Weymouth.

The 1,849-ton Norwegian SS *Einar Jarl* (1915 – Det Nordenfjeldske Dampskibsselskab, Trondheim) was captured and scuttled with explosives 10 miles from Start Point; she was voyaging in ballast from London for Fowey and North America. The fishing cutter *Reindeer*, of 52 tons, was captured and sunk by gunfire 15 miles from Berry Head. The 36-ton fishing cutter *Forget Me Not* also received the same treatment, 12 miles off Portland Bill. The 3,203-ton steamship *Memnon* (1906 – Elder Line Ltd, Liverpool), was inbound from Dakar, Senegal on the west coast of Africa to Hull with a general cargo when Pustkuchen torpedoed her without warning; she sank with the loss of six men.

THE MEN WHO DIED

Hughes, William James, 35yrs, Donkeyman
Irwin, John, 56yrs, 4th Engineer Officer
Peter, Tom, Trimmer
Thomas, Alfred William, 29yrs, 2nd Engineer
Washington, George, 29yrs, Fireman
Williams, Thomas, 31yrs, Fireman

Next morning, the 34-ton British fishing cutter *Try* was 10 miles south of Wolf Rock, when she was captured and sunk by gunfire. Early in the morning of 14 March, *UC 66* laid six mines off Daunt lightship and six more off the Old Head of Kinsale; then soon after midnight on the 15th, the remaining mines were placed off Galley Head. (Galley Head was regularly patrolled by mine-seweeping sloops of the 10th Flotilla. These vessels, which came under the aegis of Vice Admiral (Queenstown), had been fitted with the 'Skipjack pattern bow defence'. This equipment was to prove their undoing.)

At 0930hrs on the 17th, the 1,250-ton Arabis Class sloop HMS *Mignonette* (Lt Arthur Evans) detonated one of the mines laid on the 15th. The explosion caused the ship to break in two but she did not sink immediately. At the time of the explosion, *Mignonette* was sweeping in company with HMS *Rosemary* (Lt Cdr Mayne). The bulkheads were not shored up causing the vessel to sink the following morning. It was later established that the offending mine had been caught between the Skipjack defence and the bows of the ship. At the time of her loss HMS *Mignonette* carried a crew of ninety-three.

THE MEN WHO DIED IN THE EXPLOSION

Allan, Ernest, ERA 4th Class RN
Bruce, Richard Wilson, ERA RNR
Carriage, Henry, Stoker 1st Class RN
Evans, Walter, Signalman RN
Gosnell, Charles Albert, Ordinary Seaman RN
Hodson, Fred, Stoker 1st Class RN
Hopper, George Hobday, Leading Stoker RN
Kemp, Herbert William, Stoker 1st Class RN
Law, James Henry, Ordinary Seaman RN
Lillys, Cecil Benjamin, Leading Stoker RN
Millum, Charles Thomas, Stoker 2nd Class RN
Perham, George, Stoker 1st Class RN
Skewis, Edwin Henry, Boy Telegraphist RN

On 18 March, a second Arabis Class sloop, HMS *Alyssum* (built by Earle's Shipbuilding Co. Ltd, Hull in 1915), also detonated a mine and sank in the same area; she was under the command of Admiral Sir Lewis Bayly and serving as a convoy escort vessel based at Queenstown, however no one was killed. Once again the Skipjack equipment had trapped the mine against the bows. Following this second minesweeper sinking, the Skipjack equipment was removed from all British minesweepers.

On 17 March, the 5,252-ton US freighter SS *City Of Memphis* (1902 – Ocean Steamship Co. of Savannah, Savannah) was voyaging from Cardiff to New York in ballast when she was captured, shelled and sunk 33 miles off Fastnet; the loss of personnel is unknown, but she also carried a crew of ninety-three.

Pustkuchen captured the 261-ton wooden French sailing vessel, *Armoricain* (1911 – Louis Girard) off Dodman Point on 19 March and sunk her with explosive scuttling charges.

Just after midnight on 21 March, the 12,002-ton liner HMHS *Asturias* (1908 – Royal Mail Steam Packet Company, Belfast), which was serving as a hospital ship and voyaging from Avonmouth to Southampton, was attacked with torpedoes and damaged off Start Point. The ship grounded at the entrance to Salcombe harbour, was re-floated and towed to Plymouth where she arrived on 20 April. However, although the ship did not sink, many men and women of the Mercantile Marine were killed in the explosions or died of their injuries later:

THOSE WHO DIED

Anderson, John Aitken, 6th Engineer
Andrews, Arthur Charles, Waiter
Crook, William Henry, Fireman
Cross, Stanley Henry, Greaser
Doncom, Edward Thomas Baden, OA
Earl, James William, Trimmer
Flux, Henry Charles, Fireman
Glasspool, Edwin Alexander, Assistant Baker
Gosney, Thomas Henry, Trimmer
Hall, Charles Henry, Fireman
Harvey, George Bevis, Engineroom/StrKpr
Humby, Arthur Edward, Fireman
Hunr, Reginald Ernest, 1st Assistant Pantryman
Jones. George Robert, Scullion
Kimber, Herbert George, 1st Assistant Cook
Kneller, Albert Isaac, Mate of Hold
Lawes, Randolph Blair, Waiter

Manger, Charles Robert Prioux, Trimmer
Orman, Victor Charles Mafeking, DrsBoy
Paxton, George Edward, 6th Engineer
Pitfield, J. W., 5th Engineer
Reeves, Ernest Hemy, Butcher's Mate
Robinson, John Bertram Ernest, Assistant Laundryman
Seaborn, Walter William George, Fireman
Shaw, W.D., Waiter
Shore, Harry Edwin Gerald, Seaman
Stone, Harold Thomas, Steward
Stone, Robert, Fireman
Tillyer, James John, Able Seaman
Trenberry, Bridget, Stewardess
Tubb, Percy Newton, Fireman
West, Henry Seymour, 5th Engineer
White, John Albert, 3rd Assistant Cook

While transporting coal from the Tyne to La Rochelle on the 20th, the 1,964-ton defensively armed steamer *Hazelpark* (1916 – Denholme Line Steamers Ltd, Greenock) was torpedoed and sunk without warning 3.5 miles southeast of Start Point. The 57-ton fishing cutter *Advance* was 25 miles off Portland Bill when Pustkuchen sunk her with gunfire on 21 March 1917.

Pustkuchen's last victim during the patrol was the 569-ton wooden-hulled Norwegian schooner *Efeu* (1907 – A/S Efeu, Skien) off Dungeness; she was in ballast on 22 March and en-route from Falmouth to Porsgrund when she was sunk by gunfire.

UC 66 returned to Zeebrugge on 23 March.

(4) Leaving Flanders on 15 April 1917, *UC 66* sailed to the Irish Sea and North Channel for operations; she then proceeded around the west coast of Ireland. During the outward journey on 17 April, Pustkuchen torpedoed and damaged the SS *Clan Sutherland* (1896 – Cayzer, Irvine & Co., Glasgow) off Start Point; she was travelling from Cochin in southwest India to London with a general cargo. The vessel was beached at Dartmouth, but re-floated; unfortunately, however, at least thirteen foreign merchant crewman died in the incident.

SOME OF THOSE WHO DIED

Abdul Aziz Kalimuddin, Lascar
Abdulaziz Kalimuddin, Lascar
Asar Ali Musawwir Ali, Fireman
Azhaullah Nazar Muha Mmad, oilman
Chulam Rasul Pir Bakhsh, General Servant

Faizullah Muha Nnad Yasin, Cassaub
Hahinhullaalla Shakur Ahmad, Trimmer
Idrisullah Qasimullah, Fireman
Miyan Muha Mmad Qasiruddini, Trimmer
Mobassir Ali Nazw Myan, Fireman
Saiyedaali Muhammad Kalim, 1st Tindal
Usman K. Sakhi, Bhandary
Wahabullah Muhammad Mansur, 2nd Tindal

The British 1,279-ton steel barque *Arethusa* (1891 – Ship Arethusa Co Ltd, Liverpool) was captured off Eagle Island light and sunk by explosive scuttling charges on 23 April 1917. She was under the command of Captain S.W. Burnley and delivering pitch-pine from Gulfport, on the Mississippi Sound, to the Clyde. Also on the 23rd, the RN trawler *Rose II* (ex-*Rose*, GY.321 (1907)) detonated a mine in Belfast Lough and sank, while under the command of Captain T. Allison; she had been requisitioned in December 1914 and converted to Admiralty Minesweeper No.592.

THE FOUR MEN WHO DIED

Adam, Samuel Stepney, Trimmer RNR
Wright, James, Tempory Skipper RNR
McAteer, James Kennedy, Deckhand RNR
Steven, William, Leading Seaman RNR

The 4,470-ton defensively armed SS *Quantock* (1910 – Tatem Steam Navigation Co. Ltd, Cardiff) was incoming from St Johns, New Brunswick with timber when a torpedo fired without warning, damaged it off Mizzen Head; two crewmen were killed in the explosion: fireman and trimmer James Boyle and fireman Sam Williams; the steamer was taken in tow and reached port.

On 1 May 1917, three vessels were attacked and sunk by *UC 66*: while transporting coal from the Clyde to Naples, the defensively armed SS *Bagdale* (1904 – Thomas Smailes & Son's Steamship Co. Ltd, Whitby) of 3,045 tons, was torpedoed and sunk without warning, 13 miles from Creach Point, Ushant and twenty-three hands were lost.

SOME OF THE MEN WHO DIED

Abdal Ibrahim, Fireman and Trimmer
Adams, Alfred Thomas, 22yrs, Boatswain (Bosun)
Bakhshullah, Fireman and Trimmer
Brown, John, 27yrs, Carpenter
Caudia, Jose, 25yrs, Sailor
Chhotu Muha Mmad, Fireman and Trimmer
Dowdall, Charles Henry, Able Seaman RNVR (DAMS)
Ismail Ilahi Bakhsh, Fireman and Trimmer
Kemble, John Rhys, 26yrs, 2nd Engineer
MacDonald, John, 17yrs, Sailor
Martins, Joseph, 30yrs, Fireman and Trimmer
McDougall, John, 20yrs, Sailor
McLennan, Marcus, 19yrs, Mess Room Steward
McNeil, Donald 23yrs, Able Seaman
McNeil, M., 24yrs, Able Seaman
Mennell, Frederick James, 23yrs, 2nd Mate
Mennell, Henry, Master
Petheram, Joseph Thomas, 31yrs, 3rd Engineer
Rowe, Arthur Leslie, 28yrs, Chief Engineer
Steel, Nathan Hewson, 28yrs, Steward
Terry, Walter Joseph, 18yrs, Apprentice

The 76-ton British sailing vessel *John W. Pearn* was captured and then sunk with explosives 40 miles SSE from Start Point; the crew had to abandon ship, while en-route from Granville in Normandy to Plymouth in ballast. Off Guernsey, on the homeward leg, Pustkuchen captured and sank the 335-ton French sailing vessel *la Manche* (1886) with explosives off Guernsey; she was travelling from Granville, Normandy in ballast to Cardiff.

UC 66 arrived back at Zeebrugge on 3 May.

FINAL PATROL

(5) *UC 66* sailed from Zeebrugge on 22 May 1917; her mission was to lay mines off Swansea and Milford in the Bristol Channel and attack Allied shipping off the south coast of Ireland. Three days after sailing, Pustkuchen sunk the 1,405-ton Danish steamship *Sjaelland* (1872 – 'Damskibsselskabet Tom', Copengagen), 18 miles off Start Point, while she was voyaging from Le Havre to Barry Roads in ballast. At 0435hrs on 25 May, *UC 66* opened fire on the steamer from a range of 150 yards and the 30-year-old master, Alexander MacPhee, was killed, plus two men badly wounded when the bridge was hit. Forty rounds were fired before the vessel stopped and the surviving crew of seventeen abandoned ship at 0540hrs in the only boat left undamaged; the *Sjaelland* sinking at 0540hrs, the U-boat made off towards another vessel. Twenty minutes later, the survivors were resued by the 349-ton SS *Seaforth* (1891 – Alfred J. Smith Ltd, Bristol) and landed at Torquay.

On 3 May, a torpedo from *UC 66* hit the 1,754-ton Italian steamer *Portofino* (1912 – Italian Government requisition – Ferrovie dello Stato, ops, Genoa), voyaging from Penarthe to Blaye. The master tried to beach her in Mounts Bay, but the ship sank off Penzance (Lloyd's), according to Adm. Spindler's charts: 20 miles northwest of Lundy Island, with considerable loss of life. (*Portofino* was originally German, but had been seized by the Italians.)

(U-boats often bottomed out on the seabed between Kynance Cove and the Lizard and it was a common ploy for patrol boats to drop random depth charges in this sector, in the hope of damaging a submarine. (Trawler crews were not averse to netting the many fish killed in these attacks either.)

On 11 June 1917, Cdr Godfrey Herbert DSO (*see* vols 1 and 4) was in command of the Falmouth-based HMT *Sea King*, one of three armed trawlers sent to investigate reports of U-boats 'bottoming out' in the area. Herbert, an arch survivor, was fresh from the *K13* disaster at Gareloch. A submariner of significant experience, he had earlier commanded the Q-ships *Baralong* and *Carrigan Head*. For his role in the notorious 'Baralong incident' (or outrage, depending upon the reader's perspective) the Germans had denounced Herbert as a war criminal.

Once again, Godfrey Herbert found himself in the thick of the action. Cdr Herbert noted:

> At 23.30 on 12 June I spotted, about 400 yards away, two or three points on my port beam, the periscope, stanchion and jumper-stay of a submarine travelling westwards. I concluded that her captain had been taking a bearing from the Lizard and as I turned towards her, she dived…we wasted not a second and let go sixteen large depth charges and sixty-four smaller ones. To leeward of the enemy there rose up a quantity of oil. The depth charges had, beyond all questioning, burst the U-boat and set off her mines and torpedoes…After the sea had regained its calm from the underwater disturbance, we stopped engines and listened on our hydrophones. It was ideal for hearing any movement but nothing came through. Had she survived, our expert listeners would have detected her under way. The depth at this spot was forty fathoms and she could not have rested on the bottom voluntarily.

(Quoted by Keble-Chatterton in *Amazing Adventure*.)

Godfrey Herbert was credited with sinking the boat. He was made up to full Commander and awarded a Bar to his DSO. The crew of *Sea King* received the usual prize money. However, close analysis of material evidence tends to undermine the case that *Sea King* destroyed *UC 66*. As *UC 66* failed to return, post-war historians tended to favour the *Sea King* sinking, however with the benefit of hindsight (and German records) the evidence is far from convincing.

(Launched by Cochrane at Selby in 1916, the *Sea King* was again requisitioned in August 1939 and converted to Admiralty minesweeper No.3321; she joined the 40th M/S Group at Grimsby, but was lost to an underwater explosion in the Grimsby Roads on 9 October 1940.)

Michael Lowrey – Observations on the loss of *UC 66*:

> If patrol length calculations are made, based on a typical UCII boats operating through Dover Strait from Flanders (an average derived from 145-patrols to the English Channel, Irish Sea, or Bay of Biscay) most patrols are from 12 to 17 days in duration. The record patrol is 20 days. *UC 66* was supposedly sunk on her 21st day at sea. If the *SEA KING* attribution IS accepted, this boat would be the record holder for longest Flanders-based UCII patrol at the time of her loss. Even at this juncture, supposing the boat was off the Lizard, she would have been a good 3 days' sailing from home. It is very likely therefore, that *UC 66* was lost elsewhere and for other reasons.

NARA Series T-1022, Roll 109, PG 61987 ADM 137/2962 U-Boot-Ehrenmal Möltenort

THE FOLLOWING MEN PERISHED WITH UC 66

Ahls, Karl U-F.T.Gast
Assmussen, Nikolaus U-Matrose
Baumann, Richard U-Maschinistenmaat
Beitzel, Gustav U-Heizer
Berthold, E. Maschinistenmaat der Reserve
Biegon, J. Leutnant z.S.d.Res
Briesemeister, U-Bootsmannsmaat
Baack, Richard U-Steuermann
Gefäller, Bernhard U-Matrose
Gottschewski, W. U-Oberbootsmannsmaat der
  Reserve
Günther, Hans U-Matrose
Heber, H. Bootsmannsmaat
Hondrich, Emil U-Maschinistenmaat
Koch, Otto Heizer

Lausen, Ernst U-Maschinistenmaat der Reserve
Leban, Alfred U-Obermaschinistenmaat
Merkel, Otto Oberbootsmannsmaat
Müller, Egon Marine Ingenieur Asp
Nitzschner, W. U-Oberheizer
Obermeyer, L. U-Heizer
Oppenländer, P. Maschinistenmaat
Peters, D. U-Maschinist Anw
Pustkuchen, Herbert Oberleutnant zur See
Rochnia, J. U-Heizer
Schwandt, August U-Matrose
Schön, Walter U-Obermaschinist Anw
Smolka, Albert U-Matrose
Wildenhain, R. U-F.T.Maat
Witteler, Bernhard U-Heizer

WRECK SITE

The wreck of *UC 66* has never been located to date (September 2007).

ANALYSING THE LOSS OF U 95, U 93, U 84 AND UC 50 IN JANUARY 1918 BY MICHAEL LOWREY

Since the war, researchers have struggled to understand German submarine losses in January 1918. At the core of the problem is that four U-boats, *U 84, U 93, U 95* and *UC 50*, sailed for overlapping patrol areas in the English Channel and Bay of Biscay and did not return home. The boats accounted for fifteen ships and damaged two more, but it has always been uncertain which submarine sank certain of these vessels or how, when, and where the submarines were lost.

The only particularly strong submarine sinking claim came on 7 January 1918, when the steamer *Braenil* rammed and apparently sank a U-boat off Lizard Point (49° 57'N 05° 09'W) at 0415hrs. The crew of the ship heard voices in the water, but no survivors were rescued. The Admiralty's analysis at the time was that the submarine sunk was *U 93*. The official German history, however, thought this was extremely unlikely. *U 93* had exchanged recognition signals with *UC 17* off Penmarc'h in the Bay of Biscay at 0830hrs on 5 January. That night a convoy was attacked in the area and four ships were sunk. *U 93* would have had neither enough time after this action to reach the Lizard by the next morning at normal cruising, nor a reason to be there, as her assigned patrol area was along the French coast. As an alternative, Admiral Spindler suggested that the submarine rammed could have been *U 95*, which had been ordered to patrol the western English Channel.

The wreck of a large Germania-built U-series submarine, believed to be *U 95* based upon pro-peller markings, has recently been located off Hardelot, France in the eastern English Channel. The submarine has damage at the extreme stern, but is otherwise intact.

This would leave *U 84* as the only possible boat that *Braenil* could have rammed. The loss of *U 84* has traditionally been linked to a depth charge attack on 26 January in the Irish Sea. However, upon closer review of primary source documents, there is little evidence to show that a submarine was actually sunk on this date. It was extremely rare for a German submarine to cut through the Irish Sea on their way to, or from, the Bay of Biscay and *U 84* had never done this in her previous patrols to the area.

Any attribution that *U 95* was responsible for the sinking of of the steamer *War Song* (The Shipping Controller, London) requires that *U 95* survived to that date. Both *U 93* and *UC 50* should still be classified as missing; it's possible, but by no means certain, that one of the unidentified UCII wrecks is *UC 50*.

U 95 sailed on 27 December 1917; she sailed through the Dover Straits and was to operate in the western entrance of the English Channel. Last radio contact was on 30 December 1917, although it's clear she was operating at least through 2 January. Return would have been through the Dover Straits again. Ships sunk by *U 95* include:

AREA	VESSEL'S NAME	FLAG	TONS	D	M	YEAR	LOCATION
English Channel	*Vigrid*	NOR	1,617	31	12	1917	Sunk 10 miles WNW of Rundelstone Buoy, Lizard
Irish Sea	*Christos Markettos*	ITA	3,084	2	1	1918	Sunk about 4 miles NW of Gurnards Head
English Channel	*Gallier*	GBR	4,592	2	1	1918	7 miles ENE of Wolf Rock

U 93 sailed on 29 December, 1917. She also sailed through Dover and was to have returned the same way. Her assigned patrol area was the French north and west coast between the Channel Islands and Penmarc'h. The last contact with *U 93* was at 0830hrs on 5 January 1918 when she exchanged recognition signals with *UC 17*. Ships sunk by her include:

AREA	VESSEL'S NAME	FLAG	TONS	D	M	YEAR	LOCATION
English Channel	*Veda* (fishing smack)	GBR	25	2	1	1918	By gunfire 30 miles SSW of Eddystone Lighthouse
English Channel	*Goeland II MN*	FRA	235	4	1	1918	Sunk off Penmarc'h, en-route Brest-Lezardrieux
Bay of Biscay	*Dagny*	DAN	1,220	6	1	1918	About 4 miles SW of Penmarc'h
Bay of Biscay	*Harry Luckenbach*	USA	2,798	6	1	1918	2 miles NNW of Penmarc'h, 6 miles off Armen
Bay of Biscay	*Henri Le Cour*	FRA	2,488	6	1	1918	Sunk SW of Penmarc'h 47°45'N 0428'W
Bay of Biscay	*Kanaris*	GRE	3,793	6	1	1918	Sunk off Penmarc'h
English Channel	*War Song*	GBR	2,535	15	1	1918	12 miles W of Ile de Sein, near Brest

U 84 sailed on 1 January 1918 (exact time unknown). Like *U 93* and *U 95*, she was assigned to the Emden-based IV Flottille. Her routing would have been through Dover Straits outbound, with the return trip from her station between Permarch and Ile de Ré to have been around Scotland.

We know *U 84* signaled from the western end of the Channel. The official German history by Admiral Arno Spindler lists this as being on the 6th. Robert M. Grant in '*U-boat Intelligence*' notes that a message from *U 84* was intercepted; the approximate location 30 miles south of Prawle Point (an estimated distance based on the map in *U-boat Intelligence*). Grant gives the date as 3 January, which may not be reasonable given the date when *U 84* sailed.

UC 50 sailed on 7 January 1918 and was to operate off the Loire and Gironde estuaries. There was no contact with her after she sailed and it is unclear whether she laid her mines. *UC 50* would have gone through Dover Straits both outbound and inbound. The 4 February attack off Dungeness generally listed as sinking *UC 50* was in fact made against *UC 79*. (*UC 79* survived this engagement.)

Vessels sunk by *U 93* or *UC 50*:

AREA	VESSEL'S NAME	FLAG	TONS	D	M	YEAR	LOCATION
Bay of Biscay	*Bayvoe*	GBR	2979	9	1	1918	10 miles S of Iles des Glenans
Bay of Biscay	*Cardiff*	GBR	2808	10	1	1918	Damaged about 20 miles SW of Lorient
Bay of Biscay	*Messidor*	GBR	3883	11	1	1918	Damaged 2 miles E ½ S of Penmarc'h
Bay of Biscay	*Voltaire*	FRA	2651	11	1	1918	About 140 miles NE of Cape Ortegal
Bay of Biscay	*Château Lafite*	FRA	1913	12	1	1918	Sunk SW Penmarc'h
Bay of Biscay	*Babin Chevaye* (s/v)	FRA	2174	14	1	1918	30 miles WSW of Penmarc'h at 47°36'N

A SERIES OF RADIO INTERCEPTS MADE BY BRITISH NAVAL INTELLIGENCE DECEMBER–JANUARY 1918

For the most part, these fragmentary snatches of U-boat W/T transmissions provide us with the only evidence of the last known locations of the missing boats.

29 December at 1227hrs *U 93* out Weg Gelb
29 December at 1937hrs −*U 95* in 49 44'N/02 40'W
30 December at 0335hrs *U 95* in 49 00'N/0403'W
31 December −*U 93* one bearing in Channel
3 January at 2036hrs −*U 84* in 49 57'N/03 48'W
(5 January at 0820hrs −*U 93* W Penmarch ES *UC 17*)
6 January at 0110hrs −*U 84* in 49 30'N/03 36'W
6 January at 1000hrs −*U 84* in 48 03N/05 36'W
(7 January at 0417hrs −*U?* rammed 49 59'N/05 12'W)
8 January −*U 84* 'one directional places her apparently still in the Channel'
9 January at 1045 −*U 84* in 49 51'N/05 08'W
17 January at 0800hrs −*U 95* in 48 35'N/05 13'W
18 January at 0700hrs −*U 84* in 51 13'N/04 15'W
(26 January at 0610hrs −*U?* rammed 51 53.30'N/05 44'W)

ADM 137/3914

U 95, SM IMPERIAL U-BOAT

DATE OF LOSS: **Approximately 7 January 1918**
REFERENCE: withheld on request
LOCATION: off the French coast

Type: Mittel–U Class (U.I Project) ocean torpedo attack boat   **Builders**: Germaniawerft, Kiel for Kaiserliche Deutsche Marine   **Ordered**: on 15 September 1915, within the batch of *U 93–U 98*   **Keel laid**: as Yard No. 259 on 29 March 1916   **Launched**: on 20 January 1917   **Commissioned**: by Kapitänleutnant Athalwin Prinz on 19 April 1917

TECHNICAL SPECIFICATIONS

Hull: double   **Surface displacement**: 838 tons   **U/Dt**: 1,000 tons   **LBDH**: 71.6m × 6.30m × 3.90m × 8.70m   **Machinery**: 2 × 1,200ps MAN diesels   **Props**: 2 bronze   **S/Sp**: 16.8 knots   **Op/R**: 9,020 nautical miles at 8 knots   **Sub/R**: 52 nautical miles at 5 knots   **U/Power**: 2 × 600ps electric motors gave 8.6 knots   **Batteries**: AFA lead/acid/accumulators.   **Fuel/Cap**: 47 + 60 tons   **Armament**: 4 bow and 2 stern 50.04cm torpedo tubes   **Torpedoes**: 12 or 16 × 50.04cm (19.7in).   **Guns**: 1 × 105mm (4.13in) forward deck gun   **Ammo**: 500 rounds of 105mm   **Mines**: none   **Diving**: max-op-depth 50m (164ft) and 45 sec to crash-dive   **Complement**: 35

U 95 was assigned to IV.U-Bootflottille at Emden on 24 May 1917, with Kplt. Athalwin Prinz the commander from 19 April 1917, Oblt.z.S. Erich Ross and Oblt.z.S. Hans Weber the watch officers and Oblt.Ing. Paul Wandel the engineering officer.

U 95 made the following war patrols:

On 29 May 1917, *U 95* left Emden and sailed for operations off the west and south coasts of Ireland, travelling via the Isles of Shetland. Prinz sank three British steamships in the Atlantic on the boat's first war patrol, the first ship being the defensively armed 4,221-ton *Hollington* (1912 – F.S. Holland, London) by a torpedo attack following a 1-hour gunfight, south of the Færoe Islands, on 3 June; it was bound from Liverpool for Archangelsk, Russia in ballast and thirty men, including the master, were lost.

THE MEN WHO DIED

Burnett, J., Wireless Operator
Byrom, W., 33yrs, Donkeyman
Cameron, W.H., 46yrs, Chief Engineer
Christensen, C., 28yrs, 4th Engineer Officer
Conroy, Michael, 46yrs, Able Seaman
Elliott, Christopher, 36yrs, Fireman
Foster, H., 16yrs, Assistant Steward
Foster, T.W., 58yrs, Chief Steward
Hamilton ?, 31yrs, Able Seaman
Hannan, Robert, 17yrs, Assistant
Harrigan, George, 26yrs, Fireman
Hayday, Harry, 17yrs, Fireman
Hogan, John Joseph, 45yrs, Carpenter
Kay, Joseph, 18yrs, Ordinary Seaman
Kirk, S., Master
Mills, John William, 35yrs, 3rd Engineer
Mills, Walter, 21yrs, Able Seaman
Mitchell, T.J., 64yrs, Ship's Cook
McCabe, Thomas, 27yrs, Fireman
Owen, W.J., 54yrs, 2nd Mate
Pennock, George, 35yrs, 1st Mate
Ralston, J., 41yrs, Fireman
Reid, Thomas, 35yrs, 2nd Engineer
Roberts, Edward, 53yrs, Boatswain (Bosun)
Ryan, Thomas, 28yrs, Fireman and Trimmer
Sanders, John Richard, 26yrs, 3rd Mate
Teviotdale, Frederick William, 20yrs, Seaman
Turner, William, 31yrs, Fireman
Weaffer, Charles, 34yrs, Fireman and Trimmer
Doyle, Herbert Lawrence, 757218 Able Seaman, M.F.A. 'Purdy' MMR
Hayes, James Robert, 44yrs, 912465 Boatswain (Bosun) M.F.A. 'Purdy' M.MR
Heron, Thomas, 820426 Greaser M.F.A. 'Purdy' M.MR
Woodruff, Leon Stanislaus, 25yrs, 887591 Donkeyman, M.F.A. 'Purdy' M.MR
MacDonald, Murdo, Leading Seaman RNR
Bridger, Arthur Robert, Able Seaman RNVR

U 1195 powering through the Atlantic waves (see page 108). (Photo taken by Matr. Ob. Gfr Rudolph Wieser)

On 9 June, *U 95* opened fire on the defensively armed 641-ton *Achilles* (1900 – J. & P. Hutchinson Ltd, Glasgow), 75 miles west by south of Fastnet, however the steamer was already under attack by *U 55*, which sunk *Achilles* with a torpedo after she surrendered. The ship's master and a DAMS gunner were taken prisoner, probably by *U 55* as this is not mentioned in *U 95*'s KTB; the ship was on passage from Cadiz for Liverpool and Glasgow with general cargo.

The British submarine *K7* (Cdr Kellett) attacked *U 95* with six torpedoes east of Fair Isle on 16 June, however only one hit the U-boat and failed to explode. *U 95* fired her gun against the conning tower of K7, which was breaking the surface, but the shell/s missed too.

The defensively armed SS *Polyxena* (1896 – Ocean Steam Ship Co. Ltd, Liverpool) of 5,308 tons was attacked with two torpedoes without warning and finished off by gunfire 75 miles off Fastnet Rock on 12 June; she was on a voyage from Australia to Queenstown, Ireland with a cargo of wheat and seven of her crew were drowned.

THE SEVEN MEN WHO DIED

Clark, Charles Lancaster, 21yrs, 4th Engineer Officer
Deane, John, 37yrs, Donkeyman
Jonsson, K., 24yrs, Fireman and Trimmer
King, Martin Patrick, 50yrs, Greaser
Logan, Michael Hugh, 25yrs, Fireman and Trimmer
Vangelete, George, 26yrs, Fireman
Webb, W.H., 24yrs, Fireman and Trimmer

On 16 June a most interesting encounter took place between *U 95* and the British fleet submarine *K7* (*see* vol. 3). At the time *K7* (Cdr Gilbert Kellett) was engaged in an anti-submarine sweep coded 'Operation BB'. At 1512 hrs *K7* was patrolling the Fair Isle Channel at periscope depth when a U-boat was spotted. Care with identification was needed as Kellet knew that *K2* was operating in the same sector. The submarine was the returning *U 95*. At 1520hrs the range had closed sufficiently for Kellet to fire a beam torpedo at his target, which missed. Kellet now turned the boat, bringing all four bow tubes to bear on *U 95*. At 1529hrs he gave the order to fire. Surely one would hit home. The third torpedo was seen to strike the U-boat squarely amidships. It failed to explode. *K7* surfaced to pursue but at 1530hrs *U 95* retaliated with her gun. Steam was quickly raised and the fleet submarine belched into action with Kellet manoeuvring to bring his starboard tube within range. The torpedo was fired at 1534hrs but it missed. *K7* was now entering her stride. Shells were exploding in her wake but she was rapidly overhauling the U-boat, her crew training their guns on the German boat, eagerly waiting for the range to close.

KTB of *U 95*:

> The submarine came as far as the conning tower deck out of the water. Both conning tower and control room periscopes extended. (The enemy boat is) Running at high speed. Shot at with artillery. A hit was observed between the periscopes. Boat disappears after 7th shot.
>
> The second torpedo attack was perceived by Prinz to be at extreme long range. One torpedo didn't even reach *U 95*, the other was evaded and passed astern. No periscope was seen from the second boat.

Prinz, fully aware that he could not outgun the monstrous machine hotly pursuing him, dived to safety. So ended the 'K' boats' day of near glory. The rest is history.

U 95 returned to Borkum Roads on 18 June and arrived at Emden on the 19th.

(2) Leaving Germany on 11 July 1917, *U 95* sailed to an operational area about 250 miles off the southwest coast of Ireland. On 24 July, lookouts reported a three-masted barque and a torpedo was fired at it, however it missed. She was the Swedish *Bellville*, a 992-ton iron barque that was built in 1877 and owned by AB Bellville, Landskrona. After surfacing, Prinz stopped the ship with gunfire; one shell made a direct hit and damaged her, but two Allied destroyers arrived on the scene and *U 95* was forced to dive, leaving the *Bellville* to make her escape. The 3,877-ton turret-hulled steamer *Belle of England* (1905 – Arctic Steamship Co. Ltd, Newcastle) was armed for defence and transporting iron ore from Algiers to Barrow when Prinz torpedoed and sunk her without warning, 155 miles off Fastnet (51° 00'N 14° 30'W) on 27 July.

The *Whitehall* (1905 – Whitehall Steam Navigation Co. Ltd, Liverpool (Cardiff), a 3,158-ton defensively armed British steamer, was bound for Ipswich from Montreal with a cargo of wheat and flour when she was unexpectedly hit with a torpedo and sank on the 29th at 49° 35'N 16° 10'W. Edward George Ford, the 16-year-old mess room steward was drowned, but seventeen of the survivors were rescued by USS *Winslow*.

In the Atlantic on 30 July, the Italian steamer, *Eolo* (1877 – Chiarelle & Carbone, Genove) of 1,679 tons was torpedoed and sunk without any warning at: 53° 54'N 15° 15'W; she was bound for Genoa with coal from the Clyde and three men were killed. (In an earlier incident on 15 June 1917, the *Eolo* was attacked by an unknown submarine and left damaged, 12 miles south of The Old Head of Kinsale, while transporting iron ore from Melilla to Glasgow; she was towed into Queenstown on 16 June.)

On 31 July, *U 95* was involved in a gun battle with the 4,237-ton British steamer *Beacon Grange*, which was travelling from Liverpool to Rio de Janeiro with coal. At position 53° 46'N 16° 39'W, two direct hits resulted in the death of Ordinary Seaman Thomas Morgan on board the steamer. *U 95* gave up the chase because of fuel shortage and she returned to Emden on 5 August.

(3) *U 95* departed Emden on 25 August 1917 and travelled to the North Channel for operations, going via the Isles of Shetland. Prinz captured the 3,063-ton Norwegian SS *Majoren* (1887 – Aktieselskapet Solgran, Stavanger) and after an unsuccesful torpedo shot he fired about thirty shells at her, which set her on fire; the ship sank at 0730hrs on 3 September, aproximately 25 nautical miles west off the Tory Island at 55°14'N-08°56'W, however the whole crew survived. She had been transporting 2,800 tons of lubricating oil from Philadephia, USA to Glasgow.

At 1530 on 12 September, a stern torpedo fired from the British submarine *D7* (Lt Hallifax) off the North Channel missed *U 95* and she in turn then unsuccessfully aimed her gun at *D7*'s periscope. Earlier that day *D7* had efficiently disposed of *U 45* (*see* vol. 4).

On 17 September, *U 95* joined the gunfight of *UB 62* and the defensively armed 4,278-ton steamship *Queen Amelia* (1905 – Dunlop SS Co. Ltd, Glasgow). The steamer, which stopped after three hits from *UB 62* (Bernhard Putzier), was travelling with a cargo of flax from Archangelsk, Russia to Dundee. *UB 62* finished the steamer off with a torpedo, while *U 95* captured the master and two other men.

The *U 95* arrived back in Germany on 20 September 1917, travelling via the Shetland Isles.

(4) On 23 October 1917, Kplt. Prinz made a sortie to the St George's Channel area with *U 95*, going around the Isles of Orkney on the outward and return journeys. The US steamer *Rochester* (1912 – Kerr S.S. Line) of 2,551 tons was voyaging from Manchester to Baltimore in ballast when she was torpedoed after her convoy dispersed on 2 November; then she was shelled and sunk, 325 miles west of Tory Island at position 55° 17'N 17° 44'W.

At 2040hrs on 10 November, *U 95* sank an unknown sailing vessel with gunfire, 11 miles southeast of Coningbeg light vessel, which was probably the missing 110-ton British schooner *Lapwing*, voyaging from Waterford to Cardiff with pit props.

THE CREWMEN WHO DIED

Merrigan, Patrick, Able Seaman MM
Kearon, Edward Victor, Mate MM
Kearon, George Roberts, Ordinary Seaman MM
Kearon, Joseph, Master MM
Tyrrell, George, Boy MM

On 11 November 1917 the small Admiralty trawlers *Thuringia* and *Harlech Castle* were engaged in escorting the tanker *Alchymist* towards a local convoy route. All three vessels were 12 miles south of Mine Head on a southwest course when *Harlech Castle* was suddenly rocked by an explosion which emanated from the direction of *Thuringia*. There was not the slightest sign of the little vessel or her crew. The convoy later reported spotting a submarine some 3 miles astern of the convoy. This was later confirmed by the armed yacht *Beryl*.

U 95's KTB states:

> 07.10h Anlauf gegen S/T 'Alchymist' in Geleit HMT 'Thuringia', Kurs 250°, S Irland (023 eps. I) 07.39 hversenkt brit. Trawler 'Thuringia' (Skipper Thornham), 297 BRT, U-Torpedoschuß
>   18 sm SSO Mine Head, 14 Tote, keine Überlebenden meldet Geleit 2 S/S, Torpedo gegen S/S – 4000 BRT, explodiert, sofort gesunken.

All fourteen hands were lost.

THE MEN WHO DIED

Amis, George Alfred, Deckhand RNR
Anderson, George Patrick, Trimmer RNR
Blakelock, John William, Deckhand RNR
Cann, William, Engineman RNR
George, Llewellyn, Stoker RNR
Greenacre, William Hart, Deckhand RNR
Grew, Albert Edward, Deck Boy RNR
Harris, Charles, Leading Seaman RNR
Hurst, Thomas Joseph, Trimmer RNR
Jenkins, Ernest, Deckhand RNR

Noel, William, Deckhand RNR
Sandham, Robert, Deckhand RNR
Thornham, Albert William, Temp/Skipper RNR

(The 297-ton steam trawler *Thuringia*, built by Cook, Welton & Gemmell in 1913, was requisitioned in 1915 and converted to Admiralty auxiliary patrol vessel No. FY 1624.)

In St George's Channel and 7 miles off Coningbeg light vessel, the 3,040-ton steamship *Carlo* (1913 – Wilson Line Ltd, Hull), which was bound for Liverpool from Carthagena, Colombia with general cargo, was torpedoed and sunk at 0128hrs on 13 November.

THE TWO CREWMEN WHO DROWNED

Hughes, Arthur Charles, 19yrs, Assistant Cook
Radford, Henry, Fireman MM

The second vessel to be sunk in the Irish Sea on the 13th was the *Ardmore* (1909 – City of Cork Steam Packet Co. Ltd, Cork), a 1,304-ton British steamer armed for defence. She was torpedoed and sunk without warning 13 miles off Coningbeg light vessel at 2329hrs, while transporting general cargo from London to Cork; nineteen crewmen were drowned.

SOME OF THE MEN WHO DIED

Ahern, Dan, 26yrs, Fireman
Barry, Pat, 39yrs, Trimmer
Best, John, 54yrs, Quartermaster
Collins, D., 49yrs, Able Seaman
Good, M., 53yrs, Quartermaster
Griffiths, H.Y., 35yrs, Carpenter
Healy, James, 49yrs, Fireman
Herlihy, D., 34yrs, Trimmer
Horgan, John, 50yrs, Able Seaman
Jago, Richard, 54yrs, Mate
Leahy, M. 42yrs, Fireman
O'Sullivan, Michael, 42yrs, 1st Engineer
Smith, Thomas, Leading Seaman RNR (DAMS)
Tobin, Michael, 55yrs, Able Seaman
Twomey, John, 53yrs, Fireman
Twomey, Patrick, 33yrs, Steward
Twomey, Timothy, 34yrs, Fireman
Twomey, Timothy, 70yrs, Donkeyman
Walsh, Joe, 33yrs, Fireman

(*U 95* reported the *ARDMORE* as a steam-tanker of approximately 5,000 tons)

U 95 arrived back in Germany on 20 November.

FINAL PATROL

(5) *U 95* sailed from Emden on 27 December 1917 and headed for the western end of the English Channel, but this time Kplt. Prinz took the perilous route directly through the Dover Strait. On 31 December Prinz torpedoed the *Vigrid* (1915 – Dampskipsselskapet Aktieselskapet Vigrid, Bergen) at 0130hrs; she was a 1,617-ton Norwegian steamship on passage from Barry Docks for Rouen with 2,102 tons of coal; she sank 10 miles off the Runnelstone Buoy.

HM Drifter *Hawthorne* rescued thirteen survivors, but six men were drowned.

THE SIX MEN WHO DIED

Hansen, Hans, Stoker from Skien
Johansson, Werner, Stoker from Sweden
Melin, Otto, Sailor from Sweden
Nilson, Ludvig, 2nd Engineer from Sweden
Paulsen, Sverre, Sailor from Bergen
Søderman, Oskar, Sailor from Sweden

At 0230hrs on 2 January 1918, the 679-ton British steamer *Kingsley* (1881 – W. Eccles & W. Ball, Newcastle) was attacked with gunfire 3 miles east of Runnelstone Buoy (50°00'N-05°40'W) and eight shells scored direct hits. Five men were killed in the shelling and four more were wounded but the steamer escaped to Penzance, however she claimed one hit on the conning tower of the U-boat, from six shots of her 13-pounder gun.

FOUR OF THE MEN WHO DIED

Baile, H., Mate MM
Eerzeneek, Martin, Donkeyman MM
Hydera, R.D., Fireman MM
McGoverin, George, 2nd Engineer MM

The second vessel attacked on 2 January 1918 was the 4,592-ton defensively armed steamer *Gallier* (1914 – Lloyd Royal Belge (Great Britain), Ltd, London) commanded by Cpt. Goodwin. Off Wolf Rock, one of *U 95*'s torpedoes detonated without warning in the No.2 hold at 0345hrs. After firing five rounds of ammunition from the deck gun to attact attention, thirty-three of the crew got clear away from the ship in the boats at 0415hrs; only the master, boatswain and chief engineer remained on board. However, the three men abanded ship soon after when another torpedo exploded against the No.1 hold and the ship sank 5 minutes later at position 49° 59.30'N 05° 38'W, at 0415hrs. The ship had been travelling in ballast from Le Havre to Swansea. HM Trawler *Reeve* picked up all of the crew at 0510hrs and landed them at Penzance.

At 1445hrs, also on 2 January, the Italian steamer *Christos Markettos* (1892 – Italian Government requisition- managed by Ferrovie dello Stato) of 3,084 tons was torpedoed and sunk in the Irish Sea at 50° 13'N 05° 42'W, while on passage from Bilbao for Newport, Monmouth with iron ore. HM Drifter *Primrose* rescued the crew of twenty-six.

The last radio contact was on 30 December 1917 and *U 95* was never heard from again. Robert Grant claimed the last W/T was intercepted by the British on 17 January at 0800hrs in approximately 48° 35'N 05° 13'W, west of Ouessant, but that attribution could be in doubt.

NARA Series T-1022 Roll 38 ADM 173/6267 ADM 137/3291 ADM 137/3262
ADM 137/1693 U-Boot-Ehrenmal Möltenort CWGC Swedish Archives

THE MEN WHO PERISHED IN U 95

Ackermann, R. U-Bootsmannsmaat
Anders, Otto F.T. Maat
Baum, Franz U-Maschinistenmaat
Bieth, Georg U-Heizer
Blass, Otto U-Matrose
Dürkop, Harry U-Obermatrose
Erler, Kurt U-Obermatrose
Frey, Lothar U-Bootsmannsmaat
Hageböck, Adolf U-Obermaschinistenmaat
Heidemann, Fr. U-Obermatrose
Heinrich, Emil U-Heizer

Jänsch, Georg U-Obermatrose
Jordan, Karl U-Heizer
Krebs, K. U-Obermaschinist Anw
Krüger, Otto U-Maschinist Anw
Martens, W. U-Maschinist d.Seew.I
Munderloh, A. U-Maschinistenmaat
Pfeil, W. U-Obermaschinist Anw
Prinz, Athalwin Kapitänleutnant
Rabenstein, G. U-Obermaschinist
Rechel, Hans U-Maschinistenmaat
Reuter, Friedrich U-Matrose

Ross, Eric Oberleutnant zur See
Rossmayr, Johann U-Maschinistenmaat
Scheer, Anton U-Heizer
Schmidt, Friedrich U-Heizer
Schütte, Hermann U-Matrose
Sillis, Dietrich U-Obermaschinistenmaat
Spiegele, Johann Conrad U-Steuermann
Steigleder, O. U-Heizer
Stührmann, H. U-Maschinistenmaat der
   Reserve

Voigt, Erwin Ed. U-Obermaschinistenmaat
Wagner, Paul U-Maschinist Anw
Wagner, Max U-Obermatrose
Woleszcyk, R. U-Maschinistenmaat
Wandel, Paul Marine Ober Ingenieur
Weber, Hans Oberleutnant zur See
Wellmann, W. U-F.T.Gast
Wienecke, G. U-Oberbootsmannsmaat der
   Reserve
Woithe, R. U-F.T.Gast

WRECK SITE

The wreck of *U 95* lies off the French coast.

U 93, SM IMPERIAL U-BOAT

DATE OF LOSS: January 1918
DEPTH: 31m
REFERENCE: withheld on request
LOCATION: Dover Strait, off Hardelot, France

Type: Mittel-U Class (U.I Project) ocean-going torpedo attack boat   *Builders*: Germaniawerft, Kiel for the Kaiserliche Deutsche Marine   *Ordered*: on 15 September 1915, within the batch of *U 93–U 98*   *Keel laid*: as Yard No.257 on 12 January 1916   *Launched*: on 15 December 1916   *Commissioned*: by Kapitänleutnant Freiherr Edgar Spiegel von und zu Peckelsheim on 10 February 1917

TECHNICAL SPECIFICATIONS

Hull: double   *Surface displacement*: 838 tons   *U/Dt*: 1,000 tons   *LBDH*: 71.6m × 6.30m × 3.90m × 8.70m   *Machinery*: 2 × 1,200ps MAN diesels   *Props*: 2 bronze   *S/Sp*: 16.8 knots   *Op/R*: 9,020 nautical miles at 8 knots   *Sub/R*: 52 nautical miles at 5 knots   *U/Power*: 2 × 600ps electric motors gave 8.6 knots   *Batteries*: AFA lead/acid/accumulators   *Fuel/Cap*: 47 + 60 tons   *Armament*: 4 bow and 2 stern 50.04cm torpedo tubes   *Torpedoes*: 12 × 50.04cm (19.7in)   *Guns*: 1 × 105mm (4.13in) forward deck gun   *Ammo*: 500 rounds of 105mm   *Mines*: none   *Diving*: max-op-depth 50m (164ft) and 45 sec to crash-dive   *Complement*: 35

U 93 was formally assigned to IV.U-Flottille at Emden on 5 April 1917, with Kplt. Von Spiegel commander from 10 February 1917 until 30 April 1917, when he was washed overboard. (Von Spiegel was born on 2 October 1885.)

Oblt.z.S. Wilhelm Ziegner stood in to deputize until 22 May 1917 when Kplt. Helmuth Gerlach took over command on 23 May 1917.

U 93 was ordered to sail for her first war cruise on Friday 13th, but the crew was agitated at the thought of her putting to sea on such an unlucky date. Kplt. Edgar Spiegel von und Peckhelseim persuaded them that the boat was only sailing from Emden to Heligoland to provision, the mission proper would actually commence on the 14th.

Fortunately many of the crew had served under Peckhelseim earlier in *U 32*, while *U 93* was fitting out in the Kiel-Germania yard.

On Saturday 14 April 1917, *U 93* sailed from Heligoland for her operations sector; a zone situated about 200 miles between the Irish coast and western entrance of the English Channel, known as the Celtic Sea. The route would take them past the Isles of Shetland, before traversing Atlantic coast of Ireland. Unrestricted submarine warfare had been declared since February and U-boats had been devastating Allied traffic, each day destroying a few more ships. Von Spiegel and his crew were impatient to join the hunt.

The first opportunity came next day when Ltz.S. Wilhelm Ziegner spotted a sail on the horizon and altered course, while alerting his commander. As the sailing ship approached, it was recognized as a schooner and in this zone of the North Sea there was good reason to think she must be British, or at least belonging to a country that was trading with Britain. Two shots from the deck gun were enough and the schooner heaved to. Minutes later the crew responded to the submarine's warning by lowering a rowing boat – although Von Spiegel was so alarmed by the appearance of this rowing boat that he intially dived, but returned to the surface a few minutes later. Suspicious, he was careful to keep the rowing boat between *U 93* and the sailing ship in case it was a Q-ship. However, this vessel was the *Fram*, a 105-ton Danish vessel en-route from Hull to Aarhus in Denmark with 156 tons of coal. The crew were informed they had 20 minutes to abandon ship before their vessel would be sunk; 30 minutes later, *FRAM* was sunk by gunfire. *U 93* approached the Shetland Isles to enter the Atlantic and time and time again Allied patrol boats forced her to submerge.

On the morning of 18 April 1917, *U 93* was 50 miles west of the Shetland Isles when a three-masted vessel appeared on the horizon. In a repeat of the earlier encounter with *Fram*, von Spiegel destroyed the *West Lothian* (1882 – A/S West Lothian, Sandefjord), an iron-hulled 1,887-ton Norwegian barque which was en-route from Buenos Aires to Kristiania with maize and oilcake. Some hours later Von Spiegel attacked the 1,459-ton Norwegian steamer *Troldfos* (1912 – Aktieselskapet Manchester, Kristiania), en-route from New York for Kristiania with agricultural equipment. Despite desperate attempts to turn her helm and avoid the torpedo, the missile struck home. With a black plume of smoke and the scream of steam, the ship began to sink. It was all too slow for Von Spiegel, who surfaced the U-boat. Once the crew had abandoned ship, the *Troldfos* was sunk using the deck gun. Despite the misgivings over leaving on Friday 13th, this patrol seemed to be going very well indeed.

On 22 April and at the entrance to the North Channel, *U 93* intercepted the full-rigged, iron-hulled Norwegian ship *Vestelv* (1880 – Henschiens Rederi A/S, Tvedestrand), transporting pitch pine from Mobile, Alabama to Liverpool. This time a scuttling party was sent on board armed with explosive charges, adding 1,729 tons more to the tally!

Pursuing a course down the west coast of Ireland, two days passed before a further opportunity presented itself. By 25 April, having reached her designated operational zone some 200 miles southwest of Fastnet Rock, a large fast steamer suddenly appeared, heading west. Von Spiegel may have misjudged the steamer's speed because the torpedo missed, so he surfaced and attacked the ship using the deck gun. Strangely, more shells appeared to be striking the vessel than *U 93* was firing – the reason being that, *U 43* (Hellmuth Jürst) was also blasting away. The steamer finally outpaced them and the two submarines were forced to break off the pursuit. In fact the 6,373-ton *Swanmore*, which was armed for defence, had not escaped, because *U 50* (Gerhard Berger) was waiting for her and by the end of that day, 230 miles into the Atlantic from Fastnet Rock, the ship was torpedoed without warning and then shelled and sunk. *Swanmore* (1913 – Johnston Line Ltd) was transporting general cargo and ordnance from Baltimore, Maryland for Liverpool and eleven of the crew perished.

THE MEN WHO DIED

Alvarez, Jose, 21yrs, Trimmer
Bello, Custodio, 26yrs, Fireman
Cole, John, 32yrs, Fireman and Trimmer
Corcoran, John Thomas, 19yrs, 2nd Steward
Coredo, Eduardi, 34yrs, Greaser
Greene, Lawence, 35yrs, Sailor
Jones, David, 19yrs, Able Seaman and Quartermaster
Marfil, Castro, 26yrs, Fireman
O'Connor, Edward, 19yrs, Seaman
Talbot, Frederick Arthur, 17yrs, Appentice
Turner, Arthur Glendenning, 17yrs, Apprentice

Meanwhile the two U-boat skippers Jürst and Spiegel exchanged information and greetings before parting. Such fortuitous meetings were always a welcome respite.

At 0600hrs on 28 April, the Danish *Diana*, a 207-ton, wooden-hulled (oak), three-masted schooner, owned by C.W. Clausen, Marstal, was attacked by *U 93*, 200 miles southwest of Fastnet Rock. The *Diana* was transporting eighty standards of timber on a voyage from New Brunswick to Newport, Monmouth when Von Spiegel fired a warning shot over the top of her; the schooner then stopped and a boat was lowered with provisions and the crew's effects. Captain Rasmussen of *Diana* was ordered on board the submarine with the ship's papers. The captain, together with three men carrying two explosive charges from *U 93*, then rowed back to the schooner, whose crew was ordered to abandon ship. The Germans were on board the sailing boat for about 1 hour before they returned to the U-boat, after which the sailing vessel was shelled and they left her sinking. *U 93* towed the lifeboat with the Danes in it for about 80 miles on an easterly course until 1830hrs, when they stopped; the Danish sailors were then given the longitude and latitude coordinates, together with course and distance to Fastnet Rock, before *U 93* parted company. The sailors rowed the boat until 0300hrs next morning when the British trawler *Lolist* from Lowestoft picked them up. However, the *Lolist* had just arived at the fishing grounds, so the people were transfered to a Belgian trawler, which was bound for Milford Haven that same day. After five days, the *Diana*, which was by then just floating on her cargo of wood, was found and towed to Queenstown, Ireland by a British Man-of-War and beached on 4 May; the vessel was afterwards written off as a constructive total loss.

The next day was fruitful indeed: *Comedian* (1903 – Charente Steamship Co. Ltd, Liverpool), a defensively armed 4,889-ton steamer, was torpedoed and sunk without warning, while en-route from St John, New Brunswick to Falmouth with Government stores and three men died, including a DAMS gunner.

THE MEN WHO DIED

Ledson, John, 39yrs, Storekeeper and Greaser
Muirhead, Duncan, Leading Seaman RNVR (DAMS)
Whitney, Robert, 17yrs, Ordinary Seaman

U 93 approached the lifeboat containing the survivors to discover the name of its victim. As the captain had not survived, Von Spiegel decided to take a DAMS gunner prisoner. That night (29th) *U 93* was surfaced and Von Spiegel torpedoed the 5,434-ton SS *Ikbal* (1894 – Elder, Dempster & Co. Ltd, Liverpool), which was armed for defence and on passage from St John, New Brunswick for Falmouth with ammunition. The master and two DAMS gunners were taken prisoner; the ship was sunk without warning.

A full moon on the night of 29/30 April assisted Von Spiegel in torpedoing the 2,949-ton defensively armed SS *Horsa* (1894 – Herskind & Co., West Hartlepool) without warning, which was en-route from Port Breira, Algeria to Cardiff with iron ore. Frustratingly the ship remained afloat and once again *U 93* resorted to the deck gun. Suddenly the lifeboat containing the twelve survivors overturned and ten crewmen were drowned.

THE MEN WHO DIED

Rushton, Charles, Sailor
Soares, M., Sailor
Stonehouse, Edward Knaggs, Master
Tibbo, Peter John, Sailor
Casey, James, Chief Boatswain (Bosun)
Elliott, Arthur, Fireman
Farrant, Walter, Engineer's Steward
Josphson, J., Donkeyman
Nash, Alfred, Chief Engineer
Casey, James, 3rd Engineer

Von Spiegel sunk ships because it was his role in wartime, but he was also a humane person who would do everything in his power to preserve life, where possible. Not only did he tow the lifeboats of *Vestelv* towards the shoreline of the Shetland Isles, he also ordered his crew to rescue the *Horsa* survivors from the water. First aid was given and the survivors were nursed as carefully as conditions allowed. The master, eleven crewmen and one gunner were taken prisoner. Evidently the submarine must have been somewhat crowded by this stage, but the commander had planned on transferring them to another ship.

Later that morning, the British steamer *Huntsmoor* (1901 – The Shipping Controller, London) encountered *U 93*, but this time the U-boat was in an unfavourable position for firing. *U 93* surfaced and at a distance of 7,000m opened fire. *Huntsmoor* (ex-4,972-ton German *Rostock*) returned fire with the stern cannon and made its escape. (*UB 40* eventually torpedoed and sunk the *Huntsmoor* without warning on 20 February 1918, 23 miles from Owers light vessel; twenty crewmen including the master were lost.)

Fortunately for *U 93*, a second steamer appeared and *U 93* torpedoed the Italian *Ascaro* (Edoardo Mazza, Savona) heading from Almeria to Ardrossan with iron ore; it sank in less than 5 minutes, taking all of the crew down with it. The steamship had hardly sunk when a three-masted ship came into view. On course to make an attack, another submarine was spotted on the surface, also heading towards the ship, and was about to open fire on it. Von Spiegel had lost this one to his friend, Kptn. Hersing in *U 21*. Nevertheless, a full moon was due and this sector was frequented by dense maritime traffic. Von Spiegel took advantage of the situation to transfer his twelve British survivors into lifeboats, but he was determined to hold onto his three prisoners. As large numbers of prisoners were an unwelcome encumbrance, the skipper shouted at the British sailors he had rescued, '*Go tell King George that we didn't take you lot because we've already got plenty of your kind and they are all much better than you!*'

The competing submarines never got a chance to attack because the 91-ton armed drifter *Begonia II* appeared, firing her 6-pounder. *U 21* dived immediately, but *U 93* made her escape on the surface. On spotting the survivors in the life rafts, *Begonia II* broke off the pursuit, besides, *U 93* was just a speck on the horizon by this stage and the armed boat could not hope to hit the submarine at that distance.

The afternoon of 30 April proved a fruitful time for *U 93*, but a fatal episode for the Greek steamer *Parthenon* (D. A. Stathatos, Ithaca) off the southwest coast of Ireland, voyaging from New York for Havre with general cargo; one torpedo sent her quickly to the bottom. Von Spiegel ensured that the survivors had all the essential provisions to wait for a rescue and then he returned to the hunt, because the weather was good and the moon was full. At 2035hrs the lookouts caught sight of a schooner flying Swedish colours.

The German skipper had just retired to his little 'cabin' when the call came down from the bridge: 'SAILING SHIP AHOY!'

There was far more to this little vessel than met the eye. In reality, the schooner was the Q-ship *Prize*, alias HMS *Q 21*. *Prize* was an iron and steel, 200-ton three-masted, topsail schooner, built by Smit & Zoon shipyard at Westerbrock, Germany in 1901 and launched as the *ELSE*. She was registered at Leer and was 37.33m (122ft 6in) in length. On 4 August 1914 and within hours of the outbreak of the First World War, she had been captured in the English Channel and provided with a destroyer escort to Britain. *Else* therefore became the very first ship to be captured by Britain during the First World War. Following an auction under the 'prize laws', she was bought by the Marine & Navigation Co. and renamed *First Prize*. Admiralty was always on the lookout for vessels suitable of carrying out decoy work and requisitioned the ship as a Q-ship. She was now officially listed as HMS *Prize* or *Q 21*. The managing director of the Marine & Navigation Co., being very patriotic, waived any compensation rights, loaning her to the Admiralty unconditionally. The company was never to see its ship again. The little warship was armed with two Lewis machine guns and two large deck guns. One was positioned forward and concealed by a collapsible deckhouse, the second was fixed on an imaginative vanishing mount beneath the hatchway covers of the aft-hold.

Prize was stationed at Milford Haven, with a brief to engage marauding enemy submarines in the southwestern approaches. Her commander, Lt William Sanders RNR (35), had previously served as mate on the Q-ship *Heligoland*. Born in Auckland, New Zealand in 1883, Sanders was a real sailor, having worked on steam and sailing ships since 1897. The outbreak of the First World War found him in Britain, having just survived the wrecking of his barque in the North Sea, and he spent the next year serving on the troopships *Moeraki* and *Willochra*. In June 1915 Sanders was gazetted an acting lieutenant in the RNR. His crew was largely drawn from Milford Haven reservists.

Prize had earlier left Milford Haven on 26 April 1917 for a patrol off the west coast of Ireland. She had been nearing the end of her patrol area (between 44° 49'N 11° 42'W and 49°40'N 11° 40'W)

Lt William Sanders.
(Private collection)

making about 2 knots under full sail and steering on a northwesterly course, when her lookouts observed the U-boat steering a parallel course on her port beam. Sanders called 'Action Stations!' The crew of *U 93* could not believe their luck. Unsuspecting, the U-boat moved to intercept the little sailing vessel. Once the distance closed to 5,000m, Von Spiegel ordered the firing of two warning shells, one short, one over. The crew of *Prize* played their parts well. Under the command of Skipper Brewer, men charged about on deck in mock panic, while the gun crews quietly took up their prearranged positions. Lt Sanders and Skipper Meade ducked down behind the steel companionway cover as the shells straddled *Prize*. At 2045hrs Sanders ordered the helmsman to turn the bows into the wind (with a view to slowing *Prize* down) thus enabling the six-man 'panic crew' to lower the lifeboat and row clear of the ship. *U 93* continued to fire while approaching from dead astern at half speed. Von Spiegel, examining the ship through glasses, found no cause for suspicion, but well aware of the British practice of using Q-ships against submarines, he decided to watch and wait.

At 2105hrs Von Spiegel made his move. *U 93* closed in on the ship's port beam. Once range had closed to 75 yards they stopped dead in the water. The U-boat's gun opened up again. This time the shells were being aimed at the waterline. The time for subterfuge was over. Lt Sanders stood up and yelled: '*Right boys now's your time. Raise the Ensign, Down Screens. Open Fire.*'

The aft gun screen fell away, the gun rose and locked into position. Two seconds later, the second 12-pounder, concealed under the dummy deckhouse, chimed in. Both vessels opened fire simultaneously and neither could miss at this range. Shells exploded within the Q-ship injuring the mechanic and putting one of the diesel engines out of action. A second shell exploded within the wireless cabin, wounding the operator. Von Spiegel's instincts were to ram. He ratcheted up the U-boat's speed then had the helm put at hard a port. Sanders anticipated the move, maintaining sufficient motive power to keep *Prize* outside the U-boat's turning circle. Just at that moment, a shell fired from the schooner's aft-gun, struck and ruptured the U-boat's compressed air tank under the gun, destroying its optics and killing Bts.Mt. Bahr. What follows is an extract from the British account of the engagement:

> The second round from *Prize* hit the base of the conning tower rendering diving impossible. The next round destroyed the gun and its crew. Remaining hits were on the aft part of the boat, her stern being turned towards *Prize*. Numerous casualties were caused amongst the German crew by *Prize's* Lewis gun. The three survivors were blown overboard. The submarine proceeded for 3,000 yards before the engines stopped and they sank. An explosion with black smoke occurred.

Shells from the schooner found their mark and *U 93*'s bow was seen to rise shortly before slipping away beneath the swell, leaving behind just a few whiffs of smoke. In this short, savage engagement, the Q-ship had fired thirty-six rounds in just 4 minutes. For those involved, however, it must have seemed that the battle had raged forever.

The 'panic crew' rowed around looking for survivors. Von Spiegel was dragged out along with Knappe, the navigating officer and Stoker Petty Officer Deppe. Initially covered by Skipper Brewer's pistol, Von Spiegel offered his word as an officer and a gentleman that he would not make any attempts to escape. Von Spiegel later gave this account of his meeting with the enigmatic Sanders:

> '*Where is the U-boat Captain?*' Spiegel asked. 'I stood up, and he came to with a good friendly smile and grasped my hand.' '*My dear fellow,*' he said, '*I am sorry for you. Please feel that you are my guest, but,*' he exclaimed apologetically, '*I am sorry I can't give you better quarters – especially as we are about ready to sink*'.

If the ship had won her battle with the U-boat, it looked as if she would lose her struggle with the elements. *Prize* was holed portside, level with the waterline. The decks were flooding and the pumps could not keep pace with the volume of water entering the ship. The masts were smashed to match-wood, the sails in shreds. Neither engine could be made to work and to cap it all, the W/T cabin had received a direct hit. The nearest land was some 120 miles to the northeast. Lt Sanders was desperate enough to ask his German prisoners to help save the ship. Remarkably, they agreed.

Holes were plugged using a combination of hammocks and blankets. The starboard lifeboats were filled with coal then turned out. The shift in weight was sufficent to ease the severe list to port. At last the pumps gained control over the flooding. Despite all the attention lavished on them, the engines refused to start. PO Deppe, the U-boat survivor, volunteered his services and within minutes the three men had managed to start one of the engines.

Prize pressed painfully on and after almost three days and nights of constant pumping and struggling against the elements, the Irish coast was sighted on 2 May. Five miles west of Old Head of Kinsale, HMM L161 (Lt Hannah, RNVR) met the ship and towed her into Kinsale harbour, where the wounded were taken ashore. On 4 May *Prize* departed Kinsale for her Milford Haven base (under tow from HM drifter *Rival II*). In the course of this voyage a surfaced UC boat was spotted by the *Prize* crew, about 2 miles away to the south. The crew of the Q-ship immediately went to action stations. The enemy boat travelled on a parallel course for almost an hour before it finally disappeared.

On arrival at Milford Haven, the prisoners were taken ashore. Sanders shook hands with Von Spiegel and the two men exchanged friendly words. Lt Sanders wished the Baron 'God-Speed' before handing him over to the waiting authorities. The three German survivors were transferred to the Donnington Hall PoW camp, in Leicestershire. Under interrogation, Von Spiegel offered the name of his boat, plus the names of vessels he had sunk and prisoners taken.. When he admitted that *U 93* had indeed sunk the SS *Horsa*, much to his astonishment the British interrogation officer heaped praise on him for assisting the crew and saving them from certain death.

Like all good stories there is a twist in this tale. All on board *Prize* believed the U-boat had been sunk. In fact *U 93* had levelled off beneath the surface, her presence masked by the heavy swell and the welcome cloak of darkness. With the pressure hull pierced, Lt.z.S. Ziegner, now officer in command of the boat, realised the submarine was severely damaged and limited in terms of the avoiding action it could take. Large sections of the casing had been torn off the submarine. Air tanks were ruptured beyond repair and the periscopes had been shattered. Shell fragments had penetrated the oil tanks, marking the submarine's track with a viscous tell-tale slick. Gauges and other instruments in the control centre were broken and useless and the boat's drinking water was contaminated with seawater. Miraculously and against all odds, Lt.z.S. Ziegner succeeded in sailing *U 93* back to Wilhelmshaven, arriving home on 11 May 1917. Upon arrival, Ziegner desribed how Von Spiegel had been worshipped by his crew and that all concerned had reacted badly to his death.

A month later, Von Spiegel and the two other survivors learned that *U 93* had in fact limped home. In turn, the Red Cross informed the KDM that the three men blown off the bridge had survived too. The Red Cross were also able to inform the families of British merchant seamen that their men were interned in German PoW camps but very much alive. There was good news for the crew of *Prize* too. All crewmen received the DSM. Lt Beaton RNR was awarded a DSO. Lt Sanders received the highest award for courage, the Victoria Cross, plus the rank of 'Temporary' Lt Commander, RNR.

It would be pleasing to be able to end this account on such a positive note but the First World War holds few happy endings and this is no exception. Lt Sanders was offered a safer command but he turned down all offers and returned instead to the patched-up *Prize*, now based at the Irish port of Killybegs. The vessel was operating anti-U-boat patrols in conjuction with a number of 'D' Class submarines based on HMS *Platypus*. This was a 'livebait' operation. The 'D' Class submarines were the hunters and HMS *Prize* was the bait. On 12 June there was an inconclusive scrap with a U-boat and once again the battered old schooner suffered damage. Sanders too was slightly wounded in the course of the engagement. By August 1917, *Q21* was back in action and Lt Sanders now bore the ribbon of a DSO in addition to his VC. In the months that followed, the KDM patiently built up a picture of Q-ship operations and identities. Rather than tackling suspicious vessels on the surface, the U-boats were increasingly attacking them while submerged at periscope depth. August was to be a bleak month for the Q-ships.

On 13 August 1917 *Prize* was working in company with *D6*. What follows is an extract from the KTB of *UB 48*. The U-boat was on passage to the Mediterranean via the *nordweg* at the time of the attack. Steinbauer wrote:

13.8. [CT] Northwest Ireland. Wind and sea north strength 3, cloudy.
    1630 3-mast schooner with Swedish flag, about 500 t. observed. Forced the crew to leave the schooner after more hits with shells, thereafter we dived. 8 crew members observed leaving in a lifeboat and nobody left on the schooner. Could observe all of the schooners deck without seeing anything suspicious. Dived again at a range of 1000 m. Then the lifeboat was heading back towards the schooner and we signalled 'abandon ship'. With our deckgun manned we sailed nearer to the schooner. Suddenly we observed people on the deck and the Swedish flag was changed with the British White Ensign. From the foredeck they opened fire with a small calibre gun and on the afterdeck they they were turning a heavier cannon towards us. After I ordered 'Alarm' and before we dived, my deck crew scored a hit close to the heavy gun on the afterdeck on the schooner. This hit maybe saved us, because there was no fire from this cannon, they only hit us with one shell from the small gun before we disappered. Then we left, but stayed in the area because we were determined to sink this ship.

The crew of *UB 48* were exceptionally fortunate in that *D6* had become separated from HMS *Prize* and was some distance astern. What follows is an extract from the log of HMS *D6*:

1550 Observed shells falling close to Prize. Group up. Stand by bow tubes. Proceeded to port side of Prize. Flag signal immediately. Enemy submarine seen to be there.
1616 Observed submarine on starboard side of Prize. Speed up and make towards enemy.
1625 Enemy disappears. Prize having opened fire.

The submarine hailed *Prize* and Lt Sanders gave an account of what had transpired. He reiterated his belief that the U-boat had been shelled but not sunk. Lt Sanders was absolutely correct. Close by, lurking at periscope depth and observing every movement, lay *UB 48*.

Steinbauer:

In the dusk we closed in on the schooner, first on the surface and then submerged. The schooner sailed slow and was zigzagging towards the wind without changing the spread of canvas, which showed us that it was motordriven. On both sides of the schooner were two small boats, but I couldn't see if they were motorboats or submarines in the darkness.

D6 kept astern of *Prize*, charging batteries 500-700 yards away, leaving Steinbauer to stalk his prey. Steinbauer observed:

4.8. Dark, cloudy, rain shower, strong phosphorescence, wind NW strength 3–4.
    0135hrs. It was too dark to fire a torpedo submerged, we then surfaced. The schooner was heading NE at high speed. At 0305hrs we fired a torpedo at a distance of 400m but the torpedo missed. The torpedo was not observed from the schooner. At 0325hrs we fired a second torpedo at a distance of 700m. The torpedo hit the schooner midships which resulted in a very big explosion. After the explosion the schooner had vanished from the surface.

The log of *D6* contains this entry:

> Dark night, rough sea, low visbility
> 0130hrs Violent explosion on board *Prize* (observed to have sunk) Proceeded over spot. Noone to be seen in water. Dived and kept in vicinity until daylight. Observed enemy submarine 3–5 miles distant but unable to get within range.
> 15 August moored alongside *Platypus*

THE CREW OF HMS PRIZE

Clemo, Charles Reginald, Shipwright 2nd Class
Ferguson, James, Deckhand RNR
Iinch, John Lumsden, Temp/Skipper RNR
King, Nicholas, Seaman RNR
Lake, Frederick, Temp/Skipper RNR
Portch, Henry Herbert, Temp/Lt RNVR
Ravey, Thomas, Deckhand RNR
Sanders, William Edward (VC, DSO), Temp/Lt Cmdr RNR
Stobart, Walter Percy, Motor Mechanic RNVR
Tarraway, Robert, PO RN
Thacker, Tom, Deckhand RNR
Vincent, William Robert, Deckhand RNR
Watson, Harold Leslie, Motor Mechanic RNVR
Williamson, Alexander, Deckhand RNR
Wilson, Gilbert John, Deckhand RNR

The men of HMS *Prize* are remembered on Panel 23 of the Plymouth War Memorial. The church at Milford Haven also preserves a memorial tablet to Lt Sanders VC and his crew.

Meanwhile, back to the patrols of *U 93*:

Oblt. Wilhelm Ziegner remained CO until 22 May 1917, when Kplt. Helmut Gerlach assumed command of *U 93* and Ziegner returned to his job as second officer.

(2) After a complete refit and the damage repaired, Helmut Gerlach left Emden on 18 June 1917 and sailed for the North Channel, the Irish Sea and an area 300 miles west of Ireland, going via the Shetland Isles and Cape Wrath. Gerlach torpedoed and sunk the 645-ton, wooden-hulled, Norwegian barque *Louise* (1876 – A/S Louise, Fredrikstad) on 19 June, 135 miles ENE from Hook Point, Hartlepool, which was on passage Hartlepool for Kristiania with coke. The defensively armed SS *Baron Ogilvy* (1909 – Hogarth Shipping Co. Ltd, Ardrossan) of 4,570 tons, was torpedoed and sunk on the 27th without warning, 172 miles off Tory Island; she was on passage from Montreal for Liverpool with wheat and two men were killed.

THE MEN WHO DIED

Leong Wong, Fireman
Wybar, Robert Winnings, 24yrs, 4th Engineer Officer

The 308-ton, wooden-hulled, three-masted Danish schooner *Kodan* (1897 – H.C. Ryhave, Fredensborg) was sunk on Wednesday 4 July 1917; she was en-route from Fleetwood to Reykjavik, Iceland with 441 tons of coal. At 1700hrs, a periscope was observed and all hands were mustered on deck and the lifeboats launched. The submarine crossed the bow of *Kodan* on a SSE course; then after 45 minutes she came alongside and ordered the crew into the boats, informing the men that their vessel was going to be scuttled. The master, Captain H. R. Christensen, the 2nd mate and an able seaman rowed to the submarine and handed over ship's papers. One German officer and three submariners returned to *Kodan* and put dynamite-cartridges into the hold. Twenty minutes later these exploded and the vessel sank at about 56° 24' N 9° 9' W. The Danish crew sailed with the boats in a southerly direction, until 1600hrs on Saturday, when a British patrol boat picked them up and landed them at Oban, Scotland on the Sunday morning.

U 93 put back into Emden, travelling via the Isles of Orkney.

The U-boat had suffered some damage during the voyage, but put back out to sea after repairs. Off Terschelling light vessel, U 93 narrowly missed being sunk when a submarine, possibly a British one, fired two torpedoes at her and missed.

U 93 returned to Emden on 13 July 1917.

(3) Gerlach sailed from Emden with U 93 on 4 August, travelling around the Isles of Orkney, down the southwest of Ireland to the western end of the English Channel and Bay of Biscay. In three weeks, Gerlach sank nine steamships during the war cruise and one sailing vessel. The Norwegian SS *Bestum* (1895 – D/S Aktieselskapet Bestum II, Kristiania) was captured, then shelled and sunk while en-route from Baltimore, Maryland to London with flour on 12 August.

The 5,642-ton steamer *ASTI* (1896 – Italian requisition – operated by Ferrovie dello Stato, Genoa) was torpedoed and sunk without warning on 13 August, 220 miles southwest of the Isles of Scilly; she was transporting coal from Barry to Taranto.

Four men were lost on the defensively armed 3,558-ton steamship *Elswick Lodge* (1900 – Elswick Steam Shipping Ltd, Newcastle) which was torpedoed and sunk without warning 260 miles off Ushant while travelling from the Tyne to Naples with maize on the 20th.

THE MEN WHO PERISHED

Arnott, Benjamin, 16yrs, Mess Room Steward
Beyarano, T.G., 33yrs, Fireman and Trimmer
Sheehan, Jeremiah, 19yrs, Sailor
Wordingham, Albert Victor, 24yrs, 4th Engineer Officer

The next day ten crewmen, including 1st Mate Charles John Angus, were drowned on the defensively armed 5,689-ton SS *Volodia* (1913 – Cunard Steam-Ship Co. Ltd, Liverpool), which was torpedoed without warning, while travelling from Montreal to London.

The 898-ton US sailing ship *Carl F. Cressy* (Percy & Small, Bath, Maine) left La Pallice on 22 August, 1917, but at daylight the next day she was intercepted by U 93 and sunk by gunfire at 45° 53'N 11° 13'W; her crew of nine were able to launch the boat and make their escape. She was en-route from La Pallice in ballast to New York. On 25 August the *Heatherside* (1909 – Charlton Steam Shipping Co. Ltd, Newcastle), a defensively armed steamer of 2,767 tons, was torpedoed and sunk without warning while voyaging from Milford Haven to Malta with coal; twenty-seven men were drowned.

SOME OF THE MEN WHO DIED

Batchelor, H., 17yrs, Ordinary Seaman
Bell, Alexander, 17yrs, Fireman and Trimmer
Besley, Albert John, 51yrs, Ship's Cook
Bolam, John William, 39yrs, 1st Mate
Cairns, John, 29yrs, Fireman and Trimmer
Caplin, Joseph Harry, 17yrs, Mess Room
  Steward
Carrick, John, 48yrs, 2nd Engineer
Curtis, Ivor Leslie, 17yrs, Sailor
Foster, Robert, 33yrs, Fireman and Trimmer
George, Arthur Reuben, 27yrs, Carpenter
Golightly, Matthew, 26yrs, 3rd Engineer
Goodall, William, 62yrs, Sailor

Grey, Edward James, 24yrs, Sailor
Harland, William Sowerby, 24yrs, Sailor
Harrison, James Grainger, 16yrs, Apprentice
Johnson, Charles, 24yrs, Sailor
Lilburn, William, 24yrs, Fireman and Trimmer
Lockey, John Brown Baker, 44yrs, Fireman
McKenzie, John, 44yrs, Boatswain (Bosun)
Mitchell, Peter, Able Seaman RNVR
Mitchell, Peter, Able Seaman RNVR (DAMS)
Morgan, Charles Hiram, 35yrs, Steward
Ross, Harry Lamond, 15yrs, Apprentice
Thomas, William Richard, 33yrs, 2nd Mate

The 1,650-ton steamer *Ovar* (1903 – Portuguese Government requisition – Transportes Maritimos do Estado, Lisbon) was next to sink by a torpedo strike without warning later that day at position 46° 05'N 11° 15'W; the ship was en-route from Milford Haven to Lisbon with coal.

The SS *Marmion* (1912 – Pyman Steamship Co. Ltd, West Hartlepool) of 4,066 tons and defensively armed, was torpedoed without warning 300 miles from Ushant on 26 August, while transporting oats and steel from New York to Bordeaux; seventeen crewmen were drowned.

SOME OF THE MEN WHO DIED

Abde Hasan, Fireman and Trimmer
Ali Muha Mmad, Fireman and Trimmer
Buchell (or Brickell), W., 20yrs, Sailor
Carbaltlo, S., 37yrs, Sailor
Cooke, Henry, 42yrs, 2nd Engineer
Corbett, Robert, 17yrs, Apprentice
Davies, Thomas Hector, 23yrs, 3rd Engineer
Dinitre, A., Fireman
Ghulam Muha Mmad, Donkeyman
Gosling, William George, 16yrs, Assistant Steward
Hasan Liaqat, Fireman and Trimmer
Jamal Ali, Fireman and Trimmer
Kemp, William, Leading Seaman RNVR (DAMS)
Merriman, Joseph William, 27yrs, Boatswain (Bosun)
Prendergast, Maurice William, 28yrs, 2nd mate
Stuart, Robert William, 30yrs, Ship's Cook
Young, James Reginald Bullen, 17yrs, Apprentice

Later that same day, the wooden, three-masted barque *Minas Queen* (1916 – Minas Queen Shipping Co Ltd, Parrsboro, Nova Scotia) of 492 tons, was on passage from Tonnay Charente in France for New York, when she was captured 350 miles from Cape Finisterre; Gerlach then sunk her by gun-fire and five men were killed.

THE MEN WHO DIED

Gardner, Henry, Able Seaman
Johnson, King David, Able Seaman
Kay, George Alfred, Mate
Marner, or Warner, F., Cook
Pitts, William, Able Seaman

Before he returned to Emden, Gerlach torpedoed and sunk the 3,071-ton defensively armed SS *Treloske* (1902 – Hain Steamship Co. Ltd, St Ives) without warning, 145 miles from Cape Finisterre on 29 August; the ship was taking coal from Barry to La Spezia in Italy and William Charles Edward Garrod, a 20-year-old able seaman, was drowned.

U 93 returned home via the Orkney Isles, arriving on 7 September.

During September 1917, *U 93* moved to the shipyard at Wilhelmshaven for a minor refit.

(4) On 9 October 1917, *U 93* departed Emden with Kplt. Gerlach and sailed via Kiel and the Baltic Sea around the Isles of Orkney and down to an area 300 miles southwest of Ushant, off Brittany. Gerlach shelled, torpedoed and sunk the 3,557-ton Brazilian steamer *Mação* (1912 – Brazilian Government, Rio de Janeiro) on 18 October and 170 miles northwest of Cape Ortegal; the vessel was inward bound from Rio de Janeiro with coffee and cocoa and was lost with all hands. On 27 October, the American steamer *D. N. Luckenbach* (1883 – E.F. Luckenbach) of 2,929 tons was torpedoed and sunk while it was travelling from New York to Le Havre; eight of her crew of thirty-three were lost. Next day, *U 93* torpedoed and damaged the 12,222-ton US cargo ship *Finland* (1902 – International Mercantile Marine Co., New York), but she eventually reached port safely and was salvaged. On the 29th, the Uruguayan sailing ship *La Epoca* (1893 – Dodero Hnos) of 2,432

tons was on passage from New York for Bordeaux when a torpedo sunk her in the Gironde Estuary, about 30 miles from Cordouan lighthouse.

The 2,521-ton Norwegian SS *Liff* (1913 – Skibs-Aktieselskapet 'Liff', Kristiania) sank on the 30th after being captured and shelled 70 miles west of Penmarc'h, France; it was bound from Norfolk, Virginia to Bordeaux with general cargo.

U 93 sailed back to Emden on 8 November, returning via the Orkney Isles.

FINAL PATROL

(5) On 29 December 1917, *U 93* sailed out of Borkum Reede with Gerlach for operations at the western end of the English Channel. Oblt.z.S. Wilhelm Ziegner, the hero who brought the boat home in May 1917, was forced to disembark through illness. Gerlach is known to have taken the more dangerous route directly through the Dover Straits. The 25-ton fishing smack *Veda* (Cocks & Davies, Swansea), skippered by Walter Hewett, had left Brixham light/empty for Swansea on 31 December 1917 in heavy seas and a moderate gale. About 30 miles off the Eddystone light on 2 January 1918 at 0700hrs and position 49° 40'N 04° 21'W, a U-boat was sighted at 4,000 yards range; when a shell was fired, she was brought up into the wind and the crew abandoned ship in a small sail boat. The *VEDA* was sunk by gunfire and went down burning, by the head. After six days at sea in their small craft, the destroyer *Cockatrice* picked the men up at about: 49° 12'N 05 20'W, west of the Scilly Isles.

The 235-ton armed French patrol boat *Goeland II* followed her to the bottom on 4 January. At 1945hrs on Saturday 5 January and 25° north of Ushant light, the 2,459-ton US steamer *A.A. Raven* (1912 – American Transportation Co., Inc., Philadelphia) was in a convoy from Brest to The Lizard, when a man on a raft was heard shouting and whistling for help. The ship swung out of the convoy and manoeuvred, until the raft was located and the man picked up. Unfortunately, he was in an unconscious state and his whole body had to be rubbed and then rolled in blankets before he came round properly. Afterwards, the man said he was 24-year-old Ronaud Pierre Marie, a Navy-fireman (Military No.81732) from the French Navy patrol boat *Goeland II* of Brest. Fireman Marie asserted, that *Goeland II* was escorting a three-masted schooner off Ile de Vers at 0900hrs on 4 January when his vessel encountered a U-boat (*U 93*), which they engaged in combat. The second and third shots from the submarine exploded the boilers. After the explosion, they managed to lower a boat, but he and another man, Fireman Mateo Louis Bureoux Aqation, got on a raft. Fireman Marie stated that the other man had died 10 hours previous and his body was still on the raft when he was picked up by the steamer. (Mr Marie was handed over to the Naval Authorities at Penzance on 6 January.)

On that day, the *Evening News* recorded:

> *Goeland II* was bombarded at night by a submarine at point blank range with two guns. Although the French ship had received her death blow, the crew took up their fighting positions and two men who were serving the guns at the bows, were killed. The quartermaster gunner joyously gave the order to open fire. His second shell put the gun at the stern out of action. The submarine then submerged after having fired three times with her forward gun. The *Goeland II* then sank and the crew abandoned her under the orders of the second officer, who was seriously wounded, the commander of the patrol boat having gone down with his vessel.

At 2330hrs on 5 January, the French 2,488-ton steamer *Henri Le Cour* (1917 – Chargeurs de l'Ouest, Nantes) was in convoy from Cardiff to Nantes when a torpedo fired by *U 93* sank her 9 miles west of Penmarc'h at 47° 44'N 4° 33'W. Armed with two guns of 90mm model 77 on 1918 mountings, she had departed Cardiff with 4,067 tons of coal on 3 January 1918, the master, Captain Adolphe Caudal, having received his last instructions in Bay of Roscanvel, near Brest. She was steering S80W (260°) on a straight course from Roscanvel Bay and travelling at 7/8 knots. The master ordered hard to starboard when submarine was sighted, but the ship sank before the order was completed, however other ships from the convoy were still in sight, the closest being the leader of the outside column, steering abeam. An SOS was sent out three times before the electricity ran down, but no reply was received. One torpedo detonated about 15m from the rear in No.4 hold. On board was a crew of thirty-two Frenchmen, one British engineer, one passenger and a pilot. The gunners were named as Louis Riou, chief servant, G. Sauvage, Leon Harcouet, J. Gavard, Leon Gilles and L. Boudeau.

The steamer sank at once, leaving just enough time to lower two large boats and one jollyboat, in which the men abandoned ship. The master took command of the boats on starboard side (one boat and the jollyboat), which contained eleven other men, including the British engineer; later those in the jolly were taken on board the master's boat and the jolly was abandoned. Those men were all rescued by the destroyer *Temeraire*, some 3 hours after the ship sank, at around 0230hrs; they were landed at Nantes. The second boat, commanded by the first officer, contained eighteen men, however, at the time when this report was made there was no trace of those men. A Naval Administration Officer at Quimper just reported that fishermen had found a boat marked '*Henri Le Cour*' with nobody on board and they towed it to Penmarc'h.

In the Bay of Biscay on 6 January, Gerlach sent three more steamers to a watery grave: early that morning the 1,220-ton Danish *Dagny* (1901 – Aktieselskabet Dampskibsselskabet Selsk. Heimdal, Copenhagen) was destroyed by a torpedo, while transporting 1,587 tons of coal from Port Talbot to Bordeaux and two crewmen were drowned.

The 2,798-ton US steam freighter *Harry Luckenbach* (1881 – Luckenbach Steam Ship Co.) was on charter to the American Forces when *U 93* torpedoed and sunk her without warning on 6 January 1918. Commanded by Captain Fred S. Jones, the unarmed *Harry Luckenbach* departed Brest for Cardiff in a convoy of fifteen vessels in two lines, on the afternoon of 5 January; she was the first one in the right column, with *Henri Le Cour* first ship in the left column, roughly steering east and heading for Glenans Roads. The torpedo slammed into her amidships on the starboard side at 0010hrs on 6 January and she sank immediately, on bearing S60W (240°) and 2 miles from Penmarc'h. The explosion was so violent that many of the thirty-three were thrown overboard, although some managed to lower a boat and seven clambered into it. Seven other men clung to floating wreckage and the other survivors kept swimming, but luckily, the escort HMS *Wanderer* (1895) arrived almost immediately. *Wanderer* picked up twenty-five men and landed them at Quiberon, but eight others had perished. The two escorts, *Kanawaga* and *Harward*, remained on the spot for a further 2 hours. Captain Jones, who had a serious head injury, later stated that one of the officers lost with the ship, had reported seeing a submarine 25 minutes before the incident, but nobody else saw it.

The 3,793-ton Greek ship *Kanaris* (1901 – N. Embiricos Sons, Andros) was in convoy and carrying 4,435 tons of coal from Barry to Bordeaux when she too was torpedoed off Penmarc'h, on 6 January.

Gerlach was probably on his return voyage home with *U 93* when the SS *War Song* (1917 – The Shipping Controller, London) was sunk by gunfire on 15 January; she was en-route from Bilbao to Brest with iron ore and sixteen men were drowned.

SOME OF THE MEN WHO DIED

Abdaullah Saleh, Fireman and Trimmer
Abdus Hamid, Bhandary
Ali Ju Mma, Fireman
Audigier, Charles Lombard, 16yrs, Boy (W/T Op.)
Brown, M.T., Ship's Steward
Fleming, Alfred Stalker, 41yrs, 1st Engineer
Goulding, William Patrick, 52yrs, 2nd Officer
Hollingsworth, J., 29yrs, 2nd Engineer
Ramsay, James Rankine, 48yrs, Mate
Rasmussen, A., 25yrs, Carpenter
Said Umar, Donkeyman
South, J.G., 47yrs, Master
Tepsich, J., 30yrs, Boatswain (Bosun

The identity of the U-boat responsible for sinking *War Song* remains conjectural.

Nothing was ever heard of the U-boat again. In common with the crew of their adversary HMS *Prize* and many other sailors before and since, the sailors of *U 93* were brave men who had simply pushed their luck a patrol too far.

NARA Series T-1022, Roll 38, PG 61676 M.1581 – S.1.O. Cardiff 9-1-18, GOELAND II ADM 173/1086
U-Boot-Ehrenmal Möltenort CWGC

THE MEN WHO PERISHED WITH U 93

André, R. U-Obermaschinistenmaat
Belger, Friedrich U-Oberheizer
Burchardi, Friedrich Kapitänleutnant
Böxkes, Karl U-Oberheizer
Gerlach, Helmut Kapitänleutnant
Goldalmer, E. U-Maschinistenmaat
Graef, Franz U-Maschinist
Gromczik, W. U-Bootsmannsmaat
Gutschmidt, K. U-Matrose
Hahn, Hermann Leutnant zur See der Reserve
Hanke, Hermann U-Steuermann
Hartmann, G. U-Matrose
Haussmann, H. Marine Ingenieur
Heidner, Karl U-Maschinistenmaat
Hölscher, Heinrich U-Heizer
Jeddicke, Karl U-Maschinistenmaat
Just, Arthur U-Oberbootsmannsmaat
Karl, Emil U-F.T.Maat d.Res
Kranz, A. U-Heizer
Kunkel, Karl U-Heizer
Kyritz, Karl U-Maschinistenmaat
Köhler, Konrad U-Obermaschinistenmaat

Meyer, Karl U-Oberheizer
Munder, Paul U-Obermatrose
Nieden, Johann U-Bootsmannsmaat
Pannermeyer, T. U-Heizer
Peters, M. U-Maschinistenmaat der Reserve
Petzold, Max U-Heizer
Robrecht, Joseph U-Heizer
Schemm, von W. U-Heizer
Scherfose, August U-Maschinistenmaat
Schmidt, Peter U-Heizer
Schmidt, Kurt U-Matrose
Schönawa, J. U-F.T.Gast
Schröder, Peter U-Maschinistenmaat.d.Ers.
   Reserve
Schröder, P. Friedrich U-Matrose
Schulze, Karl U-Obermatrose
Schuster, Georg U-Oberbootsmannsmaat
Seiberlich, Otto U-F.T.Gast
Strohmeyer, A. U-Maschinistenmaat
Thurau, Heinrich U-Matrose
Usedom, von H. Oberleutnant zur See
Wefer, Friedrich U-Matrose

WRECK SITE

French and Belgian divers have just recently identified this wreck as that of *U 93*. It lies on a seabed of rocks, sand and gravel, in a general depth of 31m (102ft), being the lowest astronomical depth. The wreck is upright and intact and in quite reasonable condition, with the hatches all still closed. The upper sections also have a covering of anemones. Divers report that there is no obvious damage to the boat externally, so it was presumably an operational loss, probably caused by some sort of diving accident, a surprising fate for such an experienced crew. The wreck is also classed as a war grave.

U 84, SM IMPERIAL U-BOAT

DATE OF LOSS: after 15 January 1918
DEPTH: Unknown
REFERENCE: Unknown
LOCATION: Unknown

Type: Mittel-U (Improved Type *U 65*) ocean torpedo attack boat   **Builders**: Germaniawerft, Kiel for Kaiserliche Deutsche Marine   **Ordered**: on 23 June 1915, within the batch of U 81–U 86   **Keel laid**: as Yard No.254 on 25 October 1915   **Launched**: on 22 July 1916   **Commissioned**: by Kapitänleutnant Walter Roehr on 7 October 1916

TECHNICAL SPECIFICATIONS

Hull: double   **Surface displacement**: 808 tons   **U/Dt**: 946 tons   **LBDH**: 70.10m × 6.30m × 4m × 8.70m   **Machinery**: 2 × 1,200ps Maschinefabrik-Augsburg-Nürnberg diesels   **Props**: 2

bronze   *S/Sp*: 16.8 knots   *Op/R*: 11,220 nautical miles at 8 knots   *Sub/R*: 56 nautical miles at 5 knots   *U/Power*: 2 × 600ps electric motors gave 9.1 knots   *Batteries*: AFA lead/acid/accumulators   *Fuel/Cap*: 81 + 38 tons   *Armament*: 2 bow and 2 stern 50.04cm torpedo tubes   *Torpedoes*: 8 × 50.04cm (19.7in)   *Guns*: 1 × 105mm (4.13in) forward deck gun and 1 × 88mm (3.46in) 5m aft of conning tower   *Ammo*: 276 rounds *Diving*: max-op-depth 50m (164ft) and 45 sec to crash-dive   *Complement*: 35

U 84 was formally assigned to IV.U-Bootflottille at Emden on 3 December and began training operations with Kplt. Walter Roehr, the commander from 17 October 1916. Oblt.z.S. Keysers was 1WO; Ltz.S.d.R. Hunlich was 2 WO and Mar.Oblt.Ing. Keiser was chief engineer.

(1) The first patrol of *U 84* was a training run into the North Sea in December 1916. However Roehr still captured two steam ships: the 1,359-ton Norwegian *Aamot* (1907 – Rederi Aktieselskapet Orkla, Trondheim) on 14 December, which was voyaging from Skien to the UK with nitrate, and the 1,200-ton Swedish *Malcolm* (1879 – Rederi AB. Malcolm, Landskrona) on the 18th. She had loaded up with 520 standards of pit props at Sandesund, Norway and departed with a crew of eighteen on 17 December, heading for Grimsby, under the command of Captain C.A. Karlsson. The vessel was captured by *U 84* at 0940hrs the very next day at position 57° 10'N 7° 35'E. The prize crew ordered the *Malcolm* to go to Cuxhaven and from there to Hamburg. The *Aamot*, however, was condemned for her actions by a prize court and requisitioned as a store ship for the Kaiserliche Deutsche Marine in April 1917. (In 1919 the vessel became Deutsches Reich – Reichskommissar für die Seeschiffahrt.)

(2) On 1 January 1917, *U 84* left Heligoland for operations off the west and south coast of Ireland, going via the Isles of Orkney. On the 9th Roehr torpedoed and damaged the SS *Alexandrian* (1901 – F. Leyland & Co. Ltd, Liverpool) of 4,467 tons without warning, southwest of Fastnet Rock; the vessel was transporting a general cargo from New Orleans to Liverpool and was beached twice, but re-floated both times.

Roehr sank the 3,606-ton Norwegian SS *Bergenhus* (1899 – A/S D/S Bergenhus, Bergen) on 10 January, which was captured in the Atlantic and scuttled with explosives, while voyaging with coal from Newport, Monmouth to Portovecchio in France. The 3,908-ton SS *Auchencrag* (1903 – Auchen Steam Shipping Co. Ltd, Glasgow) was captured on the 12th, 20 miles off Ushant, then torpedoed and sunk while en-route from La Plata, Argentina to Cherbourg with wheat.

THE FOUR CREWMEN WHO DROWNED

Lee Yao, Fireman
Nicholas, James, 53yrs, Chief Steward
Platts, Frederick Cecil, 50yrs, Able Seaman
Subg Low, Fireman and Trimmer

The 1,944-ton, steel-hulled, three-masted, British sailing vessel *Kinpurney* (1902 – John Stewart & Co, of 26-28, Billiter Street, London) was commanded by Captain J.S. Davidson and en-route from Cardiff for Port Nolloth, South Africa with coal and coke on 15 January, when Roehr captured and then torpedoed and sank her, 110 miles west of Bishop Rock. Also on the 15th, the 1,574-ton Danish SS *OMSK* (1884 – Det Forenede Dampskibs Selsk., Copenhagen) was captured and then shelled and sunk, 93 miles west of Bishop Rock; she was voyaging from Leith to Genoa with coal and fish.

A torpedo fired without warning by Roehr sunk the SS *Bulgarian* (Ellerman Lines, Ltd, Glasgow), of 2,515 tons, southwest of Ireland, which was armed for defence and transporting iron ore from Cartegena, Spain to Garston on the River Mersey; twenty-two men, including the master, drowned.

THE MEN WHO DIED

Begley, Richard 39yrs, Able Seaman
Bridgewater, William Fred 17yrs, Mess Room Steward
Burnell, Louis 17yrs, Trimmer

Burns, P. 30yrs, Fireman
Devine, Mat 22yrs, Fireman
Edward, James Peter 28yrs, Greaser and Fireman
Ellis, Henry Oscar 27yrs, Chief Steward
Evans, L. 30yrs, Fireman and Trimmer
Fryer, Charles Frederick 52yrs, 1st Mate
Gambling, William Robert 18yrs, Assistant Cook
Holden, N. 25yrs, Fireman
Humphries, John William 24yrs, 3rd Mate
Irvine, W. 17yrs, Trimmer
Jones, Lewis 24yrs, Carpenter
Kelly, Richard 43yrs, Donkeyman
Lewis, H.H. 35yrs, Lamps and an Able Seaman
Libby, F.W. 36yrs, Able Seaman
Mackenzie, William 33yrs, Sailor
Miller, Harold Victor 26yrs, 2nd Engineer
Pigram, C. 36yrs, Greaser and Fireman
Rourke, James 36yrs, Sailor
Streamer, J. 28yrs, Fireman

Eighteen men were drowned, including the master when the 3,583-ton SS *Neuquen* (1913 – Buenoa Ayres Great Southern Railway Co. Ltd, London) was captured and sunk 20 miles from the Skelligs. She was making 9 knots and transporting a 5,900-ton cargo of maize from Rosario, Argentina to Belfast when *U 84* opened fire on her at 1430hrs, from about 2–3 miles astern. The master, Captain Phillip Thomas Evans, zig-zagged the ship every few minutes in an attempt to escape, but after two shells made direct hits, he stopped at 1640hrs and instructed his crew of thirty-four to abandon ship in two boats. *U 84* then torpedoed the ship and questioned the crew about their cargo and destination. Roehr also said they would send a radio message to Queenstown for someone to come to their rescue, before allowing the boats to move away. The boats got separated at about 0100hrs and the one holding the master and seventeen other men was never seen again, having presumed to have sunk; the second boat however, holding sixteen men, were picked up by RN trawlers, three days later.

THE PEOPLE WHO PERISHED

Alvarez, Manuel, 31yrs, Able Seaman
Binns, Ridley Bertram, 28yrs, Able Seaman
Christensen, A., 48yrs, Steward
Dixon, Thomas Basil, 33yrs, 2nd Mate
Eguen, Jose, 56yrs, Fireman
Ekstrom, H., Sailor
Evans, Phillip Thomas, 36yrs, Master
Feen, Michael, 41yrs, Able Seaman
Hansen, Martin, 27yrs, Donkeyman
Jossa, J., 20yrs, Fireman and Trimmer
Karistino, Pedro John, 44yrs, Able Seaman
Mahood, John, 21yrs, Assistant Steward
Morachis, Peter, 28yrs, Fireman
Newman, Percy, 29yrs, 3rd Engineer
Stewart, Gordon, 34yrs, Chief Engineer
Suarez, Jules, 28yrs, Fireman
Thorkildsen, Thomas Andrea, 43yrs, Carpenter
Torbensen, Otto, 27yrs, Fireman

U 84 returned home to Heligoland via the Orkney Isles, arriving on 25 January.

(3) *U 84* departed Heligoland on 15 February and sailed through the Dover Strait for operations off the south coast of Ireland. Ten miles off Portland Bill, Roehr torpedoed and sunk the defensively armed 2,548-ton SS *Romsdalen* (1895 – G.B. Harland & Co., West Hartlepool) without warning; she was transporting a 3,500-ton cargo of coal and patent fuel oil from Swansea to Calais. That same day and 25 miles off Start Point, the Rouen registered 2,589-ton steel-hulled, three-masted, French sailing ship *Bayonne* (1901 – Société Anonyme des Voiliers Normands) was captured and sunk with three explosive charges; she was under the command of Captain Thoumyre and en-route from New York to Ipswich with 1,000 tons of maize and 2,300 tons of barley. (Interestingly, after having lost his vessel, Captain Thoumyre, born in St Malo, met the young French naval lieutenant Trinité-Schillemans in Rouen while both of them were very much engaged in future anti-submarine activities. Lying in Rouen at this time was the unused barque *Nomandy* and they both decided that it would be a good idea to have it back at sea as a Q-ship. This they did until 25 June 1917, when they saw gunfire action in the mid-Channel against SM *UC 71*. During this encounter between the barque and the U-boat, Lt Trinité-Schillemans was killed by a shell but the U-boat evaded any damage. After the war, the name of Trinité-Schillemans was given to *UB 94* of the French Navy.

Walter Roehr attacked four vessels on 18 February: the 11,137-ton SS *Berrima* (1913 – Peninsular & Oriental Steam Navigation Co., Greenock) was between Start Point and the Lizard when she was hit with a torpedo and left damaged, while en-route from Fremantle to London with Australian produce; three men were killed in the explosion.

THE THREE MEN WHO DIED

Brown, Amos, Troop Cook
Grist, William Henry, Boatswain (Bosun)
McCarthy, James, Trimmer

The SS *Hunsworth* (1911 – Admiralty requisition, London) was heading for Karachi from the Clyde, when a torpedo damaged her 6.5 miles off Portland Bill; the ship was towed into Portland Roads, however the explosion, killed two men in the engine room.

THE TWO MEN WHO DIED

Thornhill, Prince Albert, Fireman
Whittaker, Allan Arthur St. Clair, Fireman

The iron-hulled 2,416-ton Norwegian steamer *Juno* (1888 – Aktieselskapet Vera, Kristiania) was en-route from New York to Le Havre with general cargo, which included copper ingots, autos, machinery and provisions, but *U 84* captured her off Start Point; the ship was then scuttled with five explosive charges.

While travelling from Manchester to Cherbourg with flour and hay, the 2,233-ton steamer *Valdes* (1914 – Avetoro S.S. Co. Ltd, Liverpool) sank off Portland Bill after a torpedo strike and eleven men drowned.

THE MEN WHO DIED

Clay, David, 39yrs, Fireman and Trimmer
Davis, Edward Day, 45yrs, Fireman and Trimmer
Hall, John, 54yrs, Able Seaman
Herbert, William, 37yrs, Fireman and Trimmer
Malpus, Joseph, 18yrs, Storekeeper
Marsters, Frederick Arthur, 22yrs, Seaman
Morris, Samuael, 56yrs, Boatswain (Bosun)
Robinson, William Henry, 43yrs, 1st Mate
Seaton, M., 24yrs, Fireman and Trimmer
Spence, William, 35yrs, Chief Engineer
Tuaminen, J., 26yrs, Carpenter

In the Atlantic, Kplt. Roehr captured, shelled and sunk the *Dukat* (1903 – Dampskipsselskapet Aktieselskapet Dovre, Drammen) a 1,408-ton Norwegian steamer hauling coal from Barry to Fayal in the Azores.

On the 22nd and 22 miles off Mine Head, Co. Waterford, the 1,416-ton, steel-hulled, British barque *Invercauld* (1891 – Marine Navigation Co. Ltd) was captured while transporting wood/timber from Gulfport to Fleetwood. The crew of twenty-three were ordered to abandon the vessel and it was then torpedoed. However, according to the master's report at Queenstown, Kplt. Roehr first boarded the barque and removed the ship's bell and chronometer, for which he gave the master a receipt. The master, chief officer and cook had remained on board and, when the torpedo exploded, the cook was blown overboard, followed by the other two men who jumped over the side. *U 84* then fired three shells into the half-sunken barque, but being full of wood, she stayed afloat and drifted eastward; however, soon after, witnesses saw her capsize. The survivors were landed at Queenstown, where the master made his report. (An interesting tale about this ship is, that, in the late twentieth century, a fisherman got his pots entangled in a wreck and asked a local diver to retrieve them for him; in doing so, the diver recovered a bell from the wreck, which identified her as the *Invercauld*, and dated 1891.)

Soon after the barque incident, *U 84* sustained serious damage in a gunfight with the Q-ship HMS *Penhurst*. The U-boat managed to escape and limped back into Heligoland on 28 February, travelling via the Isles of Shetland.

(4) Following repairs, *U 84* sailed from Emden with Kplt. Walter Roehr on 5 April 1917 and proceeded around the Isles of Orkney, to patrol areas in the Atlantic, west and southwest of the Isles of Scilly. Roehr attacked two ships on 13 April: the defensively armed 3,547-ton SS *Argyll* (1901 – Routhi S.S. Co. Ltd, London) was struck by a torpedo without warning and sunk 110 miles from Bishop Rock; she was shipping iron ore from Port Kelah, Algeria to Middlesborough and twenty-two crewmen (all hands) were drowned as a result.

THE MEN WHO DIED

Barry, William Christopher, 16yrs, 2nd Steward
Bryant, Frederick Benjamin, 23yrs, 2nd Engineer
Cabena, Frank, 34yrs, Fireman
Cameos, Francis, 23yrs, Fireman
Cook, Donald McQueen, 17yrs, Mess Room Steward
James, George, 43yrs, Fireman
Jones, David, 28yrs, 1st Engineer
Manderson, John, 52yrs, Chief Steward
Martin, Alexander, 29yrs, Fireman
Mutford, H.Y., 60yrs, Carpenter
McConologue, Neil, 24yrs, Sailor
McCormick, Denis, 24yrs, Fireman
McGall, Thos, 32yrs, Sailor
McGalliard, James, 48yrs, Ship's Cook
McLean, Hugh, 29yrs, Sailor
Pouliet, Jos, 54yrs, 2nd Cook
Richardson, Daniel, 22yrs, Sailor
Smith, Alexander Miller, 41yrs, Fireman
Spedding, Samuel Christopher, 23yrs, 4th Engineer Officer
Williams, John Parry, 23yrs, 3rd Engineer
Williams, John Patrick, 22yrs, Chief Engineer

The 5,379-ton defensively armed *Lime Branch* (1902 – Nautilus Steam Shipping Co. Ltd, Sunderland) was carrying nitrate and general cargo from Callao, near Lima, Peru to London, when a torpedo from *U 84* damaged her and she put into Plymouth for repairs.

Two ships were destroyed on 18 April 1917: a torpedo fired without warning sunk the 3,235-ton defensively armed SS *Cragoswald* (1899 – Lunn & MacCoy, Newcastle) 60 miles off Bishop Rock; the ship was carrying maize from Buenos Aires to London and two men drowned.

THE MEN WHO DIED

Ghani Bin Qaisar, Sailor
Owen, Albert 52yrs, Boatswain (Bosun)

Walter Massingham (51yrs), a fireman and trimmer, drowned when the SS *Rowena* (1988 – Herskind & Co., West Hartlepool), a 3,017-ton steamer armed for defence, was torpedoed and sunk without warning 95 miles off Bishop Rock; she was transporting general cargo to Hull from Alexandria, Egypt.

The 3,943-ton *Elswick Manor* (1900 – Elswick S.S. Co. Ltd, Newcastle), a steamship armed for defence, was hit by a torpedo without warning on the 19th and she sank 180 miles west of Ushant, while on a heading for Naples from the Tyne with coal.

The 7,653-ton defensively armed SS *Malakand* (1905 – T. & J. Brocklebank, Liverpool) was first captured 145 miles from Bishop Rock on 20 April, then she was torpedoed and sunk; the ship was proceeding from Calcutta, India to Dundee with a jute and general cargo, unfortunately Edward Jones (35yrs), the ship's second engineer, was killed in the explosion.

U 84 travelled back to Heligoland via the Isles of Shetland and arrived there on 22 April.

(5) On 18 June 1917, *U 84* sailed out from Heligoland and around the Isle of Shetland for operations in the Atlantic, off the west coast of Ireland, the Bay of Biscay and Northern Ireland. Kplt Roehr sank three steamships and a Norwegian sailing vessel on this patrol: the 2,184-ton Spanish *Bachi* (1893 – Hijos de Astigarraga, Bilbao) was sunk by a torpedo on 1 July, west of Sables d'Olonne, while en-route from Newport, Monmouth to Bilbao. That same day, a torpedo damaged the 11,484-ton British liner *Demerara* (1912 – Royal Mail Steam Packet Co., Belfast) 6 miles from Sables d'Olonne, while transporting general cargo from Liverpool to Buenos Aires; she was beached at Ile de Ré, but re-floated later; sadly, a fireman and trimmer, Vasili Crasikov, died in the explosion. The ship was also armed for defence and the torpedo fired without warning. Ten miles south of Belle Ile, Kplt Roehr sank the SS *Goathland* (1906 – Headlam & Rowland, Whitby) with a torpedo fired without warning on 4 July; she was a 3,044-ton steamship, armed for defence and voyaging in ballast from St Nazaire to the Gulf of Mexico; twenty-two men were either killed or drowned.

SOME OF THOSE WHO DIED

Abdul Muha Mmad, Fireman and Trimmer
Burnley, William Arthur 18yrs, Ordinary Seaman
Casha, Laurene 42yrs, Donkeyman
Davies, Evan Lewis 26yrs, 3rd Engineer
Davies, John Llewellyn 30yrs, Sailor
Hanson, Francis 42yrs, Steward
Harrison, Thomas 32yrs, 2 Engineer
Jackson, Ernest 29yrs, Ship's Cook
Jansen, Wilfred Thomas 24yrs, Mess Room Steward
Jones, Thomas Enoch 24yrs, 2nd Mate
King, Frederick 25yrs, 1st Mate
Marsay, Norman McDonald 16yrs, Apprentice
Mordey, James 16yrs, Apprentice
Nagi Ali, Fireman and Trimmer
Rodger, R.G. 42yrs, 1st Engineer
Roe, John, Master
Romero, Juan 26yrs, Sailor
Shea, John 45yrs, Able Seaman

The 8,557-ton SS *Condesa* (1916 – Furness-Houlder Argentine Lines Ltd, Liverpool), a vessel armed for defence, went to the bottom of the Atlantic following a torpedo hit, fired without warning on the 7th; she was on her maiden voyage, transporting frozen meat from Buenos Aires to Liverpool. Roehr also captured and then torpedoed the 831-ton, iron-hulled, Norwegian barque *Oxø* (1876

– Skibs-A/S Oxø Kristiansand) on 7 July, 90 miles from the Scilly Isles; she was carrying logwood from Montego Bay to Le Havre.

U 84 returned to Emden, via the Isles of Shetland, arriving home on 15 July 1917.

(6) Departing Borkum on 4 August 1917, *U 84* sailed across the North Sea and around the Isles of Orkney to patrol off the west coast of Ireland and in the North Channel.

In the Atlantic on 12 August, Roehr attacked the 623-ton, wooden-hulled, Norwegian barque *Ursus Minor* (1890 – Heinrich Biørn Jr., Kragerø) with gunfire and set it ablaze; she was voyaging from Fleetwood for Reykjavik, Iceland with coal.

On 13 August, the 1,290-ton Royal Navy sloop HMS *Bergamot* (built in 1917 by Armstrong Whitworth) was torpedoed and sunk without warning. It is believed that at the time of her loss she was disguised as a merchantman and carried a complement of ninety-eight.

SOME OF THE CASUALTIES

Allen, Philip Henry, Able Seaman RN
Caplin, Frank, Leading Stoker RN
Collingham, David Arthur, Stoker 1st Class RN
Dyer, Richard Edward, Stoker 1st Class RN
Glasson, William Ewart, Officer's Steward 2C RN
Harding, Wallace, PO 1st Class RN
Letouze, Frank Charles, Chief ERA RNR
Mather, Ernest, Ordinary Seaman RN
Morton, William, Chief PO RN
Silvester, William Edwin, Stoker 1st Class RN
Stevenson, John, Temporary Lt RNR
Turner, George William, (MiD) Acting Temp/Paymaster RNR

U 84 returned to Emden on 1 September, travelling via the Shetland Isles.

(7) After a long stay in port, *U 84* departed Emden on 12 November 1917. Roehr had orders to go via the Orkney Isles to patrol off the west and southwest ends of the English Channel and down into the Bay of Biscay. On the 24th, the 4,999-ton American freighter *Actaeon* (US Shipping Board, New York) was destroyed 150 miles from Cape Finisterre, following a torpedo attack, after travelling from Bordeaux. The *Antonio Stathatos* (1901 – C. Stathatos, Ithaca), a Greek steamer of 2,743 tons, was also torpedoed and sunk in the Bay of Biscay, off Iles du Pilier, on 1 December, while on passage from Bordeaux for the UK.

Chief boatswain (bosun) Charles Frederick Butler was killed when the 2,821-ton defensively armed steamer *Birchgrove* (1894 – S.S. Mary Co. Ltd, Glasgow) sank on 2 December, 10 miles off Groix, after being hit by a torpedo without warning; she was transporting coal from Penarth to Bordeaux.

Roehr took the short route back to Emden in *U 84*, going through the Dover Strait, and arrived home on 12 December 1917.

FINAL PATROL

(8) On New Year's Day 1918, *U 84* departed Emden with her crew of forty and sailed into the North Sea, for operations in the Bay of Biscay. The skipper took the more perilous route through the Dover Strait, but *U 84* never returned. However, a message was intercepted, to the effect that *U 84* had reached the Channel on 3 January, but Emden never received that message. Roehr seemingly continued to try to communicate, then *Rugia* at Emden received a distorted message from *U 84* on the 6th, saying she had reached the western end of the Channel; no further messages were received.

U 84 was assessed to have torpedoed and sunk the 2,979-ton defensively armed steamer *Bayvoe* (1894 – Bay Steam Ship Co. Ltd, London) without warning on 9 January. The *Bayvoe* was transporting wheat from Portland, Maine via Halifax to Bordeaux. She had arrived at Brest from Halifax in convoy on 7 January 1918 and left in convoy for Bordeaux on 8 January. At 0230hrs on Wednesday 9 January, the ship was 10 miles south of Iles de Glaenean, between Penmarc'h Point and Belle Ile, with the second mate in charge on the bridge, the master having gone to the chart room on the lower bridge. Just as the master switched on the electric light, which went out again, there was a grating sound, followed by a heavy explosion. On arrival at the bridge and discovering his ship had been torpedoed in the engine room, amidships on the port side, he ordered everyone to the boats. Unfortunately, the explosion had destroyed the two boats on the port side and the engine room was full of water, so the master ordered the two starboard boats lowered and then he blew the steam whistle. After being satisfied that no one alive was still on the vessel, the boats pulled clear; the *Bayvoe* sank 8 minutes after the explosion. Her crew had been in the boats about 10 minutes when the submarine surfaced and the men were asked who was in charge. A reply was made by the 'second mate' (who was in fact the master); the U-boat commander said: '*come on board, second mate*'; when he did so, he was questioned about the ship, etc. and whether it had a gun on board. Particulars of the vessel were offered, but the master denied there was any gun on board, after which he was ordered back to the lifeboat and told to steer for Glaenean Island. Both boats were picked up by a French patrol vessel, one at 1000hrs and the master's boat at 1030hrs. The survivors were landed at Lorient at 1300hrs.

THE FOUR MEN WHO DIED

Balled, Michael E., 40yrs, 3rd Engineer
Magesan Nayudu, Fireman and Trimmer
Nissim, Loya, 19yrs, Mess Room Steward
Sevastiadis, E.O., 38yrs, Cook

At 0230hrs on Thursday 10 January, a violent explosion on the port side abreast of the stokehold, when about 20 miles SW of Lorient, rocked the 2,808-ton SS *Cardiff* (1989 – R.W.J. Sutherland & Sons, Cardiff). She was in convoy and transporting coal from Cardiff and Brest for St Nazaire, with the master in charge on the bridge, two lookouts forward and gunner on the platform aft. The shock from the explosion threw the master half way across the bridge, which flooded with warm water, possibly from the boiler. The order was given to abandon ship, but while lowering the port lifeboat, the davit snapped, throwing the boat and occupants into the sea. Nineteen hands lowered and manned the port boat, which then pulled clear. About 1 hour later, the U-boat appeared and Kplt. Roehr asked for the master or any officer, but he was informed that they had been killed. Roehr then asked for someone to step aboard the submarine and the second engineer volunteered, without divulging his identity; he was then questioned about the ship, cargo and gun calibre, before being sent back to the boat and the U-boat left in the darkness. The lifeboat waited until daylight before heading to shore, landing at the small village of Douean at 1020hrs on the 10th; from there they were sent by train to Lorient and discovered that their ship had been towed into Lorient Bay, where it grounded. French patrol vessels that towed the *CARDIFF* in, had also found and rescued a donkeyman still on board, his door having jammed in the explosion. When the master left Lorient, his ship was submerged up to the bridge at high water; it was re-floated later. Eight of the crew of twenty-eight died.

THE MEN WHO DIED

Annes, James, Fireman and Trimmer
Brien, James, Sailor
Dows, Herbert Cyril Surtees, Mess Steward
Gatt, Guiseppe, Sailor
Rodgers, Thomas, Fireman
Stanton, John Richard, Fireman
Sumari, Amadon, Fireman
White, Walter, Sailor

On 11 January, a torpedo fired without warning killed Fireman Juan Llanilos and damaged the *Messidor* (1904 – Plisson Steam Navigation Co. Ltd, London), a 3,883-ton steamship armed for defence, 3 miles off Penmarc'h; the ship was transporting coal from Blyth and Brest for Quiberon, France; either *U 93* or even *UC 50* may have fired the torpedo. (This ship was finally sunk by a torpedo fired without warning by *UB 50* on 23 July 1918.)

In the Bay of Biscay and southwest of Penmarc'h, Roehr torpedoed and sunk the 1,913-ton French steamer *Château Lafite* (1914 – Worms & Cie., Havre) on the 12th, which was voyaging from Bordeaux to Dunkerque. On 14 January 14 and 30 miles west, southwest of Penmarc'h, the 2,174-ton French sailing ship *Babin Chevaye* (1901 – Bureau Frères & Baillergeau) was captured and sunk with explosives, while travelling from Antofagasta, Chile to Nantes, France.

Time was running out for *U 84*. Quite simply we cannot be certain what became of her. The traditional view is that on 26 January 1918, the British patrol boat HMS *PC62* observed a U-boat on the surface in St George's Channel, at position 51° 53'N 05° 44'W. *PC62* turned towards the submarine and increased speed. The U-boat tried to escape, but *PC62* slammed into her just aft of the conning tower. The U-boat sank to the bottom, leaving just a large oil slick and no survivors. It is perfectly feasible that *U 84* was in this location at this very time. It is equally possible that she was somewhere else. It is worth pointing out that no wreck has ever been discovered in this position.

NARA Series T-1022, Roll 9, PG61666 ADM 53/56692 ADM 137/2961 Board of Trade M.7787 – M.7353
U-Boot-Ehrenmal Möltenort CWGC

THE MEN WHO PERISHED WITH U 84

Albrecht, Gustav U-Matrose
Bender, Heinrich U-Heizer
Bernhard, H. U-Matrose
Beutner, Max U-Obermaschinistenmaat
Bredenkamp, U-Maschinistenmaat
Böttcher, Fritz U-Bootsmannsmaat
Farchmin, E. U-Obermatrose
Franzke, Hellmut U-Heizer
Goltz, Gustav U-Steuermann
Hünlich, Paul Leutnant zur See der Reserve
Höflich, Rud U-F.T.Ober Gast
Keiser, Albert Marine Ingenieur
Keysers, Ernst Oberleutnant zur See
Kinder, Gottlieb U-Maschinistenmaat
Klussmann, Otto U-Heizer
Kröger, Georg U-F.T.Ober Gast
Kunz, Johann U-Heizer
Kämmler, H. U-Oberbootsmannsmaat
Lange, Karl U-Maschinistenmaat
Lessing, Emil U-Obermatrose
Lopp, Erich U-Matrose

Lücht, Jann U-Obermatrose der Reserve
Mohauft, H. U-Maschinistenmaat
Mohr, Bruno F.T.Maat
Müller, E. U-Oberheizer
Naujokat, F. U-Obermaschinistenmaat
Niemann, F. U-Obermaschinistenmaat der Reserve
Ossenberg, R. U-Maschinistenmaat
Rehberger, M. U-Obermatrose
Reichelt, W. U-Maschinistenmaat
Roehr, Walter Kapitänleutnant
Rühmer, R. U-Obermaschinist Anw
Schneider, Erhard U-Heizer
Schroeder, W. U-Heizer
Schütz, Johann U-Oberheizer
Schöning, Johann U-Matrose
Vogt, Wilhelm U-Obermaschinist Anw
Voss, A. U-Bootsmannsmaat
Wille, Henry U-Heizer
Woitschanske, U-Obermatrose
Wünsch, Bruno U-Obermaschinist Anw

WRECK SITE

The wreck has never been located.

U 103, SM IMPERIAL U-BOAT

DATE OF LOSS: 12 May 1918
DEPTH: 83m
REFERENCE: 49 15'.950 N, 04 51'.085 W
LOCATION: Approx. 45 nautical miles SSE of the Lizard

Type: Mittel-U (improved Type *U27*) ocean torpedo attack boat   **Builders**: AG Weser, Bremen for Kaiserliche Deutsche Marine   **Ordered**: On 15 September 1915, within the batch of *U 99–*

U 104 **Keel laid**: as Yard No.254 on 8 August 1916 **Launched**: on 9 June 1917 **Commissioned**: by Kapitänleutnant Claus Rücker on 15 July 1917

TECHNICAL SPECIFICATIONS

Hull: double **Surface displacement**: 750 tons **U/Dt**: 952 tons **LBDH**: 67.58m × 6.31m × 3.80m × 8.0m **Machinery**: 2 × 900ps Maschinefabrik-Augsburg-Nürnberg diesels. **Props**: 2 bronze **S/Sp**: 16.7 knots **Op/R**: 10,100 nautical miles at 8 knots **Sub/R**: 45 nautical miles at 5 knots **U/Power**: 2 × 600ps electric motors gave 8.8 knots **Batteries**: AFA lead/acid/accumulators. **Fuel/Cap**: 46 + 68 tons **Armament**: 2 bow and 2 stern 50.04cm torpedo tubes. **Torpedoes**: 7 × 50.04cm (19.7in) **Guns**: 1 × 105mm facing forward and 1 × 88mm aft of conning tower **Ammo**: 220 rounds **Diving**: max-op-depth 50m (164ft) and 45 sec to crash-dive **Complement**: 35

It is universally known that *Olympic* was the sister ship of the doomed *Titanic*. What is less well known is that the razor-sharp bows of this beautiful ship accounted for a U-boat.

U 103 was formally assigned to II.U-Flottille at Heligoland on 26 August 1917.

Previous history of *U 103*:

During July and August acceptance trials were carried out from Kiel, after which the boat joined 2nd U-Flottille based on Heligoland, with Kplt. Claus Rücker as her only commander.

(The daily fuel consumption tables in a notebook captured from the engine room warrant officer, give 6 September 1917 as the departure date for the first patrol.)

Rücker took the boat on the following five patrols:

U 103 proceeded directly across the North Sea and then round Muckle Flugga. About 50 miles SW of the Færoes the 943-ton SS St Margaret (1913 – North of Scotland and Orkney and Shetland Steam Navigation Co., Aberdeen) *of Aberdeen was sunk by torpedo and five men were lost with her while on passage from Leith for Reykjavik with a general cargo.*

THE THREE MEN WHO DIED

George Brady, Fireman
Patrick Edward Loughran, Donkeyman
John Bradford Meadley, Chief Engineer

Further west, when approaching 10°W, a British auxiliary cruiser was sighted, but no attack could be carried out owing to the fact that the officer in charge flooded the wrong tubes!

Shortly after this, *U 103* returned to her base, arriving about 27 September. No other vessels were sunk on the cruise, which was only intended to be of a short duration, giving the crew a chance to shake down before attempting anything more ambitious.

(2) Starting on 1 November, 1917, *U 103* proceeded across the North Sea and round Muckle Flugga and the west coast of Ireland to the Bay of Biscay, where she reached the latitude of Bordeaux. On the outward journey she sighted a number of British battle cruisers near the Shetlands, but they were some way ahead, and their superiority of speed made any attack impossible. In the Bay of Biscay *U 103* operated mostly close inshore. Several Spanish vessels were stopped, but subsequently allowed to proceed. A few British ships were sunk, either in these localities or when passing the Channel entrance on the return voyage.

The 4,121-ton French SS *Depute Pierre Goujon* (1894 – French Government, St Nazaire) was sunk with all hands when a torpedo struck her off Belle Ile, in the Bay of Biscay on 12 November. Four days later (16th) the 1,933-ton defensively armed SS *Garron Head* (1913 – Ulster Steamship Co. Ltd, Belfast) was struck by a torpedo and sunk, 40 miles off Bayonne, while en-route from Bilbao to Barrow and Maryport with iron ore; twenty-eight crew were killed, including two DAMS gunners.

THE MEN WHO DIED

Burnley, William, 24yrs, Fireman and Trimmer
Creighton, Edward Henry, 32yrs, 1st Engineer

Crowley, James Edward, 40yrs, Able Seaman
Davison, Charles, 37yrs, Greaser
Devine, Thomas, 38yrs, Fireman and Trimmer
Grandin, Alfred, Leading Seaman RN (DAMS Gunner)
Green, Archibald, 18yrs, 3rd Steward
Hanna, John Glendenning, 25yrs, 2nd Engineer
Hay, William James, 19yrs, Sailor
Hodkinson, Arthur, 35yrs, Fireman and Trimmer
Holmes, Charles Adair, 26yrs, 3rd Engineer
Kennedy, Matthew John, 27yrs, 2nd Steward
Lewis, James, 39yrs, Fireman and Trimmer
Lyttle, John 20yrs, Sailor
Maxwell, James, 36yrs, 2nd Mate
McDonald, William, 38yrs, Ship's Cook
McIlwaine. James, 22yrs, 4th Engineer Officer
McaKay, Patrick, 34yrs, Boatswain (Bosun)
McMordie, Leslie William Watt, 28yrs, 1st Mate
Moore, Alexander, 37yrs, Chief Steward
Porter, James, 41yrs, Fireman and Trimmer
Ritchie, James, 21yrs, 3rd Mate
Runnette, William John, 28yrs, Carpenter
Shaw, Thomas Molyneux, 18yrs, Sailor
Skilling, James, 46yrs, Able Seaman
Taylor, Edwin Lough, 22yrs, Wireless Operator
Turlington, George Bertram, AB RNVR (DAMS Gunner)

On the return voyage, *U 103* proceeded via the Isles of Orkney and arrived in port on 1 December 1917.

(3) *U 103* departed Helgoland on 14 January 1918 and proceeded to the North Channel and Irish Sea, travelling via the Orkney Isles. On the 26th, the *CORK* (1899 – City of Dublin Steam Packet Co. Ltd, Dublin), which was 1,232 tons and armed for defence, was voyaging from Dublin to Liverpool with passengers and general cargo when she was torpedoed and sunk 9 miles off Lynas Point and twelve people drowned.

SOME OF THE MEN WHO DIED

Byrne, James, 40yrs, Seaman
Doyle, Thomas, 29yrs, Quartermaster
Henry, Olivia, 55yrs, Stewardess
McGrath, Michael, 42yrs, Fireman
Phillips, Thomas, 33yrs, Greaser

The defensively armed SS *Ethelinda* (1911 – The Harrowing S.S. Co. Ltd, West Hartlepool) of 3,257 tons sank after a torpedo attack on the 29th, 15 miles off the Skerries, while carrying iron ore from Bilbao to Barry and twenty-six people (all hands) were lost.

SOME OF THE MEN WHO DIED

Ali Abdullah, Fireman and Trimmer
Ali Muha Mmad, Fireman and Trimmer
Ashford, William, 15yrs, 2nd Cook
Ching, L.L., Ship's Cook
Cuthbert, A., 39yrs, Master
Davey, Walter Ernest Rose, Seaman RNR (DAMS)
Hansen, W., 51yrs, Able Seaman
Hayashi, K., 20yrs, Mess Room Steward

Henrikson, G., 32yrs, Able Seaman
Ikitoni, K., 31yrs, 3rd Engineer
Inskuchi, N., 31yrs, Donkeyman
Kingston, Robert, 43yrs, 1st Engineer
McKean, James, 17yrs, Wireless Operator
Morgan, Morgan, 19yrs, Apprentice
Nagi Hasan, Fireman and Trimmer
Nyland, Waldemar, Sailor
Pallo, 32yrs, Able Seaman
Rundle, William Middleton, 52yrs, 1st Mate
Sakomoto, K., 26yrs, Steward
Saleh Ali, Fireman and Trimmer
Sandys, Ed, 40yrs, Able Seaman
Severs, James, 45yrs, 2nd Engineer
Tilley, John Edward, 65yrs, 2nd Mate
Zachler, Paul, 37yrs, Sailor

U 103 arrived back in Germany on 9 February, going via the Skagerrak and the Baltic.

(4) The U-boat departed Heligoland on 3 March 1918 and Kplt. Rücker took to the North Channel and west coast of Ireland by going via the Isles of Orkney. Rücker sank two vessels on 17 March: the 150-ton yacht *CRESSIDA* (1884 – Inglis, Pointhouse) was en-route from Preston to Dublin with coal when she a torpedo sunk her without warning, 16 miles from Skerries, and three men were killed.

THE MEN WHO DIED

Edwards, William Fireman
Owen, David Cook and Boatswain (Bosun)
Wright, John Chief Engineer

Later that day, the master and nineteen crewmen were drowned off the Skerries when the 976-ton defensively armed SS *Sea Gull* (1899 – Leach & Co. Ltd, London) was torpedoed and sunk without warning while on passage from Le Havre for Liverpool with general cargo.

THOSE WHO DROWNED

Barrand, George 28yrs, Fireman
Bellhouse, Arthur 47yrs, Master
Burns, William Hugh 23yrs, Sailor
Campbell, Stewart Kidd 19yrs, Able Seaman
Corner, Clement William 23yrs, Fireman
Crosby, William Thurlow 25yrs, Fireman
Darragh, Bernard 20yrs, Steward
Darragh, James, Fireman
Dunthorne, A., Sailor
Grainger, Thomas 50yrs, Donkeyman
Lipsberg, Paul, Able Seaman
MacDonald, Archibald 29yrs, 2nd Engineer
McBride, William 21yrs, Mess Room Steward
O'Grady, Joseph 36yrs, 2nd Mate
Perrello, V., Sailor
Shelley, Samuael 42yrs, Engineer
Smith, Perct Willaim 33yrs, Chief Engineer
Smith, Thomas 39yrs, Able Seaman
Weller, Sidney George James 23yrs, 3rd Engineer

On the 18th, and without any warning, Rücker torpedoed the 6,042-ton SS *Grainton* (1911 – Cambay SS. Co. Ltd and Carlton SS. Co. Ltd, Newcastle) and left the ship badly damaged; she was armed for defence and transporting coal from Birkenhead to Lough Swilly, however she reached Dublin Bay safely.

Two days later on 20 March, Rücker torpedoed and sunk the defensively armed 3,015-ton steamer *Kassanga* (1899 – S.S. Kassanga Co. Ltd, Glasgow) without warning, 23 miles from South Arklow light vessel; the ship was voyaging to the Clyde with coal.

U 103 returned to Wilhelmshaven, going via the Skagerrak and Baltic Sea and arrived in port on 1 April 1918.

FINAL PATROL

(5) On 28 April 1918, *U 103* left Wilhelmshaven – putting in at Heligoland, she remained in harbour there for several days awaiting her escort. On the afternoon of 3 May, she commenced her cruise, in company with *U 70* and convoyed by a half flotilla of destroyers and three mine-sweepers, the latter boats probably being 'A' boats. Course was altered several times whilst passing the mine area, the general direction being NNW from Heligoland. Somewhere near the North Dogger Bank light-vessel *U 103* and her escort parted company. Apparently *U 70* proceeded independently at the same time, but she remained in wireless communication with *U 103* a short while longer, while the latter was still in the North Sea. It was originally intended to pass through the channel south of Fair Isle, but, on reaching the entrance, the presence of patrol craft and the strength of the tidal streams induced *U 103* to turn back and await nightfall, before making the passage. She then decided, in view of the set of the tidal streams, to pass north of Fair Isle, and did so between 11 and 12 midnight (5 May) on the surface. In the morning a few trawlers and destroyers were sighted W.S.W. of Foula, but no attack was made. Course was then shaped to pass between St Kilda and the Hebrides, after which *U 103* continued on round the west course of Ireland, keeping well clear of the land and proceeding mostly on the surface at speed, sometimes with one, sometimes with both engines. Subsequently, course was shaped direct for the Scillies. At a point a little to the south of these islands, a seaplane was sighted on patrol. *U 103* immediately dived to a depth of about 45m, but two well-aimed bombs exploded uncomfortably close to her, though without causing any damage. Ushant light was picked up in a SSW direction at 1230hrs on the night of 11/12 May, the weather being misty at the time. From this position (about 48° 43'N, 5° W.) the submarine steered due north, with the object of intercepting ships passing in or out of the Channel on the English side. At 0437hrs the navigating warrant officer, who was officer of the watch, sighted a black patch on the horizon on the port side and slightly abaft the beam. He at once altered course two points to port, and increased the speed from 'Slow' to 'Utmost'. At the same time he called the captain. Soon he was able to make out one destroyer ahead of the vessel sighted (SS *Olympic*) and a second destroyer passing across the wake of *U 103* on an easterly course.

The dazzle-painted 46,359-ton *Olympic* (Admiralty requisition) was bound for Southampton, carrying 9,000 American servicemen, in company with an escort of four Queenstown-based American destroyers. Rucker attempted to determine *Olympic*'s track from periscope-depth but the prevailing conditions rendered depth keeping impossible. The inevitable happened. *U 103* broke surface in full view of the big ship and her consorts:

> …She then turned onto a course roughly parallel to that of her target. Shortly afterwards, or about 20 minutes after she had been sighted, the merchantman, which was not recognized as being the Olympic, fired two shots in rapid succession. *U 103* at once dived to 30m, continuing on a parallel course.

U 103 had just broken surface one and a half points on the starboard bow, about half a mile away, when Captain Bertram Hayes spotted her from the *Olympic*'s bridge. Immediately Hayes turned to ram at a speed of 24 knots, no mean feat considering the size of the vessel concerned and the complexity of the operation. Lookouts on the U-boat reported that they could see the bow-wave of a very large steamer heading towards them and Rücker was unaware that the ocean-liner was due. He tried to take *U 103* down quickly, but the prevailing conditions made it difficult for the boat to maintain periscope depth. Twice the submarine broached. Nothing seemed to go right.

Interrogation report of Kplt Claus Rücker:

> The stern tubes were prepared for firing at a four funnelled merchant at 2,000 yards range. – Olympic, fired two shots in rapid succession. – There was a delay in flooding the stern tubes and the boat got within this range before the tubes were really ready.

The initiative now passed to the wily Captain Hayes and his great ship. Claus Rücker tried to turn *U 103* inside the liner's turning circle with a view to buying enough time to get a torpedo attack in. At 0305hrs Captain Hayes foiled this move by wrenching over *Olympic*'s helm, hard a port. The interrogation report continues:

> *U 103* turned on a course parallel to the target. *U 103* dived to 30m. Immediately after, a violent impact was felt on the port side just abaft the conning tower and *U 103* listed over to starboard. I believe this damage was caused by the big ship's propellers having sucked in *U 103*. Ballast tanks were ripped open and external fittings destroyed. At the same time she began to sink by the stern. Water penetrated the control room because a number of rivets started to spring. Once the engine room started to flood, chlorine gas fumes were detected. To add to our discomfort the motors packed in. We sank to 50m before the boat levelled off. Fortunately the emergency lighting was quickly restored. The undamaged tanks were blown, the boat surfaced, but she was well down by the stern. On emerging onto the bridge I fired a distress signal using a very light. At the same time the vents were opened and the submarine sank rapidly.

In his book *Hull Down* (Cassell 1925), Bertram Hayes described the considerable satisfaction all felt at hearing the grinding noise caused as *Oympic*'s paravane chains tore into the U-boat's pressure hull. American soldiers cheered as the lolling submarine was swept astern by the leviathan's wash, like a broken toy. *Olympic* sped away to disembark her troops at Cherbourg, leaving the destroyers to 'clean up'.

Fortunately, the USS *Davis* was able to rescue twenty-seven men out of the thirty-six who escaped from *U 103*, including Claus Rücker.

(Rücker was indicted as a war criminal for sinking the 155-ton Fleetwood trawler *Victoria* in St George's Channel on 1 June1915, while he was commander of *U 34*. The skipper of *Victoria* tried to make a run for it, refusing to stop, after *U 34* fired on his vessel. Not surprisingly, *U 34* kept on firing and six of the crew of ten were killed, including the skipper, Captain J. Stevenson, before the trawler eventually stopped; it was then scuttled with explosive charges by the Germans. The four survivors were taken on board the U-boat, but next day the trawler *Hirose* was captured and sunk by *U 34* and the four men from *Victoria*, were placed in her lifeboats. Six men died on the *Victoria*.

SOME OF THOSE WHO DIED

McCarthy, D., Mate
Rudge, G. J., Cook
Slate, F. ,Trimmer
Stevenson, J., Skipper
Coles, A.G., 1st Engineer

ADM 186/38 ADM 186/39 U-Boot-Ehrenmal Möltenort CWGC

THE MEN WHO PERISHED IN U 103

Dorka, Wilhelm U-Maschinistenmaat der Reserve
Geb, J. U-Maschinist Anw
Kiesow, K. U-Obermatrose
Kunze, Hermann U-Maschinistenmaat
Lauxmann, E. U-Bootsmannsmaat
Mügge, A. U-Obermaschinistenmaat
Reppert, Philipp U-Maschinistenmaat
Reumann, K. Oberleutnant zur See der Reserve

Rudloff, Otto U-Obermatrose
Schröder, Heinrich U-Oberbootsmannsmaat

WRECK SITE

To date, the wreck of *U 103* has never been located (September 2007).

U 399, KRIEGSMARINE U-BOAT

DATE OF LOSS: 26 March 1945
DEPTH: 56m
REFERENCE: 49 56'.433 N 005 22'.472 W
LOCATION: 5.37 nautical miles from Rill Point, near Kynance Cove

The unprecedented concentration of Second World War U-boat wrecks in the deep waters off Land's End demonstrates the near impossible odds which confronted the Kriegsmarine in the closing stages of the war.

Type: VIIC ocean-going attack boat   *Builders*: Howaldtswerke AG, Kiel-Gaarden for Kriegsmarine   *Ordered*: on 25 August 1941, within the batch of *U 399–U 400*   *Keel laid*: as Yard No.114 on 12 November 1942   *Launched*: on 4 December 1943   *Commissioned*: by Oblt.z.S. Kurt van Meeteren on 22 January 1944   *Feldpost No*: M 46 386   **Badge:** a Witch

TECHNICAL SPECIFICATIONS

See page 342.

OTHER SPECIFICATIONS OF U 399

GSR: Fliege and drum-shaped aerials, probably 'Tunis' was fitted and the *schnorchel* head was fitted with an anti-radar rubber covering.

Kurt van Meeteren was born on 13 March 1908 in Bremen and commenced his naval career in 1939. He was first appointed commander of VP-boat *Hornisse* between May 1940 and August 1942 and was promoted to Oberleutnant zur See (R) on 1 February 1944.

Following the commissioning, Van Meeteren carried out two Baltic training programs with the boat and left with the whole crew on 2 July 1944; he took command of a Type XXI boat at Bremen. Oblt.z.S. Heinz Buhse then assumed command of *U 399*. (Heinz Buhse was born on 3 January 1917 in Heideberg and began his naval career in 1939. He was appointed ADC Kriegsmarine Depot (Aalborg) between May 1940 and August 1940 and was promoted to Oberleutnant zur See (R) on 1 January 1944 – Oblt.z.S. van Meeteren went on to command the Type XXI boat, *U 3021*, from January 1945 until May 1945.)

U 399 was assigned to 5.U-Flottille as *Ausbildungsboot* until 31 January 1945. However final adjustments were carried out at Kiel and lasted until the end of October 1944. During the period, *schnorchel*, Hohentwiel radar and a 37mm gun were fitted. *U 399* lay in the Strander Bucht before leaving on her patrol.

U 399 left Kiel on 25 January 1945 and arrived at Horten (59° 24.45'N 10° 29 08'E) near Oslo in Norway on the 28th. As a frontline boat, *U 399* formally transferred to 11.U-Flottille, Bergen, in southwest Norway, on 1 February 1945, with Oblt.z.S. Buhse in command.

FINAL PATROL

(2) Departing Horten on 6 February 1945, *U 399* proceeded to the English Channel and, by March, was operating at the western entrance. Northeast of the Eddystone Rocks, convoy TBC 103 was sighted at 1335hrs (CT) on the 21st and Buhse fired a torpedo at the 7,176-ton steamer *James Eagan*

Hedgehogs ready for throwing. (Author's collection)

Layne, which damaged her at position 50° 13'N 04° 05'W; the ship was voyaging from Barry to Ghent in Belgium, carrying US Army engineers' stores and twenty-seven US military gunners, who were all passengers. The torpedo detonated between Nos 4 and 5 holds on the starboard side, causing a large crack in the hull. Her prop shaft had broken and the shaft-tunnel flooded and steering gear put out of action. Holds 4 and 5 and the engine room flooded and she sank by the stern until the sea was between the mainmast and accommodation, then she steadied. The ship was abandoned 10 minutes after being attacked and HMS *Flaunt* and a minesweeper took her in tow; the vessel was beached in Whitsand Bay near Plymouth and became a total wreck.

Buhse was not finished. Just west of the Lizard, at 0530hrs on the 26th, he torpedoed and sank the 362-ton Dutch motor vessel *Pacific* (C. Tammes, Groningen) in convoy BTC 108 at position 49° 54'N 05° 17'W; she was on passage from Maryport for Penryn, Cornwall with 350 tons of coal. Five of her crew of ten were killed. It seems probable that the unfortunate vessel ran into a torpedo aimed at a much larger member of the convoy. The strike had the effect of alerting the EG 3 frigates(Lt Cdr R.G. Mills), HMS *Rowley* and *Essington*. The vessels responded by dropping depth charges aimed at cutting off the U-boat's line of retreat.

The famous frigate, HMS *Duckworth* (Lt Dennis Jermaine) then swiftly acquired a good ASDIC contact. Jermaine knew what it was like to be torpedoed, having lost his previous command HMS *Manners* to a *zaukonig* (*see* Chapter 3). The U-boat was deduced to be moving across the tidal flow at a depth of 60m, so Hedgehogs were deployed and *U 399* was destroyed. A large bubble of air rose to the surface, containing two men, one of whom was rescued alive, but the other drifted away on the tide. Captain Jermaine made the following observation:

> ...at first there was a typical sailor's reaction towards the survivors. When they first surfaced the bloodlust was up and the gunners had to be restrained from firing. By the time we were alongside the reaction had set in and our men had to be held back again, this time from jumping overboard in their zeal to help

fellow sailors in distress. 'They are only some mother's sons' was the cry. When one of the Germans died, a sense of deep gloom ran through the ship.

The warships then pounded the wreck with Hedgehogs and depth charges, until the kill was established.

The German perspective – Oberbootsmannsmaat Gerhard Pflock:

After the attack on the ship we dove the boat to a depth of 50m in order to get out of the danger area. Unexpectedly, we suddenly received a close depth charge barrage against the stern. Water immediately came into the boat and we sank to the bottom. The commander tried to the last to save the boat. The flooding was so rapid, however, that most of the sailors found a quick Seemannstod (literally: mariner's death. I was at my station in the control room, as the water quickly rose around me. With two others I climbed into the conning tower. As the pressure equalised, I opened the hatch and was forced out by water pressure and escaping air bubbles. I could see none of my mates on the surface. When I was picked up I was told that I was the only survivor from the boat.

THE MEN LOST WITH U 399

Ahlke, Paul Gfr. (Born 16-06-1925)
Appel, Günter Gfr. (1-01-1926)
Bengsch, Kurt Ob.Gfr. (4-2-1924)
Bielefeld, Albin Gfr. (23-12-1925)
Bohle, Manfred Gfr. (15-9-1926)
Braunstein, Wenzel Gfr. (17-2-1925)
Buhse, Heinz Oblt.z.S. (3-1-1917)
Chifkowski, Bruno Gfr. (18-10-1925)
Chojnacki, Max Maat. (6-5-1923)
Dalluege, Günter-Heinz Gfr. (7-8-1925)
Engler, Werner Ob.Strm. (30-3-1920)
Filz, Heinz Gfr. (23-4-1926)
Godau, Günther Maat. (6-8-1920)
Griesel, Siegfried Gfr. (27-8-1925)
Gundel, Julius Ob.Strm. (27-6-1917)
Häger, Georg Ob.Gfr. (2-1-1922)
Himmer, Waldemar Gfr. (23-1-1925)
Hollmann, Hans LtIng (7-12-1922)
Jarzina, Alois Gfr. (3-7-1925)
Jöchel, Erwin Ob.Masch. (17-8.1916)
Klenke, Heinz-Georg Ob.Gfr. (16-12-1924)
Koch, Gerhard Ob.Gfr. (12-12-1924)
Köhler, Horst Ob.Gfr. (1-4-1923)
Lewark, Erich Maat. (17-7-1913)

Liesenfeld, Josef Ob.Mt. (14-12-1919)
Marotzki, Willi Ob.Mt. (29-7-1920)
Matzke, Rudi Gfr. (22-2-1926)
Mayer, Max Maat. (8-1-1923)
Messerschmidt, Wilhelm Maat. (1-10-1919)
Michels, Johann Ob.Masch. (11-3-1918)
Murr, Walter Maat. (7-1-1923)
Nakonzer, Joachim Gfr. (21-5-1925)
Nicolai, Gerhard Gfr. (28-10-1925)
Oberkofler, Willibald Gfr. (22-6-1925)
Plank, Rupprecht Oblt.1st WO. (6-1-1923)
Reichelt, Fritz LtIng [date unknown]
Reinitz, Lothar Ob.Gfr. (25-5-1923)
Röder, Gerhard Gfr. (15-9-1921)
Rohrdanz, Werner Gfr. (3-6-1925)
Schäfer, Adolf Ob.Gfr. (22-12-1920)
Schenk, Heinz Ob.Gfr. (14-7-1923)
Schlosser, Werner Maat. (4-2-1920)
Schobner, Hans-Alfred Maat. (21-10-1919)
Spillner, Herbert Ob.Gfr. (5-7-1924)
Taube, Alois Ob.Mt. (10-5-1921)
Theeden, Kurt Maat. (2-12-1921)
Wichmann, Franz Ob.Gfr. (20-9-19)

ADM 1/30348 CB 04051 (103) NARA Series T-1022, Roll 3900, PG 31752 U-Boot-Ehrenmal Möltenort

WRECK SITE

The wreck, probably that of *U 399*, lies on a seabed of sand and shingle, in a general depth of 56m (184ft), being the lowest astronomical depth. It is reported as being upright and intact, with the propellers half buried and the casing badly damaged in a number of places. The upper half of the wreck has a well-established colony of soft corals attached and lots of fish shoal around the conning tower. The wreck is also a war grave.

U 1018, KRIEGSMARINE U-BOAT

DATE OF LOSS: 27 February 1945
DEPTH: 53m
REFERENCE: 49 56'.728 N 05 20'.239 W
LOCATION: 4 nautical miles WSW from Rill Point, near Kynance Cove

Type: VIIC/41 ocean-going attack boat   *Builders*: Blohm & Voss AG, Hamburg for
Kriegsmarine   *Ordered*: on 23 March 1942, within the batch of U 1013–U 1018   **Keel laid**: as
Yard No.218 on 16 April 1943   *Launched*: on 1 March 1944   *Commissioned*: by Kapitänleutnant
Ulrich Faber on 24 April 1944   *Feldpost No*: M 22 623

TECHNICAL SPECIFICATIONS

See page 342.

OTHER SPECIFICATIONS FOR U 1018

Two Type GW F46 diesel/oil engines manufactured under licence by Blohm & Voss AG and fitted
with *Gebläse* (super-chargers), powered the two propellers. During September/October 1944 the
boat was fitted with *schnorchel* during final adjustments at Kiel.

U 1018 was also equipped with 'Seelilie', which indicated if the boat was being detected by aircraft or surface radar. Contacts were indicated on a dial, like a voltmeter and a receiver was built into
a small stand on the bows. She was the third boat to carry 'Seelilie', the first two were presumed lost,
which may lead the reader to question the efficacy of this device.

Ulrich Faber was born in Stuttgart on 10 October 1918 and commenced his naval career in 1937.
Between February 1942 and March 1943 Faber was Instructor of the Mine Warfare School at Kiel
before commencing U-boat training and was promoted to Kapitänleutnant on 1 April 1944.

U 1018 was assigned to 31.U-Flottille at Hamburg as *Ausbildungsboot* from 24 April 1944 to
30 November 1944, with Kapitänleutnant Ulrich Faber the commander.

From 20 to 30 June 1944, the boat stayed at the Holm Yard at Danzig and lost three of its crew
members due to a training accident on the 27th.

Kplt. Ulrich Faber became ill and Kplt. Walter Burmeister assumed command of U 1018 on
1 December 1944. Walter Burmeister was born on 9 February 1919 in Aerzen, Hameln and commenced his naval career in 1937. He was Works Officer at the Naval Ordnance Office at Kiel
between May 1940 and June 1940; on 1 January 1945, he was promoted to Kapitänleutnant.

U 1018 was formally assigned to 11.U-Flottille on 1 December 1944 for operational duties, with
Burmeister as commanding officer.

(1) U 1018 left on Kiel on 7 December 1944 and arrived at Horten (59° 24.45'N 10° 29 08'E)
near Oslo in Norway on the 10th.

(Note: The boat remained at Horten for a month, which was unusual because normal *schnorchel*
training at Horten only lasted ten days.)

FINAL PATROL

(2) U 1018 moved independently from Horten to Kristiansand on 20 January 1945, arriving
early the next morning. Later in the day the boat sailed together with U 868 for operations in the
English Channel and British coast waters. After passing between the Shetlands and Færoe Isles (and
50 miles to the westward of Rockall), U 1018 reached her first operational area, approximately
midway between the Scillies and Brest. Burmeister had permission to move to the convoy route
near Devonport and Falmouth should his initial billet prove barren. So far the U-boat had been
unmolested, though on one occasion screw noises from ships had been heard. Following one day
of tedium in the first patrol zone, U 1018 moved to the second area, as ordered. A convoy was
sighted, to the westward, on the first day in the second area, but it was too far away. On the third day
Burmeister fired a spread shot of two Lut torpedoes and then a T5 at a corvette, believed to be part
of a convoy, at about 700 yards range; these missed and the attack was not renewed.

After the eighth day, Burmeister wanted to turn back, but was overruled by the other officers, with good reason. The return from patrol was not due to start until about 3 March and the boat still had 44 tons of fuel left. The submarine was performing well. The only problem encountered to date had been the oil pressure system for raising the *schnorchel*; the entire system had mysteriously been adulterated by water, making both *schnorchel* and periscope difficult to raise, low-level sabotage being endemic in the Norwegian harbours. On 25 February, Control informed Burmeister that two Allied ships had been torpedoed in the Lizard area, shortly before he had arrived. Burmeister was warned that Allied hunter-killer groups would be consequently alert. On the 26th, a convoy passed close by, but *U 1018* was unable to attack because a destroyer surprised her from astern. By the middle of February, *U 1018* was operating at the western entrance to the Channel. She was sailinging at position 49° 56'N 05° 20'W by the 27th. At about 1015hrs on the 27th *U 1018* sighted a convoy and fired a spread of two torpedoes; after 25 seconds, detonations and then sinking noises were heard. It was presumed that a freighter had been sunk (although this could not be confirmed as a destroyer intervened). *U 1018* crash-dived under the convoy and stood away from the coast. Meanwhile…

Official Report of the Second Escort Group's Patrol – 25 February to 23 March 1945 Lt Cdr Rodgers:

> The Second Escort Group, HM Ships, *Wild Goose* (Senior Officer), *Loch Fada, Dominica, Labuan* and *Loch Ruthven* left Liverpool on 25 February 1945. On entering the Plymouth Command, the First Division; consisting of *Wild Goose, Dominica, Loch* Ruthven patrolled and trailed convoys between the Lizard and Pendeen; *Loch Fada, Labuan* carrying out the same duties between the Lizard and Start Point.
>
> At 1013hrs on 27 February 1945 the destroyers were following convoy BTC 81 when the 1,317-ton Norwegian freighter CORVUS (Det Bergenske Dampskibsselskab, Bergen) was struck by a torpedo in No.2 hold, starboard side at position 49° 55'N 05° 22'W.

The steamer blew up, capsized and sank before they could get the lifeboats out, although some managed to get a raft off; eight of her crew of twenty-five were killed and four were taken to hospital.

THE MEN WHO DIED

Årås, Peder Magnus 2nd Mate
Nygjerde, Nicolai 1st Engineer
Onzols, Petris Stoker
Hegg, Arne Leonard Stoker
Kristensen, Nordal Steward
Boniface, Thomas Albert 16yrs (British)
Thomas Sillet, Charles, DAMS Gunner (British)
Baker, Dennis DAMS Gunner (British)

Built in 1920 by Kjøbenhavens Flydedok & Skibsvft., Copenhagen, the *CORVUS* was on passage from Garston and Mumbles for Plymouth, with 1,800 tons of coal. According to the Second Escort Group's Patrol Report of 25 February to 23 March 1945:

> The convoy escorts counteracted with a barrage of 150 depth charges and detected the U-boat at 164ft (50m) and 16ft from the bottom. On the bridge of HMS *Loch Fada* commanded by Lt Cdr B Rodgers, the order rang out: 'Action Squid!'
>
> At 11.24 *Loch Fada* obtained contact in position 26 degrees from Lizard Light, 6 miles 2.1 miles. 006 degrees from the wreck of CORVUS and attacked with squid at 11.29 to be rewarded with the sight of five Germans breaking surface in a large air bubble beside the swirl. *Loch Fada* recovered two of them, an officer and a rating, but the others drifted away and were not seen again. Two of the Germans seemed to be barely alive and were being supported by a third wearing a Mae West Jacket.
>
> At 0930hrs/27 the First Division had left Convoy BTC 81, which it had trailed from Pendeen to Wolf Rock, to join convoy ONA 287. Forty minutes later, when midway between the two convoys, the Senior Officer saw a ship in BT.C.81 torpedoed… EG14 (HMS *Hesperus*, Senior Officer), which was supporting ONA 287, came streaming in from the south-eastward and a little later *Loch Fada* and *Labuan* joined.

The two groups then began a co-ordinated search, EG 2 sweeping in line abreast northward into Mounts Bay from close westward of the wreck.

Contacts and attacks were numerous in all directions. At 1124 *Loch Fada* obtained contact in position 261° Lizard Light 6 miles-2.1 miles 006° from-the wreck – and attacked with Squid at 1129, to be rewarded 8 minutes later by the sight of five Germans breaking surface in a large air bubble beside the swirl. She recovered two of them, an officer and a rating, but the others drifted away and were not seen again. She continued to hold the contact though – with difficulty, and delivered three more Squid attacks, during which the contact never moved. After this the echo was lost. No further evidence whatever came to the surface.

It was not until several hours later that *Duckworth* was able to hold the contact firmly enough to attack it, but neither she, *Wild Goose*, nor *Labuan* could firmly obtain any results and at 1913/27 the hunt was abandoned. EG2 spared no pains to obtain conclusive evidence and during the next 10 days the ships never passed through the area without giving the matter their attention…On 1 March the First Division, making contact after an intensive search and holding it with great difficulty, made fruitless depth charge attacks. A week later *Loch Fada* approaching the position, observed an oil slick and obtained contact with a bottomed object which echo-sounder traces, showed to have a length of 60ft. and heights varying between 10 and 20ft. She and *Labuan* attacked with Squid and depth charges, which produced nothing but air bubbles. On 10 March EG2 eventually got what it wanted. *Loch Fada* and *Labuan* found a long oil slick and their fourth attack produced, among other things, two inflatable dinghies, a German novel, and a pair of oilskin trousers. This hunt was a good illustration of the conditions that are found in coastal waters, even when ASDIC and weather conditions are good…

The U-boat was probably destroyed by *Loch Fada*'s first Squid attack, delivered while she was deep but still moving and not on the bottom. Had it not been for the appearance of the five Germans some minutes later, few would have thought this a submarine contact. The U-boat was a very indifferent ASDIC target giving poor recorder trace and no contact on the 147B ASDIC set. In the subsequent hunt the U-boat was swept over from every direction and a great number of firm contacts, not one of which was the U-boat, was obtained.

Loch Fada's Squid pattern apparently tore a large hole in one side of the pressure hull, but the tanks could still be blown and the boat was momentarily brought up from 165ft to 65ft. Flooding caused the boat to sink back. Apart from the five men who were in the conning tower and were able to open the hatch and escape, all the crew had by that time either, been killed or knocked unconscious. Possibly the U-boat settled with her torn side against the ridge of shingle …and it was not until this had been blown away or the wreck had been completely shattered – that the desired evidence of success was obtained.

Before a motorboat took the two survivors off to Plymouth, the escapees confirmed the identity of the U-boat as *U 1018*. The two survivors, Bank and Merling, described the scene inside the boat. It was truly horrific. It appears that a Squid exploded against the pressure hull, flooding the bow, stern and control room, killing most of the crew.

ADM 1/30334 NND: 83941 NARA Series T-1022, Roll 3981, PG 30360 Roll 3900, PG 31752 CWGC
U-Boot-Ehrenmal Möltenort

Except for Ltz.S. Werner Bank and Maat. Merling, who were both picked up, all of the crew, including Kplt. Walter Burmeister, were lost.

THE MEN WHO DIED IN U 1018 WERE

Asmus, Gunther Gfr. (born: 5-8-1923)	Burmeister, Walter Kplt. (9-2-1919)
Backeberg, Helmut Mt. (9-7-1923)	Doblinger, Johannes Ob.Gfr. (9-6-1924)
Bauer, Heinrich Ob.Gfr. (29-1-1923	Eggert, Reinhold Gfr. (8-7-1924)
Bethke, Gunter Ob.Gfr. (29-12-1925)	Ehlert, Leo Ob.Mt. (12-4-1920)
Bettinger, Hermann Ob.Gfr. (22-7-1921)	Flemmisch, Karl Gfr. (6-8-1924)
Binderat, Horst Ob.Gfr. (19-4-1925)	Gehrmann, Walter Ob.Strm. (13-12-1920)
Born, Helmut Ob.Gfr. (24-2-1922)	Gerstberger, Wolf Ob.Mt. (9-4-1921)
Buck, Herbert Ob.Gfr. (27-8-1925)	Halama, Siegmund Gfr. (10-2-1925)
Buck, Wolfgang Oblt.Ing. (22-12-1923)	Hardt, Horst Gfr. (26-5-1924)

Heinrichs, Paul Haupt.Gfr. (14-7-1921)
Hotes, Heinrich Gfr. (14-2-1925)
Huttl, Siegfried Ob.Gfr. (27-6-1925)
Klaubert, Ulrich Oblt.z.S. (31-12-1921)
Kobl, Josef Mt. (19-1-1923)
Kuhfeld, Wilhelm Mt. (30-7-1923)
Kukielka, Horst Mt. (5-12-1924)
Kusters, Josef Ob.Gfr. (17-12-1923)
Kwiatkowski, Gustav Gfr. (7-12-1925)
Lango, Karl-Heinz Ob.Gfr. (31-7-1923)
Lehmann, Heinz Mt. (23-12-1923)
Lehmann, Kurt Ob.Gfr. (16-10-1924)
Maliska, Kurt Mt. (16-11-1920)
Meyer, Rudolf Haupt.Gfr. (26-1-1923)
Mith, Johannes Matrose (11-4-1925)
Panek, Stefan Ob.Gfr. (4-8-1923)

Rackebrandt, Wilhelm Ob.Gfr. (8-4-1923)
Raster, Friedrich Gfr. (24-5-1924)
Rotschke, Fritz Haupt.Gfr. (25-8-1921)
Ruick, Kurt Ob.Masch. (22-2-1918)
Rybka, Richard Ob.Gfr. (25-2-1924)
Schmidt, Karl St.Obstrm. (25-3-1916)
Schnabel, Wilhelm Haupt.Gfr. (26-6-1922)
Schumann, Heinz Mt. (3-11-1921)
Strauch, Alois Ob.Mt. (31-10-1920)
Struck, Herbert Mt. (8-6-1921)
Winkhaus, Helmut Ob.Masch. (1-5-1919)
Winkler, Emil Mt. (20-1-1922)
Wullenweber, Theodor Ob.Gfr. (13-1-1923)
Wurster, Ernst Ob.Gfr. (8-11-1925)
Zahn, Karl-heinz Ob.Gfr. (16-91925)
Zimmermann, Gustav Ob.Gfr. (8-11-1924

WRECK SITE

The wreck, most probably that of *U 1018*, lies on a seabed of sand and shingle, in a general depth of 53m (174ft), being the lowest astronomical depth. It is upright, but the casing is broken open and full of holes in many places. Numerous types of fish and crustaceans have also adopted the remains. This wreck site is a war grave and should be treated with the utmost respect.

U 1169, KRIEGSMARINE U-BOAT

DATE OF LOSS: probably 29 March 1945
DEPTH: 57–60m
REFERENCE: 49° 58.1'N 05° 25.1'W
LOCATION: approximately 8 nautical miles W by S of the Lizard

Type: VIIC/41 ocean-going attack boat *Builders*: Danziger Werft AG, Danzig, for Kriegsmarine *Ordered*: on 2 April 1942, within the batch of *U 1167–U 1170* *Keel laid*: as Yard No.141 on 9 April 1943 *Launched*: on 2 October 1943 *Commissioned*: by Oblt.z.S. Heinz Goldbeck on 9 February 1944 *Feldpost No*: M 50 520

TECHNICAL SPECIFICATIONS

See page 342.

Heinz Goldbeck was born in Berlin on 10 February 1914 and commenced his naval career in 1936. He began his service as divisional officer and watch officer on board auxiliary warship *Ammerland* between October 1939 and February 1942. On 1 September 1943 Goldbeck was was promoted to Oberleutnant zur See (R).

U 1169 was assigned to 8.U-Flottille, Danzig as *Ausbildungsboot*, from 9 February 1944 until 31 January 1945 with Goldbeck the CO. *U 1169* was involved in two accidents during training exercises in the Baltic, in which three crewmen were killed and two others injured.

On 1 February 1945, *U 1169* formally transferred to 11.U-Flottille, Bergen, for frontline duties.

On 8 February 1945, *U 1169* left Kiel and sailed to Horten (59° 24.45'N 10° 29.08'E) near Oslo in Norway, where she arrived on the 13th.

U 1169 departed Horten on 2 February and moved down to Kristiansand, in southern Norway (58° 08.41'N 7° 59.54'E), arriving there the following day.

HMS *Duckworth* at Belfast. (Courtesy of the Imperial War Museum)

FINAL PATROL

(3) On 20 February 1945, Oblt.z.S. Heinz Goldbeck took *U 1169* out of Kristiansand for operations in British coastal waters. On 6 March the boat was ordered to proceed via AM 78, AM 79
and AM 87. Very little else is known about the U-boat, but her engines were apparently damaged
early in March. A *Passiermeldung* was transmitted by the boat on 8 March. (the location could not
be logged but was almost certainly AM 40). The boat was expected to leave patrol on or around the
second week of April. She failed to return and was regarded as lost with effect from 5 April. Post-war
assessors concluded wrongly that the boat had been mined in St George's Channel. *U 1169* had
not been ordered into this sector. There is one intriguing possibility. On 21 March the frigate HMS
Cosby (EG15) was carrying out an A/S sweep in the Mounts Bay area following the torpedoing of
the *James Egan Layne*. A torpedo detonated astern of the ship, causing minor damage. The Royal
Naval Historical Branch concluded this attack must have been the work of *U 1169*. [Author's note:
At 0822hrs on 29 March 1945 *U 315* 'gnatted' HMCS *Teme* (K 458) (Lt D.P. Harvey, RCNVR).
The ship, which was engaged in escorting convoy BTC-111 off Land's End, lost some 60ft of her
stern. She was towed to Falmouth and declared a total loss, proof, if any was needed, that a cornered
U-boat was always a dangerous adversary. *U 1169* now faced their nemesis in the form of Dennis
Jermain and HMS *Duckworth*.

Narrative of the attack by HMS *Duckworth* (Lt D Jermaine) – 29.3.1945:

> At 0830hrs HMS *Rowan*, one of the close escorts [saw a] a plume of water 264° Lizard Head 11.2 miles.
> This was assumed to have been a second U-boat patrolling in Mounts Bay.
>
> *Rowley* and *Duckworth* left E.G.6 searching for the U-boat which had torpedoed HMS *Teme* at 0724hrs,
> in 347° Longships 3.6 miles, and followed up this fresh scent.
>
> A probability firing area radius 6,000 yards from *Rowan*'s position at the Northern edge of the swept
> channel in the centre of Mounts Bay. This sector was taken as an arbitrary datum. The rough appreciation
> being that the U-boat would remain bottomed or make North into Mounts Bay.
>
> A sweep of the narrow western end of the bay was completed by 1500, when *Duckworth* joined and a
> sweep of the Eastern half of the bay was begun from very close inshore. After numerous 'non-subs' had
> been investigated, *Duckworth* made firm contact with a stationary target at 1815. An Echo-Sounder run
> showed the object to be 24ft high. *Duckworth* turned and made a Hedgehog attack, resulting in a major

explosion two seconds after the pattern hit the water, and followed by the remainder of the pattern on the bottom, five seconds later.

A wide spread disturbance about 15ft high, about the size of a shallow depth charge explosion, came up, but there was no evidence of a U-boat surfacing. A further Echo-Sounder run showed what was apparently the same object 24ft high and about 170ft long, in its original position.

Duckworth and *Rowley* carried out Hedgehog and depth charge attacks, none of which produced any evidence. A survey of the taget and examination of the recorder trace merely served to confirm the impression that it might well be a bottomed U-boat. The swell running at the time made Echo-Sounder results unreliable, thus the target was buoyed, and *Duckworth* held contact, whilst the rest of the Group patrolled further to seaward between the Lizard and Wolf Rock. From daylight on the 30th, further fruitless attacks were made on *Duckworth*'s contact, but their accuracy was doubtful, due to the state of the sea and no results were achieved.

S.O.'s opinion: '*Duckworth's attack on 29 March, was not on a U-boat and the cause of the premature detonation of the Hedgehog pattern has not been explained*'.

C-in-C Plymouth's opinion: '*…it is now considered probable that a U-boat was attacked and destroyed on this occasion*'.

ADM 199/1786 – Ref: A.U.D. 785/45
NARA Series T-1022, Roll 3981, PG 30360, Roll 3900, PG 31752

Note: in the post-war period the Staff History of Mining concluded *U 1169* had fallen victim to one of the 'CH' series minefields, CH(N) in position 52 03N, 05 53W to the south-east of Tuskar Rock. This unfortunate boat is now believed to be *U 242*.

ADM 199/1786 – Ref: A.U.D. 785/45 NARA Series T-1022, Roll 3981, PG 30360, Roll 3900, PG 31752
U-Boot-Ehrenmal Möltenort ADM 1/30528 Awards of Mention in Despatches to 6 officers and men of HMS *Duckworth* for sinking U-boat southeast of the Lizard – 29 March 1945

THE MEN WHO PERISHED WITH *U 1169*

Becker, Werner Masch.O.Gfr. (26-1-19250
Bothe, Horst Mtr.O.Gfr. (30-4-1925)
Brachvogel, Gottfried Ltz.S. (21-8-1923)
Breunig, Erwin Masch.Mt. (20-4-1923)
Dultz, Kurt Mtr.I.Gfr. (16-1-1923)
Elsperger, Ernst Masch.OGfr. (27-10-1924)
Emich, Karl Mech.O.Gfr. (2-5-1925)
Fischer, Ludwig Mtr.Gfr. (18-3-1925)
Freundl, Markus Masch.Mt. (9-12-1919)
Galts, Hans Masch, Mt. (4-1-1923)
Geiger, Alfons Mtr.Gfr. (29-12-1925)
Goldbeck, Heinz Oblt.z.S. (10-2-1914)
Graaf, Martin O.San.Mt. (21-6-1921)
Heitsch, Karl Bts.Mt. (18-8-1915)
Hundt, Erich Mtr.O.Gfr. (2-6-1925)
Jansen, Wilhelm O.Masch. (8-8-1920)
Kleiner, Herbert O.Masch. (25-10-1906)
Kortlepel, Peter Fk.O.Gfr. (22-2-1925
Kotzur, Kurt Mtr.O.Gfr. (23-5-1924)
Kühne, Rudolf Masch.Gfr. (16-10-1924)
Ladage, Hans Bts.Mt. (15-1-1922)
Legien, Hans Masch.O.Gfr. (2-11-1925)

Liebig, Willy O.Mech.Mt. (8-11-1920)
Linke, Heinz Mtr.O.Gfr. (6-5-1923)
Lüning, Engelbert Fk.Mt. (18-9-1922)
Mayer, Franz Mtr.O.Gfr. (16-12-1923)
Meißner, Paul Masch.Mt. (27-5-1922)
Müller, Henry Masch.Gfr. (15-10-1925)
Nimtz, Erhard LtIng. (20-11-1922)
Pahl, Horst Masch.O.Gfr. (2-2-1925)
Pastofski, Rudi O.Strm (18-2-1917)
Pirdssun, Horst Fk.O.Gfr. (11-10-1924)
Plainer, Johann Masch.O.Gfr. (28-1-1925)
Polster, Heinrich Masch.O.Gfr. (3-7-1925)
Postl, Franz Masch.Gfr. (18-8-1925)
Przytulski, Karl-Heinz Mtr.H.Gfr. (9-3-1923)
Reutermann, Fritz Mtr.O.Gfr. (24-11-1925)
Rolf, Friedrich Masch.O.Gfr. (10-12-1922)
Saliger, Otto Mech.Gfr. (22-6-1925)
Schmidt, Hans-Gerhardt Masch.Gfr. (30-5-1924)
Schmidt, Wilhelm Mech.O.Gfr. (8-8-1924)
Senff, Kurt Mtr.O.Gfr. (2-6-1924)
Siegner, Rudolf Bts.Mt. (17-12-1923)
Stoob, Hermann Fk.Mt. (12-7-1922)

Thiel, Jodef Mash.Gfr. (16-8-1924) Veh, Otto Masch.Mt. (25-2-1923)

Tschepe, Werner Ltz.S. (23-12-1923) Voigt, Werner Fk.O.Gfr. (7-5-1923)

WRECK SITE

The wreck of *U 1169* has never been identified to date, September 2007.

U 1199, KRIEGSMARINE U-BOAT

DATE OF LOSS: 21 June 1945

DEPTH: 67m

REFERENCE: 49 57'.808 N 005 42'.704 W

LOCATION: 4.47 nautical miles SSW from Gwennap Head, near Land's End

Type: VIIC ocean-going attack boat *Builders*: F. Schichau GmbH, Danzig (now Gdansk, Poland) for Kriegsmarine *Ordered*: on 16 October 1941, as *U 1199* **Keel laid**: as Yard No.1569 on 23 March 1943 *Launched*: on 12 October 1943 *Commissioned*: by Kapitänleutnant Rolf Nollmann on 23 December 1943 *Feldpost No*: M 42 161 **Badge:** A fish underwater in a shield and a man's hat

TECHNICAL SPECIFICATIONS

See page 342.

OTHER SPECIFICATIONS

U 1199 had deck containers fitted for 13ft rubber dinghies.

Rolf Nollmann was born on 29 December 1914 in Wollmeringen, Lorraine and commenced his career in 1936. He was ADC with 1 E-boat Flottille between February 1941 and April 1941 and then moved to the battleship *Gneisenau* for three months. On 1 November 1943 Nollmann was promoted to Kapitänleutnant.

U 1199 was assigned to 8.U-Flottille at Danzig as *Ausbildungsboot* with Rolf Nollmann the CO from 23 December 1943 to 31 July 1944. The 1st lieutenant was Ltz.S. Helms and 2nd Lieutenant Obersteuermann Winterfield.

Pre-tactical exercises were carried out at Pillau. The boat also did manoeuvre practices here before proceeding to Hela for about seven weeks *Agrufront*. During the *Agrufront*, Leutnant zur See Schmitz replaced Winterfield as 2nd leutnant and Winterfield became 3rd watch officer. While she was at Hela the boat spent sixty days at sea with engineering officers on board, under instruction. *U 1199* then proceeded to Libau for torpedo firing and returned to Hela for an additional three weeks, as Nollmann considered the ship's company needed extra training. *U 1199* then moved to Swinemunde for AA firing practice, which lasted about a week; from there she carried out ten days' tactical exercises off Gdynia. Ltz.S. Helms left the boat at Gdynia and Oblt.z.S. Fuesslein succeeded him as 1st leutnant. At the beginning of July 1944, *U 1199* entered Howaldt's yard at Kiel, where *schnorchel* was fitted. Final adjustments were completed by the beginning of September 1944 and fitting-out at Kiel was completed by mid-September. The boat and crew then transferred to 1.U-Flottille at Brest as a frontline boat.

On 18 August 1944, *U 1199* left from Kiel and on the 20th arrived at Horten (59° 24.45'N 10° 29 08'E) near Oslo, Norway, where she carried out *schnorchel* trials.

U 1199 departed Horten on 8 August and proceeded via Kristiansand in southern Norway (58° 08.41'N 7° 59.54'E), to Bergen (60° 23 17'N 5° 19.54'E), where she arrived on the 25th.

Leaving Bergen on 14 August 1944, the boat sailed for operations off the Scottish northeast coast. The *schnorchel*-equipped *U 1199* spent seven and a half weeks patrolling off the Moray Firth, Aberdeen and Peterhead, during which time she remained submerged for fifty days (probably something off a record). The BdU Diary for 5 November 1944 contains this entry:

U 995, the Second World War Type VIIC/41 Kriegsmarine U-boat on display at the Marine Memorial (Marine-Ehrenmal) located near Laboe, Germany. (Courtesy Kevin Belcher of Swindon)

> *U 1199* has returned from her first operation off Bergen. Her short report shows that the operation lasted 50 days, of which 31 were spent in the operational area off Peterhead and Aberdeen (AN 1895, 0131) close under the coast. Boat ran submerged the whole time, crew most enthusiastic about schnorchel…

Control was understandably keen to milk any positive experience at this grim stage of the war. The following transmission was broadcast to all U-boat crews on 3 December 1944:

> Experience report 193: Radio to all boats: Text is last paragraph of summary from log of *U 1199* (Boat has operated 30 days in area AN 01).
>
> Shallow water is best protection against search gear. Boat was not intercepted and we felt absolutely safe on the bottom. Schnorchel completely tested, 50 days submerged without surfacing. I have a feeling of complete superiority with the schnorchel. Unfortunately the possibilities for hydrophone listening along the coast are poor, which results in unfavorable tactical positions to the enemy if picked up by hydrophones. Morale of the crew good and conviction that the U-boat arm again has superiority over the enemy.

U 1199 returned to Bergen on 11 November and joined 11. U-Flottille as a frontline boat.

FINAL PATROL

(4) *U 1199* departed Bergen on 1 January 1945, unaccompanied and carrying provisions for about nine weeks. She proceeded through the Rosengarten and off the west coast of Ireland, the last position noted by the sole survivor, Chief Petty Officer Clausen, being somewhere to the southwest of the Scillies, as they were approaching the Channel from the Atlantic.

Convoy TBC43 was allegedly encountered off Wolf Rock on the 21st and Nollmann badly damaged the 7,176-ton American Liberty ship *George Hawley* with a torpedo; she was in ballast on passage from Cherbourg for Mumbles and the USA and two of her crew of sixty-eight were killed. The ship was towed to Falmouth by the tug *Allegiance*, where it was declared a total loss and scrapped.

Soon after the attack on the *George Hawley*, the escorting corvette HMS *Mignonette* (Lt H.H. Brown) located the U-boat. *Mignonette* and HMS *Icarus* (Lt Cdr R. Dyer) then depth charged it to destruction.

Position: 49 57' 8 N 05 42 7 W
Escorting Convoy: HXA331

At 1320, Convoy course 285 degrees an explosion was heard and SS *George Hawley* the second ship in the starboard column was seen to be holed amidships on the starboard side. *Migonette* closed to 3000 yards on the starboard side of the torpedoed vessel and commenced an 'observant' dropping depth charges and frequently changing course and speed as a precaution against gnats. At 1335 a contact was gained at 600 yards and immediately attacked with depth charges.

Icarus later joined the hunt:

Meanwhile *Mignonette* gained another contact about 1000 yards East of *Icarus* which produced an echo sounder trace indicating a wreck or a bottomed U-boat. This was attacked with depth charges and a very heavy explosion was heard after the last depth charge of the pattern. *Icarus* made an excellent depth charge attack at 1720, the target showing no movement. Her second attack was broken off at 1741 when a survivor, Oblt. Friedrich Claussen, was sighted floating with the aid of escape apparatus: he was picked up. At 1746 a very large air bubble, circular in shape and about 100ft in diameter was observed on the port bow. The area inside the circle gave the appearance of boiling water. The noise of the bubbles was reported by ASDIC and it was thought that the U-boat was endeavouring to surface. *Icarus* carried out another depth charge attack at 1805 and by this time a quantity of diesel oil and large bubbles were observed.

Chief Quartermaster Friedrich Claussen escaped from the boat and was later found on the surface. During the interrogation, Claussen mentioned that his commanding officer was called 'Norman' and the boat was '19'; the British soon deduced that the boat sunk in this encounter was *U 1199*.

AUD 177/45 ADM 1/30262 NND 873041 NARA Series T-1022, Roll 4066, PG 30362
U-Boot-Ehrenmal Möltenort

THE MEN WHO DIED IN U 1199

Arnold, Fritz Mtr.Ob.Gfr. (1-5-1925)
Baack, Klaus Fk.Gfr. (10-8-1924)
Behrens, Gustav Mtr.H.Gfr. (12-12-1921)
Boldt, Walter Fk.Gfr. (13-1-1926)
Brinkmann, Johannes Mech.Mt. (13-12-1922)
Buchwald, Günther Mtr.Gfr. (28-1-1925)
Bux, Walter Ob.Masch. (9-8-1919)
Claussen, Friedrich Ob.Strm.
Dietrich, Leonhardt Fk.Mt. (13-11-1922)
Dietzmann, Kurt Bts.Mt. (13-4-1923)
Drechsel, Werner Masch.Mt. (21-3-1922)
Eisenmenger, Willi Bts.Mt. (24-4-1923)
Füsslein, Rainer Oblt.z.S. (12-7-1919)
Galke, Horst Masch.Gfr. (15-10-1926)
Gewildat, August Mtr. (11-5-1920)
Giese, Karl-Heinz Oblt.Ing (12-7-1922)
Hampel, Helmut Ob.Fahnr.Ing (26-6-1923)
Heine, Helmut Mech.Ob.Gfr. (30-3-1925)
Heinemann, Rudolf Mtr.Gfr. (1-2-1922)
Jußen, Johann Mtr.H.Gfr. (5-9-1919)
Kienzler, Wilhelm Fk.Ob,Gfr. (11-9-1924)
König, Fritz Masch.Gfr. (8-1-1925)
Krems, Heinz Bts.Mt. (30-1-1921)
Kupfer, Helmut Masch.Ob.Gfr. (6-11-1923)
Lindner, Willi Masch.Mt. (20-11-1919)

Litzinger, Heinrich Masch.Mt. (29-6-1922)
Löffler, Josef Mtr.Ob.Gfr. (6-1-1925)
Mörkelsberger, Franz Osan.Mt. (19-4-1902)
Müller, Friedrich Mech.Gfr. (11-10-1924)
Nollman, Rolf Kplt (29-12-1914)
Pätzold, Hans Mtr.Ob.Gfr. (11-8-1921)
Peppmöller, Hermann Mtr.Ob.Gfr. (26-4-1925)
Rathke, Franz Ob.Masch.Mt. (5-3-1921)
Schröder, Wilhelm Ob.Masch. (13-2-1914)
Smits, Hans Ltz.S. (12-10-1922)
Sprung, Karl Ob.Fk.Mt. (30-11-1919)
Tanz, Helmut Masch.Gfr. (27-1-1926)
Vogel, Heinz Masch.Gfr. (29-8-1924)
Volmari, Josef Masch.Mt. (3-5-1922)
Walther. Adolf Masch.Ob.Gfr. (25-3-1922)
Watterott, Hans Masch.Gfr. (11-8-1924)
Wehner, Josef Mtr.H.Gfr. (15-1-1922)
Weidemann, Walter Masch.Ob.Gfr. (16-8-1924)
Weissenburger, Albert Mtr. (23-7-1926)
Werrmann, Franz Masch.Ob.Gfr. (26-9-1924)
Wetzig, Johann Masch.Ob.Gfr. (30-11-1922)
Wilhelm, Werner Mtr.Ob.Gfr. (23-4-1923)
Winterfeld, Walter Ob.Strm. (23-2-1918)
Wunder, Arthur Mech.Gfr. (22-2-1925)

WRECK SITE

This wreck is possibly that of Nollmann's *U 1199*, but as far as the authors are aware, there has been no positive identification. The wreck at this location lies on a seabed of sand, shingle and pebbles, in a general depth of 67m (219.8ft), the lowest astronomical depth. It is upright and intact, with considerable damage to the outer casing, where soft corals have established themselves. Tidal streams are quite brisk. The wreck is also a war grave.

U 1209, KRIEGSMARINE U-BOAT

DATE OF LOSS: 18 December 1944
DEPTH: 68m
REFERENCE: 49° 55'N 05° 48'W
LOCATION: ESE from Wolf Rock in English Channel

Type: VIIC ocean-going boat   *Builders*: F. Schichau GmbH, Danzig (now Gdansk, Poland) for Kriegsmarine   *Ordered*: on 2 April 1942, within the batch of *U 1205–U 1210*   *Keel laid*: as Yard No.1579 on 14 July 1943   *Launched*: on 9 February 1944   *Commissioned*: by Oblt.z.S. Ewald Hülsenbeck on 13 April 1944   *Feldpost No*: M 28 716   *Badge*: a coronet over two crosses in a shield

TECHNICAL SPECIFICATIONS

See page 342.

OTHER SPECIFICATIONS

Two 375hp Allgemeine Elektricittäts-Gesellschaft electric motors powered her for running submerged. Armament consisted of one 37mm (1.46in) gun fully automatic on lower bandstand plus 1,195 rounds and two twin 20mm (0.79in) Flak guns on upper bandstand with 4,380 rounds. She also had five torpedo tubes (one stern and four at the bow) and carried ten torpedoes, stowed as follows: T3 Lut in tube I, II and IV, T5 in tube II, four torpedoes two (T5 and two T3) in bilge. Aft: one T5 loaded in tube V, and one T5 spare. 'Hohentwiel' was fitted, but never used. *U 1209* also had a wooden Schorchel head for anti-radar protection.

Ewald Hülsenbeck was born on 21 December 1919 in Milspe, Ruhr and commenced his naval career in 1938. From March 1942 to May 1941, Hülsenbeck was Comp. Officer 2.UAA and was promoted to Oberleutnant zur See on 1 April 1942.

   U 1209 was assigned to 8.U-Flottille, Danzig as *Ausbildungsboot* from 13 April to 31 October 1944 and Hülsenbeck was the boat's only commander.

   U 1209 was a shoddily built vessel and at 120m (394ft) some of the tanks started to leak because of badly fitting valves, etc. In consequence, she never dived beyond 120m.

   Training completed, the boat formally transferred to 11.U-Flottille at Bergen (60° 23 17'N 5° 19.54'E), in southwest Norway for frontline service on 1 November 1944.

   On 14 November 1944 the senior officer of the 5th.Flottille gave a short address and 'send-off' to the crews of *U 1209* and *U 1020* and at about 0830hrs (CT), both U-boats left Kiel together. *U 1209* proceeded on the surface from Kiel to Horten (59° 24.45'N 10° 29 08'E) near Oslo, Norway, carrying out *schnorchel* trials and arrived at Horten on the 17th.

   (2) On completion of these, she sailed from Horten on 22 November, in company with another 500-tonner and proceeded, surfaced to Kristiansand in southern Norway, where she arrived on about the 23rd.

   (3) On 23 November, *U 1209* left Kristiansand and arrived at Farsund in southern Norway (58° 05 42'N 6° 48 00'E) on the 25th.

FINAL PATROL

(4) At 1605hrs (CT) on 26 November 1944, the boat left Farsund accompanied by another U-boat (possibly *U 1020*) and some patrol boats, and sailed for operations in the English Channel off Cherbourg. *U 1209* set course between the Færoe Isles and Scotland, instead of following the usual passage through the Rosengarten. Off the north coast of Scotland, a signal was received from control, reporting the exact position of two Allied convoys, which were being escorted by heavy surface units. Although *U 1209* was in a position to attack, Hülsenbeck for some reason was disinclined to strike and signalled that he was nowhere near the position of the ships reported.

(Prisoners later said that he was very near one convoy and could hear the noises of ships on their hydrophones. One Telegraphist also stated that signals were received, warning U-boats of an area in which the British Fleet units were operating. According to this source, U-boats were ordered to avoid this area and were not to attack independent ships. The BdU Diary contains no supporting prohibitions.)

After passing the Færoe Isles, *U 1209* proceeded south of Rockall. From Rockall she crossed and made for the Irish Coast at a point opposite Donegal Bay; from there she proceeded down the west coast of Ireland, keeping close inshore and submerged throughout most of the journey.

It was stated that a special signal from Dönitz was received, ordering the U-boats to stay close inshore, because of the better chance of intercepting convoys there than in mid-ocean. This probably referred to 'Experience Report' 193, an exerpt from the log of *U 1199* which had recently returned (*see U 1199* above).

During this period two signals were received, which the Telegraphists believed gave *U 1209* her operational areas, but these could not be deciphered as Hülsenbeck had left the cipher books for the commanding officer's codes behind in Kiel. According to survivors, Hülsenbeck pretended that he had understood the signals and acknowledged them because he did not dare admit his error. The BdU Diary provides the following patrol projections for *U 1209*: AN35, AN28, AN23, AF79, AF76, AF75, AF74, AF77, the last being reached on 3 December. Thence AM32, AM31, AM33, AM24, AM25, AM27, AM29, AM43, AM49, reaching AM75 on or around 15 December. *U 1209* was next expected to proceed through the following zones: BF11, BF12, and BF16. Given the proximity of this route to the known plot which the boat followed, the allegation that Hülsenbeck forgot the cipher books must be in doubt.

U 1209 was searching for an aircraft carrier. One prisoner later said that *U 1209* followed an aircraft carrier from Donegal Bay down the coast and sighted her again at a point approximately off Black Sod Bay. However Allied records confirm that no Allied aircraft carrier was operating in the area stated, which would have been Irish territorial waters. When *U 1209* was south of Queenstown, sighted three merchant ships. However they were not attacked because *U 1209* was still following the mythical carrier which was apparently seen for the last time off Milford Haven. For the three days before she was sunk, the boat was at about 130ft patrolling off Land's End. As *U 1209* proceeded to her billet, the boat struck submerged rocks at Wolf Rock on 18 December 1944.

The German perspective – excerpt from Interrogation Report:

> Early on 18 December a steamer was sighted. The boat was about to attack when an argument broke out between the Captain and the Navigator. The Navigator was convinced that the boat was heading straight for Wolf Rock but the Captain was convinced that the boat was well to the west of it. At the height of the argument *U 1209* struck bottom. She grated along and was thrown off again, then hurled back onto the rock by the swell.

A 19 year old German survivor gave skipper Richard Perrin (commanding Rescue Marine Launch 542) this account:

> The commander decided to go to periscope depth but found the sea so rough, so we went down again. That's when it happened. We landed on a rock and water was coming in all over the place. Still the commander decided to go up again, to periscope depth. However, the leading engineer was of a different opinion: the tanks would have to be blown or else we would all drown. My job was to destroy the secret documents and then abandon ship. When I climbed up to the tower, half of the boat was already under water. I wondered what to do now. A big wave came along and that was me in the water.

HMCS *Ribble*
launching a boat to
rescue the crew of
U 1209. (Courtesy
Ian Smith)

Extract kindly provided by Vin Edwards.

At 1030hrs on 18 December, Wolf Rock Lighthouse reported a U-boat washed up on the rocks
and immediately afterwards signalled that the U-boat had slipped off and was underway proceeding westwards with one man on the conning tower. At 1045 the boat was reported on an eastward
course, sinking fast. Crew was abandoning ship. At 1101 the lighthouse signalled that the boat
had sunk. At 1238hrs HMCS *Montreal* signalled that the U-boat had sunk 155°, 1½ miles off Wolf
Rock.

Excerpt from Interrogation Report continued:

Finally the boat was badly holed aft and water began to rise in the diesel and motor rooms. The boat soon
became stern heavy. Hülsenbeck found it impossible to open the conning tower hatch and the U-boat
submerged again. Fuel oil had to be pumped out before she surfaced again. This time the conning tower
hatch was opened and the commanding officer was already on the bridge before he gave the order to

Crewmen of HMCS *Ribble* picking up survivors from *U 1209*.

Survivors of *U 1209* oboard HMCS *Ribble* at the burial at sea ceremony of a colleague. (Courtesy Ian Smith)

abandon ship. Georg Claussen, the engineer officer, who was the most popular office on board, was the only one to remain below. He remained below to scuttle the boat and was blown out of the conning tower hatch shortly before the boat sank.

Royal Navy motor launches and the two Canadian frigates, HMCS *Ribble* and *Montreal* of hunter-killer Group 26, were diverted and raced to the scene. Despite the heavy seas, 1½ hours later, they rescued forty-four crewmen, but seven men were lost. Amongst the survivors were Oblt.z.S. Ewald Hülsenbeck and Hans-Georg Claussen the chief engineer, but both died shortly after being rescued. The British report said that Hülsenbeck had died of a heart attack on HMCS *Montreal*, while Claussen, who had also been picked up by the Canadian ship, died in hospital. During interrogations it was discovered that three other crewmen had failed to clear the submarine before she sank.

Later cross-examination of the crew demonstrated that they despised Oblt.z.S. Hülsenbeck, believing him to be an inept coward. One rating even claimed that Hülsenbeck had physically hurled him from the life raft to make room for himself.

News of the wrecked U-boat and capture of her crew was released by London and even broadcast by the BBC. British Naval Intelligence (wrongly) having assumed the Germans would have previously intercepted the lighthouse-keeper's un-coded running commentary. An emergency Enigma key change was then ordered by the German High Command to take affect by noon of 21 December.

> According to an enemy radio broadcast report early on 18.12., *U 1209* ran onto rocks off Wolf Rock Lighthouse. Boat then surfaced and the crew took to rubber dinghies. The boat must be assumed lost, as according to dead reckoning she was in this area. Although the crew apparently had sufficient time to destroy confidential books, the key-word will be altered at 1200 on 21.12. Besides this, *U 181* and *U 843* have instructions to make their rendezvous with greatest caution.
>
> BdU Diary 19 December 1944

Later, on Christmas Eve, Information Report No. 203 was broadcast to all U-boats:

> According to an English broadcast a German submarine ran on rocks south-west of England near 'Wolf-Rock' and sank. The report is considered reliable. Only by painfully exact navigation can such accidents and losses be avoided. Navigation off enemy coasts is more difficult than navigation in the Baltic As astronomical fixes must not be taken in enemy coastal waters, the fullest use must be made of terrestrial navigation; very precise dead reckoning, taking into account the current as shown in the current atlas; and sounding (line of soundings). Basic principle: If exact position is not known, always assume that the boat is in the most unfavorable position possible, and in navigationally dangerous waters proceed with appropriate caution.

All the survivors of *U 1209* were held in the UK and many were not set free until 1948, however quite a number happily settled in Britain after their release.

Oblt.z.S. Ewald Hülsenbeck lies in Cannock Chase, Block 7 Row 3 plot 66. The grave of Lt Hans Claussen can be found in Block 5 Row 12, plot 265.

ADM 199/2061 NID/PW/REP/1 19 NID/PW/TEC 1-9, NND 873041 NARA Series T-1022 Rolls 4066, 3981 – PG 30358-30361 CPMB B-787 G2 Intelligence Division

WRECK SITE

The wreck of *U 1209* is believed to lie at the position offered above, but it has never been positively identified to date. A wreck is reported as sitting upright and still intact, with a heavy covering of nets. Little else is known about the wreck. Tidal streams are fairly brisk.

U 247, KRIEGSMARINE U-BOAT

DATE OF LOSS: 1 September 1944
DEPTH: 68m
REFERENCE: 49 53.9N 05 49.7W
LOCATION: 1 nautical mile SW of Wolf Rock

Type: VIIC ocean-going attack boat   *Builders*: F. Krupp Germaniawerft AG, Kiel-Gaarden for Kriegsmarine   *Ordered*: on 5 June 1941, within the batch of *U 247–U 250*   *Keel laid*: as Yard No 681 on 16 December 1942   *Launched*: on 23 September 1943   *Commissioned*: by Oblt.z.S. Gerhard Matschulat on 23 November 1943   *Feldpost No*: M 53 355   *Badge*: A submarine travelling through a letter 'U'

TECHNICAL SPECIFICATIONS

See page 342.

Gerhard Matschulat was born in Berlin on 25 May 1920 and commenced his naval career in 1938. Following U-boat training, Matschulat served as 1st watch officer with *U 458* between December 1942 and July 1943, during which time he was promoted to Oberleutnant zur See on 1 April 1943.

U 247 was assigned to 5.U-Flottille at Kiel as *Ausbildungsboot* (training boat) from 23 October 1943 to 31 May 1944, with Matschulat the commander.

On 18 May 1944, *U 247* left Kiel for Arendal (58° 27 41'N 8° 46 21'E) following orders of the 5.U-Flottille. Later that day however, *U 247* received orders from 11.U-Flottille that *U 999* and *U 247* would be taking part in special sea-trials for comparisons with the *Alberich*-coated boat *U 480*. On 20 May 1944 *U 247* put into Arendal, near Kristiansand in southern Norway.

Leaving Arendal on 27 May 1944, *U 247* put into Bergen (60° 23 17'N 5° 19.54'E), in southwest Norway, on the 28th.

On 31 May 1944 *U 247* left Bergen following the mission orders of 11.U-Flottille and headed for British coastal waters around northern Scotland. However on 1 June *U 247* formally transferred to 1.U-Flottille, Brest (according to the monthly organizational summaries of Kdr. Adm. der Unterseeboote).

> *U 247* situation from North Minch: 18.6. triple miss at ship of King George Class with two destroyers, course S. 5.7. *AM 3682* T5 miss at 'Agathe' (escort vessel). Shot missed because speed too slow. Double T1 avoided by trawler. 'Noreen May' (207 GRT) sunk with flak. Finishing shot T3 failure. On 6.7. auxiliary carrier with 3 destroyers in *AM 3539*. Observed by aircraft at 1313. The boat neither sighted convoys nor heard them in her hydrophones. A few small independently-routed ships. Boat has been ordered to return to W. France.
>   BdU Diary 9 July 1944

The 207-ton British fishing boat *Noreen Mary* had been journeying to the fishing grounds from Ayr and Oban; two men survived, but eight crewmen were killed.

THE MEN WHO DIED

Allen, Wilfred, Deckhand
Barnet, Alexander Annan, Second Deckhand
Coates, James Findlay, Apprentice
Flockhart, John, Skipper
Gordon, George, Fireman
Jackson, William, Chief Engineer
Lindsay, Charle,s Cook
McKenzie, Alexander, Fisherman

It was a questionable action, because anti-submarine aircraft regularly patrolled the skies around Britain, and especially off northern Scotland. It was later stated, however, that Matschulat not only sank the fishing boat, but also fired at, and killed, most of the trawler's crew as they tried to make their escape. This is believed to have been the last gun attack made on a trawler in the Second World War. This event formed the basis one of the war crimes charges brought against Admiral Dönitz at the Nuremberg War Trials. On 10 July 1944, *U 247* was ordered to go to western France, then on 12 July she was ordered to go to Brest, where she arrived on the 28th and came under the jurisdiction of 1.U-Flottille

FINAL PATROL

(3) On 26 August 1944, *U 247* left Brest for operations in the English Channel. The boat was expected to commence patrol in BF24 on 30 August and remain there until 20 September.

Meanwhile, in response to an aircraft radar report, six Canadian frigates of the 9th Escort Group, which were patrolling off Land's End on 31 August, were instructed to move to the area off Trevose Head on Cornwall's north coast. At 1845Z, the frigate *Saint John* attained a good sonar reading, 15 miles east of Wolf Rock. Commander-in-Chief at Plymouth then ordered three of the ships, HMCS *Stormont, Meon* and *Monnow*, to carry on north and pursue the aircraft radar subject, while HMCS *Saint John, Swansea* and *Assiniboine* remained and pursued the *Saint John* contact. At 2115hrs HMCS *Swansea* made an ASDIC contact and a single depth charge was dropped, but the crew thought it could have been a shoal of fish. However the men on *Saint John* claimed to have seen oil bubbling up, so the attack was pressed home with more depth charges and Hedgehog until 2300Z when the contact was lost.

The Group continued sweeping across the most likely path of the target and were south of Wolf Rock in the early hours of 1 September when HMCS *Saint John* picked up an interesting ASDIC reading at 0115hrs.

HMCS *Saint John*: Acting Lt W.R. Stacey RCNR commanding officer's report to senior officer on *Swansea*:

> …ASDIC reported a contact at 2,050 yards range. As this target had no movement, Doppler or H.E., it was assumed to be on the bottom, depth of water 42 fathoms. I ran over the trace with an Echo Sounder at 0205hrs. This trace had all the characteristics of a bottomed submarine, with a hard sharp peak on the centre of the hull trace.
>
> At 0300hrs, after further investigation, I passed over target again by Echo Sounder and dropped five depth charges from the rails, settings 'y' (three heavy and two light) according to a pattern developed within the 9th E.G. This pattern brought up a heavy flow of oil after a heavy tearing explosion.
>
> At 0320hrs, after I passed over the target by Echo Sounder and dropped another 5-charge pattern as above. Unfortunately the E/S trace was inadvertently destroyed. This pattern produced a terrific tearing explosion with a further heavy flow of oil, which soon extended over an area 2½ miles long and a mile wide, but no wreckage was seen due to darkness. At 0345hrs, hedgehog pattern was fired and a further flow of oil produced.

Saint John stood by the oil slick until daybreak, but due to the previous attacks, had great difficulty in holding the contact. The ship investigated many other wrecks and non-sub contacts in the vicinity until 1350hrs, when the original source was located again.

> At 1404B, a five depth charge pattern, as previously stated was dropped over the E/S trace. The E/S was broken down and the ship was placed over target on centre bearings and E/S. This pattern produced a heavy tearing explosion and brought forth a further flow of oil, wreckage was seen rising from the explosion, and a whaler was lowered to collect evidence.
>
> As the wind and sea were rising the whaler had difficulty in seeing the wreckage, which was rising all around the ship and spreading rapidly in all directions in the oil slick.

In fact the wind was blowing Force 8, west, northwest.

Amongst the flotsam and jetsam recovered was part of the Engine Room Log of *U 247*, Engineering Maintenance Book (Type 'U'), marked U-247. – Certificate celebrating the 10,000,000th engine revolution on *U 247*. – Diagram of German Radio Set. – Light List of Bay of Biscay area – part of a crewman's typewritten diary – German Death Notice – part pages of Torpedo Dept. Inventory for *U 247* – photos of German Officers and families and Personal letters in German – German Rubber raft – Leading Tel. ? Jacket complete with buttons and insignia (souvenir hunters took some of the buttons) – shirt with Insignia – undershirt – sock – German Leather Coat – leatherette cushion – small wooden locker doors, complete with lock and key (the door was burnt through panel) – broken piece of woodwork with 'RADIEL' talley and a wooden shelf.

The sea however was so rough that many other articles could not be recovered and just drifted away in the tide and oil.

> At 1730hrs, the 'C' Class frigate HMCS *Assiniboine* (ex HMS *Kempenfelt*), was detailed by Senior Officer E.G.11, to assist, but both ships experienced major difficulties in obtaining and holding contact, in spite of the oil still rising and definite radar fix of the target from Wolf Rock Light. At about 2025, *Saint John* dropped a ten-charge pattern of depth charges, followed by another ten-charge pattern by Assiniboine, and these brought more oil to the surface.
>
> At 1050hrs on the 2nd, *Assiniboine* ordered *Saint John* to rejoin E.G.9 and at 1604N *Saint John* joined HMCS *Monnow* and continued the patrol.

U 247's projected track during the period in question was; *BF24 (30/8) AE47, AE42, BF24, BF16 (20/9), BF15, BF14 BF36, BF32, BE31 (25/9), AL99, AL95, AL67, AL92 (30/9)*. It will readily be seen that the U-boat was in the sector where the attack described above took place. Of course BdU was oblivious to her loss and made the following diary entry on 20 September:

> *U 247* was ordered to move away to westward and report situation in operations area around Land's End. Boat has been at sea for 4 weeks already and still has long return passage to Norway. If possible boat will be stationed as weather boat until fighting capacity expended.

The BdU Diary contains this entry for 31 October 1944:

> *U 247* must be presumed lost. She left Brest on 26.8 for an operations area south of the Scilly Islands and Land's End. After all boats had left the Channel, Operations Control had no information on the state of affairs there and the boat was therefore ordered to move off to the West and report the situation. So far no situation reports, weather reports or position reports ordered have been received. According to her supplies, she should have entered port by now. Loss presumably occurred in the Western Channel (probably already on her way out to her operations area) due to anti-submarine activity. No further information.

There is an interesting postscript. On the night of 12/13 March, HMS *Loch Ruthven* and *Wild Goose* of 2-EG made an attack on a bottomed, stationary target. The location was described as '198 degrees Wolf Rock, 3.2 miles' although the assessors initially dismissed the claim to have destroyed a second U-boat (on the grounds that the vessels had attacked the dead *U 247*). In August 1945 '*in the light of information obtained from German records*', the assessors pronounced that a second U-boat had been present, assumed to be *U 683* and had been duly destroyed by 2-EG. However it is known that 2-EG revisited the location on 15 March and carried out yet another can opener. Among the detritus was a letter addressed to Maschinenmaat Werner Genzel. As will be seen, this unfortunate sailor was one of *U 247*'s crew. The fate of *U 683* remains a mystery.

ADM 1/30162 NARA Series T-1022, Roll 4066, PG 30225, 30353-30357 U-Boot-Ehrenmal Möltenort CWGC

All of the crew of *U 247* were lost.

THE MEN WHO DIED

Barchfeld, Kurt Gfr. (Born: 13-6-1924)
Bratfisch, Waldemar Ob.Gfr. (31-3-1924)
Brune, Friedrich Mt. (13-2-1920)
Cornelius, Heinz Mt. (27-5-1922)
Dengeler, Oskar Ob.Gfr. (19-11-1923)
Dittmann, Alfred Ob.Mt. (2-9-1921)
Dürr, Josef Mt. (2-3-1920)
Ewert, Alfred Ob.Gfr. (12-4-1923)
Faifer, Stanislaus Gfr. (11-8-1925)
Fischer, Erwin Ob.Gfr. (18-3-1922)
Floth, Heinz Ob.Gfr. (2-6-1924)
Gast, Anton Ob.Gfr. (16-3-1924)
Genzel, Werner Mt. (26-2-1922)
Göhring, Fritz Mt. (25-6-1923)
Graf, Gottfried Gfr. (18-7-1925)
Hoffmann, Berthold Ob.Gfr. (11-9-1923)
Höher, Wolfgang-Gerhard Ob.Gfr. (19-11-1924)
Holz, Herbert Ob.Gfr. (22-2-1925)
Huwe, Hermann Ob.Gfr. (13-12-1924)
Jeschke, Hans Ob.Gfr. (3-3-1925)
Kanthak, Horst Ob.Gfr. (13-11-1923)
Keller, Heinz Ob.Gfr. (27-8-1923)
Kilimann, Willi Ob.Strm. (2-12-1917)
Klaussner, Georg Ob.Mt. (10-11-1919)
Köhler, Karl Ob.Gfr. (7-6-1925)
Lang, Aloysius Gfr. 28-2-1924)
Lepach, Reinhold Ob.Gfr. (8-10-1923)
Lüchtemeier, Johann Mt. (5-9-1920)
Matschulat, Gerhard Commander
Meyer, Ernst Ob.Gfr. (21-3-1925)
Meyer, Hans Ob.Masch. (1-9-1914)
Misch, Hans Mt. (14-8-1920)
Mittag, Oswin Gfr. (18-9-1924)
Netzsch, Johann-Richard Gfr. (6-4-1924)
Neyses, Walter Ob.Gfr. (29-8-1924)
Nottbohm, Helmut Gfr. (29-11-1924)
Papesch, Georg Mt. (11-10-1922)
Penzkofer, Franz Ob.Gfr. (22-1-1924)
Peschke, Walter Mt. (19-8-1917)
Philipp, Johannes Ob.Gfr. (23-3-1924)
Rosenstock, Heinz Ob.Strm. (24-9-1919)
Röttger, Josef Ltz.s. 2ndWO (9-5-1923)
Rüdiger, Max Ob.Mt. (8-8-1919)
Schenk, Otto Ob.Gfr. (22-5-1922)
Schindler, Gerhard Ob.Gfr. (8-3-1925)
Schulze, Horst Gfr. (13-11-1921)
Sirek, Karl-Heinz Gfr. (11-8-1923)
Stiebner, Heinz Oblt.z.S. 1stWO (4-8-1922)
Stoffregen, Hans St.Ob.Masch. (11-8-1910)

For the destruction of *U 247* and holding the target in poor ASDIC conditions for 12 hours, Lt Cdr William Roland Stacey and Lt James Richard Bradley were awarded a DSC, while Leading Seaman William Edward Royds RCNVR of Toronto and Able Seaman Lloyd Palmer Haaganson of Sanctuary, Sask., were awarded the DSM. The following four other crewmen received a 'Mention in Despatches': Lt Henry Blair Blanchard RCNVR of Nova Scotia, Chief Engine Room Artificer Hawer Liabo RCN of Haugisund, Norway, Petty Officer Robert William Warburton RCNVR of Hamilton, Ontario and Able Seaman Thomas Alexander McCullen RCNVR of Sydney, Nova Scotia.

WRECK SITE

The wreck lies on a seabed of sand and shingle, in a general depth of 68m (223ft), being the lowest astronomical depth. It is reported as being reasonably intact, but the outer casing and conning tower are badly damaged and the wreck is covered in soft corals. The site is also a war grave.

U 327, KRIEGSMARINE U-BOAT

DATE OF LOSS: 27 February 1945
DEPTH: Unknown
REFERENCE: 49° 46'N 05° 47'W (historic position)
LOCATION: Unknown

Type: VIIC/41 ocean-going attack boat   *Builders*: Flender Werke AG, Lübeck-Siems for Kriegsmarine   *Ordered*: on 16 July 1942, within the batch of *U 323–U 328*   **Keel laid**: as Yard No.327 on 15 April 1943   *Launched*: on 27 May 1944   *Commissioned*: by Kapitänleutnant Hans Lemcke on 18 July 1944   *Feldpost No*: M 36 449

TECHNICAL SPECIFICATIONS

See page 342.

Hans Lemcke was born on 9 December 1918 in Pragsdorf, Mecklenburg and commenced his naval career in 1937. He served on board the destroyer *Z 4 Richard Beitzen* between April 1939 and June 1940 and was then seconded to the Luftwaffe for the next three years. On 1 July 1944 Lemcke was promoted to Kapitänleutnant.

U 327 was assigned to 4.U-Flottille at Stettin as *Ausbildungsboot* from 18 July 1944 to 31 January 1945, with Kplt. Lemcke the CO.

U 327 left Kiel on 20 January 1945 and transferred to Horten (59° 24.45'N 10° 29 08'E) near Oslo in Norway, where she arrived on the 24th.

On 28 January 1945, *U 327* moved from Horten and the following day arrived at Kristiansand in southern Norway (58° 08.41'N 7° 59.54'E).

On 1 February *U 327* formally transferred to 11.U-Flottille at Bergen for frontline service.

FINAL PATROL

(3) Departing Kristiansand with Kplt. Lemcke and a crew of forty-six on 30 January 1945, *U 327* proceeded to the western entrance to the English Channel, for operations in British coastal waters.

U 327 was never heard from again.

On 27 February 1945 however, a VPB Liberator sighted a U-boat leaking oil and running submerged at *schnorchel*-depth, 112 miles south of Wolf Rock. A message was quickly relayed to the hunter-killer 2nd Escort Group, consisting of veteran frigates HMS *Loch Fada, Wild Goose* and *Labuan*, which raced to the scene. After searching the area a contact was found and an attack was made using depth charges, Hedgehog and Squid. The British frigate HMS *Labuan* carried out an attack in the dark.

Official report of the Second Escort Group's patrol – 25 February to 23 March 1945:

> In the evening of 27 February EG.2 was ordered to home on an aircraft which had sighted a periscope in a position to the south-westward. By 2024/27 the Group was approaching the marker and searching at 8 knots. There was no lack of contacts; at one moment four separate ones were being investigated – and there was also a strong smell of oil near one of the markers.
>
> Within a short time, however *Labuan* had selected one of these contacts for her target. After her second attack the Senior Officer again smelt oil and sighted what looked like an oil drum floating low in the water. – An attempt was made to pick it up, but it was heavy and difficult to get hold of and the Senior Officer, thinking that it was the cause of the reported oil slick and of the smell of oil, left it where it was.
>
> Nearly 12 hours later, having searched in vain to the east and northeast of the datum, EG.2 was on the way back to its starting point when the drum was sighted again. The Senior Officer had another look at it and, finding it no ordinary drum, hoisted it in by means of the foxer-davit. It was opened and found to contain a collapsible dinghy.
>
> Intended to save life, this container instead ensured the destruction of the U-boat in which it had been fitted. The ships proceeded to the position where it had first been seen, *Labuan* obtained contact at the head of a long oil streak and, with a depth charge attack, which increased the flow of oil, left no doubt as to the destruction of the enemy.

ADM 1/30334 NARA Series T-1022, Roll 3900, PG 31752 U-Boot-Ehrenmal Möltenort

The Admiralty were still not totally convinced of a kill and later classified the attack as 'B' – 'U-boat probably sunk'.

THE MEN WHO DIED IN U 327

Akuszewski, Fritz Gfr. (6-6-1925)
Andrae, Wolfgang Maat. (5-9-1923)
Apel, Artur Maat. (24-2-1919)
Blaschek, Walter Maat. (2-4-1922)
Bornemann, Werner Mtr. (11-10-1925)
Brabender, Franz Ob.Masch. (15-12-1916)
Cordes, Werner Gfr. (22-10-1924)
Engeler, Günter Ob.Masch. (9-1-1920)
Fecker, Kurt Gfr. (20-12-1925)
Geisler, Josef Ob.Gfr. (6-12-1921)
Gohlke, Herbert Ob.Gfr. (26-7-1922)
Hanske, Wolfgang Maat. (21-6-1921)
Hohn, Paul Mtr. (5-11-1921)
Kähler, Willi Ob.Strm. (20-11-1920)
Karow, Kurt Gfr. (1-8-1925)
Keller, Franz Ob.Gfr. (16-4-1924)
Kollmann, Martin Ob.Gfr. (3-4-1923)
Krenz, Fritz Ob.Mt. (5-2-1921)
Krüger, Gustav Maat. (1-3-1920)
Kümmel, Heinz Ob.Gfr. (23-11-1923)
Lefreve, Heinrich Ob.Strm. (25-3-1915)
Lenthe, von Georg-Wilhelm-Helmut Ltz.s. 2nd (15-12-1922)

Lieder, Kurt Gfr. (12-9-1925)
Lis, Theodor Gfr. (5-10-1925)
Lohmann, Franz Gfr. (20-9-1925)
Lohr, Siegfried Gfr. (11-8-1925)
Mauczik, Herbert Ob.Gfr. (12-6-1924)
Mehner, Günther Gfr. (9-1-1925)
Meyer, Hermann Gfr. (22-9-1924)
Mölders, Josef Maat. (17-5-1922)
Neitzel, Herbert Ob.Gfr. (23-7-1925)
Ochner, Raimund Ob.Mt. (5-10-1914)
Pieritz, Karl-Heinz Ob.Gfr. (9-5-1925)
Prussas, Hans Oblt.z.S. 1st WO (31-7-1917)
Riediger, Heinz Ob.Gfr. (24-10-1924)
Römmling, Ernst Ob.Mt. (21-12-1920)
Sandkämpfer, Johannes Gfr. (21-6-1926)
Sandmeyer, Hans Ob.Gfr. (6-8-1923)
Schätz, Franz Maat. (8-7-1924)
Schwarz, Paul Gfr. (24-4-1925)
Stein, Siegfried Maat. (18-1-1924)
Wiech, Willi Maat. (16-2-1921)
Witte, Walter LtIng. (1-1-1921)
Wörle, Fritz Gfr. (19-11-1925)
Wössner, Erich Gfr. (11-1-1925)

WRECK SITE

At the time of writing, the location of this U-boat wreck is unknown.

U 1208, KRIEGSMARINE U-BOAT

DATE OF LOSS: 27 February 1945
DEPTH: 65m
REFERENCE: 49 51'.820 N 06 06'.806 W
Also suggested: 49 51'.783 N 06 06'.750 W
LOCATION: 10 miles SE of the Isles of Scilly

Type: VIIC ocean-going attack boat   ***Builders***: F. Schichau GmbH, Danzig for Kriegsmarine   ***Ordered***: on 2 April 1942, within the batch of *U 1205–U 1210*   ***Keel laid***: as Yard No.1578 on 30 June 1943 ***Launched***: on 13 January 1944   ***Commissioned***: by Korvettenkapitän Georg Hagene on 6 April 1944   ***Feldpost No***: M 05 973   **Badge**: A knight in armour holding a sword and shield, in a shield

TECHNICAL SPECIFICATIONS

See page 342.

Georg Hagene was born on 24 July 1908 in Niederschöneweide, Teltow and commenced his naval career in 1927. He served aboard the heavy cruiser *Blücher* between September 1939 and April 1940 and was promoted to Korvettenkapitän on 1 April 1944.

Georg Hagene was the boat's only CO and during his brief command sank no enemy vessels.

U 1208 was assigned to 8.U-Flottille, Danzig as *Ausbildungsboot* from 6 April 1944 until 31 December 1944. On 1 January 1945, the boat and commander formally transferred to 11.U-Flottille, Bergen, for frontline service.

On 30 December 1944, *U 1208* left Kiel and sailed to Horten near Oslo in Norway, where she arrived on 2 January 1945.

On 13 January 1945, *U 1208* departed Horten and moved to Kristiansand in southern Norway, arriving on the 14th.

FINAL PATROL

(3) *U 1208* left Kristiansand on 16 January 1945 for operations off the south west coast of England. The Allies intercepted her *Passiermeldung* passage report on 31 January from AM 4855. By early February the boat was patrolling the waters south of Ireland. *U 1208* and her crew of forty-nine never returned and were presumed lost through unknown causes with effect from 5 March. What can we piece together about her last patrol? Only fragments. On 24 February, Georg Hagene torpedoed and sunk the 1,664-ton British steamer *Oriskany* (ex-*la Ceiba*) (Wallem & Co., Hong Kong), between Land's End and the Scilly Isles, at position 50° 05'N 05° 51'W; she was in coastal convoy BTC 78, comprising nine ships and en-route from Newport, Monmouth to London with coal. The master, Captain David Souter Morrison, Commodore Commander Ian Neil Macmillan RNR, the crew of twenty-one, seven naval ratings and four DEMS gunners were lost.

THE CREWMEN WHO DIED

Abdo Syeed Abdul Malik, Fireman
Avery, Leslie Ernest Francis, Sailor
Azi Abdul, Fireman
Cossey, William Sidney, Sailor
Fenn, Sidney Walter James, Chief Engineer Officer
Fenton, Michael, Boatswain
Gooch, George Alfred, Cook
Harris, Frederick Osborne, Able Seaman
Hashim, Said Ali, Fireman
Haworth, Wilfred, First Radio Officer
Hayward, Leslie William John, Cabin Boy
Jakeman, William, Able Seaman
Mackenzie, George Fingal, 3rd Engineer Officer
Meagan, Albert, Able Seaman
Morrison, David Soutar, Master
McGhee, John Irwin, 2nd Officer
O'Donovan, John, Able Seaman
Razak, Abdul, Donkeyman
Roberts, John, Chief Officer
Tribe, Isaac, Cook Steward
Voitsehovits, Boris, 2nd Engineer Officer
Williams, Kenward, Boy (16yrs)

THE DEMS GUNNERS WHO DIED

Hare, Harold Leslie P/JX 235727 Leading Seaman HMS *President III*
Terry, Reginald D/JX 333951 Able Seaman HMS *President III*
Tomlinson, Ernest D/JX 619209 Able Seaman HMS *President III*
Wright, Kenneth C/JX 556526 Convoy Signalman HMS *President III*

The names of seven naval ratings could not be found.

The two frigates and convoy escorts, HMS *Duckworth*, commanded by Cdr R.G. Mills and HMS *Rowley* by Lt Cdr F.G.J. Jones, immediately set about hunting the U-boat.

Official Report of 3rd Escort Group – 49 55'N 06 08'W – U 1208:

At 1020/24 *Rowley* in the centre of the line reported very good contact, which she stopped and held whilst *Duckworth* (next to starboard) closed. Target showed a definite southerly movement. At 1025 *Rowley* attacked with Hedgehog. *Duckworth* then attacked with Hedgehog, remainder forming 'observant' … at 1100 *Duckworth* classified target as positive U-boat by echo sounder trace showing submarine silhouette 30ft clear of bottom, some 2ft high by 100ft long.

The contact was lost and regained throughout the afternoon yet despite the attacks, echo sounding indicated the U-boat to be 'still serenely underway'. At 1255 *Duckworth* carried out a devastating attack on the apparently bottomed U-boat.

This attack was assessed as lethal as there was no further movement from then onwards. On the other hand the trace became so woolly that it was uncertain whether it was just another 'non-sub', which had been hit.

From 1530hrs *Rowley* carried out a 'scientific' can opener. In other words, a line of closely packed depth charges was used to blow the unfortunate submarine to smithereens. Among the debris was a fine oil slick, several tins of German dried milk showing signs of a terrific battering. Loaves of brown bread floated to the surface, followed by a forage cap, complete with Nazi badge. All forty-nine crew perished with the boat. Post-war assessors mistakenly identified this U-boat as *U 246*.

THE MEN WHO PERISHED WITH U 1208

Bauroth, Roland Mech.O.Gfr. (26-4-1925)	Lindemann, Friedrich Ltz.S. (24-4-1922)
Beyer, Markus Fk.O.Gfr. (8-2-1925)	Macherey, Hans Bts.Mt. (20-9-1922)
Claußen, Hans-Georg Ob.Strm. (13-3-1920)	Michaelis, Max Mtr.O.Gfr. (14-3-1923)
Cybulla, Heinz Masch.O.Gfr. (16-12-1925)	Niegel, Josef Bts.Mt. (30-3-1922)
Deger, Sebastian Masch.O.Gfr. (7-2-1924)	Nowak, Hans Mech.O.Gfr. (4-9-1924)
Engel, Willi Masch.Mt. (10-12-1921)	Piethe, Werner Mech.Mt. (23-8-1919)
Faßhauer, Joachim Mtr.Gfr. (28-5-1926)	Radlsböck, Karl Masch.O.Gfr. (20-6-1924)
Fehler, Gerhard Masch.Gfr. (7-9-1926)	Scheuing, Karl Masch.O.Gfr. (13-11-1925)
Fehr, Walter Ob.Masch. (14-2-1916)	Schmitz, Johann Masch.Mt. (25-12-1922)
Fichtner, Joachim Mtr.O.Gfr. (10-6-1925	Schorm. Gerhard Mtr.O.Gfr. (31-12-1925)
Fickbohm, Erwin Masch.O.Gfr. (21-6-1923)	Schreiber, Erich Mtr.O.Gfr. (31-10-1924)
Gärtner, Werner Masch.O.Gfr. (27-3-1925)	Schubert, Kurt Ob.Bts.Mt. (18-8-1918)
Glorius, Otto Masch.Gfr. (19-9-1925)	Schulten, Johannes Mtr.O.Gfr. (4-8-1924)
Gromotka, Herbert Ob.Masch. (14-12-1919)	Schwertz, Friedrich St.Ob.Strm. (20-7-1908)
Haase, Walter Ob.Masch.Mt. (5-11-1921)	Simon, Kurt Mech.Gfr. (30-8-1925)
Huhk, Heinrich Fk.O.Gfr. (5-1-1925)	Sölter, Harald Fk.O.Gfr. (21-2-1924)
Jörchel, Gerhard Masch.O.Gfr. (26-2-1925)	Sweeren, Alfred Fk.Mt. (24-12-1923)
Kiwitt, Johann Masch.Mt. (9-5-1923)	Weigmann, Lorenz Masch.O.Gfr. (16-8-1925)
Krüger, Karl-Heinz Ob.Fk.Mt. (12-10-1919)	Wendlandt, Siegfried Mtr.O.Gfr. (19-1-1922)
Künne, Heinz Masch.Gfr. (6-8-1925)	Werner, Wolf Oblt.Ing. (28-9-1920)
Lange, Ewald Ob.San.Mt. (26-1-1913)	Wetzel, Wilhelm Mtr.O.Gfr. (13-10-1921)
Lange, Klaus Ltz.S. (28-3-1921)	Wiezorrek, Franz Mtr.O.Gfr. (9-1-1926)
Langguth, Franz Mtr.O.Gfr. (20-1-1924)	Zierenberg, Rolf Mtr.O.Gfr. (1-8-1924)
Leunert, Gerhard Masch.O.Gfr. (11-4-1925)	

ADM 1/30321 ADM 217/292 ADM 1/30334 NARA T-1022, Rolls 3900, 4066, PGs 30361-30362 and 31752
U-Boot-Ehrenmal Möltenort CWGC

WRECK SITE

The wreck lies on a seabed of sand and shingle, in a general depth of 65m (213ft). It is reported as being intact and upright, with the gun still in place. The casing is broken open and the interior looks badly silted up. Nets also cover much of the conning tower and aft section of the boat. This site will also be classed as a war grave.

U 681, KRIEGSMARINE U-BOAT

DATE OF LOSS: 10 March 1945
DEPTH: 86m
REFERENCE: 49 52'.433 N 06 38'.633 W
LOCATION: W of the Isles of Scilly

Type: VIIC ocean-going attack boat   *Builders*: Howaldtswerke AG, Hamburg for Kriegsmarine   *Ordered*: on 25 August 1941, within the batch of *U 681–U 683*   **Keel laid**: as Yard No.830 on 21 October 1942   *Launched*: on 20 November 1943   *Commissioned*: by Oblt. z.S. Helmut Bach on 3 February 1944   *Feldpost No*: M 49 036   *Badge*: under Bach, the U-boat badge was an elephant standing on its hind feet poised on a mine. This motif was retained as cap badge under Gebauer

TECHNICAL SPECIFICATIONS

See page 342.

OTHER SPECIFICATIONS

U 681 was fitted with *Hohentwiel* radar. *Tunis with Fliege and Mücke. U 681* had six containers of which four were filled with 6-man dinghies with sails and compressed air-bottles, etc. (The other two were empty because no more dinghies were available at Kiel).

Helmut Bach was born on 5 December 1906 in Helfda, Mansfelder Seereis, Saxony-Anhalt and commenced his naval career in 1939. Bach served on the infamous merchant raider *Pinguin* between February 1940 and May 1941. He was promoted to Kapitänleutnant (R) on 1 April 1945.
　　U 681 was assigned to 31.U-Flottille, Kiel as *Ausbildungsboot* from 3 February 1944, with Oblt. z.S. Helmut Bach the commander.
　　After her commissioning at the Howaldt Werke, *U 681* proceeded to Kiel for U.A.K. trials. While there, on or about 10 February, she rammed a freighter, and had to proceed to Rostock for about three weeks for repairs. The boat's ill fortune continued, because she also collided with a patrol boat, then, on another occasion, with a mole.
　　U 681 finally moved to Sönderborg for silent running trials, which took place there for one day and at Roenne; thence she proceeded to Swinemuede, for A.A. practice with the 20mm. On passage however, she was again delayed, this time by heavy weather, which caused her to spend four or five days for repairs in Gdynia.
　　Just before Easter the boat went to Pillau for pre-tactical exercises. These lasted about 10 to fourteen days, after which *U 681* proceeded to Hel for five months' *Agrufront*. Here, one of her hydroplanes was damaged when another U-boat rammed her, which necessitated a ten- to fifteen-day refit in Danzig.
　　From Hel the boat went to Libau, arriving about 14 July and carried out torpedo firing. At the end of July, a few days were spent in Gdynia and at the beginning of August *U 681*, she proceeded to Pillau for twenty days' tactical exercises, after which she entered Howaldt Werke at Hamburg for overhaul. During this period the crew were accommodated in the depot ship *Veendam*. On one occasion a bomb fell between *U 681* and the dock, but did no damage.
　　Oblt.z.S. Bach, left the boat on 2 August, on account of night-blindness, which rendered him unfit for sea service; the engineering officer and 1st lieutenant were also relieved.
　　Oblt.z.S. Werner Gebauer assumed command on 2 August 1944. Gebauer was born on 10 September 1922 in Bad Soden and commenced his naval career in 1939. He served as 2nd watch officer on board *U 212* between April 1942 and August 1943 and was promoted to Oberleutnant zur See on 1 December 1943.

When Oblt.z.S. Gebauer took over, some of the trials had to be carried out again. On 1 October 1944, *U 681* was formally assigned to II.U-Flottille, Bergen in southwest Norway, as a frontline boat.

Towards the end of October, after adjustments had been made to the *schnorchel*, *U 681* returned to Swinemunde for a further ten days' A.A. practice with the 37mm, which had been mounted at Hamburg. She then proceeded to Hel for two weeks, having to spend four or five days at Danzig for repairs to one of the pumps. From Hel *U 681* moved to Pillau, spending about three weeks for further torpedo firing and tactical exercises.

Towards the end of December she again returned to Howaldt Werke, Hamburg for refit. About 22 January 1945 she proceeded to Kiel for fitting out for about three weeks; during this period, the U-Flottille S.O. Fregattenkapitän Topp had to deal with the drunk and disorderly conduct of her crew ashore. The Gauleiter of Berlin was entertained on board, and presented each member of the crew with a fur-lined waistcoat. Some of the crew went to Berlin to bring these back. On 4 February 1945 the crew received a security lecture from a Kapitänleutnant or (according to other prisoners) by Freg.Kpt. Topp himself. Curiously, at the same time they were compelled to watch a six-act play depicting the tricks and temptations they would be confronted with at any Allied interrogation centre they might come to. Prisoners' opinions were that the play was not particularly effective…

British Naval Intelligence document NID 1/PW/REP/20 quotes disturbing orders allegedly given to the crew of *U 681*:

> Before *U 681* left Kiel [7 February 1945] the Senior Officer of the 5th Flotilla said in his farewell speech that there were unwritten orders that U-boat commanding officers should destroy all survivors from sunken ships and shot down aircraft. As these orders were unwritten, he said he must leave their execution to the conscience of the individual C.O. He said he himself would carry out such orders. When survivors are destroyed this is not to be logged and no ratings are to be present if it can be avoided. The fact that these orders are believed to emanate from Dönitz himself tends to shake the high opinion which all COs formerly had of their chief.
>
> [Gebauer] said he did not know any CO's who would carry out these orders. He himself on passage to his operational area sighted two fishing boats…which he should, if carrying out his orders, have sunk without trace, but he decided not to do so.

On 7 February 1945, *U 681* left Kiel in company with *U-Holpert*, *U-Struebing*, *U-Mueller-Baetge*, *U-Boos*, *U-Becker* and *U-Lauth*. Most of these still had their *Agrufront* exercises before them. After a two-day passage, during which she dived for 4 hours to escape aircraft, which did not actually attack, she spent one night off Friedrickshaven, then proceeded to Horten, going up the fjord further inland than the town itself. Two or three days were spent here doing *schnorchel* exercises, and practicing deep diving up to 80m in the fjord. She provisioned for a twelve-week patrol, and embarked equipment for an Arctic patrol. When the operational area was later changed to the Channel, there was insufficient time to land this equipment. *U 681* then proceeded to Kristiansand, where the 37mm gun was fired at an aircraft during a night air raid in the Skaggerak. One prisoner mentioned seeing one VIIC U-boat and one IXC in Kristiansand, in addition to a damaged U-boat. During the passage of the Skaggerak a message was received by W/T warning them of possible MTB activity in those waters, but no hostile craft were encountered.

Note: the account of the last patrol of *U 681* is drawn from prisoner interrogations quoted in NID 1/PW/REP/20 and NND 873041. While some scepticism as to the contents of this account may be justified, the information does largely correspond with known facts concerning this particular patrol.

FINAL PATROL

A few hours after arriving at Kristiansand, *U 681* sailed again, this time for her operational area, which was to be on the convoy route between the Scilly Isles and Ushant, sailing east of Land's End if the more westerly regions proved unfruitful. The commanding officer later said his intention had been to enter Plymouth harbour, sink all he could and then, withdrawal being impossible, scuttle his boat. The U-boat left harbour in convoy, consisting of two minesweepers preceding three or four munitions ships bound for Stavanger, an escorting U-boat and finally *U 681* and another U-boat setting out on patrol. When ready, the two U-boats dived to *schnorchel* depth without notifying the convoy, and parted company. For navigation, the commander of *U 681* depended almost entirely on Echo-Sounder and *Elektra-Sonne* fixes; the accuracy of *Elektra-Sonne* was supposed to be 0.3 miles with a good cut, but the boat very rarely achieved anything approaching this figure.

U 681 proceeded submerged, *schnorchelling* at night. Course was set between the Shetlands and the Færoes; then close inshore along the west coast of Scotland and Ireland. The 100 or 200m line was followed, soundings being taken every half hour, but on one occasion off the Shetlands bearings were lost, and the U-boat found herself only about 40m off shore. At about this time, too, the presence of aircraft was detected by the radar fitting on the *schnorchel* head.

U 681 dived and about 4 hours later heard distant depth charge explosions. A navigational miscalculation near the Hebrides brought the U-boat 60 miles off course and into a British minefield. The position approximately 56°N 09°W screw noises were heard, intermittently, apparently from three escort vessels. (These were probably fishing vessels.)

Considerable trouble was experienced with the *schnorchel*. Exhaust gas emissions rendered some of the engine room personnel unconscious. Indeed the fumes were so unpleasant, even the donning of drager sets made the task impossible. This contrasts sharply with the optimistic picture of the apparatus painted by BdU in November 1944 (*see U 1199*). There were machinery failures too. For two weeks during the patrol the the electrically driven compressor broke down. One diesel was also unserviceable, a cylinder being damaged, but was later repaired. As if to compound an already bad situation, low pressure (400-500 millibars below normal) burst cans of food, which went bad. Rations were cut as a consequence.

On 6 March, *U 681* was cruising at periscope depth off Galway, when three anti-submarine vessels hove into view. Gebauer decided to attack. Tube V was prepared and a T5 fired. At the same time the target stopped dead in the water. Nine minutes later the torpedo was heard to explode. Reloading took an hour, as mishandling the valves admitted water into the boat instead of the tube. Later, when all was quiet, the U-boat surfaced to transmit news of the apparent sinking. It was incorrect, the anti-submarine trawler had not been sunk and had steamed away, quite oblivious to the presence of *U 681*.

Radar provided evidence that aircraft were patrolling nearby and dived again. She had been using the opportunity to secure the guns, which the weather had loosened on their mountings, and to dump accumulated rubbish ['gash' in naval parlance]. A depth charge attack developed, but was too distant to be effective, depth charges being apparently dropped on the rubbish. Later *U 681* sighted a large merchant ship proceeding independently. Range was so short that the name *CAIRO* was visible, and the tubes were once again made ready: T5s in tubes III and V, Lut in II and IV. Orders were given to fire tube II, but the Lut setting gear jammed. When tube III also failed to fire, Gebauer judged it useless to attempt further action, unsure whether to blame sabotage or bad drill.

Interrogation Report – the loss of *U 681*:

> Early on 11 March she was off the Scilly Isles. The Captain's intention was to enter St Mary's Road and at 0800hrs he took cross bearings on the Bishop Rock Light and on the disused lighthouse, which stands on St Agnes. He put himself 3 miles south of land in about 40-fathoms of water. He apparently intended to pass through St Mary's Sound for he set a course of 020-degrees. At about 1100 he ran on a rock. In his efforts to get off, he damaged the U-boat's propellers and hull. An excess pressure was set-up in an inner fuel tank, from which oil poured into the control room and electric motor compartment. The bulkhead doors had to be closed and soon the men in the control room were splashing about in 2 or 3ft of oil.
>
> The boat was at about 80ft. when she went aground and after getting off was brought up to periscope depth. The Captain wanted to proceed at this depth, but by that time he had 7 tons of oil and water in the boat and after 5 minutes gave the order to surface. He soon found that the boat could not dive, but he no doubt hoped to be able to get close to the Irish coast before abandoning ship. In a calm sea he drove the damaged boat as hard as he could and might have succeeded in his object had not a Liberator of 103 Squadron, USN sighted him, in a position about 3 miles west-north-west of the Bishop Rock.

It was bad luck for Gebauer and his men that US Navy Squadron VB 103 *B-24* ('N') spotted the boat limping towards Irish waters. Lt Norman R. Field made two attacks from at an altitude of 100ft, dropping eight depth charges on the second run from astern.

The order to abandon ship was immediately given and, while 38 men got out the dinghies, others made a vain attempt to keep the aircraft off by firing the 37mm gun. The Liberator ran in from astern and straddled the boat with a stick of depth charges, finishing her off with a second attack. She then homed other aircraft and ships of the Second Escort Group, which picked up most of the crew, but 11 died.

Soon afterwards the charges detonated and the U-boat disappeared beneath the surface stern first, about 4 miles northeast of the Isles of Scilly. Thirty-eight survivors, three officers, five senior rates and thirty junior ratings were rescued by British naval vessels of Support Group 2, including that U-boat scourge, HMS *Loch Fada*.

ADM 199/2062 NID 1/PW/REP/20 NND 873041 NARA Series T-1022 Roll 3900, PG 31752 CPMB B-794 G2 Intelligence Division U-Boot-Ehrenmal Möltenort

THE MEN WHO DIED IN U 681

Beck, Heinrich Mtr.H.Gfr. (22-10-1920)
Frank, Ernst O.Strm (6-8-1914)
Graichen, Willi Mtr.H.Gfr. (14-8-1920)
Gruber, Josef Masch.O.Gfr. (22-2-1924)
Grundmann, Max Mech.O.Gfr. (30-9-1924)
Krakowski, Kurt Fk.O.Gfr. (15-1-1924)
Kupka, Gerhard Masch.O.Gfr. (23-9-1924)
Öhlaann, Rudolf Masch.Mt. (10-2-1921)
Thomann, Ernst Ltz.S. (7-11-1919)
Vogel, Werner Mtr.H.Gfr. (14-3-1923)
Weder, Karl Mtr.H.Gfr. (21-9-1919)

THOSE WHO SURVIVED

Berger, Karl-Heinz Ob.Mech.Mt.
Buergel, Alfred Masch.Ob.Gfr.
Bundt, Kurt Matr.Ob.Gfr.
Ehring, Heinrich Masch.Gfr.
Fehnert, Werner Matr.Ob.Gfr.
Förster, Richard Bt.Smt.
Friedrichsen, Hans Oblt.Ing
Fuchs, Ernst Matr.Ob.Gfr.
Gebauer, Werner Oblt.z.S.
Hermann, Willi Mech.Gfr.
Hoffmann, Rudolf Fk.Mt.
Klein, Erich Bt.Smt.
Klose, Willi Masch.Ob.Gfr.
Kordick, Johann Mtr.Gfr.
Kröll, Willi Mech.Gfr.
Lauterbach, Eduard Ob.Mech.Mt.
Lehniger, Heinz Ob.Masch.
Leithold, Helmut San.Mt.
Liesack, Manfred Masch.Gfr.

Michalak, Josef Masch.Ob.Gfr.
Muelier, Karl Fk.Mt.
Nehring, Alfred Masch.Ob.Gfr.
Nowak, Stefan Mtr.Gfr.
Pallasch, Alfred Fk.Ob.Gfr.
Pipal, Günther Ltz.S.
Rechner, Ernst Ob.Mech.Mt.
Rieger, Willi Masch.Mt.
Rudolph, Helmut Masch.Mt.
Schweinforth, Karl Matr.Ob.Gfr.
Sonnewald, Günther Matr.Ob.Gfr.
Stephant, Rudi Matr.Ob.Gfr.
Themer, Karl Stbs.Ob.Masch.
Tohen, Heinz Masch.Gfr.
Uhlig, Johannes Masch.Gfr.
Vogel, Ernst Bt.Smt.
Von Gehr, Walter Fk.Ob.Gfr.
Wegner, Hans Masch.Gfr.
Wirths Horst Masch.Gfr.

WRECK SITE

The wreck of *U 681* lies on a seabed of sand and gravel, in a general depth of 86m (282ft), being the lowest astronomical depth. It is upright and intact, with the stern broken up. Shoals of fish have adopted the wreck, which is covered in soft corals on the upper sections.

TECHNICAL DETAILS OF THE KRIEGSMARINE VIIC AND VIIC/41 U-BOATS (COURTESY AND COPYRIGHT OF DR AXEL NIESTLÉ)

DIMENSIONS

The VIIC boat became the 'workhorse' submarine of the Kriegsmarine during the Second World War. The official tonnage of the original design as per 22 March 1941 was 761.89 tons on the surface and 864.69 tons submerged. However the figure may change to a very small degree with later modifications. Usually 769 tons and 871 tons are given as the standard official figures throughout the war. Boats from different yards may also have varied to a certain degree due to small design variations. The overall general dimensions measured 67.1m in length overall, 6.22m in beam, 4.8m-draught and 9.60m in height around the conning tower.

MACHINERY

Two diesel/oil engines powered the two propellers, originally designed in bronze, but a shortage of non-ferrous metals led to the use of steel propellers during the war. Boats already ordered before the war were fitted either with engines manufactured by Maschinefabrik-Augsburg-Nürnberg (MAN) or by the Germaniawerft (GW). After the start of the war, other companies or yards manufactured these two diesels types under licence. Front-line experience soon showed the more rigid GW construction, being superior and new constructions were gradually fitted with GW-type diesels only. Both types were fitted with *Gebläse* (super-chargers) and developed 1400ps each at 475 revolutions per minute continuous power, or 495 revolutions maximum power for 30 minutes developed 1600ps, which give a maximum surface speed of 17 knots. The boat had a calculated operational range of 9,700 nautical miles at 10 knots, or 6,500 nautical miles at 12 knots and carried a maximum fuel/oil capacity of 113 tons.

For running submerged, two 62-cell lead/acid batter/accumulators usually manufactured by Accumulatoren-Fabrik-Aktiengesellschaft (AFA) powered the two electric motors that developed 375ps at 295 revolutions and gave her a maximum speed of 7.6 knots. The four electric motors manufacturers were:
AEG (Allgemeine Elektricittäts-Gesellschaft)
BBC (Brown, Boveri & Cie.)
GL u. Co. (Garbe, Lohmeyer & Co.)
SSW (Siemens-Schuckert-Werke)
These companies all produced more or less very similar designed motors and sometimes under licence (GL). Using battery power the boat had a calculated operational range underwater of 80 nautical miles at a steady 4 knots.

ARMAMENT

TORPEDOES

The VIIC boat was designed with five torpedo tubes, four at the bow and one at the stern.

Initially fourteen torpedoes were carried until Summer 1943, with two of them in the upper-deck reserve containers. These were later then removed to save weight and because it became too dangerous to reload them in North Atlantic waters. In 1944 the number was reduced to ten to increase living conditions in the bow room when the boats stayed submerged for long times.

From Autumn 1944 onward, on boats operating in the Atlantic, or British coastal waters, the ten torpedoes usually consisted of five T5 and five Lut, often stowed as follows: T5 one in forward tube, three in forward bilges and one in aft tube. Five Lut stowed: three in forward tube, one in forward bilges and one in the aft bilges.

MINES

Mines were only carried on special order and in exchange for torpedoes and not in addition.

The figures for mines offered in reference books are theoretical numbers and have nothing really to do with operational realities.

There were three different types of U-boat mines, which were called Torpedominen and these were delivered through the torpedo tubes:

TMA – moored floating mines, designed for, but never actually used on U-boats.

TMB – small ground mines with various fuses and an explosive charge of 1,276lb (578.7kg).

TMC – large ground mines with an explosive charge of 2,200lb (997.9kg).

The exchange ratios of mines/torpedo were:

One torpedo – three TMB

One torpedo – two TMC

GUNS

Initially, the VIIC gun specifications consisted of: one 88mm (3.46in) deck gun, plus 220 rounds and one 20mm (0.79in) AA Flak gun, plus 4,380 rounds of ammunition. On Atlantic boats the deck gun was removed in Summer 1943. The single gun bandstand aft of the bridge (model 0) was modified in early 1943, by adding a second, lower bandstand with another single 20mm gun (this was then called conning tower modification II). The Type I modification (two 13.2mm twin machine gun mounts on upper bandstand, single 20mm on lower bandstand) was abandoned when tests showed that the machine guns were not powerful enough. From May 1943, modification – IV was introduced, showing at first two single 20mm mounts on the widened upper bandstand and a quadruple 20mm mount on the enlarged, lower bandstand. After 20mm twin mounts became available in July 1943, twin mounts replaced the single mounts. From October 1943 onward, the 37mm mount replaced the quadruple mounts. This represented the final variation of the Type IV conning tower modification. Later in the war 37mm twin mounts were tested experimentally on a few boats, but the snort had already reduced the threat from aircraft, by then. This was a summary of standard AA modifications on Atlantic boats.

Other experimental modifications were carried on some boats however, but they never became a standard form. Modifications were done to all front-line or working-up boats regardless of their date of commission and boats were continuously up-graded to the latest version during yard layovers.

DIVING DEPTHS

The operational diving depth of a VIIC boat was 100m (328ft), with a maximum depth 165m (541.33ft) and a crush depth of 200m (656ft). A crash-dive to 20m took 30 seconds on average.

The VIIC/41 boat was almost the same in all respects as the VIIC, but was designed with a stronger pressure hull, which gave the boat an operational diving depth of 120m (394ft) and a crush depth of 250m (820ft).

COMPLEMENT

Both VIIC and VIIC/41 boats carried between forty-four and fifty-two crewmen. With increased AA-armament in 1943/44, the crews reached the highest figures. Following the introduction of the *schnorchel* the crews were often reduced to forty-six to fifty crewmen.

Each Type VII U-boat carried thirty-six *unteroffiziere* and ratings, generally two *unteroffiziere* to every three ratings. Apart from the officers, the crew of a U-boat was divided between technical personnel and seamen. The technical division comprised of specialist personnel: diesel machinists, electricians, radio operators and torpedo mechanics. There were four senior NCOs.

APPENDIX

Additional information on the movements of HM S/M Sidon, from page 184

SIDON commenced working up trials on 23 November , prior to joining the 3rd Flotilla, attached to HMS *FORTH* at Holy Loch. On 20 January, the boat accidentally rammed her stable-mate *TURPIN*, while submerged during exercises. *SIDON* came off worse with serious damage to her bow casing. On 8 March 1945 the boat left Lerwick for her sole war patrol off the Norwegian coast. The patrol was plagued by snow storms preventing the boat from obtaining any navigational fixes for three days. Apart from a fleeting glimpse of a JU 88, the remainder of the patrol was uneventful. On 23 March, the boat tied up at Lerwick, before returning to Holy Loch next day.

On 7 April 1945, *SIDON* was dispatched to the Far East (Eighth Flotilla) under the command of Lt Henry Carty-Gowan. Engine problems forced a detour to Freemantle in Australia. On 12 July *SIDON* departed Onslow enroute for the Lombok Straits. In company with USS *HAMMERHEAD* the boat made a frantic search off Saigon for survivors of a downed Liberator bomber. On 27 July a miracle occurred. The boat was about to break off the search when, following the navigator's hunch, *SIDON's* lookouts spotted 2nd Lt S. Reed USAAF. Lt Reed had drifting alone for five days and had drifted over 250 miles from the ditching point. As the patrol report states: '*The joy on his face when he saw Sidon amply repaid all the fruitless searching and false hopes we had experienced*'.

On 3 August 1945 the boat arrived at Subic Bay in the Phillipines. The boat later relocated to Hong Kong to view the surrender of Japanese forces. With the war now over, the boat arrived at Portsmouth on December 6th 1945. Her career can thus be summarised:

27th December 1945: Paid off into Reserve Group 'S' at Portsmouth (Fifth Flotilla)
28th January 1946 to the 9th March 1946: Repairs to armaments.
26th February 1948 to 18th June 1948: Refit, returned to Reserve Group 'G' at Portsmouth.
1st August 1948 to 24 January 1950: Reserve Group 'M' at Portsmouth followed by refit.
31st August 1950: Allocated to Second Submarine Flotilla, Portland.
19th April 1951: Took part in search for HM S/M *AFFRAY*.
11th November 1951 Reserve Group 'F' (Fifth Flotilla) Devonport prior to major refit
21st November 1951: Major refit. Removal of the 4-inch gun and gun tower and the installation of a
    snort-mast and Type 267MW radar. Refit completed by 27th June 1952. HMS Sidon re-commissioned
    into the 2nd Submarine Squadron, based at Portland for submarine and anti-submarine training.
1st February 1954: Boat joins Fifth Submarine Squadron, at Portland.
9th February 1954: Refit at Cammell Laird, Birkenhead.
30 March 1954: Lt. Cdr. Hugh Verry, aged 30yrs, assumed command of *SIDON*
3rd November 1954: Boat returns to Second Submarine Squadron, Portland.

Additional information on the sinking of LLANDOVERY CASTLE by SM U 86 from pages 61 to 65:

Statement by Captain Sylvester:

> *The second officer found a lifeboat with the after end lowered in the water and the fore made fast, the bow hanging in the air by the tackle. With the assistance of a steward, the second officer lowered the boat in the water, and the remainder of those on board went down the ropes into her. I went down a life line into the boat and we pulled off from the ship, pulling away just in time to avoid the suction as she went down stern first. This was not more than ten minutes from the time she was torpedoed. We pulled over the spot as soon as the turmoil had subsided, and succeeded in picking up eleven men from rafts and wreckage.*

There is clear evidence that the lowering of the boats was not entirely successful. The account of Steward Burgess provides an intriguing angle on the sinking:

When I first got on deck, I cut my foot among the mass of broken glass from lamp and windows that was lying about, but I managed to get to my station alongside the boat I was allotted to. As I was going down to the port side, I saw two or three boats hanging up in their davits with nothing but their ropes left – they were just skeleton boats, all the sheafing having been blown away by the explosion. As my boat was being lowered, I jumped into the stern and somebody who was standing on the ship's deck let go of the fall, causing the boat to drop suddenly into the water. The fastening at one end of the life boat was not loosened and this caused the bows to swing away from the ship, and she filled and broke up, the shop dragging her along. We were all thrown into the water, except for one or two who managed to cling to the life lines hanging from the davits. I got one and had a thirty foot climb back to the ship. The lifeline I was holding swung away from the ship, but a sailor pulled me on board, and I scrambled in. I am afraid most of those who were in that boat were drowned. I went across to the opposite side of the ship, looked over and saw another lifeboat alongside. I went down the rope ladder, and had just set foot on the boat, when she went from under me and filled. I held on to the rope ladder and had just got half way up when I felt my strength going, but I just managed to get on board the ship, which was then sinking fast and listing to starboard.

After I got on board again, I found that one of the chaps who was in the other boat had escaped too and we were intending to get into the launch but on second thoughts we concluded she would be sucked under when the ship sank and so we changed our minds and got a raft out. There were several of these rafts and each was designed to keep twenty or thirty afloat. We found the second engineer aft in his pyjamas: he had just rushed out of bed; and we helped him on with his lifebelt. He assisted us in getting the raft over but I lost sight of his after that. The sailor who was with me got over the side onto the raft and then a soldier medic turned up and they shoved off. I was standing on the ship up to my knees in water and concluding she would soon go down, I dived over the side and joined them in the raft. We had a difficult job to keep the raft from being sucked under the ship but we managed to clear and we got about a hundred yards astern, when she blew up and sank with her bows upright in the water. There was a terrible roar of things falling as she went.

Well after the ship went down we were busy clinging tight to save ourselves from getting taken off the raft by the wash the ship made but we saw a light in the distance and heard the captain's voice. He was picking up men and we called to him. He said 'All right I will be with you in a minute' and he came alongside in a lifeboat and picked us off the raft. Amongst those our lifeboat picked up, was a fireman who had been in the Canadian nurses' boat and he told us it filled up and they all went under. I saw myself two or three boats go under. That was because the ship's engines could not stop and she dragged them all under.

As the fate of the nurses would later pre-occupy Allied propagandists, it is interesting to note here we have evidence that they may have succumbed to botched lifeboat drill rather than 'Hun atrocity'. Eye witnesses claimed to have seen three boats in the water, the captain's boat, the first officer's boat with six people on board and Chapman's boat. Purser Evans would later testify to having seen 'several boats and rafts' having escaped the vortex. *Steuermannsmaat* Walther Popitz recalled seeing 'two or three as well as the captain's boat'. It is nevertheless unclear as to how many boats survived the botched lowering and the question remains as to what happened to them? So far Patzig had given orders to torpedo a British hospital ship, which was in itself against international law. However the charges laid at the door of Helmut Patzig were about to get much worse. Popitz testified at Leipzig that Patzig had addressed the men in the control room with these words: '*You know what has happened and I beg you to keep silent about it. I take the responsibility for sinking the hospital ship on my own conscience.*'

Having sunk the ship, Patzig urgently needed evidence that the vessel had indeed been engaged in unlawful activity to justify his actions.

Captain E.A. Sylvester again:

…We were pulling down to a man who was calling out from the water ahead of the boat when the submarine appeared and ordered the boat alongside. The second officer replied, 'We are picking up a man from the water', as the order was not promptly obeyed, two rifle shots were fired over the boat, and someone on the submarine shouted, 'Come alongside or we will shoot with the big gun'.

The boat accordingly proceeded alongside the submarine. I was taken onboard to the conning tower. An officer, who appeared to be in command, asked me what ship it was. I replied, 'The hospital ship Llandovery Castle'. He said, 'Oh yes but you were carrying eight American flight officers. I answered, 'I beg your pardon; we were not. We have seven Canadian medical officers on board and the ship is chartered by the Canadian government to carry sick and wounded men from England to Halifax'. To this his reply was, 'You have been carrying American flight officers'. I answered, I have been running to Canada for six month with wounded and give you my word of honour that we have carried none except patients, medical staff and crew and sisters'. The officer asked if any Canadian officer was in the boat and on receiving the reply 'yes' ordered him on board. The officer [submarine] said to him, 'You are an American flight officer'. I said, 'No he is not, he is a Canadian medical officer'. The submarine officer then asked the Canadian officer what he was and on receiving a similar reply ordered him back to the boat. I was also ordered back to the boat and warned to get away as soon as possible. The boat was let go, oars got out and we proceeded to pull away from the submarine The submarine then circled round through the wreckage at full speed, twice coming close to the boat; the occupants of the boat shouted out 'same boat'. The boat was again ordered alongside the submarine and the second and fourth officers were taken aboard.

Second Officer, Leslie Chapman:

The German officer asked me who I was and if we were carrying American flight officers. I said 'No' and then he said, 'You had ammunition on board; there was a loud explosion' I explained to him that it was the boilers had burst as the water reached them. He then told us to go back to the boat. We were then ordered to cast off again.

Note: Chapman was in one of the other lifeboats before being ordered onboard the U-boat. Afterwards he was put into the Captain's boat.

Major Thomas Lyon:

…when the call came for a Canadian officer to go on board the submarine I responded smartly. I jumped for the submarine and just as I was landing on the deck, a German officer pulled my arm, with the result that I fell heavily, and broke my right leg just above the ankle. I was taken to the conning tower where the commander of the submarine was standing talking to the captain. The commander said to me 'You are an American flight officer'. I said I was not and that was a Canadian medical officer. The German officer asked me whether we carried ammunition. I said 'No' we never carried anything except patients'. We were then told to get back into the boat.

The Major's unfortunate leg injury was later embroidered by British newspapers into a deliberate German assault. All told, Patzig obtained no evidence of American servicemen or any other illegal activities from the survivors of *LLANDOVERY CASTLE*. The only activity contrary to the Hague Convention had been *his own* deliberate sinking of a hospital ship in waters wherein Germany had guaranteed such vessels immunity from attack. Patzig now ordered '*Klarmachen zum Tauchen*' – 'diving stations' as events reached a climax. Oberleutnant Patzig, Lts Ludwig Dittmar and IWO Johann Boldt remained on the bridge. Ominously, *Bootsmannsmaat* Meissener the gunner was ordered to remain at his post. Below, in the control room, Walther Popitz saw nothing but all on board could hear the gun firing: '*I had a suspicion at the time that they were firing at the boats but the only men who knew what was going on were the fellows on the bridge. Nobody dared say a word about it afterwards but we all made our assumptions.*'

Captain Sylvester was equally unsure what was going on as the U-boat commenced to zig-zag past the lifeboat: '*The submarine after circling round again just missing the boat twice, the last time by about two feet, went a short distance away and appeared to stop. From this position she opened fire at unseen targets and fired about 12 shells. One shell passed near the boat.*'

Having discussed the matter with submarine officers, it seems highly unlikely to the author that these evolutions of the U-boat marked a serious attempt to ram the lifeboat. Had Patzig sought to sink the captain's boat, he could have accomplished this with ease. Submariners were equally surprised that a U-boat would even attempt to use its gun against such small targets in darkness and were of the opinion that a gun of this era would prove difficult to depress. The purpose of these actions remains speculative. By this time the sea was cloaked in darkness and the men in the lifeboat could not see what target the U-boat was firing at. At the trial it was established that the surviving lifeboat was a quarter of a mile from the U-boat at the time the firing commenced. There are conflicting accounts of how long the firing carried on. Popitz said it lasted ten minutes, Chapman said it carried on for half an hour. When it did end *U 86* resumed her patrol. The KTB and the track chart for 27 June later proved to have been falsified. The remainder of the patrol was eventful and the incidents are given below.

Next morning the surviving lifeboat containing twenty four people was found by the destroyer HMS *LYSANDER* drifting 41 miles off the Irish coast. Eighteen crew plus six men of the Canadian Medical Corps had survived and they were anxious to tell their rescuers what had transpired, before they were landed at Queenstown.

The survivors of *LLANDOVERY CASTLE*:

Abraham, Ward Attendant
Barton, D. 4th Officer
Chapman, L. 2nd Officer
Cooper, Orderly
Davies, Painter
Evans, H. Purser
Goodridge, Able Seaman
Heather, Deck Steward
Hickman, Orderly
Knight, Sergeant
Lyon, T. Major
McVey, Fireman
Mounsey, Trimmer
Murphy, Able Seaman
Pilot, Orderly
Record, Lamp Trimmer
Savage, Steward
Schroeder, Able Seaman
Scott, Ordinary Seaman
Sylvester, R. Captain
Taylor, Orderly
Tredigian, Firemean
Ward, Able Seaman

In response, the sloop HMS *SNOWDROP* and four American destroyers raced to the area where the *LLANDOVERY CASTLE* had sunk. There were no survivors and no wreckage apart from one undamaged lifeboat recovered some 9 miles from where the captain's boat had been found. By the 2 July, the newspapers were permitted access to survivors. If Patzig had been aiming to expose British mendacity, he had instead handed the allies a priceless propaganda coup. 'Hun frightfulness' screamed the headlines. Artists competed to produce ever more lurid imagery capturing the last stoic seconds in the lifeboats before the machine guns tore into them. Taste the flavour of this account by the Sgt E Knight, which appeared in various newsapers in July 1918 under the caption '*Without Complaint or Murmur*':

> *Unflinchingly and calmly, as steady and collected as if on parade, without a complaint or a single sign of emotion, our fourteen devoted nursing sisters faced the terrible ordeal of certain death--only a matter of minutes--as our lifeboat neared that mad whirlpool of waters where all human power was helpless.*
>
> *The fourteen nurses and eight crewmen were placed in No. 5 lifeboat and sergeant Knight took charge. He said they were lowered to the water's surface and found great difficulty in breaking free from the ropes that held them to the ship's side. Two axes were even broken trying to cut them-selves away, without success. All the time the heavy swell and choppy sea pounded the boat against the ship's hull and the oars that they used to fend themselves off with, all broke. Sergeant Knight stated that eventually they broke free and commenced to drift away towards the stern of the ship. Nursing Sister M.M. Fraser, the matron, turned to Sergeant Knight and asked 'Sergeant, do you think there is any hope for us?' to which he purportedly replied, "no". It was just about then, that the poop deck appeared to break away and the vacuum it caused as it sank pulled the lifeboat into it. The boat tipped over sideways and all the occupants fell into the sea. Knight recalled that everyone was sucked under in seconds, even though they were all wearing lifebelts. That was the last time he saw any of the nursing sisters. Sergeant Knight said, he remembered going down and coming up three times before finding some wreckage to cling to. Fortunately for him he was eventually picked up by the captain's boat; the only one to escape…*

Not only had he attacked and sunk an inviolate hospital ship, Patzig had apparently tried to hide the evidence by massacring the survivors. Every major newspaper in the English speaking world listed the names of those that perished.

SOURCES OF INFORMATION

SOURCES OF GENERAL INFORMATION AND OFFICIAL HISTORIES

A Precarious Existence, R. Mackay, Periscope Publishing
Allied Submarine Attacks of World War Two, J. Rowher, Greenhill Books
Amazing Adventure, E. Keble, Chatterton, Hurst & Blackett
Axis Successes of World War Two, Jürgen Rohwer, Greenhill Books
Beating the U-boats, E. Keble, Chatterton, Hurst & Blackett
Beneath the Waves, A.S. Evans, William Kimber
Blue Guide to Scotland, John Tomes (1992)
Britain's Maritime Memorials and Mementoes, D. Saunders, Patrick Stephens
British and Commonwealth Merchant Ship Losses to Axis Submarines 1939–1945, A.J. Tennent,
    Sutton Publishing
British Merchant Ships Sunk by U-boats in the 1914–1918 War, A.J. Tennent, Starling Press
British Submarines of the First World War, Paul Kemp
By Guess and by God, W. Carr, Hutchinson
Convoy, J. Winton, Hutchinson
Crash Dive, Dickinson
Damned Un-English Machines, Jack Hool and Keith Nutter, Tempus Publishing
Der Krieg sur Zee: Der Handelskrieg mit U-booten, Konteradmiral Arno Spindler, 5 volumes, Mittler
    & Son
Dictionary of Disasters at Sea During the Age of Steam, Charles Hocking FLA, Lloyd's Register of
    Shipping
Die Deutschen Kriegsschiffe, Erich Groner, 2 vols, Lehmanns Verlag
Die UB-Boote der Kaiserlichen Marine 1914–1918, Harald Bendert
Dive Kent, Dive Sussex, Dive Hampshire and the Isle of Wight, Dive South Devon, all by Kendall
    McDonald, Underwater World Publications
Encyclopaedia of British Submarines, Paul Akermann, Periscope Publishing
Endless Story, 'Taffrail', Hodder & Stoughton
Far Distant Ships, J. Schull
Few Survived, E. Gray
Fighting the U-boats, E. Keble, Chatterton, Hurst & Blackett
Find and Destroy, Dwight R. Messimer, Naval Institute Press
FIPS – Legendary U-boat Commander, G. Brooks, Leo Cooper
German U-boat Commanders of World War II, Rainer Busch & Hans-Joachim Röll, Greenhill Books,
    Naval Institute Press.
German U-boat losses during World War II, Dr Axel Niestlé, Greenhill Books
Historic Almanac Of Italian Warships 1861–1995 (Official branch of the Italian Navy – Roma)
History of the Great War: Naval Operations, Corbett and Newbolt, 5 vols, Longmans
Hitler's U-boat War – the Hunters, Clay Blair, Weidenfield and Nicholson
HM U-boat, J. Drummond, Wyndham
HMS Dolphin, Keith Hall, Tempus Publishing
Hull Down, Sir Bertram Hayes, Cassell
Italian official sources and Navi Mercantili Perdute, Roma, 1997, last edition
Jane's Fighting Ships of World War II – Jane's Publishing
Liverpool and the Battle of the Atlantic 1939–1945, Paul Kemp, Maritime Books
Lloyd's War Losses, The First World War, Lloyd's of London

Lloyd's War Losses, The Second World War, 2 vols, Lloyd's of London
Lost Patrols, Innes McCartney, Periscope Publishing
Memoirs of a Swedish Seafaring Family, Eva Ternström-Lidbetter-Sessions, Ebor Press
Merchant Fleets 1939, Roger Jordan, Naval Institute Press
Military History
Mines, Minelayers and Minelaying, Capt. J.S. Cowie, OUP 1949
Mit dem Einhorn Gegen Engelland, Franz J. Fröwls
Neither Sharks nor Wolves, T. Mulligan, Naval Institute Press
One Man Band, B. Bryant
Q Ships and their Story, E. Keble, Chatterton, Conway Press
Records of Armstrong Whitworth, Tyne Wear Archive
Records of Messrs Cammell Laird, Birkenhead
Records of Messrs Vickers, Barrow
Royal Dockyards, P. Macdougall, Shire
Royal Navy Trawlers Part 1, Gerald Toghill, Maritime Books
Royal Navy Trawlers Part 2, Requisitioned Trawlers, Gerald Toghill, Maritime Books
Ships of the Royal Navy vol. 2, J.J. Colledge, David and Charles
Shipwreck Index of the British Isles, 6 vols, Richard and Bridget Larn, Lloyd's Register – Fairplay
    Cook, Welton & Gemmell, Shipbuilders of Hull and beverley 1883–1963, Hutton Press
Shipwrecks of North East Norfolk, Stephen Holt, Ayer Tikus
Shipwrecks of North Norfolk, Stephen Holt, Ayer Tikus
Shipwrecks of the East Coast, 2 vols, Ron Young, Tempus Publishing
Shipwrecks of the Forth, Robert Baird, Nekton
Shipwrecks of the Isle of Man, Adrian Corkhill, Tempus Publishing
Shipwrecks of the North East Coast, 2 vols, Ron Young, Tempus Publishing
Shipwrecks of the North of Scotland, Robert Baird, Birlinn
Shipwrecks of the West of Scotland, Robert Baird, Nekton
Shore Establishments of the Royal Navy, Lt Cdr Warlow, Maritime Books
Staff History; Submarine Operations: Home Waters
Starke Schell, The World Ship Society
Submarine Operations: Mediterranean vol. 2
Submarines, War Beneath the Waves, Robert Hutchinson, Janes
Subsunk, W. Shelford, Harrap
Swept Channels, 'Taffrail', Hodder & Stoughton
The 'K' Boats, D. Everitt, Airlife Publishing
The Admiralty Regrets, Warren and Benson
The Auxiliary Patrol, E. Keble, Chatterton, Lauriat & Co.
The Battle of the East Coast, J.P. Foynes
The Clyde Submarine Base, Keith Hall, Tempus Publishing
The Codebreakers of Room 40, Admiral Sir William James
The Cross of Sacrifice vol. I, S.D and J.B. Jarvis
The Cross of Sacrifice vol. IV, S.D and J.B. Jarvis
The Cross of Sacrifice vol. V, S.D and J.B. Jarvis
The Dover Patrol, 2 vols, Admiral Sir R. Bacon, Hutchinson
The German Submarine War 1914–1918, R. Gibson and M. Prendergast, Periscope Publishing
The Illustrated Guide to Britain, Automobile Association
The Isle of May, J. Allen
The Log of a U-boat Commander, Ernst Hashagen, Putnam
The Paravane Adventure, Cornford
The Saint and the Sparrow, Richard W. Skinner, Historic Military Press
The Shipbuilder
The Sinking of U 309, Richard W. Skinner, Historic Military Press
The Tin Openers, Kendall McDonald, Historic Military Press
The U-boat: Evolution and Technical History, Eberhard Rössler, Cassell & Co.
The U-boat Commanders Handbook, Thomas reprint
The U-boat Offensive 1914–1945, V.E. Tarrant, Arms & Armour

The U-boat War in the Atlantic, G. Hessler
The World's Merchant Fleets 1939, Rodger Jordan, Naval Institute Press
Thetis, Secrets and Scandal, D. Roberts, Avid
This Dangerous Menace, A. Jeffrey, Mainstream
This Present Emergency, A. Jeffrey, Mainstream
This Time of Crisis, A. Jeffrey, Mainstream
Type VII U-boats, R. Stern, Naval Institute Press
U 995: *Das Boot von Laboe*, E. Wetzel, Motorbuch Verlag
U-297, Richard W. Skinner, Historic Military Press
U-boat bases and Bunkers, G. Williamson, Osprey
U-boat Crews 1914–1945, G. Williamson, Osprey
U-boats of the Kaiser's Navy, G. Williamson, Osprey
U-boat Fact File, Peter Sharpe, Midland Publishing
U-boat Hunters, R. Grant, Periscope Publishing
U-boat Intelligence, R. Grant, Periscope Publishing
U-boat *Operations of the Second World War*, 2 vols, Kenneth Wynn, Chatham Publishing
U-boats Destroyed, R. Grant, Periscope Publishing
U-boats: The Illustrated History of the Raiders of the Deep, David Miller, Pegasus Publishing
Verschollen, Dwight R. Messimer, Naval Institute Press
Watchdogs of the Deep, Jones
We Dive at Dawn, Lt Cdr K. Edwards, Rich and Cowan

WEBSITES

www.ubootwaffe.net
www.warsailors.com
www.uboat.net
www.yorkshire-divers.co.uk/forums/
www.diverforum.co.uk
members.iinet.net.au/~eadej/homepage.html
www.multimap.com/index/NO1.htm
users.hunterlink.net.au/~maampo/militaer/glenn/marine/kaiserliche_marine_1914.htm
www.u-boot-net.de/
www.british-merchant-navy.co.uk/U-BOATS.htm
www.britsub.net/
web.ukonline.co.uk/chalcraft/sm/page6.html
www.dropbears.com/w/ww1subs/index.htm
www.usmm.org/ww1merchant.html
users.pandora.be/tree/wreck/wrecksite/wrecksite.html
www.gwpda.org/naval/sml00003.htm
www.dropbears.com/w/ww1subs/jclass.htm
www.rnsubmus.co.uk/losses.htm
www.cwgc.org/
www.gwpda.org/naval/n0000000.htm
www.royal-naval-reserve.co.uk/
www.cronab.demon.co.uk/wss.htm
www.harry-tates.org.uk/
www.world-war.co.uk/index.php3
www.hazegray.org/
www.feldgrau.com/
www.combinedfleet.com/ss.htm
www.usmm.org/ww1merchant.html
www.voy.com/65298/
www.irishwrecksonline.net/
www.numa.net/expeditions/north_sea_and_english_channel_hunt.html

ubootwaffe.net/quadrant.cgi
www.periscopepublishing.com/images/Deadlight per cent20gallery per cent20pages/OD per cent20exhibition.
tmg110.tripod.com/3reich1.htm
www.deutsche-marinesoldaten.de/lebenslaeufe/liste-ritterkreuztraeger-t-z.htm
www.deepimage.co.uk/wrecks/vandal/vandal_pages/vandal-mainpage.htm
www.ukdiving.co.uk/
www.miramarshipindex.org.nz
www.2worldwar2.com/knights-cross.htm
www.mysticseaport.org/Library/Initiative/ShipRegister.cfm?BibID=179721885
www.ubootkameradschaft-kiel.org
www.uboat-memorial.org

INDEX